Heralding a Renaissance:
Women & Leadership
in the
Catholic Church

Published in 2019 by Connor Court Publishing Pty Ltd
Copyright © Christine Cameron 2019

All rights reserved. No part of this book may be reproduced or transmitted in any form or by any means, electronic or mechanical, including photocopying, recording or by any information storage and retrieval system, without prior permission in writing from the publisher.

Connor Court Publishing Pty Ltd
PO Box 7257
Redland Bay QLD 4165

sales@connorcourt.com
www.connorcourtpublishing.com.au
Phone 0497 900 685

ISBN: 9781925826692

Front Cover Design: Ian James

Printed in Australia

Heralding a Renaissance: Women & Leadership in the Catholic Church

Christine Cameron

Connor Court Publishing

Contents

Acknowledgements	9
Foreword by Ms Kerry Alys Robinson	13
(Global Ambassador, Leadership Roundtable)	

FIRST MILLENNIUM: Setting the Context

1. Introduction — 17
2. Mary – Leading the Way — 25
   Part I: Church Honouring Mary
   Part II: Profile of the Historical Mary
3. The Role of Women Leaders in the Early Church — 49
   Part I: St Mary Magdalene (Apostolorum Apostola)
   Part II: Women Officeholders – Deacons & Teachers
4. Leadership as a Call to Service — 85
   Faith, Values & Leadership Practices
5. Profile of St Monica (4th Century) — 107
   Mother of St Augustine – Doctor of the Universal Church

SECOND MILLENNIUM: Profiles of Selected Women Leaders
& their Response to the Call of the Gospel

6. St Hildegard of Bingen (12th Century) — 133
   Doctor of the Universal Church
7. St Clare of Assisi (13th Century) — 157
   Co-founder of the Order of Poor Clares

8. St Catherine of Siena (14th Century) — 187
   Doctor of the Universal Church

9. St Joan of Arc (15th Century) — 213
   Patroness of France and of soldiers

10. St Angela Merici (15th – 16th Centuries) — 247
    Foundress of the Ursuline Order

11. St Teresa of Ávila (16th Century) — 287
    Doctor of the Universal Church

12. Caroline Chisholm (19th Century) — 319
    Philanthropist & "Emigrants Friend"

13. St Thérèse of Lisieux (19th Century) — 337
    Doctor of the Universal Church

14. Blessed Frances Siedliska (19th – 20th Centuries) — 371
    Foundress of the Sisters of the Holy Family of Nazareth

15. St Mary of the Cross MacKillop (19th – 20th Centuries) — 433
    Co-founder Sisters of St Joseph of the Sacred Heart

16. St Josephine Bakhita (19th – 20th Centuries) — 461
    Patron Saint of Victims of Slavery & Human Trafficking

17. Dorothy Day (19th – 20th Centuries) — 485
    Servant of God & Social Activist

18. St Teresa of Kolkata (20th Century) — 509
    Foundress of the Missionaries of Charity

THIRD MILLENNIUM: Current & Emerging Global Trends

19. Voices of Selected Women in the Contemporary Church   545

20. Voices of the Future – The Youth of the Church   567

21. Conclusion   583

   A Living Church – Changes & Grows

   Voices from the Past to the Present – Challenge Future Leaders

References   601

Appendices   643

Acknowledgements

It is with sincere and profound appreciation that I acknowledge the incredible support I have received over the past eighteen months, which has resulted in the publishing of my third book in the leadership series "Heralding a Renaissance: Women & Leadership in the Catholic Church". I acknowledge the outstanding contributions from the following sources:

- Ms Kerry Alys Robinson (Global Ambassador, Leadership Roundtable) for graciously agreeing to write the Foreword to this book. Kerry's kind words and impressive assessment are very much appreciated.

- Dr Dan Riley for once again providing such amazing support and encouragement and utilising his very considerable editing skills and advice regarding the book as it evolved over months of writing and research.

- Mr Brian Hanley, Principal of St Monica's College, Epping, Melbourne Victoria Australia for sharing the charism of the Monican spirit with the author and readers of this book.

- Ms Bernadette Harris, Deputy Principal (Identity, Mission & Administration) and her students at St Monica's College for their outstanding work and responses to the questionnaires which addressed the topics of "Faith, Service, Inspiration, the Catholic Church, and Voices of the Future".

- Mr Frank Cumbo, Liturgy, Faith & Mission Coordinator at St Monica's College, a colleague of Ms Harris. Frank very generously shared his time and talents. His support has been invaluable.

- Mrs Patricia McRae who shared her experiences with Mother Teresa when the saint was in Australia with her sisters, the Missionaries of Charity.
- Maria and Robert McRae who contributed their thoughts and experiences when visiting Mary MacKillop Penola Centre South Australia.
- Brother Robert E. O'Connor FMS for his wonderful insight and notes into Mary's faith journey and the provision of resource data on the "Historical Mary".
- Sr Lois Ann Richardi CSFN for providing outstanding research information on Blessed Frances Siedliska, Foundress of the Sisters of the Holy Family of Nazareth.
- Sr Helen Tereba CSFN a good friend from my early teenage years who encouraged me to become the best I could be.
- Sr Miriam Joseph CSFN who inspired me in my love of learning.
- Sr Catherine Duxbury OSU who mentored and offered advice during the early days of my leadership experiences and who has been supportive during the research process providing information on St Angela Merici, Foundress of the Ursuline Order.
- Ms Jennifer Harman a colleague and friend who was most supportive during my time working in the Armidale Diocese in New South Wales Australia.
- Gail and John Orman for their confidence that the book would be written and that I was the person to complete the task.
- Mrs Lorraine Jones a dear friend for contributing to the collection of data for the research.

- Dr Anthony Cappello Publisher at Connor Court Publishing and his Team for their contribution to the publication of this book.
- Professor Greg Craven Vice-Chancellor ACU and Ms Simone Chetcuti, Director, Office of the Vice-Chancellor and President ACU, for providing ongoing email and library access/support during my months of research.
- Library Staff at ACU, particularly staff at the North Sydney, Brisbane, Strathfield and Melbourne Campuses, for organising intercampus and interlibrary loans. Their support has been outstanding.
- Twelve women who contributed to the chapter on the "Voices of Selected Women in the Contemporary Church", for sharing their experiences and their faith journeys while engaged in various ministries within the Church.
- Mr John Cameron a loving and very patient husband for being so supportive and providing sound feedback and giving encouragement especially when the task seemed endless and progress too slow.
- Mrs Theresa Cameron a much-loved twin sister who provided wise advice and very capable proofreading skills.
- Mr Michael Daly a loved brother for his support and insight into suggested titles for the book.
- Camille and Tom Swanton a beloved sister and brother-in-law who did what they could to enhance the research.
- Father John Daly a dear cousin who kindly wrote a tribute to Servant of God Dorothy Day, which enriched the chapter on her life and works.
- Mrs Maureen Mary Daly a beautiful mother for gifting me life and who showed great strength and courage

by challenging the status quo of her generation – an extraordinary woman who lived before her time and who died too soon.

- Fourteen amazing women across centuries of Church history, who responded to the Gospel's call to service, and who gifted the charism of their legacy to future generations of leaders within the Church.
- Eve "mother of all the living" (Gen 3:20) and *"witness to the biblical beginning"* (Pope St John Paul II, 1988:para.11).

Finally, and most importantly Mary, Mother of God and Mother of the Church – a model and inspiration for all generations of leaders to emulate, as they engage in a ministry of leadership, "illumined by the Living Light" of her Son Jesus Christ!

Foreword

In early May of this year (2019), 250 women religious from Zimbabwe, Nigeria, Malawi, Zambia, Uganda and the United States met in Harare. They are part of a network formed at the height of the HIV/AIDS pandemic in Africa known as All Africa Conference: Sister to Sister. Each woman is a vital leader in her community. Their ministries are myriad: providing healthcare, education, catechesis, pastoral care, nourishment, shelter, safety, skills training, and care for children, including orphans. A week later, 820 women comprising the membership of the International Union of Superiors General traveled from 80 countries to Rome for their general assembly and to meet with Pope Francis. Their discussions touched on matters urgent to the health and vitality of both the church and world.

The Catholic Church is the largest global humanitarian network with enormous potential to address human suffering and complex global challenges. It is also the vehicle through which the Catholic faith is transmitted to 1.3 billion of the world's population covering every region of earth, even the Arctic circle. In every part of the world, conversations and convenings about the Church, its mission, its challenges, its potential and its future seem to center on one crucially important element: the role and opportunity for leadership and decision-making of women in the Church.

For those who value the Church's mission and vitality, concern about the role of women in the Church is one of urgency. How compromised is the Church by failing to include women at the highest levels of leadership and at the tables of decision making in the Roman Curia and throughout the institutional Church? Nearly every institution in the world has accommodated and incorporated women in leadership – often reluctantly at first – only to admit the practical, tangible value of having done so.

To be sure, women have played a crucial role in the life of the Church from the moment of Jesus's conception. But the Church, understood to be both holy and sinful, has been influenced over time by cultures that consciously or unconsciously served to devalue the role of women, de-emphasize their agency and leadership, write them out of history, and subscribe roles for them subservient to men.

Dr Cameron has offered us a profound gift with **Heralding a Renaissance: Women & Leadership in the Catholic Church.** There is something for everyone in this considerable and comprehensive resource. Even the reader most keenly knowledgeable and passionate about the role of women in the Church will find something new and inspiring. Dr Cameron's combination of historical reference, scriptural exegesis, commentary from theologians, historians, sociologists and poets, all the while illuminating the myriad roles women have played over millennia is a feast for the mind and heart.

It becomes abundantly clear with each succeeding chapter just how impoverished the church would be without the contribution of women. In offering us this retrospective replete with prominent examples of compelling women across millennia and alive today, Dr Cameron sounds a clarion call for ever greater levels of participation in leadership and decision making for women, alongside of men, in the church.

Dr Cameron takes particular care to include the voices of young adults. She notes the deleterious impact that failing to be a good steward of the leadership contributions of women has on the transmission of faith to their generation.

We are blessed by Dr Cameron's comprehensive approach to such a crucial, perennial concern, the role of women in the church, published not a minute too soon. Each woman held up within these pages is a reminder of how tenaciously and creatively women over millennia have managed to respond to the responsibility of their baptism, and how faithfully they have heeded the Spirit's invitation to act, despite the gratuitous obstacles often laid in their paths. We are treated to beautiful insights into the lives of remarkable saints from Mary, the Mother of Jesus to St Monica; St Hildegard of Bingen to St. Catherine of Siena; St Joan of Arc to St Teresa of Ávila to St Thérèse of Lisieux; St Josephine Bakhita to Servant of God Dorothy Day to St Teresa of Kolkata and others; as well as contemporary, remarkably faith-filled women alive today. One is left with profound gratitude for the witness, courage, fidelity, servant leadership, integrity, compassion and faith of the women illuminated within these pages. It is a celebration of women and their voices, actions, service, leadership and indelible contributions.

Today is the Feast of St Mary Magdalene, Apostle of the Apostles, on whose faithful witness all of Christianity rested. I can't think of a more appropriate date to commend this rich and inspiring resource, a gift to all women and men who care deeply about the role of women in the Church over millennia and especially now in the 21st Century.

July 22, 2019
Kerry Alys Robinson
Woodbridge, Connecticut, United States of America

FIRST MILLENNIUM:

Setting the Context

1

Introduction

The Catholic Church in the third millennium is on the threshold of change. Forces from within and without are gathering momentum. Change is inevitable. Therefore, now in the twenty-first century leaders are needed who listen to the Spirit, and who are prepared to step outside their comfort zone and challenge the status quo! Thus inspirited, and serving as change agents, they can respond to the Gospel's call to service and engage in active discipleship. These contemporary leaders are stewards of the legacy gifted by women and men of previous generations, whose charism has been embedded in their leadership practices and in their lived response to the Gospel.

While acknowledging and respecting the great efforts of many charismatic leaders in history, the book honours in a special way, Mary Mother of God and all women who have served and graced the Church in leadership positions across three millennia. The analysis includes an investigation into the lives and works of significant female leaders in the Catholic Church throughout the centuries and is followed by an emphasis on current and emerging global trends, with selected women leaders giving voice to their role within the contemporary Church. Implications for the future regarding change and growth in the Church, highlight the voices of the youth and reference the Apostolic Exhortation *Christus Vivit* "Christ is Alive" (Pope Francis, 2019), the Post-Synodal response to the XV Ordinary General Assembly of the Synod of Bishops on "Young people, the Faith and Vocational Discernment" (2018). Finally voices from the past to the present – challenge future leaders!

Structure

The book is divided into three sections covering three millennia. The First Millennium comprises Chapters 1 to 5. Discussion commences with the Introductory chapter which states the overall purpose of the study, followed by a brief outline of the content of all twenty-one chapters. Chapter 2 is divided into two parts: Part I – honours the leadership of Mary with acknowledgement by the Church of her status as "Mother of God", and "Mother of the Church" (CCC, 1997:para.963); and Part II – comprises a profile of Mary that emphasises the "Historical Mary", describing images and doctrine from the post-Vatican II Church, and includes various interpretations of Marian and feminist theologies. Mary's faith journey is depicted through the Gospel narratives, and the perceived model of her leadership, reflects the Gospel's call to service (Mark 10:43-45), thus setting the scene for the remainder of the book, which highlights the very significant contribution of selected women leaders throughout the history of the Catholic Church.

Chapter 3 is also divided into two parts: Part I – explores the concept of St Mary Magdalene as "Apostolorum Apostola" (Apostle of the Apostles), and is a precursor to Part II – which involves a discussion on the active role of women officeholders, including female deacons and teachers in the early Church. In Chapter 4, there is a brief digression from the focus of the overall research, to present arguments regarding leadership practices that are analysed in the ensuing chapters. In this chapter service is described as "the essence of leadership", and the discussion centres on how faith and values determine leadership and behaviour. Reference is given to appropriate publications that highlight servant leadership, and values-based leadership as Christ-centered approaches, that may appeal to leaders of faith-based organisations and communities.

Chapters 5 through to 18 commence with a background and profile, followed by a "Leadership as Service" section, in which the lives and works of fourteen significant female leaders throughout the centuries are investigated, according to the seven pillars of servant leadership, using selected attributes as a guide (see Appendix A) and incorporating the values of dignity, respect, fairness, justness and equality (see Chapter 4 for the terms of reference).

Role Models

The role models for the *First Millennium* were decided quickly. I knew that Mary as Mother of God and Mother of the Church would be the forerunner, and her model of leadership in responding to the call of the Gospel, would serve as a guide for women leaders in the Catholic Church. I then investigated the origins of Christianity, and identified St Mary Magdalene and the women office holders, including female deacons and teachers, as leaders who performed significant roles in the early Church. Finally, the concluding chapter in this first section incorporates the profile of one of the "great women" of antiquity, St Monica – wife, saint, and mother of St Augustine, Doctor of the Universal Church, and considered by many scholars, to be one of the greatest theologians and teachers that the Catholic Church has produced.

The *Second Millennium* section comprises Chapters 6 through to 18. These chapters profile the lives and works of thirteen female leaders, whose service to the Church has transcended the centuries and whose leadership capabilities have inspired and continue to inspire contemporary leaders and followers. In Chapters 6, 8, 11 and 13, I investigate the lives and works of the current (2019) four women doctors of the Catholic Church: St Hildegard of Bingen, St Catherine of Siena, St Teresa of Ávila and St Thérèse of Lisieux. In these chapters I have included, and revised, information written previously in my first two publications on the four women: "Leadership as a call to service The life and works of Hildegard of Bingen" (2015), and "Leadership as a call to service The lives and works of Teresa of Ávila, Catherine of Siena, and Thérèse of

Lisieux" (2012). Please note in this book, the women doctors of the Church are investigated according to the year of their birth, and not according to the year of their proclamation as Doctors of the Universal Church.

Following considerable thought, prayer and discussion with colleagues, I eventually formulated the remaining list of nine significant female leaders, whom I believed would be representative of the many women who have graced the Church, with their service and leadership qualities and practices. Hence the selection of women leaders throughout the ages is not random but consists of leaders who have inspired me throughout my educational and academic career. I acknowledge that other researchers may have their own ideas on whom they would have chosen to honour in this way, and indeed, if circumstances permitted a study of all women throughout the lens of time (from creation until the present day) – female members of religious orders, married women, mothers, single women, female saints, doctors of the Church and others – I suggest that the findings would reveal, that the number of women who have given service to God, Church and humanity, would be close to infinite and therefore beyond the scope of this book!

Consequently, I opted to profile and investigate the lives and works of the following women, whose charism is embedded in the legacy of their service to others: St Clare of Assisi, Co-founder of the Order of Poor Clares; St Joan of Arc who is mentioned (along with St Monica, St Catherine of Siena, St Teresa of Ávila and others), in the 1988 Apostolic Letter of Pope St John Paul II *Mulieris Dignitatem* on the "Dignity and Vocation of Women"; St Angela Merici, Foundress of the Ursuline Order; Caroline Chisholm who was involved in philanthropic work in Australia, England and India; Blessed Frances Siedliska who was the Foundress of the Sisters of the Holy Family of Nazareth, the Congregation of nuns that I entered at the age of 14 and left at 21, a year prior to making final vows; St Mary of the Cross MacKillop, Australia's first canonised saint and Co-founder of the Sisters of St Joseph of the Sacred Heart;

St Josephine Bakhita, who is the patron saint of victims of slavery and who has been singled out as a role model by Church authorities in their efforts to raise awareness of human trafficking – a global problem in the 21st Century; the American social activist and Servant of God, Dorothy Day, who has always held my interest as an ordinary 'modern' woman who lived an extraordinary life; and finally Mother Teresa, now referred to as St Teresa of Kolkata, Foundress of the Missionaries of Charity – a contemporary saint who so influenced a personal friend of mine that she shared her experiences of meeting the Saint and her sisters in the early 1980s at their mission in Bourke North West NSW Australia.

Please note the chapters in the Second Millennium section are of varying lengths depending on existing resources and the availability of significant data that address *Leadership as a call to service*, regarding research on women and leadership in the Catholic Church.

Leadership Roles & Implications for the Future

The *Third Millennium* section comprises Chapters 19 through to 21, with the focus on "Current and Emerging Global Trends". Chapter 19 emphasises the "dignity, roles and rights of women" (Pope St John Paul II, 1995b) within the contemporary Church. Selected women leaders give voice to their role in relation to their faith journey in the Church, thus following in the *Footsteps* of the significant women leaders throughout the centuries. Implications for the future call for "greater involvement of women in leadership, decision making, and ministry roles in the [life of the] Church" (Women Matter, 2017, September 28). Implicit consideration is given to the question: "Will listening to the spirit, and developing a growing awareness of *Spiritual, Cosmic* and *Existential* realities", herald a renaissance for women leaders in the Catholic Church?

Chapter 20 is dedicated to the "Voices of the Future – the Youth of the Church", in which senior college students (female and male), have generously provided this researcher with their thoughts on faith, service, and leadership regarding the role of women and leadership in the contemporary Church. Implications and recommendations for the future are included in the chapter. Responses have been collated and summarised, and due to the lengthy number of submissions, copies not included in the chapter, are available from the author upon request. It is possible that this initial project on *Voices of the Future*, may be considered as pilot research and later used as a springboard for further investigation involving female and male student leaders at selected local, national and global colleges and universities! In this chapter there is also mention of the XV Ordinary General Assembly of the Synod of Bishops on "Young People, the Faith, and Vocational Discernment", that was held in Rome in October 2018.

Finally, Chapter 21 summarises the findings that have emerged from the various discussions, and information presented over the preceding chapters. There is reference to the 2019 Post-Synodal Apostolic Exhortation *Christus Vivit* "Christ is Alive", which includes an emphasis on life, change and growth in the Church. The women leaders from the past give voice to those in the present with a message, challenging future leaders (female and male) to step up and be the leaders God wants them to be. In sum, "When God created humankind; he made them in the likeness of God. Male and female, he created them, and he blessed them, and named them 'Humankind' when they were created" (Genesis 5:2). And again, "Whoever wishes to become great among you must be your servant ... For the Son of Man came not to be served but to serve" (Mark 10:43-45). Hence, whether we are called to lead or to follow we have a mandate from Christ to serve. For it is in this way, that we are called to action (Pope Francis, *Laudato Si'*, 2015).

To recap, the initial chapters prepare the reader for the subsequent chapters spanning decades, centuries and millennia, whereby women leaders in the Catholic Church, including not only those who have been honoured with sainthood and doctoral status, but seemingly ordinary women living extraordinary lives, who while loyal and committed members of the Catholic Church, an organisation that is hierarchical in nature and structure, could lead and serve within their own milieu, while challenging the status quo and calling for dignity and respect through fairness, justness and equality; thus paving the way for greater acknowledgement and involvement of women leaders in the Catholic Church in the twenty-first century.

With this book I hope to inspire, inspirit and empower the next generation of female Catholic leaders – and indeed all leaders, regardless of gender and/or religious affiliation, so that those who lead and serve others, will work together in a spirit of solidarity and communion. Hopefully then, by acknowledging diversity and inclusion, these leaders will emulate the servanthood of Jesus Christ, by living the Gospel values and engaging in a mission of ongoing active discipleship!

Let us begin our leadership journey commencing with Mary, a woman who is incomparable and "without sin" (CCC, 2000:para.491), but who was – nevertheless, a human being, who experienced love, pain, suffering and loss, and who was and is a role model for leaders and believers – past, present and future!

2

Mary – Leading the Way

In the *Catechism of the Catholic Church* (CCC) we read that "Mary truly became the Mother of God by the human conception of the Son of God in her womb" (2000:para.495). The Church refers to this event as the "Incarnation" when "the Word Became Flesh". Initially in this chapter it was my intention to emphasise this defining moment, which became the pivotal point in the focus of my research on the leadership role of Mary. However, in my naivety I assumed that the study would be straightforward and would reinforce the concept of Mary that had accompanied me throughout my childhood, young adulthood and into the twilight years of my life – that is the image of a gentle, elegant beautiful lady, serene in appearance and surrounded by a luminescence – an image perhaps similar to how I envisaged Mary would have appeared to St Juan Diego in 1851 (Our Lady of Guadalupe), to St Bernadette in 1858 (Our Lady of Lourdes), to the three children of Fatima in 1917 (Our Lady of Fatima) and to possibly others over the centuries.

Yet, my research has given me a renewed understanding of the image of the Mother of Jesus Christ, and new-found perspectives have enlightened my previous narrow concepts of Mary's faith journey – all touching on areas that transcend my thinking as a lay person – a lay woman within the Catholic Church. This chapter is divided into two parts. The first part investigates how the Church has honoured Mary, and the second part explores the concept of the historical Mary.

Part 1

Church Honouring Mary

As I researched the chapter on Mary, I began to realise the enormity of the task I had set myself and my dilemma was how to present Mary as a role model for leaders of the Church and other faith-based organisations in the twenty-first century, while still maintaining the mystique that has enveloped and continues to envelop a woman, so extraordinary and unique that as early as the year 431 during the Council of Ephesus the presiding Christian Bishops proclaimed that Mary was truly the Mother of God – *Theotokos* [God-Bearer], (CCC, 2000:para.495).

This formal recognition by the Church of the divine motherhood of Mary, is but one of four Marian dogmas, defined as revealed truths by the Catholic Church. The remaining three dogmas include (1) the *Perpetual Virginity of Mary* where the Church maintains that Mary was a virgin before, during and after Christ's birth (Council of the Lateran, 649); (2) the *Immaculate Conception* proclaimed by Pope Pius IX in his Apostolic Constitution 'Ineffabilis Deus', December 8, 1854 which states that "The most Blessed Virgin Mary, from the first moment of her conception, by a singular grace and privilege from Almighty God and in view of the merits of Jesus Christ, was kept free of every stain of original sin" (Catholic News Agency [CNA], 2017:2); and (3) the *Assumption* which was proclaimed by Pope Pius XII on November 1, 1950 in the Apostolic Constitution 'Munificentissimus Deus' and states that "Mary, Immaculate mother of God ever Virgin, after finishing the course of her life on earth, was taken up in body and soul to heavenly glory."

The proclamation of the four Marian dogmas signify Mary's relationship with God and the Church, and thereby demonstrate her leadership model potential, with which contemporary leaders (female and male) may want to identify and emulate in their leadership practices. However, though my research incorporated contacting Marian academics and accessing several Marian resources including Marian libraries, I found that while there was a great volume of data on Mary there was a dearth of information that explicitly referred to Mary's leadership role within the Church. Hence the paradigm of leadership associated with Mary in this book is based on my own previous leadership experiences, and on my interpretation of the available information on Marian doctrine and Marian theology investigated during the research.

In addition, while analysing and investigating the available data on Mary as an effective leadership model for the contemporary Church, I was very conscious of following the rules of hermeneutics whereby when interpreting biblical texts, that I analyse the texts critically "to know what the author wanted to communicate, to understand intended meanings, and to place documents in a historical and cultural context" (Richard Palmer, 1969, cited in Michael Patton, 2002:114). I was aware also that my present-day approach to interpreting the texts should not be an excuse for distorting the information or "reading into the material what was not intended" (Cameron, 2012a:171), particularly if there was a need to discern fact from myth.

My investigation then led me to the beginning – to the first book of the Bible – Genesis (Gen 2:4-24; Gen 3:1-24). This awareness of Genesis had been prompted by a publication that engaged my interest early in the research, when I noted that the author equated Mary with the biblical Eve. The work was entitled: *God's Mother, Eve's Advocate* (Tina Beattie, 2002) and Beattie's treatment of the topic throughout the book is from a feminist perspective. Beattie (2002:183) posits that "Together Eve and Mary provide symbols of time and eternity, of history and eschatology, of the present reality and the future promise of life in Christ and the Church for women." Interestingly, I found that the imagery of Mary as the New Eve had been raised by some of the early Church fathers, though I had been previously unaware of this analogy, and the likely significance of the interplay and duality of the roles of Mary and Eve.

However, Beattie's publication and the Apostolic Letter *Mulieris*

Dignitatem (Pope St John Paul II, 1988), soon enlightened me regarding the comparison between Mary and Eve. In his letter, the Pope reflects on the Eve-Mary dichotomy emphasising that apparently it was a theme "frequently taken up by the Fathers, ecclesiastical writers and theologians" (para.11). The Holy Father compares Eve and Mary stating that Eve as "the mother of all the living (Gen 3:20), is the *witness to the biblical 'beginning'*, which contains the truth about the creation of man, made in the image and likeness of God and the truth about original sin" (para.11). The Pope then refers to Mary as a witness but a witness to "the new *'beginning'* and the 'new creation' (cf 2 *Cor* 5:17), since she herself, as the first of the redeemed in salvation history, is 'a new creation': she is 'full of Grace'" (ibid.). Though this missive of the Pope explains in part Mary's role in the history of salvation, I was still a little perplexed as to the relationship between Eve – a 'sinner', and Mary – Mother of God!

Mary Hines (1991:283) offers some explanation regarding this enigma: "In the parallel between Eve and Mary, Eve is depicted as the woman whose disobedience brought sin into the world, while Mary's obedience, in the words of Irenaeus, 'became the cause of salvation both for herself and for the whole human race.'" The article also posits that as the image of the 'disobedient' Eve and the 'obedient' Mary "entered into the tradition, real women became more and more associated with Eve, while Mary became increasingly idealized, as both virgin and mother, a model impossible for real women to achieve" (ibid.). From a leadership perspective I considered how would a 'real' female leader looking for a model to emulate, view this scenario? Would contemporary women leaders identify with Mary 'the Mother of God' as the 'New Eve' or with Eve 'the sinner'? And Why? These questions are addressed in the following section of this chapter on the "Profile of the Historical Mary".

It is interesting to note however, that to reinforce her statements on the attitude of some of the early church fathers to Eve's part in the 'fall story', Hines includes a message to women from Tertullian, who was a noted North African and Christian theologian in the second century

(Cameron, 2009:21). In the quotation Tertullian is reminding women not only about how they should dress but he also gives his perception on how their 'folly' led to the fall of humankind, and the subsequent need for redemption and salvation:

> I think you should be dressed in mourning garb, neglecting your appearance, filling the role of mourning and repentant Eve in order to expiate more fully by all forms of penitential dress what women derive from Eve – I mean the ignominy of original sin and the odium of being the cause of the fall of the human race ... The sentences of God on this sex of yours lives on even to this day and so it is necessary that the guilt should live on. You are the one who opened the door to the devil, ... you are the one who persuaded man whom the devil was not strong enough to attack ... Because of your desert, namely death, even the Son of God had to die (Tertullian, cited in Hines, 1991:283).

Harsh words to the women of the time and beyond – but are they just?

Within the Church opinions vary (Personal correspondence, 2017), but for some, the Eve-Mary analogy is just one of the many images of Mary together with her prolific titles that are projected in this chapter (and elsewhere) all of which serve to highlight the leadership model potential of the Mother of God for aspiring women leaders in the Church in the twenty-first century. Prior to and since the proclamation of Mary as the Mother of God in the first century, Marian devotion has spread throughout the eastern and western Churches. Hines (1991:284) writes that "Medieval times saw the development of ever-increasing marian devotion, leaning toward extravagance."

Indeed, through the centuries, devotion to Mary seemed to hit a crescendo with the building of cathedrals and churches in the name of the Blessed Virgin Mary and the organising of Marian pilgrimages. Marian treatises and books were written; Marian icons, sculptures and art were created; and various prayers, litanies, pious and devotional practices (including an emphasis on the regular recitation of the Holy Rosary) were followed religiously. However, from about the 16th Century and following the Reformation, the protestant churches were not impressed with this emphasis on Mary. Hines tells us (reinforcing the words of St Paul) that "The Reformers moved to reassert that there is only one mediator between God and human beings, Jesus Christ" (1991:284). And because of the widespread increase in devotion to Mary in the "post-Reformation period Mary was almost eliminated from the Protestant traditions, while marian devotion became a rallying symbol of Roman Catholicism" (ibid.).

The dogmas on Mary and her reported apparitions at Guadalupe in 1851, Lourdes in 1858 and to the three children at Fatima in 1917; reinforced the Marian themes that were becoming so popular with believers. Popes wrote at length on the Mother of God (refer to the Vatican website to access the numerous documents on Mary) and spoke often of the Mother of God "who occupies a place in the Church which is the highest after Christ and yet very close to us" (Pope St Paul VI, *Lumen Gentium*, 1964:para.54, Ch.8).

In 1959, during the latter half of the second millennium, Pope St John XXIII spoke about an inspiration that came to him to call a Council – an "Ecumenical Council" (Joseph A. Komonchak, 1995:6). The inspiration became a reality when he convoked the Second Vatican Council in 1963. The major theme of the Council was the Church and the document on the Church was referred to as the "Dogmatic Constitution on the Church" – *Lumen Gentium*. My point in discussing the convocation of the Council is because prior to Vatican II, Pope St John XXIII had organised for a "Marian preparatory theological Commission ... to incorporate the conciliar teaching on Mary in a separate document" (Sr Thomas Mary McBride, 2003:1) to that on the Church. Several drafts on the proposed document were prepared but were then rejected during the Council.

Though the Council fathers recognised Mary's "central role in the work of redemption ... A substantial minority ... had expressed the desire that the Council not promulgate any new Marian doctrines, particularly because of the ecumenical implications" (Komonchak, 1995:257/260) for the members of the commission were conscious of the "theological implications of 'mariology' for the ecumenical world" (Walter M. Abbott, 1967:446). Yves Congar, a Council father, had even referred to a "galloping mariology" and so there was a concern that if there were to be advances towards unity then there should be no new dogmas on Mary (Komonchak, 2000:369). The dialogue became heated as the Council fathers argued whether to situate Mary in the document on the Church, or to introduce a separate document that would celebrate her unique role within the Church.

Though the debates were at times intense, the Council fathers continued to reinforce the high esteem in which Mary was held. Those who wanted a separate document on Mary wanted to respect her dignity, "As the Most Holy Mother of God ... [Mary] was, after her Son exalted by divine Grace above all angels and men" (Abbott, 1967:94), and those who wanted Mary included in the document on the Church were very conscious of the ecumenical trends of the day and for the sake of unity, wanted Mary to be acknowledged and be viewed more favourably by the various Christian churches (McBride, 2003:5). The Council wanted to produce a document that would "satisfy all the fathers" (ibid.).

The deliberations swayed 'to and fro' with very little progress – first a decision was made to go one way and then after further discussion, the majority of the fathers opted to go another way. And so, heated debates continued – in time, however, it became apparent that there were "Two issues [that had] become the touchstones of the argument involving Mary – the titles of Mediatrix, and that of Mother of the Church" (Komonchak, 2003:55). The title of Mediatrix for Mary was not popular with some of the fathers who argued that St Paul's directive regarding

Christ as the one and only Mediator was quite clear (p. 56). Pope St Paul VI, who was elected Pope following the death of Pope St John XXIII on 3 June 1963, was in favour of bestowing on Mary the title of 'Mother of the Church', however this was not an idea that appealed to the majority of the Council fathers.

One of the most inconsequential arguments against the title of Mother of the Church was from a bishop who stated that: "If Mary is the Mother of the Church and the Church is our Mother, then Mary must be our grandmother; if Mary is the mother of the Church and Mary is a member of the Church, then Mary is her own mother" (cited in Komonchak, 2003:59). Such an outlandish statement was promptly dismissed but it does give some idea of the length to which some of the Council fathers were prepared to go to prove their point. Finally, on 29 October 1963, after much deliberation, the Council fathers opted by a slight majority to include Mary in the document on the Church and not in a separate document. The title of Mother of the Church was not used in the document and the title of Mediatrix was to be included in a litany of Marian titles and not listed separately so as not to detract from Christ as being the "one [and only] mediator".

Surprisingly however, when Pope St Paul VI concluded the third session of the Council on 21 November 1964, he declared that Mary would be given the title of *Mater Ecclesiae* "Mother of the Church" – a move described as perhaps more of a 'personal action' rather than a collegial action on behalf of the Council, and it was noted that the title was not an infallible "doctrine on the spiritual maternity of Mary" (cited in Komonchak, 2003:447). The Holy Father had been keen for the Council Fathers to include the title in the Constitution on the Church but when this did not eventuate, he decided to act on his own initiative and as Bishop of Rome he made the decision to give Mary the title regardless of opposition from several Council fathers.

Interestingly, the title "Mother of the Church (*Mater Ecclesiae*)" was not new for it had been used by Berengaud, Bishop of Treves (d.1125) in his writings. Later authors such as St. Antoninus, Archbishop of Florence (d.1458) and St. Lawrence Justiniani (d.1455) also invited the church to venerate Mary as her Mother" (Matthew Mauriello, 1996). Hence there was some pre-history as it were, regarding Mary and the title of "Mother of the Church"! The Catechism (2000:para.964) emphasises Mary's role in the Church as being "inseparable from her union with Christ and flows directly from it. 'This union of the mother with the Son in the work of salvation is made manifest from the time of Christ's virginal conception up to his death.'" The Catechism also states that "We believe that the Holy Mother of God, the new Eve, Mother of the Church, continues in heaven to exercise her maternal role on behalf of the members of Christ" (St Paul VI, CPG § 15, cited in CCC, 2000:para.975).

In her maternal role as Mother of Christ, Mother of the Church and Mother of the people of God, there is no disputing the leadership qualities of Mary. However, it appears that since Vatican II, there has generally been a decrease in Marian devotion globally. Many factors may have precipitated this decline – for example, possible fall-out from the debates that surrounded the Vatican Council's decision on *Lumen Gentium* or indeed perhaps the "re-emergence of the woman's movement" (Hines, 1991:286), for "according to feminist historiography, the feminist movement was riding the crest of its 'second wave' [1950s-1980s]", (Cameron, 2009:14). Hines posits that "The feminist movement awakened a suspicion on the part of women that Mary had contributed to their oppression and marginalization in society as well as the church" (1991:289).

If you remember earlier in this section, Mary was compared to Eve and it was suggested that real women would associate more with Eve the 'sinner', than Mary in her 'idealized' form. In the initial paragraphs to this chapter I also referred to a Mary who is generally depicted by the Church as visually 'immaculate' – a beautiful woman surrounded by light, who projects perfection and prosperity but seemingly not adversity or poverty! To view Mary then from the perspective of history, the following section on the "Profile of the historical Mary", will portray the mother of God as a 'real woman' – a woman with whom other women can identify and empathise – a woman whose leadership qualities are evident in her faith journey through the gospel stories that sequence the life, death and resurrection of her divine Son Jesus Christ.

Part II

Profile of the Historical Mary

I approached this section with confidence and enthusiasm – again with preconceived ideas of a historical Mary – and once again I was otherwise enlightened! My image of the child Mary and her family was that of a young child and an older couple. I was aware that Mary's Mother was called Anne and her father Joachim. Surprisingly, I found that there is no recorded information in the scriptures regarding Mary's parents. However according to tradition (Catholic News Agency [CNA], 2017:1), "documents outside of the Biblical canon do provide some details. Although these writings are not considered authoritative in the same manner as the Bible, they outline some of the Church's traditional beliefs about Joachim, Anne and their daughter."

These documents which include information that may or may not be authentic, are referred to as apocryphal gospels and include the "Protoevangelium of James", which is the First Gospel of James – though not believed to be referring to the James in scripture who is portrayed as a relative of Jesus (Catholic Bible, NT:228). This Gospel is sometimes referred to as the "Infancy Gospel of James" and it is thought to be from the second century. There is also the "Evangelium de nativitate Mariae – Gospel of the Nativity of Mary", which may have been written around the third century (Encyclopaedia Britannica website).

The above documents reveal that Anne, the mother of Mary was born in Bethlehem, Judea and that Mary's father Joachim, was a member of the twelve tribes of Israel. Apparently, the couple lived in Nazareth and were wealthy, though childless and desperate to have a baby. In time their years of prayer and fasting were rewarded by the appearance of an angel, whom it is written informed Anne that she would soon become a mother, and that "all generations would honor their future child" (CNA, 2017). When the baby was born, she was given the name "Mary" – and her parents rejoiced at this miracle from God.

In the Protoevangelium of James (ibid.), there is reference to Mary being presented as an offering to God at the temple in Jerusalem, when she was a young child. On the Western Church calendar, this is celebrated as a liturgical feast – the Presentation of the Blessed Virgin Mary (21 November). Additional Liturgical feasts established, because of the Protoevangelium, have included the Nativity of the Virgin Mary (September 8) and the Immaculate Conception (December 8).

According to tradition and legend, information in the Protoevangelium reveals that, "Mary's parents, along with the temple priests, subsequently decided that she would be offered to God as a consecrated Virgin for the rest of her life, and enter a chaste marriage with the carpenter Joseph" (p.1). Now in the Protoevangelium of James there is mention that Joseph was an older man also living in Nazareth, and having been previously married, was widowed and the father of sons (cited in Walker [Trans.], 1886:4). However, in the pastoral Letter on the Blessed Virgin Mary "Behold Your Mother: Woman of Faith" (1973) by the National Conference of Catholic Bishops in the United States, there is reference to a change in opinion regarding the age of Joseph, and it is now thought that at the time of his marriage to Mary which was arranged by her parents, that Joseph may have been about 18 years old and Mary around 14 years of age.

There are few references to Mary in scripture. Interestingly, Ludwig Hageman (cited in Irarrazabal, Ross and Wacker, 2008:67) maintains that

"Mary is accorded more space in the Koran than in the New Testament, and as far as biographical details are concerned, the Koran has more to relate about Mary than the New Testament writings. What the Koran says about Mary's birth, childhood, and the signs that she was divinely chosen (cf. Koran 3.33) are very reminiscent of what is related in the New Testament, apocrypha, especially in the infancy gospels." However, though Mary is recognised as the Mother of the prophet Jesus and though she is well-respected and a greatly admired woman in Islamic tradition, she is not venerated as the "'Mother of God' for the Koran does not acknowledge Jesus as the son of God" (p.73).

Sister M. Danielle Peters tells us that there are "four different occasions when Mary's words are recorded in the Bible." These include the *Annunciation* (Luke 1:26-38); the visit of Mary to her cousin Elizabeth where she recites the *Magnificat* (Luke 1:46-56); finding the child Jesus in the Temple (Luke 2:41-52); and the *Wedding at Cana* (John 2:1-11). Peters (ibid.) states that there are several occasions where Mary is mentioned in the scriptures particularly, in the Gospels of Luke and John. In these instances, she is referred to as Mary or the Mother of Jesus. Father Bertrand A. Buby (Marian Library, Dayton University) writes that though there is little recorded information on Mary in Scripture some relevant passages can be found in the four Gospels, the Acts of the Apostles, Revelations and selected letters of St Paul.

Thus, how does the world perceive Mary? Mary was a real human being – she was born and grew to adulthood. She loved, suffered, aged and died? However, perceptions of her appearance vary. Johnson (2003:205-206) maintains that early artistic representations may be inappropriate:

> Miriam [Mary] of Nazareth's physical appearance ... [it is] obvious that not only are the blond hair and blue eyes typical of so much European and North American art inappropriate, but so too is the delicate, unworked physique of a privileged, teenage beauty queen. Art critics note that Renaissance portraits depict women with exquisitely

beautiful features whether they were actually beautiful or not ... Was Miriam of Nazareth beautiful? Perhaps. Perhaps not. Along with the women of her class and ethnic heritage, she had Semitic features, Mediterranean dark hair and dark eyes. Given her everyday life, she also would have had a muscular body shaped by the routines of hard daily labor.

The poet Kathleen Norris (cited in Johnson, 2003:206) supports this description of Mary. Norris "identifies the need for artists today to produce more work that envisions Mary as a strong peasant woman 'capable of walking the hill country of Judea and giving birth in a barn,' a woman with a robust physique both in youth and in old age." Recently in an email to a Marist Brother I expressed my thoughts (refer to the beginning of this chapter) as to how I perceived Mary. The response (Personal correspondence, 2017) was as follows: "In recent years we Marist Brothers have actually committed ourselves in some places, to commissioning where feasible, images that speak more directly to our young of the post-Vatican 2 Church. Images such as that of the village peasant girl in St Stephen's Cathedral in Brisbane [please note this statue of Mary has since been moved to St Stephen's Chapel]" is one such example.

Some cultures depict the Madonna (Mary) and child with the features of their ethnicity – which would perhaps lead to their communities identifying more with Mary and her son in a religious and spiritual sense. We can all conjure up images in our mind of how we perceive historical figures such as Mary, however, is a preoccupation with "the cosmetic dimensions of how Mary looked or was dressed" (Personal correspondence, 2017) important? Let us retrace our steps back to the first century in Galilee to the home of a young Jewish peasant girl who followed the Torah religiously, lived in relative poverty and who was betrothed to Joseph. This ordinary individual was soon swept up in the most extraordinary experience that has been gifted to humankind, whereby she (Mary) became the "the Mother of the Saviour in the economy of salvation" (*Lumen Gentium*, 1964:para.55).

In Luke (1:26-28) we read that the angel Gabriel was sent "by God to a town in Galilee called Nazareth to a virgin engaged to a man whose name was Joseph, of the House of David. The virgin's name was Mary." The heavenly messenger greets the young woman before him and reassures her that there is no need for fear, "for you have found favour with God. And now, you will conceive in your womb and bear a son, and you will name him Jesus …" (ibid.).

Mary showed much courage in her response. What was this apparition that had appeared before her? Why was she singled out from all her peers? Did Mary cower in fear at the intrusion of a stranger or beg for her life (if feeling threatened) or indeed was she so submissive of a perceived patriarchal authority that she felt she had to confer with her husband Joseph before responding – No! She kept her cool as it were and had a rational response and was perplexed as to how such a phenomenon could happen since she was a virgin. Some may question why would Mary be married and still be a virgin? The following offers one explanation. Apparently, the Jewish marriage has two parts:

> Betrothal: The first part of the two-part process of Jewish marriage, which creates the legal relationship without the mutual obligations. In Hebrew it is called: *kuddushin* (sanctification). *Kiddushin* is far more binding than an engagement as we understand the term in modern English. Once *kiddushin* is complete the woman is legally the wife of the man. The relationship created by *kiddushin* can only be dissolved by death or divorce. However, the spouses do not live together at the time of the *kiddushin*, and the mutual obligations created by the marital relationship do not take effect until the *nisuin* is complete. The *nisuin* (elevation) finalizes the marriage process. The husband brings the wife into his home where they begin their married life together.

(From the *Glossary of Jewish Terminology* – refer to http://www.jewfaq.org/glossary.htm#B)

Hence though Mary was legally the wife of Joseph they had not yet lived together as husband and wife, so Mary was somewhat confused by the message from the heavenly visitor. The angel affirmed that: "The Holy Spirit will come upon you, and the power of the Most high will overshadow you; therefore, the child to be born will be holy; he will be called the Son of God" (Luke 1:35-38). Mary responded in faith "Here am I, the servant of the Lord; let it be with me according to your word" (ibid.). As mentioned earlier it doesn't appear as if Mary felt the need to ask permission of Joseph or her elders regarding such a momentous decision that would affect not just her own life but that of the child she would conceive. Hence, one moment – one decision in time – changed history! Mary's marriage and life with Joseph was forever transformed. Indeed because of her faith response, Mary "became the cause of salvation for herself and for the whole human race" (St Irenaeus, cited in CCC, 2000:para.994).

Nevertheless, there may be some unbelievers (or even believers) who may query the circumstances of the Incarnation. For example, regarding the actual conception of Jesus, Raymond Brown (1977:527, cited in Johnson, 2003:227) speculates after reading the Gospel of Matthew, that:

> [P]eople remembered that Jesus was born too early after his parents started to live together ... While the evangelist emphasizes that despite the scandal this child is the fruit of the action of the Holy Spirit from earliest times reading the historical nucleus of the tradition of this too-early birth, present also in Luke's infancy narrative, thinkers from the second century onward have endorsed four different options.
>
> First Joseph was the biological father who conceived Jesus with Mary while they were in the betrothal stage of their marriage.

Second, an unknown man seduced Mary and committed adultery with her.

Third, a Roman soldier, usually given the name Panthera forcibly violated Mary, rape not being an unknown behaviour in the Roman army.

Fourth, it was a physical, biological miracle, the Holy Spirit of God causing the genesis of the child in Mary's womb in the absence of any human biological father.

This last position, technically known as the virginal conception of Jesus, became and remains the official teaching of the Catholic Church, giving rise to the ancient appellation of Mary as Virgin Mother.

As reiterated by Johnson (above) the Catholic Church affirms that "The gospel accounts understand the virginal conception of Jesus as a divine work that surpasses all human understanding and possibility. 'That which is conceived in her is of the Holy Spirit'" (CCC, 2000:para.497). Similarly, Mary Christine Athans (2013:74) cites the work of Jane Schaberg on the perceived *Illegitimacy of Jesus* stating that "Schaberg's interpretation ... on the illegitimacy of Jesus [possibly from rape], is strongly grounded in feminist hermeneutics." Schaberg posits that the father of Jesus was a soldier called Pantera. However, Athans (2013) maintains that Schaberg's interpretation is "highly speculative ... [and] even Schaberg [herself] admits that her proposal is conjecture" (p.75).

What is important and what is acknowledged, is the concept of God becoming man – the Incarnation – an extraordinary event that has led to the redemption of humankind. And where did such a significant event occur – in a palace – in a church – in a grand city or in a very large town? No! When "The Son of God assumed human nature and became man to accomplish our salvation" (CCC, 2000:883), he chose as his mother a poor Jewish, peasant girl who lived in a humble dwelling in a small village called Nazareth in Galilee.

The village of Nazareth is located within the area known as "Lower Galilee" in Palestine and is built on the side of a soft rocky incline. There are fertile valleys and fresh water in the area. Hence, agriculture and farming often supplement the income of the inhabitants (Jean-Pierre Isbouts, 2016:11). If Joseph farmed as well as utilised his carpentry and craft skills, then this may explain the reference to agriculture in some of the parables of Jesus (ibid.). Johnson maintains that archaeological evidence has uncovered "olive presses, wine presses, and millstones for grinding grain, indicating the rural character of this village", but she also emphasises that no obvious signs of "wealth" were revealed in the archaeological finds within the village environs, thus indicating that poverty was prevalent (2003:13).

Isbouts writes that, "Most Galilean farmers lived with their families and relatives in multifamily dwellings, grouped around a courtyard that usually featured a [communal] clay oven" (2016:11). Johnson supports this description and adds that the small buildings were grouped together, "three or four ... around a courtyard open to the sky" (2003:142). The absence of archaeological evidence however "leads scholars to conclude that the roofs were thatched, constructed of thick bundles of reeds tied over beams of wood, and most likely covered with packed mud for additional protection" (ibid.), and hence due to the weakness in structure, the dwellings would not stand the test of time!

Towards the end of BCE and the beginning of CE, Galilee was "deeply affected by the arrival of the Herodian dynasty" (Isbouts, 2016:8), and the occupation of the Roman army. Herod the Great was appointed King of Judea by Rome, and history records that his reign was violent. According to Johnson (2003:14) he was ably supported by the Roman legions whenever the Jewish community, many of whom hated their king, decided to rebel. "In 4 BCE [Herod died and] three legions put down a Jewish uprising; they crucified two thousand men around Jerusalem and, marching on Sepphoris, four miles from Nazareth, 'burned the city and enslaved its inhabitants.'"

In a culture of poverty, exacerbated by an economy sapped by heavy taxes imposed by violent rulers; living in a society over-run by a foreign power, and fighting for survival in a land where the burning of villages and the slaughter of devout Jewish residents was a reality; this is the scenario where we situate the historical Mary. Johnson (2013) informs us that:

> Living in Nazareth, Miriam [Mary] would have been around fifteen or sixteen years old at the time [during the uprising and slaughter following Herod the Great's death in 4 BCE], a young married woman with a new baby. She obviously survived the damage inflicted on her neighbourhood by brutally efficient, rampaging Roman legions. Did she hide with other village women in a cave in the Nazareth ridge as the tidal wave of violence come sweeping down? What terror, what loss from deaths, rapes, and looting had to be coped with? How much rebuilding absorbed their energy when psychically they were at a low ebb and materially, they had so little to begin with?
>
> Sad to say, the wretched wars of the late twentieth and early twenty-first centuries, reported in the press and shown on television, leave little work for our imagination. Watching village women over the years in Vietnam, El Salvador, Bosnia, Indonesia, Congo, Afghanistan, and elsewhere flee, hide, be injured, all the while trying to protect their children from forces intent on their destruction conjures their courage and suffering in real time. The world of Miriam of Nazareth was no stranger to such violence and social disruption (p.153).

During her lifetime Mary endured pain and oppression. As I write this chapter, I am viewing a map (historical in origin) showing "The Ministry of Jesus in Lower Galilee" (Isbouts, 2015:18-19). On the right-hand side of the map and in the lower corner the country of Syria can be located. This morning (Friday 9 February 2018) media reports described bombings and atrocities occurring in present-day Syria. As a woman and a mother, Mary, who experienced indescribable pain and suffering at circumstances that led to the death of her son as a convicted criminal, would surely identify with, and understand the pain and anguish that many people – women, in particular, are experiencing globally today, and in countries that are so close to her own?

Yet there are some who say they cannot identify with Mary because they cannot see the human side of one who is 'without sin', for the Church emphasises that Mary "was preserved from all stain of original sin and by a special grace of God committed no sin of any kind during her whole earthly life" (CCC, 2000:para.411). Astrid Lobo (cited in Johnson, 2003:9-10) who is "a young Christian woman in India … expresses the frustration of many of her peers who find Mary too high, too holy, and too innocent to be of much use for their own spiritual growth":

> As a human being constantly struggling through difficult choices, I could find no comfort in this docile Mary who said 'Yes' so easily to God. As a young woman faced with the challenge of taking up my rightful role in society, I just could not understand this Mary tucked away inside her four walls. She was the 'virgin most pure' with whom I could never share the excitement of my flowering sexuality. What could this sinless woman understand of my weakness and failure?

What are the inferences here regarding virginity and purity? Can a person be pure and yet not be a virgin? Is there a universal definition for virginity? "Marianne Katoppo in Indonesia and Rita Mateiro in India … [argue] that virginity refers to the state of being whole in oneself rather than biological abstinences from sex." Cunneen (1996, cited in Athans, 2013:70) refers to "Asian Christian women [who] insist that 'virgin' symbolizes Mary's autonomy, not her sexual celibacy." Warner (1983, cited in Athans, 2013:67) "believes that the image of Mary as both virgin and mother, in whom opposites are reconciled, is responsible for women's frustration. 'By setting up an impossible ideal, the cult of the Virgin does drive the adherent into a position of acknowledged and hopeless yearning and inferiority.'"

But what really is the issue here? Those of us who are females, let us celebrate our womanhood – Virginity, purity, sexuality – and all that this entails. Cunneen (1996, cited in Athans, 2013:70), "challenges readers not to put Mary on a shelf, but to appreciate her in all her humanity." Whether female or male we all make choices and generally most of us live out our humanity each day according to our response to our own inner and outer needs and realities. Pope St John XXIII (*Pacem et Terris*, 1963:para.41) reiterates the importance of contemporary women 'flexing' their humanity: "Women are gaining an increasing awareness of their natural dignity. Far from being content with a purely passive role or allowing themselves to be regarded as a kind of instrument, they are demanding both in domestic and in public life the rights and duties which belong to them as human persons." The Pope is emphasising that women are calling for dignity and respect. Rosemary Radford Ruether (1974, cited in Athans, 2013:67-68) argues that such a justness in the attitude towards women was not always the case. According to Athans:

> In her [Ruether's] chapter "Misogynism and Virginal Feminism in the Fathers of the Church," she opened the eyes of many women to the radically dualistic teachings of revered saints and scholars whose negative attitudes toward women in the early centuries affected the church for years to come. Their writings influenced the formulation of teachings on the virginity of Mary and on sexuality in general. In a world with a dualistic perspective, and some such communities exist even today, the spiritual and the material are in opposition. Men are identified with the higher elements of life: the spiritual, the intellectual, light, and good. Women are identified with the material (the body

as opposed to the spirit), emotion and will (as opposed to intellect), darkness (as opposed to light), and evil (as opposed to good). In the patristic era the only way a woman could rise above her carnal condition was to commit to a life of virginity (ibid.).

Athans maintains that in the early Church: "Statements of Augustine, Tertullian, Jerome, and even Clement of Alexandria regarding women shocked many readers" (ibid.). You may recall in the first section of this chapter I cited a quotation from Tertullian that I consider would be offensive to the women of the time and indeed to women of any era. Have these theologians perpetuated emphasis on the virginal state of Mary, rather than celebrating Mary for her womanhood and her motherhood?

Mary "is the representative and the archetype of the whole human race: she *represents the humanity* which belongs to all human beings, both men and women" (Pope St John Paul II, *Mulieris Dignitatem*, 1988:para.4). Mary serves therefore she leads. Her leadership of service is reflected in the leadership of her son for "The Son of Man came not to be served but to serve" (Mk 10:45). Pope St John Paul II in his Apostolic Letter on the Dignity of Women (1988:para.5) emphasises that:

> From the first moment of her divine motherhood, of her union with the Son whom "the Father sent into the world, that the world might be saved through him" (cf. John 3:17), *Mary takes her place within Christ's messianic service*. It is precisely this service which constitutes the very foundation of that Kingdom in which "to serve ... means to reign". Christ, the "Servant of the Lord", will show all people the royal dignity of service, the dignity which is joined in the closest possible way to the vocation of every person.

Many contemporary women want to see, to visualise Mary as a real woman who experienced life at its best and at its worst. I suggest that

Mary lived such a life! She was born during the tyranny of Herod the Great; she experienced poverty all her life; she had to face her husband Joseph when he became aware of her impending motherhood and the realisation that he was not the father; she witnessed her son being treated like a criminal then crucified and finally dying on a cross. She held her dead son in her arms. Admittedly Mary is not alone in her pain – somewhere in the world today there are women who are suffering unbearable pain – because of human trafficking and bondage; racial prejudice; verbal and physical abuse; rape; sexual degradation; poverty; alcohol and drug addictions; abuse because of their sexual orientation and much, much more. These women are crying out for respect and dignity though fairness, justness and equality. Who will listen to so many voices calling out (in agony and despair) to be heard? Who, but Mary (Mother of God and Mother of the Church), can lead these women on a faith journey in which they might find some solace in their hour and time of need?

Mary's leadership can be traced through her faith journey in the Gospels, where the various events in her life as depicted in the Gospel are emphasised. For example you may recall in Luke (1:26-38), when Mary as an inspirited teenager asked "the tough questions of the heavenly visitor"; and again when she faced the village gossips and their derision while "protecting her beloved Joseph about her unexplained pregnancy"; then when she visited her cousin Elizabeth to share the news of her impending motherhood and "her singing [of] Hannah's beautiful prayer from 1 Samuel from which the Magnificat (Luke, 1:39-56) clearly comes; indeed, a young woman … [who remained] always the faithful and practising Jewess who does Torah and takes her child to temple and to synagogue, and whom we can assume, teaches the budding Jesus his prayers and Torah practices and who finds his behaviour inexplicable and painful when he goes missing at the age of 12 [Luke, 2:41-51] in the bustling city of Jerusalem" (Personal correspondence, 18 August 2017).

As her son grew Mary realised that his teaching, parables and miracles would bring him to the attention of the Jewish and Roman authorities. At the Wedding at Cana she spoke with authority to her Son and he agreed to her demands even though he didn't think that he was ready to begin his public life (John, 2:1-11). John's Gospel places Mary at the foot of the Cross and even if she was not physically present on this occasion, she would have experienced every nail being driven into his body, as if it was piercing her heart (19:25-27). And finally, in Acts (1:14-15) there is reference to Mary being included in the group assembled in the room at Pentecost – "the beginning of the new 'age of the Church'" (CCC, 2000:893). As the mother of Jesus, Mary participated in the ministry of leadership of her Son. She was not just a token leader. Her faith journey resulted in a paradigm of leadership that was a discipleship of love.

What leadership does the contemporary Church require of us (women in particular)? What do women leaders in the Church in the 21st century ask of the Church? Mary was graced and favoured by God and so with Mary leading the way, let our leadership serve to reflect our values as we continue our own faith journey!

Turn now to Chapter 3 and participate in the narrative of some inspiring women leaders who have graced the pages of the Old and the New Testaments. The chapter is divided into two parts in relation to the role of women leaders in the early Church with Saint Mary Magdalene *Apostolorum Apostola* being introduced in Part 1 and Women office holders including women deacons and teachers comprising the content in Part II.

3

The Role of Women Leaders in the Early Church

There are many inspiring women who grace the pages of both the Old and the New Testaments (cf Catholic Bible Press, 1990) and undoubtedly, we all have our favourites. However, the sheer magnitude of the numbers of biblical women preclude the listing in this chapter of all but a few – selected significant women in the New Testament, who held an active leadership role in the early Church. To date Mary, Mother of God has led the way with her own faith journey and there has been the Mary-Eve analogy (see Chapter 2). Hence, prior to addressing the topic of this chapter, I have collated the following list of selected names from the Old Testament of women with whom I have been most impressed over the years, and whose names would be familiar to biblical scholars and interested readers alike. Information available regarding the narrative of their lives combined with the challenges associated with the faith journey of these amazing women, reveal that their extraordinary courage and strong leadership contributed to the transformation of Jewish history, and ultimately paved the way for the advent of Christianity:

Sarah (Abraham's wife) [Genesis 11:27-30]	Rebekah (Isaac's wife) [Genesis 25:19-28]	Rachel (Mother of Joseph – Egypt) [Genesis 30:22-24]
Miriam (Sister of Moses & Aaron) [Exodus 1:7-8; 15:20-21]	Deborah (Prophetess – Judge) [Judges 4:4-23; 5:1-31]	Ruth (Wife of Boaz – genealogy of Jesus) [Book of Ruth]
Hannah (Mother of Samuel) [1 Samuel 19-28; 2:1-10]	Bathsheba (Mother of Solomon) [2 Samuel 12:24-25]	Queen of Sheba (Gifts to Solomon) [1 Kings 10:1-13]
Judith (Wealthy Widow) [Book of Judith]	Esther (Queen) [Book of Esther]	Anne (Mother of Mary) [Protoevangelium of James – refer to Chapter 2 – Part II]

(Catholic Bible Press, Old Testament, 1990)

This chapter is situated in the "First Millennium" of the Catholic Church and is divided into two parts with Part I emphasising the role of St Mary Magdalene (*Apostolorum Apostola*) and Part II concentrating on "Women Officeholders – Deacons & Teachers".

Part 1

St Mary Magdalene (*Apostolorum Apostola*)

Perhaps one of the most recognisable names within the New Testament is that of Mary Magdalene (cf Catholic Bible Press, 1990); hence, I decided to allocate a separate section of this chapter to the faith journey of this remarkable woman. But who was Mary Magdalene? You may be aware that she was one of several women who provided support for Jesus and his disciples (ibid.). Scholars maintain that Mary Magdalene came from the ancient town of "Magdala". In his National Geographic magazine publication on "Jesus and the Origins of Christianity", Jean-Pierre Isbouts includes a map depicting historic sites in relation to the "Ministry of Jesus in Lower Galilee" (2016:18-19). The map reveals that Magdala is located on the left-hand side of the Sea of Galilee, with Nazareth perhaps some days walk to the south-west and Capernaum situated to the north-east of Magdala further around the Sea of Galilee. It is feasible then, that during his ministry and travels Jesus would have passed through Magdala on his way to Capernaum which, at the time, was considered to be an "important trade route" and therefore, a good base for his Galilean ministry (p.19).

Other routes along which Jesus may have travelled during his ministry are included on Isbouts map, together with a citation from Luke's Gospel (8:2-3), which recounts the times when Jesus was travelling from town to town proclaiming "the good news of the kingdom of God ..." And that during this time the "twelve were with him, as well as some women who had been cured of evil spirits and infirmities [including] Mary, called Magdalene, from whom seven demons had gone out" (ibid.). Some scholars highlight this "demonic" experience of Mary Magdalene, but there is little evidence in the scriptures apart from a description of the incident, with no reason given for her condition.

Mary Jane Chaignot (2018) in her article on "Mary Magdalene and Seven Demons" posits that "In J.B. Phillips the interpretation of the seven devils are seven evil spirits" (para.2). However as mentioned, there is little evidence to support this in scripture. Interestingly Chaignot (para.4) associates "demon possession ... [with] mental illness" so it is possible that Mary suffered from a psychological illness but again such a diagnosis would just be conjecture. Suffice to say that Mary Magdalene may have been "possessed", but would have been cured prior to accompanying Jesus, his disciples and the other women, as they traversed the countryside on their mission of preaching and spreading the good news.

The surname 'Magdalene' identifies Mary "with [Magdala] the place of her birth, just as Jesus was called 'the Nazarene' because of his association with Nazareth" (Bible Gateway, 1988). Unfortunately, though "We have no record of Mary's parentage, her marital status or her age. That she was free to follow Jesus in His journeyings would suggest that she had no home or family obligations" (para.2). Further research reveals that, "in the time of Christ the town of Magdala was a thriving, populous town … [and the industries included] Dye works, and primitive textile factories [that] added to the wealth of the community" (para.1). However, the following quotation describes a downside to this ancient town with its seemingly affluent economy:

> The Jewish *Talmud* affirms that [the town] Magdala had an unsavory reputation, and because of the harlotry practiced there was destroyed. Doubtless it was from this tradition, and from the fact that Luke's first reference to her follows the story of the sinful woman, that the idea developed that Mary was a prostitute, but there is not an iota of genuine evidence to suggest such a bad reputation (para.3).

Ancient Magdala was thought to have been destroyed by Roman forces during the Great Jewish War in 67 CE, and according to the Magdala website (2018), the destruction of the town was "punishment for its wickedness." Jennifer Ristine, contemporary Director of the Magdalena Institute in 2018, quotes from her book *Mary Magdalene: Insights from Ancient Magdala*, and states that in "A Jewish writing called the Lamentations Rabbati refers to three towns that were destroyed for their sinfulness, among them [was] Magdala" (Personal correspondence, 2018).

Ristine (ibid.) emphasises that though she is using "the Jewish Talmud … in … [her book] … some historians question the validity of its use." She offers two reasons for this – it (the Jewish Talmud) may not reflect the reality and/or, "it could be referring to a different Magdala."

However according to Ristine, "Ancient Magdala was uncovered in 1970 and again in 2009" (ibid.), and the site is still in evidence today with pilgrims "flocking to St Mary Magdalene's hometown" (2016).

As a young child I recall reading bible stories, and believing that Mary Magdalene was a sinner, who washed the feet of Jesus with her tears and then wiped his feet with her hair, but the Gospel of John (12:1-8), reveals that it is Mary of Bethany the Sister of Martha and Lazarus, who anoints the feet of Jesus with perfume and then wipes them with her hair. Matthew (26:6-13) and Mark (14:3-9) recount a similar incident occurring in Bethany but they do not identify the woman.

Given my recent research I conclude that my childhood memories of the Gospel passage may have come from Luke (7:36-50), but again in this Gospel the woman is not named. She washes the feet of Jesus with her tears, anoints them with ointment and wipes them with her hair: "he [Jesus] said to her, 'Your sins are forgiven ... Your faith has saved you; go in peace'" (ibid.). Was this woman Mary Magdalene, a repentant sinner? Had she lived as a prostitute and upon meeting Christ was so profoundly affected by his teaching and his example that she chose to follow him as a disciple? The scriptural passages cited in this paragraph do not identify Mary Magdalene as the sinner.

Understandably then, there has been some controversy, particularly during the early centuries of the Church regarding Mary's role in the scriptures (Richard Covington, 2008). Apparently three "'characters' were cited in this controversy: (1) Mary Magdalene, follower of our Lord (John 20:11-18); (2) The anonymous penitent woman (Luke 7:36-50); and (3) Mary of Bethany, the sister of Martha and Lazarus (Luke 10:38-42)", (Father William Saunders, 2004). Interestingly, in the early Eastern Church, the three characters were regarded as three different women, but in the western Church especially during the time of Pope St Gregory the Great, the three characters were all identified by Gregory as one and the same person, namely – Mary Magdalene (ibid.).

Hence, Pope St Gregory determined that Mary Magdalene was the subject of all three biblical passages and according to Covington (2008), "reasoned that if a woman like Mary, who had fallen so low, could be forgiven, through faith and the church [and] her carnality transformed into spirituality, [then] the worst sinners could hope for salvation." You may recall the constant references in Chapter 2 (Part 1) to Eve being responsible for the fall of humankind; now once again a woman has been depicted in an unacceptable manner to enhance the faith and spiritual life of all who seek salvation. Covington (ibid.) cites Pope St Gregory's reference to Eve and Mary Magdalene in his "famous sermon in 591" where he argues that "In paradise, a woman was the cause of death for ... man; coming from the sepulchre, a woman proclaimed life to Men." Irrespective of Pope St Gregory's analogy however, the portrayal of Mary Magdalene as a prostitute, is not supported in the scriptures, where Mary Magdalene is mentioned at least a dozen times and, on all occasions, there is no suggestion that she was a harlot, a prostitute or a promiscuous woman.

The following scriptural references recount Mary Magdalene's participation during those traumatic days that culminated in the passion, death and resurrection of Jesus Christ:

The Death of Jesus

Matthew (27:55-56) writes that there were many women present when Jesus was crucified and: "Among them were Mary Magdalēne, and Mary the Mother of James and Joseph, and the mother of the sons of Zebedee." Mark (15:40-41) identifies some of the women who were present at the crucifixion: "among them were Mary Magdalēne, and Mary the mother of James the younger and of Jōsēs, and Sālomē." He mentions that other women were also present though he does not name them. Luke (23:49) maintains that the "acquaintances [of Jesus] including women" who had followed him from Galilee were present at the crucifixion, but Luke does not refer to the women by name. John (19:26) is the only one of the four to record the presence at the crucifixion of Mary the Mother of Jesus: "standing near the cross of Jesus were his mother, and his mother's sister, Mary the wife of Clōpas and Mary Magdalēne." John also refers indirectly to his own presence, "Jesus saw his mother and the disciple whom he loved standing beside her."

The Burial of Jesus

The four gospel writers verify the role of Joseph of Arimathēa as the person who organised for the tomb in which the body of Jesus was placed. Matthew (27:60-65) records that a stone was rolled across the doorway while "Mary of Magdalēne and the other Mary were there, sitting opposite the tomb." On the following morning, there was a request by the chief priests and Pharisees to have a command issued to secure the tomb: "until the third day; otherwise his disciples may go and steal him away, and tell the people, 'he has been raised from the dead' ... Pilate said to them [chief priests and Pharisees], You have a guard of soldiers; go, make it as secure as you can."

Mark (15:46-47) writes that "a stone [was rolled] against the door of the tomb. Mary Magdalēne and Mary the mother of Jōsēs saw where the body was laid." Luke (23:55-56) does not refer to Mary Magdalene when he mentions that women from Galilee "saw the tomb [of Jesus] and how his body was laid. Then they returned, and prepared spices and ointments." John (19:38-40) does not refer to women being present at the tomb. He writes that "Nicodēmus ... also came, bringing a mixture of myrrh and aloes ... [Nicodēmus and Joseph Arimathēa] then took the body of Jesus and wrapped it with the spices in a linen cloth, according to the burial custom of the Jews."

The Resurrection of Jesus

Matthew (28:1-10) recounts that Mary Magdalēne and "the other Mary" on the day following the burial of Jesus, both went to the tomb at dawn and found an angel had descended from heaven and had rolled back the stone at the door. Sensing the women would be afraid, the angel reassured them:

> Do not be afraid; I know that you are looking for Jesus who was crucified. He is not here; for he has been raised, as he said. Come, see the place where he lay. Then go quickly and tell his disciples, "He has been raised from the dead, and indeed he is going ahead of you to Galilee; there you will see him. This is my message for you." So, they left the tomb quickly with fear and great joy and ran to tell his disciples. Suddenly Jesus met them and said, "Greetings!" And they come to him, took hold of his feet, and worshiped him. Then Jesus said to them, "Do not be afraid; go and tell my brothers to go to Galilee; there they will see me."

In this passage there is a reference to Mary Magdalēne and "the other Mary". Scripture does not reveal the identity of this other "Mary". Mark (16:1-8) begins with Mary Magdalēne but informs us that she is going to the tomb with Mary the Mother of James and Salōmē to anoint the body of Jesus. As with Matthew's recount the women meet the angel who tells them not to be alarmed. They are asked to go and tell the disciples, but Mark's account differs here from Matthew's in that he states that the women are so frightened by what they have witnessed that "they said nothing to anyone". However, Mark has inserted an additional extended version in that he changes his narrative to Jesus appearing to Mary Magdalene only (16:9-11):

> Now after he rose early on the first day of the week, he appeared first to Mary Magdalēne, from whom he had cast out seven demons. She went out and told those who had been with him, while they were mourning and weeping. But when they heard that he was alive and had been seen by her, they would not believe it.

Interestingly, Chaignot (2018:para.2) writes that: "Most scholars agree that the verses 9 – 16 at the end of Mark were probably not written by the original author. Mark's gospel, for whatever reason, ended abruptly at (16:8). Someone found that totally unsatisfactory and added a better ending, borrowing most of the ideas from others."

Luke (24:1-11) tells us that the women went to the tomb with spices and that they saw not one but two men "in dazzling clothes". The message is similar to that recorded in the other Gospels where the women are asked to inform the apostles and it is here that Luke refers to Mary Magdalēne. "Now it was Mary Magdalēne, Jōanna, Mary the mother of James and the other women with them who told this to the apostles. But these words seemed to them an idle tale, and they [the apostles] did not believe them."

John (20:1-18) recounts the Resurrection of Jesus by maintaining that just one woman went to the tomb on the morning after the burial of Jesus and that one woman was Mary Magdalēne: "Early on the first day of the week, while it was still dark, Mary Magdalēne came to the tomb and saw that the stone had been removed from the tomb." John then describes Mary's encounter with Simon Peter and himself after running to find them and telling them that Jesus had been taken and that there was now no sign of him. All three then went back to the tomb and found the linen cloths in which the body of Jesus had been wrapped. After the two disciples leave, Mary Magdalēne is still distraught and weeping at the tomb. John tells us that there were two angels who ask her why she is weeping, and she told them about Jesus having been taken and that she didn't know where he was. A man approached her whom she assumed to be the gardener and she asked him where Jesus had been taken.

> Jesus said to her, "Mary!" She turned and said to him in Hebrew, 'Rabboūnī!' (which means Teacher). Jesus said to her, "Do not hold on to me, because I have not yet ascended to the father. But go to my brothers and say to them, "I am ascending to my Father and your Father, to my God and

your God." Mary Magdalēne went and announced to the disciples, "I have seen the Lord"; and she told them that he had said these things to her.

According to all four canonical gospel writers (Matthew, Mark, Luke and John), Mary Magdalene is the first witness to the Resurrection of Jesus. Heidi Schlumpf in her article "Who Framed Mary Magdalene?" – reflects on the fact that Mary Magdalene "was a woman whose name and reputation have become so misunderstood, misinterpreted, and misconstrued over the centuries that she is more commonly, though erroneously, remembered as a prostitute than as the faithful first bearer of the Good News" (2000:para.2).

Karen King, Professor of New Testament Studies and the History of Ancient Christianity at Harvard University Divinity School (1998) disclosed that recent, "Discoveries of new texts have now proven that her [Mary Magdalene's] reputation as a repentant prostitute is entirely inaccurate." Here King is referring to early Egyptian writings which include the gnostic gospel of Mary Magdalene. The gnostic gospels, "are writings by early 'Christian' Gnostics ... [and] are [considered] forgeries, fraudulently written in the names of the Apostles to give them a legitimacy in the early church" (gotquestions website, 2018). Such documents are not recognised as orthodox by the Church.

However, King (ibid.) posits that: "the newly discovered Egyptian writings ... [portray] Mary as a favoured disciple – a woman leader among the disciples ... an influential figure ... a prominent disciple and leader of one wing of the early Christian movement that promoted women's leadership", and this is also what can be interpreted from the canonical gospels. King (ibid.) reminds us that Mary Magdalene was the first witness to the Resurrection of Jesus and that as a follower of Jesus and assisting with his mission she undertook the role of apostle, "[and that] Later Tradition ... will herald her as 'the apostle to the apostles.'"

Ute E. Eisen in *Women Officeholders in Early Christianity* (2011:51) provides two examples of how "Mary Magdalene was interpreted as an apostle":

> Hippolytus of Rome (235/36) explains the gospels' description of women having been the first witnesses of the resurrection by saying that Christ met the women on Easter morning "so that women, too, would be Christ's apostles." Theologically, he proposes the events at the tomb and the women's acting as the first witnesses [see the Gospel passages above] as the antithesis of Eve's disobedience, and he emphasizes Christ's empowerment of women as apostles ... Gregory of Nyssa (ca.334-394) also interpreted the women's status as first witnesses as antithetical to the story of the Fall. He mentions Mary Magdalene as witness to the empty tomb, as recipient of the angel's message, as eyewitness to the Risen One, and finally as the bearer of the joyful news to the disciples.

In the Gospel passages regarding the Resurrection of Jesus we see that John (20:1-18) was the only author (remember that Mark or an unknown author had extended Mark's version) who acknowledges that just one woman, Mary Magdalene, approached the tomb following the Resurrection of Jesus. John writes that when Jesus appeared to Mary, he told her to go and tell the apostles and others that he had risen from the dead. If this is an actual record of the events and if Mary Magdalene was indeed the first person approached by Jesus, then in contemporary terms (2019) Jesus commissioned her to spread the good news – to evangelise. This is the mission of the Church – "the carrying forth of the Good News to every sector of the human race" (Congregation for the Clergy, 1997:para.46), and the reason why the Church exists (ibid.).

In sum, has history been kind or fair to St Mary Magdalene? Has there been justness in how her life has been depicted by scholars and writers of biblical texts? She alone, was courageous and supportive when Jesus was betrayed and arrested; when he was taken by the soldiers and denied by Peter, who refused to acknowledge him; and when it seemed as if he had been abandoned by those closest to him. Where were the apostles when their Lord was being condemned and crucified? The gospels (apart from Luke) recount the presence of Mary Magdalene when he died. She was a witness to his suffering and death and though we are also informed of the presence of other women who had followed Jesus from Jerusalem and Galilee, not all these women are identified, except a few who are recorded in the gospels of Matthew, Mark and John.

In his gospel, John also implies his own presence and recalls that of Mary the mother of Jesus. Significantly when tensions in the region were still high following the arrest and subsequent execution of Jesus, Mary Magdalene, though experiencing profound grief and perhaps fearful of a confrontation with Roman soldiers, was bold and forthright, as she demanded to know where Jesus had been taken, after it was discovered that he was no longer in the tomb.

The Risen Christ appeared to Mary Magdalene and energised as a "messenger" (an evangelist) by this experience she spread the Good News and is credited in the contemporary Church with being the first witness to Christ's Resurrection. Unfortunately, the reward for so profound a love and unwavering loyalty was to have been portrayed throughout history as a woman without morals, as one who sinned against God and about whom the "Historian Jane Schaberg coined the term 'harlotization' to describe ... [the negative interpretation of Mary Magdalene's life by the early Church], a process that disempowered a powerful leader of the faith" (cited in Covington, 2008).

In recent years however, the Church has finally recognised the tremendous impact that Mary Magdalene had on its early history. On 10 June 2016 the Holy See Press Office announced the publication of a decree honouring Mary Magdalene in her role as *Apostolorum Apostola* (Apostle of the Apostles). And as mentioned she was given this title because she was the first person to see Christ after his Resurrection. The decree states:

As expressly wished by the Holy Father [Pope Francis], the Congregation for Divine Worship and the Discipline of the Sacraments has published a new decree, dated 3 June 2016, Solemnity of the Sacred Heart of Jesus, by which the celebration of St. Mary Magdalene ... will be elevated in the general [Roman] calendar to the level of a feast day.

The Feastday of St Mary Magdalene then is celebrated on 22 July. Archbishop Arthur Roche, who as secretary of the Congregation for Divine Worship and the Discipline of the Sacraments at the time, clarifies the meaning of the decree:

[It] will enable Mary Magdalene to be "celebrated" liturgically like the rest of the apostles. The decision is situated in the current ecclesial context, which calls upon us to reflect more deeply on the dignity of women, the new evangelisation and the greatness of the mystery of divine mercy. "Precisely since she was an eyewitness to the Risen Christ, she was also the first to testify before the apostles..."

Roche (ibid.) refers to Magdalene as "an evangelist, or rather a messenger who announces the good news of the resurrection of the Lord." He emphasises that the "special mission of this woman be highlighted, as an example and model to every woman in the Church." It appears then as if the Church has gained a new perspective on its previous opinion of this woman who was once considered a sinner, but who is now a saint of the Church, and who has been formally declared *Apostolorum Apostola*. But could Roche's need to clarify the decree be an implicit reminder of how the "supposed sinful" past of Mary Magdalene, was transformed into an inspiring narrative, so that she is now regarded as a role model to be emulated and respected by all in the Church?

Now some 2000 years after her death, Mary Magdalene has been officially honoured by the Church, which is respecting her "dignity", by acknowledging her spirituality – her strength and her leadership. She led and set an example for the followers of Jesus by proudly heralding the Good News of his resurrection, even though she knew that some members of the community would disbelieve and perhaps ridicule her, for spreading what they believed to be misleading rumours – for how could one who was dead and buried – still be alive? Sister Evelina Belfiore highlights the importance of the apostolic role of Mary Magdalene: "When Jesus spoke to Mary to go [and] tell the other disciples he was risen; it shows that woman has a complementary role in the mission [of the Church] and that we need one another. It's not [just] a man's church or a woman's church" (cited in *The Gazette* by Victor Greto, 1999). As equals then, we have a role to play and regardless of our gender, we complement one another. We are – the Church!

In the next section events leading to the appointment of selected women officeholders in the early Church including women deacons and teachers, are discussed in relation to leadership opportunities and practices during the first millennium of Christianity.

Part II

Women Officeholders – Deacons & Teachers

Christianity commenced with the ministry of Jesus Christ who was born and raised in a Jewish household in Galilee (Isbouts, 2016:13). You may recall from the previous section that scripture reveals that Jesus died on the Cross but resurrected on the third day. In Acts (1:6-11) we read that he ascended to Heaven about forty days after his Resurrection. A custom in Jerusalem at the time was that around fifty days after the Passover "Jewish pilgrims from all over the Roman world would travel to Jerusalem ... for ... the feast of *Shavuot* ['Weeks' in Hebrew, or 'Pentecost' in Creek, meaning 'fiftieth']. This feast celebrated God's presentation of the Jewish

Law to Moses on Mount Sinai" (Isbouts, 2016:25-26). Significantly since the death and resurrection of Jesus, and with the birth and growth of Christianity, the above "Pentecost" celebrations also now commemorate the birth of the Catholic Church. According to the Catechism:

> The Church is born primarily of Christ's total self-giving for our salvation, anticipated in the institution of the Eucharist and fulfilled on the cross. "The origin and growth of the Church are symbolized by the blood and water which flowed from the open side of the crucified Jesus." "For it was from the side of Christ as he slept the sleep of death upon the cross that there came forth the 'wondrous sacrament of the whole Church'" (CCC, 2000:para.766).

Marshall Connolly on the *California Network* (2016), refers to Pentecost as the time when "we, as Catholics celebrate the birth of our Church." The origin of Christianity and the subsequent emergence of the Church – have given life to the Gospel, which is energised by the light of the Spirit, which illuminates the way to the Living Light of Christ:

> When the work which the Father gave the Son to do on earth was accomplished, the Holy Spirit was sent on the day of Pentecost in order that he might continually sanctify the Church. Then "the Church was openly displayed to the crowds [who had all gathered in one place] and the spread of the Gospel among the nations, through preaching, was begun" (CCC, 2000:para.767).

Johnson (2003:299) writes that "Traditional artistic depictions of Pentecost portray the Spirit descending upon thirteen figures, one woman, Mary, surrounded by twelve male apostles." However, there is no reliable evidence as to the number or identity of all who gathered in the room on that occasion. In Acts (1:14-15) we read that indeed the mother of Jesus was present with other women and men but that the number present was about "one hundred and twenty persons." Isbouts

(2016:26) describes the venue where all assembled on this occasion as being a "safe house" – a haven for a group to meet whose leader Jesus Christ was no longer with them, and who were still fearful of retaliation by the Roman forces for their association with the Jewish "Rabbi".

In Acts (2:2-4) those present in the room became inspired by inexplicable events that occurred, which signalled to them that they were in the presence of the Holy Spirit. Their courage returned, and they were motivated to leave the room and "spread the word". They were ready to assume the mantle of discipleship. Johnson (2003:300) posits that "When the leader of a messianic movement dies, the movement frequently dies too. In the case of Christianity, however, something happened that changed this local Jewish movement into a worldwide religion."

To gain a deeper insight into the role of the women leaders in the formation of this "new worldwide religion", the faith journey and discipleship of some of the more memorable personalities from scripture during this time are discussed, including the women and men who emerged from the "safehouse" at Pentecost, and who became apostles because they were on a mission to preach the Good News (Mat. 28:19-20). Barbara Reid (2006:30) defines "The word *Apostolos*, 'apostle,' [as meaning] ... 'one sent,' an envoy or a missionary."

My research revealed a solid working relationship between Peter and Paul in the early days of their mission, following Paul's conversion and name change from Saul (book of Acts). On the historical map of the *Origins of Christianity* (Isbouts, 2016:32-33), I was amazed to see the extensive area covered by Paul in times when transport by land and sea would have been treacherous, and not, without its challenges. The numerous routes included those linking Jerusalem, Damascus, Antioch, Cyprus, Tarsus, Rhodes, Asia Minor, "gateway to the greater Roman Empire" (Isbouts, 2016:6), Greece, Macedonia, Sicily, Italy and many others – indeed an area covering practically the entire length of the Mediterranean Sea. Also, what I hadn't realised previously was that the

Jewish elders wanted Paul arrested and put to death for his preaching on Christianity and his passive interaction with the gentiles (Acts). The Jewish leaders believed that Paul was abandoning his Jewish faith and favouring the gentiles which to them was an absolute betrayal of his religion.

Nevertheless, after experiencing imprisonment on several occasions and often having the threat of imminent death "hanging over him", Paul managed to continue his mission and was ably assisted in his efforts to advance the cause of Christianity. Johnson (2003:301-302) posits that much of Paul's success was due to the "discipleship and apostolic witness" of the exceptional women of the gospel – women who had been the first to discover the resurrected Lord (see Part 1 in this chapter) and women who were gathered in the room at Pentecost, and who when inspirited left the sanctuary of the "safe house" and engaged in apostolic activity, spreading the good news that they had witnessed. However, Johnson (ibid.) adds that: "Given … [the] Pentecost beginning, one would expect many stories to follow of women's leadership in preaching and prophesying. Such is not the case. Luke [as the author of the Acts] focuses instead on the deeds of Peter and Paul, with little regard for women's ministry. Even where women are mentioned, incidentally and sporadically, as building up the church, we never hear them speak."

In Acts (16:11-15) we read of Paul's encounter with Lydia "a worship[p]er of God … she was from the city of Thatīra [Asia Minor] …The Lord opened her heart to listen eagerly to what was said by Paul". It is believed that Lydia was Paul's first convert though there is little evidence to support this. Reid (2006:31) maintains that Lydia "was a devout person attracted to Judaism but [at the time of meeting Paul she was] not a full convert … scholars disagree about her cultural and economic status. Some think that although she worked with luxury items [she was a dealer in purple cloth] she herself was not rich but was rather a freed slave." Eisen (2000:2/18) makes brief reference to Lydia including her in the group of women who were active in "the Christian lives of the [early Church] communities."

It would be impossible to analyse the contribution of all women leaders who influenced the growth of early Christianity, for though there were many who may have had ministerial roles, few have been mentioned by name in the new Testament. What is known is that some were apostles, others were prophets, and still others were widows and deacons. Surprisingly, Paul refers to just one deacon by name – Phoebe.

Ministries in the Early Church – Deacons

In his letter to the Romans (16:1-2), Paul writes: "I commend to you our sister Phoēbē, a deacon of the church at Cenchrēae, so that you may welcome her in the Lord as is fitting for the saints, and help her in whatever she may require from you, for she has been a benefactor of many and of myself as well." In her article *Desperately Seeking Phoebe*, Belinda Stringer (2016:15) comments on Paul's letter to the Romans (above):

> St Paul, in his letter to the Romans written around 56 CE commends Phoebe, the *diakonos* of Cenchreae. The scripture scholars point out that the term *diakonissa* (deaconess) was not used here but *diakonos*. Some editions of the bible refer to Phoebe as a deaconess, but the more recent editions recognise that her designation was *diakonos*, a title that acknowledged her as a minister and key figure in the community of Cenchreae.

In the *New Revised Standard Version* of the Bible, Paul's Letter to the Romans (16:1) has a reference note citing "minister" as an alternative word for "deacon". Stringer reflects on the link between the deaconate and ordination but stresses that at the time the meaning of ordination differed to how we understand the term today (ibid.). Barbara Reid in her article *Leading Ladies of the Early Church* (2006:28), gives various translations of the term *diakonos* – "deacon," "minister," and "servant".

Reid emphasises that "The translation 'deaconess' is incorrect. *Diakonos* is masculine in form; the feminine form *diakonissa* did not develop until the late third or early fourth century. In Paul's day there were no set job descriptions or titles, no official ordinations, no fixed lists of different tasks for different kinds of ministers" (ibid.).

Gary Macy (cited in Macy, Ditewig and Zagano, 2011) recalls the description given by the early Christian theologian Origen in the third century on Paul's words of praise for Phoebe: "This passage teaches by apostolic authority that women also are appointed in the ministry of the church". Now Paul cites the church at Cenchreae. On the historical map (Isbouts, 2016:32) Cenchreae was situated near Corinth and was not far from Athens. Macy (ibid.) discusses another passage of Paul in scripture where Paul is referring to the requirements for deacons and there seems to be conflicting opinions by scholars as to whom Paul was directing his advice – if it was just to female deacons or to both male and female deacons. The following is Paul's list of "Qualifications [expected] of Deacons" (1 Timothy, 3:8-13):

> Deacons likewise must be serious, not double-tongued, not indulging in much wine, not greedy for money, they must hold fast to the mystery of the faith with a clear conscience. And let them first be tested; then, if they prove themselves blameless, let them serve as deacons. Women likewise must be serious, not slanderers, but temperate, faithful in all things. Let deacons be married only once and let them manage their children and their households well; for those who serve well as deacons gain a good standing for themselves and great boldness in the faith that is in Christ Jesus.

When researching the role of women leaders in the early church I came across a book titled *The Woman's Bible* that had been first published by Elizabeth Cady Stanton in 1895 (Part I), and 1898 (Part II). The publication consisted of "a two-volume edited compilation of woman-centered commentaries on biblical passages" (Abstract by Elisabeth Schüssler Fiorenza, 2009, cited in Emily R. Mace, 2009:5), which presented women's views on various books of the bible. You may recall in Chapter 2, I referred to the work of Elizabeth Johnson (2003). Elizabeth when discussing a "celebration of the genders" (p.47) regarding the mission of females and males in the Church, cites Fiorenza who describes the missionary task as "a discipleship of equals" (p.41).

Interestingly, *The Woman's Bible* was not published again until 1972. According to Fiorenza (2009) when the Bible was first published "clergymen reviled it and Stanton's fellow suffrage leaders [Stanton was an American suffragist and a social activist] disassociated themselves from it ... [and] The work was out of print until the 1970s, when *The Woman's Bible* found a new home among second-wave feminist scholars of religion, who saw in Stanton a feminist forerunner and in her *Bible* a validation of their own efforts." During the latter part of the nineteenth century, Stanton and her supporters believed that women were not well-represented in the Bible and that "the Bible could do more to dignify women" (Benjamin Wayman, 2014:541). In our contemporary society biblical scholars (female and male) around the world have voiced their own thoughts on how they interpret the role of women in the bible.

The Woman's Bible provides information on Luke of which many readers would be aware – that he was a Syrian who was called "the beloved Physician" by Paul, and that both men worked together. Stanton (p.152) writes of Phoebe and the fact that:

> CHENCHREA was the seaport of Corinth, where a separate church was founded. Phoebe was a deaconess and was probably employed in visiting the sick and in teaching the women in the doctrines of the Church. She appears to have been a woman in good circumstances, and probably had more than ordinary intelligence and education. Even Paul acknowledged himself under great obligation to her.

The data reveals little more than what is found in Paul's letter (see previous paragraphs). Eisen (2011:2) writes that "Phoebe ... was a preacher of the gospel and at the same time a businesswoman who was not defined by a male ... that is by a father, husband or brother." Reid (2006:29) summarises Phoebe's role by stating that Phoebe would have been involved in service that would have included "apostolic ministry (Acts 1:25); of the table and of the Word ministry (Acts 6:2,4), and financial ministry" (Acts 11:29). According to Reid (ibid.): "It is likely Phoebe became the leader because she had the resources to host and finance the community. Another clue to her status is that Paul calls her his *prostatis* (Rom, 16:2). The *root* meaning of that word is 'leader', and in Greek literature it has political connotations." It is interesting that Paul is calling Phoebe his leader, but more evidence or concrete examples of the type of leadership are not provided.

Corrado Marucci in his essay *History and Value of the Feminine Diaconate in the Ancient Church* (cited in Zagano, 2016:30) analyses and collates the results of "many studies on the existence of a feminine diaconate in the New Testament and in the history of the Church." Although Marucci (ibid.) emphasises that: "Some traces of feminine ministries seem to be found in the New Testament. Other than Luke's emphasis on the presence of some women among Jesus followers" (Luke 8:1-3; cf Mark 15:40ff.), "the clearest and most ancient reference should be that of Romans (16:1ff) relating to Phoebe." Phyllis Zagano in her Introduction to *Women Deacons* (2016:xvi) refers to the (2010) work of Father Corrado Marucci SJ, in which he discusses the fact that there is only one "scriptural reference to a deacon by name" and that person is Phoebe.

Darius Jankiewicz (2013, April) repeats words of praise from St John Chrysostom (c 349-407), Doctor of the Universal Church, regarding the ministry of Phoebe believing that Phoebe was indeed blessed because she had "the blessing of so favourable a testimony from Paul ... [and she also had] the power to render assistance to him who had righted the whole world?" In addition, Jankiewicz (ibid.) posits that: "The role of Phoebe in early Christianity has been hotly debated throughout the centuries, ranging from views suggesting that her ministry was nothing more than that of a helper (or patron) of the apostolic task, to those ascribing to her a significant ministerial role."

Priscilla – Teacher

Paul mentions few women by name but one such prominent woman was Priscilla also referred to as Prisca. However, there is no mention in the scriptures that Paul refers to Priscilla as a deacon. On his arrival at Corinth Paul (Acts, 18:1-4) "found a Jew named Aquila, a native of Pontus, who had recently come from Italy with his wife Priscilla, because Claudius had ordered all Jews to leave Rome." Often when Paul refers to the couple, he addresses Priscilla/ (Prisca) first. Reid (2006:30) gives one explanation:

> This likely signifies that she was of a higher status than her husband. We have no description of what Prisca's ministry included. Most likely it strongly resembled that of Phoebe: presiding over worship, overseeing the education of the community, and coordinating ministries of hospitality, service, and evangelization.

Apparently, Prisca and Aquila hosted Paul during his time in Corinth and Luke tells us that they worked together. Reid (ibid) suggests that perhaps Prisca and Aquila "founded the church in Ephesus in modern-day Turkey" but there is no evidence of this in Acts. Marucci (cited in Zagano, 2016:32) refers to Priscilla "as being a collaborator of Paul … who in (Acts, 18:2, 26) … together with her husband Aquila catechizes Apollo." The actual passage reads:

> Now there came to Ephesus a Jew named Apollos, a native of Alexandria. He was an eloquent man, well-versed in the scriptures … he began to speak boldly in the synagogue; but when Priscilla and Aquila heard him, they

took him aside and explained the Way of God to him more accurately (Acts, 18:24-26).

Elizabeth Clark (1983:158-160) asserts that 1 Timothy (2:12) contradicts the above passage in which there is "an account of the Christian matron Priscilla's instruction of the male convert Apollos." In the first letter to Timothy we read that, "I permit no woman to teach or to have authority over a man; she is to keep silent". Clark (ibid.) gives a reason for the contradiction: "Chrysostom attempted to explain why Priscilla's teaching was praiseworthy while female instruction in general was not ... The following selection is from his homily *Greet Priscilla and Aquila*, on Romans (16:3).

> Apollos was an eloquent man, skilled in the Scriptures, but he knew only the baptism of John. This woman took him, instructed him in the way of God, and made him a perfect teacher (Acts 18:24-28). The women who lived at the time of the apostles did not participate in the things women do [p.159] today, so as to clothe themselves in splendid garments, beautify their faces with paint and eye makeup ... These women of earlier times discarded all these things. They rejected worldly vanity and sought one thing only, namely to become companions of the apostles and to share in their pursuits ... But why then, when he writes to Timothy, does he [Paul] say, "I do not permit a woman to teach, nor to have authority over a man" (1 Tim. 2:12)?
>
> This is the case whenever the man is reverent, holds the same faith, shares in the same wisdom. But if the man is an unbeliever, wandering in error, Paul does not deprive her of the power of a teacher ... [1 Cor 14:33-36]. But how can a believing woman save an unbelieving husband? Quite clearly, through her instructing, teaching, and leading him to the faith, just as Priscilla did for Apollos. In a word,

then, when Paul says, "I do not permit a woman to teach," he is talking about public instruction that involves arguing in front of people and about the teaching that befits the priesthood. But he does not rule out her exhorting and [p.160] giving advice in private. For if this had been ruled out, he would not have applauded Priscilla for her actions (ibid.).

Eisen (2000:100) states that Luke in the Book of Acts (relating to Priscilla and Apollos) had "no problem in depicting a woman as a Catholic teacher of a Christian man and missionary who was already instructed in the Scriptures and filled by the Holy Spirit." However, Eisen does acknowledge that, "The first restriction of teaching to the appointed officeholders of the Church who were emerging in the second century appears in the Pastoral letters. The restrictive intent is accompanied by a general prohibition on teaching by women … [and yet] women worked as theological teachers in the first centuries of the Church in a wide variety of ways" (pp.101, 103).

Another prominent woman and one who is credited for her expertise in teaching scripture was Macrina who is referred to as a "monastic leader … an exemplary teacher of the Word, respected by men and women, and by lay people and clergy alike" (Eisen, 2000:99). Eisen writes that Gregory of Nyssa was the younger brother of Macrina and that "In his literary work he clearly acknowledges Macrina's theological superiority" (ibid.). Gillian Clark (2015:93) maintains that Macrina was "one of the very few women in late antiquity who [was] said to have taught philosophy." Macrina then could be described as a theologian, a philosopher – a teacher – and a woman! Perhaps this commitment to teaching by women of the time, involved a "creative interpretation" in their understanding of the restrictions on teaching by women as outlined in the Pastoral letters!

From my readings of Paul, I believe that he had a huge respect for women and that perhaps over time his words may have been misinterpreted or taken out of context. However, I do agree that there have been occasions when if not "overtly but covertly restrictions were [and still are] imposed" by hierarchical authorities in the Church, regarding teaching and leadership opportunities available to women. John Toews in his article (1980) on *The Role of Women in the Church: The Pauline Perspective* supports Paul's affirmation of the "equality of men and women of faith":

> Paul affirms the equality of men and women of faith before God both in terms of privilege and gifts of the Spirit. All disciples of Christ and thus all members of the new eschatological community are empowered by the spirit and given gifts of the Spirit. Nowhere in Paul, or elsewhere in the new Testament for that matter, is the exercise of the gifts of the Spirit restricted on the basis of sex.

Overall then, Paul publicly affirmed the work of women and men who were engaged in the mission of apostleship.

Junia – Apostle

In Romans (16:7-8) Paul acknowledges another couple when he announces, "Greet Andronicus and Jūnia my relatives who were in prison with me; and they are prominent among the apostles, and they were in Christ before I was." Reid (2006:30) maintains that Andronicus and Jūnia are "A Less-Known pair", compared to others who were associated with Paul. However, they "were imprisoned with him, [and] were Christians before he was, and were "prominent among the apostles." Johnson (2003:301) asks us to "Recall Paul's salutation to the deacon Phoebe, leader of the church of Cenchreae [note the difference in spelling]: and to Jūnia, outstanding among the apostles in Rome…"

In a previous paragraph, Paul's expectation of the qualifications required of Deacons (1 Timothy 3:8-13) was cited. Reid (1 Cor 9:1-27) recounts the qualifications that Paul cites, "for apostleship". She maintains (2006:31) that the qualifications emphasise that the 'apostle' should have "seen the risen Lord and been commissioned by Christ to proclaim the Good News". Reid (ibid.) tells us that early church leaders "such as Hippolytus of Rome and Origen – who both died in the 200s – regarded Mary Magdalene as 'apostle to the apostles' … but that the gospels do not give her this title or 'the other Galilean women at the tomb' even though they all fulfil Paul's guidelines for apostles." Interestingly, Reid (ibid.) states that Jūnia is the "only woman given the title 'apostle' in the New Testament", even though there were several other women who were also considered apostles at the time. Eisen (2000:55) supports Reid's statements that: "While there are no other women in the New Testament context who are accorded the title of apostle, several have central importance in the first proclamation of the Christian message, especially Mary Magdalene and the other women at the tomb. This explains why these women were regarded as apostles and evangelists in the traditions of the ancient Church and the early Middle ages."

Some contemporary biblical scholars debate the gender of Jūnia. Eisen (2000) in her chapter on *Women Apostles in the New Testament* discounts the argument that Jūnia (sometimes referred to as Julia) may have been male:

> A striking witness within the Greek tradition of interpretation to the fact that Jūnia was identified in the early Church as a woman is the work of John Chrysostom. He comments on Romans (16:7) with the words: "It is certainly a great thing to be an apostle; but to be outstanding among the apostles – think what praise that is! She was outstanding in her works, in her good deeds; oh, and how great is the philosophy … of this woman, that she was regarded as worthy to be counted among the apostles!" (p.47)

Marucci (cited in Zagano, 2016:32) discusses the former tendency among scholars to portray Jūnia as male but, "now it seems in fact more probable that she was a woman (*Jūnia*), most of all because a corresponding masculine name different from the feminine has not yet been found in any literary of epigraphic source." Unfortunately, there is little recorded information available on the ministry of Jūnia.

Several women who accepted ministerial roles in the early Church supported each other and the Church with their monetary contributions. In Book II (1898) of the Woman's Bible, Stanton recounts the names of some of these women: "the early Church was immensely indebted to the benefactions of rich widows and virgin heiresses for the means of sustaining life in its fellowship. Thecla, Paula, Eustochium, Marcella, Melanie, Susanna, are but a few of the women of wealth who gave both themselves and their large fortunes to the establishment of the ethics of Jesus" (1972:137). Philippe Delhaye in his essay on *A View of the Past and Future of Feminine Ministries within the Church* (cited in Zagano, 2016:149) emphasises that the Pauline epistles, "recognise the apostolic activity of several women" including Priscilla who was also considered a prophet (Eisen, 2000:73).

Prophets

To have foresight is a privilege given to just a few. And "until the end of the second century the prophets, male and female, were regarded in Christianity as a necessary element of the Church in possession of the Holy Spirit" (Eisen, 2000:67). Eisen writes that there are references to "early Christian prophets" in the New Testament and that women were a part of this select group (ibid.). For example, "Luke characterizes Elizabeth (1:41-45) and Mary, the mother of Jesus (1:46-55), in similar fashion as prophets. Elizabeth 'utters a prophetic cry' and Luke places the Magnificat, a text shaped by Old Testament prophecy, on the lips of Mary." Other examples are cited in "Paul's letters, the Acts of the Apostles, and Revelation" (p.69). Eisen (2000:72) maintains that it could be said that "from the beginnings of Christianity women have acted as prophets (cf. 1 Cor 11:5; Luke 1:41-45, 46-55; 2:36; Acts 21:9; Rec 2:20).

The same is true for subsequent centuries." However, Eisen (ibid.) does stress that, "On the whole we can perceive a clear decline in prophetic activity and prophets in Christian literature from the end of the second century onward."

Presbyters

It was about the third century that "the role of presbyters ... [began] to emerge" (*National Catholic Reporter*, 2013). Regarding the possibility of there being women presbyters the inference is that while women may have been considered for the role of apostle or deacon, Epiphanius, Bishop of Salamis Cyprus, established that women would never hold "the rank of presbyter, that is, priest" (p.119). However, Eisen (p.121) does cite some instances in Asia Minor in the fourth century (apparently the role of presbyters gained impetus during this century), in which "Canon II of the Synod of Laodicea ... attests to ordained women *presbyters*, called presbytides, who acted as presidents of their congregations ... This canon is a second witness, in addition to Epiphanius, for the existence of such women officeholders on the one hand, and on the other hand for attempts to repress them in the fourth-century Church in Asia Minor." In the Catechism of the Catholic Church we read that, "Today the word '*ordination*' is reserved for the sacramental act which integrates a man into the order of bishops, presbyters, or deacons" (2000:para.1538). Presbyters then are priests who have received the sacrament of ordination.

You may recall that in a previous paragraph in this section of the chapter it is stated that the concept of "ordination" in the early Church had a different meaning to that of today (Stringer, 2016). Hence, when discussing ordination, it is important to understand where it is placed "in the definition of time". Macy (2013) in response to an interview in *U.S. Catholic Faith in Real Life* maintains, that "Under the later definition of *ordination*, these historical women weren't ordained." Macy (ibid.) in his response to questions regarding the changes to the definition of ordination as it was in the early Church, states that "ordination gets redefined in the 12th and 13th centuries."

Deacons – Eastern and Western Churches

The position in the Eastern and Western Churches differed regarding the period associated with the emergence of women deacons. In the Eastern Church, Marucci (2016:32-33) maintains that, "In the third century both Clement of Alexandria and Origen, when commenting on the corresponding passages in the New Testament, often mention the widows and the women deacons." And Marucci (ibid.) emphasises that even if there were disputes regarding the presence of women deacons during this time, "It is important [to remember] that, according to Origen, 'This passage [from Scripture], [Rom 16:1] teaches on the basis of apostolic authority that even women exercised ecclesiastical ministry … and that in the Church there are women with ecclesiastical ministry.'"

The Council of Nicea, the First Ecumenical Council, was convened in 325. Canon 19 of this Council decreed, "… Likewise in the case of … deaconesses, and generally in the case of those who have been enrolled among … [the] clergy … And we mean by deaconesses such as have assumed the habit, but who, since they have no imposition of hands, are to be numbered only among the laity" (www.intratext.com). In reference to Canon 19 it appears as if women seeking to be deacons were not to receive the imposition of hands which means that the women deaconesses were not ordained and though considered to be part of the laity, were still expected to exercise ecclesiastical ministries. Note the difference with Canon 15 below from the Council of Chalcedon, which was the Fourth Ecumenical Council and "which speaks more clearly of the ordination of woman as deacons." In the Council of Chalcedon at Asia Minor in 451, the following Canon 15 was decreed:

> A woman shall not receive the laying on of hands as a deaconess under forty years of age, and then only after

searching examination. And if, after she has had hands laid on her and has continued for a time to minister, she shall despise the grace of God and give herself in marriage, she shall be anathematized [condemned] and the man united with her (www.intratext.com).

In other words, a woman was not to be ordained a deacon prior to turning 40 years of age, and if she was forty years of age or more and had been ordained a deacon, then she was not permitted to leave this position to marry. Again, I remind you that the concept of "ordination" in the early Church differs to that now held in the contemporary Church (Stringer, 2016).

Macy (2011:13) notes that: "According to the canonical Collection of the Patriarch Photius of Constantinople, there were forty women deacons in that Church in the ninth century." Remember that in the Eastern Church women deacons began to emerge about the third century, however:

> References to women deacons as such in Western Christianity first appear with certainty in the fifth century, thus much later than the Eastern Church. Ambrosiaster and Pelagius ... both referred to women deacons, but they understood this institution to be an Eastern practice, not one of their own Western Church ... The First Council of Orange [then part of the Western Roman Empire] held in 441, certainly did know of women deacons and was not thrilled about them (ibid.).

Marucci (cited in Zagano, 2016:41) also comments on the situation regarding women deacons in the Western Church and supports the above statement on the feminine ministry that "was in general less prevalent and spread slowly in the west." Marucci (pp.42-43) writes that following some prohibitions imposed on women exercising:

> [C]ertain ministries ... the extraordinary Council

of Worms in 868 renewed Canon 15 of the Council of Chalcedon [refer to the quotation Canon 15 above] and eventually three popes (Benedict VIII, John XIX, and Leo IX) granted to the respective Bishops of Porto, Sylva Candid, and again Porto the right to ordain deaconesses.

Women deacons in the Western Church were less well-known than their Eastern counterparts but according to documents from "councils ... [that include] references in wills, letters, and chronicles of women who were deacons" (Macy, 2011:15), it is understood that there was a significant number of women deacons "spread over the seven centuries". Macy (ibid.) cites a "famous woman deacon in the Western Church ... Queen Radegund, the wife of King Clothar 1 (511-58)", who demanded to be ordained a deacon upon leaving her husband the King. Her wish was granted, and she became "an extremely powerful abbess as well as a deacon" (ibid.). Additional deacons in the Western Church included:

> Anna, a woman deacon from Rome in the sixth century; Theodora, a woman deacon from Gaul buried in 539; and Ausonia, a [married] woman deacon from Dalmatia in the sixth century ... A number of references to women deacons also exist from the eighth century. Pope Gregory II wrote three Letters to women deacons between 715 and 730 ... Women deacons continued to appear in documents between the tenth and twelfth centuries (Macy, 2011:17).

As mentioned previously, women engaged in service in several ministerial activities including that of apostles and deacons. According to Macy (2011:11-13) and as has been previously reported, woman deacons, "were much more prevalent in the Eastern Church than in the Western Church." Macy lists several names citing the importance attached to their ministry. For example, "John Chrysostom wrote four letters to the woman deacon, Amproukla in Constantinople, thanking her for her support while he was in exile." There is mention of a woman deacon called Anastasia from Severus, who wrote four letters to the "bishop of

Antioch, after he was exiled in 518," and in addition there is reference to the woman deacon Celerina in Constantinople, who received a letter from Theodoret of Cyrrhus "urging her to convince the bishops she knew of the orthodoxy of Theodoret's Christology." All the women have been described as "influential and learned [particularly regarding the Bible] ... [and with Celerina] discussing the complex theology with the most learned scholars of her day" (p.12).

Marucci (cited in Zagano, 2016:39) agrees that John Chrysostom engaged in "large and devoted correspondence with various deaconesses; like many other theologians of the same period he ... [was] concerned with reconciling the restrictive affirmation in 1 Cor (14) and 1 Tim (2) with the existence of a feminine ministry." Chrysostom was supportive of the work the women were undertaking in their various ministries. Macy (2011:12) expounds the virtues of Olympias, the woman deacon whom he describes as perhaps "The most famous and influential of the women deacons ... [she was] born into a wealthy and influential family, as a child she knew Gregory Nazianzus [Doctor of the Universal Church] ... while in her thirties ... [she became] political and personal advisor ... to Bishop Nectarius." Macy (ibid.) informs us that some graves of the deacons are still extant today, and that most of these date "from the fifth through to the seventh centuries."

Elizabeth Clark (1983:176) posits that "from the early Middle Ages on ... [the role of the woman deacon] seems to have been subsumed under that of the nun", though monasteries had been established much earlier:

> In the later fourth century, when the ascetic spirit had pervaded Rome, several Roman aristocratic women renounced their worldly lives and possessions and journeyed to the Holy Land where they founded monasteries for both men and women near the sites sacred to Christians. Melania the Elder ... started a monastery for women at Jerusalem in ... the last quarter of the fourth century. Another

female monastic founder was Jerome's friend Paula, who established a monastery for women at Bethlehem in the closing years of the fourth century. Jerome's *Epistle 108* constitutes a memorial to Paula. In it, Jerome describes the organization and routine of Paula's monastery (pp.134-135).

In sum, the role of women leaders in the early Church was significant. They fulfilled their ministerial duties, including those as deacons and on occasion as "heads of house", in good faith and often with the support of their male counterparts. Macy (2011:23) writes that "in the early years of Christianity, women who were designated deacons probably did the same ... [duties] that men designated deacons did. *Diakonos* in Greek just means 'servant,' and so the 'servants' of the Church did the service jobs. They took care of the poor, visited the sick and those in prison, and generally looked to the upkeep of the fabric of the Church." However, it appears as if many of the ministries changed direction with the advent of monasteries and convents. Indeed, some abbesses became deacons and there were occasions when women deacons taught other women (p.28). The institutional situation was to change during the ensuing centuries. Caroline Walker Bynum (1987:16-17) notes that around the time of the Middle Ages:

> Holy women ... were less inclined to institutionalisation than men, and ... they often chose a "quasi-religious" status. For example, many chose to be tertiaries, "Individuals who lived in the world but were affiliated with one of the great mendicant orders (usually Franciscan or Dominican) and followed a life of penitential asceticism, charitable activity and prayer." Such women resided in the world, where they were given greater opportunity "for significant geographical mobility through pilgrimage" (cited in Cameron, 2012a:129).

This accounts for the ministerial work of women such as St Catherine of Siena (fourteenth century Italy) whose "leadership revolved around her ministry of discipleship ... She had her band of followers – her disciples – who gathered around her and listened to her spiritual direction, and who travelled the country with her, preaching and ministering to the sick and the poor" (Cameron, 2012a:247).

In this chapter we have followed the faith journey of several women leaders who have assisted the Church in its mission of evangelisation – spreading the Good News of the Gospel, but space has limited the numbers that could possibly be given a voice and formal recognition of their tremendous contribution to leadership in the early Church, so to those women (and their male counterparts) whose names have been omitted thank you for your ministry of leadership and service to the Church! In her Woman's Bible (1895 [Part I]; 1898 [Part II]) Elizabeth Cady Stanton reminds us that:

> The masculine and feminine elements, exactly equal and balancing each other, are as essential to the maintenance of the equilibrium of the universe as positive and negative electricity, the centripetal and centrifugal forces, the laws of attraction which bind together all we know of this planet whereon we dwell and of the system in which we revolve (1972:15).

Similarly, St Paul (Galatians, 3:26-28) shared his vision of the future with us: "In Christ Jesus you are all children of God through faith. As many of you as were baptized into Christ have clothed yourselves with Christ. There is no longer Jew or Greek, there is no longer slave or free, there is no longer male and female; for all of you are one in Christ Jesus." We are all members of this global planet and stewards of the legacy of previous generations. Hence whether we belong to the past, the present or the future, "we are [part of] one single human family" (Pope Francis, *Laudato Si'*, 2015:para.52).

In this section, I have been writing from the context of the twenty-first century, and so many of the details discussed within the content are dependent on reliable and viable information provided by the biblical scholars, those who have spent many hours, days, and years researching and publishing their findings. This study then, is based on my own interpretation of the data gleaned from informed scholars, and generally using secondary sources. I acknowledge that due to the absence of significant primary sources, valuable information may have been "lost in translation" as it were. Hence, I have "exercised caution in articulating what the early Church roles actually were" (Stringer, 2016:15). My approach may differ from that of my more learned colleagues; the role of women deacons in the postmodern Church will receive some attention in the final chapters in this book. While at the same time I give thanks and praise to those male deacons, who are presently performing a great and much needed service within the Church, as did their male counterparts when first called to service during the early days of Christianity (Acts of the Apostles, 6:1-6).

I now invite you to turn to the following chapter and digress somewhat from the overall theme of the book to investigate how faith and values can determine leadership behaviour, and how leaders (females and males), can respond to the mandate of Christ to serve. In Chapter 4, the leadership practices best suited to faith-based organisations and communities, are discussed, and leadership as service is aligned with a values-based leadership approach which includes a brief discussion on the relevant literature, with particular reference to the "Seven Pillars of Servant Leadership" (Sipe and Frick, 2015:4-6), which in Chapters 5 through to 18 are applied to the lives and works of selected women leaders in the Catholic Church throughout the centuries. Also, in Chapter 4 you are asked to refer to Appendix A to access the attributes used as a guide for each of the Seven Pillars of Servant Leadership. The chapter then concludes with the terms of reference with suggested indicators for five values – dignity, respect, fairness, justness and equality, which are embedded in the context of this research.

4

Leadership as a Call to Service

Pope Francis in his homily during the inauguration Mass in 2013, celebrating the beginning of his papacy, spoke about leadership as service. It is this service to others that was the focus of my two previous books on leadership, in which I reflect on the ten core characteristics of servant leadership in relation to the leadership practices of the four women doctors of the Catholic Church. "Servant leadership is a secularised approach to leadership conceptualised by Robert Greenleaf in 1970, and it is based on the maxim that the 'essence of leadership is service' [2002:17]. Interestingly, leading by serving is a paradigm that can be traced back to biblical times and even to antiquity" (Cameron, 2012a:11-13).

As this chapter unfolds, let us reflect on a period in history more than two thousand years ago when Jesus Christ, a poor Jewish carpenter from the small peasant village of Nazareth in Galilee, heralded the birth of Christianity and emerged as a leader without equal, who though "True God and True Man" (CCC, 2000:para.464), promoted servanthood in his leadership practices, by issuing a mandate to his followers to serve: "[W]hoever wishes to become great among you must be your servant, and whoever wishes to be first among you must be slave of all. For the Son of man came not to be served but to serve, and to give his life a ransom for many" (Mk 10:42-45).

"Servant" and "Leadership" appear to be two contradictory terms – in other words, a paradox, for how can one be a servant and at the same time a leader? There are theorists who suggest that the servant leadership approach is a weak form of leadership, whereby, the leader may be lacking in strength and be indecisive. Yvonne Bradley (1992, cited in Cameron,

2009; 2015a:198) suggests that leaders who display the characteristics of servant leadership, might be seen to be timid and incapable of making decisions and lacking in confidence, which may devalue their position. Bradley posits that "Leadership sometimes demands bold action, harsh decisions, courage, risks, ignoring the opinion of others ... It sometimes involves deep regrets, difficult negotiations and disappointing compromises" (p.52).

I suggest that a servant leader would respond positively to the demands put forward by Bradley, for a servant leader is serving the people they are leading by helping them to improve their performance by becoming the best they can be. Obviously, there will be occasions when the leader does have to make difficult decisions depending on the gravity of the situation, but the response will be measured, and action will be taken but only after considering the needs of all members of the team/ organisation/community. This will be done by leaders listening to others and also listening to their inner voice. Greenleaf stressed that "Listening is an attitude, an attitude toward other people and what they are trying to express ... it is an openness to communication ... openness to hear the prophetic voices that are trying to speak to us all of the time" (1977:300). "Listening to the inner voice is described by John Gardiner (cited in Spears, 1998) as being attuned to a 'quiet presence, ... [which is a place] where leadership and the Spirit meet'" (Cameron, 2009). For example:

> Listening to others and then taking time to listen to the inner voice, is a source of wisdom for the leader who then becomes conscious of the needs of followers and conscious of his or her own inner needs. The leader who becomes attuned to the inner voice develops a quiet presence in the busyness of life. Gardiner (cited in Spears, 1998:117-118) promotes this concept and emphasises that human consciousness must envelop all who are part of creation and seek its survival, "The leaders of this global revolution will be people of quiet presence, the calm ones

at the center of great corporate and global enterprise, the eyes of the storms. Robert Waterman noted that "most of the renewing companies had calm at the center." The leader in the new world will be such a quiet presence" (cited in Cameron, 2009).

Dave Ramsey in his essay *Leading Is Serving* (cited in Ken Blanchard & Renee Broadwell, 2018:196), maintains that the *servant* part of *servant Leadership* can be a problem: "When some leaders hear *servant*, they think *subservient.*" However, Ramsey (ibid.) quickly discounts this assumption and emphasises the strength needed by servant leaders in their service to others. He compares this strength to that displayed by Jesus when he met with the Sanhedrin, prior to being taken before Pilate (Luke 22:63-67), and on a separate occasion when the "moneychangers" desecrated the temple, which Jesus described as His Father's house (Luke 19:46). Yet, while having the confidence, strength and even anger to confront behaviour that was unacceptable, Jesus also had the humility to wash his disciples' feet (John 13:1-20), and the love to suffer and pay the ultimate price for that love by offering his life for humanity (1 John 3:16).

Surprisingly, in my recent research, I did find an argument where the term servant leadership may not appeal to some female leaders. As I delved into the amazing world of the historical Mary, and Marian and feminist theologies, I read where Johnson (2003:254) recorded the Gospel's response of Mary to the angelic messenger: "Behold the handmaid of the Lord. Be it done to me according to your word." In my translation of the Bible (Luke 1:38), the term *handmaid* is replaced with *servant*. Now, Johnson (ibid.) tells us that "In the original Greek of the gospels the word *doulē*, which is usually translated 'handmaid' literally means female slave girl; *kyriou* means literally 'master' or 'lord'". So, *handmaid of the Lord* could be translated as "a female slave girl of the master". Herein lies the conundrum, which according to Johnson (p.255) is the "master-slave relationship: Traditional demands for conformity to patriarchal order and for obedience to male religious authority figures, be they God, husband, or priest, make women shudder before this text and reject it as dangerous to physical and psychological health as well as to a liberating spirituality."

In a later chapter in this book, I research the faith journey and present the profile of St Josephine Bakhita, who is the patron saint of victims of *slavery* and *human trafficking*. Her life and work mirror the analogy presented by Johnson (p.255), who in this context argues that the terms – "handmaid and Lord" are:

> [T]otally abhorrent in human society and no longer suitable as a metaphor for relationship to God, certainly not in feminist theological understanding. African American women who write theology out of the heritage of slavery and subsequent domestic servitude stress this repugnance even more strongly in unmistakable terms. Slavery is an unjust, sinful situation. It makes people into objects owned by others, denigrating their dignity as human persons. In the case of slave women, their masters have the right not only to their labor but to their bodies, making them into tools of production and reproduction at the master's wish … the Spirit groans with the cries of the oppressed, prompting persons not to obey but to resist.

Such is the legacy of previous generations of many African American women and men, whose descendants lived in an era when slavery flourished, and when they were subjected to indescribable atrocities, that included being forcibly taken from their homeland; beaten and denigrated – all of which resulted in extreme suffering; the loss of freedom, the loss of human dignity and much, much more. Sadly, and perhaps surprisingly time has only exacerbated the problem to such an extent, that in a report from the Vatican (dated 9 February 2018), Joshua J. McElwee, National Catholic Reporter [NCR], Vatican Correspondent, issued the following statement: "Pope Francis urged a global coalition fighting human trafficking to examine how society has tolerated or even turned a blind eye to the exploitation of vulnerable people."

Hence, in our contemporary society the 'scourge' of slavery and human trafficking continues to be a problem, with most of the victims being female though males are included. According to an article on St Josephine Bakhita, printed in an edition of the Australian Catholic Weekly (2018, Feb. 4): "It is estimated that millions of women, girls, men and boys are trafficked annually into domestic servitude, sexual exploitation, pornography, forced marriage and forced labour ...[and] There are more than 500 different human trafficking routes across many parts of the world, according to a 2016 United Nations report" (ibid.).

When I researched the above information, I realised then that there may be some leaders in our global community, who might feel 'uncomfortable' using the terms *servant leader* and *servant leadership*, even though they may espouse the values that such leadership inspires. However, as the list of contemporary leadership paradigms is extensive, there is ample choice for the committed and effective leader. Hence, below is a list I have compiled over the years of a variety of leadership approaches (in no particular order), that I experienced as a leader in Catholic education, and as a lecturer of prospective leaders in tertiary education (cf. ACU EDLE 638 Faith Leadership Unit, 2015:PPT Slide 13). The list is by no means exhaustive. You may think of others!

Faith Leadership	Spiritual Leadership	Religious Leadership	Shepherd Leadership	Charismatic Leadership
Visionary Leadership	Ethical Leadership	Authentic Leadership	Contingency Leadership	Moral Leadership
Distributed Leadership	Parallel Leadership	Passionate Leadership	Collaborative Leadership	Ecology of Leadership
Shared Leadership	Relational Leadership	Leadership as Stewardship	Strategic Leadership	Socio-Cultural Leadership
Cultural Leadership	Situational Leadership	Instructional Leadership	Transactional Leadership	Transformational Leadership
Laissez-faire Leadership	Autocratic Leadership	Great Man/[Woman] Theory of Leadership	Engaged Leadership	Contextual Leadership
Conceptualised Leadership	Sustainable Leadership	Healing Leadership	Democratic Leadership	Constructivist Leadership
Missionary Leadership	Disciple Leadership	Servant Leadership	Authoritarian Leadership	Values-Based/Led Leadership

Some of the above leadership approaches may overlap! A leader could be partial to one style of leadership, but there could be occasions when alternative leadership styles are more suited to a particular situation, however the essence of the leadership practice will be modelled on the leader's preferred approach. For "there are similarities and differences in all the theories and models of leadership, and much depends on the attitudes, values and behaviour of the leader in ensuring effective leadership practices, regardless of which leadership theory is espoused" (Cameron, 2009). Effective leadership then is linked to our "attitudes, values and behaviour", and as the characteristics of servant leadership are aligned to our values, then an alternative leadership concept to Servant Leadership could be values-led or values-based leadership.

As mentioned in my two earlier books, the "characteristics of servant leadership can be best described as intangible qualities [generally values] that are seen in people who are most admired, and who lead by serving" (Cameron, 2012a:15; Cameron, 2015a). Larry Spears (1998:3-6) identified ten core characteristics of servant leadership: listening, empathy, healing, awareness, persuasion, conceptualisation, foresight, stewardship, commitment to the growth of people and building community; however, these core characteristics are just ten of the many traits that could be attributed to a successful servant leader. "Theorists acknowledge the variety of choices available, particularly when considering personal and interpersonal values. Joe Batten (cited in Spears, 1998:47) writes about his *Values Manifest for Tough-Minded Servant-Leaders* which lists thirty-seven values that effective leaders practise each day, and Bill Bottum (cited with Dorothy Lenz in Spears, 1998:158) bases his eight *Guiding Principles for Business* on the eight beatitudes" (Cameron, 2009).

Values are linked to our behaviour and I believe they are also linked to our principles and the cultural, religious, spiritual and moral beliefs that guide us through life. Other theorists may have differing opinions. For example, Stephen R. Covey (2004:35) maintains that "Principles are not values". He compares principles to "territory" and values to "maps". According to Covey (ibid.): "When we value correct principles, we have truth – a knowledge of things as they are. Principles are guidelines for human conduct that are proven to have enduring, permanent value. They are fundamental." Prior to writing the chapters in his successful book, *The 7 Habits of Highly Effective People*, Covey (2004:42) begins with a chapter titled "Inside-Out". He explains that "'Inside-out' means to start first with self [and] even more fundamentally, to start with the most *inside* part of self – with your paradigms, your character, and your motives." If the focus of the leader is on the inner and outer realities then "effective leadership ... [will] start on the inside" (Ken Blanchard & Phil Hodges, 2003:18). According to Aristotle: "Knowing yourself is the beginning of all wisdom" and this involves discovering the spirit within, and then leading with soul – with gentleness and strength – born out of the silence of prayer and contemplation.

We each have standards that we set for ourselves, and as leaders we also have an expectation of a standard of behaviour from the members of our teams. According to Blanchard and Hodges (2003:51): "True success in servant leadership depends on how clearly values are defined, ordered and lived by the leader." Leaders need to know themselves, and they need to know the individual members of their teams. They need to be aware of their own strengths and weaknesses, and that of their team members. As leaders, they must set an example by "walking the talk". Hence, those who lead, should not just be aware of their own values and that of their colleagues, but they must also value their people and "their performance", engaging them in open dialogue, thus leading to effective communication, and encouraging all members of the team to work together collaboratively.

Consequently, leaders need to be aware of the core values that guide behaviour and when policies are formulated including Vision and Mission Statements – the values of each member of the team should be considered and respected, and after communal discussion and reflection, values should be identified that are agreeable to all members of the team, who could then work together collaboratively to produce the required documents. In this way, the values that drive the behaviour of the group will ultimately work towards the "big picture" – a shared vision for the organisation – with everybody on the same page as it were. For "the way you as a leader serve the vision is by developing people so that they can work on that vision even when you are not around" (Blanchard & Hodges, 2003:68).

Now apart from the many styles of leadership, there are many definitions of leadership. For example, John Hoyle (2007:10) notes that "leadership scholars Warren Bennis and Burt Nanus (1985) and Ralph Stogdill (1981) found over 350 definitions and characteristics of leadership in the literature." However, a simple definition is that cited by Harry Kraemer Jr (2011:2): "Leadership, simply put, is the ability to influence others". Kraemer (ibid.) then defines values-based leadership as allowing "leaders to hold true to ...[their] values to make a difference in their lives, their organisations, and the world." He posits that there are "four principles of values-based leadership ... *self-reflection, balance, true self-confidence,* and *genuine humility* ... [and that all] are interconnected, each building on and contributing to the others" (p.5).

Earlier in the chapter, the ten core characteristics of servant leadership identified by Larry Spears (1998) were listed. Spears emphasises, "Spiritual awareness, general awareness and self-awareness as providing the holistic approach to ... servant leadership" (cited in Cameron, 2009). James W. Sipe and Don M. Frick published "Seven Pillars of Servant Leadership: Practicing the Wisdom of Leading by Serving" (2015) and maintain that readers who "are familiar with the publications of Larry Spears ... [may] recognize many parallels between our 'Seven Pillars of Servant Leadership' and his list of the ten characteristics of Servant Leaders" (p.7). Though there are fewer pillars than the ten core characteristics, the seven pillars certainly integrate many of the same qualities. For more information on the ten core characteristics of servant leadership, refer to my two previous books in the leadership series which demonstrate how the ten core characteristics are reflected in the lives and works of the four women doctors of the Catholic Church – St Hildegard of Bingen (2015), St Catherine of Siena, St Teresa of Ávila and St Thérèse of Lisieux (2012).

Dale Roach (2016) writes about a *The Servant-Leadership Style of Jesus: A Biblical Strategy for Leadership Development.* Though Roach cites various passages from scripture and offers some reliable strategies for the servant leader, I found some difficulty understanding when he cites, for instance "What Jesus Taught About Servant-Leadership ..." and "Jesus Taught That Servant-Leaders Were Not Self-Promoting (Mark 1:11)", (p.21). I do not believe that as contemporary writers we can interpret the actions of Jesus to suit our explanation of what he may or may not have thought or taught. If you remember in Part 1, Chapter 2, I referred to Hermeneutics and explained that this form of approach "offers a perspective for interpreting legends, stories, and other texts, especially biblical and legal texts" and I then stated that "To make sense of and interpret a text it is important to know what the author wanted to communicate, to understand intended meanings, and to place documents in a historical and cultural context" (Palmer, 1969, cited in Patton, 2002:114). Hence, though Jesus has been described as the "prototype of the servant leader" (Sims, 1997:17), given the times, culture, and societal influences, I doubt whether he would have described his leadership practices using the term servant leadership as a paradigm of leadership. The concept may have been implied but certainly was not explicit.

Ken Blanchard & Renee Broadwell (2018) in their published book on *Servant Leadership in Action: How You Can Achieve Great Relationships and Results* build on their past efforts. I have long admired Blanchard's approach to servant leadership. His wise counsel made a huge impression on my own leadership practices, when I realised that my own style of leadership mirrored *Servant Leadership*. Blanchard & Broadwell's book (2018) is a collection of "contributions from forty-four celebrated servant leaders ... [with] themes that include basic principles of servant leadership" (Inside front Cover) and lessons, profiles and stories of effective leaders implementing their servant leadership practices.

Christopher Branson (2009:1) promotes a values-led approach to leadership, and in his *Search for Authentic Leadership* emphasises the "Self" and its dimensions, particularly the "Self-Concept" as "indirectly influenc[ing] behaviour through the sequential dimensions of the Self [for example] of self-esteem, motives, values, and beliefs." In a previous paragraph I referred to Harry Kraemer Jr (2011) in connection with values-led leadership, and he (p.13) defines self-reflection as "the key to identifying what you stand for, what your values are, and what matters most". So, values are paramount to effective leadership relationships and behaviours, and such leaders would value themselves and others by initially reflecting on self and then setting a clear direction for all members of the team – thus sharing and serving vision.

Servant leadership and values-based leadership are the foremost leadership approaches best suited to a faith-based organisation, and hence, are the models of choice for this study, which is based on the "Seven Pillars of Servant Leadership: Practicing the Wisdom of Leading by Serving" (Sipe & Frick, 2015), who quote Proverbs (9:1): *Wisdom has built her house, she has hewn her seven pillars* (pp.4-6). The following seven pillars are identified:

- Pillar I – Person of Character;
- Pillar II – Puts People First;
- Pillar III – Skilled Communicator;
- Pillar IV – Compassionate Collaborator;
- Pillar V – Has Foresight;
- Pillar VI – Systems Thinker; and
- Pillar VII – Leads with Moral Authority.

The attributes associated with each of the above seven pillars are listed in Appendix A. These attributes are used as a guide when the lives and works of fourteen selected women leaders in the Catholic Church throughout the ages are discussed and analysed in Chapters 5 through to 18.

According to Blanchard & Hodges (2003:50), "Research shows that people can't focus on more than 3 … [to 5] values if you really want to impact behaviour." Hence, for the purpose of this study, the focus is on five values – dignity, respect, fairness, justness and equality – some theorists may consider these to be virtues; however, I am not going to differentiate here between virtues and values, as each of us has our own opinion in this regard. In addition, throughout this book many important values are emphasised, but it is the five values listed in this paragraph that are applied to the lives and works of each of the fourteen women leaders selected for study; with the information incorporated in Pillar

VII – Leads with Moral Authority – Values – which is located in the "Leadership as Service" section of Chapters 5 through to 18.

The following are the terms of reference for each of the five values listed in the above paragraph:

Dignity

The *Universal Declaration of Human Rights* was proclaimed and adopted by the United Nations General Assembly on 10 December 1948. The document comprises 30 articles and its global message affirms the human dignity and value of all people. This same message is reinforced in several Vatican documents particularly the Encyclical Letter *Evangelium Vitae*: "On the Value and Inviolability of human life" (Pope St John Paul II, 1995), which was written some 30 years after the Second Vatican Council (1962-1965), and emphasises the integrity and dignity of the human person. Paragraph 3 of the document is quite comprehensive and highlights some controversial issues that are discussed in a later chapter:

> Whatever is opposed to life itself, such as any type of murder, genocide, abortion, euthanasia, or wilful self-destruction, whatever violates the integrity of the human person, such as mutilation, torments inflicted on body or mind, attempts to coerce the will itself; whatever insults human dignity, such as subhuman living conditions, arbitrary imprisonment, deportation, slavery, prostitution, the selling of women and children; as well as disgraceful working conditions, where people are treated as mere instruments of gain rather than as free and responsible persons; all these things and others like them are infamies indeed (1995:para.3).

The Encyclical was written over two decades ago, but its message is still very relevant; for in our contemporary world – human life, freedom and security continue to be at great risk. Article 3 of the Universal

Declaration of Human Rights states that "Everyone has the right to life, liberty and security of person." The Catholic Catechism emphasises that: "The dignity of the human person is rooted in his [her] creation in the image and likeness of God" (2000:para.1700). According to the Education for Justice website (cited by Katherine Freely, n.d.), "The principle of human dignity is the foundation of all the Catholic social teaching principles." Let us rejoice then in the sacredness of human life and let us always value human dignity!

Dignity

Jesus treated all women with dignity and respect. In all our dealings with humanity let us remember:

- The Universal Declaration of Human rights
- Equal rights for all genders
- Integrity and dignity of the human person
- Human dignity should be for all
- To value our self and others
- Human life is sacred
- Dignity or freedom should not be compromised

Respect

Pope St John Paul II (1988) writes of the profound respect Jesus had for the women of his time: "In all of Jesus' teaching, as well as in his behaviour, one can find nothing which reflects the discrimination against women prevalent in his day. On the contrary, *his words and works always express the respect and honour due to women*" (para.13). Jesus was known for his tendency to go against the norm and he challenged the status quo. In a *Letter to Women* on 29 June 1995, on the eve of the Fourth World Conference on Women held in Beijing in September of that year, Pope St John Paul II, when writing of the many ways women have been exploited over time, refers to the attitude of Jesus in regard to his respect for women and his appreciation of their dignity:

> Unfortunately, we are heirs to a history which has *conditioned* us to a remarkable extent. In every time and place, this conditioning has been an obstacle to the progress of women. Women's dignity has often been unacknowledged, and their prerogatives misrepresented; they have often been relegated to the margins of society and even reduced to servitude. This has prevented women from truly being themselves and it has resulted in a spiritual impoverishment of humanity ... When it comes to setting women free from every kind of exploitation and domination, the Gospel contains an ever-relevant message which goes back to the *attitude of Jesus Christ himself*. Transcending the established norms of his own culture, Jesus treated women with openness, respect, acceptance and tenderness. In this way he honoured the dignity which women have always possessed according to God's plan and in his love (1995:para.3).

Admirable words from the Holy Father, but nearly a quarter of a century later, have attitudes really changed within the top echelons of the Church regarding one of its richest resources – its women! Admittedly, there is progress in some areas, and this is acknowledged, but are the small successes just token efforts by a patriarchal hierarchy to still the voices of women that are calling for a fair go? Are women really respected or are they just tolerated? Jesus respected women sufficiently to choose a woman, St Mary Magdalene to be the first witness to his Resurrection. This female saint is now referred to as *Apostolorum Apostola*, Apostle of the Apostles (see Chapter 3, Part I).

Let us emulate Jesus and define leaders not in terms of gender but in terms of their leadership – effective leadership! Effective leaders are asked to share and serve vision. An effective leader shows respect and values each member of the team. Jesus taught how this can be done –

"Love of God and love of neighbour"; and to do this it is necessary to follow him: "I am the way, the truth and the life" (John 14:6). The enemies of Jesus nailed him to a cross – his response was "Father, forgive them; for they do not know what they are doing" (Luke 23:34). Effective leaders will be ready to forgive those who hurt or disappoint them. They respect themselves and others enough to stand up for what they believe. Their voices will not be silenced!

Respect

Jesus' voice was not silenced. He honoured and respected women. Let us follow his example by remembering to:

- Respect self and others
- Respect the rights and property of others
- Respect the dignity of others
- Have respect for the human person – regardless of gender
- Treat others with openness, respect and dignity
- Respect all living things
- Respect and sustain the environment

Fairness

During my years in Catholic primary education, whether it was in the role of teacher or administrator, I always believed in fairness and consistency when dealing with students or colleagues. When employing staff, and in consultation with my team, it was the person best suited to the position and needs of the school, who was appointed to the position. When teaching a class, it was a willingness to enable all students to be included in the classroom activities and encouraging all to be the best they could be, by enabling staff to differentiate the curriculum to suit the individual needs of each of the students. Generally, within the school context in which I exercised my role as leader, discipline was often based on *Restorative Justice Principles*, and these involved following a fair process for the accuser and the accused. Hence, when student behaviour was challenging, or inappropriate, procedural fairness was considered to be the best process suited to achieving a just outcome. George Klosko (1997:272) writes that, "The concept of fairness is closely related to … [several] other moral concepts, such as EQUALITY, IMPARTIALITY, AND JUSTICE … it centers on how people are treated by others".

Donald DeMarco (1999) refers to *fairness* as a virtue. He repeats an adage – a response that those of us who are parents have probably heard countless times from young children, and even teenagers when they are asked to do something that is not to their liking – "That's not fair!" According to DeMarco that response "may very well be that the first moral judgment a child utters … [and that] Virtually all studies on the subject report that children as young as four already have an active and flourishing sense of fairness."

Fairness involves making decisions in the best interests of all and treating our "neighbours" equally and respectfully. As members of the global community, we are all stewards of our planet and *neighbours* to each other, and while we are all unique, we must value and respect our similarities and differences. Leaders are also custodians of those they serve, and it is important that when following established rules and laws, the needs of all people are considered regardless of their economic circumstances. Pope Francis in his Encyclical Letter *Laudato Si'* on Care for our Common Home (2015), stresses the rights of all people, "especially the poor, to have access to the Earth's goods and not to be trampled on by powerful interests and a consumerist culture that encourages taking more than a fair share" (Justice and Peace website, 2018).

Fairness

Jesus celebrated the differences of his followers. He was fair and just in his dealings with all who approached him for counsel, and healing. He was compassionate even to his captors. Let us serve others by reaching out as Jesus did to the poor and the marginalised by remembering to:

- Treat others fairly – with honesty and respect
- Have an active "sense of fairness"
- Exhibit "fairness and justice" in relationships and service
- Relate fairness to the moral concepts of – equality, impartiality and justice
- Work towards a fair and just society
- Be fair when making decisions
- Be consistent

Justness

When I first heard the term *Justness* it sounded odd! I thought justice would be a more appropriate way of expressing a *just* approach to leadership. However, during my research, I realised that in some instances the word "justness" is the more suitable word to use even though there are few references to its use, apart from in a legal sense. One such legal example was revealed when I came across a 2016 Youtube TED Talk by a Kimberley Motley. At the time, though Motley was practising law in Afghanistan, she was hosting a presentation at the San Francisco Freedom Forum. The title of Motley's presentation was "Justness for All" and the focus of her session was to emphasise "Rule of Law". Motley spoke about a young female child of 12 who had been forced into marriage with an older man and had suffered inexplicable brutality to her person. In our contemporary times it is evident that "lack of justness is a global problem" (Motley, 2016), that needs to be addressed. As mentioned previously, I will be discussing slavery and human trafficking in a later chapter.

Motley maintains that for societies to achieve justness then there is a need "to re-educate people who are unaware of their legal rights ... everybody has a right to be protected [and] a right to be free ... individual problems are now global problems". Justness is needed for all. According to Motley (ibid.), "By creating a global human rights economy and becoming global investors in human rights we can achieve justness together". However, I believe that people need to want to achieve justness in their dealings with others. Alternatively, there may be some who would be content with the status quo and would not want change regardless of the benefits to the majority!

Helen Taylor Boursier (2015) in her article *The necessity of social just-ness for a postmodern ecclesi-odicy* emphasises that "to share the salvific message of Jesus Christ (Matt 28:19) means that the Christian gospel needs to resonate with the social and existential concerns of the current people of God as well as with changing culture and emerging generations." In other words, to share in the mission of evangelisation, and to do justice to all, Christian leaders need to be aware of the problems and changes that have occurred over time and are still occurring within the global Christian community.

By his very presence and being, God shows justness to humanity! The Vatican has published a document *Compendium of the Social Doctrine of the Church*, and in Australia the Catholic Church has established the Catholic Social Justice Council [ACSJC]. The *Compendium* itself is very lengthy but its final paragraph states that:

> *Only love can completely transform the human person.* Such a transformation does not mean eliminating the earthly dimension in a disembodied spirituality. Those who think they can live the supernatural virtue of love without ... [considering] its corresponding natural foundations, which include duties of justice, deceive themselves. "Charity is the greatest social commandment. It respects others and their rights. It requires the practice of justice and it alone makes

us capable of it" (2004:para.583).

For the Church then, justice is central to its mission. Such a mission is laudable, but because of recent allegations against the Church regarding child sexual abuse, and the establishment of Commissions around the globe to investigate such abuse, it is acknowledged that justness has not always governed the actions and decisions of some members of the Church and/or her representatives? On a positive note, in Australia on 15 December 2017 the Final Report of the *Royal Commission into Institutional Responses to Child Sexual Abuse* was presented. And now with transparency, insight and hindsight, and as a result of the findings of the various global Commissions, it is an expectation that all associated agencies and networks will work together towards a just and equitable outcome, so that the first steps towards healing, though tentative and precarious at first, will endeavour to restore and make whole again – "broken bodies", "broken lives", "broken spirits" and to a certain extent – a broken Church!

Justness

Jesus preached justness for all. He was prepared to step outside his comfort zone to bring salvation to those he served. As we engage in social justness with our neighbours let us remember:

- The Justness of God
- Catholic Social Justice
- Justness for all
- Justness as a "Rule of law"
- Justness to humanity
- The importance of justness and transparency
- Lack of justness is a global problem

Equality

As a senior educated woman in Catholic education and administration at a school and tertiary level, there have been occasions when I have questioned the relevant authorities regarding possible career advancement opportunities, however, the purpose of this chapter is not to point out less favourable decisions that have affected my own life and that of many other females (and undoubtedly males also), but to discuss ways that contemporary young women (and men) can move forward with their leadership aspirations, and be able to do so, based on their faith commitment, experience and academic achievements — and not their gender, age or sexual orientation.

In the Catechism of the Catholic Church (2000:para.1935), we read "The equality of men [women] rests essentially on their dignity as persons and the rights that flow from it." And again, "There exist also *sinful inequalities* that affect millions of men and women. These are in open contradiction of the Gospel", for "Their equal dignity as persons demands that we strive for fairer and more humane conditions. Excessive economic and social disparity between individuals and peoples of the one human race is a source of scandal and militates against social justice, equity, human dignity, as well as social and international peace (2000:para.1938).

In the document *The Church and Racism: Towards a More Fraternal Society*, the Pontifical Commission on Justice and peace (1988) states the following:

> Equality does not mean uniformity. It is important to recognize the diversity and complementarity of one another's cultural riches and moral qualities. Equality of treatment therefore implies ... recognition of differences which minorities themselves demand in order to develop according to their own specific characteristics, in respect for others and for the common good of society and the

world community. No human group, however, can boast of having a natural superiority over others, or of exercising any discrimination that affects the basic rights of the person (#23).

The 1963 Papal Encyclical of Pope St John XXIII, *Pacem In Terris* – "Peace on Earth" – demonstrated that the Church was aware that the role of women in the Church needed to be changed: "[T]he part that women are now playing in political life is everywhere evident. This is a development that is perhaps of swifter growth among Christian nations, but it is also happening extensively, if more slowly, among nations that are heirs to different traditions and imbued with a different culture" (para.41). A reminder that the role of women leaders in the Contemporary Church is discussed in the Third Millennium section of this book. In *Mulieris Dignitatem* on the "Dignity and Vocation of Women", the Apostolic Letter of Pope St John Paul II (1988), reinforces the equality of the genders: "God created man [and woman] in his own image, in the image of God he created him [and her]; male and female he created them" *(Gen* 1:27) ... [therefore] *both man and woman are human beings to an equal degree,* both are created *in God's image"* (para.6).

Equality

Jesus valued the sacredness of all life. In his dealings with humanity he didn't place the importance of one person/gender over another person/gender. Let us remember:

- Equality amidst diversity and inclusion
- Equality does not mean uniformity
- Equality of treatment
- "The discipleship of equals" (Fiorenza, 2009)
- "The Equality Act" (2010)
- Equality of genders
- Equality is a "MUST" in the 21st Century

Conclusion

Obviously, there are many more Church documents and other related literature, that support the arguments addressed in this chapter. However, it is important to always remember that we are all human beings and by the grace of God, "neighbours to each other" and custodians of our global environment. Let all human beings then, whether they are leaders or followers – and regardless of gender – call for dignity and respect, through fairness, justness, and equality, in their service toward others.

The next chapter profiles the life and works of St Monica, Mother of St Augustine, Doctor of the Universal Church. The focus is on leadership as service, and how the faith and values of St Monica defined her as a person, as a woman, and as a leader in the Church. As St Monica was born in the fourth century, she is included in this section of the book on the First Millennium of the Catholic Church.

5

St Monica

In his Apostolic Letter *Mulieris Dignitatem* "On the Dignity and Vocation of Women" (1988), Pope St John Paul II commented on the "witness and achievements of Christian women" as having "a significant impact on the life of the Church as well as society" (para.27). In his letter, the Pope maintains that since the beginning of Christianity there have many women: "holy martyrs, virgins, [single women, wives] and mothers of families" from countries all over the world, and from every generation who have been "'perfect' women ... [and] despite persecution, difficulties and discrimination, they have [all] shared the Church's mission" (ibid.). The Pope then cites at least a dozen names as examples, and the faith journey of some of these women will be discussed in the coming chapters. For now, however, the focus is on one of these women – St Monica, who lived a life that bore testimony to the Gospel, and which reflected her strong faith commitment when serving and sharing in the mission of the Church.

Profile

Monica is perhaps better known as the mother of St Augustine – Doctor of the Universal Church, who is arguably one of the greatest theologians and teachers of the Catholic Church (John F. Fink, 2000:127). In support of this statement Fr Christopher Rengers, OFM Cap., quotes John Delaney (*Dictionary of Saints*): "It is the common opinion that St. Augustine was, 'with the possible exception of St. Thomas Aquinas', the greatest single intellect the Catholic Church has ever produced" (2000:131). My research on the Doctors of the Church some years ago, revealed that: "Augustine left a legacy of numerous works including his *'Confessions'* and *'City of God'* which were written c400 and 'are still regarded as classics'" (Holmes & Bickers, 1983:42; cited in Cameron, 2009:24/25). Gillian Clark maintains, "Augustine is one of the most influential theologians in western tradition and that is why Monica is one of the best-known women of classical antiquity" (2015:2).

An investigation into the life of Monica cannot be separated then from the works of her son, for what we know of Monica is generally what is recorded in the *Confessions* of Augustine which are described by Fink (2000:128) as Augustine's "spiritual autobiography". As referenced in the above paragraph, Augustine's work was written about c 400 which was approximately ten to fourteen years after the death of Monica. According to Gillian Clark (2015:3) Augustine's writings, "are the only source for her life" and so what we know about the faith journey of Monica is to be found in the writings of her son. Therefore, to obtain some idea of this woman, who was a daughter, wife, mother and saint, it is important to read the *Confessions* of Augustine which Elizabeth Clark (1983:246) maintains were also Augustine's "prayer to God". Clark tells us that we know this because Augustine addresses God as "You" in the texts (ibid.). She posits that the last section of Book 9 of the *Confessions*, "is Augustine's tribute to his mother." Apparently, the passage highlights "the emotional bond that linked mother and son" (ibid.).

Giovanni Falbo (2007:vii) concurs with both Gillian Clark (2015) and Elizabeth Clark (1983) in that, "The majority of references to St. Monica's life are found in the words of St. Augustine, especially his *Confessions* … [For] up until Book Nine of that work, and especially in Book Nine, Augustine's life is completely interwoven with his mother's". Gillian Clark (2015:2) informs us that it is in Book 9 of the *Confessions* that the name of Monica is revealed "in a prayer that concludes the book":

> So let her be in peace with her husband, before whom and after whom she was married to no one, whom she served bringing you profit by her patience, so that she could win

him also for you. Inspire, my Lord, my God, inspire your slaves, my brothers, your sons. My masters, whom I serve with heart and voice and writings, that all who read this may remember at your altar Monica, your slave, with Patricius, once her spouse, through whose flesh you brought me into this life, how I do not know (Augustine, *Conf.* 9.13.37).

Interestingly, Clark (2015:8) informs us that the spelling of the name of Augustine's mother was probably "Monnica ... Some people feel strongly that 'Monnica' links this woman more closely to her African homeland, whereas the traditional 'Monica' claims her for Roman culture and its later reception." Monica is said to have been born in Thagaste (or Tagaste) an inland town in northern Africa in about 331 or 332. Falbo (2007:1) writes that the town was situated in "an ancient Berber Kingdom [Numidia]." Today the site, "on the hills where the town of Thagaste once stood, sits the town of Souk-Ahras, which is located in modern-day Algeria on the border with Tunisia" (ibid.). A background glimpse into the world that preceded Monica's birth, shows us a country occupied by Rome, for the Roman Empire had reached the shores of North Africa, and the land of Numidia had witnessed, "the fervor of the first generations of Christians in Africa, who with their blood spilled during persecutions, both sowed and watered the seeds of Christianity" (p.2).

Two young women martyrs receive special mention in the history books – Perpetua and Felicity – both young mothers with babies, who were put to death in Carthage during the beginning of the third century (c.203). Falbo (2007) writes that "an authentic account [of their martyrdom] ... may even have been compiled by Tertullian" (p.4) who was born in Carthage during the second century. You may recall that there have been references to Tertullian in previous chapters. Now Gillian Clark (2015:4) writes that Monica was born: "late in the reign of Constantine, the first Roman emperor to give open support to Christianity, and in her lifetime, there were civil wars and uprisings and outbreaks of violent religious and social conflict, but there is no evidence that they affected Monica or her family."

As the persecution of Christians continued during the first two centuries of Christianity, heresies began to emerge, and what came to be known as the Donatist heresy, "quickly gained a substantial following." Falbo (p.5) maintains that "The Donatist heresy was the mistaken idea that the sacraments were valid only if the minister conferring them was holy ... the obvious result would be that no one would ever be able to know if the sacraments were validly celebrated ... This undermined the very foundation of the Church." Fink (2000:134) posits that: "Donatism was named after Donatus, a priest who became a schismatic bishop of Carthage in 312 ... [and that] The Donatist schism split the African hierarchy into two almost equal parts."

In later years, Augustine in his efforts to combat heresy and schism, taught "that the efficacy of the sacraments depends not on the worthiness of their ministers but on the power of Christ, who is their true minister" (Fink, ibid.). According to Falbo (2007:6): "Except for a small colony in Rome, Donatism never spread beyond Africa, but it met with astounding success in its country of origin, thanks to the personality and organizational genius of Donatus." In his later years when he was a Bishop "Augustine found himself constantly defending the church against the heresies of his day, notably Manichaeism, Donatism and Pelagianism" (Fink, 2000:133). Manichaeism "was named for a third-century Persian named Mani (or Manichaeus in Latin) and was the religious and ethical doctrine that Augustine originally embraced as a youth. It taught that there are two equal, eternal principles: one of good, light and spirit; the other of darkness, matter and evil" (pp.133/134).

Gillian Clark (2015:140) posits that though Augustine embraced Manichaeism he was only what was described at the time – a "'Hearer' the usual word for someone who attends the teaching of a philosopher but does not make a commitment to the philosopher's way of life. Manichaean leaders, the 'Elect', were celibate and would not have approved of Augustine's involvement with the mother of [his son] Adeodatus." Regarding the heresy called Pelagianism, Fink (2000:134) explains that Pelagius "was named after an Irish monk" who lived during the time of Augustine. Pelagius rejected the doctrine of original sin, denied the necessity of grace for salvation, and taught that humans can achieve salvation by their own efforts. This contrasted with Augustine's beliefs and teachings. Augustine defended the Church's doctrine that grace is necessary for salvation, and in contemporary times he has been referred to as the Doctor of Grace. Arianism (named after Arius – a 4th Century teacher) was another heresy (this cult denied the divinity of Christ), that was encountered by Augustine but Clark (2015:142) tells us that "Arian interpretation is not a theme of his [Augustine's] preaching until nearer 418."

Consequently, to focus on the world of Monica in times of antiquity, is to envisage countries being occupied by Roman forces, Christians being persecuted and heretical ideas and sects infiltrating growing Christian communities. We know from Book 9 of Augustine's *Confessions*, that his mother Monica was a Christian, and that she was married to the pagan Patricius, and that Patricius was converted to Christianity virtually on his deathbed. Monica is believed to have had two sons (Augustine and Navigius) and a daughter. There is little information on the daughter. Clark (2015:9) writes that the name of Monica's daughter is not known but that some scholars refer to her as Perpetua, "the name of the famous African martyr", who has been mentioned in an earlier paragraph in this chapter. Clark recounts that "Some years after Monica's death, her widowed daughter was the leader of a community of women at Hippo" (p.139).

History has not recorded the names of Monica's parents; however, "According to the tradition found in the breviaries of the Augustinian Order, her mother was called Faconda, but this name appears nowhere in Augustine's works" (Falbo, 2007:9), even though he indirectly refers to his grandparents when he converses with God in his *Confessions*: "…

you created her, and not even her father or mother knew what kind of child would be born from them. She was brought up to reverence you, schooled by the crook of your Christ, the shepherd's care of your only Son, in a faithful family that was a sound limb of your Church" (Augustine, *Conf* 9.8.17).

What is interesting about Augustine, including his mother and her life and her faith journey in his writings, is that during antiquity and into the Middle Ages, the general practice was for men to write about women. And so, Monica did not "own" the writings, for the source did not come from her own hand, but from that of her son. Gillian Clark (2015:3) emphasises that "For the lives of women, at all periods of classical antiquity, we depend on men writing about women. There are hardly any texts written by women, because women hardly ever wrote for an audience. Elizabeth Clark (1983:163) argues that the reason is not as has been suggested by the Fathers of the Church, that "all Christian women suffered from 'weak intellects,'" for this was "flatly contradicted by references to the scholarly activities in which some of them engaged. Education in the late Latin world was tied to class, and girls of the aristocracy apparently received the same general literary education as their brothers, even if they did not enjoy higher formal training in law, philosophy, and other specialized subjects."

Later in this section we read about Monica's participation in philosophical debates with her son, even though her own education was quite limited. Clark (1983) reinforces that there was a lack of evidence to support women's contribution to the written word for, "Unfortunately, we have almost no materials remaining from ancient Christianity that were composed by women" (p.165). Hence, to obtain more information about Monica, scholars referred to the prolific works of her son. In his writings, Augustine reveals that Monica was continually abused by her husband – his father. Elizabeth Clark (1983:246) suggests that Augustine describes, quite frankly "Monica's ordeals as a wife" but doesn't give the impression that he thinks the treatment of his mother by his father is unusual. Clark (pp.252-253) quotes from the *Confessions* where, in his conversation to God Augustine recounts the gentle and calming approach that Monica used to influence her philandering and abusive husband:

> She thus endured the wrongs to her bed, so that she never had any feuding with her husband on account of this matter ... She learned not to resist a wrathful husband, not only in deed, but not even by a word. Indeed, when she saw an appropriate moment after he was restrained and quiet, she would explain to him the reason for her behaviour, if he had been unadvisedly upset. In short, while many married women with milder husbands nonetheless bore on a dishonored face the traces of beatings, women who would in friendly conversation betray their husbands' lives, she would censure their tongues and [she would] admonish them in a dignified fashion ... [she would tell them to remember] the conditions of the marriage contract, they ought not to take the upper hand against their masters. And when these women, knowing what a fierce husband she put up with, marveled that it had never been heard or made evident by any sign that Patricius had beaten his wife nor that they had been opposed in domestic strife with each other even for a day (Augustine, *Conf.* 9.9).

Gillian Clark (2015:12) endorses Elizabeth Clark's (1983) description of the trials that beset Monica during her marriage, for she states that, "Domestic life had a darker side. Augustine cited Monica's advice to her neighbours on how not to be a battered wife" (*Conf* 9.9.19) and that she tolerated her husband's infidelity. These are admirable traits in Monica, but I suggest that her reaction would take a lot of courage and strength, and that women of our contemporary era, may react differently if confronted with such abusive situations. Obviously, this is because there are so many avenues of support available to women today, that would not have been a part of the culture and society during early antiquity.

Nevertheless, Patricius seemed to appreciate the efforts by his wife to placate him, in times of his emotional outbursts, and though a pagan he did seem to respect her religious beliefs as a Christian.

It may be difficult for us today, to understand the reasoning behind Monica's "acceptance" of her husband's behaviour to her, even though it had the desired effect at the end of his life when he converted to Christianity. There were undoubtedly vastly different societal and cultural expectations in those early days of antiquity, however, perhaps what is more difficult to understand with the contemporary mind, is the attitude of Monica's son Augustine to the treatment of Monica by his father, in that he didn't think the treatment of his mother by his father was unusual. From his writings we know that Augustine had his own 'demons', and indeed Monica spent her entire life in prayer and hope that her son would change his ways and come to know the "joys" and "peace" of converting to Christianity.

Regarding the social position of the family, Possidius – a Bishop and friend of Augustine (who wrote Augustine's biography probably not long after the saint's death around 430), writes that "Augustine's parents belonged to the class of the *Honestiores*, the upper class of Roman society … [who] enjoyed certain legal privileges … Patricius held the position of 'decurion' of the illustrious municipality of Tagaste. Decurions were municipal councilors" (Falbo, 2007:17). Regardless of their station in society, money seemed to be scarce and the family accepted the support of a friend and neighbor Romanianus, when it was time for Augustine to move away, initially to Madauros "a day's journey from Thagaste" (Gillian Clark, 2015:11) to pursue an education suited to his growing intellectual needs. Even after the death of Patricius (who died before Monica turned 40), Romanianus continued to offer financial support to the family, for the higher education of Augustine, who was a student and then teacher at Carthage, and later became a professor of rhetoric in the Italian city of Milan (p.17).

Falbo (2007:29) writes that following the death of her husband,

Monica chose not to remarry, and in her widowed state was held "in particular esteem in the ancient Church ... [for] those who strove to remain unmarried received a special consecration." However, as Monica was relatively young with children still at home, she was unable to participate in activities assisting the local Christian community, that resulted from receiving the special consecration. As a result, finances were limited and necessitated support from others, including the family friend Romanianus.

Nevertheless, according to Augustine, his mother was an exemplary widow (*Conf.* v.9.17). Following the death of her husband, Monica did not seek male company, but was content to remain a widow and "embraced an even more sober and austere way of life" (Falbo, 2007:30). And when she could, she gave alms to the poor. "She was dutiful toward the presbyters and the heads of the Church, humbly serving and seeing Christ in all those who found themselves in need." Gillian Clark (2015:6) tells us that she was "not a martyr or an ascetic. She was a good Christian who showed love of God and love of neighbour. She went regularly to Church, heard and read the scriptures, and prayed. She was a peacemaker in her household and among her neighbours, and she was charitable to the poor."

In his youth, Augustine appeared to be on the path to self-destruction. He himself states in his conversations (*Confessions*) to God (written in later years):

> My hope from my youth (Ps.71:5), where were You in relation to me, to where had You retreated? For truly, did You not make me and distinguish me from the four-footed beasts and the birds of the air by making me wiser? Yet I walked in darkness and in slippery places, and I sought You outside of myself and did not find God in my heart; I came into the depths of the sea, had no confidence, despaired at finding the truth. Already my mother had come to me, strong in her piety, following me over land and sea, secure

in You against all dangers (*Conf* 1.11, cited in Elizabeth Clark, 1983:247).

Clark (ibid:246) emphasises that "Monica spent years of her life suffering over her sexually and religiously wayward son." From a young age Augustine is said to have had "a brilliant mind and when he was about sixteen, he was sent to the major African city of Carthage (in modern Tunisia) to study law. However, he turned to literary affairs instead. He also succumbed to the temptations of youth and took a mistress ... he was faithful to her for fifteen years, until he sent her away while he was in Milan. With his mistress, he fathered a child whom he named Adeodatus (given by God) when he was seventeen" (Fink, 2000:pp.128-129).

As mentioned by Augustine in a previous quotation, Monica followed him across land and sea – in fact, from North Africa to Italy. She "Still mothered Augustine, his students and his friends" (*Conf* 9.9.22, cited in Clark, 2015:50). In Milan, Monica lived with her son and it was here that she and Augustine encountered Ambrose, who was then Bishop of Milan, and is now a canonized saint and Doctor of the Church. Monica pleaded with Ambrose to hear her son's case. She wanted Augustine to be converted and baptised by Ambrose (Falbo, 2007:61). Ambrose was impressed with Monica – with her serenity and her deeply religious behaviour (p.63). Augustine was attracted to the preaching of Ambrose but found it difficult to converse with him. And from my research it appears as if the feeling was mutual! In Ambrose however, Monica "saw the instrument of the salvation of her son" (p.67).

In time and with the guidance of the Letters of St Paul, the reading of which had been precipitated by the voice of a child urging him to read what was before him, Augustine came to the realisation (after this "mystical" experience), that he wanted to be converted to Christianity (Falbo, 2007:75-76). Having made the decision, he couldn't wait to tell his mother, and describes the moment when accompanied by his best friend Alypius: "We went indoors and told my mother, who was overjoyed ... You [God] had also converted her grief into joy far more abundant than she had desired" (*Conf* 8.12.28-30). Falbo (2007) maintains that it was "in [the] August of 386", that Augustine made his decision to convert, and leave everything behind, devoting himself to God (p.79). He had sent away his mistress (concubine) of many years and was preparing to marry a woman who was from a social class similar to his own. This union was being negotiated by Monica, but the marriage did not actually proceed due to Augustine deciding that he wanted to devote his life exclusively to God.

Gillian Clark (2015:80) writes that in the "early autumn of 386, in a borrowed villa at Cassiciacum outside Milan", Augustine, his mother Monica, his son and his brother Navigius, with some friends and students, were engaged in philosophical debates. As mentioned earlier in this chapter, "These dialogues are a major source for [information on] Monica, second only to the *Confessions*. But her part in them is unexpected: as she says, 'have I ever heard, in those books you read, of women brought into this kind of discussion?' (*Ord.* 1.11.31). She had not heard of it, because the techniques of philosophical argument belonged to higher education, which was almost always the preserve of men" (p.81). During the dialogue, Monica was able to bypass the deep philosophical discussion of the group and go to the heart of the matter. She impressed all present even her son, with her simple logic and her intelligent reasoning.

Augustine was proud of his mother and her wisdom, stating in the biography of his life: "I smiled at her with delight, and said, 'Certainly ... Mother, you have laid hold on the citadel of philosophy'" (*b. vita*: 2.10, cited in Gillian Clark, 2015:99). On another occasion "in his *De Ordine* (On Order 11.1.1), Augustine again insisted that his mother be present [at their gathering] ... He wrote that his long experience of life with her had revealed to him her sharp intelligence and the burning of her spirit for the things of God" (cited in Falbo, 2007:92). Augustine writes that he told his mother he was proud of her: "women practiced philosophy in the ancient world, and besides, your philosophy pleases me greatly. In fact, mother, you should know that the Greek word 'philosophy' means 'love of wisdom'" (*De Ordine*, On Order 1.xi.31-33).

Augustine and his son Adeodatus were baptized by Bishop Ambrose in Milan, during the Easter Vigil on 24-25 April 387, Monica's hard-fought battle was finally won. Preparations were made for the group to return to Africa, but enroute, Monica fell ill during their stay at Ostia, waiting for passage to Africa. In 387 Monica succumbed to her illness and passed away. Augustine tells us that Adeodatus witnessed the death of his grandmother, and he was so upset that he had to be helped from the room in which his grandmother had passed away. Adeodatus himself passed away when he was seventeen. The death of his son precipitated Augustine's acceptance of an ecclesial appointment, and when he was about forty-one, he was consecrated Bishop of Hippo, a position he held for almost thirty-five years (pp.132-133).

Over time, Augustine tried to control his grief at the passing of his mother, and towards the end of his *Confessions* which were written more than ten years after Monica's death, he gives vent to his grief before God:

> Then gradually did I call back my earlier feeling for your handmaid, her devout conversation with You, her gentleness to and compliancy with us in holiness, of which suddenly I was destitute. It was pleasing to weep in your sight for her and over her, for myself and over myself. And I released the tears which I had restrained, that they might flow as much as they wished, spreading them under my heart, which rested in them, since Your ears were there, not those of a man, who would interpret my weeping in a haughty spirit. And now, Lord, I will confess to You in writing. Let him read it who will, and let him interpret it as he will, and if he finds a sin in my weeping for my mother for a small part of an hour – a mother who was meanwhile dead to my eyes, who had wept over me for many years that I might live in Your eyes ...

(Augustine asks God to forgive any sins his mother may have committed [Augustine, *Conf.* IX.12, cited in Elizabeth Clark, 1983:257-258]).

According to Gillian Clark (2015:145), Monica "began to be commemorated as a saint almost eight centuries after her death." The feastday of St Monica was celebrated initially on 4 May, which was "believed to be the vigil of St. Augustine's conversion" (Falbo, 2007:122), but in the contemporary Church, her feastday is celebrated on 27 August, which is the day before the feast of her son St Augustine.

Conclusion

If you recall in Chapter 4, I mentioned that throughout the chapters in this book there is an emphasis on service as the essence of leadership, and that faith and values in the study, define the leadership practices and behaviour of significant women leaders in the Catholic Church, from the origins of Christianity, up to and including the dawn of the Third Millennium. The five values listed in the terms of reference (see Chapter 4) are: dignity, respect, fairness, justness and equality – and demonstrate how the women: "who while loyal and committed members of the Catholic Church, an organisation that is hierarchical in nature and structure, could lead and serve within their own milieu, while challenging the status quo."

Leadership as Service

We are all leaders and followers at some stage in our lives. Even though Monica lived in the 4th Century, she would have been responsible for the workings of her household, and the raising of her children. In other words, she was a leader in her home, and service was the essence of her leadership practices. According to Gillian Clark (2015:58): "The word 'served' echoes through Augustine's writings about Monica. She was given to a husband and served him as her master (*Conf.* 9.9.19). She served her parents and her son's friends: 'she cared for us as if she had given birth to all and served us as if she had been born from all'" (*Conf.* 9.9.22).

Remember that when Augustine was engaged in discussion with his mother regarding her contributions to his philosophical discussions, he defined philosophy for her as coming from the Greek, meaning "love of Wisdom". *Wisdom has built her house, she has hewn her seven pillars* (Proverbs 9:1, cited in Sipe & Frick, 2015:4). For the purpose of this analysis, the "Seven Pillars of Servant Leadership" (see Appendix A for the list of attributes) are outlined below, and the discussion on each pillar includes aspects of Monica's life and service in regard to her leadership practices.

Pillar 1 – "Person of Character"

Monica was honest and humble. She accepted her life and respected her husband, regardless of his abusive and philandering behaviour. She didn't criticize or complain to others. She lived for God and her family. Her faith was strong. She was charitable and compassionate toward others. Though she wanted to do everything in her power to see the conversion of her son before she died, Monica didn't compromise her integrity or values to do this. While demonstrating humility and serving a higher purpose, she prayed and shed tears for her wayward son.

Pillar II – "Puts People First"

Throughout her life Monica put others first. She was empathetic to other women, who had abusive husbands. She engaged in charitable works for the Church, and she cared for her husband and children. She looked after her son, his friends and others. Augustine in a conversation to God, explained that "during the hazards at sea she comforted the sailors themselves ... promising them a safe arrival, because You [God] had promised this in a vision" (*Conf* VI.I, cited in Elizabeth Clark, 1983:247).

Pillar III – "Skilled Communicator"

Monica spoke to all with whom she came in contact. She was supportive of her son and his friends. She negotiated finances to be able to ensure that Augustine could continue his tertiary studies. She was able to convince Bishops – for example, Ambrose to come to her aid in her prayers of petition for her son, and she astounded Augustine and his friends when she was able to listen to their philosophical arguments, and then respond in kind with persuasive arguments, that belied her lack of formal education. She didn't shy away from difficult situations but prayed for strength and courage to confront each challenge as it arose.

Pillar IV – "Compassionate Collaborator"

Her service to the Church, played a major role in Monica's life. She was known for her charity and her compassion. She reached out and empathised with women in abusive relationships, offering advice and helping them to cope with their situations. Falbo (2007:30-31) writes that "In essence, Monica lived a life of prayer and charity, harmoniously blending the two ideals of Martha and Mary: action and contemplation. She drew from prayer the breath she needed for her spiritual life and the energy necessary for works of charity." Monica collaborated with Ambrose, the Bishop of Milan, to influence her son in such a way, as to ensure Augustine's conversion to Christianity. She travelled to be with Augustine to look after him and his friends, during their time in Milan, and actively participated in the philosophical discussions which her son organised at the villa in Cassiciacum.

When in Milan, Monica engaged in "shared prayer and fellowship, and she even provided food for those who remained in the basilica for days at a time" (Falbo, 2007:65). On one occasion, during a tense situation when the imperial forces of the empress tried to take over the basilica for the Arians, Ambrose closed the basilica to the intruders, though Monica and the faith community were still inside. The Bishop successfully held the basilica, and the empress and her troops were forced to withdraw. Ambrose and his supporters were jubilant. "Monica had also played her part" by working collaboratively with ... [them] in a potentially dangerous and volatile situation (ibid.).

Pillar V – "Has Foresight"

Monica was able to visualise the future. She believed that her faith and prayers, would ensure that her son Augustine would be converted. According to Augustine, "She came to me ... she was certain that You [God] who had promised the whole would supply the part that remained. She replied to me very calmly and with a heart full of confidence, that she in Christ, trusted that before she left this life, she would see me a believing Catholic" (*Conf* VI.I., cited in Elizabeth Clark, 1983:248). As mentioned in Pillar II, when Augustine speaks to God in his *Confessions* and refers to her comforting the sailors "during the hazards at sea", he maintains that Monica knew that the sailors would be safe "because You [God] had promised her this in a vision" (VI.I. ibid:247).

And again, from Augustine's *Confessions*, "we daily begged from You [God] with strong cries of the heart that You would show her through a vision something about my future marriage, but you never would. She saw certain vain and phantastic things, such as a human spirit concerned with inclinations about this matter brings up. She told me about them ... You [God] had shown her something ... she said she could tell the difference, although she could not explain it in words, between Your revelation and the dreams of her own mind" (*Conf* VI.I3., cited in Clark, 1983:249). Robert Greenleaf posits that "the leader needs to have *a sense for the unknowable* and be able to *foresee the unforeseeable*" (2002:35). Monica had this gift in relation to her intuition about her son's conversion to Christianity.

Pillar VI – "Systems Thinker"

Monica's life revolved around her children, particularly her son Augustine. The "big picture" for her was to have her son "brought back to the fold" as it were. Her life decisions revolved around this purpose. Her vision was to have her son experience God, and to have the same joys and peace that her faith gifted to her. Everything Monica did – for the members of her family, the people she met and helped, including the students and friends of her son – all contributed to her quest to win back her son to God. Her regular communication with Ambrose, Bishop of Milan was a means to an end, but Monica did not abuse his friendship, but accepted his guidance regarding her son. Monica knew what she had to do, and adapted to the circumstances, and her behaviour was always ethical. Her faith journey was her plan to achieve her goal – her thoughts were not of herself but of her son.

When Augustine was keen to leave Carthage and go to Rome, Monica was deeply upset. She thought that Rome would have similar temptations, to those that were rampart in Carthage. So, she decided to go to Rome also, and be there for Augustine, but he was unhappy with this turn of events, and told her that the ship was delayed, and for her to rest and pray. Monica was devastated when she later realised that Augustine had deceived her and had actually left without her. There was an enforced separation, but "after two years ... she was finally able to embrace her Augustine once more" (Falbo, 2007:55), when she arrived in Milan.

Pillar VII – "Leads with Moral Authority"

According to Stephen Covey (cited in Sipe & Frick, 2015:157) *"Moral authority requires sacrifice"*. Monica lived her life according to her values. Even though she was in a difficult marriage, "She was a faithful and compliant wife" (Clark, 2015:4). Her love for her son was strong, and she sacrificed her life for him. However, when Augustine "became a Manichaean, believing that this was the true profound understanding of Christianity" (ibid:139), Monica was extremely distressed at her son's rebellion, and "until she was reassured by a dream that he would rejoin her, Monica thought of refusing to share a house with him or to eat with him (*Conf.* 3.11.19)."

Monica's faith was her life. And until the time that God gave her an indication that Augustine would change his ways and revert to Christianity, she believed that Augustine had betrayed her belief in God, and regardless of her profound love for her son, she was not prepared to compromise her values or her beliefs for him.

Values

Aspects of Monica's life and works are now discussed in relation to the values – dignity, respect, fairness, justness and equality (see Chapter 4 for the terms of reference).

Dignity

Pope St John Paul II in his "Letter to Women" (1995) considers:

> [T]he essential issue of the dignity and rights of women, as seen in the light of the word of God … Thank you, *Women who are mothers!* You have sheltered human beings within yourselves in a unique experience of joy and travail. This experience makes you become God's own smile upon the newborn child, the one who guides your child's first steps, who helps it to grow, and who is the anchor as the child makes its way along the journey of life (para.2).

St Monica gifted her son St Augustine – brilliant theologian and Doctor of the Church – to the Church and to humanity. She maintained her dignity throughout her life – through an abusive marriage and through her efforts to save her son, who was set on the path of self-destruction. She prayed to God for the conversion of Augustine but asked nothing for herself. Through her pain, suffering and humiliation, Monica valued the sacredness of life and faith which was a measure of her human dignity.

Respect

As we have witnessed during her lifetime and beyond, there was much respect for Monica from the Church of antiquity, and now from the contemporary Church. In 2009 during the *Angelus at the Courtyard of the Papal Summer Residence, Castel Gandolfo*, Pope Benedict XVI spoke about the celebration of:

> [T]he liturgical Memorial of St Monica, Mother of St Augustine, considered the model and patroness of Christian mothers. We are provided with a considerable amount of information about her by her son in his autobiography, *Confessions*, one of the widest read literary masterpieces of all time. In them we learn that St Augustine drank in the name of Jesus with his mother's milk, and that his mother brought him up in the Christian religion whose principle remained impressed upon him even in his years of spiritual and moral dissipation. Monica never ceased to pray for him and for his conversion and she had the consolation of seeing him return to the faith and receive Baptism. God heard the prayers of this holy mother, of whom the Bishop of Tagaste had said: "the son of so many tears could not perish" ... St Augustine used to say that his mother had "conceived him twice."

When first married, Monica lived with her mother-in-law, who initially encouraged some of the servants to be disrespectful towards Monica, however, in time because of the person she was, Monica soon gained the respect of her mother-in-law and the servants. Monica's husband was abusive, but respected her religion, and in time this led to his conversion. Initially, her son was wayward, but he still respected and loved his mother as did Adeodatus his son (Monica's grandson), and the other family members and friends. Bishop (Saint) Ambrose respected her "interior piety ... [and her] fervor at the services and by her deeply religious behaviour ... Ambrose would ... sing her praises and congratulate ... [Augustine] on the good fortune of having such a mother" (Falbo, 2007:63). Monica respected herself because she valued others before herself.

Fairness

On my initial reading of the life of Monica, as perceived by her son Augustine in his *Confessions*, I didn't feel that life had been fair to her. The tense situation in her home, and her extreme unhappiness at the lack of religious commitment from her son seemed real, but then I realised that I was observing her life from the perspective of a person living in a different century, time and place. Michael Patton (2002:284) promotes the concept of historical research in understanding societal influences. Paul Leedy and Jeanne Ormrod (2005:169) emphasise that "'history is dimensional. It has dimensions of historical time and historical space.' History does not just occur in a particular time but it 'also happens in a particular place' and it is important for a researcher to consider the dimensions of time and space when undertaking historical research and interpreting historical data" (cited in Cameron, 2009:5-6). After investigating the situation more, I realised that perhaps Monica didn't know any better – perhaps she believed that the life that she was living was the way things were supposed to be. Her reaction to the challenges certainly implies this, as she doesn't seem to criticise the abusive behaviour of her husband, to family members and friends, and in her discussions with her friends, who suffered similar treatment from their husbands, she doesn't take sides, but is fair and encourages positive thinking.

Monica never gives up hope about her son and keeps the dialogue with

God open. I must admit I do wonder at the fairness of the situation with Augustine, and Monica's two other children, but when Augustine quotes his brother Navigius in his *Confessions* – Navigius was at Cassiciacum, and Ostia with Augustine and Monica, there doesn't seem to be any indication of jealousy concerning the attention being given to Augustine. Again, that may have been the sign of the times, as perhaps also is the treatment regarding Augustine's sister, but such an argument is just supposition. In her dealings with members of the Church, and all with whom she came in contact Monica acted fairly – with empathy and with compassion.

Justness

I again felt that I had to approach this value from a contemporary stance, as a female who abhors violence. What was the justness in how Patricius treated his wife? There was the abusive behaviour to Monica and the philandering! Was this the common and accepted behaviour of the male population at the time, for many of Monica's friends bore the signs of their husbands' ill treatment? As mentioned previously even Augustine gives the impression that he saw nothing wrong with the way his father treated his mother. Did he engage in these actions with the mother of Adeodatus? "Who could bear an adulterous wife? Yet a woman is told to bear an adulterous husband! What justice! Why, I ask you, why? 'Because I am a man'" (Aug. *ser.*392.4-5, cited in Gillian Clark, 2015:76). And again:

> Do you see others rushing off to get drunk, even in holy places, where it is quite unfitting? Stop those you can, hold back those you can, frighten those you can, speak gently to those you can, but don't keep quiet. Is it a friend? Let him be mildly admonished. Is it your wife? Let her be sharply reined in. Is it your slave woman? Let her be checked, even by beating (*Jo.EV.TR.10.9*). (ibid.).

Clark (2015:79) maintains that "In Monica's hometown, where domestic violence was endemic and, it seems, unchallenged by family or neighbours, deference was a way of managing, for wives as it was for slaves." She continues: "Victims stay in abusive relationships sometimes because the culture gives them no other resources and their families would suffer if they complained, but also because they believe it is all their fault, that they deserve it" (ibid.). Sadly, we could transcend the centuries and even in our "so-called civilized" post-modern society, the cry of these women and others can still be heard – just the time, century and location are different. Nevertheless, I believe the information revealed in the research, suggests that there was a lack of justness in the behaviour of many males toward females during early antiquity, and that the women didn't really have a voice, for as mentioned earlier in the chapter, it was the men of the time who interpreted the facts and recorded the information.

God showed justness to Monica after her years of tears and prayers for her son Augustine and her years of pain were rewarded when Augustine converted to Christianity. Falbo (2007:130) writes that:

> The story of Monica's life is more relevant today than ever, because it is close to the problems we face in our own time. She had to come to terms with an adulterous, quarrelsome, and unbelieving husband. Despite her best efforts, she raised a son who ignored all moral norms and engaged in the most bizarre experiences, joining various religious sects. Although her methods of dealing with situations as a wife and mother in antiquity often vary from the kinds of solutions available to us today, Monica is still a witness for our time ... she did not run away from her responsibilities ... [she did not] lose or compromise her [values or] Christian identity.

Perhaps there was no "social just-ness" (Helen Taylor Boursier, 2015) in those days of early antiquity, but how can those of us who live in a different age, judge a society that is so far removed from our own? Irrespective of the many differences – societies and cultures have flourished over the centuries, and as we have seen with Monica – saints have emerged – women and men who have achieved justness in their dealings with humanity, and who have been honoured by the Church for their loyalty, commitment and service.

Equality

In some ways, Augustine treated his mother as an "intellectual" equal. However, there has been criticism from various quarters, of the intense relationship between mother and son. Gillian Clark (2015:170-171) maintains that the influence of Freudian and post-Freudian psychology offered a different interpretation of the tears of the devoted mother. She cites "an epigraph from Freud's lecture on femininity by Peter Walcot" (1996:114):

> A mother is only brought unlimited satisfaction by her relation to a son; this is altogether the most perfect, the most free from ambivalence of all human relationships. A mother can transfer to her son the ambition which she has been obliged to suppress in herself and she can expect from him the satisfaction of all that has been left over in her of her masculinity complex.

I suggest that it is not just females, who may want to live the lives that they really want to live through their sons, but from my experience, I believe that there are many males who would also like to live the lives they wanted to live, but for various reasons didn't have the opportunities to do so when younger, and now want to live their lives through their sons.

In his *Confessions* (IX.10.23-25) Augustine recounts a passage where both he and his mother could be classed as equals. It "would be immortalized as the ecstasy at Ostia. For one moment, the Lord permitted Monica and Augustine to contemplate, beyond the boundaries of time, the eternal happiness that comes from God himself" (cited in

Falbo:2007:106):

> Mother and son ... she with her intuition and he with his profound intellect ... Augustine recounts: Our colloquy led us to the point where the pleasures of the body's senses, however intense and in however brilliant a material light enjoyed, seemed unworthy not merely of comparison but even ... of remembrance beside the joy of that life ... we arrived at the summit of our own minds... (*Conf* IX.10.23-25, p.104).

In other words, an equal meeting of minds!! And at that time and in that place – gender would have been irrelevant! You may recall the words of Pope St John Paul II in his Apostolic Letter *Mulieris Dignitatem* "On the Dignity and Vocation of Women" taken from *Genesis* (1:27): *"both man and woman are human beings to an equal degree, both are created in God's image"* (1988:para.6).

This chapter, which has investigated and highlighted the life and faith journey of an extraordinary woman – St Monica, concludes the First Millennium section of this book. Prepare now to enter the Second Millennium, where over the next one thousand years you will meet just thirteen of an infinite number of female leaders, who graced and gifted the Church, with their unique and exceptional leadership qualities, during times of turbulence and efforts at renewal within a 'struggling' Church. The narratives of the faith journey of the selected thirteen women, describes how their lives and works reflect the seven pillars of servant leadership (Sipe & Frick, 2015), with reference also to the values that I believe have defined their leadership practices – dignity, respect, fairness, justness and equality. Monica, and the thirteen women, whose stories and voices are yet to be heard, responded to the Gospel's call to service and challenged the status quo of their day, leaving a prophetic legacy for future generations of leaders and followers in the Catholic Church.

SECOND MILLENNIUM:

Profiles of Selected Women
Leaders & Their Response to the
Call of the Gospel

6

St Hildegard of Bingen

The Second Millennium section begins with Chapter 6 which, with Chapters 8, 11, and 13 update information regarding the content of the two previous books I have written on the four women Doctors of the Catholic Church. The remaining chapters in this section, focus on selected women leaders throughout the centuries. Overall, this section profiles and investigates the lives and faith journeys of thirteen women, in light of their leadership practices, and their service to God, Church and humanity. The analysis is based on the "Seven Pillars of Servant Leadership" (see Appendix A), as identified by Sipe & Frick (2015), with particular emphasis on the five values of dignity, respect, fairness, justness and equality (see Chapter 4 for the terms of reference).

Background – Women Doctors

As of July 2019, there are four women doctors of the Catholic Church – St Hildegard of Bingen, St Catherine of Siena, St Teresa Ávila and St Thérèse of Lisieux. In mid-2012 the manuscript of my doctoral thesis on the then three women doctors of the Catholic Church, titled *Leadership as a call to service The lives and works of Teresa of Ávila, Catherine of Siena and Thérèse of Lisieux* was published, and in October 2012, the proclamation of St Hildegard of Bingen as the fourth woman doctor of the Church, led to the publication of my second book *Leadership as a call to service The life and works of Hildegard of Bingen* in 2015. Each of the four women doctors is a major study in her own right, so if you find that after reading this book, you would like to further your knowledge on one or more of the women doctors, then I recommend that you access my first two publications in the leadership series.

As defined within my previous work: "A Doctor of the Church is a person who has been honoured posthumously by the Church, and who has fulfilled the criteria of eminent doctrine, sanctity of life and acceptance [formal approval] by the Pope and/or his General Council" (Cameron, 2009:2). According to Umberto Betti (1988:282, cited in Steven Payne, 2002:27): "Candidates [for the doctoral title] are meant to be 'doctors of the Church' not merely for their own times but for all time." To date (July 2019), there are just thirty-six Doctors of the Universal Church – thirty-two males and four females.

The Church has now entered its third millennium, but it was not until 1970, towards the end of the second millennium, that Saint Teresa of Ávila was proclaimed the first woman Doctor of the Catholic Church. The proclamation was celebrated on 27 September 1970 by Pope St Paul VI and just one week later, on 4 October 1970, St Catherine of Siena was also proclaimed a Doctor. However nearly three decades were to pass before Pope St John Paul II "conferred the title of Doctor of the Universal Church on St Thérèse of Lisieux on 19 October 1997, the year that marked the anniversary of the centenary of her death" (Cameron, 2012a:8). St Hildegard of Bingen was proclaimed the fourth female Doctor on 7 October 2012, by Pope Benedict XVI (now Pope Emeritus Benedict XVI).

St Hildegard of Bingen

On Pentecost Sunday 2012, just prior to the publication of my first book on the then three women Doctors of the Catholic Church, Pope Benedict XVI announced that a decision had been made to proclaim St Hildegard of Bingen a Doctor, and that the ceremony would take place in October of that same year, when both Hildegard and St John of Ávila would be conferred with the doctoral title. With the first book ready for publication and with interest expressed from various religious communities on the possibility of producing a similar book on servant leadership regarding Hildegard, I immediately began my research and commenced writing the manuscript.

In early 2015, prior to the completion of the book, I received an invitation to attend a one-woman performance on Hildegard, by the International Mezzo-Soprano Linn Maxwell Keller, at the St Mary MacKillop Chapel in Sydney, to commemorate the 25th Anniversary of the Australian Catholic University. I was keen to attend the performance, as Linn had performed Hildegard on the international stage, and I thought that she would know Hildegard quite well, and that if I watched the performance, it would reassure me that I had covered the most important aspects of the life of the most recent female doctor of the Church.

On the evening of 5th May 2015, at least 200 people gathered to view the performance. On entering the Chapel, I met several supporters of Hildegard's healing remedies (by all accounts still being used and very popular today), and many who just loved the music of this 12th century nun – in particular, the *Canticles of Ecstasy* Album by Sequentia. The performance by Linn that evening was superb. Her costume resembled the habit of a 12th century Benedictine nun, and she acted out the life of the saint and sang Hildegard's music while playing medieval instruments.

I realised at the conclusion of the performance, that I had covered much of what was needed to bring Hildegard to life, within the pages of the manuscript of my proposed book. I contacted the university regarding the possibility of Linn writing the Foreword to my book – she was approached and replied that she would be honoured. Her contribution to the book is invaluable, well-written and very informative. Unfortunately, within a year of writing the Foreword, Linn passed away.

Therefore, at this time and now in this space, I dedicate this chapter on St Hildegard of Bingen to the incomparable Linn Maxwell Keller. Linn passed away on 18 June 2016. In the final paragraph in her Foreword to the book on Hildegard, Linn wrote:

Since 2009 I have toured with my play, "Hildegard of Bingen and the Living Light," and I have met audience members all over the English-speaking world who long to know this saint more deeply. My play touches on a few of the many aspects of her amazing and multifaceted life: her initial papal confirmation as a reliable and orthodox visionary of the Church, her music, healing, conflicts with Church hierarchy and her prophecies. Yet there is so much more to St Hildegard's message and ministry! By meeting Hildegard as a servant leader through Christine Cameron's insightful work, we may enrich our relationship to her and to each other. This book will be our guide (cited in Cameron, 2015a:x).

It was an honour to have Linn write the Foreword to my book. Linn's faith journey and leadership of service were illumined by "God" the "Living Light"! She was indeed "a feather on the breath of God" (Hildegard of Bingen). Linn, may you rest in Peace!

Let us now retrace our steps back through the centuries, to the cusp of the late Middle Ages. For the purpose of this investigation on St Hildegard of Bingen, I present a brief outline of my previous research on Hildegard, which can be found in the publication: *Leadership as a call to service The life and works of Hildegard of Bingen* (2015). I then apply aspects of Hildegard's life and works to the "Seven Pillars of Servant Leadership" as defined by Sipe and Frick (2015), and in the analysis of the final Pillar VII "Leads with Moral Authority", I also incorporate the five values of dignity, respect, fairness, justness and equality, in relation to the faith journey of Hildegard and her leadership of service to the Catholic Church.

Profile

As far as we know Hildegard was born around 1098, probably at Bermersheim in Germany, "to parents of noble lineage who were wealthy landowners" (Pope Benedict XVI, 2010a). When Hildegard was about 8 years old, her parents offered her to the church as a 'tithe' to God, because she was the tenth and youngest child. According to Cameron (2015a:12) "Scholars differ on details regarding the age of Hildegard when she was admitted to the monastery, her experiences prior to entry and whether she was admitted as an oblate or enclosed within the monastery."

Emily Sutherland (2010:1, cited in Cameron, 2015a:12-13) writes that there is a difference between the terms "oblate" and "enclosed"; for a child, oblate would be accepted into the community and live with the monks and nuns, and be "expected to participate as fully as possible in monastic life." This would involve communal living, whereby "Enclosure would mean living in isolation, sealed within an enclosed cell, attached to a church or monastery, leading an ascetic life of intense prayer, with minimal contact with the outside world or the monastic community."

Pope Benedict XVI (2010a) states that initially the young Hildegard was placed in the care of a "consecrated widow Uda of Gölklheim" and then, at the monastery at Disibodenberg she was entrusted to the care of a former noblewoman Jutta Von Sponheim, whose family members were known to Hildegard's father. Jutta was a member of the Benedictine Order, and she was an anchoress (Anna Silvas, 1998:xvii). Now an anchoress "was a deeply religious woman who chose to live a solitary life in confined quarters called an anchorage or an anchorhold, which usually consisted of a single small cell. … [An] Anchoress lived within populated communities but the anchorhold was often attached to the wall of a church" (Middle Ages website, 2015).

Besides being the spiritual mother for the monks, Jutta also became Hildegard's "spiritual mother" (Silvas, 1998:xvii). Jutta assumed responsibility for Hildegard's education teaching her "the rudiments of reading and writing", though Hildegard later credited her own theological insights with divine inspiration, stating that "her formal education was limited as she had been taught by an unlearned woman" (Cameron, 2015a:14).

Hildegard was about fifteen when she made her profession with others before Bishop Otto of Bamberg, and her cloistered life of service began in earnest. The monastery at Disibodenberg which was to be her home for many years, had separate living quarters for the women and the men. Jutta was the *Magistra* (teacher and prioress) and the rule of St Benedict was followed by the community of nuns, which "flourished under Jutta's leadership" (ibid.).

When Jutta died in 1136, Hildegard was elected *Magistra*, albeit she accepted the position reluctantly. Later, due to a growth in numbers of young women entering the religious life; lack of suitable accommodation in a monastery that housed both females and males; and increasing tension between Hildegard and Abbot Cuno/Kuno, the Abbot in charge at Disibodenberg, Hildegard left the monastery and established a convent of nuns "at Mount St Rupert [also referred to as Rupertsberg] and [later she established] … its daughter house at Eibingen where the modern Hildegard Abbey stands today" (Linn Maxwell Keller, cited in Cameron, 2015a:ix-x).

Hildegard had been a sickly child and suffered chronic ill health throughout most of her long life, with some scholars citing "severe migraines" as the cause of much of her suffering, and also inferring that the "migraines" were responsible for the visions she experienced. Hildegard died at the convent in Rupertsberg on 17 September 1179. Interestingly, "as early as 1227 AD there were moves to have her canonised and thus over the centuries Hildegard was venerated as a saint but in reality, the formal canonisation process was never completed until 10 May 2012" (Cameron, 2015a:35), some five months before she was elevated to doctoral status. The process is referred to as "equivalent canonisation", and was a special dispensation granted to Hildegard by Pope Benedict XVI. At the time it was stated in the Vatican newspaper *L'Osservatore Romano* (2012, May 12), that Hildegard of Bingen "has finally been proclaimed a saint by the Church after centuries, even though she had been venerated as such since her death particularly within the Benedictine Order."

Pope Benedict XVI described "St Hildegard of Bingen as a 12th Century Benedictine Abbess who was learned in medicine, poetry and music", and was a healer, a poet and a composer, who promoted Church reform through her writings. And during his Homily at the proclamation service for Hildegard, the Pope reflected on the many gifts of this German Benedictine nun. He emphasised Hildegard's impressive achievements, which included her "writings on theology, mysticism, medicine, science and music [she was a composer of Sacred music]", (cited in Cameron, 2015a:31). Hildegard also left a legacy of her "extensive correspondence [some 400 extant letters and replies]; her plays and poetry; and her creation of a 'new' form of language" (ibid.).

The influence of St Hildegard of Bingen regarding her service to the Church, has transcended the centuries, and her life and works continue to inspire many in the contemporary Church. In his Apostolic Letter, *Proclaiming Saint Hildegard of Bingen, professed nun of the Order of Saint Benedict, a Doctor of the Universal Church*, Pope Benedict XVI (2012a) recalled the words of Pope St John Paul II in 1979, when he referred to Hildegard as a "Light for her people and her time." Benedict reinforced the words of the late Pontiff when he stated:

> This great woman truly stands out crystal clear against the horizon of history for her holiness of life and the originality of her teaching. And, as with every authentic human and theological experience, her authority reaches far beyond the confines of a single epoch or society; despite the distance of time and culture, her thought has proven to be of lasting relevance.

Conclusion

The Pope recognised the important contribution that Hildegard's elevation to doctoral status has meant for contemporary women leaders in the Church: "In Hildegard are expressed the most noble values of womanhood: hence the presence of women in the Church and in society is illumined by her presence ... Her ability to speak to those who were far from the faith and from the Church make Hildegard a credible witness of the new evangelization" (*Apostolic Letter*, 2012a). In other words, whether we are female or male leaders in the Church, Hildegard of Bingen encourages us to let the light within us shine, so that our ministry of leadership is illumined by God's Living Light. Hildegard died surrounded by her sisters at the monastery of Rupertsberg Bingen, on 17 September 1179 at the age of 81. Her feastday is celebrated on 17 September.

Leadership as Service

Hildegard's leadership of service is encapsulated by Linn Maxwell Keller in her Foreword to *Leadership as a call to service The life and works of Hildegard of Bingen* (2015a:x):

> St Hildegard's voice as servant leader permeates her own voluminous correspondence. In the nearly 400 extant letters and replies, we meet time and again with a woman who was sought out by popes, cardinals, heads of state, frustrated abbots and abbesses, as well as anonymous monks and lay people. Hildegard consistently urged her correspondents to stay the course, to seek God's will and to do the *right thing*. She treated each person with respect and dignity, and when necessary, called someone to account for inappropriate or unwarranted actions.

In a General Audience in Rome, Pope Benedict XVI (2010b) spoke about St Hildegard of Bingen, and the "spiritual authority [wisdom] with which she was endowed." *Wisdom has built her house, she has hewn her seven pillars* (Proverbs 9:1, cited in Sipe & Frick, 2015:4). For the purpose of this analysis, the "Seven Pillars of Servant Leadership" (see Appendix A for the list of attributes) are outlined below, and the discussion on each pillar includes aspects of Hildegard's life and leadership practices.

Pillar 1 – "Person of Character"

Hildegard grew from childhood to maturity in a monastery, without the comforts of parents or home. Losing a parent or indeed losing both parents, can have "a traumatic effect on a child" (James Hamilton, 2006:1, cited in Cameron, 2015a:13). The warmth of the family home was absent and replaced with the cold walls of a monastery. Even when living within a community of people, there would be occasions when loneliness would intrude, and particularly more so when a child is separated from parents. Though her spiritual mother Jutta Von Sponheim was a presence in her life, Hildegard's major source of solace, was her time spent in prayer. Lucetta Scaraffia (2012, May 11) writes of Hildegard's "mystic childhood experiences", which continued through to adulthood. So, the warmth or light that Hildegard was seeking, became centered on her relationship with God. In her prayer life, she was serving "a Higher Purpose" (Sipe & Frick, 2015:30), which we have seen in the narrative of her life – this "closeness to God" equipped her to cope with all situations. She was an enigma – frail of body but strong of mind. My research on Hildegard revealed that she was:

> subject to "extremes of behaviour". Perhaps in the years in the "anchorhold" combined with the times in which she lived had an impact and added to the development of a multi-faceted personality which comes across [at times] as forceful but also at [other] times as self-doubting and questioning. Nevertheless, Hildegard had inner strength and not content with the status quo was prepared to step outside her comfort zone to deliver the message of the Living Light (*Scivias*, 1990; Cameron, 2015a:199:200).

Hildegard was "bold and outspoken. She had courage and she took risks. She negotiated, compromised and on occasion ignored the opinion of others" (Cameron, 2015a:198). Pope Benedict XVI recounts the time when the "Emperor Frederic Barbarossa caused a schism in the

Church, by supporting at least three anti-popes against Alexander III, the legitimate Pope, Hildegard did not hesitate, inspired by her visions, to remind him that even he, the Emperor, was subject to God's judgement. With fearlessness, a feature of every prophet, she wrote to the Emperor these words as spoken by God: 'You will be sorry for this wicked conduct of the godless who despise me! Listen, O King, if you wish to live! Otherwise my sword will pierce you!'" (2010b, cited in Eduard Gronau, 1996:412). Hildegard led by example. She walked her talk as it were.

Hildegard responded to the call to service, and her legacy is evident today in the message of her writings, which inspired popes and the faithful alike; in her music which transports listeners to another reality, and in her charism, which is embedded in the culture of the Benedictine communities.

Pillar II – "Puts People First"

When Hildegard was elected *Magistra* on the death of the saintly Jutta, she assumed full responsibility for the nuns under her care. As the numbers grew, Hildegard became concerned at the lack of suitable accommodation at the monastery at Disibodenberg and approached the Abbot about finding alternative living arrangements for the nuns. The monks were reluctant to let the nuns leave, as when the young women entered the monastery their wealthy families donated huge monetary settlements, and so it was primarily for financial reasons then that they did not give their support to Hildegard's request to leave Disibodenberg. At a General Audience in Rome Pope Benedict XVI (2010a), recalled the occasion when there were increasing numbers of young women wanting to enter the monastery, and because of this and the "dominating male monastery" at Disibodenberg, Hildegard broke away with her community and settled at Rupertsberg near Bingen.

On another occasion, the Pope (2010b) maintained that "the popularity that surrounded Hildegard impelled many people to seek her counsel. It is for this reason, that we have so many of her letters at our disposal. Male and female monastic communities turned to her for advice, as did several Bishops and Abbots." Hildegard was compassionate and empathised with the needs of those who sought her guidance.

Pillar III – "Skilled Communicator"

As is evidenced from the almost 400 letters that are still extant, Hildegard had little difficulty in communicating with others. In her letters and dealings with popes, archbishops, kings, emperors, queens, abbesses, abbots, nuns, monks, laywomen and lay men, she encountered challenges with strength and with determination. In fact, letter writing was not the only area in which she was proficient. In his Apostolic Letter proclaiming Hildegard a Doctor of the Church, Benedict (2012a) emphasises that "Her main writings are the *Scivias* ["You Know the Ways"], the *Liber Vitae Meritorum* ["Book of the merits of life"] and the *Liber Divinorum Operum* ["Book of the divine works"], also called *De operatione Dei*. Her works relate her visions and the tasks she received from the Lord to transcribe them." We know that Hildegard was a prolific writer, and her many works also include 58 sermons, and her books on medicine (*Physica* and *Causae et Curae* "a medical compendium"), which unlike her visionary works are not considered divinely inspired.

At the age of 60 and for the next ten years or so, when many would consider slowing down, Hildegard embarked on four preaching tours travelling across the country, along the Rhine to Trier and Metz and then Cologne and finally to Zwiefalten. Benedict (2010b) asserts that "in the last years of her life Hildegard set out on journeys, despite her advanced age and the uncomfortable conditions of travel, in order to speak to the people of God." Hildegard had a gift for communication and for getting her point across to others. Her "persuasion techniques are evidenced by testimonials from witnesses to her life and works; through her influence in persuading others to support her endeavours; through her charismatic personality and through her persuasive letter writing" (Cameron, 2015a:98).

Pillar IV – "Compassionate Collaborator"

During her lifetime, Hildegard worked with several secretaries who initially assisted her with her writings, and eventually commenced collating correspondence and other information, towards the eventual writing of her *Vita* – life story. The most loved – a true friend and her spiritual advisor, was the monk Volmar (on occasion ably assisted by her close friend Sr Richardis di Strade), and when Volmar died in about 1173 he was replaced as secretary by another monk Gottfried [Godfrey], who died some three years after Volmar. Then a "learned" monk Guibert assumed the role of secretary (Silvas, 1998:xxi), until his departure a year or so following Hildegard's death. According to Baird (2006:135), Guibert *"was ... her last intimate associate and secretary."* Hildegard collaborated with her secretaries, sharing her notes and her correspondence. However, it was not until some years after her death that her *Vita* was finally completed (Cameron, 2015a).

There were occasions when Hildegard experienced conflict. There was the emotional conflict when she continued to have visions and doubted the source, and so initially tried to keep these experiences to herself. There seemed to be continual conflict with the monks at the Disibodenberg monastery, particularly when Hildegard initiated the idea of a change of living quarters for the growing numbers of nuns, and eventually relocated with her sisters to Rupertsberg. Hildegard was concerned that the monks would want to "usurp a right over the estates of St Rupert" (Silvas, 1998:147), so she approached the Bishop's office at Mainz and was approved and given the rights to the property."

Benedict (2012a) often emphasised, that "Hildegard was committed to caring for the spiritual and physical 'well-being' of the members of her community [her team]: 'Within the walls of the cloister, she cared for the spiritual and material well-being of her sisters, fostering in a special way community life, culture and the liturgy'" (cited in Cameron, 2015a:145). However, Hildegard was mindful of the weaknesses of human nature, and was every ready to support her sisters and assist their spiritual, physical and emotional growth. Silvas (1998:113, as cited in Cameron, 2015a:146) quotes from Hildegard's *Vita* stating that: "When there were rebels in the community, she [Hildegard] did not immediately reproach them sharply or cut them off. Instead she used to overlook, warn, put up with, and patiently bide the time, until through a revelation from God she received counsel as to what she should do about them."

The Pope (2012a) stressed that besides her empathy for her sisters, Hildegard possessed a deep compassion for the Church and its people. She collaborated with all groups "In the outside world she devoted herself actively to strengthening the Christian faith and reinforcing religious practice, opposing the heretical trends of the Cathars, promoting Church reform through her writings and preaching and contributing to the improvement of the discipline and life of clerics." Hildegard was empathetic to the needs of others.

Pillar V – "Has Foresight"

Hildegard experienced visions from her early childhood. But it was in 1141 that she experienced a spiritual awakening that would change her life forever.

> When I was forty-two years and seven months old, heaven was opened, and a fiery light of exceeding brilliance came and permeated my whole brain, and inflamed my whole heart and my whole breast, not like a burning but a warming flame, as the sun warms anything its rays touch. And immediately I knew the meaning of the exposition of the Scriptures, namely the Psalter, the Gospel and other Catholic volumes of both the Old and the New Testaments

(*Scivias*, 1990:59, cited in Cameron, 2015a:88).

It was at this time that Hildegard developed awareness of the meaning of all the visions that she had experienced since the "age of five" (*Scivias*, 1990:60). In his Apostolic Letter proclaiming St Hildegard a Doctor of the Universal Church, Pope Benedict XVI (2012a) refers to Hildegard as the "mystic of Bingen". He suggests that it is her "acute wisdom-filled and prophetic sensitivity" that focuses "her attention on the point of revelation … and in her visions and her subsequent reflections she presents a compendium of the history of salvation from the beginning of the universe until its eschatological consummation" (ibid.). The Pope (2010a) refers to her as the "Teutonic prophetess … [which] is the seal of an authentic experience of the Holy Spirit, the source of every charism." He also spoke about Hildegard's early years as "a superior at the Monastery of Disibodenberg … [when she] began to dictate the mystical visions that she had been receiving for some time, to the monk Volmar, her spiritual director, and to Richardis di Strade, her secretary" (ibid.).

Initially, Hildegard was reluctant to discuss her visions. She was plagued with self-doubt, and in all humility was worried about how her visions would be interpreted. However, she needed to get the message out there. Eventually St Bernard of Clairvaux consulted with Pope Eugene III who read Hildegard's work and requested that she record her visions and present them publicly (ibid.). Centuries later another Pontiff – Benedict XVI (2010a), who as Pope held the title 'Servant of the Servants of God' stated that:

> this great woman, this 'prophetess' who also speaks with great timeliness to us today, with her courageous ability to discern the signs of the times, her love for creation, her medicine, her poetry, her music, which today has been reconstructed, her love for Christ and for his church which was suffering in that period too, wounded also in that time by the sins of both priests and lay people.

"Hildegard demonstrated foresight through her visionary leadership and her prophetic gifts" (Cameron, 2015:185).

Pillar VI – "Systems Thinker"

The "big picture" for Hildegard was building community with her sisters in religion and following the Rule of St Benedict, which Sr Philippa Rath OSB (1996) maintains in her article "is more than 1400 years old." Hildegard also built up community by her efforts at Church "reform through her apostolic, pastoral activities and through establishing two monasteries during her lifetime" (Cameron, 2015a:156). The monasteries were at Rupertsberg near Bingen and Eibingen, which was not far from Rüdesheim. Please note (as per the practice of some of the historical scholars) that the terms 'convent' and 'monastery' are often used interchangeably (p.161). However, I believe that it was the practice in those early years for some nuns (and monks) to live in monasteries while some priests resided in convents.

It was during her time at Rupertsberg, that Hildegard completed the first in her trilogy of visionary works – the *Scivias*. According to Newman, "This intense burst of activity directed toward [her work and] her daughters, was complemented by an ever-widening correspondence with the outside world. Hildegard's growing fame brought a constant stream of pilgrims and miracle-seekers, as well as prospective nuns, to the Rupertsberg gates" (1990:13-14, cited in Cameron, 2015a:160).

Pillar VII – "Leads with Moral Authority"

Hildegard had confidence in her nuns and their abilities. She was firm but flexible. She set her standards, and she empowered the members of her community to think for themselves. However, her often "unorthodox" leadership methods were at times criticised by others. One such lengthy letter of criticism to her, was from a Mistress Tengswich (Baird, 2006:24-26, cited in Cameron, 2015a:151) which is cited, in part, below:

We have, however also heard about certain strange and irregular practices that you countenance. They say that on feast days your virgins stand in the church with unbound hair when singing the psalms and that as part of their dress they wear white, silk veils, so long they touch the floor. Moreover, it is said that they wear crowns of gold filigree into which are inserted crosses on both sides and the back, and with a figure of the Lamb on the front, and that they adorn their fingers with golden rings. And all this despite the express prohibition of the great shepherd of the Church, who writes in admonition: Let women comport themselves with modesty "not with plaited hair, or gold, or pearls, or costly attire" [1 Tim 2.9].

Hildegard's equally long response was not one of denial, however, she did tend to justify her reasons for allowing the virgins in her care to reveal the beauty of their person and soul to their divine bridegroom. Part of her response was to emphasise that: "Virgins are married with holiness in the Holy Spirit and in the bright dawn of virginity, and so it is proper that they come before the great high priest as an oblation presented to God … it is appropriate for a virgin to wear a white vestment the lucent symbol of her betrothal to Christ" (p.152).

Hildegard's "collection" of writings included the "Play of Virtues" (*Ordo Virtutum*). Butcher (2013:69, as cited in Cameron, 2015a:154) elaborates:

> *The Play of Virtues* is a medieval musical drama and "a splendid staging of the Soul's struggle with the Devil. It is also the earliest surviving morality play." The play narrates a struggle between seventeen virtues and the devil for possession of a human soul … The play is about choices and would have been a good lesson for the nuns in their interaction with one another" teaching them to make decisions for the common good.

"As the leader and spiritual mother of her nuns ... [Hildegard considered her role] to be her highest responsibility and her moral duty" (Linn Maxwell Keller, cited in Cameron 2015a:x).

Values

Aspects of Hildegard's life and works are now discussed in relation to the values – dignity, respect, fairness, justness and equality (see Chapter 4 for the terms of reference).

Dignity

Pope Benedict XVI recalls the Apostolic Letter *Mulieris Dignitatem*, "On the Dignity and Vocation of Women" by Pope St John Paul II, who wrote on "the precious role that women have played and [continue to] play in the life of the Church" (2010a). Benedict emphasises that, "Various female figures stand out for the holiness of their life and the wealth of their teaching even in those centuries of history that we usually call the Middle Ages." The Pope speaks highly of the sanctity of Hildegard of Bingen, who possessed integrity and human dignity. She responded to the call of the Gospel and engaged in active discipleship in her time, and the fruit of her endeavours (her writing, music, healing remedies to name a few) has lasted through the centuries.

Silvas (1998:209) also reminds us of the holiness of this women, who was loved by her community. She celebrated the sacredness of womenhood, and many of her writings reflect this particularly in her approach to sensitive female medical issues, in her role as a physician and in her understanding of the workings of the female anatomy. She treated with respect and dignity all who sought her healing advice and remedies. However, Hildegard's own health was quite poor, and several historical scholars believe that her visions were caused by migraines, which on occasion, resulted in her being unable to function or leave her sick bed. However, this condition did not affect her relationship with her daughters, who respected her dignified struggle to cope with the challenges of severe ill-health throughout her life. Silvas (ibid.) writes that Hildegard "had waged battles for the lord with many difficult struggles ... She had labored in illness for some time, when in the eighty-second year of her life ... she departed with a happy passage to her heavenly spouse. Her daughters, to whom she had been all joy and solace, wept bitterly as they took part in the funeral rites of their beloved mother" (Cameron, 2015a:201).

Many miracles were performed in Hildegard's name following her death. So much so that in 1228 Pope Gregory IX informed his "ecclesial colleagues" that the Benedictine nuns had petitioned the Church to have Hildegard canonised a saint. An investigation was conducted, and witnesses called, however, it would be many years before this honour was bestowed albeit following a process referred to as "equivalent canonization" (Scaraffia, 2012, May 11), which is explained in a previous paragraph in this chapter.

In life and in death, Hildegard influenced her fellow human beings. In fact, after her death there were many complaints regarding the large number of people who visited her tomb in the hope of having the saint perform miracles. Apparently, their presence at the tomb caused disruptions to the daily lives of the nuns (Silvas, 1998:269, cited in Cameron, 2015a:102). As a result, the Archbishop personally went to the tomb and ordered Hildegard "to stop the signs" (ibid.). The situation then eased. The contemporary Church has honoured Hildegard by admitting her to the catalogue of saints, and almost immediately elevating her to doctoral status.

Respect

Fordham University published "The Life and Works of Hildegard von Bingen (1098-1179)" on its website. The information includes the following:

Hildegard of Bingen (1098-1179) was a remarkable woman, a 'first' in many fields. At a time when few women wrote, Hildegard, known as "Sybil of the Rhine", produced major works of theology and visionary writings. When few women were accorded respect, she was consulted by and advised bishops, popes, and kings. She used the curative powers of natural objects for healing and wrote treatises about natural history and medicinal uses of plants, animals, trees and stones.

In fact, Hildegard had a huge respect for the environment, so much so, that contemporary scholars advise caution when referring to Hildegard as a "naturalist" in regard to environmental issues. Sabina Flanagan (1995, cited in Cameron, 2015a:7) "stresses this with her emphasis that environmentalism as such would not have been a consideration in Hildegard's era."

Hildegard was respected by popes, emperors and most people with whom she came in contact. You may recall that St Bernard of Clairvaux consulted with Pope Eugene III on her behalf, and that he directed Hildegard to record her visions and then speak about them publicly. On another occasion her 'prophetic persona' resulted in Hildegard being called before the Emperor Frederick Barbarossa at Ingelheim in about 1155, "to give a prophetic oracle, the contents of which neither party ever disclosed in writing" (Newman, 1990:15, cited in Cameron, 2015a:129). Nevertheless, Frederick seemed to be extremely happy with the outcome, and having much respect for Hildegard, asked for her continued prayers and those of her sisters (ibid.).

Fairness

Recall the situation in Pillar IV "Compassionate Collaborator", when Hildegard engaged in dialogue with the monks regarding her purchase of the property at Rupertsberg. You may remember that the monks were less than pleased when Hildegard wanted to relocate her nuns, for their families had paid huge sums for their daughters to be accepted into the order. Hildegard was quite fair in her resolution of the situation for she:

> Explained why she was compelled to come, and, while there, separated the place of her new monastery along with some other properties belonging to her community from the brothers of that monastery, but left to them the larger portion of possessions which had been given to it when the sisters had been first received, and in addition left them a not inconsiderable sum of money so that there might remain no just cause for complaint (Silvas, 1998:148-149, cited in Cameron, 2015a:159).

There was a time towards the end of her life, when Hildegard may have believed that she was being treated unfairly by Church bodies, when the Diocese of Mainz accused her and her sisters of burying the body of a nobleman, whom they (the Church authorities) maintained had died "excommunicate", and therefore, was not entitled to be buried in the monastery grounds. Hildegard refused to abide by the order, agreeing that the nobleman had been excommunicated from the Church, but that he had been reconciled prior to this death. The community was soon placed under an ecclesiastical interdict, which included being forbidden the reception of the Eucharist, and in addition all forms of liturgical music were prohibited. In time, Hildegard was proven to be correct in her version of the events, but she was over 80, and the unjustness of the situation and its consequences took their toll, and within six months of the episode, Hildegard would pass to eternal life.

Justness

Hildegard's communication with so many people from all walks of life, necessitated that she be fair and just in her dealings with them. In particular, Hildegard was quite concerned about the need to reform the clergy. "She called ... all the monastic communities and the clergy to a life in conformity with their vocation" (Pope Benedict XVI, 2010a). Scaraffia (2012, May 11) maintains that Hildegard was, "certain of being the bearer of the divine message, [and so] she dedicated herself to preaching, travelling around Germany, and even speaking in churches. She urged the Popes to reform, harshly criticizing them and explaining that the Holy Spirit spoke through her, a woman, because the Church, led by men, had betrayed in many ways ... its nature and ... its mission."

In a poignant reminder of past injustices by the Church, in regard to the behaviour of some members of its clergy, Pope Benedict XVI in his address to the Roman Curia on 20 December 2010 (midway through the celebration of the "Year for Priests"), recalled with deep sorrow the sins of those who had abused children, and in doing so had betrayed the children and the Church. "We were all the more dismayed then, when in this year of all years and to a degree we could not have imagined, we came to know of abuse of minors committed by priests who twist the sacrament into its antithesis, and under the mantle of the sacred profoundly wound human persons in their childhood, damaging them for a whole lifetime" (2010e).

On this occasion, the Pope (ibid.) recalled the words of Hildegard, in her efforts to fight for justness for those who suffered injustice at the hands of members of the Church. Benedict informed the assembled group:

> [A] vision of Saint Hildegard of Bingen come to my mind, a vision which describes in a shocking way what we have lived through this past year. [Hildegard recounts] "In the year of our Lord's incarnation 1170, I had been lying on my sick-bed for a long time when, fully conscious in body and in mind, I had a vision of a woman of such beauty that the human mind is unable to comprehend. She stretched in height from earth to heaven."

The Pope (ibid.) then narrates Hildegard's description of the beautiful woman – how she appeared and how she was dressed. He then repeats what Hildegard then noticed about the woman that "her face was stained with dust, her robe was ripped down the right side, her cloak had lost its sheen of beauty and her shoes had been blackened." The woman is identified as the betrothed of the Son of Man, "who was conceived and born in virginity, [and who] poured out his blood" (ibid.). The Pope continues Hildegard's dialogue of her vision:

> For my Bridegroom's wounds remain fresh and open as long as the wounds of men's sins continue to gape. And Christ's wounds remain open because of the sins of priests. They tear my robe, since they are violators of the Law, the Gospel and their own priesthood; they darken my cloak by neglecting, in every way, the precepts which they are meant to uphold; my shoes too are blackened, since priests do not keep to the straight paths of justice, which are hard and rugged, or set good examples to those beneath them. Nevertheless, in some of them I find the splendor of Truth (ibid.).

The Pope reveals that the voice Hildegard heard was from heaven, and that the image she saw in her vision was the Church. Benedict is reinforcing the message of Hildegard, which was given so many centuries ago to an ailing Church, so that the contemporary Church, will accept accountability for any transgressions committed by members – its clergy, and understand that for healing to occur there needs to be justness and compassion for all!

Equality

If we refer to the *Apostolic Letter* (2012a) proclaiming St Hildegard of Bingen, a Doctor of the Church, we find that the Pope had immense respect for Hildegard and her works:

Human beings are seen as a unity of body and soul ... Our bodies, like the body of Christ, are oriented to the glorious resurrection, to the supreme transformation for eternal life ... The human being exists in both the male and female form. Hildegard recognized that a relationship of reciprocity and a substantial equality between man and woman is rooted in this ontological structure of the human condition.

Equality means many things – basic human rights, diversity, inclusion, awareness – and much, much more. Finally, whether the candidate is female or male, the criteria for consideration to be proclaimed a Doctor of the Universal Church are the same. St Hildegard of Bingen fulfilled each of the three criterions – eminent doctrine, profound sanctity, and the acceptance and [formal] approval by the Pope and/or his General Council (all of which comprise the criteria necessary for admittance to the select group of Doctors of the Catholic Church).

In Chapter 7, we fast forward to the thirteenth century where we meet St Clare of Assisi, Co-founder of the Order of Poor Clares.

7

St Clare of Assisi

Pope Francis visited Assisi and the Basilica of St Clare, on 5 October 2013, praying at the crypt where the saint is buried, and then meeting with the cloistered nuns of the order, which is said to be co-founded by St Clare and St Francis of Assisi. Please note that some documents while acknowledging the contribution of St Francis, cite St Clare as the Foundress. However, according to other scholars, "there are clear indicators in ... [Clare's] writing that St Francis alone is the founder of her Order" (Personal correspondence, 19 June 2019). Hence, due to inconsistencies in data researched and for the purpose of this chapter, St Clare will be referred to as the Co-founder of the Order of Poor Clares.

During his visit and at an open discussion with the assembled religious at Assisi, Pope Francis spoke about external perceptions of the cloistered way of life and stressed that though their lives of prayer and contemplation are experienced in isolation and austerity, their consecrated lives signified much more than that. The Pontiff emphasised that prayer and contemplation lead to love of the crucified Christ, and a desire to pray for the needs of humanity. He also spoke about the value of communal living: "Forgive and support each other, because community life is not easy ... Make sure that the monastery is not a purgatory, but rather a family ... Cherish community life, because when the community is like a family, the Holy Spirit is among the community" (Ester Regina Blog, 2013). It is this emphasis on contemplation and community life, that is at the heart of the message of St Clare of Assisi, whose faith journey commenced more than eight centuries ago.

Profile

It was around 16 July in the late twelfth century, that Chiara Offreduccio was born in Assisi, Italy, to Favarone di Offreduccio a wealthy nobleman, and his devout wife Ortulana. There is some discrepancy regarding the year of Chiara's birth, as various historians cite 1194, while others quote 1193. In the acts of the process of canonization of Clare of Assisi, it states that "The date of her death is certain, August 11, 1253. Yet that of her birth, eighteen years before her entrance into religious life ... is obscure ..." (Franciscan Intellectual Tradition, 2017:145).

It is believed that Chiara, or as we have come to know her – Clare – was the eldest of three daughters. The women of the family were often engaged in pious practices, feeding the poor, and caring for the sick. Later in our narrative you will discover that in time, sisters Catherine, Beatrice and their mother Ortulana, all joined Clare in the religious life. Also some historians refer to Catherine as Agnes, and suggest she received the name from St Francis, when she joined Clare some days after Clare's conversion, and subsequent flight from the family home, when Clare decided to surrender her life to God, to live a life inspired by the Gospel.

However, if Catherine received the name Agnes on entering the religious life, one might then ask why did Clare and Beatrice, and other members of their community, retain their baptismal names on entry? Nevertheless, some Catholic records show that Agnes has since been declared a canonised saint of the Church, and is referred to as St Agnes of Assisi, while Clare's mother Ortulana is given the title of Blessed (Kevin Knight, 2017). Clare's younger sister Beatrice is also sometimes referred to as Blessed. Unfortunately, I could find no evidence to support the beatification of either Ortulana or Beatrice. Evidently, "in those early centuries, it was common practice to call holy people 'beata – Blessed', but many were not officially beatified" (Personal correspondence, 19 March 2015). This may have been the case with Ortulana and/or Beatrice!

Unfortunately, little is known of the early life of Clare, and what information is available is found in the testimonies of the witnesses, given during the process of her canonisation (Franciscan Intellectual Tradition, 2016). Joan Mueller (2010:18) writes, "Although Clare says nothing about her life in the Offreduccio household in her writings, the process of canonization offers direct testimony concerning Clare's youth." The process commenced just two years after Clare's death, with fifteen witnesses from the convent interviewed (including friends who joined the order); plus, five additional witnesses, including neighbours of the family. Clare's written legacy includes her *Forma Vitae* (Form of Life), which was the Rule written by Clare, and is acknowledged as the first rule that was written for religious women by a woman in the Church (Bill Short, 2009).

Background

Clare was born on the cusp of the 13th century, and Italy at that time, was "a cauldron of political and military strife. Society was divided into two groups: the maiores and minores. The maiores were the nobility. The minores were former serfs, who had become merchants, craftsmen and field workers. These two groups were continually fighting for power among themselves" (Sister Claire André Gagliardi, n.d.). Clare and her family lived in a "palazzo", which was situated close to the church of St Rufino. The families of the nobility, besides having their residences in the town, also "owned country castles and land, that provided them with revenue and resources" (Mueller, 2010:11).

In Assisi at the time, the nobility and their families, including Clare, her parents and her sisters: "lived on the upper regions near S. Rufino and the Merchant families (including the family of St Francis) lived in the strata below S. Rufino." Mueller (ibid.) maintains that at the "beginning of the 13th Century, economic predictability of the old feudal law was being challenged." The merchants were increasing their trade, and with their growing wealth, were becoming a threat to the nobility, who were forced "to borrow to maintain their lifestyle" often from the merchants (ibid.).

Dissatisfied with the situation, merchants who were opposed to the ruling nobility, fought for control. The noble faction was exiled, and many found refuge in Perugia (*Key to Umbria* website). Thus, Clare and her mother and sisters, were exiled along with other members of nobility. While her father Favarone and the other knights and noblemen, were engaged in fighting wars, Clare and her mother and sisters were assisting the poor and destitute, bringing them food and visiting the prisoners. Some scholars suggest, that Clare may have even visited St Francis, who as a merchant's son and soldier, had been captured and jailed in Perugia for twelve months, and following a ransom paid by his father, returned to Assisi an ill man. It is also suggested, that his conversion may have commenced about this time (ibid.).

Perugia declared war on Assisi in 1202, and then around 1204, an "uneasy peace" existed between both warring factions (*Key to Umbria* website). Consequently, it was about 1205, that Clare and her family returned to Assisi. At this time, Francis was engaged in rebuilding the Church of San Damiano. Regis Armstrong (2006:15) maintains, that there is little information available, as to when Clare may have met Francis – it could have been when he was in Prison in Perugia, or perhaps she heard of his preaching at the Cathedral of San Rufino?

In 1211 or 1212, when Clare was about eighteen years of age, following the Palm Sunday service, Francis and the brothers received her at the chapel of St Mary of the Angels (the Portiuncula), after she had absconded from the family home. Her biological sister Beatrice testified at the process of canonization of Clare that:

> Saint Francis gave her the tonsure [shaving off her hair] before the altar in the church of the Virgin Mary, called the Portiuncula, and then sent her to the church of San

Paolo de Abbadesse. When her relatives wanted to drag her out, Lady Clare grabbed the altar cloths and uncovered her head, showing them that she was tonsured. In no way did she acquiesce, neither letting them take her from that place nor remaining with them (Franciscan Intellectual Tradition, 2017:183).

Clare's family upon discovering that she was "missing", searched and found her in the Church. However, by showing her "cropped" head to her family, Clare was demonstrating that she was no longer available, to be given in matrimony to an earthly suitor; for now, as Christ's bride, she was engaged in service to Him. Mueller (2010:34) maintains that "the cutting of her hair made her worthless as a bride and made her choice irrevocable":

A papal bull of [Pope] Innocent III on May 5, 1201, granted numerous privileges to the Benedictine nuns including broad rights of asylum and forbidding the use of violence under the pain of excommunication. Therefore, in San Paolo, St. Clare was safe from any violent reaction on the part of her family (Franciscan Intellectual Tradition, 2017:183).

Hence, finding Clare in the church of San Paolo, Clare's family could not retaliate, under threat of excommunication, as per papal directives. St Francis and his brothers, then took Clare to the church of Sant'Angelo di Panzo, where holy laywomen (Beguines), who belonged to no particular religious order resided. Clare's younger sister Catherine joined her after a few days, and the family again reacted with hostility. After an unpleasant confrontation, and unsuccessful attempts to abduct Catherine to return her to her home, the family finally accepted, that Clare and now Catherine were forever lost to them. In time, Francis brought Clare, Catherine (now referred to as Agnes), and a small group of their followers to the church of San Damiano, and it was at the monastery in this location, that Clare was to spend the next forty and more years of her life. The order became known, as the Order of Poor Ladies, "a monastic religious order for women in the Franciscan tradition" (Mueller, 2010).

The first witness for the process of Clare's canonization, was a Sister Pacifica de Guelfuccio, who was a nun at the monastery of San Damiano, where we have said that Clare lived her entire religious life. Under oath, Pacifica testified that, "she knew Saint Clare while that holy woman was in the world in her father's house; and that she was considered by all those who knew her [to be a person] of great honesty and of very good life; and that she was intent upon and occupied with works of piety." Pacifica also stated, "that Saint Clare began the Order that is now at San Damiano, through the admonition of Saint Francis." She acknowledged, that she was a neighbour and distant relative of Clare and her family (Franciscan Intellectual Tradition, 2017:144).

Pacifica (p.146) also testified that "Lady Ortulana came to that same Order as her holy daughter, blessed Clare, and lived in it with the other sisters in great humility." Unfortunately, the notes (ibid.) suggest that "the date of Ortulana's entrance into San Damiano is not known." Clare, her sister Agnes, Pacifica and others, who become known as the "Poor Ladies of San Damiano", were followers of Francis, and "he provided them [initially] with a 'form of life' [a rule – referred to as *forma vitae*]. It is a very simple statement [see below], describing the Trinitarian foundations of the life at San Damiano, as well as the close ties that would bind the Poor Ladies with Francis and his brothers" (Armstrong, 2006:16):

> Because of divine inspiration you have made yourselves daughters and handmaids of the most High, most exalted King, the heavenly Father, and have taken the Holy Spirit as your spouse, choosing to live according to the perfection of the holy Gospel, I resolve and promise for myself and for my brothers always to have the same loving care and special solicitude for you as for them.

It was in this way, that Clare and Francis responded to the call of scripture: "If you wish to be perfect, go, sell your possessions, and give the money to the poor, and you will have treasure in heaven; then come, follow me" (Mat 19:21). The "Poor Ladies" and the Brother, chose to live their lives according to the Gospel. The order of brothers was called Friars Minor, or Franciscans, and was established by St Francis in 1209 (Short, 2009), and became involved with the San Damiano monastery, following the arrival of Clare and her Sisters. Mueller (2010:52) writes that the "brothers played a pivotal role in begging for the needs of the sisters, keeping the monastery in basic repair, and providing the sisters with spiritual care."

Now in her testimony, "Pacifica testified that Clare ... [three years after her conversion and] at the insistence of Francis accepted the direction and governance of the Sisters" (Mueller, 2010:51). However, according to the *Legend of Saint Clare*, "she declined the name and office of abbess, willing to be a servant to her sisters" (p.52). Nevertheless, Clare was to lead the group of nuns at San Damiano, for over forty years until her death in 1253.

According to tradition, "Pope Innocent III had issued a privilege enabling Clare and the Poor Ladies of San Damiano to live more in accord with the poverty envisioned by Francis" (Armstrong, 2006:86), but the authenticity of this information is questioned. And it was not until the election of Pope Gregory IX, that the "Privilege of Poverty", was issued on September 17, 1228. The following is taken from Gregory's letter to Clare:

> Gregory, Bishop, Servant of the servants of God, to his beloved daughters in Christ, Clare and the other servants of Christ gathered together in the church of San Damiano of the diocese of Assisi, health and apostolic benediction. As is evident, you have renounced the desire from all temporal things, desiring to dedicate yourselves to the Lord alone. Because of this, *since you have sold all things and given them to the poor,* you propose not to have any possessions

whatsoever, clinging in all things to the footprints of Him, *the way, the Truth, and the Life* Who, for our sake, was made poor ... He Who *feeds* the birds *of the heavens* and clothes *the lilies of the field* will not fail you in either food or clothing ... Therefore, we confirm with our apostolic authority, as you requested, your proposal *of most high poverty,* granting you by the authority of [those] present that no one can compel you to receive possessions... (Armstrong, 2006:87).

Armstrong wonders, if Gregory was fully aware of the implications of the Decree, as in later years he was inclined "to offer relaxations and dispensations to the Poor Ladies at San Damiano and elsewhere" (ibid.). However, Clare steadfastly refused all offers, as she strongly believed in maintaining absolute poverty in accordance and obedience to the Gospel.

Sister Beatrice, Clare's biological sister, was the twelfth witness, and in the notes of the process of canonization of Clare, it states that Beatrice "was the third and youngest daughter of Clare's family. She entered the monastery of San Damiano in 1229 and died there in 1260" (Franciscan Intellectual Tradition, 2017:183). Beatrice spoke effusively about the "Lady Clare of holy memory whose life was, from her childhood, almost angelic; that she was a virgin and remained always so. She was careful about good deeds of holiness so her good reputation was spread about among all who knew her" (ibid.). Prior to entering religious life, Clare's fame and holiness grew, and Beatrice testified, that Francis became impressed, and visited her often at their home, preaching his Gospel message. Gagliardi (n.d.) suggests there was, "Some speculation that women were asking to join his movement and Francis needed a strong woman to lead the others ... [and he considered Clare] ... would be the perfect leader."

Beatrice testified, that Clare responded to the preaching of Francis, by renouncing, "the world and all earthly things and went to serve God as soon as she was able. After that she sold her entire inheritance and part of that of the witness and gave it to the poor" (Franciscan Intellectual

Tradition, 2017:183). This is an interesting statement by Beatrice. She is suggesting that apart from selling her entire inheritance, Clare also sold part of Beatrice's inheritance!

Sister Benvenuta of Perugia was the second witness called to testify on Clare's behalf and, "was the third companion of St. Clare to enter San Damiano. She knew St. Clare as a young girl when the family of Favarone had to flee to and reside in Perugia" (ibid.). Benvenuta repeated similar comments to Sister Pacifica (the first witness). She was questioned about the time when Saint Clare entered religion, stating that Clare, "was eighteen years old or so ... She was a virgin in spirit and in body and held in great veneration by all who knew her even before she entered religion. This was because of her great honesty, kindness, and humility" (Franciscan Intellectual Tradition, 2017:183). Benvenuta was asked how she came to know these things, and she responded, that she had known Clare prior to her entry to religion, "and had stayed in the same house", and that she had lived with her at the monastery, until her death almost forty-two years later (ibid.).

Benvenuta also commented on the harsh mortifications and extreme penances, to which Clare subjected her body, for she was, "so severe toward her body that she was content with only one tunic of *Iazzo* [a type of home-spun cloth made of inferior wool and used by country folk], and one mantle. If she ever saw, that the tunic of another of the sisters was worse than what she was wearing, she took it from her for herself and gave the better one to that sister" (Franciscan Intellectual Tradition, 2017:151). Regarding Clare's penitential practices Benvenuta said that:

> Blessed Clare at one time had a certain shirt made of boar's hide. She wore it secretly under her woollen tunic with the skin and its bristles close to her skin. Likewise, another time, she had another shirt made of horsehair, knotted with certain cords. She tied it around her body and thus afflicted her virgin flesh (ibid.).

Benvenuta was questioned how she knew this, and she admitted that she had seen the shirts, and when Clare was taken ill, the sisters removed the shirt to ease her suffering. Benvenuta also testified that Clare, "always fasted on bread and water, except on Sundays when she drank a little wine when there was some. Three days a week, Monday, Wednesday and Friday, she did not eat anything until Saint Francis commanded her" (Franciscan Intellectual Tradition, 2017:151). When Francis commanded Clare to eat something every day, she complied by partaking of a little bread and water. The information provided by Sister Benvenuta, is similar to information provided by many of the witnesses, including Sister Pacifica, who was mentioned earlier. However, Pacifica also stressed, that because of Clare's severe abstinences, "she developed a certain illness" (p.146). The testimony reveals that "While Sister Pacifica claims that St. Clare was sick for twenty-nine years, other recorded information maintains [the length of time was] twenty-eight years" (p.149).

The third witness called to testify, was Sister Filippa, daughter of Lord Leonardo di Ghislerio. Filippa was a nun of the monastery of San Damiano and had entered the monastery four years after Clare entered. Filippa testified, that "She too was a member of an aristocratic family of Assisi that undoubtedly fled to Perugia at the same time as Clare" and her family (Franciscan Intellectual Tradition, 2017:156). She stated, that none of the sisters including herself, ever doubted the sanctity of Clare, "she was considered a saint by all those who knew her. And this was due to the righteousness of her life, her many virtues and graces which the Lord had placed in her" (p.155). Filippa stressed Clare's love of poverty: "Noble by her birth and upbringing and rich in worldly goods, she so loved poverty that she sold her entire inheritance and distributed it to the poor. She so loved the Order, she never wanted to neglect the slightest detail of the Order's observance, even when she was ill" (pp.161-162):

> [W]hen the begging [brothers] of the monastery brought back whole loaves of bread as alms, she reproachingly asked: "Who has given you these loaves of Bread?" She

said this because she could never be persuaded by the Pope or the Bishop of Ostia to receive any possessions. The *Privilege of Poverty* granted to her was honored with great reverence and kept well and with great diligence since she feared she might lose it (p.158).

Clare passed away on August 11, 1253 and depending on whether the year of her birth was 1193 or 1194, she would have been 59 or 60 years of age, at the time of her death. The feastday of St Clare of Assisi, is celebrated on August 11.

Leadership as Service

As their leader, Clare wanted to serve her sisters. She never used the title Abbess for herself, even though she was Abbess and mother to her sisters in religion, for over forty years. Armstrong (2006:25) states, that while Clare understood the role that Francis had "almost forced upon her", her understanding was:

> [N]ot in a hierarchical sense but in one of subservience characterized by a ministry and service more in keeping with the [life of poverty and] minority of Christ as Francis himself had done. The title [of Abbess] however appears only in Clare's *Rule* in which it refers to her successor. In all her other writings she refers to herself as the "handmaid", "mother", or "servant". "Let the Abbess ... be so familiar with [the sisters]," she declares in the *Form of Life*, "that they can speak and act with her as ladies do with their servant. For this is the way it should be: the Abbess should be the servant of all the sisters" (ibid.).

Clare believed that to lead was to serve. She didn't lead with "power" or with "domination", for "Clare envision[ed] the abbess servicing the others through manifesting tenderness, consoling the afflicted, and being 'the last refuge for those who are troubled'" (ibid.). Clare emulated

Christ, the greatest of all servant leaders. She lived "the Gospel".

The Ninth witness to be interviewed for the process of the canonization of Clare, was Sister Francesca, Daughter of Sir Capitaneo of Col de Mezzo. Francesca lived with Clare in the monastery of San Damiano, for more than twenty-one years. She testified that even if "she [Francesca] had as much wisdom as Solomon as much eloquence as Saint Paul, she did not believe she could tell fully of the goodness and holiness that she saw in Lady Clare" (Commission on the Franciscan Intellectual Tradition, 2017:174). To radiate such virtues to others (Francisca's testimony is repeated by the other witnesses), indicates that Clare was in touch with her inner reality, and according to Aristotle, this is "the beginning of all wisdom".

Wisdom has built her house, she has hewn her seven pillars (Proverbs 9:1, cited in Sipe & Frick, 2015:4). For the purpose of this analysis, the "Seven Pillars of Servant Leadership" (see Appendix A for the list of attributes) are outlined below, and the discussion on each pillar includes aspects of Clare's life and leadership practices.

Pillar 1 – "Person of Character"

Clare's profile reflects her profound humility, and desire to live a life of poverty and self-sacrifice. She emulated Christ in his service to others. She lived the Gospel. Pope Emeritus Benedict XVI (2010c) stated:

> In the Convent of San Damiano, Clare practiced heroically the virtues that should distinguish every Christian: humility, a spirit of piety and penitence and charity. Although she was the superior, she wanted to serve the sick sisters herself and joyfully subjected herself to the most menial tasks. In fact, charity overcomes all resistance and whoever loves, joyfully performs every sacrifice.

Sister Claire André Gagliardi (Franciscan Media, 2018) wrote that "Clare's Character Challenges Us". Gagliardi gave her reasons: "Clare was a woman of prayer", who was a contemplative who lived simply. She embraced "inner poverty", which besides referring to a poverty of spirit, also refers to a poverty of possessions. Clare was also courageous – she embraced the cross but was "no victim-martyr. She did not go out searching for suffering" (ibid.) but faced the suffering that came her way.

Cardinal Hugolino was elected pope in 1227, taking the name Pope Gregory IX. He was "not happy with the intense poverty embraced by Clare and her sisters at San Damiano and attempted to dispense her from following her ideal" (p.19). Mueller (2010:74) maintains that after the canonization of St Francis of Assisi in 1228 (two years after his death):

> Gregory himself visited the monastery of S. Damiano, and because of the "current events" and the "dangers of the world," tried to persuade Clare of the need for a regular income from landed endowments ... Clare resolutely resisted and would in no way acquiesce. Gregory assured Clare that she should not fear being unfaithful to her original vow since he had the power to dispense her. Clare remained undeterred: "Holy Father, I have absolutely no desire ever to be absolved from the following of Christ" (ibid.).

Clare's argument was that when she and her sisters entered religion, they "followed the gospel path by selling everything and giving it to the poor" (p.75). She struggled throughout her life, to maintain the "privilege of poverty", because of ongoing opposition from ecclesiastical authorities.

Pillar II – "Puts People First"

Clare was not a leader who delegated, and then waited for the 'job' to be done. She worked with her team of sisters, performing even the most mundane of tasks. The seventeenth witness for the process of canonization of Clare, a Lady Bona, daughter of Guelfuccio of Assisi, and herself the biological sister of Sister Pacifica, the first witness, spoke of the great holiness of Clare, that was witnessed prior to her entry to the convent, for she [Lady Bona] knew Clare, and had stayed in her home and that Clare "used to send to the poor the food she was supposed to have eaten" (Franciscan Intellectual Tradition, 2017:192).

The nineteenth witness Pietro di Damiano, of the city of Assisi, also said under oath, that he lived near Clare and her family. "He knew Lady Clare when she was in the world and [he] knew her father, Lord Favarone, who was noble, great and powerful in the city ... Asked what sort of life she led, he replied: 'Although their household was one of the largest in the city, and great sums were sent there, she nevertheless saved the food they were given to eat, put it aside, and sent it to the poor'" (p.195). This empathy, love and compassion, that Clare displayed to the poor and needy, prior to entering religious life, was endorsed by the many witnesses called to testify at the process of her canonization.

The Gospel discipleship Clare displayed before her conversion (meeting and hearing the preaching of Francis; then renouncing the world and selling her inheritance), continued when she entered religion. According to Mueller (2010:226), Clare did not believe that becoming an abbess in the monastery was just "a personal achievement, but a responsibility not only of service, but of the very souls of the sisters who ...[were] under her care." Clare, "supported the sisters psychologically as well as physically" (p.242). The sisters were "directly involved in the decision making ... and consensus was the norm" (pp.226/228). Clare did not make decisions on behalf of all her sisters, for she believed that, as they all belonged to the same community, it was important that they had their say. Mueller (p.229) maintains that "The roles were simply positions of service". Everybody worked together, and "work was not defined by an individual agenda but pertained 'to the integrity and service of the community'. In work, therefore one's love of God was love of neighbour" (p.239).

Pillar III – "Skilled Communicator"

Communal living meant that each of the Sisters, as part of the community, "was responsible for the quality of virtuous living, not just the abbess. There was admonition and correction of behaviour, but this was done in a positive manner. Any "lapse of charity" (Mueller, 2010:244) was given a gentle reminder with "private correction", rather than public humiliation. Clare's attitude to the disobedience of a sister, was likened to her own behaviour, "If ... [she] could refuse the pope, a sister could certainly refuse her abbess" (p.250). In addition, Clare "identifies the instruction of the sisters as the abbess's primary responsibility, '... needing to spend time LISTENING'" (p.249), and this form of listening, concerns, not just what is being said but what is left unsaid, by a person who may be 'suffering' in silence.

Following the granting of the "Privilege of Poverty" by Pope Gregory IX to Clare's community at San Damiano, there were other communities that wanted "to model their lives on that of Clare and her sisters" (Armstrong, 2006:19), but most of these communities, were in Tuscany and Lombardy. However, according to Armstrong, "news of their commitment reached Prague. Agnes, the daughter of the King of Bohemia (and the future Saint Agnes of Bohemia), began a correspondence with Clare in 1234. Unfortunately, just four of Clare's letters to Agnes remain" (ibid.).

Benedict XVI, at a General Audience in Rome (2010c), cites from the first of four letters, sent by Clare to Agnes, "who wished to follow in Christ's footsteps":

> [Clare] speaks of Christ, her beloved Spouse, with nuptial words that may be surprising but are nevertheless moving: "when you have loved [him] you shall be chaste; when you have touched [him] you shall become purer; when you have accepted [him] you shall be a virgin. Whose power is stronger, whose generosity is more elevated, whose

appearance more beautiful, whose love more tender, whose courtesy more gracious. In whose embrace you are already caught up: who has adorned your breast with precious stones ... and placed on your head a golden crown as a sign [to all] of your holiness."

Agnes was keen to enter religion, and renounce her life of wealth and luxury, giving all her possessions to the poor. She wanted to model her life, on that of Clare and her sisters, so she asked Clare for advice. The two never met, but their written communication is revealing. Gregory XI: "who had intervened when Agnes sought to avoid marriage in order to enter religion, balked at the idea of her embracing the same way of life as Clare and the women of San Damiano. Between 1234 and 1238, he wrote a series of papal documents directing Agnes and responding to her concerns" (Armstrong, 2006:19). Clare encouraged Agnes to ignore the papal decrees. Her reasons for this, were that although Gregory and St Francis had been friends, "Gregory did not understand the Franciscan imperative to be poor as the essence of the Franciscan vocation" (Mueller, 2010:79/80). Armstrong (2006:19) states that:

> [O]n August 6, 1247, Gregory's successor, Innocent IV, provided a new *Form of Life* for all the monasteries of the Order of Saint Damian [for example those following the Franciscan rule] and on August 23, 1247, bound the women of these monasteries to its observance with the papal bull, *Quoties a nobis*. Innocent's *Form of Life* was a milder form than that given by Hugolino (The late Pope Gregory IX). This document mitigated fasting obligations and even allowed possessions. There is no documentation tracing Clare's immediate resistance to Innocent's demands.

Interestingly, just three years later, Innocent "declared in another papal bull *Inter Personas*, June 6, 1250, that no sister could be forced to accept his initial document. At about this time, Clare, once again courageous and determined, began to write her own *Form of Life*" (p.20).

You may recall that earlier in this chapter, it was stated that Clare's *Forma Vitae* – Form of Life – Rule, was the first canonically approved monastic legislation, written by a woman, and bearing the papal seal, it was finally received by Clare on her death bed.

Pillar IV – "Compassionate Collaborator"

According to Armstrong (2006:26), there is an "obvious sense of freedom and flexibility with which Clare approaches the daily life of the Poor Ladies and [we] are left with the impression that she had a great respect for the workings of the Spirit of the Lord in her sisters. This is also obvious in …[the] frequent encouragement of the abbess … [when using] 'discernment.' The word and its derivatives appear sixteen times in Clare's writings, most frequently in her *Form of Life*." Armstrong (ibid.), emphasises the "sense of reverence and respect in Clare's attitude toward her sisters, one that prompted her to treat them as mature spirit-filled women whose principal desire was to live fully the Gospel life."

Sister Filippa, who you may recall, was the third witness for the process of canonization, maintains that: "from the time Saint Clare entered Religion, the Spirit increased her virtues and graces. She knew Saint Clare was very humble and devout, kind and very enamored of poverty, with compassion for the afflicted. She was persevering in prayer. Her manner of life and speech was always concerned with the things of God, so she never gave her tongue or ears to worldly things" (Franciscan Intellectual Tradition, 2017:156).

Now, Sister Agnes, the daughter of the Mayor of Assisi, Oportulo de Bernardo of Assisi, was a nun at the monastery of San Damiano. Agnes said that: "if Lady Clare ever saw any of the sisters suffering some temptation or trial, she called her secretly and consoled her with tears, and sometimes threw herself at her feet. Asked how she knew these things, she replied she had seen some of those she had been called to console" (p.178). Many of the witnesses testified to Clare's great compassion for her sisters in religion. Sister Cristiana was the daughter of Sir Bernardo da Suppo of Assisi, and was a nun at the monastery of San Damiano. There is evidence to support the fact, that the families of Clare and Cristiana were friends. Questioned about the virtues of Clare, Cristiana responded:

> The lady Clare was thoroughly inflamed with charity and loved her sisters as herself. If she at times heard something that was not pleasing to God, she would try to correct it with great compassion and without delay. Because she was like this and so holy and adorned with virtue, God wanted her to be the first mother and teacher of the Order. She protected the monastery, the Order, and herself from every infection of sin so her memory will be eternally held in reverence (p.186).

Again, as with most of the testimonies, Cristiana cites the many virtues of Clare, and the profound love, care and compassion, that their mother in religion had for her sisters.

Pillar V – "Has Foresight"

Armstrong (2006:31) refers to Clare's vision as a "unique feminine expression of the Franciscan ideal." He believes that Clare and her vision, may never have really been understood. The very first sentence of "The Form of Life of Saint Clare (1253) reads, 'The last years of Clare's life were characterized by her struggle to have her vision of religious life [*form of life* for the Poor Ladies] approved by the Church'" (p.106). Armstrong (p.31) asserts that Francis had a great respect for, and was "in awe of Clare's poverty that was far more demanding than his own, a poverty dependent on the providence of God, the generosity of others, and the care and attention of the brothers charged with begging for their needs ... Clare's vision of a life *sine proprio* [without property], without anything of one's own, is more expressive of dependence, upon and receptivity of God's providence" (ibid.).

Sister Filippa, as third witness, recounted a prediction of future events, regarding Clare. Apparently, Clare "told the sisters how her mother, when she was carrying her, went into the church. While standing before the cross, and actually praying for God to help and protect her during the danger of childbirth, she heard a voice telling her, 'You will give birth to a light that will shine brilliantly in the world'" (Franciscan Intellectual Tradition, 2017:161). Filippa also narrated the following that occurred one Christmas evening:

> [B]ecause of her serious illness ... [the Lady Clare] could not get up from her bed to the chapel. All the sisters went as usual to Matins and left her alone. The Lady then said with a sigh: "Lord God, look, I have been left here alone with you." She immediately began to hear the organ, responsories, and the entire Office of the brothers in the Church of Saint Francis, as if she were present there (ibid.).

As an interesting aside, the previous quotation is why St Clare of Assisi has now in our contemporary era, been given the title: "Patroness of Television". In fact, there is an Apostolic Letter (written in French), published by Pope Pius XII in 1957, proclaiming St Clare the Patron Saint of Television.

Sister Filippa recounts another "miraculous" occasion, when Clare is said to have freed the monastery from the Saracens.

> At the time of the war of Assisi the sisters were very much afraid of the arrival of those Tartars, Saracens, and other enemies of God and the Church. The blessed mother began to comfort them saying, "My sisters and daughters, do not be afraid because, if the Lord is with us, the enemy cannot harm us. Have confidence in our Lord Jesus Christ because He will free us. I want to be your hostage so that you do not do anything bad. If they come, place me before them."

> One day, when the enemy had advanced to destroy Assisi certain Saracens scaled the walls of the monastery and went down into the enclosure. The sisters were greatly afraid. But the most holy mother comforted all of them, looked down on the troops, and said "Do not be afraid, because they will not be able to hurt us." After saying this, she turned to the help of her usual prayer. The strength of the prayer was such that the hostile Saracens departed as if driven away without doing any harm nor touching anyone in the house (Franciscan Intellectual Tradition, 2017:159).

In the *Legend of Saint Clare*, the above information is included with a slight change, in that Clare, "ordered that she be brought, sick as she was, to the door and placed there before the enemy, while the silver pyx enclosed in ivory in which the Body of the Holy of Holies was most devotedly reserved, preceded her …" (Armstrong, 2006:301/302). In the notes on the cited pages there is reference to the "attack upon San Damiano by the 'Saracens,' a band of Moslem soldiers of fortune or mercenaries in the pay of Frederick II" (ibid.). Nine references to the incident, are cited in the acts of the process of canonization, however, there is no historical record of this event, and though "Iconography often depicts Clare holding a monstrance, … [this] is not verified here" (Armstrong, 2006:301).

Benedict XVI, speaking about St Clare of Assisi, at a General Audience in Rome (2010c), emphasises that it was incidents similar to the above, and the many miracles reported during her lifetime, and after her death that, "prompted Pope Alexander IV to canonize her in 1255, only two years after her death." Indeed, Clare is an inspiration to all who are willing to live their faith, inspired by the Gospel!

Pillar VI – "Systems Thinker"

The "Big Picture" for Clare, was to have her own *Forma Vitae* – Form of Life (Rule), and to have it resonate with the message of her love of the

"Privilege of Poverty". Sister Filippa testified, that at the end of Clare's life, she called the sisters together, and "entrusted the *Privilege of Poverty* to them":

> Her great desire was to have the *Form of Life* of the Order confirmed with a papal bull, to be able one day to place her lips upon the papal seal, and, then, on the following day to die. It occurred just as she desired. She learned a brother had come with letters bearing the papal bull. She reverently took it even though she was very close to death and pressed that seal to her mouth in order to kiss it. On the following day, Lady Clare passed from this life to the Lord (Franciscan Intellectual Tradition, 2017:162).

The papal bull brought to Clare, as she was near death, was the *Solet annuere* sent by Pope Innocent IV. Her legacy to succeeding generations of the Order of Poor Ladies, now known as the Order of Poor Clares, consists of a dearth of written evidence, regarding her life and works for what little is known of her early life, and that of her religious life is found in the acts of the process of her canonization. As mentioned previously, in addition to Clare's *Forma Vitae*, there are four extant letters (generally regarded as authentic) that Clare sent to St Agnes of Prague.

Armstrong (2006:420) cites a "Letter of Saint Clare to Ermentrude of Bruges" but calls into question its origin. There is also a document called *The Testament,* which is said to contain autobiographical information by Clare, but scholars question its authenticity (Mueller, 2010:14; Armstrong, 2006:59). Armstrong though, maintains that during Clare's struggle to have the Pope approve her Rule, the Testament, "may have been written as a statement of the essential values she perceived in the daily life of San Damiano. It was her farewell message, her 'last will' that would guide her sisters after her death" (ibid.).

It was just two months after the passing of Clare, on 11 August 1253, that "Pope Innocent IV issued the papal bull, *Gloriosus Deus*, October 18,

1253, in which he entrusted Bishop Bartholomew of Spoleto with the responsibility of promoting the Cause of her canonization" (Armstrong, 2006:139). The account of her life was then written in poetic form – *The Versified Legend of the Virgin Clare* (1254-1255). Armstrong (p.272) posits that, when a saint was canonised in the Middle Ages, part of the process was to organise the composition, of an official biography: "For the most part it was a work undertaken by a writer familiar with the data gathered to establish someone's sanctity either through personally interviewing eyewitnesses or reviewing the transcripts of official ecclesiastical investigations." *The Legend of St Clare* was composed in 1255. Its author is unknown, though some scholars believe the person to be Thomas of Celano.

Pillar VII – "Leads with Moral Authority"

Because of the 'Privilege of poverty' Clare and her sisters were not "forced to accept landed endowments ... Clare affirmed that she and her sisters followed the gospel path by selling everything and giving it to the poor" (Mueller, 2010:75). They never wavered from this position, even in the face of incredible opposition from Popes, Cardinals and Bishops. According to Mueller (p.76) "Throughout the [years of] controversy, Clare drew strength from the words of Francis himself. At the end of her life, she would archive Francis's words to her concerning poverty, at the very center of her *forma vitae*":

> I, little brother Francis, want to follow the life and poverty of our Most High Lord Jesus Christ and of his most Holy Mother and to persevere in this until death. And I beg and counsel you, my ladies, always to live in this most holy life and poverty. Guard yourselves carefully that you never, in any respect, whatsoever, turn away from this because of the teaching or advice of anyone.

It was "In 1228, [that] Clare interpreted Francis's 'anyone' as the pope himself. She kept her promise of absolute poverty for her monastery, knowing full well that she risked papal confrontation and contempt" (ibid). Over the years various popes and cardinals tried to dissuade her from the tenaciousness of her stance, but to no avail. Eventually, after several years of remarkable resilience Clare's efforts were rewarded, when Pope Innocent IV approved a Franciscan Rule for women, "with the privilege of poverty at its core on Clare's deathbed in 1253" (Mueller, 2006). The sisters struggled to come to terms with the passing of Clare. They wrote a text, notifying Sisters within the various monasteries, and those in distant communities of her death. Their sadness and tears graced the document that they tried to write. They found great difficulty in reconciling "to the loss of their mother Clare" (Franciscan Intellectual Tradition, 2017:135).

Values

Aspects of Clare's life and works are now discussed in relation to the values – dignity, respect, fairness, justness and equality (see Chapter 4 for the terms of reference).

Dignity

Clare was a member of a noble family. The witnesses to her life, testified that it was with grace, dignity and presence, that prior to entering religion, she spent many hours feeding the poor, and providing them with clothing. Benedict XVI, (2010c), reminds us, that Clare "belonged to a wealthy, aristocratic family ... [and] renounced her noble status and wealth to live in humility and poverty." Indeed, when she entered religion, Clare upheld the dignity of all, and served her sisters in religion by caring for them when they were sick. She did their washing and catered to their toiletry needs. She covered them at night, when she noticed they were cold. She substituted her own clothing for that which was worn, and not in as good condition, and provided much comfort to her sisters.

Such information and more has been gleaned from the testimonies of witnesses during the process of Clare's canonization. "Human beings are created in the image of God", (Genesis 1:27); hence according to Mueller (2010:132), Clare treated everybody as if she was in the presence of Christ. In her writing "Clare speaks of herself as the unworthy servant to Jesus Christ and the useless handmaid of the enclosed ladies of the Monastery of S. Damiano." She respected the sacredness of life, and the value of human dignity. Clare maintained her dignity, throughout the years of controversy when she had Popes, Cardinals and Bishops, advising her to consider exemptions and dispensations for her "Privilege of Poverty", so that the sisters could receive possessions, and own property (landed endowments), but Clare resisted all efforts to convince her otherwise. The Catholic Catechism informs us that "The human body shares in the dignity of 'the image of God': it is a human body precisely because it is animated by a spiritual soul, and it is the whole human person that is intended to become, in the body of Christ, a temple of the spirit" (CCC, 2000:para.364).

Respect

Benedict XVI (2010c) emphasises that, "Clare's testimony, shows us how indebted the Church is to courageous women, full of faith like her, who can give a crucial impetus to the Church's renewal." Such words of respect for a strong, humble, and courageous woman! Pope St John Paul II (2003b) also gives praise and respect to this saint of Assisi (note the Holy Father's reference to Clare as "the founder of the Poor Clares"):

> [T]he message left 750 years ago by the founder of the Poor Clare Sisters is more important than ever for a world characterized by superficiality. In a letter, the Pope explains that the charism of St. Clare of Assisi, "is characterized, in the first place, by a call to live according to the perfection of the holy Gospel, with a decided reference to Christ, the

only and authentic program of life. 'Is not this a challenge for the men and women of today?'"

A few years earlier, in his Apostolic Letter *Mulieris Dignitatem*, 'On the Dignity and Vocation of Women", Pope St John Paul II (1988), writes of the profound respect Jesus had for the women of his time: "Transcending the established norms of his own culture, Jesus treated women with openness, respect, acceptance and tenderness. In this way he honoured the dignity which women have always possessed according to God's plan and in his love" (1995:para.3).

Mueller (2010:63) writes that "Clare deeply respected church leaders. She did not allow this respect, however, to overshadow her responsibility as a leader of women and courageously countered even the Pope himself when she felt her religious life threated. Her dissent revolved around the coveted 'privilege of poverty' that Clare, and especially the first sisters who entered S. Damiano with her, defended as their most fundamental spiritual treasure." In humility and with reverence, Clare showed respect to all, her sisters in religion, and the ecclesiastical authorities. She showed this respect by never wavering from what she believed to be a "privilege of poverty", living the Gospel which she "tenaciously defended throughout her life" (Pope St John Paul II, 2003b).

Fairness

Possibly in her dealings with the ecclesiastical authorities, Clare gives the impression of a strong-willed, stubborn woman – but should it have taken a lifetime, to have her *Form of Life* (Rule) approved? Was this fair to the community, or to Clare? There would have been many occasions during her forty or so years in the religious life, when she probably thought that the canonical acceptance and seal of the Pope regarding her rule, would not be forthcoming! Nevertheless, in her service to the sisters in her community, and in her service to the Church, Clare demonstrated justice and fairness.

She accomplished all the above, by her service of love to others. She treated everybody fairly and equally. As a leader, she did not ask her sisters in religion to do what she herself was not prepared to do. She washed, cleaned and looked after the sick. "Clare though Abbess, considered herself the servant of all" (Mueller, 2010:63). She worked collaboratively with her sisters and involved them in decision making. Her reasons for doing this were: "Because the work done was for the service of the community, and it was this communal love and shared service among the sisters that preserved the spirit of prayer and devotion, it was the community that needed to discern the work to be done, and who was best to do it" (p.239). Sister Beatrice, who you may recall, was the twelfth witness of the process of the canonization of Clare, and Clare's biological younger sister, when asked:

> [I]n what Lady Clare's holiness consisted, she replied: "in her virginity, humility, patience, and kindness, in the necessary correction and sweet admonition of her sisters; in the continuous application to her prayer and contemplation, abstinence and fasting; in the roughness of her bed and clothing; in the disregard of herself, the fervor of her love of God, her desire for martyrdom, and, most especially, in her love of the Privilege of Poverty" (Armstrong, 2006:184).

It is interesting to note in the above quotation, that sisters who are to be corrected receive "sweet admonition", that is, gentle reminders of behaviour that is expected. In her *Form of Life*, Clare catered for the diversity in her order, by showing understanding and fairness. For example, regarding the "Divine Office and Fasting, Confession and Communion" (Armstrong, 2006: 112). The sisters who could read, were to say the Divine Office. Those sisters who couldn't read, were to say the *Our Father* several times, depending on the time of prayer – Matins, Lauds, Vespers, Compline. All sisters were expected to fast; however, there were exceptions – on festive occasions, or when a sister was weak or ill, or if the sister was very young. According to Clare, "Fairness involves making decisions in the best interests of all and treating our 'neighbours [sisters]' equally and respectfully."

Justness

Clare assisted the papacy, whenever she was able to do so. Mueller (2010:60) writes that "Clare's involvement in the larger community included even the papacy itself. The *Legend of Clare* states that Pope Gregory IX requested Clare's prayers during times of difficulty, both when he was the Bishop of Ostia, and later while he served as pope. He would request Clare's assistance by letter and relied upon her help." Yet, even though Clare considered herself a servant to all, as we have been able to discern from this chapter, "she was a woman of courage, challenging familial knights, popes and Saracens alike" (p.63).

Armstrong (2006:332) lists a collection of documents, in reference to St Clare of Assisi. One of the documents is titled: "A Dossier for the Order of Saint Damian" (p.333). The very first paragraph leads the reader to interpret the papal decrees, by considering justness, not solely for Clare's community, but for the many communities of religious women, that experienced growth in the Middle Ages.

> In reading the documents by, to, or about Clare of Assisi, it quickly becomes obvious that the popes of her lifetime – with the exception of Pope Celestine IV, who died within a month of his election – issued a number of decrees concerning her, and those inspired by her. These papal documents offer a provocative perspective on the development of Clare's feminine expression of the Gospel inspiration of Francis, and on medieval religious women in general. Some historians have interpreted the canonical documents of this period negatively, as the papacy's way of manipulating or confining these women; others tend to see

them as positive efforts to foster, clarify and protect their ideals (ibid.).

When Gregory IX was elected in 1227, he was considered "one of the most influential supporters of women's religious movements during the Middle Ages" (p.344). By October 1232, there was:

> [I]ncreasingly tight papal control over the developing monasteries. A number of documents emerge providing directives to Agnes in Prague [you may recall that Agnes was the daughter of the King of Bohemia and is today a canonised saint]. These [documents] are important because they frequently relate to Clare's letters to Agnes and because, once again, they show the widespread papal scrutiny of enclosed women. Because Agnes was a royal princess and because her father, Ottokar I, and her brother Vaclav III, were successively Kings of Bohemia, her political influence was potentially beneficial to the papal court. Real questions persisted regarding the financial and material provisions for enclosed communities. It took four years for Agnes and her sisters to receive papal approbation to live without common property in the manner of Clare (ibid.).

Mueller (2010:126) maintains that Clare and Agnes "received their wish when Innocent IV approved Clare's *Forma Vitae* on August 9, 1253, just two days before Clare's death." Agnes survived Clare by thirty years (ibid.). Reasons given why some of the "women's monasteries were placed under papal authority, [were] to protect them from predatory interests of local bishops and avaricious laypeople" (p.92). When the sisters "were encouraged to endow their monasteries with their own dowries and inheritances ... [they] were frequently implicated in secular lawsuits" (p.228). Many of these lawsuits could be protracted, particularly those involving the estates of families. However, was there justness in the approach of the Church, to resolving the challenges the women in monasteries faced in the 13th century? When the properties (landed endowments and possessions) of women and their monasteries were accepted, "under the law and patrimony of the Roman Church" (p.92), it is obvious that it was the Church which benefited from such an arrangement.

Equality

No gender has superiority over another. Each person has basic human rights, that must be respected. Regarding the treatment of women leaders, and particularly those living within religious communities, during the Middle Ages, there seems to be some discrepancy between the treatment of the genders. St Francis of Assisi founded the male version of the Franciscans in 1209, and St Clare of Assisi co-founded the female version of the Order (the Poor Ladies later renamed the Poor Clares) with Francis around 1212. In the notes accompanying Armstrong's work on Clare of Assisi (2006:90), we read that "Pope Innocent [III] thus acknowledges the *Rule* of St. Francis and the *Form of Life* as the way of life of the Poor Sisters." The *Later Rule* of St. Francis was solemnly approved by Pope Honorius III in the bull *Solet annuere*, November 29, 1223.

Admittedly, Francis died in 1226, however, he and/or his order did not have to wait nearly forty-two years, as did Clare and her community, to have their *Form of Life* canonically approved. Also, it would be interesting to know, if the male communities of the middle ages, were subjected to the same intense scrutiny by the papal authorities, as that experienced by their female counterparts? Based on my research for this chapter – I think not? Both St Clare of Assisi and St Francis of Assisi lived their lives based on the Gospels, and both rejoiced in the privilege of poverty. Both were created in the image of God (Gen 1:27), and therefore both are equal in the eyes of God!

In the following chapter, we fast forward to the fourteenth century where we meet St Catherine of Siena, the second woman to be proclaimed a Doctor of the Universal Church.

8

St Catherine of Siena

During a visit to Rome in 2002 to undertake doctoral research, I was fortunate to meet with Sr Giuliana Cavallini, who at the time, was in her nineties and had held the position of Director of the International Centre for Catherinian Studies (CISC) for more than twenty years. Prior to my trip to Italy, I had corresponded with Cavallini, and she shared with me some of her knowledge and wisdom regarding Saint Catherine of Siena: "Catherine had, we might say, a natural bent towards Truth. While still a child, ... [she came] to understand that St Dominic's aim in founding his Order had been to share with people the priceless gift which Truth is". Cavallini then explained Catherine's devotion to "Truth":

> [S]he cherished for some time a childish project: to put on masculine clothing and go and ask for admittance to a Dominican convent in a distant country. But it did not take her long to understand that it could not do. But love of truth and desire to share it with her fellow beings never failed her. Her favoured substitute for the name of God is Truth, "First sweet Truth". "God's Truth" can mean both God's plan for the welfare of humankind and Christ, its performer (Personal correspondence, 2002).

As Catherine's life unfolds in the following pages, we will see that her personality and her Dominican spirituality, inspired her in all her endeavours.

On 26 April 2003, some twelve months after my trip to Rome, Pope St John Paul II sent a formal message of congratulations to Professor Cavallini, when "on the occasion of the European Symposium on St

Catherine of Siena", a decision was made to award her the *Targa d'Onore* (Plaque of Honour) of the *Angelicum*. The Pope stressed his admiration to Cavallini, "for the merit you have acquired during your long life, much of which you have spent in studying and disseminating the thought of this saint of Siena, a Patroness of Europe." He also praised her for her tireless efforts to present Catherine to the world: "As a devout spiritual daughter of St Catherine, you have illustrated the riches of her teaching ... Your tireless cultural and scientific activity has crossed the boundaries of Italy, giving rise to far-reaching echoes and growing appreciation in various countries, which have recognized you as a Catherinian expert of international fame" (ibid.).

The Holy Father concluded his message with one of thanksgiving: "I rejoice in taking part in the initiative of the Pontifical University of St Thomas Aquinas to honour an expert scholar who has never ceased to work to make people love and imitate St Catherine, an outstanding Doctor of the Church" (Vatican, 2003). Cavallini's remarkable contribution to the studies of Catherine, is also recognised in the following statement by Suzanne Noffke, a Dominican Sister, and international authority on St Catherine of Siena, who was personally acquainted with Cavallini, and who in the introduction to her [Noffke's] English translation of *The Dialogue* maintains that: "[Cavallini's] scholarship [over many years] has produced critical editions of 'The Dialogue' and 'Prayers of Catherine of Siena' as well as a number of analytical and interpretive works on the saint in Italian" (1980; cited in Cameron, 2009:10). Such are the works that comprise Catherine's eminent doctrine, but what of the life of this Saint of Siena?

Profile

Catherine de Benincasa and her twin sister Giovanna were born around 25 March 1347, in 14th Century Siena Italy. Sadly, Giovanna died shortly after birth, and her parents Giacomo Benincasa and Lapa di Puccio di

Piacenti later gave her name to the next and youngest of their twenty-five children. Unfortunately, "the second Giovanna did not survive to adulthood" (Conleth Kearns, 1980:27; cited in Cameron, 2012a:49). In those early years, the family was reasonably well-off and engaged as wool dyers in the textile industry.

In his biography of her life, the now Blessed Raymond of Capua, who became Catherine's Confessor, and later Master General of the Dominicans, states that, "She was an engaging child and was well-liked by all" (cited in Kearns, [ibid.]; Cameron, [ibid.]). It was when Catherine was about 7 years of age, that she had her first mystical experience which occurred on an occasion when she was in the company of her brother Stefano, after they had visited their sister, Buonaventura "the wife of Niccolo," and were returning to their home. Cameron (2012a:144) recounts Raymond's version (Kearns, 1980:29) of these events, "Catherine's vision was of Jesus Christ seated on a throne with the apostles Peter, Paul and John standing in his presence." The experience so affected Catherine, that Raymond maintains from that time onwards she committed herself to God – vowing her virginity to him. Perhaps a surprising decision for so young a child, but Caroline Bynum (1987:24; cited in Cameron, 2012a:130) explains that for women in late medieval times this type of commitment at such a young age was common:

> In their recent quantitative study of saints' lives, [Donald] Weinstein and [Rudolph M.] Bell, (1982) have demonstrated that in general, women's saintly vocations grew slowly through childhood and into adolescence; a disproportionate percentage of female saints were certain of their commitment to virginity before age eight.

The vow had repercussions for the entire family, particularly as Catherine grew to marriageable age (which at time, was approximately twelve to fifteen years). Catherine's parents were becoming less prosperous, and with their finances "dwindling" they "urged her to pay more attention to her appearance, so they could find a suitable husband for her" (Cameron, 2012a:130). Catherine resisted their demands, for she was determined to keep the vow she had made to God (Raymond, cited in Kearns, 1980:37) as a young child. Her parents did everything to cajole her, but their efforts were in vain. Catherine began to withdraw from the outside world. Raymond tells us that "she made for herself a secret cell within her own heart and she retreated to this private place whenever she needed to be alone and reconnect with her inner self" (cited in Kearns, 1980:54).

Fink (2000b:106) recounts, "Years later, Catherine wrote in *The Dialogue* that God had shown her how to build in her soul a private cell where no tribulation could enter. She was to call this private place 'the cell of self-knowledge.'" In time, her parents became reconciled to Catherine's decision, and organised a small room for her within the family home, where she could spend her time in solitude and silence. Catherine immersed herself in prayer and contemplation, only leaving her quarters to attend Mass at "the nearby Church of San Domenico" (Suzanne Noffke, 1980:4).

Catherine had a dream from early childhood which "centered … [on] a life of quiet union with God'" (Noffke, 2000:xiii). Her biographer Raymond refers to Catherine's dream, in which she visualised the various religious orders and their founders, trying to decide which order would be best for her to serve Christ. One of the Founders she visualised in her dream was St Dominic. He approached Catherine and spoke the following words to her "Dearest daughter, be of good courage; do not lose heart, no matter what the odds against you. Be assured that you will one day wear this habit which you long for" (cited in Kearns, 1980:50).

You may also remember from a previous chapter, that "holy women during Catherine's era were less inclined to institutionalisation than men and that they often sought 'quasi religious' status." Consequently, many chose to be tertiaries who lived in the world, but who "were affiliated with one of the great mendicant orders (usually Franciscan or Dominican) and followed a life of penitential asceticism, charitable activity and prayer"

(Bynum, 1987:16-17; cited in Cameron, 2012a:129). Catherine was keen to gain admittance to one such group – the *Mantellate* – "a group of women assumed to be widows ... who were affiliated with the Order of Saint Dominic and wore the habit but lived in their own homes, serving the needs of the poor and sick under the direction of a prioress and ultimately under the direction of the friars" (Noffke, 1980:4; Cameron, 2012a:131). However, these women were initially reluctant to accept Catherine because of her youth, and perceived single virginal status, and it was only after Lapa, Catherine's mother pleaded with them on her behalf, that around 1365 when she was about eighteen years of age, Catherine was finally accepted into the order as "a member of the lay division of St. Dominic's Order of preachers" (Benedict Ashley, 1981:43).

Yet, "rather than immediately involving herself in serving the needs of the sick and the poor as was the practice of the *Mantellate*" (Noffke, 1980:4), Catherine continued to restrict herself to the confines of her home for the following three years. She occupied herself by learning to read, and she continued with her severe austerity and penance, devoting her life, time and body to God, who spoke to her within the inner silence of her soul. Raymond (cited in Kearns, 1980:76-77; Cameron, 2012a:132) explains:

> I had it from herself that as soon as she began this life of seclusion in her cell, our Lord Jesus Christ began in his goodness to appear to her, and to give her full instruction on every aspect of her spiritual life ... these apparitions for the most part took place in her imagination; but sometimes they were perceptible externally also, by her bodily senses, so that she actually heard his voice sounding audibly in her ears.

It was during this time of isolation, that Catherine experienced visions, ecstasy, spiritual aridity and extraordinarily – a mystical marriage to Christ (Noffke, 1980:4; Cameron, 2012a). However, the time was fast approaching for her to abandon her incarceration, but Catherine was apprehensive, for she was content with the status quo and disinclined to venture out into the public arena. Nevertheless, Raymond (Kearns, 1980:114-116; Cameron, 2012a:133) soon persuaded her that it was God's will that she "begin to trade with the talents he has entrusted to her, so as to give them back to him enriched with interest" by her service to others. Catherine prayed for guidance:

> [N]ot my will be done, Lord, but yours ... But may I ask you, Lord, if it be not presumptuous, how can what you say be done? How can one like me, feeble and of no account, do any good for souls? My very sex, as I need not tell you, puts many obstacles in the way. The world has no use for women in such work as that, and propriety forbids a woman to mix so freely in the company of men (ibid.).

According to Raymond (ibid.) God alleviated her fears by responding, "Nothing shall be impossible with God."

Catherine realised then, that the time had come for her to combine her contemplation with active service; hence, responding to the divine request, she left the confines of her small room and the security of her home, to engage in a public life of service "to the poor and the needy". Noffke (1980:4) recounts some of the "tales that have come down to us from these years of 'social work' in Siena [stating that they] are full of the warmly human side of Catherine. She served as nurse in homes and hospitals, looked out for the destitute, [and sadly also] buried her father." Noffke posits that regardless of her "busyness" Catherine still sought solitude, silence and contemplation, whenever the opportunity arose (ibid.).

During the following years, Catherine travelled through many areas, tending the needs of the poor, sick and dying, and in time attracted a group of followers – her disciples – women and men who became her spiritual family and called her "Mamma". However, over time her seemingly "unorthodox activities" (Cameron, 2012a:50-51) drew the attention of the Dominican hierarchy and circa the spring of 1374, Catherine was summoned "before the Dominican General Chapter [in Florence] for examination, presumably of her orthodoxy" (Ashley, 1981:43). Ashley maintains that "The examining theologians [eventually] approved her manner of life, provided she receive direction from an official confessor" (ibid.). As a result, Catherine met Raymond of Capua for the first time. He was appointed her confessor, and became her lifelong friend and supporter, writing her biography after her death.

Catherine's prolific letter writing career started around 1375 (Noffke, 1980:5). However, though she had mastered the rudiments of reading between the ages of 18 to 21, her writing skills were still quite underdeveloped, so she dictated her numerous letters to scribes (generally her disciples). It was also at this time, that the political situation between the republics and the papacy began to deteriorate. The independent city states were rising in rebellion. Noffke (1980:5) writes that though Catherine was heavily involved with political affairs and the challenges associated with "the antipapal rebellion … [she] continued to attend to more homey and intimate matters as well". For instance, when Catherine was in Pisa in 1375, she received the stigmata. Raymond recalls:

> It happened in the city of Pisa, and I was present at it myself and witnessed it all … I had celebrated Mass … Suddenly, before our eyes, her emaciated body, which had been prostrate on the ground, rose up to a kneeling position; she stretched out her arms and hands to their full length; her face grew radiant … of a sudden she pitched forward on the ground as if she had received a mortal wound. A few minutes later she returned to her senses … she sent for me … "Father," she said, "I must tell you that by his mercy, I now bear the stigmata of the Lord Jesus in my Body" (cited in Kearns, 1980:185-186; Cameron, 2012a:51-52).

This mystical experience resulted in Catherine experiencing the pain of the five wounds received by Christ (hands, feet and heart), for the remainder of her life until her death. However, at her request "the wounds were visible only to herself" (Cameron, 2012a:52). Bynum gives her interpretation of the stigmata in light of medieval times, explaining that there were many "holy" women who received the stigmata, "these women wanted to 'imitate Christ' by participating in his experiences of pain, for the stigmata 'mystical wounds' represent the five wounds of Christ. 'To medieval people themselves, what modern eyes see as self-punishment or psychosomatic manipulation was *imitatio Christi* – a fusion with Christ's agony on the cross'" (1987:211-212).

Raymond (Kearns, 1980:56) emphasises the "extreme" ascetical practices practised by Catherine during her lifetime, stressing that she was motivated by a desire to have the spirit dominate the flesh. "For a bed she set aside a couple of wooden beams or planks on top ... At one time she wore a hairshirt. But ... she ... exchanged ... [this for an iron] chain" ([ibid.]; Cameron, 2012a:139). Raymond tells us that this information was recounted to him by Catherine's "companions and spiritual daughters" (ibid.).

Stefano Maconi (a disciple of Catherine's), who testified at the process for Catherine's canonisation (Processo Castellano, ed. Laurent, p. 267, cited in Noffke, 2001:17), recounts her eating habits, which he states he had witnessed over "many years". Stefano says, that she did not enjoy eating meat or drinking wine, and that she did not like to eat meals "prepared with eggs". She ate, "raw greens ... Cheese she would eat only when it was already spoiled ... sometimes [she ate her food] with bread, sometimes without bread. She would swallow the juice of the greens and spit out the rest. Most often she drank only water" (ibid.). Bynum "compares the similarities of Catherine's experiences with the twentieth-century diagnosed conditions of anorexia nervosa and 'the closely related disorder bulimia (binge-eating)'" (1987:196-197, cited in Cameron, 2012a).

It was around 1377, some three years before her death, that Catherine travelled to Rocca d'Orcia, about twenty miles from Siena, "on a local mission of peacemaking and preaching." According to Noffke (1980:6) it was here that she learned to write, and where, while in an ecstatic trance, she dictated to scribes the *Dialogue*, "a conversation between God and ... [herself]" which was to be her major work. "This is evidenced in Noffke's (1980:366) notes which recount the closing words of Catherine following her completion of *The Dialogue*: 'Here ends the book composed by the blessed virgin, the faithful spouse and servant of Jesus Christ, Catherine of Siena, dictated in ecstasy. She was clothed in the habit of Saint Dominic. Amen.'" (Cameron, 2012a).

On 27 March 1378, Pope Gregory XI passed away. He was succeeded by Pope Urban VI. Noffke (1980:6) states that, "Urban was keen to continue to work towards reform but his instability soon became apparent. [He started] exercising his authority with tactlessness and even violent suppression of any opposition, whether clerical or lay." Unfortunately, the mental condition of Urban VI seemed to deteriorate, and the Cardinals who had elected him started to realise that they had committed a grave error in electing such an "unbalanced" candidate, and announced that they would elect a second pope, stating that their first election had been invalid (Fink, 2000b:113). An antipope was duly elected – Clement VII, and while he resided in the papal palace at Avignon, Urban VI stayed in Rome.

And so, began what is referred to in Church history as "the Great Western Schism" (1998:11). Catherine "spent the remainder of her life supporting and promoting Urban VI as the legitimate Pope while urging him to practise self-control and moderation. The Great Western Schism continued until some decades after ... [her] death" (Cameron, 2012a:55). Catherine died at the age of thirty-three years on 29 April 1380, and her feastday is now celebrated on the date that marks the occasion of her passing to eternal life – 29 April.

Leadership as Service

Catherine's leadership was one of service. She was given a mandate (*Dialogue*, Noffke, 1980:38; Cameron, 2012a:127) from God to serve:

> All I want is love. In loving me you will realize love for your neighbors, and if you love your neighbors you have kept the law [Cf. Mt. 22:37-40]. If you are bound by this love you will do everything you can to be of service wherever you are ... I have told you how to serve your neighbors, and how that service proves your love for me.

Throughout her life and in her work, Catherine followed this mandate to serve (Noffke, 1980:159). Bynum (1987:26) emphasises that "charitable service, particularly care of the poor and sick, was especially common among Italian women affiliated with the Dominican and Franciscan orders." Elizabeth Dreyer (2014:45), recalls that in 1970 in his bestowal statement, conferring the title of "Doctor of the Universal Church" on St Catherine of Siena, Pope St Paul VI praised Catherine for her qualities. In his conferring of the doctoral title on Catherine the Holy Father spoke of her "infused wisdom" and

> [H]er gifts of exhortation and "wisdom in discourse". He explained that "The first quality points to her work in Church reform [and] The second points to her theology, a wisdom that weds knowledge to love [for] in the background of Catherine's theology is the female figure of Wisdom (*Hokmah* in Hebrew; *Sophia* in Greek – Proverbs 8 and 9; Wisdom 7), and the Wisdom/Sophia/Logos Incarnate of Matthew and John (Matthew 11:19; 12:42; 13:54; John 1).

Wisdom has built her house, she has hewn her seven pillars (Proverbs 9:1, cited in Sipe & Frick, 2015:4). For the purpose of this analysis, the "Seven Pillars of Servant Leadership" (see Appendix A for the list of attributes), are outlined below, and the discussion on each pillar includes aspects of Catherine's life and leadership practices.

Pillar 1 – "Person of Character"

At my meeting with Giuliana Cavallini, in Rome in September 2002, and in response to my query regarding Catherine as a role model for women and men in the twenty-first century, Cavallini's response was enthusiastic, stating that Catherine was constantly in touch with God. "She was concerned more with the universe – God and Man. She was courageous, honest and humble." Raymond (cited in Kearns, 1980:10) praises Catherine's humility, and emphasises that in her decisions she was "principle-centered", and governed by virtuous actions:

> For myself I am far from being a man of virtue, yet I have known many virtuous persons in my time. But I do not remember ever to have seen nor do I think I ever shall see, another of such universal excellence in every virtue as this maiden obviously was. Let me begin with the foundation and the support of all the other virtues, humility. So perfectly did she possess it that not only did she invariably choose to be made lower than the lowest of all, man or woman, and to be regarded as beneath everyone else, but she was also unshakably convinced that she herself was the cause of all the evils which others suffered.

Here Raymond refers also to Catherine's self-deprecation, which was not a ruse by Catherine to gain sympathy or to impress others for as evidenced throughout this work, she was conscious of her role in promoting "God's Truth".

My investigations into Catherine's life and works, have revealed that she was not prepared to compromise her values. Noffke (2000:546) recounts an occasion when Pietro del Monte Santa Maria, a "senator of Siena" and respected and trusted by Catherine, because of his loyalty and trustworthiness, was praised 'in Florentine circles' for his values and integrity, at the same time was criticized for "his excessive loyalty to the papacy." Catherine advises in a letter (T148) sent in "August 1375":

> I don't want you to be afraid, no matter what you may experience, my dear son in Christ Jesus, because God has so favored us that he himself is our helper, and he has given us good armor ... Let us follow in his footsteps, driving out vice by virtue: pride by humility, impatience by patience, injustice by justice, impurity by perfect chastity and continence, vainglory by God's honor and glory – so that whatever we do and accomplish may be for the glory, praise, honor, and spread of our Jesus' name (cited in Noffke, 2000:151).

Catherine was counselling Pietro del Monte Santa Maria, to avoid situations in his political career, where he might have to compromise his values ostensibly for the common good, but often just for the benefit of a few. She was advocating integrity and honesty. This letter to Pietro del Monte Santa Maria is just one of many examples, where Catherine chose to offer advice, and be of service to others rather than indulging in self-serving aspirations regarding her own faith journey.

Pillar II – "Puts People First"

Catherine's entire life revolved around her service to the Church and its members. She valued others, and it is the "spiritual welfare" of those she served that was important to her. Noffke (1980:xi) states that "the aim of the *Dialogue* was the instruction and encouragement of all those whose spiritual welfare was her concern, for there is reference to all their situations in its pages."

Catherine offered advice to all, particularly the poor and the marginalised, and while she did not condone the practices of those whose lifestyles might conflict with the teachings of the Church, she was prepared when the necessity arose, to put their needs first, showing compassion and love, and assisting them in their spiritual and personal growth. From her letters we know that Catherine was inclusive and understood that diversity was part of human nature. And indeed, her actions mirrored those of Jesus Christ himself, who reached out to the poor and the marginalised. Noffke (2001:144-148) refers to a letter (T21) from Catherine around early 1376 to a "nameless" person thought to be "engaged in homosexual practices":

> Catherine's attitudes toward homosexuality are typical of her age ... she does not hesitate to write lovingly and frankly to one whose behaviour she admits finding it hard to even talk about: "[D]earest brother! Sleep no longer in the death of mortal sin. Don't be cruel to yourself ... Run back to your Creator ... I assure you, if you decide to reform your life in the bit of time that is still left for you, God is so gracious and merciful that he will have mercy on you and receive you graciously into his arms" (Noffke, 2001:144-148).

There are many such letters to people from all walks of life. People known to her, and others she hadn't met. Now, Catherine loved the members of her spiritual family, and looked after them; mentoring, nurturing and offering spiritual advice – she felt responsible for them (Cavallini, 1998:14). She nursed the sick and the dying during the plague and attended the needs of her sisters in religion – the *Mantellate* – nursing many of them during times of illness, when for some, not just their bodies but their minds were also affected (Cameron, 2012a:141).

Catherine taught and nurtured the members of her team, and this mentoring and collaboration built a "sense of community" within their ranks. Following God's instructions in *the Dialogue*, Catherine promoted charity amongst her followers. "Every perfection and every virtue proceeds from charity. Charity is nourished by humility" (cited in Noffke, 1980:118). Consequently, in a letter (T61) to a Monna Agnesa Malavolti, and members of the *Mantellate* in Siena" (Noffke, 2000:2), Catherine discusses how important it is to be humble, charitable, and to persevere in "obtaining virtue and finding God":

[O]h, my dearest daughters, learn ... from the holy virgin Agnesa [Saint Agnes of Montepulciano], learn true holy humility. She kept this virtue alive within her ... submitting to everyone, giving God the credit for every grace and virtue. And I tell you, she was afire with the virtue of charity, ever seeking God's honor and the salvation of souls ... her other virtue was her constant zealous perseverance (cited in Noffke, 2000:3-4).

Cavallini (1998:10) maintains "that Catherine understood the needs of others and knew how and when to praise or to blame, to spur or to soothe."

Pillar III – "Skilled Communicator"

During her lifetime Catherine wrote numerous letters (close to four hundred are still extant) which you may recall, she dictated to scribes as her writing skills were just being developed. Noffke (1980:10-11) describes "Catherine's letters [as being] ... the better window to her personality, growth, and relationships with others ..." Her influence extended beyond class distinction, and this is evident in her many letters which, "She addressed ... [to] every imaginable class of people – popes and cardinals; monarchs, princes, and governors; priests, nuns, and pious laity; mercenaries, prisoners, prostitutes and [intimate friends and those not so intimate]" (ibid.). Though her letters were scribed by others, they revealed Catherine's determination to get her message across. At our meeting in Rome, Cavallini in addressing my query regarding Catherine's "candid approach" in her letters responded:

The heading of her letters, "In the name of Jesus Christ ... I, Catherine write to you ..." is a clear hint that her message is not her own, but is what in her familiarity with God, she understands she had to transmit to that particular person, and is what makes it possible frankly to praise or to reproach any kind of person, from the pope to a peasant or even to a prostitute (Personal correspondence, 2002).

As is evident from the above, and the content of many of her letters (Cameron, 2012a), Catherine didn't hold back, regardless of the identity of the recipient, who was either being praised or reproached, for she believed that her message had the approval of a 'Higher Being'. For example, when the hostilities between the papacy and "factions" within the papal states escalated, Catherine entreated the Holy Father to return the papacy to Rome from his residence in Avignon (the popes had resided in France since the beginning of the fourteenth century). She wrote an urgent message to Pope Gregory XI, who, on the advice of his relatives who feared for his safety, was reluctant to return the papacy to Rome.

> My dear babbo ["a name of endearment for one's father"] ... I hope you will not love yourself selfishly, nor your neighbors selfishly, nor God selfishly ... Let us concentrate no longer on friends or relatives or on our own material needs ... Pursue and finish with true holy zeal what you have begun by holy intent – I mean your return [to Rome] and the holy crusade. Delay no longer ... Up, father! No more irresponsibility! ... Courage! (Catherine, cited in Noffke, 2000:246-249).

The Pope's fears were not without foundation, for soon divisions within the Church widened so much, that Catherine petitioned God (Noffke, 1980:16) for the "reform of the Church and for peace in the whole troubled world" (Cavallini, 1998:3). She did all that she could to support the Church during this time and "her letters describe her involvement in ecclesiastical matters and other relevant issues of the day" (Cameron, 2012a:54).

Pillar IV – "Compassionate Collaborator"

As a young single woman on her own travelling the country-side, and engaging freely with the public, Catherine did attract some "notoriety", but then there were others, as is evidenced in previous chapters, who were so impressed with her way of life, that they became her "Spiritual family", and began to join her on her escapades around the country. She referred to her supporters as "la bella brigata – the beautiful brigade" (Noffke, 1980:1). She became their "spiritual mother". Catherine was building her team – her disciples! She valued the diversity of these supporters who were:

> [D]rawn from many levels of society and many religious traditions, and they regarded her as teacher and spiritual guide. And through her influence on Raymond of Capua she was to be a major force in Dominican reform even after her death. Even those who exploited her saw her as a woman to be reckoned with (ibid.).

However, at the time, the Church itself was not without its problems. Noffke tells us that in the fourteenth century "church and society and ... [the] Dominican Order were in chaos ... [but then] it was a great century for mysticism" (ibid.) and Catherine, while utilising a practical approach to confronting "political' situations, also found time as we had seen through this study, to action her mysticism (Wendy Brennan, 2003:8). During my discussion with Cavallini in Rome, September 2002, she emphasised that "Catherine was an uncommon kind of mystic. When experiencing ecstasy most people cannot see, speak or move. Catherine could speak."

During her public life, Catherine's reputation began to spread around the countryside, and while she had a powerful influence on her followers, she also had her critics. Fink (2000b:108) points out: "Public opinion about Catherine was understandably divided at the time. Some people revered her as a saint, but others thought she was a fanatic or a little crazy because of her extreme penitential practices." Nevertheless, her leadership practices had a powerful influence on her followers. She was compassionate, and empathised with the needs of the Church, her spiritual family, the members of the mantellate, and all whom she believed suffered poverty or injustice.

Pillar V – "Has Foresight"

Catherine was a visionary who possessed the gift of foresight, and the charism of prophecy. She demonstrated these skills through her intuitive insight, which Raymond (Kearns, 1980:258) recollects: "Those of us who lived with her could not in her absence do anything of any moment, whether good or bad, but she was aware of it. This we knew by experience repeated again and again." Raymond also emphasised, that "Catherine possessed the charism of prophecy in so perfect a measure, and it was so continuously present in her that, as far as we could see, nothing was hid {sic} from her that concerned herself or those about her, or those who sought her help for the salvation of their souls" (cited in Kearns, 1980:258). Bynum advises that "one should be aware of the practice in medieval times of confessors of saintly women, 'embellishing' their stories and putting their own interpretation on events that may or may not have occurred" (1987:28).

In *the Dialogue* God informs Catherine that "souls who reach union with him through the state of 'perfect tears' are able to receive the 'spirit of prophecy': how sweet is this union to the soul who experiences it! For in the experience she sees my secrets, and from this she may often receive the spirit of prophecy, knowing the future. It is my goodness that does this" (cited in Noffke, 1980:165-166).

Catherine possessed the skill of foresight. This is evidenced in her life and her works (particularly her letters), and from witnesses to her faith journey. Raymond (cited in Kearns, 1980:337) maintains that Catherine foretold what she would do following her passing to eternal life: "I make this solemn promise: that I will be more helpful to you after I have passed away than I have ever been or ever could be while still with you in this world with all its troubles" (cited in Cameron, 2012a:233).

Pillar VI – "Systems Thinker"

Catherine was not just aware of the "big picture" – the vision for the future – but she was also aware of the needs of the present. Cavallini (1998: 8) explains, "Concern for great problems such as the Hundred Years War or the Great Schism does not prevent her from being aware of everyday events, such as that of a monastery in grave need of help or of the situation of a sick member of her spiritual family." DeGraaf et al. (2001:15) emphasise the need to accept "the challenge of responding to the issues of the present", and to be flexible enough to be open to change, while creating a vision for the future. As we have seen in previous paragraphs, one grave concern Catherine had was that the Holy Father resided in Avignon rather than Rome, and that his absence did not augur well for the priests, who were left without a shepherd. In a letter (T 206) to Pope Gregory, Catherine exhorts the Pope to return to Rome (cited in Noffke, 2001:61-63). Finally, on 13 September 1376, Gregory XI left Avignon for Rome (p.243).

One of the questions I put to Cavallini during our meeting in Rome in 2002, was to ask, "How many monasteries did Catherine found?" The response was, "Catherine founded one convent – Our Lady of the Angels". In a letter (T12) written in 1376, Catherine wrote to Abbot Giovanni di Gano da Orvieto asking him to assist in establishing a suitable monastery for women [and emphasised that] "if you can, locate a suitable place for establishing a really good monastery, and put a few good leaders there – as far as members are concerned, we have plenty" (cited in Noffke, 2000:274). Noffke informs us that it was not long after Pope Gregory's return to Rome, that Catherine returned to Siena, and "shortly afterwards founded a women's monastery of strict observance outside the city in the old fortress of Belcaro" (1980:6) for it had been "on 25 January 1377 ... [that she had] obtained leave from the Commune of Siena to convert ... [a] former military installation into a monastery ... [called] Santa Maria degli Angeli (Saint Mary of the Angels)", (Noffke, 2001:272).

To lead is to serve – and in Catherine's *Letters* "there are over three hundred references to service, particularly service in relation to God, Church, neighbour, self and created things" (Noffke, 2001:799). Writing (T282) to Pope Gregory XI's secretary, Nicola da Osimo in late 1377, Catherine stresses the importance of service to the Church, by revealing God's words to her, "I am inviting you and my other servants to exert yourselves ... no one who serves her [holy Church] will go unrewarded, so much do I value that service. They will never see eternal death" (Noffke, 2001:685).

You may recall from previous paragraphs, that Cavallini (2002) admired the courage and strength of Catherine, whom she described as a real woman. "She possessed the qualities of a man and a woman. She was strong and courageous." Bynum (1987:26-27) maintains that:

> A study of the women's own writings [medieval times] suggests that women who lived in the world (either as tertiaries or beguines or as laywomen) ... differed from nuns raised in convents by having a sharper sense of male/female differences ... They were more aware of the prohibition of sacramental functions and teaching to women, more likely to see the female as weak and vulnerable, more male-oriented (i.e. more dependent on confessors or powerful male religious leaders) ... and more concerned with male power and male roles.

Hence, the male influence in the writings! Bynum (1987:27) in her work singles out Catherine of Siena, and states that "this tertiary was a leader and adviser of men." In addition, Catherine was concerned with reform in the religious orders, because many of these orders had suffered a radical loss in numbers, "after the Black Death had ravaged Tuscany in [the] spring of 1347 and again in summer of 1374. Recovery, both of numbers and of morale and discipline, was slow and difficult" Noffke (2001:274).

Pillar VII – "Leads with Moral Authority"

Catherine inspired trust in her followers as she taught them about God. Drucker (2001, as cited in Hunter, 2004:123-124) stresses the importance of trust to a leader: "the final requirement of effective leadership is to earn trust. Otherwise there won't be any followers – and the only definition of a leader is someone who has followers." Catherine did have her followers, and people gravitated towards her. Raymond (Kearns, 1980:227) recalls:

> I myself, more than once, have seen a crowd of a thousand or more men and women ... crowding in from the mountains and the country districts around Siena, just to see her and hear her. And when they heard her, or even only had sight of her, their hearts were pierced by sorrow for their evil deeds. Weeping and grieving for their sins they ran in search of confessors – Of whom I myself was one.

Catherine's love for "God's Truth", her faith, and for her spiritual family, knew no bounds. She was prepared to die for her beliefs – to pay the ultimate price. And indeed, such a situation arose, when she was forced to make a choice and she came close to being martyred. Noffke recounts "It was in June 1378, [that] mobs of the Florentine Ciompi (guildsmen of Florence) rose up ... against the powerful Guelfs [supporters of the Church] whom they saw as the instigators of the woes inflicted on the city ... Over the next several days they would murder many of them and burn their houses. The victims included a number of Catherine's disciples" (2007:147). Catherine, who was living nearby at the time, was advised to leave with her disciples, but she chose to stay, because she wanted to be a martyr. "She took her followers [disciples] with her into the garden to pray, and when the rioters broke in she calmly went to meet them, asking only that they not harm her companions. Too astounded to kill her, the attackers backed off, leaving Catherine to grieve over having been cheated of 'the red rose' of martyrdom" (ibid.).

Catherine's principles would not allow her to bypass a situation, in which she might be able to sway to the common good. One such occasion involved a mercenary soldier John Hawkwood, who according to Noffke (2000:79-80): "vacillated between the warring factions, fighting with the 'rebellious' groups and then transferring his troops to the 'service' of the papal supporters; in fact, generally hiring his troops out 'to the highest bidder.'" Catherine (T140) wrote to Hawkwood in mid-1375:

> Oh dearest gentlest brother in Christ Jesus ... consider how much pain and anguish you have endured in the devil's service and pay ... change your course and enlist instead in the service and cross of Christ crucified ... Then you would be one of Christ's companies, going to fight ... the unbelievers (cited in Noffke, 2000:80).

Apparently, Catherine was finding it "difficult to understand how Christians could be fighting each other when they could be joining forces in a crusade to recover the Holy Land from the 'infidels' ... it was commonly believed in Catherine's day that the Holy Land belonged by right to the Christian world" (Noffke, 2000:80).

Values

Aspects of Catherine's life and works are now discussed in relation to the values – dignity, respect, fairness, justness and equality (see Chapter 4 for the terms of reference). Please note that the abbreviation "T" that you have seen listed next to the number indicating a letter of Catherine's, stands for – *Lettere di S. Caterina da Siena*, ed. Niccolò Tommasèo (Florence: Barbera, 1860, cited in Noffke, 2000).

Dignity

You may recall the growing tension between the Independent city states, and the papacy. In a letter (T28) from Catherine to a Bernabò Visconti of Milan, who was regarded as a tyrant, and who was violently opposed to "the papacy" (in fact, he was excommunicated from the Church in 1362, and again in 1373), Catherine writes about the importance of the soul, which she refers to as "a city in which the all-good God dwells ... [the soul] is never lost except through deadly sin. And in that event, we become servants and slaves of sin; we become nothings, bereft of any dignity we had" (cited in Noffke, 2000:131-133). Noffke (ibid.), explains that Catherine is emphasising "that it is our sin which makes the human person a 'nothing'. By virtue of creation out of God's love, human beings have great dignity, though it is a contingent dignity" which must be valued and respected, for what is from God is sacred.

Respect

Pope St Paul VI (*L'Osservatore Romano*, October 15, 1970) emphasises the "deep respect ... and passionate love that Catherine had for the Roman Pontiff". Catherine valued and respected God, the clergy, the Church and others. Circa late 1376 or early 1377, she wrote (Letter T191) to Tommaso d'Alviano, who was a "mercenary fighter", and later "appointed ecclesiastical administrator of Orvieto and commissary of Pierre d'Estaing, Cardinal of Ostia" (Noffke, 2001:228-230). According to Noffke, "Catherine is asking Tommaso to come to the aid of the Church with his material possessions as well as his military service" (ibid.).

In her letters Catherine refers to the church "as a glorious garden", in which workers who are faithful Christians can serve by engaging in humble prayers and following true obedience. "I mean they must be obedient and respectful to holy Church" (Catherine, cited in Noffke, 2001:229-230). In addition:

those who are appointed to work in this garden as ministers, whose duty it is to administer the sacraments of holy Church, to feed and nourish us spiritually ... must nourish us with [their] teaching and example. But if their example were no mirror of virtue, it does not diminish the life we derive from these sacraments so long as we receive them worthily. Nor should any fault or bad example of the shepherds lessen the respect we owe them, since the power of the sacrament is in no way impaired by any defect in them. So we ought to respect them in virtue of the sacrament and because they are God's anointed, called by the scriptures his christs (ibid.).

Catherine served the Church and the people of God with respect, using the gifts given to her by her Divine Spouse.

Fairness

Catherine invariably equated fairness with justice, when dealing with various organisations – including the Church hierarchy, religious communities, political allies and opponents, royalty and others. Pope St Paul VI (*L'Osservatore Romano*, October 15, 1970) when conferring the doctoral title on Catherine stated that she "hungered for justice". In her letter (T196) addressed to Pope Gregory XI, in Avignon in February 1376, prior to his return to Rome, when the "tensions between the republics of the Italian peninsula deepened as the pope's representatives there exercised their authority through increasingly oppressive measures" (Noffke, 2001:18) Catherine entreats the Holy Father:

> Oh my dear most holy *babbo!* I see no other way, no other help for getting back your little sheep who have left the fold of holy Church as rebels disobedient and unsubmissive to you their father. So I am begging you in the name of Christ crucified, and I want you to do me

this favor: use your kindness to conquer their malice. We are yours, father, and I know for certain that all of them realize they have done wrong. And even though there is no excuse for wrongdoing, still, because of all the suffering and injustice and unfairness they were enduring from bad pastors and administrators, it didn't seem to them they had any alternative. They smelled the stinking lives of these bad administrators (who you know are devils incarnate) and they became so terribly fearful that, like Pilate, who killed Christ so as not to lose his authority, they attacked you rather than lose their position. So I am asking your mercy for them, father (cited in Noffke, 2001:20).

Here Catherine is asking for mercy for those who have turned against their Church because of the "corrupt" behaviour of their leaders. A second example is noted in a letter (T125) sent by Catherine in 1377, to "Monna Nera, prioress of the *Mantellate* of Siena" (Noffke, 2001:443).

You know, dearest mother, that a superior who is too in love with herself never gives correction, because she is always afraid. And if she does correct, her correction is often dictated not by the truth but by what people will think, or by her own selfish opinion, her own dislike for certain people's ways. This is not right since God has many ways with his servants and leads them along many paths … If your correcting is dictated by your own opinion it is more likely to be unfair rather than just. You ought simply to correct according to the faults you see, gently raising your own will to God's honor and looking with understanding at those in your charge, giving each one what she needs (cited in Noffke, 2001:444).

Catherine addresses Monna with respect, but her message is clear. She is asking the prioress to be fair and just in her dealings with the members of her community.

Justness

In many of her letters, Catherine writes about divinity, justice and love. So, in effect, she is emphasising that divine justness is available to everybody, and that this is because of the justness of God. Everybody has a right to be protected. There is reference here to two letters that support this statement. One letter mentioned in the previous discussion on "Fairness", is letter T196, which was addressed to Pope Gregory XI, in Avignon in February 1376, prior to his return to Rome in September of that same year. After formally addressing the Holy Father Catherine tells us that in love God gave us "the Word, his only-begotten Son … But justice wants vengeance for the wrong done to God. So along comes divine mercy and ineffable charity, and to satisfy justice as well as mercy, condemns his Son to death, once he had clothed him in our humanity … So, by his death the Father's anger is appeased and justice is satisfied by the sentence passed on the person of his Son." Perhaps an extreme example of the justness of God!

Regarding a Letter (T261) sent to Mariano, priest of the Casa della Misericordia (hospital) in Siena circa 1374 (Noffke, 2000:58) Catherine refers to the all-knowing God:

> There is nothing so hidden that God does not see it. He repays both good and evil, and there is no one who can escape this judgment. So rouse yourself … when the time of your death arrives, you can speak those sweet words Paul spoke "I have run; I have finished [the race], always keeping my faith in you, Lord. Now I am asking you for the crown of justice." One must persevere, then. Take up your place at the [open]side of Christ crucified and bathe in his precious blood."

Consequently, the just will be rewarded with eternal salvation. Such is the application of divine justness for all!

Equality

From her writings and her faith journey, we know that Catherine treated everybody equally. The Catholic Catechism (2000:para.1935) tells us that, "The equality of men/[women] rests essentially on their dignity as persons and the rights that flow from it. 'Every form of social or cultural discrimination in fundamental personal rights on the grounds of sex, race, color, social conditions, language, or religion must be curbed and eradicated as incompatible with God's design.'" God gave Catherine a mandate (*Dialogue*, Noffke, 1980:38) to serve everybody equally, and this she did with fairness and justness. Catherine empathised with everybody, regardless of their social status. Her letters were addressed to a diversity of recipients including the Pope, kings, queens, priests, religious and many others. She served by nursing the ill, sick and dying, even when she was ill and bedridden herself. In fact, Raymond tells us of a time when she "rose from a sick bed to tend a widow and her family who were suffering from hunger" (Kearns, 1980:127; Cameron, 2012a).

In the Dialogue (Noffke, 1980:330) God tells Catherine: "I created you without your help, without your ever asking me, because I loved you before you even existed, but I will not save you without your help". We are all created in the image of God, and "equally endowed with rational souls, all men [and women] have the same nature and the same origin. Redeemed by the sacrifice of Christ, all are called to participate in the same divine beatitude: all therefore enjoy an equal dignity" (CCC, 2000:para.1934). Catherine was unique and expressed her love of God and her communion with Him through her scribes, and through her emphasis on treating her disciples and others with dignity and respect.

In the next chapter, let us fast forward to the fifteenth century, where we meet St Joan of Arc Patroness of France and of soldiers.

9

St Joan of Arc

At a General Audience in Rome on 26 January 2011, Pope Emeritus Benedict XVI spoke to the assembled audience, about a young French woman Joan of Arc, who is now a canonised saint of the Church. Joan lived during the late Middle Ages and was put to death on 30 May 1431 at Rouen France, when she was just nineteen years of age. You will notice in the later Chapter on St Thérèse of Lisieux, that Joan featured in several poems and plays written by Thérèse, who had a fascination with the "military imagery" of Joan. Surprisingly, given that it was the latter part of the nineteenth century, there exists photographs of Thérèse (taken by her sister Céline, using a camera she had brought from home), dressed as Joan, acting in a play she had written on the French Saint. Benedict (2011a) refers to the connection between the two young saints:

> I like to recall that St Joan of Arc had a profound influence on a young Saint of the modern age: Thérèse of the Child Jesus. In the context of a completely different life, spent in the cloister, the Carmelite of Lisieux felt very close to Joan, living in the heart of the Church and participating in Christ's suffering for the world's salvation. The Church has brought them together as Patronesses of France, after the Virgin Mary.

The Pope spoke of Thérèse's desire to die as Joan did, with the "Name of Jesus on her lips" (ibid.). Interestingly, this utterance of Joan's as she died, is recorded in the Catechism of the Catholic Church (2000:para.435). Who then is the enigma that was Joan of Arc? It is appropriate at this point, to provide some historical background prior to presenting a profile of this great saint and female French "icon" of the Catholic Church.

Background

Two major world events occurred during the lifetime of Joan of Arc. One was Church related, and the other, was the outcome of political warfare. The former, involved the Great Western Schism (1378-1417) in the Catholic Church. You may recall that this Schism, commenced prior to the death in 1380 of St Catherine of Siena, when there was an elected Pope in Rome, and an anti-pope residing in Avignon France. Benedict (2011a) confirms that when Joan was born around 1412, that there was a Pope in Rome as well as two antipopes located elsewhere. During the years 1415-1417, no valid Pope was in residence in Rome, but at the end of the Schism in 1417, Pope Martin V was elected and served until succeeded by Pope Eugene IV in March 1431.

The second world event was the Hundred Years War (1337-1453), which historians maintain, actually lasted more than a hundred years (David Green, 2015). The war itself involved "a series of conflicts between England and France over succession to the French throne". The war had been raging for close to eighty or so years, when in 1415, "King Henry V of England invaded northern France. After delivering a shattering defeat to French forces [at the Battle of Agincourt], England gained the support of the Burgundians in France" (Biography.com Editors, 2014). This confrontation led to the signing of the Treaty of Troyes in 1420. The outcome of this pact meant that King Charles VI, who is said to have suffered from a mental illness, announced that Henry V of England, would accede to the French throne and would be ruling as regent until such time, as he would ascend the throne as king. The Treaty signified that Charles VI now recognized Henry V of England (and his heirs) as his successor, in lieu of his own son the Dauphin Charles (17 years of age at the time), whom he had disinherited by his actions at Troyes. At the time Charles VI also approved a union between his daughter Catherine of Valois to Henry V of England.

However, best-laid plans can tend to go astray, even for royalty, and in

1422, both Henry V and Charles VI died within a couple of months of each other, and as a result, Henry's infant son (grandson of Charles VI), who at about 9 months of age, became King of both England and France. Charles' son, the dauphin prince (uncle to the young Henry VI) was just 19 years old, and his supporters believed the unexpected circumstances were now ideal, to enhance their war efforts to have a French monarch crowned. The dauphin Charles was influenced by his advisors, for he was considered by many to be weak and indecisive (Victoria [Vita] Sackville West, 1948:109), and hence prone to manipulation by others.

Consequently, France was ready for a charismatic military leader, one who could inspire and motivate the French to victory, in an age of strategic warfare. According to Green (2015):

> The Hundred Years' War saw some major developments in military strategy and technology. Indeed, some historians have argued that these changes amount to a 'military revolution'. Among such developments, the evolution of gunpowder weaponry was particularly significant. That evolutionary process was, however, a slow one. At Agincourt, for example, it appears that French artillery accounted for a solitary English archer during the battle, and in 1431 Philip the Good, duke of Burgundy, fired 412 cannonballs into the town of Lagny and succeeded only in killing a chicken. Nonetheless, as the war entered its final phase such weapons were becoming increasingly effective. They played important roles in a number of Joan of Arc's battles and sieges, and the 'Maid' was considered particularly adept in aiming the weapons.

Note the reference to the "Maid" – Joan of Arc. In French she was called "La Pucelle" – the virgin/maid (Warner, 1981:12). Joan of Arc is often also referred to as "La Pucelle Orléans" – the Maid of Orléans, in honour of her contribution to the French victory in this large city. Regarding the last sentence of the quotation, in which Green writes of the military prowess of Joan and her adeptness in "aiming weapons"; however, she always carried her standard (sometimes referred to as her banner) into battle, "to avoid killing anyone; she says she never did kill anyone" (Daniel Hobbins, 2005:69). According to Hobbins: "much of our knowledge of Joan's life, revelations, and character depends on the text of her trial" (ibid.), at which she was found guilty of heresy, and condemned to be burnt at the stake in the marketplace at Rouen on 30 May 1431. She was about 19 nineteen years of age. A life that ended too soon! But how did it begin and why did it end so violently?

Profile

Joan was born sometime in early January, about the year 1412, in Domrémy, a small village "in the eastern French frontier region of Lorraine. Sackville-West (1948:30) writes that Domrémy was situated in the Meuse valley and located half in France and half "in the duchy of Bar ... [which] formed part of the duchy of Lorraine." Her father was "a peasant farmer named Jacques d' Arc and her mother was named Isabelle Romée" (Stephen W. Richey, 2003:25). Régine Pernoud and Marie-Véronique Clin (2000:221) write that: "Joan's parents had about twenty hectares (roughly fifty acres) of land in the village, of which twelve hectares (nearly thirty acres) were fields – either plowland or meadow – and four were woodland. They owned their house and their furniture and had some money in reserve." Both parents have been described as good, hard-working Catholics "pious and decent ...[though] in no way remarkable" (Sackville-West, 1948:33). Jacques was respected in the community, and carried out some official responsibilities, because of the high regard in which he was held. It is believed that five children were born to Jacques and Isabelle – three boys – Jacquemin, Jean and Pierre and two girls "Catherine ... who it is presumed to have died young" and Joan (p.35).

It was in the village of Domrémy, in late medieval France then, that

Joan, as a young peasant girl spent her childhood. She received no formal education, though her mother and the local parish priest assisted with teaching her the basics of the Catholic faith. "Her days were filled up with helping her mother spin thread, mend clothing, and cook, and with helping her father in the fields. Like all the other children in the village, she was periodically assigned duties of watching over grazing livestock and of herding the livestock from one pasture to another" (Richey, 2003:26). During her trial, Joan spoke about her skills with spinning, but gave the impression it was not often that she assisted in the fields with the livestock (Hobbins, 2005).

It was at the tender age of thirteen, that Joan first began to hear voices. "The voice came around noon in the summer, in her father's garden" (ibid.). Initially, it was just the voice of Saint Michael the Archangel, and later two other voices were added – Saint Catherine of Alexandria and St Margaret of Antioch. Over time, the voices become insistent, convincing Joan that she had been chosen by God to "lead the French army to victory over the English invaders", and that she would be the means by which the Dauphin would be crowned King of France (Richey, 2003:26). Therefore in 1428, when Joan was about sixteen, she decided that she had to go to "France to find the Dauphin" (Sackville-West, 1948:62).

However, she was now of marriageable age, and her parents were actively looking for suitors for her. Her father in particular, was concerned about his daughter. Sackville-West (ibid.) tells us that a couple of years prior to Joan hearing the voices for the first time, her father had experienced dreams during his sleep, of his daughter being taken away by soldiers, and he said to her brothers: "If I believed that the thing I have dreamed of her should come to pass, I should want you to drown her; and if you did not do so, I would drown her myself" (pp.62-63). Joan either overheard, or was later informed of this conversation, and was saddened by her father's continual anguish and concern.

During her trial, Joan was asked, "about instruction from the voice for her soul's salvation, 'She said that it taught her to behave herself and go to Church'" (Hobbins, 2005:54). Apparently, as mentioned in a previous paragraph, the voice told her two or three times a week that she must leave her home and go to France. At the trial Joan testified that the voice told her that:

> [S]he must raise the siege of the city of Orléans. She said next that the voice told her that she, Joan, must go to Vaucouleurs to find Robert de Baudricourt, the captain there, and he would supply her with men; she answered that she was a poor girl who knew nothing of riding or waging war. She went to her uncle [Durand Lassois, referred to by some authors as Durand Laxart, a kinsman – Marina Warner, 1981]) and he told her that he wanted her to stay with him for a little while, and she stayed for about eight days; then she told her uncle that she had to go to Vaucouleurs, and he took her there (ibid.).

When Joan reached Vaucouleurs, she approached Robert de Baudricourt, the garrison commander, requesting his assistance, in her efforts to travel to the royal court at Chinon, to inform the dauphin of God's plans for him and for France. Baudricourt was initially annoyed by the girl-child and her outlandish request, but soon became amused, and after threatening to share her favours with himself and his men, sent her on her way back home.

It was not long after Joan returned from her unsuccessful attempt to recruit the services of Robert de Baudricourt, that during an attack on the village from the Burgundians, the family was forced to leave Domrémy for Neufchâteau. Richey (2003:26) writes that, "Domrémy was one of several villages and towns that comprised a small isolated pocket of territory that was loyal to the Dauphin. This pocket of pro-Dauphin ground was completely surrounded by many miles of territory that supported the Burgundian faction" (ibid.), which continued to have an on-off relationship with the British. Hence, the threat of war was never far from the D'Arc household.

It was during the family's sojourn at Neufchâteau, that a suitor for Joan's hand in marriage was revealed, and "he dragged her off to Toul, the centre of the diocese, to answer in a breach-of-promise action before the episcopal court" (Sackville-West, 1948:73). Sackville-West maintains, that the existence of this young man, would have been unknown "but for Jeanne's judges having chosen to mention him, in the ninth article of their accusation, as an additional example of how badly she had behaved" (ibid.). In Article 9 of the Trial, it states, that "Joan dragged a young man before the magistrate in Toul for breach of promise ... the young man refused to marry her and died while the case was pending" (Hobbins, 2005:127). In earlier testimony, prior to the compilation of the articles, Joan was asked by the judges "what persuaded her to summon a man from Toul in an action for marriage ... she answered: 'I didn't have him summoned; he had me summoned'" (pp. 91-92). Joan claimed that she had sworn to tell the truth, but when the judges collated her testimony, they recorded Joan's responses, according to their own interpretation of the facts presented.

Joan denied the young man's claims, because she said that from the moment that she first heard the voices, she had vowed her virginity to God and was promised to no man. It was during this time that the young man (who is not named) died unexpectedly. Joan, her parents and family members returned to Domrémy, to find that their house, which was built of stone, had been left intact (Richey, 2003:26), after a particularly vicious attack on the village by the Burgundian invaders.

In 1429, without informing her parents, Joan at seventeen years of age, set off for Vaucouleurs, to again seek out Robert De Baudricourt, to try to persuade him to organise an armed escort for her to travel to the royal court at Chinon. Sackville-West (1948:77) posits that: "nothing but the commands of God himself could have superseded the authority of her parents in her dutiful mind ... She said that sooner than go to France without God's permission she would be torn to pieces by horses. She recorded, also, that her parents nearly went out of their minds when she left them." Unfortunately, her entreaties to De Baudricourt were again rejected. It was during this time that, "the English ... laid siege to Orléans. On February 12, 1429, the English inflicted yet another crushing defeat on the French army in a battle fought in the open field at Rouvray, not far from Orléans" (Richey, 2003:30).

Joan approached de Baudricourt again, and though he had "twice turned her away and rebuffed her ... heeded her on the third attempt" (Hobbins, 2005:54), but to prove that Joan was in fact from God, and not being manipulated by an evil spirit, he organised for a priest to perform an exorcism, which "Joan passed ... proving her purity and sanctity to all" (Richey, 2003:30). As a result, De Baudricourt "agreed to provide Joan with an arms escort of six men ... [S]ome citizens of Vaucouleurs provided Joan with the male clothing she requested ... [and] she cropped her hair short and round in the male fashion of the time. She was provided with a horse of her own, so she could keep up with her six mounted escorts" (ibid). De Baudricourt also presented Joan with a sword as a parting gift. She carried no other weapons.

Thus, on February 23, 1429, the party set out for the dauphin's castle at Chinon, in the Loire Valley. On the journey "They would have ... to travel about 350 miles across France, much of it through hostile Burgundian territory" (ibid.). Fortunately, there were no major incidents along the way, and prior to their arrival at Chinon, Joan dictated a letter to a scribe which was addressed to Charles, informing him of their intending arrival and that she wanted to meet with him. At her trial:

> She said that she sent letters to her king in which it was stated that she was sending them to know if she were to enter the city where her aforesaid king was and if she had done well to travel 150 leagues to come to him, to his aid, and that she knew many good things for him to hear. And it seemed to her that in those same letters it was stated that she would recognize her aforesaid king among all the others (Condemnation Trial, session of Tuesday, February

27, 1431), (cited in Pernoud & Clin, 2000:248).

Various historians give different arrival dates; these range from late February to early March (Richey, 2003:149). Hence, it was about 6 March 1429 that Joan and her party arrived in Chinon; however, she was not immediately presented to the dauphin. Charles sent his advisors to speak with her, to ascertain the genuineness of her quest (p.31). According to Sackville-West (1948:110), at first Joan "refused to reply, saying that she would speak only to the Dauphin, but, when they explained that they had come to her in the Dauphin's name, she relented and said that the King of Heaven had sent her with a double mission, first to raise the siege of Orleans, and second to lead the Dauphin to Reims for his coronation."

Having Robert de Baudricourt's "written endorsement", was a plus, and eventually permission was granted for a meeting with the dauphin, but it seems that Charles tried to deceive Joan by wearing a disguise to confuse her, as to whom she should approach when admitted to his presence, in the company of his advisors. Joan was not fooled, and directly approached Charles and curtseyed before him, acknowledging his title, and informing him of her mission. In a later private conversation, she is said to have discussed matters with him, that no one knew apart from Charles and God; the dauphin then began to believe, that her incredible quest was divinely inspired.

Nevertheless, Charles still harboured some doubts regarding Joan, and he wanted to assure himself that she was not being influenced by the devil; hence, he organised for her to be taken to "the city of Poitiers to undergo three weeks of questioning by a panel of eighteen theologians and learned churchmen. These men asked Joan many probing and sophisticated questions on points of Christian faith" (Richey, 2003:34). Joan received a favourable report from the clerics. However, there was still another test to endure:

> Charles and his advisors required another form of proof that Joan's inspiration was divine, not diabolical.

According to the beliefs of the time, a woman became a witch by having sexual intercourse with either Satan or one of his demons. Joan had to endure not one, but two, intrusive physical examinations by ladies of the Royal court to confirm that she was a female and a virgin. The ladies found Joan's maidenhead to be intact on both occasions and duly reported to Charles that she could never have consorted with the Devil and his minions (ibid.).

During these intrusive examinations of mind and body, Joan was already planning ahead and dictated a letter to the commanders of the English forces at Orléans, which according to Richey: "must rate as one of the most ringing ultimatums in history" (ibid.).

Eventually Joan's mission was approved, and she set her sights on joining the fight for the besieged city of Orléans. Sackville-West (1948:133) lists Joan's possessions as set out to deliver Orléans from the English:

> We can thus compose a fairly complete inventory of Jeanne's personal possessions at the time she set out for the deliverance of Orleans. She had her suit of armour, humbly made without any blazon whatsoever. She had her horse. She had her standard [banner] – a proud standard, bearing the image of Christ, the world, two angels, and the lilies of France. She had a lance. She had a pennon [pennant]. She had a small battle-axe, which she sometimes carried in her hand. She had her two rings ... One of them had been given to her by her brother, the other either by her father or her mother.

The words JHESUS MARIA were written on the standard that floated above Joan's head, as she held it in one hand, and led her horse out of Poitiers bound for Orléans, which had been under siege for over six months.

Richey (2003:46) states, that Joan: "made her debut as a warrior leader in the series of battles that broke the English siege of the city of Orléans." The city of Orléans was surrounded, and "protected by high castle-like walls that completely enclosed the city" (ibid.). Strong towers fortified the walls, with the river protecting the French to the south. Several of the forts built around the enclosure, were held by the English. Richey (p.49) writes that: "The critical weakness of the English deployment around Orléans was the huge gap between their forts northeast of the city. As long as this gap in the English chain of forts existed, the French could still, with great difficulty, get supplies and reinforcements into Orléans." According to Sackville-West (1948:135), the English had not surrounded the city completely, and at one point there was enough of a gap "for the entry of provisions and munitions into the town", and this proved beneficial to the French.

Sackville-West (p.136) also asserts that after six months of fighting, the English had lost their enthusiasm, and that Joan arrived at a time when, "the English no longer had the heart or the means to stage the conclusive attack." Joan's achievements were "psychological rather than military ... her personal example and confidence were worth ten thousand men ... [her] real achievement was not the relief of Orléans, but the regeneration of the soul of a flagging France" (ibid.). Indeed, the Maid of Orléans was an inspiration to all the men, who fought for France under her standard. "At the sight of Joan on her horse with her banner, at the sound of her voice shouting encouragement over the din, the French around the north east fortress of Saint Loup rallied and went back on the attack with renewed ardor" (Richey, 2003:57). Joan was victorious in her first battle. However, as she surveyed the carnage across the fields, "she grieved equally for the French and the English dead" (ibid.).

Joan prophesied that she would be wounded in the battle for Orléans, a month or so before it occurred. The Tourelles were considered "the most important of the English forts that encircled Orléans" (Richey,

2003:60), and it was on "May 7 ... that [Joan] played the decisive role in capturing" this most important English bastion (ibid.). Unfortunately, it was also the setting where she was wounded. Her "most authentic prophecy had been fulfilled: she was hit by an arrow just above the left breast. It penetrated into her flesh to a depth of six inches. The pain frightened her, and she wept" (Sackville-West, 1948:170). Joan was taken away, and had her wound attended to, then she "returned to the fight to lead the final frenzied assault that stormed the Tourelles. The following day the English were prepared to continue fighting but Joan forbade her soldiers from following up their victory of the previous day and the English retreated." Sackville-West (1948:178) maintains that Joan held the English in her power, and that she made a huge tactical blunder in "allowing the English army to retreat after [their] defeat at Orléans." Joan's reasons were that she had allowed them to escape, because it was a Sunday – the sabbath day – a day that was "important to her".

Decisive battles were then fought at Jargeau, Meung, Beaugency, and Patay. And it was at Patay that "Lord Talbot, England's foremost warrior leader after the death of King Henry V" (Richey, 2003:71), found himself a prisoner-of-war of Joan, her right-hand man, and very good friend, Duke Jean d'Alençon (cousin of the dauphin Charles), and the French army. Richey (p.75) emphasises that even if "Joan's co-commanders handled the tactical details at Jargeau, Meung, Beaugency, and Patay, it was Joan herself who drove the overarching strategy of *forcing* a battle to take place at each of those locations ... [and] After the decisive triumph at Patay, it was time to get Charles to Reims." Hence, less than five months after Joan left her village of Domrémy: "On July 17, 1429, beneath the soaring vaulted ceiling of Reims cathedral, Charles felt the crown come to rest on his head, while the warrior girl who put it there stood beside him, magnificent in her shining armor" (p.77). With Charles VII of France now crowned, Joan and d' Alençon were keen to march on Paris:

> [T]o take back France's capital. The English and

Burgundians were in panicked disarray and the city was weakly defended. Instead, the timid and easily duped Charles immobilized the army and Joan while he entered into negotiations with the enemies of his people and his country. Weeks dragged by while the English and Burgundians used the negotiations as a cover to massively reinforce the garrison of Paris and to refurbish the city walls. Joan and d' Alençon could only seethe in fury (Richey, 2003:77-78).

Charles finally gave approval for Paris to be attacked on 8 September, the feast of the Nativity of Our Lady, but the time for victory had passed. Joan was again wounded, this time with an arrow through her thigh. She was rescued, and was fully prepared to continue an onslaught on Paris, but Charles refused (he was negotiating an agreement with representatives of the Duke of Burgundy), and "ordered a retreat ... he disbanded the great army with which Joan [and her comrade in arms] had saved France" (p.80), with one of his reasons being lack of funds. The king then retreated to "Gien on his beloved Loire ... [and] on receiving the King's final command to abandon Paris and to accompany him in his retreat, ... [Joan] discarded her armour, symbol of conquest, and ... left it lying before the image of Our Lady in the cathedral of Saint Denis" (Sackville-West, 1948:209). Nine months passed, in which Joan spent time attending the royal court, and keeping company with the King and Queen. At times there were opportunities, "to carry on the war as an independent captain, leading such meagre troops as the king allowed her, plus what she could raise on her own [mostly] ... non-French mercenaries" (Richey, 2003:81). As a reward for Joan's efforts, "Charles conferred titles of nobility ... [on her] and her family" around Christmas 1429 (p.82).

Joan's movements "from December 1429 to April 1430 are sparsely recorded" (Sackville-West, 1948:219). Though Joan was victorious in a battle at Lagny in April 1430, this was to be her final victory (Richey,

2003:83). Pernoud and Clin (2000:84), declare that "It was not until May 6 [1430] that Charles VII acknowledged his error and admitted that he had been duped by his cousin ... [the duke] of Burgundy ... [and] while the duke of Burgundy was setting in motion a carefully conceived battle plan and could count on the reinforcement of the English army, Charles VII had prepared nothing. His greatest resource was Joan the Maid." Unfortunately, in the month following her victory at Lagny, Joan was attacked by a "swarm of Burgundians [who] yanked her out of her saddle in a melee fought beneath the city walls of Compiègne. Ahead of her lay the ever-darkening road to captivity, torment, and martyrdom" (Richey, 2003:83). She was considered a major prize, and "locked up in the castle of Beaulieu en Vermandois."

The following is an account by Pernoud and Clin (2000:89), on the circumstances surrounding Joan's capture and imprisonment:

> Taken prisoner at Compiègne on May 23, 1430, Joan did not reach Rouen, the place appointed for her trial, until Christmas Eve of that year. The seven intervening months were filled with negotiations concerning her ransom, which turned into a sale price – anything but a ransom – of 10, 000 pounds paid by the English crown. The primary agent of that negotiation was Pierre Cauchon, formerly rector of the University of Paris and bishop Beauvais ... and hence an exile, since Beauvais had welcomed Charles VII ... Single-minded and tireless, Cauchon arranged to have himself appointed chief judge of Joan's ecclesiastical trial. Charles VII made no effort to ransom or free Joan.
>
> Hostile as they must have been to her, her captor, John of Luxembourg ... and his lord, Duke Philip of Burgundy ... seem to have hesitated to hand Joan over to the English and the Paris university faction: the influence of three ladies ... with whom Joan spent over three months in the fortress of Beaurevoir (and perhaps also that of the Duchess Isabelle of Burgundy) ... may account for the delay. Joan tried several times to escape but was chided by her "voices" for those efforts.

Sackville-West (1948:234) is scathing of the efforts of Charles VII, regarding the circumstances of Joan's capture, and subsequent imprisonment, trial and death sentence: "Charles owed everything to Jeanne. Admittedly, he had his difficulties to contend with. He had his own weak character, and his own strong false friends ... He had his own poverty to consider. But all the same ... there still remains a residue of contemptible treachery which must for–ever be associated with his name. He ought to have made some attempt to rescue Jeanne." As per the long quotation in the previous paragraph, Joan did develop a rapport with the Luxembourg women, but even their kindness did not shield her from the ignominy of captivity. She wanted desperately to escape, because she did not want to fall into the hands of the English, but her voices tried to dissuade her. "Finally, she took the law into her own hands, commended herself to God, and threw herself off the top of the castle tower" (p.237). Fortunately, she was not seriously injured.

In December 1430, plans were progressing rapidly to bring Joan to trial. Pierre Cauchon (as mentioned above), was negotiating for a suitable location for Joan's trial, and Rouen "a sympathetic city in pro-English France" (Pernoud and Clin, 2000:209) was selected. As Cauchon was the bishop of Beauvais, where Joan had been captured, he was required to "ask the ecclesiastical authorities of Rouen" for permission to be granted a "commission of territory", which allowed him to head the tribunal of the Inquisition for Joan's trial at Rouen (ibid.). Joan was taken under guard and arrived at the city on Christmas Eve 1430 (p.101). Joan was not taken to a women's prison, but to a military prison. "'I saw her in the prison of the castle of Rouen, in quite a dark room, chained and with leg irons', declared Isambart de La Pierre, a Dominican of the convent of Sant-Jacques at Rouen and an assessor at her trial" (p.104). Another witness was an usher, Jean Massieu, "whose responsibilities included accompanying the prisoner from the place where she was detained to the place where the tribunal met ... I know for certain that at night she slept with two pairs of irons on her legs, attached by a chain very tightly to another chain that was connected to the foot of her bed, itself anchored by a large piece of wood five or six feet long" and guards at the door (p.104).

At her trial, Joan stated that "she had always been told [by the voices that] she must be taken prisoner" (Hobbins, 2005:87), and would be tried for heresy. According to Pernoud and Clin (2000:103):

> *Joan's trial* [was held] *by an inquisitorial court composed of dozens of professional experts directed by the hostile presiding judge, Pierre Cauchon ... From January 9 until the end of May 1431, they tried to confuse and entrap this barely literate peasant girl, against whom they had not formulated a charge – a procedural flaw that would later make this trial easy to nullify. She stood them off until the very end, finally confused by her judges' decision that she had refused to submit to the Church Militant* [the Church on earth] *on the matter of wearing men's clothes. Joan had agreed to sign a document abjuring her "voices" on the understanding that she would be transferred to an ecclesiastical prison in the custody of women, rather than remain in a military prison guarded by hostile English soldiers who threatened her virginity. Betrayed on this point by Cauchon, she resumed men's clothes, was thus declared a "relapsed heretic," and was burned at the stake in the public marketplace at Rouen on May 30, 1431 ... She was nineteen years old.*

Legend reveals that Joan's heart did not burn, and that it was thrown with her ashes, when they were scattered in the Seine (Sackville-West, 1948:300).

The hundred Year's War continued for another two decades or more after Joan's death. King Charles VII eventually reclaimed his throne and ordered an investigation into the legitimacy of Joan's Trial and "*[i]n 1449, he called for the pope to authorize a new trial*" (Pernoud and Clin, 2000:139). Pope Callixtus issued a "transcript authorising the new trial with the close family of Joan acting as plaintiffs" (p.156). When the retrial began, on November 7, 1455 Joan's mother Isabelle Romée was present, and spoke on her daughter's behalf. Pernoud and Clin (ibid.) maintain that at the retrial in 1456, the original trial verdict was nullified after a *"lengthy interrogation of 115 witnesses, many of whom had been involved in the trial that condemned Joan in 1431."* Following the nullification of the first trial on 7 July 1456, Joan was officially exonerated, and cleared of all heretical accusations. Joan of Arc was beatified in 1909 and canonised a saint of the Church on 16 May 1920. The feastday of Saint Joan of Arc is celebrated on 30 May.

Leadership as Service

In her role as a military leader, Joan served God and her country. She has the confidence of the contemporary Church, and her words of wisdom are recorded in the Catechism. At a General Audience in Rome (2011a, January 26), Pope Emeritus Benedict XVI spoke of the profound love, that enveloped and radiated from this "icon" of French spirituality, who was a soldier, first for Christ, then for her king and country: "This Saint had understood that Love embraces the whole of the reality of God and of the human being, of Heaven and of earth, of the Church and of the world. Jesus always had pride of place in her life, in accordance to her beautiful affirmation: 'We must serve God first' (CCC, 2000:para.223). Loving him means always doing his will." The "Voices" called Joan and she responded, and "declared with total surrender and trust: I entrust myself to God my creator, I love him with my whole heart" (Benedict, 2011a).

Wisdom has built her house, she has hewn her seven pillars (Proverbs 9:1, cited in Sipe & Frick, 2015:4). For the purpose of this analysis, the "Seven Pillars of Servant Leadership" (see Appendix A for the list of attributes) are outlined below, and the discussion on each pillar includes aspects of Joan's life and leadership practices.

Pillar 1 – "Person of Character"

Hobbins maintains that "In many ways the character of Joan of Arc still eludes historians, perhaps in part because of the many roles she is made to play – pious peasant, mystic, martyr-saint, French patriot, protofeminist and others" (2005:26). Joan accomplished what she set out to do. She raised the siege of Orléans, leading the French army to victory over the English invaders, and she witnessed the crowning of King Charles VII of France. Sackville-West (1948:312) writes that, "Her courage and conviction were superhuman. They were of the quality which admits no doubt and recognizes no obstacle. Her own absolute faith was the secret of her strength." And, as I have expressed in previous paragraphs, "her psychological value as a leader … far surpassed [her superior] tactical or strategical value. It was her single-mindedness which enabled her to inspire disheartened men and to bend reluctant princes to her will" (ibid.).

Joan prized her virginity, which she offered to God, from the moment she first heard the voices at the tender age of thirteen years. Benedict (2011a) informs us that: "Virginity of soul is the *state of grace*, a supreme value, for her more precious than life. It is a gift of God which is to be received and preserved with humility and trust." One of the best known texts of the first *Trial*, concerns precisely this: "Asked if she knew that she was in God's grace, she replied: 'If I am not, may it please God to put me in it; if I am, may it please God to keep me there'" (CCC, 2000:para.2005).

When Joan was imprisoned, she was denied the comforts of the Church. Her spiritually and the Church were her life. Her faith journey was nurtured by the voices she heard and by her love for Jesus and Mary. Pope Benedict XVI (2011a) emphasises that: "[The] spirituality [of Joan] was Christocentric and Marian". You may recall from previous paragraphs, that the names Jesus and Mary were included on all the letters she dictated to scribes and the words "JHESUS MARIA" were written on the standard, that she carried into battle – the standard that inspired an army – the French army.

Pillar II – "Puts People First"

In an earlier paragraph I referred to the fact, that when Joan engaged in battle and men were killed, she grieved for both sides – the enemy plus her countrymen. As mentioned however, in the introductory paragraphs, Joan admitted at her trial that she never killed anyone and that this is why she carried the standard into battle. Joan testified that whatever she did she did at God's command (Hobbins, 2005:69).

Her leap from the tower at Beaurevoir was one of desperation but also one of sorrow for the people in her country whom she knew would be made to suffer. "She had been told that everyone in the town over the age of seven would be put to fire and blood, and stated that she would sooner die than continue to live after such a destruction of good people ... she had no desire to commit suicide – she had only the desire to get away ... [and] it was in vain that her voices sought to restrain her" (Sackville-West, 1948:236). But her action was to no avail. At her trial Joan said: "that following her leap from the tower, she had no desire to eat for two or three days ... Yet she was comported by Saint Catherine, who told her to confess and ask forgiveness from God for leaping and [if she did this] without fail the people of Compiègne would receive help before the winter feast of Saint Martin. Then she began to get better and to eat and was soon healthy" (Hobbins, 2005:100).

Joan inspired a whole army. She trusted them, and they in turn trusted her, and were prepared to follow her standard into battle. Richey (2003:45-46) cites a Simon Charles who "served as president of the chamber of accounts to Dauphin and King Charles VII ... in the retrial, testified that 'Joan was very simple in all her actions, except in war, in which she was very expert'". A knight named Thibault d'Armagnac stated: "Apart from the doings of war, she was simple and innocent; but, in the moving and disposition of troops, in the doings of war and in the organization of combat and encouraging the troops, she behaved like she was the most skillful captain in the world, trained in all times of war" (ibid.). D'Alençon in his testimony agreed and added that Joan was especially adept in the placing of artillery, in which she was excellent (ibid.).

Pope Benedict XVI (2011a) discusses the great love Joan had for "Jesus and for her neighbour in Jesus…" As mentioned in earlier paragraphs Joan died calling out the name of Jesus. In the contemporary world, close to six hundred years after her death, this French icon is still very much remembered. In *The Economist* (2000:83) we read that "The female warrior-cum-saint holds a central place in the French imagination. Statues of 'the maid of Orleans' adorn churches and public squares, and there is a rue or a place Jeanne d'Arc in almost every French town."

Pillar III – "Skilled Communicator"

Joan was not a learned person. She couldn't read or write, and when letters had to be written she dictated what she had to say to scribes. And often she had plenty to say! Earlier in the chapter, I referred to a letter that Joan dictated and then sent to the English at Orléans, prior to her leading her troops to raise the siege of Orléans. The following is an excerpt from the letter which gives some indication of Joan's thought processes prior to engaging in battle. It is taken directly from Article 22 of her Trial, where it was presented on Tuesday 27 March 1431: "With regard to this article … [Joan] says she did not produce the letter out of arrogance or presumption, but by our Lord's command (cited in Hobbins, 2005:134-135):

> King of England, and you, Duke of Bedford, who call yourself regent of France; you, William de la Pole, Count of Suffolk; Sir John Talbot, and you, Sir Thomas Scales who call yourselves lieutenants of the Duke of Bedford: do right by the Kingdom of Heaven and surrender to the

Maid sent by God, the King of Heaven – the keys of all the good towns you have taken and violated in France. She has come in God's name to proclaim the blood royal, wholly ready for peace if you wish to do right by her, to abandon France and pay for what you have taken. And all of you before the town of Orléans, archers, companions-at-arms, you of gentle birth, and others, depart in God's name for your own country.

If you do not, wait for word from the Maid, who will come see you shortly ... I am sent by God, the King of Heaven, to chase you one and all from France ... you shall never rule the kingdom of France ... Charles the true heir will rule it. God wills it, and has revealed it to him through the Maid, and he will enter Paris ... Duke of Bedford, the Maid prays and requests you not to destroy yourselves. If you do right, you can still come join her company, where the French will perform the finest action ever seen in Christian lands. Answer, if you wish to make peace in the city of Orléans. If you do not, prepare yourselves soon for a great loss. Written Tuesday of Holy Week.

Quite an articulate letter from an illiterate peasant girl! A girl warrior, who according to Richey (2005:36), was about to go to the rescue of Orléans and that "about 4,000 men would march with Joan to that beleaguered city." She was listening to God, and to her voices. During her Trial Joan was asked "whether her voices ever called her daughter of God, daughter of the Church ... she said that before the lifting of the siege of Orléans, and every day since, when they spoke to her they frequently called her Joan the Maid, daughter of God" (ibid.).

Pillar IV – "Compassionate Collaborator"

Joan reached out in compassion to all the soldiers in her care, and to those who were wounded regardless of whether they were friend or foe. She prayed for them all. Often not leaving the site of a battle, until she had prayed for those on both sides, who had participated and paid the ultimate price. Richey (2003:57) maintains that the army was not really "Joan's army" for she "was under escort of a clique of high-ranking French warrior nobles who still considered themselves to be the true leadership of the army." Nevertheless, though she wasn't officially the leader of the army, Joan still gave the impression she was in charge. "First she made them all go to confession, and then decreed that all their loose women should be left behind" (Sackville-West, 1948:143), even swearing was frowned upon!!

Joan believed that it was her mission to have the rightful king of France crowned. She was aware of his weaknesses but trusted in God and the voices to carry out her objective. Sackville-West (1948:108) writes that Charles himself was "not an impressive figure ... physically he was weak ... [and] mentally twisted. His own mother had, in so many words declared him a bastard. Charles ... had been brought up to regard himself as the rightful heir to France ... then [he found himself] stigmatised by his own mother with illegitimacy", and therein lay the conundrum; for, was he the rightful heir to the French throne? Historians agree, that there was some speculation regarding his parentage and that his paternal uncle may have been his father, but with little evidence to prove to the contrary, he was keen to claim his heritage, for though his mother Isabeau de Bavière, produced twelve children (some died in infancy and the others barely survived young adulthood), Charles VII survived them all (ibid.).

Pillar V – "Has Foresight"

During her trial, Joan was asked about the voice she first heard at the age of thirteen. Joan said that "It seemed a worthy voice and she believed that the voice was sent by God; after she heard the voice three times, she knew it was the voice of an angel" (Hobbins, 2005:54). Joan also identified the angel, and said that: "Saint Michael, when he came to me, told me that Saint Catherine [of Alexandria – an early Christian martyr] and Saint Margaret [of Antioch – also an early Church martyr] would come to me and that I should act by their advice, that they were bidden to lead me in what I had to do and that I should believe in what they would say to me and that it was by God's order" (Maid of Heaven website).

Sackville-West (1948:57) maintains that "Whatever the nature of the voices, and however they arrived, they had come to stay. Once they had begun, they never left her." What we know of Joan's visions, come from Joan herself, and her responses at her trial: "Standing alone, a girl of nineteen, before the formidable array of judges of the Ecclesiastical Court and the Holy Inquisition, she spoke as her voices had told her to speak" (p.59).

At the trial Joan was asked many questions regarding the appearance of the angels, what they looked like, and how they were dressed. Some of her responses included:

> The spirits who habitually appeared to her were three in number – the Archangel Michael, Saint Margaret, and Saint Catherine. She claimed also to have seen the Archangel Gabriel and several hundreds of other angels, but it was with her three familiars that she was chiefly concerned. She saw them with her bodily eyes, and wept when they left her, wishing that they could have carried her away with them. They came always accompanied by the cloud of heavenly light. She could touch them and embrace them. Asked whether she embraced them round the neck or round the lower parts of their bodies, she replied that it was more seemly to embrace them round the lower part, by which I presume that she meant round the knees, and that she herself was on her knees before them (ibid.).

Joan disclosed that when they appeared to her the angels: "spoke very well and beautifully ... with soft and humble voices. They appeared to her several times a day ... Whenever they came, they brought guidance and comfort" (p.60). Joan sincerely believed in the voices – they were her link to God.

On occasion Joan was said to prophesise. She foretold when she would be injured in battle, for example during the siege of Orléans. She did say, "she would take Paris, ... [though] this promise, accepted as a divinely inspired prophecy, had been broken" (Warner, 1981:64). Also, there is the message that Joan revealed to the dauphin, as proof that she had been sent from God. Charles believed her, for what she relayed to him, was known only to himself and God. According to Warner: "At Chinon, Joan made the bold and amazing statement that she had come from God; it is only after her victory at Orléans in May that year, just two months after Chinon, that the chroniclers of the period openly agree with her" (p.51).

As a prophetess, Joan combined the roles of visionary and military leader (Hobbins, 2005). Sackville-West (1948:301) asserts that Joan "forces us to think". She asks the question: "Does God on occasion manifest Himself by direct methods? Is it possible that certain beings are born with a sixth sense, a receptivity so far beyond that of their duller fellows that in order to explain it we take refuge in such words as 'miraculous' and 'supernatural'" (ibid.)?

Pillar VI – "Systems Thinker"

Joan had a mission to accomplish. The "big picture" for her, was to ensure that Charles VII was crowned King of France, and that she would lead the French army to victory in the besieged city of Orléans. With assistance, she was able to mobilise an army. Thousands of soldiers were inspired by this young woman, dressed in armour, who led them into battle riding her horse and carrying her standard. Hobbins (2005:2) writes that "The failure to take Paris in early September marked the end of

Joan's successful campaign." You may recall from a previous paragraph that after a few minor victories Joan was captured outside the walls of Compiègne on May 23, 1430. She became a prisoner of war and was also charged with heresy" (ibid.). Charles VII owed his throne to Joan, but when she was captured, he turned a blind eye to her dilemma, and at the time showed absolutely no support, maintaining silence and keeping his distance. According to Hobbins (2005):

> No account is more critical to our understanding of Joan of Arc than the contemporary record of her trial in 1431. Convened at Rouen and directed by Bishop Pierre Cauchon the trial culminated in Joan's public execution for heresy. The trial record, which sometimes preserves Joan's very words, unveils her life, character, visions, and motives in fascinating detail. One of the richest sources for a medieval woman ... The trial of Joan of Arc began on 9 January 1431 and ended with her execution on May 30 (p.1).

According to Hobbins: "Some scholars have dismissed Joan's trial as a travesty of justice, in the words of a respected historian, 'the best-known example of a ... court violating generally recognized inquisitorial procedures.' The judge Pierre Cauchon has been denounced as a tool of the English who was willing to sacrifice Joan to further his own career" (p.17). However, Hobbins (ibid), does argue that he believes that Cauchon followed "correct procedures".

Richey (2003:46) writes from his own military experience, when analysing Joan's skill as a "Military Commander". He praises Joan's enthusiasm and inspirational behaviour on the battlefield:

> Joan's military role as an inspiring creator of the will to fight is obvious and indisputable. Establishing to what degree she was more than just a 'super cheerleader' – to what degree she was a true commander who made

decisions and gave orders concerning the strategic and tactical conduct of the war – is much more problematic. What complicates this question is that the French army of Joan's day had nothing that modern military professionals call a chain of command. Whether it was a case of strategic decisions made at the royal court, or of tactical decisions made in a tent in the field, decisions seem to have been made in an extremely loose committee fashion, with the most forceful speaker present able to make his *or her* view carry the others along.

Richey (ibid.) recommends that the reader follow the testimony of Joan's retrial, to determine the truth of what actually transpired on the battlefield, where a young girl became a warrior. Also, "it is a standard characteristic of the warrior nobility of any culture to possess a large measure of egotism. Why would men ... [soldiers, knights and royals] have made up stories that exaggerated the role of a teenage peasant *girl* telling them what to do? The very improbability of them saying what they did leads one to conclude that they were saying things that were remarkable but true" (p.87). Here, Richey is referring particularly to testimony given at the retrial for Joan by two high-ranking men, who knew her well, and could testify about her military prowess – one was Jean, duke of D'Alençon whom we have met before, and Jean, count of Dunois, who had the unenviable title of "Bastard of Orléans" (p.37).

Pillar VII – "Leads with Moral Authority"

The travesty of the trial that convicted Joan of Arc is "a distressing page in the history of holiness and also an illuminating page on the mystery of the Church which, according to the words of the Second Vatican Council is 'at once holy and always in need of purification' (Lumen Gentium, n.8)", (Pope Emeritus Benedict, 2011a). The Pope here is critical of the judges and their decision: "The Trial was the dramatic encounter between this Saint and her judges, who were clerics. Joan was accused and convicted by them, even condemned as a heretic and sent to the terrible death of being burned at the state ... these judges were theologians who lacked charity and the humility to see God's action in this young woman" (ibid.).

Benedict emphasises, that the theologians who convicted Joan, seemed to be unaware of the beauty of her soul, and didn't understand or know that "they were condemning a Saint." These men disregarded Joan's pleas uttered on 17 March and 2 May, to be taken to the Pope. She told them that if they granted her request, "then she would answer all the necessary questions" (Hobbins, 2005:23). Unfortunately, her request was denied!

The members of the tribunal were appalled by Joan's male attire (which she continued to wear, more so as protection in a military prison surrounded by males), and in addition, when collating the information from the trial, they changed some of Joan's responses to suit their own agenda. "At the royal inquest of 1450, the notary Guillaume Manchon stated that while taking notes during the trial, 'he was sometimes pressed by the bishop Beauvais and the judges to write according to their understanding, contrary to Joan's meaning'" (p.7).

However, Benedict (2011a) states that "about 25 years after Joan's death the *Trial of Nullity*, which opened under the authority of Pope Callixtus III, ended with a solemn sentence that declared the condemnation [trial] null and void (July 1456) ... This long trial, which collected the evidence of witnesses and the opinions of many theologians, all favourable to Joan, sheds light on her innocence and on her perfect fidelity to the Church. Joan of Arc was subsequently canonized by [Pope] Benedict XV in 1920."

Values

Aspects of Joan's life and works are now discussed in relation to the values – dignity, respect, fairness, justness and equality (see Chapter 4 for the terms of reference).

Dignity

A young nineteen-year-old woman, standing before a tribunal comprising numerous clerics and theologians – who were relentless in their questioning, would present a challenge for the most hardened of prisoners. Joan showed tremendous dignity and "extraordinary courage" in what Hobbins (2005:32) describes, as a "hostile setting. She transcended her world to become an 'image of female heroism.'" What indignities she must have suffered, being placed in a military prison, rather than in a cell with other women. You may recall, that she was shackled in chains day and night, and had male guards at the door of her cell in the evenings. Throughout the long months of her trial, Joan was stoic, and maintained her dignity throughout what seems to be inhumane treatment by her captors.

According to the Education for Justice website (cited by Katherine Freely, n.d.): "The principle of human dignity is the foundation of all the Catholic social teaching principles" (see Chapter 4 for the terms of reference – Dignity). Was the human dignity of Joan of Arc, a priority during her initial trial? For example when her testimony was recorded not on fact, but according to how the tribunal interpreted her responses; also during the subsequent brief abjuration, when she was coerced into changing her testimony in favour of what the members of the tribunal dictated to her demanding that she acknowledge that she was a sinner, who had engaged in sorcery and heresy and to beg forgiveness of the Church.

In addition, Joan was told that if she abandoned her male attire for female clothing, she would be permitted to hear Mass, and be relocated to another cell where she would be in the company of women. Eventually, Joan caved in, to the pressure, but the promises given to her were not honoured. Overnight Joan viewed her abjuration as a "personal failure, spoken in a moment of weakness, out of fear of the flames – a transgression against her voices that put her in danger of damnation" (Hobbins, 2005:25). Consequently, she reneged on her decision; resumed wearing men's clothing and prepared to fight her last battle in a court that had virtually already decided her fate!

Respect

Though she answered some questions respectfully; others Joan dismissed out of hand: "Do you want me to tell you what is intended for the king of France? Many things do not concern the trial" (Hobbins, 2005:75). And again "She asked the voice to counsel her how to answer and told the voice to seek counsel from the Lord; and the voice told her to answer boldly and God would help her ... The voice comes from God; and I believe I am not telling you all I know. I fear to fail by saying something that may displease the voices more than I fear answering you" (p.59-60).

Richey (2003:142) highlights the respect that Joan was held by her companions in the battlefield. While all of Joan's military comrades swore in her retrial that they never felt sexual arousal when they were around her, Knight Jean de Metz hastened to add that, "I was on fire with her words, and with what I believe was her divine love ... Joan commanded the chaste love and devotion of the men ... she [was a strong] healthy country girl-next-door [person]. It was her [approachability] ... *in combination with* her raw courage that *compelled* her companions to respect her as their warrior equal and to chastely love her as their Pucelle."

Fairness

By all accounts Joan was not treated fairly by those who participated in the tribunal. As mentioned, once she was captured the decision had already been made to put her to death. For if she would have been found innocent, then the English wanted to have her released to their custody, where they would have given her the death penalty. During the trial, Joan made simple requests that were denied. She asked on two occasions to be taken to the Pope. The celebration of Mass was very important to her, and on 20 February 1431, a day prior to the first public interrogation:

> Joan was summoned to appear "in the royal chapel of the castle of Rouen at 8 o'clock in the morning of Wednesday February 21 to answer the truth to the articles and questions and other accusations … Joan said she would appear and answer the truths to questions about her. She also requested 'that you would assemble as many clergy from France as from England' and further asked to hear Mass tomorrow before her appearance, and that the bishop be informed of these requests. [However], given the crimes of which she was accused and the shameful attire she insisted on wearing, they had decided … [to] postpone permission for her to hear Mass or attend divine office" (Hobbins, 2005:48).

It is obvious, that there was little fairness in the way the members of the tribunal treated their prisoner, for they had already determined her guilt.

Justness

The entire trial of Joan of Arc could be referred to as a travesty – a mockery of justice and has been described as such by several historians (Hobbins, 2005). Joan had a right to be protected by the Church. There should have been justness at her trial, but instead, there was condemnation, imprisonment and death. On the biography website (2018) for Joan there is emphasis on the fact, that instead of being "held in a church prison with nuns as guards, she was held in a military prison.

Joan was threatened with rape and torture though there is no record that either actually occurred ... Frustrated that they could not break her, the tribunal eventually used her military clothes against her, charging that she dressed like a man."

Warner (1981:125) quotes Deuteronomy (22:5): "The woman shall not wear that which pertaineth unto a man, neither shall a man put on a woman's garment; for all that do so are abomination unto the Lord thy God." However, did the crime deserve such a violent death as burning at the stake? Joan was warned that there was no reason for her to be still wearing men's clothes in prison (though this could be disputed as she was in a military prison guarded by men). Joan's reply was that: "When I have finished what God sent me here to do, I'll wear women's clothes" (Hobbins, 2005:176). You may recall, when reading through the chapter, that there were occasions when Joan was subjected to tests to determine her virginity – would (or indeed could) a male have been exposed to such an "intrusive examination"? Admittedly females and males both have rights whereby justness for both should be the objective.

In previous paragraphs, there is mention that the members of the Tribunal, when collating what had transpired during the trial, changed many of Joan's responses to suit their own interpretation of what they believed to be the "correct" response that would lead to a conviction. Was there justness in this for Joan? Hobbins (2005:19) maintains that if "Joan had been returned to the English had there been no trial at all she would almost certainly have been executed." Hence, trial or no trial, the fate of Joan was sealed! In a contemporary court of law, this would be enough to have the case thrown out of court, for a person is considered innocent until proven guilty. So where was the "Rule of Law" (Motley, 2016)?

Hobbins (2005:15) records that "Joan's trial was an ecclesiastical procedure, covered under canon law, the law governing the medieval Church. Hobbins (p.2) also cautions, that Joan's trial, "was not a modern trial, nor should we judge it by how closely it approximates our own legal standards." And while acknowledging the wisdom of Hobbins in relation to the process of a medieval trial, and considering the "political, cultural, and legal world of the people who produced it" (ibid.), there is still a measure of injustice, when theologians, and ecclesiastical representatives, can all unite and use their wealth of knowledge and influence to convict one young, uneducated peasant maid.

Equality

It is important to remember, that while Joan of Arc dressed in male attire, she:

> [M]ade it clear to everyone that she was a girl, not a boy. The feminine aspect of her identity was embodied in the title she proudly invented and gave to herself: 'Jehanne La Pucelle,' that is, 'Joan the maiden.' But she was a maiden who wore men's clothes, who cropped her hair short, who rode a horse astride, not sidesaddle, and who forced her own way through the manly realm of action ... Even when she spent time at the royal court, far from the harsh necessities of life in an army camp, she still affected the appearance and mannerisms of the male (Richey, 2003:103).

Richey after quoting the above, then refers to Maria Warner's book *Joan of Arc: The Image of Female Heroism*. What is of interest is that Richey highlights Warner's description of Joan, as embodying "the idealized archetypes of the Ideal Androgyne, Knight, and Prophet ... and that Joan's acts of personifying ... [these] are key components of her military success" (ibid.). Our understanding of the Knight and Prophet concepts, have perhaps been addressed in this chapter, as has the "Ideal Androgyne" concept, albeit implicitly. For example, Joan dressed as a knight in full armour, and carried into battle her standard that depicted images, that she testified had been commanded by God. Also, she was accepted at the royal court dressed in her male attire. Regarding the prophet concept, you may recall some prophesies revealed by Joan – her dialogue with her voices; her victory at Orléans; the crowning of Charles VII, and her wounds in battle to name just a few. At her trial she was likened to "a prophetess with direct access to God" (Hobbins, 2005:30).

Concerning androgyny, Joan was a female who dressed as a male. She was a soldier and being with men in battle she was comfortable dressing as a man. Throughout the trial of Joan, the continual emphasis on her "male attire" seems to have been an issue. In fact, Warner (1981:129) writes that "Joan's dress formed the subject of no less than five charges, so although we know nothing [or very little] of Joan's appearance, we have detailed information about her clothes." The question is asked why was Joan so keen to "cling to apparel so obviously offensive and even dangerous to her survival" (p.131)? According to Aristotle "Knowing yourself is the beginning of all wisdom." Richey (2003:103-104) quotes Warner to emphasise his point, that Joan's "male attire" enabled her to lead an army, a feat that at the time, "no mere girl could ever do." According to Warner (1981:131):

> Through her transvestism, she [Joan] abrogated the destiny of womankind. She could thereby transcend her sex; she could set herself apart and usurp the privileges of the male and his claims to superiority. At the same time, by never pretending to be other than a woman and a maid, she was usurping a man's function but shaking off the trammels of his sex altogether to occupy a different, third order, neither male nor female, but unearthly, like the angels whose company she loved.

At her trial, Joan was asked if she had been "commanded to wear men's clothing" (Hobbins, 2005:66). Her reply was that the command had come from God and the angels. She was then asked if this command was lawful, and she replied: "All that I have done is by the Lord's command. If he commanded me to put on something else, I would do it, since this would be by God's command" (ibid.). Joan knew that she was created in the image of God and she was proud of her womanhood and her leadership, which inspired an entire army to victory, and led to the crowning of a king.

Let us remain initially in the fifteenth century and then move into the sixteenth century, as we follow the faith journey of St Angela Merici – Foundress of the Ursuline Order.

10

St Angela Merici

Within the central doors to St Peter's Basilica in Rome, and evenly spaced throughout the nave, are niches which house thirty-nine statues of saints, who have founded Religious Orders. Two of these saints are investigated in this research – Teresa of Ávila (see the following chapter) and Angela Merici who is the focus of this chapter. Angela lived in the sixteenth century around the late Middle Ages, and was the foundress of the Ursuline Order, during a period of great turbulence in the Catholic Church – a time when the Church was being attacked from within and without, by corruption and greed – which included external pressures such as the Great Italian Wars. These wars are often referred to as the Renaissance Wars, and they were fought between 1494 and 1559, and comprised "a series of violent wars for control of Italy [which were] fought largely by France and Spain but involving much of Europe" (Editors, Encyclopaedia Britannica, 2018). The Papal States and the Republic of Venice, which are places of interest in the following paragraphs, were involved in these wars.

Prior to proceeding with Angela's faith journey, some background information is required, to shed light on the situation in the Church, during those tumultuous years, for that was a time when religious orders were founded to make a difference, and to assist the Church in its efforts towards renewal. Angela Merici founded her Company of St Ursula, known as the Ursulines, for this purpose, as did St Teresa of Ávila in her reform of the Carmelite Order.

Background

During its history, the Church has had to combat heresies (you may recall the heresies listed in the chapter on St Monica), corrupt practices and corrupt clergy, simony, nepotism, and division within its top echelons, all of which contributed to a split within the Church, and resulted in the Great Western Schism and the election of two, then three anti-popes (remember there is mention of this schism in the chapters on St Catherine of Siena and St Joan of Arc). Consequently, by the late Middle Ages, the Church was spiralling out of control, and reform was badly needed. In the early sixteenth century, the situation escalated with reports of "buying and selling indulgences", whereby penitents sought to gain some remission for the punishment due to sins, by resorting to unethical practices. At the time Martin Luther, a Catholic priest in Germany, raised his concerns, and is said to have posted ninety-five theses regarding the "abuse" of indulgences, on the door of the Castle Church in Wittenburg Germany in 1517 (Editors, Encyclopaedia Britannica, 2018).

Sources indicate, that it was Luther's intention to organise for the propositions just to be sent to the Archbishop of Mainz, and the Bishop of Brandenburg. However, with the advent of printing presses, the effects were immediate and widespread, and the documents circulated very quickly, and "Became a manifesto that turned a protest about an indulgence scandal into the greatest crisis in the history of the western Church" (ibid.). Protesters of "the abuses and totalitarian control of the Roman Catholic Church, [joined forces with] ... [r]eformers such as Martin Luther in Germany, Ulrich Zwingli in Switzerland, and John Calvin in France [and] protested various unbiblical practices of the Catholic Church and promoted a return to sound biblical doctrine" (Got Questions, 2018).

Apart from the issues just cited, the catalyst for the beginning of what history now refers to as the Protestant Reformation, is generally considered to be the action of Luther (see information above) regarding the 95 theses (ibid.). Surprisingly, the response of the Catholic Church was slow; however, by around mid-century, a Counter-Reformation was instigated by Pope Paul III, to counteract the measures taken by the protestors and "to effect a religious renewal." You may recall that in previous times of unrest in the history of the Church Ecumenical Councils had been convened to "decide what were true doctrines and what were heresies" (Fink, 2000a:xvii). Hence, Pope Paul III decided to convene a General Council to address the much-needed reforms in the Church.

This decision presented many challenges for the Pontiff, and in 1534 as St Angela Merici was preparing for the foundation of her Company in 1535, "Pope Paul was struggling desperately against the obstacles which prevented the opening of the General Council" (Ledochowska, vol. 1, 1968:200). The Pope tried to organise firm dates, but on the occasions that dates were set, several bishops were uncooperative. A further complication was the outbreak of war. Nevertheless, the Pope persevered and in 1545, after some years of postponements, convened the Council of Trent. This was the 19th Ecumenical Council of the Catholic Church, and it was held in the city of Trento in northern Italy. The Council lasted eighteen years and concluded in 1563. Its purpose was to "define the doctrine on indulgences", and to work on ways to eliminate abuses in the Church, by reforming "church teaching and discipline".

History records that Angela Merici's contribution to Church renewal was to found a religious company! Hence the story of the birth of the Ursuline Order, under the umbrella of its various companies, seems complex initially, but the narrative raises awareness and an appreciation of the prophetic vision of its foundress.

Profile

It was around the year 1474, that Angela Merici was born in Desenzano del Garda, a small town "on the southern end of Lake Garda", in the province of Brescia in Lombardy, northern Italy. The exact year of

Angela's birth is unknown, but historians place the date as between 1470 and 1474. In fact, there is very little information about the early life of Angela, and what is known has been revealed by some early biographers, and by testimonies of witnesses for the *Processo Nazari*, which was established to investigate the cause for the process of her canonisation. Querciolo Mazzonis (2007:11) informs us that "the main body of information" used in his book is taken from the *Processo Nazari*".

According to Mazzonis (ibid.), Angela was born into a "family of impoverished lower nobility with urban and commercial roots." He refers to Angela's father as Giovanni Merici, whereas in volume one of her book on Angela, Teresa Ledochowska (1968:10) refers to Angela as being the daughter of "Thomas Merici", and in her notes (2) states that, "In his text, Pandolfo Nassino gives Angela's father the name of 'Tomaso', but all the documents, including the account of Angela's election as Mother General, call her daughter of John (Giovanni) Merici." Angela's mother was "Catherina nee Biancoso (or Biancosi), and she originated from Salò (situated on the western side of Lake Garda), and her brother [Ser Biancoso de'Bianchi] lived in the town and was a lawyer and member of the city Council" (Mazzonis, 2007:12). Ledochowska (ibid.) informs us that a "Dr. Jacopo Alberti, a learned Salò author … [referred to Catherina as] Biancosa Biancosi" (p.11n).

Various authors and biographers differ regarding the number of children in the Merici family. However, Mazzonis (2007:12) tells us that Angela had "one or two older brothers, one older sister, and one younger brother". Lombardi (cited in Ledochowska, vol. 1, 1968:12) testified that "Angela had three brothers", while other "witnesses in the *Processo Nazari* speak of one sister, Angela's playmate, who died quite young." The historian Mattia Bellintani, himself a native of Salò, refers to "a nephew of Angela, Dr Tracagni, so [there is the conclusion that] the Saint also had a married sister: [and] it seems that she was one of a large family" (ibid.). Ledochowska advises caution regarding Bellintani's testimony, as apparently, he tended to exaggerate (pp.12-13).

Apart from any perceived discrepancies, suffice to say that Angela had siblings, and that in her early years she lived with her father and mother, on a small property within the environs of a town called Desenzano. Mazzonis states that the family were reasonably well-off and that the records show that, "In 1489 her family had property in livestock and land in Desenzano" and that "in 1523 Angela declared a piece of land cultivated with a vineyard" (ibid.). In her "biographical novel" written to commemorate the 450th Anniversary of the Death of Angela Merici, Janice Howard (1989:8-9) cites the early occupation of Giovanni Merici, as that of saddlery-maker living in the town of Desenzano. Mazzonis (2007:10) supports this by stating that Giovanni's, "family belonged to the urban merchant stratum, which was involved in the trade of wool and leather"; however, Giovanni had a yearning to acquire property for farming, and it appears by the records presented in this paragraph that he eventually achieved this objective.

As mentioned previously, there is very little information recorded on the childhood and early adolescence of Angela. According to Mazzonis (2007:10), "Although Angela was a famous spiritual woman during her time, she had no hagiographer or group of devotees to register the deeds of her life." Ledochowska (vol.1, 1968:13) emphasises:

> [T]he depositions of her friends during the *Processo Nazari*, held twenty-eight years after her death, do provide reliable information on her early years. For instance, Antonio Romano, in whose home Angela lived for fourteen years, said under oath "She told me herself that, from the time she was five years old, after she had listened to her father reading the lives of Saints and holy Virgins, she began to devote herself to a spiritual and contemplative way of life."

It is believed that Angela's father contributed to her spiritual development by reading to her, which enabled her to meditate on the lives of the saints. Indeed, she was being nourished by the deeds of those, who had been sanctified and canonised by the Church. Surprisingly, though Angela continued to nurture her growing spiritual awareness, and broaden her intellect with her application to reading books that would also enhance her spirituality, she received little formal education, and therefore lacked rudimentary writing skills. Accordingly, when Angela grew to adulthood, she was obliged to engage the services of a secretary, whenever she wanted to dictate letters, or produce significant volumes of written advice for her spiritual daughters.

Another insight into the daily life of the young Angela, is recorded in the evidence from a young man, Tribesco, later "Canon of the Lateran at St. Afra", who disclosed what Angela shared with him during the latter years of her life, as she gave him words of encouragement regarding his spiritual life. Apparently, Tribesco related the information to a Floriano Canali, and this was submitted as evidence for the *Processo Nazari*.

> To encourage me in a love of fasting and the desire to practise it, she assured me that God never fails to help those who desire it ardently; she illustrated this belief by the example of her own life, telling me that during her girlhood in her parents' home she had worked hard at all the household tasks that usually fall to the women's share; she had done the washing, churned the butter, kneaded the dough for the bread, carried water from the spring and done other heavy work. Yet all the week she ate only a little bread on Thursdays ... about half a handful of bread. She even showed me, by putting her left hand across the palm of her right hand, the amount of bread she was accustomed to allow herself on that day (cited in Ledochowska, vol.1, 1968:14).

As a parent my first impression on reading about Angela's fasting practices during her growing years, was to have some concern as to why her parents were not aware of her tendency to restrict her intake of food, which may have had severe repercussions on her general health. Though, to give Angela the benefit of the doubt, perhaps she just meant that it was bread that she was denying herself through the week, except for Thursdays, and that she was eating other varieties of nourishing food. However, I do not believe that this is clear in the information presented by Ledochowska (ibid.).

During her late teenage years (around 18), Angela left Desenzano to live with her uncle and his family in Salò. The events that precipitated this move are unknown, though it is believed that her parents and siblings died unexpectedly. Howard (1989:22) refers to the plague while an unnamed source (n.d.) is more specific and maintains that around 1492 a new disease – typhus, was introduced into Italy by Spanish soldiers. Nevertheless, historians agree, that in the latter part of her teenage years, Angela left her home and moved to Salò. However, there are some discrepancies regarding if she went alone, or if she was accompanied by either a sister or a brother, who may have survived the tragic events that had led to the deaths of members of Angela's immediate family.

For example, in her biographical novel, Howard (p.33) embellishes her narrative stating that Angela and her sister arrived together to stay with their uncle in their mother's hometown. On the other hand, Ledochowska (vol.1, 1968:14), after noting the "successive epidemics of the plague in Italy" informs us that not only did Angela lose her parents, but her sister also, and that she was "taken under the guardianship of her uncle at Salò where she spent several years". While Mazzonis (2007:13) writes, that it was when Angela was about 18 and after the death of her father, mother and sister from "unknown causes"; leaving them orphans, that she and her younger brother went to live with their uncle in the affluent town of Salò.

Significantly, it was during this distressing time in her life, that Angela is said to have experienced her first vision (Ledochowska, 1968:16-17; Mazzonis, 2007:13). You may recall that in the chapter on St Hildegard of Bingen and later you will see in the chapter on St Thérèse of Lisieux, that there is mention of the traumatic effects the loss of a parent can have on a young person (Hamilton, 2006:1). Angela lost not only one parent but both, and probably her sister and brother/s as well. She had belonged to a close-knit family, and now she was virtually alone (though perhaps still having a brother!), and her loss was devastating. Furthermore, circumstances necessitated a move from the town in which she was born, to the town where her guardian and uncle lived. Her faith however was strong – for most of her young life and until tragedy intervened, she had lived a life in prayerful union with her interior spirit. In fact, Mazzonis (2007:12) tells us that "At the age of five or six she began to practice abstinence and to live in retirement from people, so that she might give herself wholly to prayer and devotions." It may be that this contemplation during her childhood, contributed in a significant way to Angela's visionary experience at the time, the focus of which was her young sister who had recently died!

Ledochowska's (vol.1, 1968:16-17) description of the vision is quite comprehensive. She also writes of the inspiration Angela received from her connection with her interior spirituality: "Angela's biographers have multiplied details of her childhood showing her precocious sanctity" (p.13), and they "name her adolescence as the time of what is, in their opinion, the most important event of her spiritual life. This is the famous vision which was to decide the form of her vocation" (p.16). Mazzonis (2007:13) recounts the circumstances of the vision: "While praying for her sister, she saw her in the sky among a group of angels: Where, one day, finding herself in a small field of her own near Desenzano, and there praying for her sister with the usual prayers, at midday she saw a host of angels in the air, in the midst of whom was the soul of her beloved sister, joyful and triumphant." Interestingly in his notes, Mazzonis (ibid.) refers to the fact that Angela was worried about her sister's salvation, because her sister may have had "a more rebellious nature: [and] according to the 'rasse' [cited in the notes on p. 12] ... a book to register damages caused by people to property, she was responsible for some damage to the property of the Merici's neighbours."

The testimony of Antonio Romano regarding the vision (Ledochowska, vol.1, 1968:16-17), may have influenced Mazzonis, for both versions appear very similar. However, Ledochowska (ibid.) also presents a different interpretation of the vision by Francesco Landini. She (pp.15-16) writes that "Twenty-six years after the death of the Foundress, Father Landini, Vice-Superior of the Ursulines of Brescia, sent to Milan certain information about her and her Company." Ledochowska quotes from the letter sent by Landini in 1566. As with the other versions of the vision, the letter explains that it is harvest time, and that Angela is in the fields when she sees her sister amid a procession of angels playing music and with virgins singing.

What differs in the above interpretation, is that Angela's sister is said to have spoken to her and "looking into the future … told Angela that God wanted to make use of her to found a Company of consecrated virgins; she added that the Company would grow rapidly…" Apparently, Landini had never met Angela, and hence, did not receive the information regarding her vision from her, so Ledochowska (ibid.) states that the evidence must be regarded as indirect; however, "as Superior to her Daughters he [Landini] was likely to be well informed." Nevertheless, both Romano and Landini receive positive acknowledgement from Ledochowska (p.17), regarding their reports of Angela's vision:

> It must be admitted that these reports cannot be taken in the sense that sworn testimony in a modern court of law would be taken; their authors were honest men of the sixteenth century … the two witnesses are responsible men worthy of belief and counted among the spiritual leaders of the people of Brescia … It is impossible to reject them out of hand, particularly as another witness, Agostino Gallo, a man of undoubted integrity, also says that supernatural favours had been granted to the future foundress.

Ledochowska (ibid.) makes two interesting points, regarding the differing accounts of the vision presented by Landini, who was very familiar with Angela's Company, and her daughters, and Romano, a good friend of Angela's: "Romano stressed the certainty given to Angela of her sister's salvation; Landini emphasises that the essential fact was the certainty of her future vocation as a foundress." So, the question has been asked (ibid.) by various scholars, if perhaps Angela in fact received not one, but two visions around the same time. Interestingly, Angela never took credit for her foundation, as she believed that the idea came from God (p.18). So, did her vision inspire her future life choices, or did her "epiphany" come later?

Some years after her move to Salò, and "[a]ccording to the statements of the *Processo Nazari* ... Angela asked to be admitted into the third Order of the Franciscans of the Strict Observance." She wanted the habit, so that she would be able to "go to Mass, to Confession and to Holy Communion, because at that time it was difficult for lay people to obtain permission for frequent communion" (p.22). Consequently, becoming a Franciscan Tertiary, set the course for Angela's fulfillment of what she believed to be the will of God, regarding the status of her union with Him. Mazzonis (2007:14) confirms her choice:

> Entry into the third order was also a way of acquiring an acceptable social status that made it possible to resist family and social pressure to marry. Angela's choice of the third order testifies to her preference for a religious life lived in the world rather than in a convent. Her future foundation of the Company of St. Ursula developed further this ideal.

In time, Angela's ideal became a reality. I refer you again to the biographical novel *Angela: A woman faced with two alternatives, she saw and chose the third* (1989) by Janice Howard. I must admit, when I first read the title I was slightly confused as to the connection, though having completed research for this chapter on Angela, I now realise the significance of the title, and how it aptly describes the intentions of the wise and forward-thinking foundress. For when Angela was a young woman, the only life choices open to grown women, were marriage or a monastery. This chapter reveals that Angela's choice of a third option, differed from the two presented. Her option involved single virginal young women living at home and while gifting their virginity to their divine spouse, and nurturing their contemplative lives, they engaged in an active apostolate in the world around them.

In the ensuing twenty years, following her admittance to the third order of St Francis, there is little authentic information available on Angela's activities. Mazzonis (2007:15) suggests that during that time, she returned to her property at Desenzano (the family estate) while living "in accordance to the Franciscan third order, a life of prayer, penance, and, possibly, works of mercy such as visiting the sick and comforting the dying." But, such a version of events is just conjecture. What is known is that around 1516 when Angela was about 40 years of age, she was sent to Brescia where according to Ledochowska (vol.1, 1968:30), she "engaged in a special form of apostolate called for by the pressing needs of her time."

For example Brescia during those years was described as "a city of pleasure ... [and] Not even wars, nor the outbreak of the plague which, in 1478, carried off 30,000 of the 230,000 people in the province of Brescia, could break the high spirit of the people" (p.31). There had been French invasions, but for a time these did not seem to adversely affect the morale of the people, however, before long, moral standards began to deteriorate drastically, and an incurable disease became rampant within the city environs. This illness led to the setting up of hospitals in the city, which were established solely for patients who became known as "incurables", these unfortunate souls were suffering from syphilis – a sexually transmitted disease. A religious reform movement referred to as *Divino Amore*, began to treat and care for these poor unfortunates. The members of this company were male, and comprised – priests, brothers, husbands and fathers, all keen to be involved in charitable works but equally keen to maintain their anonymity.

Unfortunately, the moral climate continued to decline. Ledochowska (p.32) maintains, that "By 1511, the friendly attitude of the Brescians had utterly changed and in 1512 the townspeople rebelled against the French occupation." Chief among several reasons, was that the Brescian nobility were being given privileges by the French, who "were inclined to favour … [the nobility] at the expense of the bourgeoisie" (ibid.). This led to social distinctions regarding class, and in later paragraphs, you will see how this would affect the Company founded by Angela.

Mazzonis (2007:15) writes, that it was in Brescia that Angela "established her reputation as a 'living saint'." She arrived in in the city in 1516, to commence her apostolate. As a Franciscan tertiary, she had been assigned to aid the wealthy Catherine Patengola, who had recently lost family members. Mazzonis describes the political situation in the city at the time, by referring to the Venetian annexation of Brescia, and that this annexation had taken place initially, "in 1426 and lasted for four centuries, except for the period "1509 and 1516 when Brescia was under French (1509-12) and then Spanish Rule (1512-1516)". He agrees with Ledochowska about the continuing moral decline, and that some reasons for this were that: "the Brescian economy had suffered several overlapping crises caused by war, famine and epidemics" (p.16).

Fortunately, however in Brescia, "the council and the laity in general actively promoted religious initiatives … public celebrations and founding hospitals; [endorsing] popular preaching … by external preachers … and hermits … [and supporting] a tradition of female mysticism" (ibid.). Actually Ledochowska praises the efforts of the mystics of the time, by emphasising, that "Thanks to these mystics, the light of faith did not die out in Brescia", and that in the years from 1520 to 1540, "they built up a centre of deep interior life … at the very time when disorganisation in the diocese had reached the most dangerous point" (vol.1, 1968:38).

Mazzonis (2007:16) stresses, that in most early sixteenth centuries Italian cities, a significant number of clergy neglected to perform their pastoral duties, and were often absent from their parishes; and this resulted in corruption which was rife in many of the monasteries, thus emphasising the need for reform. Remarkably, in those tumultuous years of the Middle Ages, several lay persons were called upon to do their part for the Church and a number of these, were the saintly men who belonged to the company of the *Divino Amore*, and though they participated in works of charity, they preferred (as you may recall) to remain incognito.

The outstanding contribution of these generous laymen was acknowledged by Antonio Cistellini when he states, that "from the middle of the sixteenth century the whole religious life of Brescia was guided and controlled by laymen, not from their desire to be independent of the ecclesiastics but from force of circumstances" (cited in Ledochowska, vol.1, 1968:40). For example, "in 1559, Pope Paul IV determined at any cost to ensure the reform of the diocese, turned to the laity and unhesitatingly nominated a nobleman, Dominic Bollani, then Governor of the City, as Bishop of Brescia. In the upshot, Bollani turned out to be the first and one of the greatest reforming Bishops that Brescia ever knew" (p.41). And so, it was on those occasions, when a Bishop of the diocese was absent for prolonged periods, that a layman was often called to replace him, and generally performed the task admirably. Such was the case again, when the "gentle and kindly layman, Ven. Alessandro Luzzago, magistrate of Brescia" (ibid.) acted on behalf of Bishop Morosini of Brescia, during his many absences in Rome.

This was the social, political and religious climate, in which Angela found herself in Brescia in the early sixteenth century. She had an enormous affection for the people, and the town itself. And though there were occasions, in her travels, when she was invited by many high-profile personages to remain in their cities, she rejected all offers; even that of Pope Clement VII, who when Angela was in Rome in 1525 for "the great jubilee ... pressed her [to stay and] to take over responsibility for the 'Places devoted to Good Works'" (Ledochowska, Vol.1, 1968:73). Angela while honoured by the Pope's offer, graciously declined, for she was keen to return to her work in Brescia.

Hence, Angela's apostolate commenced when she was around 40, and her experiences with the wealthy Patengola family, brought her into contact with some influential spiritual figures in the town; soon, as depicted in the evidence from the *Processo Nazari*, young people began to seek her spiritual guidance. Ledochowska (vol.1, 1968:53) suggests that these young people were connected with the Company of Divino Amore." Angela stayed with the Patengola family for some months, then she moved to the home of Antonio Romano, the rich Brescian merchant. You may recall, that Romano had provided evidence to the *Processo Nazari*, regarding Angela's vision of her sister. Angela stayed nearly fourteen years at Romano's house, in the centre of the city.

Angela continued to fulfil her obligations, regarding her duties as a member of the Franciscan third order with humility, and an infinite love for all who sought her out for her spiritual guidance – she extended empathy and compassion to those less fortunate than herself. Ledochowska (vol.1, 1968:78) informs us that Angela's "visitors, both friends and protégés, came from all classes and walks of life." She was friends with students, merchants, businesspeople, professionals, nobility, religious priests and nuns, and ecclesiastical leaders. She dedicated herself to reaching out to the poor, and the marginalised, and was considered a "peace-maker" restoring peace to couples, families and siblings, and caring for "the poorest and most abandoned of mankind" (ibid.).

Mazzonis (2007:24) writes, that "Between 1522 and 1532 Angela undertook a series of pilgrimages." In 1522, she visited the tomb of the Dominican tertiary Blessed Osanna Andreasi, a stigmatic and mystic. You may recall, from the chapter on St Catherine of Siena, that Catherine received the pain of the five wounds of Christ (referred to as the stigmata), but that "the wounds were visible only to herself" (Cameron, 2012a:52). Ledochowska (vol.1. 1968:40) posits that "There is no evidence to show that Angela and Osanna [ever] actually met", and that the exact date of the pilgrimage is unknown, but that "Osanna ... died in 1505 [and] Pope Leo X ... authorized her public cult and her tomb attracted crowds of devout Christians, on account of miracles worked there" (p.83). Mazzonis (2007:24) cites the following pilgrimages, undertaken by Angela to Jerusalem, Rome and Varallo:

> In 1524 she embarked on a long and dangerous pilgrimage to Jerusalem with Romano. This pilgrimage was marked by a number of miraculous events: during the trip she became temporarily blind (she saw the holy places "with inner eyes as if she had seen them with her outward eyes") and on the way back, according to Romano, Angela's prayers saved their ships from pirates (a strong wind suddenly blew their ship away). The following year, Angela went to Rome for the holy year and met Clement VII. In 1529 ... Angela went to Varallo to see the "Sacro Monte" [Sacred Mount] with the reproduction of scenes (with sculptures) from the life of Christ. She undertook this trip a second time [1532] with a group of women who became the first members of her company.

As per the quotation, Angela lost her sight temporarily in Jerusalem; however, she was never again inflicted with this infirmity (Ledochowska, vol.1, 1968:85). Regarding her pilgrimage to Jerusalem, it is stated "In an ancient record 'at this time a servant of God called Angela of Desenzano graced with her presence the *Convent of the Tertiaries of Mount Sion of Jerusalem*" (p.85).

You may recall from a previous paragraph, that Angela met with Pope Clement VII, during her trip to Rome. He "had heard of Angela and his Chamberlain had sung her praises; he also seems to have [been] informed ... about her work at the 'Incurabili' [hospital] of Brescia and her connection with the Divino Amore", which are the reasons given for the Pontiff asking her to remain in Rome (pp.87-88). However, there is no evidence to suggest that Angela worked at the "Incurabili", though we know that "Elizabeth Prato ... who later became her disciple, her future assistant, and finally, Mother General of the Company of St. Ursula [did work in the hospital for the incurables] with all her friends" (p.71).

When Angela returned from her pilgrimage to Rome, the continuing threat to Italy, of escalating tension between France and Spain was apparent.

> Charles V [Ruler of the Holy Roman Empire and the Spanish Empire] had conquered Lombardy ... [and] Pope Clement, disturbed by Charles' victories and seeing his armies encircling the Papal States ... began to negotiate an alliance with France. War broke out. The Imperial Army then marched on Rome ... The sack of Rome ... followed ... The soldiers of Charles V pillaged the palaces and churches and tortured the helpless citizens to extort money from them ... In the same year, 1527, in which Rome was given over to the mercenaries of Charles V, blasphemous processions were organised at Brescia and priests, famous preachers among them, went over to Protestantism (Ledochowska, vol.1, 1968:88-89).

The situation continued to deteriorate. Francesco Sforza II, Duke of Milan, who had previously entreated Angela to "take him as her spiritual son" (p.90), and who had become a close friend, decided to leave with his court for Cremona. Angela's friends, "Agostino Gallo and Girolamo Patengola (nephew to Catherine Patengola whom you met earlier), were keen to find a place of refuge for Angela (ibid.)", and eventually she was persuaded to take refuge with them in Cremona. Here, Angela continued her apostolate, meeting with all who sought her counsel. It was not until 1529, however, that a treaty was signed, and Angela was able to return to Brescia, with Gallo and his family. After a time spent living in one of Gallo's houses, Angela moved "to a small flat annexed to the Church of St. Afra" (Mazzonis, 2007:25).

You may remember Antonio Romano from a previous paragraph – Angela had lived in his home for about fourteen years. Romano had travelled with her on some of her pilgrimages and was in later years called to be a witness for the process of her canonisation. It was the testimony of Romano, Gallo, Nassino, Tribesco and Bellintani to name a few witnesses, with whom we have become acquainted during the chapter, that provided some insight into Angela's penitential practices, which are summarised below by Ledochowska (vol.1, 1968:76-77):

> Angela never slept in a bed; the only furniture in her room was a chair and a table. She slept on the ground on a straw mat, which during the day was rolled up and put away in a corner of the room. A stone or a block of wood served her as a pillow. Usually she ate vegetables and fruit and she took bread only twice a week. "I have never seen her eat meat", said Romano. She did not even allow herself wine, which in Italy is drunk even by the poorest. Her fasts were stricter in Lent and also from Ascension to Pentecost, following an ancient Church tradition in Brescia ... She did not spare herself other penances; after her death her discipline and hairshirt were carefully kept in a silver reliquary in the Church of St. Ursula in Brescia ... now they are to be found in the Ursuline House in Desenzano.

This severe punishment of her body may have undermined Angela's health, and perhaps even shortened her life; but possibly prepared her for the harsh realities associated with founding her Company and organising for its survival in the years prior to her death. Interestingly, after her return from Cremona in 1529, there is little mention of Angela's connection with the Order of Franciscans, where she served as a tertiary, and both Mazzonis (p.26) and Ledochowska (p.81) refer to her petition in 1532, "to be relieved of the obligation to be buried as a Franciscan tertiary."

Angela realised, that her apostolic work was very much an ongoing exercise. Ledochowska (vol.1, 1968:100) posits, that "Angela, in 1530, was nearly sixty years old [or there abouts] and felt her age; for the last of the wars and [a] ... long sickness that had brought her near death [in Cremona]" had resulted in thoughts of death. She longed for a permanent union with her divine spouse, and so experienced a certain indecisiveness, about what the future held, and God's mission for her? Angela prayed and drew her inspiration from within. She contemplated ways, that she could actively fulfil her mission regarding God's plan for her, while being strengthened by the inner light of the burning fire of her love for Him (p.72).

In 1532, a group of young women were invited to participate with Angela on her second pilgrimage to the "Sacro Monte" at Varallo. Mazzonis (2007:25) maintains that the exact circumstances that led to Angela wanting to establish a foundation are unknown, though in 1533, Angela "shared her apartment at Sant' Afra with Barbara Fontana [one of her first daughters] ... [and then] she met regularly with [a group of] women 'maidens and widows', at first in her house, and then in a small house (later transformed into an oratory) provided by the aristocratic Brescian widow, Elisabetta Prato, a future member of the Company's government", and whom you may recall, was associated with the hospital of the 'Incurabili'.

With the Church calling for reform, Angela decided to challenge the status quo, and found an order that was "to legitimise a religious life that was lived without official recognition" (Mazzonis, 2007:45). Mazzonis describes the status of the Brides of Christ living in the world, emphasising that they "did not exist among the ecclesiastical institutions and that it ... [codified] a spiritual experience of union with the divine that was lived by women at a personal level" (ibid.).

Angela was reluctant to give her own name to the proposed Company, and alternatives included that of St Ursula. For the oratory, where Angela and her group met regularly, had been renovated and painted and frescos decorated the walls, and these works of art included a painting of St Ursula who was "a legendary princess ... and daughter of a Christian British King ... [who] travelled in the company of either eleven or eleven thousand ... maidens ... [It is uncertain if a copyist may have misread the term 11M to mean the Roman numeral for M rather than reading 11M for 11 martyrs]. Ursula and her companions were tortured and martyred in order to get them to renounce their faith" (Catholicsaints. info web, 2018, 4 June).

Another saint who was very popular during that era, was St Catherine of Alexandria, a martyr who is said to have been wedded to Christ. Remember that St Catherine of Alexandria was one of the saints that St Joan of Arc said appeared to her in her visions. There is a copy of a painting by Girolamo di Romano, depicting the Christ child presenting a ring to Catherine, in the presence of Saints Lawrence, Ursula and Angela Merici – in the Colour Plate: "The Mystic Marriage of St Catherine", which you will find on p.137 of Janice Howard's book (1989) on St Angela.

As she prepared for the establishment of her foundation, Angela facilitated meetings with her companions, and spoke about recommendations for a possible rule. She wanted everybody to contribute – to "own" the rule as it were. In contemporary leadership practices, such collegial meetings would be described as collaborative! It is believed that both widows and maidens were present at these meetings, and all participants were encouraged to contribute to the discussions. Angela is said to have "dictated the rule to a Brescian notary, Gabriele Cozzano, who became her personal secretary and the Company's Chancellor as well as its defender and legal representative" (Mazzonis, 2007:27).

On 25 November 1535 (the Feast of St Catherine of Alexandria), twenty-eight virgins were admitted to the newly founded Company of St Ursula, taking the name of the legendary saint and her companions in martyrdom. Ledochowska (vol.1, 1968:106) informs us that the 25th November, also had significance in that it was "the 11th anniversary of ... [Angela's] return from the holy Land and presumably she wanted to emphasise the coincidence, since it was given prominence in the books of the company."

Some months after the foundation, on 8 August 1536, ecclesiastical approval was given for the rule by the Vicar General of Brescia, Monsignor Lorenzo Muzio, and as the rule had been approved, elections were organised. Consequently, on 18 March 1537 Angela was elected head of the Company (Ledochowska, vol.1, 1968:109; Mazzonis, 2007:27), and Mazzonis details its rapid growth, "in 1537 it counted 75 Ursulines and ... in 1540 it had reached 150 members" (ibid.). Angela Merici died just four years after founding the Company of St Ursula, on 27 January 1540. She was canonised by Pope Pius VII, on 24 May 1807. Her feast day is celebrated on 27 January (p.29). Other dates on which the Feast was celebrated initially include 31 May and 1 June.

Leadership as Service

The motto on the Ursuline badge for contemporary school students reads – Serviam – "I will serve". This motto reflects the spirit of St Angela Merici, foundress of the Ursuline Order. Angela responded to the call of the Gospel and lived a life of service. It is this commitment to service, which is reflected in the legacy of her works – the Rule, the *Arricordi* and the *Testamento* (Mazzonis, 2007:27) written a few months before her death. These writings are embedded in the charism of the Ursuline Order. Mazzonis (2007:20) writes that "it appears from her writings for the Company of St. Ursula, ... [that Angela] interpreted ... sacred knowledge in a personal manner. Indeed, Angela became known for her wisdom ... [and all] marveled at the great wisdom in her, because they saw that she converted many to change their lives."

Wisdom has built her house, she has hewn her seven pillars (Proverbs 9:1, cited in Sipe & Frick, 2015:4). For the purpose of this analysis, the "Seven Pillars of Servant Leadership" (see Appendix A for the list of attributes) are outlined below, and the discussion on each pillar includes aspects of Angela's life and leadership practices.

Pillar 1 – "Person of Character"

Angela was extraordinary, inspiring and remarkable (Howard, 1989), a woman of insight who was forward thinking and, rather than marry or live a conventual life, decided to challenge the status quo, and found a Company that while ministering to the needs of society, existed within the world and not within the confines of a monastery. Through her Company of St Ursula, Angela supported the Church in its efforts at renewal. She had an innate presence that drew people to her. She associated with all classes of society, offering spiritual advice and guidance whenever it was needed. She lived in war and plague-ravaged cities, travelled to holy places, conferred with Popes and various ecclesiastical leaders and clerics, worked to improve conditions for the orphans, the poor and the marginalized, and she assisted the Company of Divino Amore – whenever the opportunity arose. Such was the magnitude of her apostolate.

The amazing strength and courage of Angela came from the essence of her being – her spirit. Her profile reveals that she lived at a time, when there was a plethora of mystics, a time when being a contemplative signified an awareness of the sense of self and a sense of the sacred. Angela's awareness of self and others, and her concept of the Sacred within a transcendent reality, gave her the wisdom, courage and strength to engage in active discipleship, while maintaining her independence and Christ-centred approach to life.

This description is supported by Mazzonis (2007:176), who affirms that: "Merici's spirituality was highly mystical, emphasizing fusion with the divine and constant contact with the transcendent." He quotes Gabriele Cozzano, whom you may remember was Angela's secretary, and who describes the importance of "Angela's pedagogy as reflecting 'her personality and type of sanctity … [regarding her] daughters and the people who asked for her help'":

[A]mongst them all [the virgins of the company] … She

had such gratitude and gentleness that it seemed to her that it could not ever [sufficiently] reward with courteous acts those who did even a small but heartfelt service for her. She so thirsted and yearned for the health and well-being of her neighbour ... with motherly love she embraced every creature" (p.130).

Angela translated her personal experience into a lived reality, whereby, she chose to remain in the world, and fulfil her mission of service towards others. She offered a third option to lay single women, to follow her example. Nevertheless, Angela's faith journey is not simple. According to her biographers, and from the testimonies of her friends and from her own writings, the complexity of her character is revealed. For as mentioned in the previous paragraphs, and early in Mazzonis' book: "She was both contemplative and active, mystical and practical, learned and aware of the matters of everyday life. Her personality was human, independent, and determined" (2007:17). These qualities formed her character which comprised the essence of her spirituality:

> [S]ocial recognition derives from her mysticism, sacred knowledge, humanity, and participation in civic life. Angela's originality and genius, however, reside above all in the foundation of the company of St. Ursula, because there she put her theology into practice: she translated her spiritual ideas and experience into a defined model of religious life for other women (p.x).

Throughout her life, Angela was loyal to Christ and the Church. She was a spiritual leader and guided and counselled all who sought her help. She responded to the Gospel's call to service, by founding the primitive Company of St Ursula, which became "a new religious model for women" (p.1) – the first of its kind!

Pillar II – "Puts People First"

Angela's mission was one of service. Her counsel, charity and love were directed to all. Agostino Gallo in his testimony, affirmed that Angela was used to:

> [C]ounseling and consoling each person as much as she could, in such a way that her works had more of the divine than the human and stated that "to hear from her such an interpretation [of the sacred books, listeners] were struck with amazement, so that one could say that this woman had more of the divine than the human" (Mazzonis, 2007:134).

Gallo was certainly effusive in his praise of Angela. He, as did others, noticed a distinctive presence that radiated from her. The members of the Company of St Ursula did not consider their own needs but fulfilled the commandments of "Love of God and Love of neighbour". Interestingly, the company "was not specifically directed toward girls who were poor or unable to marry or enter a convent, but was open to women from every social stratum" (Mazzonis, 2007:pp.x-xi), as long as the proposed entrant had reached the age of twelve years and was a virgin. Regarding the rule which is mentioned in Pillar III, Angela did not lay down the law or the rule with her daughters. She wanted them to think for themselves, and to make decisions that would best suit their own daily needs. For, "by entering the company, [the] women became responsible for their secular life ... [and were] no longer subject to familial authority" (p.58). Nevertheless, to maintain good relationships with the families of those wanting to enter the company, Angela organized in the conditions of entry, that the applicant have parental approval (p.35n).

The consecration of the women, "in the midst of the world ... [was] an alternative to monasticism. Merici's form of religious life was innovative [and personal to each of her daughters] ... because it was individual, inward-looking, a-institutional, and transcendent" (p.x-xi). On entering the order, the Ursulines were able to retain their possessions: there was "no prohibition concerning property" in the rule. Also, they were able to own houses, earn money and keep inheritances from family (p.150).

Angela redefined womanhood in her day. Mazzonis (2007:52) maintains that she "actually empowered women. Furthermore, the emerging female ideal – a virgin living in the world, without protection – anticipated the single woman." This foresight and vision of Angela's "was attacked by sectors of Brescian society and … a period of turmoil began after Angela's death" (ibid). There were several reasons for this including the influence of members of the Brescian aristocracy, who were very reluctant to allow their daughters to become members of the Company. In his testimony Gabriele Cozzano stated that "the main reason was that the members' virginity was not protected as in the convent … The upper classes had stricter conditions for honor that the company, due to its secular nature, did not satisfy." The aristocracy were also of the opinion, that with the daughters of artisans entering and other girls who did not belong to the noble classes, then "they didn't want their daughters to mix with girls from the lower social classes. Cozzano maintains that the aristocracy despised the company because of the presence of members belonging to the classes involved in manual or 'vile' work" (pp.84-85). Several ecclesiastical administrators held similar views.

Pillar III – "Skilled Communicator"

Angela was aware of the needs of the Church of her time. She established a company of women, who would remain in the world and engage in active discipleship. Angela moved with grace and decorum, among the war-ravaged lands, guiding, advising, and offering spiritual solace. With Her wise and gentle demeanor, she was welcomed by friends and strangers whether at home or abroad, and she always seemed to know what she could do, to ease potentially volatile situations, when dealing with the homeless, orphans and troubled dysfunctional families. The grace of her presence ensured that peace enveloped those who sought counsel from her.

As mentioned in her profile, Angela did not receive any formal education, and as has been mentioned, when she founded her Company, she engaged the services of a Gabriele Cozzano, secretary, and later chancellor, who recorded her dictations, which included: the *Regula* – Rule (12 chapters and a preface); *Arricordi* – 9 Counsels for the Colonelle (maidens), and *Testamento* – 11 Legacies for the Matrone (widows). Mazzonis (2007:88) maintains that these "writing[s] for the company … have always been a manifestation of Angela's spirituality." The fact that Cozzano was given the sole responsibly of recording Angela's ideas, presents somewhat of a conundrum: "As historians of female religiosity have frequently pointed out, the problem of the mediation and alteration of the men who wrote down women's words is serious and must be considered" (ibid.). Did Cozzano copy word for word, what was dictated to him by Angela, or did he change her dialogue to suit his own interpretation of the facts? You may recall similar instances of male scribes recording the written words and works of the female characters in the Chapters on St Monica, St Catherine of Siena and St Joan of Arc among others. Mazzonis provides examples and concludes "that Angela was in fact the author of the works" (ibid.).

It appears as if there is little doubt, that Angela wrote the *Arricordi* and the *Testamento*, for according to Mazzonis, Cozzano informed us that the evidence suggested that the letters were "written in an oral style and the first person and Angela mentions her own name throughout these writings. Neither the Churchmen responsible for her canonization nor later historians have ever questioned her authorship" (p.89). However, Mazzonis does admit, that there are "Some contradictions regarding the circumstances in which the Rule was written" (ibid.). One of the reasons given is Angela's lack of education, for there is a complexity in the Rule, that bespeaks of some grounding in theological knowledge, and that the language is more formal than that of the other documents.

Did Angela then have help formulating the Rule? From our reading of the profile we know that she worked collaboratively with members of the team to ascertain their ideas, so that all the shareholders had ownership of the document. Angela's authorship is based on a letter by Cozzano, where he affirms the Rule was dictated to him by Angela alone. Therefore, Mazzonis (p.94) argues, "The synthesis of the ideas, the elaboration of the project, and the organization of the spiritual concepts, however, were distinctly Angela's" so she "should be regarded as the author of the rule." Angela was empathetic to all, and she, as Agostino Gallo testified, had "a caring way of communicating" (Mazzonis, 2007:22).

Pillar IV – "Compassionate Collaborator"

Angela affirmed her daughters and worked with them in their efforts to engage fully with the religious life. For Angela the key to successful participation was the [human] will. For "the will was a condition for entry into the company: 'She must enter joyfully and *of her own will*'" (Mazzonis, 2007:171):

> Since Angela required the individual's will in accepting the religious life, she tried to convince her sisters of the utility of the rule rather than impose it ... The rule did not dictate strict rules but exemplified, inspired, exhorted, warned and directed. It was written to be read often: Angela prescribed that the Ursulines occasionally meet and discuss the rule and compare their own behaviour with it. Her pedagogy, too, was based on the encounter between God's grace and the Ursuline's will. She explained to the Matrone: "And above all, be on your guard not to want to get anything done by force; because God has given the free will to everyone, and wants to force no one, but only proposes, invites and counsels" (p.173).

As mentioned, there was a restriction that the young women joining the Company had to be virgins, and over the age of twelve years, with the intention of wanting to serve God. Their very acceptance and entry into the Company gave them the prestige of being the Brides of Christ who were living in the world and "married to Christ without ritual, vows or a distinctive habit." Another bonus was that a dowry was not required. The life proposed by the company, was considered as parallel, or even alternative to conventual life. For "in the sixteenth century, convents had absorbed unmarried women. These, however, as they required substantial dowries, were mainly reserved for the aristocracy, and Brescia was no exception" (Mazzonis, 2007:81). "However, the Company was open to all women who wanted to live a religious life in the secular world" (p.76), and "during Angela's lifetime, the majority of Ursulines belonged to the lower-middle class and especially the craftsman's strata of society" (ibid.). And unlike the other religious orders of the time, as a dowry was not a requirement for entry to the Company of St Ursula, there was no discrimination between the "haves" and the "have nots". Consequently, when building her company, Angela considered all the needs of her daughters, not just their spiritual well-being, but their financial situation as well:

> [T]he Company of St. Ursula protected the honor of women at both a material and an ideological level ... [it] defended the sexual honor of the artisans' daughters because by entering the company women were committed to maintaining their virginity and their secular behaviour was supervised by the Colonelle and the Matrone. The Company also offered material assistance – economic, legal and medical (Mazzonis, 2007:81).

Angela's discernment of the needs of the members of the Company, was centered on the individual's concept of self, in relation to their love of God and their treatment of others. The rule emphasised that the members value each other, and that they refrain from contentious situations by keeping "the heart pure, and the conscience clear of any evil thought, of any shadow of envy or ill-will, of any discord and evil suspicion, and of any other wicked desire or purpose ... not answering haughtily. Not doing anything grudgingly. Not staying angry. Not grumbling. Not repeating any malicious gossip" (Mazzonis, 2007:170). It was Angela's belief, that as she approached others with gentleness and humility, the expectation was that her daughters would follow her example.

Pillar V – "Has Foresight"

Angela Merici had extraordinary insight into the future. She foresaw a need and responded. Ledochowska (vol.1, 1968:133) writes that "In her vision Angela ... envisaged the raising of the whole tone of family life, by the presence of a consecrated maiden at the centre of each home. This stage of her planning necessitated an innovation which was destined to involve her in bitter opposition, yet to be of incalculable value to the Church, for here was the seed of the future Active Congregations of Women [the first of their kind]" – the first teaching Order of women religious. Mazzonis (2007:52) concurs, "Angela employed some mainstream ideals regarding the construction of 'womanhood' (such as modesty and virginity)". You may recall that Angela founded the company on 25 November 1535 and died on 27 January 1540. Therefore, she had just over four years to implement her rule, and to anticipate potential problems with the intention of solving them. There is some evidence (below) that Angela knew when she was going to die. Ledochowska writes that:

> Evidence is not lacking that Angela predicted the day of her death. In the "Book of the Dead" Bernardino Faino (author and superior general of the Company of St Ursula in Brescia in the seventeenth century) and Carlo Doneda (a secular priest, librarian, author and one of the experts in the canonization process of St Angela Merici) saw and copied down the following note "The Madre, Sister Angela, died on January 27th, 1540, having foretold the day of her death" (vol.1, 1968:207/XXII).

Mazzonis (2007:28) tells us that there was a dispute regarding the final resting place for Angela, for she had left a petition "to be relieved of the obligation to be buried as a Franciscan tertiary" (Mazzonis, 2007:26; Ledochowska, vol., 1968:81), but this took a while to locate and so it was some time before her burial could take place; surprisingly the delay did not lead to the decomposition of her body. Also, you may recall from her profile, the amazing recount of the visionary experiences of Angela, following the death of her sister. Romano and Landini certainly presented vivid interpretations of the vision, which may have been the catalyst for the later establishment of the Company of St Ursula by Angela. So, it is not just Ledochowska (vol.1, 1968:16-17) and Mazzonis (2007:17), who recount the visions that Angela experienced as a young adult but several others, for after her death "Hagiographers and witnesses (including Gallo) reported episodes of visons and of supernatural phenomena in Angela's life" (Mazzonis, 2007:17n) and "numerous miraculous recoveries" were recorded (p.28).

One particular interesting event, that occurred during her lifetime, was based on the testimony of "A certain Master Bertolino de Boscoli de Ottalengo" given during the process for the canonization of Angela. This witness said that he went to a Church where a crowd of people had assembled, and as the "Madre Angela ... [was] standing in a group of other women ... she was raised up about a hand's breadth and remained there for a considerable time, to the amazement of the crowd" (Ledochowska, vol. I, 1968:191).

A vision recorded by Agostino Gallo in his testimony, shows Angela's response to temptation and the solid strength of her faith: "Satan appeared to Angela in the form of an angel who was so beautiful that no person could believe or imagine it ... [Angela] immediately lay down on her face crying out: 'Go to hell, enemy of the cross' and so it disappeared immediately" (cited in Mazzonis, 2007:14). Other visions have been attributed to St Angela Merici, some of which, have received mention in her profile. Apparently, "female visionary activity during the Middle

Ages was not unusual for it was encouraged by Churchmen who believed that 'it was seen to be discovering God's will'" (p.98).

Pillar VI – "Systems Thinker"

Initially, the "big picture" for Angela was that her community "be democratic and meritocratic [with] no rigid hierarchy. [It was to be] self-sufficient, catering to the needs and problems of its members to allow them to persevere in their religious life" (p.30). It was also Angela's intention to have her foundation, "Entirely composed and managed by women. Angela wanted to give her institution as much autonomy as possible from external interference, both lay and ecclesiastic. Autonomy from men and from the Church. Hence [unlike the situation existing in the convents] no religious orders or prelates were involved with the order at an institutional level" (p.32). According to Mazzonis:

> The company of St Ursula was an organization that existed in the world, with its own regulations, legal representatives and governors and that offered its members various kinds of protection. It offered economic help for the poorer virgins, found jobs for those who wanted to work, provided legal assistance in case of disputes and assisted those who were sick or dying (p.37).

Unfortunately, the death of Angela, just four years after she established the Company had enormous repercussions. Ledochowska (vol.2, 1968:7) writes, that when Angela Merici passed away "the structures were not yet firmly established; nor was the Rule definitively approved. She had left her work unfinished." And even though Angela had named her own successor – a wealthy widow Lucrezia Lodrone, "one of the great ladies of the Brescian aristocracy" – division in the ranks resulted and it would be some years before the various conflicts were resolved.

In her eleventh legacy to the Matrone, Angela gave permission that if in the future changes were required to the rule, she gave her blessing.

St Charles Borromeo, Archbishop of Milan had heard of the work of the Ursulines in Brescia and founded "the company in Milan in 1567 with a new rule and a different organization" (Mazzonis, 2007:201). The year previously, he had enquired about the "Brescian Company of St Ursula and was sent a copy of the Rule" (p.202). Then in 1582, he set about reforming the company: "he codified the new organization in a new rule and put the institute under the authority of the bishop" (p.201). Apparently, this decision was necessary for the survival of the Company, and its sustainability into the future. Mazzonis (2007:197-198) writes on its evolution:

> The history of the evolution of the Company of St. Ursula is complex and diverse. In the second half of the sixteenth century, the survival of the Company was due mainly to support from the bishops of the Tridentine Church [you may recall the Council of Trent], and in particular that of the Archbishop of Milan Carlo Borromeo who reformed the Brescian Company and promoted its foundation in the Milanese territory. Subsequently the Company expanded in other Italian cities and in France.

In time, the Ursuline Order spread further than Europe, crossed an ocean to the New World, and established a community in the Americas. Interestingly, in our contemporary era, there are communities of Ursulines now fully active in six major continents including: Indonesia, Australia, Africa, South China, America, Europe and many other areas of the globe (Personal correspondence, 20 November 2018).

Pillar VII – "Leads with Moral Authority"

The Ursulines participated in the election of those who governed the Company, and they could decide on the person they wanted as their spiritual director, and where they wanted to attend Mass. They were given the freedom to work out how they wanted to live their lives. Angela

Merici was an amazing woman with incredible foresight. She empowered the young women in her founding Company of St Ursula. Her charism is embedded in the culture of all the Merici schools, colleges and various institutions in our contemporary era. Angela's legacy continues and is a rich heritage for aspiring women leaders, in fact for all leaders who are prepared to step outside their comfort zones and "be the difference that makes a difference". Mazzonis (2007:48) tells us that her "pedagogy was a direct expression of her spirituality." She encouraged her daughters to take full responsibility, for their own spirituality and their relationship with God, which was considered personal (p.58).

Values

Aspects of Angela's life and works are now discussed in relation to the values – dignity, respect, fairness, justness and equality (see Chapter 4 for the terms of reference).

Dignity

Pauline Kneipp (1982:8; Ledochowska, 1968:260) refers to the timelessness of the inspiration of the foundress St Angela Merici, who valued and empowered her daughters with dignity and respect. Certainly, such respect for human dignity is "[N]o less applicable in the twentieth [and twenty-first] centuries than it was in the sixteenth. One important aspect of it, which speaks clearly to the world of today is Angela's belief in the worth and specialness of each person. She left only a very small volume of writings, a great deal of which is devoted to this truth. She urged the members of the Company who were caring for others in any way" to take everyone into account by having:

> [E]ach and everyone deeply fixed in their hearts and minds, and not just their names, but their background and everything concerning them. This will not be difficult, if you surround them with real love ... if you love these

dear ... [children of ours] with true and selfless charity, it will be impossible for you not to have them all clearly present in your memory and in your heart (Second Legacy – Testamento).

Angela treated the young women joining her Company with dignity and respect, regardless of their circumstances. Mazzonis (2007:82) maintains that "entering the Company gave lower-middle-class women a higher status because they were considered Brides of Christ. As Merici explains in the Prologue to her rule ... [irrespective] of their social condition, life in the company gave women a new dignity that was greater than that of powerful secular people." The benefit to the women of the lower-middle-class joining the order was, that unlike conditions for acceptance into the convents, a dowry was not required for entry to the Company of St Ursula. This was an enormous advantage to those applicants who had a vocation to such a life, but who had no way of meeting the monetary costs which might prohibit entry to say a convent (ibid.).

Hence the gift of being able to serve their divine Spouse, elevated the lives of the Ursulines. "You have to thank Him infinitely that, to you especially, He has granted such a singular gift. For *how many important persons* and others of every condition *do not have* nor will be able to have such grace!" (Mazzonis, 2007:82). The Prologue of the Rule, which is also quoted by Ledochowska (vol.1, 1968:277) refers to the Preface of the Primitive Rule of Saint Angela (with the text taken from 1569, as the original text has been lost):

> Therefore, my sisters, I exhort you, or rather I beg and entreat you all, that having been thus chosen to be the true and virginal spouses of the Son of God, you be willing to recognize what such a thing this is, and what a new and *astonishing dignity* it is ... we are called to so *glorious a life* as to be spouses of the Son of God and *to become queens in heaven* ... not only shall we easily overcome all dangers and adversities, but also, to our *great glory and jubilation*, we shall

defeat them ... and our every sorrow and sadness will be turned into joy and gladness, and we shall find thorny and stony paths *blossoming for us, and covered with paving of finest gold* (Mazzonis, 2007:82).

If you recall from the Gospel, Jesus respected the dignity of all persons. He affirmed the dignity and value of his people, as did St Angela Merici with her rule to her daughters.

Respect

Dignity and respect go "hand in hand". As mentioned above, Jesus respected all, including the women with whom he came in contact. Growing up, he had the perfect example of womanhood – Mary his mother – who nurtured and guided him. Jesus challenged the status quo of his day and in all his teachings "as well as his behaviour, one can find nothing which reflects the discrimination against women prevalent in his day. On the contrary, *his words and works always express the respect and honour due to women* ... [His] way of speaking to and about women, as well as his manner of treating them, clearly constitutes an 'innovation' with respect to the prevailing custom at the time" (*Mulieris* Dignitatem, Pope St John Paul II, 1988:para.13). Jesus was humble as he performed his leadership practices. Humility is an asset that can lead to effective leadership. Angela served with humility, and she "did not impose a rigid hierarchy on the Ursulines because she deemed the individual needs of the virgins more important than respect for positions of command" (Mazzonis, 2007:35).

Angela respected her daughters as individuals, both in their spiritual lives and in their material lives, and this was reflected in her rule, which considered the Ursuline "as a complex human being with inner feelings, a will, and an intellect ... it treated her ... as an independent subject since it accorded her great freedom and responsibility in her relationship with God and everyday life" (p.190). The complex nature of human beings was acknowledged by Angela and "her writings evince no common prejudices on female psychology and interiority ... and manifest a profound respect for human beings, whose complexity she acknowledged and which she refused to judge: 'who can judge the heart and the innermost secret thoughts of any creature?'" (Mazzonis, 2007:59; Ledochowska, vol.1, 1968:251 – 8th Counsel in the *Arricordi*).

Fairness

In all her dealings in her service to others, including the members of her company, Angela acted with fairness. As we have seen in her profile, she treated everybody she met equally, regardless of their station in life. She was always approachable and wise in her decision making and gave spiritual counsel and treated fairly all who asked for her assistance, be they members of the aristocracy, ecclesiastics, clergy, merchants, professionals, artisans, the poor, the sick and the neglected. Using a contemporary expression – Angela had a 'sense of fairness'. She gave her daughters the freedom to be themselves. She gave equal opportunities to the young women from the aristocratic families, and those from the artisan families; for to Angela, they were all brides of Christ. In her rule, she celebrated the uniqueness and value of each of her daughters. She did what she could when she could. However, following her death changes occurred, and though expected, for you may recall that Angela did say that future changes would have her blessing, if implemented for the good of the Company, the events which occurred following her death were unfortunate, and not in the best interests of all, for at the time, there was little cooperation and therefore little fairness!

The events under discussion centered around the appointment of a matron-widow, Lucrezia Lodrone "one of the great ladies of Brescian aristocracy" (Ledochowska, vol. II, 1968:7), who was in fact chosen by Angela as her successor (which is surprising due to the fact that Lucrezia was not a virgin, but a widow and she was not elected through the normal processes). Unfortunately, as Angela had died just four years after the

Company was founded, the structures were not yet firmly in place and the Rule was not "definitively approved" (ibid.). You may recall that the members of Angela's Company were not required to wear a habit however:

> After 1545 the company split in two factions following the decision to introduce a black leather cincture as the exterior distinctive sign of the Ursulines. The decision was taken by a group of Matrone led by Lucrezia Lodrone, the Mother General of the Company ...[but] Another group of Matrone and virgins, led by Ginevra Luzzago and Cozzano opposed the cincture to remain faithful to Angela's original ideal. Eventually the dispute was won by the "cincture party", which in 1546, managed to obtain papal approbation [issued by Pope Paul III] for the company (Mazzonis, 2007:198-199).

Changes continued to occur, and as more and more noble women entered the Company, the administration became more hierarchical, thus deviating from the original aim that Angela had envisioned for her primitive Company, which was not to have a rigid hierarchy.

Justness

As perhaps can also be argued in our contemporary society, there was a perceived lack of justness regarding the rights of women living in the Middle Ages. Mazzonis (2007:6) asserts that due to the constraints of their time, "women were often confined within the family or the convent; they were excluded from politics, ecclesiastic roles, and public offices; they were deemed inferior to men in law, philosophy and medicine; they were not allowed to study in universities and suffered restrictions in the world of work and in access to property." This patriarchal attitude towards women, was not just a consequence of those particular times in history, for "Ancient philosophers (like Aristotle), church fathers (for example, Tertullian [whom you may remember from previous chapters]), humanists (for example, Vives), and theologians (both Catholic and Protestant) all saw a natural incompatibility between women and positions of command" (p.105). In his notes, Mazzonis (n27), quotes John Knox who in 1558 affirmed:

> To promote a woman to bear rule, superiority, dominion or empire above any realm, nation, or city is repugnant to nature, contumely to God, a thing most contrarious to his revealed will and approved ordinance, and finally it is the subversion of good order, and all equity and justice (*The First Blast of the Trumpet against the Monstrous Regiment of Women*, in Aughterson, *Renaissance Woman*, 138).

Angela was a product of this sixteenth century attitude, that did not favour social justness towards women. Her ideals and inspirations were fostered in a society that encouraged extreme views about the leadership capabilities of women. It was within this 'intimidating' environment, that Angela Merici introduced her revolutionary idea of establishing a foundation of young virginal women who would become Brides of Christ. They would not profess formal vows or wear a habit but would live a contemplative life of prayer and penance while engaged in an active apostolate. Mazzonis (2007:198) writes that "the unusual religious status of [Angela's] company; in particular, the idea of virginity in the secular world became a target of criticism", particularly following her death. "This period saw several virgins abandon the company in the face of public disapproval. Some Ursulines became nuns and some married, while others turned to 'heretical' ideals" (ibid.). Brescian society wanted their "virgin" daughters protected from the realities of life!

Equality

Angela Merici was inclusive of all – "She chose her friends, protegés and helpers wherever God indicated them to her ... [and] neither age, nor sex, nor social standing influenced her decisions" (Ledochowska, vol. I, 1968:196-197). She treated everybody equally. This is evident in her accepting into her company young maidens from all classes in society and treating them as equals. They were all virgin brides of Christ. For: -

> A virgin was a powerful type of woman because virginity freed women from male dominance and secular links. Through virginity women refused the role of wife and childbearer, which was viewed as the symbol of human slavery. Jerome affirmed that virgins overcome their female status and become men and Aquinas said that, as nuns, virgins possess the dignity of men and are liberated from subjection to men (Mazzonis, 2007:62).

An interesting argument! Mazzonis (p.102, n.18) cites Jerome's explanation: "As long as a woman is for birth and children, she is different from man as body is from soul. But when she wants to serve Christ more than the world, then she will cease to be a woman, and will be called man." (*Commentarius in Epistolam ad Ephesios* III.5, in PL 26:567a). Jerome's reasoning can be directed towards the equality of male and female in the eyes of God, for they have been created in his image and likeness (Genesis 1:27).

In the 8th Counsel of the *Arricordi*, Angela exhorts the Colonelle, whom you may recall are the local leaders of the virgins in the company, to "Love all your daughters equally and do not show preferences for one more than another, because they are all God's children and you have no idea of what He wishes to make of them" (Ledochowska, vol. I, 1968:251). These words of wisdom reflect the empathy of a loving, gentle mother, who loved her daughters with a passion, and who bequeathed to them stewardship of her vision.

The Company of St Ursula has survived division and conflict over the centuries, and early in the seventeenth century, it evolved into the Ursuline Order. This transformation occurred because of the norms and reforms of the Council of Trent, which signified that the Ursulines "would be 'true nuns' in the full canonical sense of the term. This meant they had to take solemn vows, adopt strict cloister, wear a habit and live according to one of the ancient rules of the officially recognised orders of the church" (Kneipp, 1982:11). Other changes to occur over the years, included that of reconsidering the need for strict cloisters for the nuns who had to be able to leave the enclosure of their communities, to engage in their teaching and other apostolate practices. Kneipp emphasises that because "the religious were determined to carry on their apostolate of teaching, which would have been inhibited by their rules of cloister, they took a fourth vow of instruction of girls. This allowed the rules to be mitigated to a certain extent to allow their pupils to enter the monastery area where the school was situated" (ibid.).

As a result of the evolution of the Ursuline Order, the Paris Ursulines selected the rule of St Augustine, which was ratified by Pope Paul V, with the new constitutions in 1612 (ibid.). Interestingly, in the First Legacy of the Testamento to the Mother-General, and to the Matrone, Angela Merici quotes St Augustine: *"Ama, et fac quod vis* ... *'Love and do what you will.'* That is to say have love and charity and then do what you wish, which is the same as saying explicitly, 'love cannot commit sin'" (Ledochowska, vol. I, 1968:259-260). The extraordinary love that enveloped the actions of St Angela Merici and her vision, have created a legacy, that has transcended time and given spiritual nourishment to her religious daughters – past, present and future – and enabled generations of recipients to benefit from the ministry of service provided by the members of the Ursuline Order.

I invite you now to remain in the sixteenth century and to participate on the faith journey of St Teresa of Ávila the first woman to be proclaimed a Doctor of the Universal Church.

11

St Teresa of Ávila

During a visit to Rome in September 2002, I was pleased to learn that information on St Teresa of Ávila, and St Thérèse of Lisieux could be found at the Teresianum, which at the time was a Library Institute of Spirituality, run by the Discalced Carmelites. There was also a library at the Institutum Carmelitanum, which was within walking distance of St Peter's Basilica, and the Castel S. Angelo. I was fortunate during that time to be able to undertake research at the library, with the permission and assistance of the Carmelite librarian.

In 2012, I was approached by a colleague, to write an essay on St Teresa of Ávila and Simone de Beauvoir. This proved to be an interesting project, as Teresa was a product of sixteenth century Spain, and Simone lived in twentieth century France. Later in this chapter, I investigate the background of Teresa in her profile, and I discuss her leadership practices, in relation to her ministry of service to others, but for your information, and to see another side of the Saint of Ávila, I digress a little here, to reveal the connection between Teresa, a canonised saint and Doctor of the Church, and Simone, a French philosopher, who though her mother was Catholic, embraced atheism from her adolescent years.

Simone de Beauvoir wrote "about religion, spirituality and mysticism and there are a number of references to St Teresa of Ávila in … [her] seminal work *The Second Sex* [1953] which is considered 'a classic treatise of feminist literature'" (Cameron, 2012b). According to Cameron: "Simone de Beauvoir is remembered today, as an existentialist, intellectual, philosopher and writer – a person who engaged in political activism. She was also a social theorist, a feminist and one who was instrumental in 'bringing new ideas to women's lives'" (ibid.).

De Beauvoir was interested in mysticism, and Chapter 3 in Part VI of her book (1972 edition) is titled *The Mystic*. Here she refers to an occasion in Teresa's life when the saint experienced a vision, one which Stephen Clissold describes as "'the orgasm of the mystic nuptials' … [which] was immortalised in marble by Bernini, the sculptor and architect of Italian Baroque in the seventeenth century. This marble sculpture is known as *St Teresa in Ecstasy* and is still to be seen in the Church of Santa Maria della Vittoria, in Rome" (Cameron, 2012a:102). You may recall that St Catherine of Siena experienced a mystical marriage to Christ – Teresa also experienced this spiritual phenomenon, and other visionary experiences, which included what is referred to by Teresian scholars as, "a vision known as the *Transverberation of the Heart* … 'the piercing of the heart'" (ibid.):

> By her [Teresa's] side she saw an angel. He was small, very beautiful, his face radiant. In his hand he held a long golden spear tipped with flame. This he seemed to plunge several times into her heart, and when he drew it out, it left her all aflame with a great love of God. So sharp was the pain that she groaned aloud, yet so sweet that she wished it could last forever, for she knew that now her soul would never rest content with anything but God (Clissold, 1979:59; cited in Cameron, 2012a:102).

De Beauvoir's response to Teresa's ecstatic vision is illuminating – she transcends the human reality of the experience and compares the encounter to a spiritual reality where the soul merges with the divine.

> St Theresa in a single process seeks to be united with God and lives out this union in her body; she is not the slave of her nerves and her hormones: one must admire, rather, the intensity of a faith that penetrates to the most intimate regions of her flesh. The truth is, as she herself understood, that the value of a mystical experience is measured not according to the way in which it is subjectively felt, but

according to its objective influence. St Theresa poses in a most intellectual fashion the dramatic problem of the relation between the individual and the transcendent Being (1972:683; cited in Cameron, 2012b). [Note De Beauvoir's spelling of Teresa]

De Beauvoir (1972:687) also stresses, that such inner experiences as those mentioned above – the "ecstasies, visions, talks with God", all encourage the recipients to transmit into action, what they have experienced during contemplation – and she refers to the example of strong courageous women, such as St Teresa of Ávila, St Catherine of Siena and St Joan of Arc (encountered in this and previous chapters). Here we have a 20th Century French philosopher and atheist, who held a 16th century Carmelite nun in such high esteem, that her fascination for the saint led her to place Teresa in "the category of powerful people, a sainted soul, a mystic whose acts and writings 'rose to heights that few men have ever reached'" (p.161; Cameron, 2012b). To become acquainted with the faith journey of the remarkable woman, who inspired Simone de Beauvoir, 20th century philosopher and atheist, let us journey back through the lens of time to 16th century Spain, and the focus of this chapter – St Teresa of Ávila.

Profile

Teresa was born in Spain on 28 March 1515. Previously, her birthplace was given as Ávila but, now some Teresian scholars reveal, that she was born in a place called Gotarrendura, which is some 15 miles from Ávila. Apparently, the family had a summer residence there (Keith Egan, 2011). Teresa was born into a large family. Her father Don Alonso Sánchez de Cepeda had previously been married to a Doña Catalina del Peso y Henao, and the marriage had produced three children – though some scholars refer to just two children from this marriage. On the death of his first wife Alonso married a very young Doña Beatriz de Ahumada and Teresa was the third of 9 children born to this second marriage. According to Edgar Allison Peers (1963a:10), and other scholars there were twelve children in all in the combined families, however, there is a difference of opinion regarding the composition of the numbers.

It was not until the 1940s that Teresa's Jewish ancestry was revealed (Alison Weber, 1990:8). Evidently, in order to conceal their Jewish origins, her paternal grandfather, Juan Sánchez, "won ... a legal petition that granted him the status of *hidalgo*, or gentleman" (Cathleen Medwick, 1999:12; Cameron, 2012a:41) but this was a 'title of convenience', and the reality was, that the family members were descendants from "*conversos* – Jews who had converted to Christianity to avoid persecution in the fourteenth century" (Medwick, 1999:11-12). *Conversos* feared the Inquisition [a Tribunal established so that persons accused of heresy could be investigated and judged according to the severity of their crime]" (ibid.).

In the sixteenth century, Spain was enjoying prosperity – the economy and finances were such that Egan (2011) refers to the era as the "Golden Age of Spain". Teresa's family was wealthy, and highly regarded in society, and growing up she enjoyed the privileges that such a position entailed. However, in her early teenage years (around 13 years of age), following the death of her mother in childbirth, Teresa started to rebel against her *ordered* existence, "I began to deck myself out and to try to attract others by my appearance, taking great trouble with my hands and hair, using perfumes and all the vanities I could get" (cited in Peers, 1963a:13). According to Teresa "[This was] the wickedest and most worldly period of [my] life" (cited in Clissold, 1979:17; Cameron, 2012a:42).

Teresa's teenage escapades alarmed her father Alonso, who became increasingly concerned by his daughter's seemingly inappropriate behaviour, and he organised for her to attend a finishing school at an Augustinian convent *Our Lady of Grace* Ávila. It was here that Teresa met Dona Maria de Briceno, a nun who was to change her life. Their conversations lit a fire in the depths of Teresa's heart, and she began to consider that she might have a calling to the religious life. However, even though the thought of being consecrated to God was appealing, at the same time Teresa was also still attracted to worldly pursuits, "I began to say a great many vocal prayers and to get all the nuns to commend me to God and pray that He would bring me to the state in which I was to serve him" (cited in Peers, 1963a:17).

Unfortunately, Teresa's stay at the school lasted only about two years, as she became quite ill and was sent home to recuperate. As part of her convalescence, she spent time with her paternal uncle, Pedro de Cepeda who was encouraging in his spiritual dialogue with her, and after time spent with her uncle, and following prayer for guidance, Teresa reached a decision to become a nun. "Her choice of convent was influenced by her desire to enter the Carmelite monastery of the Incarnation where her good friend, Doña María Suárez already resided" (Peers, 1963a:18; Cameron, 2012a:43). Alonso refused permission for his daughter to enter the convent, but this did not deter Teresa who as Egan (2011) so aptly said, "What Teresa wanted; Teresa got" and so in her twenty-first year (around 1535), and without parental permission she left home to join the Carmelites.

Alonso eventually became resigned to Teresa's decision, and supported his daughter, particularly when her vocation was threatened several times over the ensuing years, by continual ill-health, which on at least one occasion, necessitated her father having to bring her back home to recuperate, when she became gravely ill. Teresa (Peers, 1963a:22) explains: "The change in my life, and in my diet, affected my health; and, though my happiness was great, it was not sufficient to cure me. My fainting-fits began to increase in number, and I suffered so much from heart trouble that everyone who saw me was alarmed. I also had many other ailments."

Teresa's spiritual health was just as fragile as her physical health. Cameron tells us (2012a:97) that she began to experience difficulty with prayer. The convent of the Incarnation followed a mitigated rule, and there was such a laxity in its observance, that enclosure restrictions were virtually non-existent. Hence, the nuns were able to go beyond the confines of the convent to enjoy social get-togethers and leisure activities and/or spend time with their families and friends. Teresa's difficulties with prayer, enabled her to succumb easily to temptation and so she joined her sisters in their frivolous activities: "I began, then, to indulge in one pastime after another, in one vanity after another and in one occasion of sin after another ... I was failing thee [my Lord] ... I began to be afraid to pray" (cited in Peers, 1963a:37).

Teresa's father was aware of the struggles she was experiencing with prayer, but she convinced him that her problems were associated with her failing health. The situation continued until after Alonso's death in 1543, when she met his confessor P. Vicente Barrón, a Dominican priest and "with his support and encouragement, she returned to the practice of prayer and vowed never again to abandon it" (Peers, 1963a:45; Cameron, 2012a:98).

Teresa soon developed a preference for mental prayer: "though the Church at the time advocated vocal prayer for the Church in the sixteenth century did not designate any time 'in the legislation [of the Orders] for mental prayer'" (Kieran Kavanaugh and Otilio Rodriguez, 1987:19). These practices were strictly adhered to, for the Inquisition was always on the lookout for "transgressors", and so there was danger and risks associated with promoting this form of prayer. A persistence in engaging in contemplative prayer, eventually led to Teresa experiencing a spiritual awakening:

> Entering the oratory one day, I saw an image ... It represented Christ sorely wounded ... when I looked at it I was deeply moved to see Him thus, so well did it picture what He suffered for us. So great was my distress when I thought how ill I had repaid Him for those wounds that I felt as if my heart were breaking, and I threw myself down beside Him, shedding floods of tears and begging Him to

give me strength once and for all so that I might not offend Him (cited in Peers, 1963a:54; Cameron, 2012a:100).

Such a profound spiritual awareness heralded the onset of visions and levitations (Kavanaugh and Rodriguez, 1987:173-174). Teresa could not control her body when she had the levitations, and she was so embarrassed by her reaction, that she asked her sisters if they saw that she had begun to levitate to hold her down.

There were occasions when Teresa became depressed and was worried because she couldn't discern if the favours she was receiving were from God or from the devil (Clissold, 1979:45-49). As a result, she consulted a network of confessors from various religious communities, and they offered support and spiritual comfort. Ahlgren (1996:101) maintains that Teresa's visionary experiences had Augustinian influences (you may remember Augustine from a previous chapter on St Monica, the mother of St Augustine). "Describing a spiritual vision of Christ, Teresa writes: 'Although this vision is imaginary, I never saw it or any other vision with my bodily eyes, but with the eyes of the soul'" (Cameron, 2012a).

As with St Catherine of Siena, Teresa also engaged in severe penitential practices which according to Ahlgren (1996:161): "destroyed her health", Teresa "beat herself often with disciplines, and many times with keys or with nettles until the blood ran ... She subjected her body to iron chains, from which protruded iron points ... She engaged in these and many other penitential practices."

Over the years, Teresa produced several written works, which included her autobiography – the Story of her *Life* (Vida); *The Way of Perfection* for her sisters; *The Book of her Foundations*; the *Stages of Prayer* and what is arguably her greatest work *The Interior Castle*, which Peers refers to as "one of the most celebrated books on mystical theology in existence" (1963b:189-196; Cameron, 2012a:88). In this book Teresa gives an insight into the "seven mansions of the soul":

I began to think of the soul as if it were a castle made of

a single diamond or of very clear crystal, in which there are many rooms, just as in Heaven there are many mansions. These mansions are not arranged in a "row one behind another" but variously – "some above, others below, others at each side; and in the centre and midst of them all is the chief {sic} mansion, where the most secret things pass between God and the soul" (ibid.).

Teresa believed that the door to the castle was through "prayer and meditation". You may recall that Cavallini (2002), when questioned about the comparisons between St Teresa and St Catherine stated: "Catherine was concerned more with the universe, God and man" while "St Teresa was concerned chiefly with mysticism and prayer". Egan (2011) posits that "prayer binds us together ... and that Teresa's model of a praying Church was bound by love and prayer", and that this was her ecclesiology. It was this great love that Teresa had for the Church, that influenced her decision to seek reform in her convent. As we have mentioned previously, during Teresa's years as a Carmelite, the Order "followed a mitigated rule which permitted many liberties" (Peers, 1963a:38-41; Cameron, 2012a). This laxity in rules had filtered down from the very top "echelons of the Church". Glazier and Hellwig (1994:722) provide some explanation for this growing lack of discipline in the Church:

> The Church at the beginning of the sixteenth century stood in great need of purification and reform at every level. The Renaissance popes frequently lived more like secular princes than like spiritual leaders. Their personal lives were sometimes scandalous ... the roman Curia, the central administrative body of the Church, was top-heavy, inefficient, and corrupt; positions were frequently sold to raise funds for a depleted papal treasury (cited in Cameron, 2012a:45).

Fink (2000b:1-2) cites simony – the buying and selling of Church positions as a contributory factor to the ongoing decline. When Teresa entered the convent of the Incarnation around 1535, the nuns followed a mitigated rule which "was not observed in its primitive rigour but, as throughout the Order, according to the Bull of Mitigation ... published by Pope Eugenius IV on February 15, 1432" (Peers, 1963a:218). As Teresa's prayer life improved, she began to contemplate ways to reform the Order. Her "reading of the hermit tradition and early founders of the Carmelite order, gave her ideas about how to reformulate religious life, so that it would support the nuns' contemplative vocation" (ibid.). Teresa advocated a return to previous practices. She wanted the nuns to "observe the rule of our Lady of Mt. Carmel and keep it without mitigation as ordained by the Friar Cardinal Hugo of Saint Sabina and given in 1248, in the fifth year of the pontificate of Pope Innocent I" (Kavanaugh and Rodriguez, 1987:321).

By returning to the *Primitive Rule*, Teresa was hoping that her nuns would follow the example of their forebears in the thirteenth century, and live a life of "austerity, penance and prayer" (ibid.). However, it was not Teresa's intention for the nuns "to embrace the *eremitical life* but to pray and meditate – and to engage in contemplation" (Ahlgren, 1996:35; Cameron, 2012a:94). Ahlgren maintains that scholars do not know when Teresa made the decision to replace the mitigated rule with the primitive rule:

> [A]lthough the idea had attracted her for many years. According to several contemporaries, the decision to reform the order was born of her near-death experience in 1538-39 ... Other witnesses describe conversations at the Encarnacion (Incarnation) in which Teresa spoke of the lives of the earliest Carmelites and suggested a return to the primitive rule of Carmel (ibid.).

According to Medwick (1999:67), "no one really expected women to initiate reform. They were too suggestible, too weak-minded, to make such changes unless under the rigorous surveillance of men." This did not deter Teresa, who wanted to found a new community, that embraced the values of the past, and emphasised poverty, austerity and penance. Teresa knew her sex was an issue, in her desire to reform her order, but she had faith, courage and great strength, which she believed would stand her in good stead for "It is obvious that God has given me more than a woman's share of it" (p.38).

Teresa founded the convent of St Joseph's in 1562 in Ávila, which was to be the first of 17 convents for nuns, and two monasteries for priests that she would establish during her lifetime. Once her first convent was established, "Teresa was known simply as Teresa of Jesus, mother of the reform of Carmel. The nuns were strictly cloistered under a rule of poverty and almost complete silence. They wore habits of coarse serge and sandals instead of shoes, and for this reason were called the 'discalced' or shoeless Carmelites" (Fink, 2000b:123). In the course of founding her convents, Teresa was referred to as "The contemplative [who] became a 'gadabout'" (Cameron, 2012a:47-48), however, when establishing her foundations, her constant travelling was not done in comfort. She endured much criticism for time spent away from the convent enclosure, and she also experienced: "the harsh climatic conditions [travelling over rough terrain], unsavoury accommodation, poor health, delays and was often involved in altercations with civic and ecclesiastical authorities all in … [an] effort to establish her convents of reform" (Peers, 1963c:87-88; Cameron, ibid.).

As with St Catherine of Siena, ill-health plagued Teresa all her life; nevertheless, she accomplished much and overcame many challenges during her lifetime. Teresa died at the age of sixty-seven years, on 4 October 1582 at the convent of Alba de Tormes (Peers, 1963a: xxxvi; Cameron, 2012:49). Her feastday is celebrated on 15 October.

Leadership as Service

Teresa's approach to leadership, was one of service to others. She accepted the responsibilities of leadership with reluctance for she believed that there were others more capable than herself to lead a community of nuns. Father Domingo Báñez (Peers, 1963c:337; Cameron, 2012a:111) in his report, following Teresa's death recounted her address to the nuns at the convent of the Incarnation, when she was appointed Prioress in 1571:

> My ladies, mothers and sisters: Our Lord has sent me to this house, by virtue of obedience, to hold this office, which I had never thought of and which I am far from deserving … [you have been given] a prioress who would be accomplishing a great deal if she could succeed in learning from the least of you here all the good that is in her. I come solely to serve and please you in every possible way that I can … I am a daughter of this house and a sister of you all. I know the character and the needs of you all, or, at least, of the majority of you.

Teresa was humble in her approach to her position, and keen to serve her sisters to the best of her ability. At a General Audience on 2 February in 2011, Pope Emeritus Benedict XVI remarked that "She reformed the Carmelite Order with the intention of serving and defending the 'Holy Roman Catholic Church' and was willing to give her life for the Church (*cf. Vida*, 33,5)." Egan (2011) refers to St Teresa of Ávila as a "Wisdom figure for our age" because of the great wisdom she has left us which is evident in her life and works. Pope St Paul VI in *L'Osservatore Romano* (1970:12) stated that when Pope Gregory XV canonised Teresa a Saint of the Church in 1622, just 40 years after her death, this signified that "the charism of wisdom of the Saint of Avila was proclaimed useful for the whole Church".

Wisdom has built her house, she has hewn her seven pillars (Proverbs 9:1, cited in Sipe & Frick, 2015:4). For the purpose of this analysis, the "Seven Pillars of Servant Leadership" (see Appendix A for the list of attributes) are outlined below, and the discussion on each pillar includes aspects of Teresa's life and leadership practices.

Pillar 1 – "Person of Character"

On 27 September 1970, St Teresa of Ávila became the first woman Doctor of the Catholic Church. As early as 1923 Pope Pius XI was presented with a "memorial" by the Discalced Carmelites, requesting Teresa's elevation to doctoral status. The Pope's response was "obstat sexus" which translates approximately to "her sex is an obstacle" (*L'Osservatore Romano*, 1970:12). The Pope did not proceed with the submission on that occasion but said he would leave the decision to his successors. Almost half a century was to pass before what was previously considered "an all-male club" (Fink, 2000b:xiv), admitted its first woman in 1970, when St Teresa of Ávila was proclaimed a Doctor of the Universal Church (Cameron, 2012a:8-9), the first woman in the history of the Church to be given this title.

You may recall from previous chapters, that for a candidate to be proclaimed a Doctor of the Church, three criteria must be fulfilled – eminent doctrine, sanctity of life and acceptance and approval by the Pope and/or his General Council. Now, the second criteria of "sanctity of life" is satisfied if the candidate has been canonised a saint, for when undergoing this process, it is determined whether or not the candidate has lived a virtuous life. Hence, if the candidate is canonised than that candidate is said to be a virtuous person – a person of character! According to Pope Emeritus Benedict XVI at a General Audience on 2 February (2011b):

> St Teresa proposed the evangelical virtues as the basis of all Christian and human life and in particular, detachment from possessions, that is, evangelical poverty, and this concerns all of us; love for one another as an essential element of community and social life; humility as love for the truth; determination as a fruit of Christian daring; theological hope, which she describes as the thirst for living water. Then we should not forget the human virtues:

affability, truthfulness, modesty, courtesy, cheerfulness, culture.

It is obvious that Teresa possessed virtues in abundance, which she actioned during her lifetime. When the cause for her canonisation was being conducted, a Mother Maria De San Jeronimo, was asked to give testimony regarding Teresa's character. The nun commented on Teresa's ability to "humbly serve while maintaining her position as 'first among equals – primus inter pares'" (Hunter, 2004:99): "In those early days there were no lay sisters, and we each took a time in the kitchen. Despite all her numerous occupations, the holy Mother would take her week like the other sisters; and it gave us no small happiness to see her in the kitchen, for she worked very gaily and took great care to look after us all" (cited in Peers, 1963c:338; Cameron, 2012a:108).

Weber (1990:4) maintains that, "More recent historians have ... expressed the opinion that it was not the orthodoxy of Teresa's ideas but the force of her personality and her influence among powerful nobles that permitted her to survive." Weber argues, that even though Teresa had the support of "noble or royal patronage ... [this] alone would have been insufficient to save her had she failed to convince the theologians who examined her in person through her writings" (ibid.). So, Teresa held her own when examined by members of the Inquisition, who could be intimidating. Weber (ibid.) extols the "personal powers of Teresa" whom she asserts "was a captivating individual who was able to win over even hardened adversaries with her great charm, humour, and humility."

When Pope St Paul VI proclaimed St Teresa a Doctor of the Church, his opening address praised St Teresa for her uniqueness:

> We see Teresa appear before us, an exceptional woman and a religious. Veiled with humility, penitence and simplicity, she radiates the flame of her human vitality around her. Then we see her as the reformer and founder of an historical and eminent religious Order, a fertile

writer of great genius, a mistress of the spiritual life, an incomparable contemplative who was tirelessly active. How great she is, how unique! How human, how attractive is this personality (cited in *L'Osservatore Romano*, No. 41, 1970:6).

Consequently, both during her lifetime and after her death, Teresa presents as a 'larger than life' character!

Pillar II – "Puts People First"

You may remember that within two years of her religious profession, Teresa became very ill and because the convent had relaxed enclosure restrictions at the time, her father Alonso was able to take her home to recuperate. She was seriously ill, and in fact nearly died. Teresa stated that on her return to the convent, "a grave ... [had been] dug for her at the Incarnation ... [and] Instead of the dead body they had expected, the nuns received a living soul" (Peers, 1963a:32/45). The nuns welcomed her back, and Teresa was determined to be a good example to them, "I never spoke ill of anyone in the slightest degree, for my usual practice was to avoid all evil-speaking. I used to remind myself that I must not wish or say anything about anyone which I should not like to be said of me" (cited Peers, 1963a:33).

Weber (1998:59) tells us that, "The affection she inspired in other nuns only increased her [Teresa's] sense of unworthiness for God's affection." Teresa (Peers, 1963a:214) knew her faults, and there were occasions when she tried to hide her failings from others by not asking their help because she didn't want them to see her in less than a favourable light. However, "God [soon] enlightened Teresa in her efforts to bond with her fellow religious, 'Once God opened my eyes a little, I would ask the other girls' opinion even when I knew something but was the slightest bit in doubt about it ... [also] I was bad at singing ... when I ceased caring if my ignorance were known or not, I got on much better'" (Peers, ibid.).

Even though Teresa was the recipient of many visionary experiences including, "raptures, ecstasies and levitations", her message to her daughters in religion was simple – one of love and prayer. She advised them to think in terms of starting at the beginning, when developing their spirituality: "My sisters ... we must not build towers without foundations, and that the Lord does not look so much at the magnitude of anything we do as at the love which we do it" (cited in Peers, 1963b:350). She taught them the importance of daily prayer, and if they experienced difficulties with prayer as she once did, to just recite an Our Father or a Hail Mary.

Clissold (1979:34) emphasises the profound influence Teresa had on others.

> Her fellow nuns came to her for advice on both spiritual and practical matters. A group of younger nuns gathered around her admiringly; she referred to them as her friends, but they were in reality more like disciples. Her conversation was so natural, so vivid, so spiced with wit; she spoke of holy things with an authority and lack of sanctimonious jargon which captivated her listeners.

Teresa demonstrated that she valued her nuns and put their needs first. "She sought to enrich their lives by sharing with them her perception of human and spiritual realities" (Peers, 1963b). Weber maintains that Teresa wrote the book on her life – *Vida* at the directive of her confessors, however, "her second book the *Way of Perfection* was published in response to a request from the nuns of the convent of San Jose [St Joseph] in Avila" (1990:77).

Pillar III – "Skilled Communicator"

When I was first undertaking the research on Teresa, two current English translations were invaluable – *The Complete Works of Saint Teresa of Jesus*, translated by E. Allison Peers and *The Collected Works of St Teresa of Avila*, translated by Kavanaugh and Rodriguez (Cameron, 2012a:79). As Peers had the earlier publication, I opted to focus on that edition while referring also to the work of Kavanaugh and Rodriguez. According to Peers (1963a:xlii): "at the time of writing and first publishing his translations of St Teresa's works in 1946, most of the originals of St Teresa's major works were extant and the original autographs, including those of the *Life*, the *Way of Perfection* and the *Foundations* were to be found at the Escorial Library in Spain, with the autograph of the *Interior Castle* being preserved in the convent of the Discalced Carmelite nuns in Seville" (Cameron, 2012a:79). Ahlgren informs us that there are "approximately four hundred and fifty letters of St Teresa which are extant" and that Teresa reveals much of herself in her letters (1996:77).

The testimonies (Peers, 1963c; Cameron, 2012a), "which were given in preparation for the cause of Teresa's beatification and eventual canonisation reveal that she had the power to influence others." Ahlgren (1996:151) believes that the witnesses, including her confessors, called to give testimony were influenced by Teresa's "persuasive writing":

> The testimony of many of Teresa's confessors is also very strong on the quality of Teresa's prayer life, although their main concern was its orthodoxy. Their statements often reflect the fact that Teresa won them over from scepticism to confidence about the veracity of her prayer, often because … "she knew things it was impossible to know without revelation."

As is evident from her writings, Teresa engaged in dialogue with people from all walks of life, including future saints of the Church; for example, "in 1557, a Father Francis, formerly Duke of Gandía, and the future St Francis Borgia, revisited Ávila in his capacity as Commissary of the Society of Jesus in Spain" (Peers, 1963a:154; Cameron, 2012a:91), and he was so impressed with Teresa, that he said she "was being led by the Spirit of God". He was later reported as having spoken of "the spirituality, life and sanctity of Mother Teresa of Jesus" (ibid.). Another future saint was Father Peter Alcántara, a Franciscan priest, whom she met when invited to the home of her friend Doña Guiomar de Ulloa, who had gotten permission for Teresa to meet with the saintly man, who "kept the Primitive rule of the blessed Saint Francis in all its rigour" (Peers, 1963a:194-195; Cameron, 2012a:91). In fact, Peter Alcántara advised Teresa when she was establishing St Joseph's her first convent: "She continued to discuss various matters, spiritual and those to do with her foundations with him and after his death in 1562, he reportedly appeared to her ... [and continued to] advise ... [her] on many subjects" (cited in Peers, 1963a:177; Cameron, ibid.).

Another good friend was the future St John of the Cross (Cameron, 2012a:91-92). Though there was a significant age difference, the two met and bonded and became friends for life. John of the Cross and a Father Antonio de Jesús, worked with Teresa "to found the first house for Discalced Carmelite Friars" (Cameron, 2012a). "Teresa was keen to have monasteries for discalced friars established so that the friars could follow the primitive rule. However, there was much friction as a result of the fact of a woman being involved in the foundation of a monastery for men ... with the Bishop's support Teresa was sent "a licence for the foundation of two monasteries" (Peers, 1963c: 6-7). One was established in Durelo (later transferred to Mancera) in 1568, and another in Pastrana in 1569 (p.xxviii-xxxvi). When making her foundations, Teresa had to deal with lay and ecclesiastical authorities, and often the meetings were challenging and fraught with problems. On those occasions, she prayed and offered sacrifice for a successful outcome, and generally her prayers and sacrifices were rewarded, for her actions were prayer-based and were therefore "an exercise in love" (Egan, 2011).

Pillar IV – "Compassionate Collaborator"

Teresa had an unconditional love for the Church. At a General Audience in Rome (2011b, February 2), Pope Emeritus Benedict XVI spoke of this love of Teresa for the Church, emphasising that: "she ... [showed] a lively '*sensus Ecclesiae*', in the face of the episodes of division and conflict in the Church of her time. She reformed the Carmelite Order with the intention of serving and defending the 'Holy Roman Catholic Church' and was willing to give her life for the Church" (*cf. Vida*, 33,5).

Teresa cared for her nuns. She was always alert to their needs, and her concern for their ongoing formation in prayer, "enabled her to offer assistance to the Church in its 'hour' of need during 'the spread of Protestantism'" (Ahlgren, 1996:36). Also, Teresa's charity, and "her care and compassion for the sick and needy were qualities that received prominence in the testimonials given at the process for her canonisation" (Peers, 1963c:339). Though she often exhibited "power and decisiveness" in her dealings with others (Ahlgren, 1996), she was also caring and compassionate.

However, not just the spiritual but the physical health of her nuns was always important to Teresa. In the sixteenth century, there was evidence of an affliction similar to what in contemporary terms would be referred to as "depression", but which Teresa referred to as "melancholy". On an occasion when she was at her convent, St Joseph's Salamanca "she responded to requests from her sisters to issue some instructions regarding the treatment of melancholy." According to Teresa, "a person is not always aware of it until it is past remedy ... the principal characteristic of this temperament is that it dominates and blinds the reason" (cited in Peers, 1963c:36). Teresa did understand ... for there were occasions when she herself suffered from severe depression (Fink, 2000b:122), and as such she was able to identify the symptoms in others, and try to transform their lives for the better, as a result of her healing experiences. "Such is the experience of 'the wounded healer' whose own healing is transformed by healing others" (Daneault, 2008:1219; cited in Cameron, 2012a:99).

Teresa empowered her nuns to be the best they could be. To assist their spiritual formation, she heeded their request to write down guidelines for them to follow. She was confident of the response of the nuns to her publication, "As this book [*Way of Perfection*] is meant only for my daughters, they will put up with everything I say" (cited Peers, 1963b:48-50). Teresa wanted her nuns: "to strive for perfection without complaining: Be very careful about your interior thoughts ... 'But I am her senior [in the order]; but I am older; but I have worked harder; but that another sister is being better treated than I am'" (Cameron, 2012a:120). It was important for Teresa as a leader, to have her nuns not just value themselves but that they also valued each other.

Pillar V – "Has Foresight"

Ahlgren (1996:151) writes that "the Carmelites who were witnesses and gave testimony at Teresa's cause for canonisation believed that the intensity of Teresa's prayer life was rewarded by numerous spiritual gifts, including that of prophecy. Many of them mentioned instances of Teresa's foreknowledge of events, [and] for her gift of knowing someone's interior state." Ahlgren (1996:151) "refers to Teresa's prophetic gifts and [that] her foreknowledge of events [was] testified by witnesses at the process for her canonisation."

As evidence to be used for the process of canonisation for Teresa, a Father Pedro Ibañez was asked to produce documents, that portrayed her sanctity and influence. He responded, "If we would begin to describe the great spiritual fruit obtained by those who have to do with this servant of God, we should never come to an end" (Peers, 1963c:330-333; Cameron, 2012a:99). Ibañez recorded some of the miraculous cures performed by Teresa:

> [T]his servant of God visited one of her kinsfolk, who was very ill of an incurable disease, and was so sorry for him that she began to opportune our Lord to restore him to health. He at once recovered and has never suffered from that complaint again ... On another occasion, she was earnestly importuning Our Lord on behalf of a person to whom she was beholden and who had suddenly lost his

sight ... he [our Lord] appeared to her and told her ... that she would never ask His Majesty anything which He would not do for her. Then this person immediately recovered his sight. So this saint has worked miracles even in people's bodies (ibid.).

Ahlgren (1996:150) maintains, that one hundred and forty-four witnesses were called to give testimony during the canonisation process for Teresa, and that "the process involved two stages: 1591 to 1592 and 1595 to 1596" (cited in Cameron, 2012a:104):

> Witnesses were asked a series of questions to focus their testimony in several categories: the quality of Teresa's prayer life; her motives for reforming the Carmelite order; how she embodied the Christian virtues ... her ability to overcome difficulties through perseverance; the circumstances of her death (especially the incorrupt state of her body); and any miracles performed during her lifetime or after her death (ibid.).

You may recall from previous paragraphs, that Teresa experienced a spiritual awakening (Peers, 1963a:54): "This spiritual awareness resulted in visionary experiences" (Ahlgren, 1996:101), and increased in Teresa her desire for her nuns to concentrate on developing their self-knowledge and hence their self-awareness so that they would enrich their prayer lives. Consequently, Teresa's visionary experiences, "enabled her to cultivate the spiritual life of her nuns" (Cameron, 2012a:102-103). Whenever she was at prayer, reading, looking at images of Christ, or imagining she was praying with him in the "Garden prior to his passion", Teresa was conscious that she received many favours from God, and hence she was "aware of a sense of God within her and that she and the Divine presence were one ... [she emphasised that] 'This was in no sense a vision: I believe it is called mystical theology'" (cited in Peers, 1963a:58; Cameron, 2012a:101):

The testimonials that were produced for her beatification and canonisation, "revealed the influence of Teresa's literary work on the theological climate of the late sixteenth century" (Weber, 1990:5). Teresa's persuasive tactics were utilized in the establishment of her foundations (Peers, 1963c), and in her charismatic appeal (Ahlgren, 1996:8) and charismatic experience, which according to Ahlgren (1996), contributed to the quality of her writing. For Teresa had the "ability not only to rewrite her own life but in effect to rewrite charismatic experience ... [so that it could be viewed not] as a potential danger to the institutional church but could instead be an important source of Roman Catholic identity" (pp.30-31).

Pillar VI – "Systems Thinker"

You may recall in the introductory paragraphs in Teresa's profile, that the term Inquisition was mentioned, and described as a tribunal whereby persons accused of heresy, were brought to trial and judged innocent or guilty and an appropriate punishment applied. Often the members of this tribunal were ruthless! Teresa was always conscious of "the Inquisition 'hovering' in the background" (Ahlgren, 1996). However, she was confident of the "orthodoxy of her work in relation to the Church's teaching" (Peers, 1963b:200), and stressed, "If I should say anything that is not in conformity with what is held by the Holy Roman Catholic Church, it will be through ignorance and not through malice" (ibid.). Teresa's response to the perceived threat of the Inquisition examining her works was one of calm amusement (Cameron, 2012a:80):

> [T]hey only amused me and made me laugh, because I never had any fear about this. I knew quite well that in matters of faith no one would ever find me transgressing even the smallest ceremony of the Church, and that for the Church or for any truth of Holy Scripture I would undertake to die a thousand deaths ... for my soul would

be in a bad way if there were anything about it which could make me fear the Inquisition (cited in Peers, 1963a:225-226).

In 1559, the Valdes Index (Index of forbidden books), was introduced by the Grand Inquisitor of the Spanish Inquisition, Fernando de Valdés y Salas (Peers, 1963a:32). This document prohibited the use of "spiritual treatises for nuns to read or to meditate on or to use for prayer. The only books that were not prohibited were written in Latin, and as women had been forbidden to read Latin, only 'learned men' were able to benefit from this imposition by the Inquisition" (Cameron, 2012a:80-81).

The big picture for Teresa, was the establishment of her foundations, which as we have witnessed was not without its challenges from both ecclesiastical and local authorities; for example, written permission (in the form of a licence) for each of the foundations was needed from the Bishops, and from the local city councils. However, on occasion, to expediate matters, just verbal permissions were given, and this resulted in lawsuits and headaches for Teresa (Cameron, 2012a). Also, "when Teresa was establishing her first convent – St Josephs in Ávila, many of the nuns at the Incarnation were not happy – they were from aristocratic families, and were reluctant to change from the mitigated rule back to the perceived "harshness" of a primitive rule, whereby they would be required to engage in additional ascetical practices; be removed from their comfort zone; and have their income threatened" (ibid.). In addition, the townspeople "rejected Teresa's idea of founding the convent without an endowment, since there was no guarantee that the nuns could support themselves and the municipal resources were dwindling" (Cameron, 2012a:112).

Pillar VII – "Leads with Moral Authority"

Teresa inspired respect. When making the foundations she travelled with her sisters, and showed great strength and resilience during the trials and tribulations that beset them on their long journeys: "There were times when it did not stop snowing the whole day long; others when we lost our way; and others when we had to contend with numerous indispositions and fevers" (cited in Peers, 1963c:87). Teresa believed that it was important not to succumb to "her physical comforts [which] were ignored when she was establishing her houses, and throughout it all she maintained her affable nature in an effort to brighten the spirits of those who accompanied her on her journeys" (Cameron, 2012a:117). According to M. Maria de San Jeronimo (Peers, 1963c:346, Cameron, ibid.), Teresa would travel with her sisters in wagons over rough terrain, and in all kinds of weather that when extremely inclement forced the travellers to spend the night at an inn, "where there was no fire, and no means of making one, and nothing to eat, and the sky was visible through the roof of her , and the rain would come through into the room" (ibid.).

Sister Teresa de Jesus, a niece of Teresa, stated in her testimony in 1596 (Peers, 1963c:366) that there were many occasions when Teresa made her foundations, that she endured a lot of pain and tribulation: "she suffered great trials and inconveniences, and was often ill, but this never sufficed to deter her from what she had begun, nor would she postpone a journey by so much as a day." Teresa was accountable for those sisters entrusted to her care, though "Her own human condition [often] provided many obstacles" (Cameron, 2012a), and she was given no choice, but to submit to the ministrations of the members of her community, who could assume responsibility for her care.

For example, Teresa's cousin, the Venerable Mother Maria De San Jeronimo (Peers, 1963c:345; Cameron, 2012a:117) recalls: "one night [Christmas, 1577] she fell downstairs ... she was carrying a light in her hand and after having climbed the stairs ... suddenly her head began to swim, and she staggered and fell backwards. She dislocated her arm so badly that she was never able to use it as before." The accident necessitated Teresa delegating responsibilities for various activities which she had formerly taken for granted:

> This was a great trial both to her and to us; for one thing she was never again able to dress or undress without help or even to put a veil over her head; and, for another, she was prevented from writing letters at a time when there was so much need for her to do so, and her communities, knowing that she was in this condition, were very much grieved (cited in Peers, [ibid.]; Cameron, [ibid.]).

Consequently, when her deteriorating physical condition reversed the roles, Teresa was obliged to accept with humility and grace, the support both of an intimate nature (see the above quotation), and in regard to her many administrative duties.

When witnesses were called to give their testimonies at the process for her canonisation, the number of questions asked of them, was "organised around the key aspects of saintliness as they emerged in the Christian tradition and were evaluated in the sixteenth century" (Ahlgren, 1996:150). Ahlgren maintains, "that many of the testimonies reveal the tremendous impact that Teresa's books had on the general public [and that] the power of Teresa's books confirmed Teresa's role as a moral and spiritual teacher" (ibid.; Cameron, 2012a).

At a General Audience in Rome (2011b, February 2), Pope Emeritus Benedict XVI spoke of St Teresa of Ávila stating that though she did not have an "academic education ... [she] always set great store by the teachings of theologians, men of letters and spiritual teachers. As a writer, she always adhered to what she had lived personally through or had seen in the experience of others (*cf. Prologue to The Way of Perfection*)." The Pope emphasised that Teresa based all her experiences on first-hand knowledge, and indeed this is evident in her writings, which highlight the importance of self-knowledge which is the first stage of the four stages of prayer she inspired – which also included the prayer of quiet, followed by union of the soul with God, and finally the transcendent destination of "divine union" (Peers, 1963a:62-118).

Values

Aspects of Teresa's life and works are now discussed in relation to the values – dignity, respect, fairness, justness and equality (see Chapter 4 for the terms of reference).

Dignity

During preparations for the 500th anniversary celebrations of the birth of St Teresa of Ávila in 2015, Pope Francis spoke to the consecrated religious, and "praised the Spanish mystic and reformer for her witness of self-gift to God" (Catholic News Agency, CNA, 2014). The Pope emphasised the primacy of prayer in the life of Teresa and stated that "the discovery of Christ's humanity was central to her experience." He also expressed concern about the "danger of individualism in fraternal life" (ibid.). Pope Francis maintained, that to emulate the Saint of Ávila, it is important that a person is aware of one's own dignity and the dignity of others by having "missionary courage, gratitude and trust in God" (ibid.).

Teresa was conscious of the value of human dignity. She and her nuns had a right to live in accommodation, that was adequate and habitable. Unfortunately, when dwellings became available for the foundations, "an additional unforeseen burden ... was that most of the houses which were able to be purchased or rented for convent use were often unsuitable" (Cameron, 2012a). Teresa (Peers, 1963c:11-12) describes the nuns' arrival at the foundation site of Medina del Campo:

> We arrived at Medina del Campo at midnight ... and went to the house on foot ... it was just at that time that they were shutting in the bulls which were to take part in the next day's bullfight ... Having reached the house, we entered the courtyard. The walls seemed to me in a very tumbledown condition and by day they appeared worse still ... when I looked at the porch I saw that we should have

to remove some of the earth from it; there were holes in the roof and the walls were not plastered ... we nuns set to work to clean the floor; and we all worked so quickly that, by daybreak, the altar was set up and bell hung in a gallery, so that Mass was said immediately.

"Teresa as cultural custodian of the Discalced Carmelites was responsible for the human and institutional resources entrusted to her care" (Cameron, 2012a). She valued the sacredness of life and held the dignity and respect of her nuns in high regard. As for her own dignity, as a human person, though she often used self-deprecatory remarks "to allay suspicion when writing to evade censorship [from the inquisition]", (Ahlgren, 1996:4), she found this "deception" a challenge, because she knew her own worth, but needed to appear "humble and obedient" before the intense scrutiny and demands of the powerful Tribunal.

Respect

The Catholic Catechism tells us that there is a need to have "Respect for the human person [and that this] entails respect for the rights that flow from his [her] dignity as a creature" (2000:para.1930). There were some occasions when Teresa lost respect for herself, and this affected her prayer and community life: "Teresa abandoned God and prayer to listen to and indulge in what the world had to offer, 'I think it was a very bad thing for me not to be in a convent that was enclosed ... It seems to me, then, that it is a very great danger for women in a convent to have such freedom'" (Peers, 1963a:38; Cameron, 2012a:97). Teresa "was in a quandary. She listened to God and wanted the things of God; she listened to the world and wanted the things of the world" (ibid.):

> Oh, what terrible harm, what terrible harm is wrought in religious (I am referring now as much to men as to women) when the religious life is not properly observed; when of the two paths that can be followed in a religious

house – one leading to virtue and the observance of the Rule and the other leading away from the Rule – both are frequented almost equally! No, I am wrong: they are not frequented equally, for our sins cause the more imperfect road to be the more commonly taken (Teresa cited in Peers, 1963a:39; Cameron, 2012a:97-98).

The world showed its great love and respect for Teresa and her writings, when, within forty years of her death, her teaching had spread across many continents including: Europe, America and Asia – and that, "spiritualistic thinkers looked for them and searched them to find an answer to the great questions of the mystery of union with God" (Pope St Paul VI, *L'Osservatore Romano*, No. 40, 1970:12). In fact, in his Proclamation conferring the doctoral title on Teresa in 1970, Pope St Paul VI said that as early as 1622, when Teresa was canonised, as per "the bull of Gregory XV ... her 'doctorship' began with this affirmation which won more and more recognition, thanks to the authority that the works of the Reformer of the Carmelite Order acquired in a short space of time" (ibid.).

Fairness

It is important that Church workers, and all who belong to the Church – the clergy, religious, and lay people, "exhibit justice and fairness in relationships and service" (National Committee for Professional Standards, 2011). This was not always the case during the lifetime of Teresa.

"During the establishment of her foundations additional problems arose because of the interference of civic and state authorities and ordinary citizens, but many came from within the Church. Perhaps one of Teresa's most difficult occasions of conflict occurred when there was a cessation to her foundations over a period of four years (1576 – 1580)", (Cameron, 2012a:123-124). Reasons for this involved the "very sudden beginning of the great persecution which both friars and nuns of the Discalced Reform had to endure" (Peers, 1963c:149, Cameron, ibid.). Ahlgren (1996:127) states that, "The struggles between the Calced and Discalced were increasingly vindictive." In his account of the events, Peers (ibid.) attributes the conflict to problems caused by the "calced" friars [fathers of the mitigated rule].

The problem was that "The calced friars strongly influenced the new nuncio, Filippo Sega, who did not espouse the reform and, according to Teresa: 'This nuncio appointed a superior from among the mitigated friars to visit our convents and monasteries; and, if he had found in them what he expected, our troubles would have been great'" (Peers, 1963c:150; Cameron, 2012a:124). Nevertheless, "it took the intervention of King Philip II of Spain, a Catholic and committed to the cause of the Discalced Orders; the problem soon dissipated, and the communities existed side by side, if not in perfect harmony, then in relative peace" (ibid.). Teresa also had her detractors and critics' reasons for debating her 'authority' included the fact that they:

> [T]hey understood the teaching office to be denied to women scripturally ... [there was] Paul's prohibition of teaching for women ... a Juan de Lorenzana commented: "Teresa of Jesus would do well to take St. Paul's advice" ... In effect, the critics were arguing that as soon as Teresa entered the public realm of theological discourse, she overstepped the proper boundaries of the female role (Ahlgren, 1996:120-121; Cameron, 2012a: 83).

Ironically, Pope St Paul VI (*L'Osservatore Romano*, no. 41, 1970:7), refers to St Paul's advice when proclaiming St Teresa, a *Doctor of the Universal Church* in 1970. Regarding the decision to proclaim Teresa a doctor, the Pontiff stated categorically that it did not violate St Paul's precept (cf 1 *Cor.*14:34): "No! ... really [it is] not a title entailing hierarchical functions of teaching, but we must point out at the same time that this does not in the least signify less appreciation for the sublime mission which woman has in the People of God" (*L'Osservatore Romano*, No.41, 1970:7; Cameron, 2012a:66).

Justness

Justness should be available for all! When Teresa established her foundations, she was a 'change agent' – a disciple – spreading the Good News and mission of the Church. However, each foundation seemed to be plagued with problems, that perhaps could have been avoided, if the ecclesiastical and local authorities appreciated her plans more, and applied justness to her cause. Some of the difficulties which plagued Teresa during the establishment of her foundations included:

> [H]aving to wait for Episcopal permission and licences; negotiating in secret because many of the towns already had convents and did not want additional convents that were without revenue; objections from mayors, councils and ordinary citizens; numerous lawsuits and inadequate accommodation. [However] regardless of the impediments, Teresa was eventually able to cajole priests, bishops, ecclesiastical and state officials, and most who initially objected to her foundations to agree to her demands and so she was eventually able to proceed with her plans (Peers, 1963c, Cameron, 2009).

In addition, "Teresa's attempts at building community were not without complications. For example, her manuscript – *Life*, was denounced to the Inquisition by an aggrieved former member of the Discalced Order (the widow, Doña Ana de Mendoza, Princess of Éboli), and it was only due to the diligence of Father Báñez, who 'fearful for the result, made a few small emendations in the manuscript and then himself laid it before the Inquisitors'" (Peers, 1963a:7, Cameron, 2012a:123). The unjustness was, that even though Judgement on the manuscript cleared Teresa of any "subversion", the manuscript was not returned to her during her lifetime.

Thankfully, the original 'autograph' was eventually returned to the order some years after Teresa's death, "to be copied further and circulated among the communities of the Reform" (ibid.).

In his article on Teresa, Pérez-Romero (1997:114) stresses "the importance for contemporary interpreters to be aware of the fact that 'verbal camouflage' ... [was] practiced by the most celebrated Golden Age authors." Hence when they are interpreting such texts, he cautions interpreters to "devise methods of historical and literary decoding". Unfortunately, the same rule of law was not applied equally. Ahlgren (1996:118), "responds to the above sentiments when she posits that 'the arguments assembled by Teresa's critics make it clear that Teresa was well aware of the hostility toward women who dared to teach'" (cited in Cameron, 2012a:82). Justness should be for all, regardless of gender!

Teresa used her intelligence to great advantage. According to Cameron (2012a:107): "Did she intentionally set out to manipulate others by the subterfuge of her rhetoric, or did she generally believe that the 'power' of her influence lay in her ability to project the image of an 'unlettered' person who just happened to be a woman?" Ahlgren (1996:30) maintains "that Teresa had the ability to know what to write to satisfy the Inquisitors":

> Recognition of the censors' suspicions is readily apparent in Teresa's work ... [she] was very careful about the literary and theological sources she mentioned. Many of her favorite authors appeared on the Valdes Index ... she employed a series of rhetorical devices to justify her right to write as an "unlettered woman." Finally, and most important, Teresa practiced a sort of self-censorship.

Equality

Inés San Martín, a Vatican Correspondent, quotes Pope Francis (Cruz, 2017) and his insistence "that among the threats to life looming in the

21st century is a continuing inability to acknowledge and promote the full equality of women." If this is the situation in the 21st century, then in the 16th century, the situation would have been dire, though the concept of the term 'equality' was probably just emerging. Ahlgren (1996: 8-9) posits that: "the climate of [sixteenth century] Spain seemed to encourage women visionaries yet to accord them an increasingly ambivalent reception ... the sixteenth century gender ideology was critical to the attempts to maintain religious, social, and political order. Women were at once virtuous and evil in ways that men were not." Teresa is described as a visionary, who because of her gender faced much opposition. Ahlgren (1996:1) states that: "The challenges Teresa encountered, and the very climate of sixteenth-century Spain shaped both her message and the way she expressed it."

Teresa undertook an active role within the Church – her life and works imply, that it was her intention to share equally with males in the saving mission of the Church, without undue emphasis being placed on the fact that her "sex ... was an obstacle". Nevertheless, she overcame many "obstacles" during her lifetime, and in 1970, became the very first women to be proclaimed a doctor of the Universal Church.

In the following chapter, we fast forward to the nineteenth century where we meet Caroline Chisholm, philanthropist and "Emigrant's Friend".

12

Caroline Chisholm

Caroline Chisholm House in North Sydney, Australia, was opened and blessed in 2016. I was intrigued by the naming of this Catholic University building after a woman of exceptional foresight, a social reformer and a renowned philanthropist, who demonstrated a selfless love for all human beings, as she engaged in active discipleship in her service to others. During the official Opening ceremonies of Caroline Chisholm House, Professor Marea Nicholson, then Associate Vice-Chancellor (NSW/ACT) of the Australian Catholic University, spoke highly of Caroline and her contribution to improving conditions as a result of her humanitarian work in the nineteenth century: "The new building has been named in honour of Caroline Chisholm, a strong, independent woman who respected the dignity of all, especially the marginalised and those in need, and was effectively one of the first social workers in Australia" (ACU Staff News, 2016).

My interest was engaged, and I decided to organise a trip to Sydney, to locate the structure which housed information on this famous woman who had a profound influence on early Australian history. On entering the thirteen-storey building I discovered that Caroline Chisholm artefacts and memorabilia were displayed in glass cabinets in the foyer. Because of the restrictive display area, the content was less than I had expected, but nevertheless invaluable and priceless treasures, of a life lived in service to the underprivileged. Apparently "All artefacts and memorabilia" on display in the building are on loan to the Australian Catholic University from the Chisholm family. So, who was this amazing woman who was born and died in another country and century, but who lives on in generations of her Australian family? Who was this woman, this leader, who has been honoured for her contribution to improving the conditions and enriching the lives of countless human beings?

Profile

Caroline Chisholm (née Jones) was born in Northampton England, circa 30 May 1808. She was the youngest of seven children born to William Jones, a successful farmer and his fourth wife, Sarah (née Allum). William had children from his previous marriages and during his younger years he worked as a shoemaker, though around the time that Caroline was born he was "a well-established pig dealer" (Carole Walker, 2011:9). Little is known of Caroline's educational experiences, but when she grew to adulthood her literacy skills were quite well-developed, so in all likelihood she would have been tutored in her early years, or been the recipient of a privately funded education, but this is just conjecture for "There is no record of Caroline's education" (ibid., p.14).

Caroline was raised in an Anglican household that promoted philanthropic values (Rodney Stinson, 2015). In 1830 she married Archibald Chisholm, a Catholic, born in Scotland in 1795, who, at the time of his marriage was on leave from the East India Company Army. The wedding took place at the Anglican Church of the Holy Sepulchre Northampton. Walker (2011:20) maintains that even though Archibald was a Catholic, "It was a legal requirement that the wedding take place in an Anglican Church. The Catholic clergy were not legally empowered to hold and register services." It is possible that such restrictions were applied because England was still recovering from the "Tudor times and the beginning of the Church of England" (ibid:21), and though the "Catholic Relief Act of 1778" was a start to emancipating Catholics, the "1581 Act against saying or hearing Mass still remained in force" (ibid.). Hence, though Caroline was aware of the animosity that still existed in some quarters of England against Catholics, she converted to Catholicism, the religion of her husband.

In 1832, Archibald returned to India and the city of Madras, which in our contemporary times has been renamed Chennai. He was given the commission of Captain of his unit. The following year, Caroline, having remained behind in England after the birth and subsequent death of their first child, a daughter, left England to join her husband in India. On her arrival in Madras, Caroline was appalled at the treatment of the orphaned and illegitimate daughters of the British soldiers. She subsequently "founded the 'female school of industry for the daughters of European soldiers', in which the children were instructed in reading, writing and religion, cooking, housekeeping and nursing. It was an admirable institution, and when the Chisholm's went to Australia … it was taken over by the government" (Percival Serle, 2015:para.2).

However, Archibald's health became a concern and in 1838 he took leave and sailed with his family to Australia. At that time, New South Wales after initially experiencing some years of prosperity was suffering a downturn, and a financial crisis was looming; in fact, a depression was close at hand, with employment difficult to find and poverty becoming the norm (Walker, 2011:45-46). On their arrival in Australia, the Chisholms settled in Windsor New South Wales, but it wasn't long before they became aware there were many problems facing immigrants, particularly the females, who when they arrived in Australia were unable to find suitable accommodation and/or employment. Also, many of these women and girls were being preyed upon by "unscrupulous older males and brothel proprietors" (Stinson, 2015), who intercepted them as they disembarked from the ships, and eventually lured them into immoral practices including prostitution. According to Stinson "Mrs Chisholm saw that reliable information, accommodation and worthwhile employment, in addition to a government ban, were essential if those practices were to be stopped" (ibid.)

Archibald was ever ready to assist his wife in her philanthropic efforts, and initially they were able to provide shelter in their home for many of the immigrants, and even assisted some to gain employment (ibid.), but as the numbers of the unemployed and destitute escalated, alternative accommodation needed to be sourced. In 1840, when "Britain's Opium War with China" (Timeline, Mrs Chisholm's website) escalated, Archibald was recalled to India. Walker posits that Eneas Mackenzie believed "that Archibald returned to India … [alone] for the health of the family and so that Caroline could stay and carry out philanthropic works" (2011:50).

Caroline remained in Australia and stoically continued the cause that she and her husband had started together. Clara Geoghegan (2011:449) informs us that Caroline lobbied Governor Sir George Gipps and the newspapers for support. In January 1841 she "wrote to Lady Gipps to ask her help" in founding a home for the immigrants (Walker, 2011:51) and it was Lady Gipps who directed Caroline to discuss the matter with her husband the Governor. Consequently, barracks (though rat infested) were made available and "in October 1841, … [Caroline] was able to establish the Female Immigrants' Home in Bent Street Sydney. It provided accommodation and an employment registry … Caroline obtained favourable wages and conditions for young female job seekers, unemployed males and family groups and made more than a thousand contracts between masters and servants" (Stinson:2015). The contracts of agreement for the placement for employment were quite organised with triplicate copies produced – "one went to the master, one to the servant and a third copy was filed" (Serle, 2015). During her time managing the quarters for the young women and being available at all hours in the event of unexpected difficulties and also to avoid the threat of infectious diseases, Caroline opted to have her three young children, Archibald, William and Henry, remain at their home at Windsor, under the care of a minder during the week, but they were able to see their mother on the weekends.

By the end of 1842 the Immigrants' Home was closed, due to an easing of the "crisis in accommodation and unemployment" (Stinson, 2015). It became apparent to Caroline then "that the real need for female immigrants was in the country" (Serle, 2015), and she used her very considerable skills to address this problem. Numerous circulars were distributed; she published her report on *Female Immigration Considered in a Brief Account of the Sydney Immigrants' Home*; and she obtained newspaper support and engaged in dialogue with Governor Sir George Gipps: "to reform the reception arrangements for new emigrants, not just those who were young and female, and to improve dispersal arrangements for those seeking work in the country, the latter benefiting from accurate labour market information and the creation of district depots" (Stinson, 2015). Serle recounts that Caroline organised groups of girls to take work placements in the country, often driving borrowed drays herself with the girls taking turns walking or being seated in the drays. On occasion, the travelling was also undertaken by steamer when trying to access "more distant or less accessible, coastal areas" (ibid.). Judith Iitis (1966) emphasises that much of what the Chisholms did was at their own expense, even though they were often financially challenged themselves.

Caroline wanted to settle families on the land with long leases, but landowners opposed this plan. Walker (2011:67) states that "by the 1850s squatters had acquired most of the land suitable for agricultural and pastoral purposes. In September 1826 Governor Darling established an area known as the Limits off Location. Settlers were permitted to take up land within this area, but not beyond its boundaries. Land outside the limits was not sold or let." Over time the boundary limits were extended but in 1847, "The squatters gained security of tenure and pre-emptive rights ... This had the effect of locking up the land and making it impossible for the emigrant, or emancipist, to purchase land for fourteen years" (ibid.). Sarah Goldman (2017:134) maintains that Caroline was keen to introduce a scheme that would settle "immigrants on private acreage outside Sydney". She campaigned to have the lands unlocked "by reducing the squatters' powerful hold and allowing small farms."

However, many of the members of the Legislative Council, were against the idea of having immigrants owning land. For example, "Landowners were reluctant to offer their unimproved property on non-financial leases; more significantly they were concerned that turning poor immigrants into landowners would adversely affect the supply of labour" (Stinson, 2015). Nevertheless, "[Caroline] arranged at her own expense the settlement of twenty-three families on land at Shellharbour given to her by Robert Towns ... The land was made available for six years rent-free in exchange for the settlers clearing and improving it. The idea was that each family would establish a small farm and at the end of the rent-free period they could either start to pay rent or purchase the land" (Goldman, 2017:135).

The Chisholm family returned to England in 1846 to promote their cause for "migration to Australia as a means of alleviating the poverty in England and the labour shortages in the colony" (Geoghegan, 2011:450). During the voyage Caroline gave birth to her fourth son, who was given the name Sydney. When they arrived in England, Caroline set up an emigration office and founded a "Family Colonization Loan Society", whereby emigrants "or their colonial relations gave their savings to the society, which lent them the rest of the passage cost. Loans were repaid in instalments to the Australian agents" (Stinson, 2015). According to Serle (2015): "A committee was formed to raise funds to help deserving emigrants, and in September 1850 the first chartered ship sailed with 250 passengers, and several other ships followed at intervals."

In order to assist with the organisation at the Australian end of the journey, Archibald having retired from the army some years before, left for Australia in March 1851 (Walker, 2011:113). Geoghegan gives the year as 1850, but regardless of the date of arrival, he returned to Australia to fulfil the role of agent for the "Family Colonization Loan Society" [FCLS], (2011:450). At the time Caroline was pregnant with their sixth child, and with five children to feed and with her husband so far away, the family endured financial hardship. Archibald was also undergoing financial difficulties for he was working "long hours without remuneration" (ibid.). Apparently, some of the emigrants when they arrived in Australia did not seem to consider loan repayments as a huge priority, and though "legal advice was sought on the possibility of obtaining repayment through legal proceedings ... Archibald was advised that agreements made in England could not be enforced in Australia" (Walker, 2011:119).

In 1854, Caroline and her five younger children left for Australia "to re-join her husband. The discovery of gold had made it unnecessary to advocate emigration from England" (Serle, 2015). Caroline visited the diggings and the experience gave her the incentive to advocate for better conditions particularly for families arriving in the goldfields. Goldman (2017:237) writes that Caroline "decided that a network of shelters needed to be built along the major routes to the goldfields, to provide temporary accommodation for travellers ... Caroline's 'Shelter Sheds' – later known as 'Chisholm's Shakedowns' were built on Crown Land, at a distance of one day's walk from each other. Each shed was designed to accommodate families, as well as up to thirty single men and ten single women."

Walker writes that "In recognition of Caroline's philanthropy, and Archibald's gratuitous works as a colonial agent, the committee [of the Family Colonization Loan Society] proposed that a testimonial be raised ... [and] the legislative Council [eventually] agreed to allocate the sum of 5,000 pounds provided half the amount was raised by public subscription" (2011:129). This money was not received by the Chisholms for some time and they were reduced to such dire financial straits that the "testimonial committee" decided to advance the family "a small sum of money" (ibid.), and in due course the Chisholms settled in Kyneton Victoria and purchased a store.

Unfortunately, around 1857, Caroline became ill with complications from a serious kidney disease and was advised to move to Sydney to a more favourable climate. While in the city she engaged in some teaching and lecturing, but her health continued to deteriorate and in 1866, Caroline and Archibald with their youngest children returned to London. In 1867, "Caroline was awarded an annual pension of 100 pounds a year from the

British Government" (Walker, 2011:149) and though Archibald received his army pension, their financial circumstances were very meagre, and they lived a frugal existence for the remainder of their lives. Caroline passed away at the age of 69 on 25 March 1877, and Archibald followed on 17 August of that same year.

Leadership as Service

It has been due to her exemplary service to others that over the years there has been widespread support for Caroline Chisholm to be added to the catalogue of saints of the Catholic Church. But her cause has yet to receive the ecclesiastical support and financial backing required for the process to remain active. Serle (2015) posits that Caroline Chisholm saw a need and acted on it. She was a great organiser and her planning and organisational skills were exceptional for she had "that divine common sense which is the best kind of wisdom."

Wisdom has built her house, she has hewn her seven pillars (Proverbs 9:1, cited in Sipe & Frick, 2015:4). For the purpose of this analysis, the "Seven Pillars of Servant Leadership" (see Appendix A for the list of attributes) are outlined below, and the discussion on each pillar includes aspects of Caroline's life and leadership practices.

Pillar 1 – "Person of Character"

Caroline was a "strong, spirited woman" (Stinson, 2017:3). She devoted her life to social reform and philanthropy, overcoming obstacles with a strength of character, and a resilience that motivated her to keep going, in her efforts to assist immigrant women and families to settle in Australia and to maintain a reasonable standard of living. She was organised and disciplined and put the needs of others before her own. She was humble in that she would not accept monetary payment for her services but suffered because of this. Dr Moya McFadzean (2013:19) asserts that she "died as destitute as some of the young women she had tried to assist."

David O'Brien SDB Salesian brother (2015:3) says, "Caroline Chisholm is 'a great role model', and he wishes 'she was still around', adding 'what a difference she would make ... especially regarding refugees, asylum seekers and trafficked persons.'" Indeed, she was an extraordinary woman – an extraordinary leader!

Pillar II – "Puts People First"

During her lifetime Caroline put others first. She converted to Catholicism when she married Captain Archibald Chisholm putting her faith and trust in God. She was only married a few short years when she experienced the loss of an infant and was determined to join her husband in Madras, even though she had never been overseas. When she arrived in India, she did not succumb to the oppressive weather as a "wilting English flower", but put her own needs aside when she saw the plight of the "orphaned and illegitimate daughters of the British soldiers", and established the *Female School of Industry* for them. Her husband's health was always a priority and she travelled with him to Australia when he was on furlough from the Army. It was in Australia that she had "serious concerns and an accompanying indecision about how best to assist young female emigrants to the Colony of New South Wales. Many of these young women had little or no money and no-one to guide them into permanent, fruitful employment and accommodation, and away from older predatory men. She wanted to afford them decent protection". Her empathy, as expressed in her following words, reached out to all:

> I now considered the difficulties and prepared my plan: for three weeks I hesitated and suffered much. I was prepared to encounter the opposition of some, the lukewarmness, or the actual hostility of others, to the plan I might suggest. I saw I must have the aid of the Press; for I could only anticipate success by soliciting public sympathy for the cause I had undertaken, notwithstanding, which, as

a female and almost a stranger in the colony, I naturally felt diffident. I was impressed with the idea that God had, in a peculiar manner, fitted me for this work; and yet I hesitated. About this time, several young women, whom I had served, advised others to write to me: I did all I could to aid them in their prospects by advice, or recommending them to situations; but the number increased, and I saw that my plan, if carried into effect, would serve all (Chisholm, 2015, cited in *The Easter Vow*).

As you may recall from her Profile, Caroline then went on to successfully found the *Sydney Immigrants' Home*. Her achievements on behalf of others were outstanding – evidence of a profound love of God and love of neighbour.

Pillar III – "Skilled Communicator"

Caroline was a skilled communicator and listened emphatically to those who offered advice and engaged her services. She showed initiative when she became aware of a problem, even when the problem/s seemed insurmountable. She was persuasive in her communication with the Governor, and other officials when the situation warranted, and she was effective when they responded positively to her requests. Serle (2015) asserts that it was "In July 1847 ... [that Caroline] gave evidence before the select committee of the House of Lords on colonization from Ireland" (ibid.). She pursued her efforts at achieving "social reforms and structural changes" in the area of emigration. Also, when she was in London, she used her home "as an information centre for emigration, [where] she met and advised many thousands of prospective emigrants and answered with her husband and sometimes their older children, an average of 140 letters a day" (Stinson, 2015). Caroline toured England, Ireland and Scotland, lecturing and writing, while advocating improved safety conditions on the emigrant ships, and highlighting the need for adequate accommodation for single people and married couples, and the importance of the provision of standard medical care.

Pillar IV – "Compassionate Collaborator"

Caroline was compassionate to those who asked for her help. On an occasion in Sydney, when she was down near the ferry, she recognised a young pregnant prostitute Flora, whom she had met previously. Caroline sensed intuitively that young Flora was on the verge of committing suicide. Her reaction was immediate: "I did not leave the place until, with subdued feelings, I heard her vow never to attempt self-destruction. I procured her lodgings; and though I had been much tried and fatigued, I was able to [later re-join my friends at the steamer]. I never thought of *human help*; I neglected no steps to conciliate; I increased my exertions; but from the hour I was on the beach with Flora fear left me" (Chisholm, 2015, cited in *Fear Left Me*). Caroline worked collaboratively with others to ensure that the best possible outcomes were achieved for her goals. She wanted to build communities and re-unite families – those separated by misfortune and chance that had led to members seeking work and a life in a country, other than that of their birth. For, from the Testimonials collected from settlers in 1845, Caroline and Archibald had "obtained information from illiterate ex-convicts and bounty emigrants that helped in locating separated wives, children and aged family members in the old countries and initiating their re-union in Australia. From 1841 to 1845, Mrs Chisholm settled 11,000 people, a third of all assisted emigrants in the period (Stinson, 2015).

Pillar V – "Has Foresight"

The social justice principles, which informed Caroline's work as a laywoman, in India, Australia, and England in the middle of the nineteenth century, were articulated by the Church in the encyclical *Rerum Novarum*, published fourteen years after her death." This document of

Pope Leo XIII (1891:para.55) on "Capital and Labor", reinforces the role of a Gospel inspired laity:

> Those Catholics are worthy of all praise-and they are not a few-who, understanding what the times require, have striven, by various undertakings and endeavors, to better the condition of the working class by rightful means. They have taken up the cause of the working man [and woman], and have spared no efforts to better the condition both of families and individuals; to infuse a spirit of equity into the mutual relations of employers and employed; to keep before the eyes of both classes the precepts of duty and the laws of the Gospel – that Gospel which, by inculcating self-restraint, keeps men within the bounds of moderation, and tends to establish harmony among the divergent interests and the various classes which compose the body politic.

Caroline was a visionary, and according to Geoghegan (2011:448) "A prophetic figure – a prophet of the laity", who engaged in transformative action to improve conditions for all, in particular, the poor and the marginalised. She lived the Gospel and engaged in active discipleship.

Pillar VI – "Systems Thinker"

The "Big Picture" for Caroline was to alleviate some of the economic problems in England, caused by the industrial revolution and the potato famine in Ireland, plus she was determined to do what she could to alleviate the labour shortage problem in Australia. In 1845, the recently retired Archibald returned to Australia, and he and Caroline "travelled together throughout the New South Wales countryside collecting testimonials from settlers regarding the way in which their fortunes had improved by migrating to Australia" (Geoghegan, 2011:450). Stinson writes that they "gathered hundreds of 'Voluntary Information' statements, which were later used to promote the advantages of emigration for the less well-off and those with limited prospects in England, Ireland and Scotland" (2015).

Pillar VII – "Leads with Moral Authority"

It was around 1853 that Caroline travelled to Europe and then to Rome, to organise for her son William to return with her to Australia. He had been enrolled as a "seminarian at Propaganda College" (Goldman, 2017:212), and was training to be a missionary when he became too ill to continue his studies. Caroline was granted an audience with Pope Pius IX who presented her with two gifts: "a twenty-four-and-a-half-centimetre alabaster bust of herself and a gold medal ... The bust remained with the family until it was recently lent by Caroline's great-great-grandson, Professor Don Chisholm, to the Australian Catholic University in Sydney for display, but the gold medal is missing, pawned in Sydney in the late 1850s when Caroline and Archibald were in desperate need of funds" (ibid.). You may recall from the beginning of this section on Caroline, that mention was made of the Blessing of Caroline Chisholm House in North Sydney. The bust is presently (2019) on display in the foyer area of that building, with the other artefacts and memorabilia. To their credit Caroline's family have assumed stewardship of the resources entrusted to their care and they are serving her vision by sharing her legacy with the world.

Values

Aspects of Caroline's life and works are now discussed in relation to the values – dignity, respect, fairness, justness and equality (see Chapter 4 for the terms of reference).

Dignity

The Universal Declaration of Human Rights "Affirms the dignity and worth of all people and the equal rights of women and men" (United Nations, 1948). Caroline Chisholm treated all human life, as sacred. Her work, whether described as humanitarian or philanthropic promoted the dignity of every person. "She helped give dignity to ... [all] in a harsh colonial society" (Iitis, 1966).

Respect

Caroline showed respect for human life. Her efforts to found the "female school of industry for the daughters of European soldiers" in India, (Percival Serle, 2015:para 2) were outstanding, and when she founded the school she "drew up the rules and regulations" (Walker, 2011:12), ensuing stability and planning into the future for the students, which aimed at developing their confidence and self-respect. She recognised and respected the needs of the immigrants, when she established the *Female Immigrants Home in Sydney*, realising the importance of suitable accommodation, regular meals and gainful employment to maintain a person's sense of self – they needed to respect and value themselves and others.

The launching of the *Family Colonization Loan Society* in England was evidence that Caroline respected the contribution, that the immigrants could make to Australia, while guaranteeing that they had assisted passage to the country and hopefully secured employment upon arrival. Even her efforts to fight to "unlock the land" and make property available for the immigrants and the establishment of the "shelter sheds" on the goldfields – all showed her appreciating the rights, and dignity of families and young single women and men. She shared her vision and respected and valued those whose lives she worked so hard to improve. In addition, there was much mutual respect between wife and husband – Caroline and Archibald. I do not believe either one would have achieved so much without the assistance of the other!

Fairness

In her dealings with authorities and others, Caroline adopted a sense of fairness. Decisions she made were in the best interests of all. She was honest and wouldn't accept remuneration for her work, even when she and Archibald travelled throughout NSW collecting the testimonials from the immigrants. Generally, she co-operated with officials even when she disagreed with them, as on the occasions when she advocated unlocking the land so that the immigrants could be given property to farm. Walker (2001:95) states that "Chisholm had often spoken of the unfairness of the squatters' monopoly of the land. The conditions she saw in Victoria resulted in her campaigning even more strongly for the "unlocking of the land" and she promoted the cause for the small farmer." Her sense of fairness dictated that she should decline Government funding (Walker, 2011:115), so that in the eyes of the public she would be treated the same as they were treated – she believed in consistency and treating everybody fairly. Walker (ibid. p.83) also added that "All ... [she] achieved ... [was] without a penny being paid out by the Colonial Government. In fact, Chisholm would not accept financial assistance, believing that to do so would jeopardise her independence, to 'serve all creeds' to the best of her ability."

Justness

In the profile mention is made of a bounty system and there was also a government scheme and a nominated system regarding emigration. Apparently, this form of payment particularly of the bounty "was not always carried out evenly, justly or correctly" (Walker, 2001:75). Regarding the bounty scheme "If the emigrant was rejected, because of ill health, deemed to be of poor character, considered the wrong age, or to have an occupation not suitable to the colony, payment of the bounty was refused. No payment was given if the emigrant died en route. The ship-owner was liable for the cost of transporting the emigrant if the bounty was not paid" (Robin Haines, 1997:273, cited in Walker, 2001:74).

The Government schemes "were those of assisted, free or selected emigration. Initially assisted passages were for those who did not qualify for a free passage in that their occupation or age was incompatible with the needs of the colony. Assistance was calculated on a scale determined by occupation, gender, marital status and age. Selected emigrants were those who applied to the CLEC [Colonial Land and Emigration Commission] or its authorised representatives. The prospective emigrant would have to meet particular requirements of age, character, health, gender and occupation" (Haines, 1997:274, cited in Walker, 2001:74). The nominated system "was the system whereby those who purchased land could nominate one to three labourers for each 100 pounds of land purchased" (Haines, 1997:275, cited in Walker, 2001:74).

Whether bounty was government or nominated, the schemes used to assist the passage for immigrants to Australia required that all parties organising the schemes needed to apply justness for all, but their success depended on the honesty and reliability of the authorised agents and ship owners, and the eradication of the problems that the emigrants also met on disembarkation when they, particularly the women were most vulnerable. Another interesting case that could be described as a matter of social justness resulted in Caroline being:

> [T]he first woman in the colony to bring a case to court when she filed a case against the Captain and Surgeon of the "Carthaginian" for the maltreatment of a passenger. "In 1842, upon hearing of the maltreatment suffered by Margaret Ann Bolton on board the immigrant ship "Carthaginian", Chisholm was determined to see justice. She approached Governor Gipps and insisted that action be brought against the alleged perpetrators, Robert Robertson and Richard William Nelson" (Matthew French, 2016:1).

In his notes (p.1), French describes the treatment of Margaret Bolton stating that she was "reportedly dragged up onto deck, handcuffed, cold water thrown over her, before being left exposed to the weather for hours until she was unable to walk by herself" (ibid.). The case could have gone against Caroline for as she was the one reporting the allegation, it was up to her to provide sufficient evidence and if not, she could have been imprisoned for bringing the case to the court. "Fortunately, the undertaking of a private prosecution was never required, as the captain and surgeon were [both] tried and found guilty of assault. The men were sentenced to six months imprisonment and fined £50" (ibid.).

Equality

What did equality mean in the nineteenth century? Caroline Chisholm is depicted as a strong, formidable woman who when she set out to do a job, didn't rest until it was done. She lived at a time when transport and communication were primitive and restricted, but she was able to accomplish much because of her ingenuity, her outstanding organisational skills, and the incredible support of a devoted and committed husband. Archibald was in tune with his wife. In other words, there was an equal meeting of minds! You may recall the words of Pope St John Paul II in his Apostolic Letter *Mulieris Dignitatem*: "On the Dignity and Vocation of Women" taken from *Genesis* (1:27): *"both man and woman are human beings to an equal degree, both are created in God's image"* (1988:para.6).

The philanthropic efforts of this amazing woman and her equally amazing husband, contributed so much to social reform, particularly in Australia. Caroline Chisholm is honoured as a remarkable and extraordinary woman, wife, mother and leader. Being human, she was probably not without her faults! And perhaps there were times when she just wanted to be with her family and be a mother and wife; however, she believed that God had given her a mission, and she responded to his call. Indeed, by virtue of her baptism, she responded to the primal call of the Gospel, which was repeated in the message of Pope Francis in *Evangelii*

Gaudium in the twentieth-first century – inviting all baptized persons to engage in active "missionary discipleship" (2013:para.120). Her life was one of service to others. I salute her stamina, her courage and her tenacious will to succeed – indeed a valiant woman! A national treasure? I believe so, and a candidate worthy to be added to the catalogue of Saints of the Catholic Church.

In the following chapter we remain in the nineteenth century and follow the faith journey of St Thérèse of Lisieux, the youngest person to date (July 2019), to be proclaimed a Doctor of the Universal Church.

13

St Thérèse of Lisieux

On 18 October 2015, Pope Francis canonised a married couple Louis Martin and his wife Marie-Azélie Guérin. As canonisation is an ecclesial process, it signifies that Louis and Marie-Azélie (Zélie) are now added to the catalogue of canonised saints in the Catholic Church. Prior to 1969, the canonisation process followed strict guidelines "and was a lengthy and complicated procedure" (Cameron, 2012a:64). However, changes initiated by Pope St Paul VI with the decree *Sacra Rituum Congregatio* (1969), began to emerge after 1969; then on 25 January 1983, with the publication of the document *Divinus Perfectionis Magister* by Pope St John Paul II, the procedure was formally streamlined into the "modern canonisation process" (Unam Sanctam Catholicam, 2015).

During his Homily at the canonisation ceremony for Louis and Zélie Martin, Pope Francis spoke highly of their individual gifts, and the family they created together: "the holy spouses Louis Martin and Marie-Azélie Guérin practised Christian service in the family, creating day by day an environment of faith and love, which nurtured the vocations of their daughters, among whom was Saint Therese of the Child Jesus" (Order of Carmelites website, 2017).

Background

Louis Martin and Zélie Guérin were born in France, and prior to meeting, both had considered entering the religious life – Louis wanted to become a priest and Zélie a nun, but these aspirations were not fulfilled, and after a chance meeting they became a couple, and soon married and settled at Alençon France. Louis worked as a watchmaker-jeweller, and

Zélie became a skilful lacemaker. In time their union produced nine children, and Louis and Zélie honoured the holy family by giving each of their daughters the first name of Marie, and Joseph was the first name given to their sons. Sadly, three children (two boys and one girl) did not survive infancy, and another daughter died before her sixth birthday. The remaining five children all daughters entered religion – four daughters became Carmelite nuns at Lisieux, and one daughter, who had previously entered the Poor Clares – left after a short time, and eventually joined the Visitandine (Visitation) Order at Caen, and after two failed attempts, re-entered and after her third and final try remained in this community until her death.

The youngest child of the family was Marie Françoise-Thérèse (St Thérèse of the Child Jesus), and in this chapter her life and works are investigated in light of her leadership of service, which she embraced on her faith journey and mission for the Church. It is interesting to note, that Marie Céline who was four years older than Thérèse, survived the longest out of all the members of her family, not passing away until 25 February 1959, and therefore would have been aware that on "March 22, 1957, the Information Process on the holiness of Louis Martin was open[ed] in Rome … [and that] of his wife Zélie followed on October 10, in the same year" (Tierney, 2015). Hence, Céline prior to her death, would have been aware that her parents were under consideration for beatification and canonisation as saints of the Catholic Church.

In addition on 24 January 2015, the French Press reported that "Bishop Jean-Claude Boulanger, Bishop of Bayeux and Lisieux announced 'the opening of the diocesan process for Leonie's sainthood'", that is, Marie Léonie Martin (Sister Françoise-Thérèse), the sister of Saint Thérèse of the Child Jesus. Because of the commencement of the canonisation process in her intention, Léonie now has the title "Servant of God". Hence, the Martin family consists of two parents and one daughter who are canonised saints; another daughter Marie Léonie Martin (Sister Françoise-Thérèse) who is under consideration for sainthood, and three remaining daughters – Marie Louise (Sister Marie of the Sacred Heart), Marie Pauline (Mother Agnès of Jesus), and Marie Céline (Sister Geneviève of the Holy Face), who like Thérèse, were all Carmelite nuns. Let us turn our attention now to 19th century France, and to the youngest Martin sister, a Saint and Doctor of the Universal Church, Saint Thérèse of the Child Jesus!

Profile

It was at Alençon France on 2 January 1873, that Zélie gave birth to her youngest child Marie Françoise-Thérèse. It was a difficult birth, and the baby almost died. As a witness for the process of beatification (the stage prior to canonisation) for Thérèse, Sister Geneviève (Céline) testified: "a most serious decline in health put … [Therese's] life in danger; so, after two months, mother was obliged to entrust her to the care of a more robust wet-nurse, a very good woman with whom she stayed for one year. Mother took her back in March 1874" (Christopher O'Mahony, 1975:110; Cameron, 2012a:182).

The family members in the Martin household were quite devout in the rigorous practice of their faith, which, according to John Clarke (1996:4), who translated the original manuscript of *Story of a Soul: The Autobiography of Saint Thérèse of Lisieux*, was "rare in an epoch when Jansenism continued its ravages." Bernard McGinn (1999:184) explains that "Jansenism was a heresy which denied free will, and 'the salvific will of God.'" However, O'Donnell (2001:106), lists four currents of spirituality in France at the time (French or Berullian, Jansenism, Quietism and Pietism) and asserts that Jansenism did not overly influence Thérèse's spirituality and suggests that the extremes of Quietism were also avoided. Quietism "emphasised a direct relationship to God, and encouraged a devotion to contemplation" (Cameron, 2012a:174-175). In his Prologue, Clarke (1996:4) emphasises that the family could be described as both "active and contemplative." Jordan Aumann (1985:200-202) portrays the Jansenists as rigid, and the Quietists passive, in their approach to spirituality. Hence this was the spiritual climate in which the faith of the young Thérèse was nurtured.

Thérèse "enjoyed her early years: 'Ah! How rapidly the sunny years of my early childhood passed by, but what sweet impression they left on my soul! Everything on earth smiled at me. I found flowers under each of my steps, and my happy disposition contributed also to making my life pleasing" (Clarke, 1996:6; Cameron, 2012a:56). Sadly, Zélie Martin succumbed to breast cancer in August 1877 aged 45, when Thérèse was about four and a half years old, and the young child became inconsolable – the light had gone out of her life!

Thérèse's emotional disposition changed drastically following the death of her mother: "I, once so full of life, became timid and retiring, sensitive to an excessive degree. One look was enough to reduce me to tears ... I could not bear the company of strangers and found my joy only within the intimacy of the family" (Clarke, 1996:34-35). She does admit however, that her father's love, and that of her "two mothers", Pauline and Marie, protected her against the traumatic effects of her profound loss. Some months after the death of Zélie in 1877, Louis decided to move his family from Alençon to Lisieux, to be closer to his wife's family – the Guerin's and the family soon settled in their new home "Les Buissonnets".

Testimonies given by her sisters at the process for her beatification, reinforce the negativity enveloping Thérèse, as she battled to regain her composure and light-hearted approach to life at this time. Geneviève (Céline) recalls, "Before my mother's death, Therese was high-spirited, lively, demonstrative, naturally proud and stubborn ... After mother's death, Therese's happy disposition changed. She was cheerful only in the family circle at Les Buissonnets ... Everywhere else she was extremely timid, and other girls, finding her ill-adapted to their games, disregarded her" (O'Mahony, 1975:111; Cameron, 2012a:183). Similarly, Sister Françoise Thérèse's (Léonie's) testimony, reinforces Céline's memory of the events: "I myself noticed the sudden contrast between the vivaciousness that was so typical of her before this bereavement and the habitual hyper-sensitiveness that followed it, something she overcame only later by dint of virtuous effort" (O'Mahony, 1975:172).

In 1882 Thérèse was informed that Pauline, the sister whom she identified as "mother", was leaving her to enter the Carmelite Order. Thérèse was devastated and grieved at the loss of one whom she considered her second mother. In her grief she cried, "Pauline is lost to me, almost in the same manner as if she were dead" (Clarke, 1996:88; Cameron, 2012a:57). The child then turned to the elder sister Marie as a substitute mother. "And so, in reality I had only Marie, and she was indispensable to me ... I loved her so much I couldn't live without her" (ibid.). Thérèse was dependent on her sisters, and being the youngest, she had been cossetted by them. They anticipated her every action, even undertaking all the chores around the house. As a result, Thérèse had little to do and found it difficult to cope.

When Thérèse was ten, she became so ill that her family thought she would die. Her condition deteriorated following a visit to her sister Pauline at Carmel, when Thérèse, who had loved Pauline so much, thought that she was being ignored when other members of the family were engaged in conversation with Pauline, as she spoke to her family from behind a grill at the convent. At the time, Thérèse repeated words that she had said on a previous occasion when she suffered despair and abandonment: "I said in the depths of my heart 'Pauline is lost to me!' It is surprising to see how much my mind developed in the midst of suffering; it developed to such a degree that it wasn't long before I became sick'" (Clarke, 1996:60).

In later years at the process for the beatification of Thérèse, Sister Françoise Thérèse (Léonie) testified (as did Céline and Marie) in relation to their growing concerns regarding the ten-year-old Thérèse's deteriorating health:

[The illness] started with violent headaches, and she began to have these almost immediately after Pauline entered Carmel (October 1882). At the end of March 1883, she became delirious and had convulsions. As if by an act of providence, the illness ceased entirely for the whole of the day on which Pauline received the Carmelite habit ... Once this happy day was over the illness returned ... until 10 May 1883 when she was miraculously cured (O'Mahony, 1975:172-173).

Sister Marie of the Sacred Heart (Marie) also recalled: "I thought she was going to die from it ... Then I knelt with my sisters at the foot of the statue of the Blessed Virgin. Three times I repeated the same prayer. At the third time, I saw Therese fix her gaze on the statue, radiantly, like one in ecstasy. She confided to me that she had seen the Blessed Virgin herself" (O'Mahony, 1975: 87; Cameron, 2012a:200). Thérèse gives her account of the vision:

> All of a sudden, the Blessed Virgin appeared beautiful to me, so beautiful that never had I seen anything so attractive; her face was suffused with an ineffable benevolence and tenderness, but what penetrated to the very depths of my soul was the "ravishing smile of the Blessed Virgin." At that instant, all my pain disappeared, and two large tears glistened on my eyelashes, and flowed down my cheeks silently but they were tears of unmixed joy (Clarke, 1996:65-66; Cameron, ibid.)

Thérèse's recovery was immediate, and she began to depend more and more on Marie. However, her social skills were virtually non-existent. In a previous paragraph Hamilton (2006:1) refers to "restricted peer interaction" as being a factor that may lend itself to having traumatic effects on young children. Thérèse attended the Benedictine Abbey, a boarding/day school (Clarke, 1996:53) as a day girl, but her formal education came to an abrupt end at the age of thirteen, when her father

Louis removed her from the school, because she was having difficulty relating to her peers. Her father organised private lessons at home for her. Thérèse commented on this period in her life: "The five years I spent in school were the saddest in my life … As I was timid and sensitive by nature, I didn't know how to defend myself and was content to cry without saying a word and without complaining even to you [Pauline], about what I was suffering. I didn't have enough virtue, however, to rise above what I was suffering" (Clarke, 1996:53; Cameron, 2012a:184). To add to her despair Marie entered Carmel in 1886, and again Thérèse grieved:

> As soon as I learned of Marie's determination, I resolved to take no pleasure out of earth's attractions … I was really unbearable because of my extreme touchiness, if I happened to cause anyone I loved some little trouble, even unwittingly, instead of forgetting about it and not crying, which made matters worse, I cried like a Magdalene and then when I began to cheer up, I'd begin to cry again for having cried (Clarke, 1996:90/97; Cameron, 2012a:57).

Pauline and Marie, the sisters she loved dearly, were in Carmel, and so Thérèse began to entertain the idea of entering the convent. However, she soon realised that not just her age, but her immaturity might prove to be an obstacle to these plans. She prayed for guidance, later stating in her *autobiography* that "God would have to work a little miracle to make me *grow up*" (Clarke, 1996:97). Remarkably the "miracle" was forthcoming, for it was around this time that Thérèse experienced a spiritual awakening, which in later years she referred to as a time of conversion, and that what she had experienced was a miracle.

The "miraculous" event occurred shortly after Marie's entrance to Carmel, and some days prior to Thérèse's fourteenth birthday. It was Christmas Eve, and traditionally in the family the younger children left their 'slippers' near the fireplace to be filled with gifts. "Therese was still of an age to anticipate finding the gifts after the family's return from attendance at midnight Mass" (Clarke, 1996:97; Cameron, 2012a:188). Louis was tired when he returned from Mass and became somewhat exasperated when he saw that Thérèse had left her slippers by the fire. He thought that surely, she was of an age when such childish practices would be beyond her, so he impatiently exclaimed – probably a little too loudly: "Well, fortunately, this will be the last year" (Clarke, 1996:98). Unbeknown to Louis, "'Therese heard his words [of impatience] and tears started to flow' (DeMeester, 1998:65). This was a defining moment for Therese, and in that instance of dawning realisation … she quickly prioritised what was happening in her life, and [soon] realised that it was 'Jesus [who] had changed her heart'" (Cameron, 2012:188).

In this one unforgettable instant, Thérèse became aware that she was no longer a child seeking the thrills childhood, she was a young woman growing in faith and courage and with confidence, she realised that the time in her life, prior to this significant moment consisted of two phases; the first phase lasted from her birth in 1873 to the passing of her mother in 1877; the second phase lasted from Zélie's death, until the conversion experience; and now, in December 1886, she had entered the third phase of her life (Clarke, 1996:98). Thérèse felt her soul strengthen and realised that this strength came from the infant Jesus: "[H]e, scarcely an hour old filled the darkness of my soul with floods of light. By becoming weak and little, for love of me, he made me strong and brave: he put his own weapons into my hands so that I went on from strength to strength" (Fink, 2000b:213).

Thérèse engaged in prayer and discussions with her sisters Pauline (Mother Agnès) and Céline, re her intention to enter Carmel. Then, when she was about fourteen and a half, she broke the news to her father gently, as he had already given 3 daughters to Christ (though Léonie would soon return home again before finally settling with the Visitation nuns). Some dialogue followed, but Louis gave Thérèse the impression that it would be an honour for him to have her enter Carmel, even though initially, he had said that she was too young to make such a decision (Clarke, 1996:108).

Hence, with her father's permission, Thérèse decided that she would set in motion her plans to enter Carmel. However, when approached, the local Bishop and the Superiors at Carmel were of the opinion that her extreme youth prevented her admittance to the Order. Though upset, "I left the rectory in tears" (Clarke, 1996:111), Thérèse's determination did not falter, and she accompanied her father Louis and sister Céline on a pilgrimage to Rome. In retrospect this was to be the only time that she ever left France. The pilgrims from Lisieux were granted an audience with Pope Leo XIII, and Thérèse took advantage of the opportunity to speak to the Holy Father of her desire to join the Carmelite Order in Lisieux.

Mother Agnès (Pauline) referred to this meeting during her testimony at the process for the beatification of Thérèse:

> In her audience with the supreme pontiff she overcame great timidity and asked him for his permission to enter Carmel at fifteen years of age. Fr Reverony was present at the audience and told the supreme pontiff that the matter was being studied by the superiors; Pope Leo XIII's answer to the Servant of God was: "Do what the superiors tell you to." She insisted: "But, Holy Father, if you were to say yes, they would all agree." "Come, come," replied the Pope, "you will enter if God wills it" (O'Mahony, 1975:28; Cameron, 2012a:193).

Thérèse was disappointed with the Pope's response to her request, however, she decided to persevere and pray; and some months after her return from Rome, the local Bishop granted his permission. Consequently, on 9 April 1888, when she was fifteen years of age, Thérèse entered the Carmelite convent at Lisieux. Though very emotional at finally achieving her heart's desire Thérèse said that nobody noticed her "inward reaction":

> My emotion was not noticed exteriorly. After embracing all the members of the family, I knelt down before my

matchless Father for his blessing, and to give it to me he placed himself on his knees and blessed me, tears flowing down his cheeks … A few moments later, the doors of the holy ark closed upon me and there I was received by the dear Sisters who embraced me (Clarke, 1996:147-148; Cameron, 2012a:210).

And so, we have an image of both father and daughter on their knees before each other; one to give a blessing and the other to receive a blessing! It was in this way that Louis Martin gave his youngest child to God. The emotional well-being of Louis was affected by the departure of his "little Queen", and he soon slipped into a mental state, whereby he suffered ongoing psychotic episodes (Clarke, 1996:154). Louis was admitted to the psychiatric institution, Le Bon Sauveur at Caen on 12 February 1889, where he stayed for three years, returning to his brother-in-law Isidore Guérin's home in Lisieux in 1892.

DeMeester (1998:150/156) describes the homecoming: "On May 10, 1892 Monsieur Martin returned home to his family, henceforth paralysed in his limbs and very gentle and harmless." Two years later, on 29 July 1894, Louis Martin passed away, and Céline who had cared for her father at home, then entered the Carmel at Lisieux at the age of twenty-five. The fifth and remaining sister Léonie, after a series of attempts to enter the convent (you may recall she had also tried the Poor Clares in Alençon), entered the Visitation Order of nuns for the third and final time. She remained in the Order until her death in 1941 (O'Mahony, 1975:108/168; Cameron, 2012a:59).

Thérèse was professed into the religious life on 8 September 1890. At her profession, she pledged: "I came to save souls and especially to pray for priests" (Clarke, 1996:149). Sister Geneviève (Céline) maintains that Thérèse discussed a similar issue in previous correspondence to her, prior to her own entry to Carmel:

> During the time she spent in the convent, she bore the

sanctification of priests in a special way in her intentions. On 14 July 1889 she wrote to me: "Dear Celine, let's live for souls, let's be apostles ... and save especially the souls of priests: these souls ought to be more transparent than glass. Alas, how many bad priests and priests who are not as holy as they should be there are! Let us pray and suffer for them ... Celine, do you understand this cry from my heart" (O'Mahony, 1975:131)?

Mother Agnès (Pauline) testified that Thérèse "was entrusted with the training of the novices, as an assistant, when she was twenty years old. She first received this charge in 1893 when I was prioress, and she retained it till her death in 1897, for Mother Gonzague confirmed her in it when she became prioress in 1896." When the judge asked Agnès how Thérèse performed her duties as an assistant novice mistress, Agnès (O'Mahony, 1975:31-32; Cameron, 2012a:207) recalls:

> [S]he corrected fearlessly, whatever the cost to herself. But she did so prudently and wisely ... she never asked the novices questions just to satisfy her curiosity; she never tried to be popular with them ... she said something to me one day which I immediately went and wrote down: "I scatter the good seed that God gives me among my little birds, and then let events take their course without worrying any more about the outcome."

Apparently, Thérèse had always entertained the idea of being a missionary: "I have the vocation of the Apostle. I would like to travel over the whole earth to preach Your Name and to plant your glorious Cross on infidel soil" (cited in Clarke, 1996:192). An opportunity did arise to undertake missionary work, "when the Carmel of Saigon which had been founded by the Carmel at Lisieux asked for members to make a foundation at Hanoi." Unfortunately, Thérèse's health which had always been fragile, deteriorated, and she was diagnosed with a very serious illness – tuberculosis – which was to eventually take her life. Hence, her missionary aspirations were thwarted to just being able to pray and offer sacrifice for her missionary sisters and brothers. She was to spend the remainder of her life, not as the active missionary (which would have been her choice), but in an enclosed convent as a contemplative. Justifiably, O'Donnell (1997:132) tells us that some thirty years after her death on, "12 December 1927, Pope Pius XI declared St Therese of Lisieux principal patroness of the missions and of all missionary men and women on a par with St Francis Xavier."

Thérèse never wanted to be a burden on the community, however, as mentioned, it was just seven years after her Profession that she became very ill with tuberculosis. Such was her concern not to be a burden on her sisters, that she approached Mother Agnès (Pauline), "I find it very sad for you and the community to have to take care of a young sick religious." While ill herself, she empathised with the needs of the members of her community, encouraging them to offer the ordinary tasks and sacrifices of their daily lives to God. DeMeester (2002:9) explains:

> Towards the end of her life she developed a highly generous, all-encompassing apostolic awareness with a primary emphasis on the neighbors whom she saw every day – her community. She was very attentive to the members of the Carmel [community]. Of course, this aspect of her spirituality has especially endeared her to all Christians, both lay people and religious.

Indeed, Thérèse fulfilled her ordinary daily tasks in an extraordinary way. Her "'Little Way – 'the way of spiritual childhood' (Clarke, 1996:xii-xiii) ... is the essence of her 'spirituality,' [and] owes its inception to sacred scripture." O'Donnell (1997:168) maintains that it was: "In autumn 1894 she discovered the texts in Celine's notebook that were to be the basis of the 'Little Way.'" Therese had discovered the information in a "scripture notebook which Celine had brought into the convent with her ... the two Old Testament texts from Proverbs [9:4]; and Isaiah [66:13.12]" (p.36). The Little Way of Spiritual childhood can be emulated by all – for it is a simple approach to living an extraordinary life of faith and love in the service of others. To show profound love for Christ does not have to involve martyrdom, or indeed great suffering. Thérèse's example of teaching her way of spiritual childhood – her "Little Way", was to offer to her divine spouse the daily "minor irritations", that she believed could be annoying and distracting.

> [F]or a long-time during meditation, I was close to a sister who never stopped rattling her beads or fidgeting in a most irritating way ... I cannot find words to express the fatigue that this caused me. I was tempted to turn toward the offender and make her stop the noise. But I felt in my heart that I should suffer this annoyance with patience, for the love of the good Lord and also to avoid giving pain to this sister (Jamart, 1961:117; Cameron, 2012a:186).

Each day, this remarkable young woman offered something beautiful to God. At times, her gift was simple, like the distractions referred to in the previous quotation, or even just dealing with the cold weather. "At the end of her life she confessed that 'I have suffered so much from the cold that I almost died from it,' Therese had never made that known to anyone" (Jamart, 1961:116). At other times, the dark night of the soul descended, and what would probably be called depression in our contemporary society, enveloped this young nun, particularly during her pain and suffering, which became so unbearable that she contemplated suicide! O'Donnell (1997:173) discusses "the suicidal thoughts of Therese: 'Suicide becomes easier when one has no faith in an after-life; Therese was being tempted precisely on this score; hence the intensity of the suicide temptation.'" He (p.83) recounts the spiritual, psychological and physical 'ailments' suffered by Thérèse:

> From May until her death on 30 September Therese suffered acutely at every level. On the spiritual level she remained in a thick darkness of faith. On the physical level she suffered enormously from tuberculosis which ate away

at her lungs and her intestines ... On the psychological level she had all the humiliations associated with the collapse of bodily functions ... Yet through all of this there was a serenity about Therese. She did not deny her suffering or seek to over spiritualise it. She displayed no self-pity and was constantly thinking of others (cited in Cameron, 2012a:185).

Thérèse's suffering was spiritual, physical and psychological. O'Donnell (2001:25-26) maintains that the "trial of faith" she experienced in the months leading up to her death ... was a time when she was plunged into 'the deepest darkness' ... [but was able to produce] 'some of her most radiant and intense writing'" (Cameron, 2012a). This "Trial of faith" endured right up to the last day of her life. O'Donnell (1997:83) refers to this final condition of Thérèse, as a "lived theology of suffering."

Conclusion

Thérèse did not complain during her last hours. "Sister Marie of the Eucharist (Marie Guérin), Therese's first cousin, in a letter (O'Mahony, 1975:269-270) to her parents, dated 21 July 1897, writes of the courage of Therese": "The Father Superior came at six o'clock and anointed her; then he brought her God [communion] ... It was a moving sight, I can assure you, to see our little patient still so calm and pure. I have never seen anyone dying so calmly. 'What do you expect?' she said. 'Why should death make me afraid? All I've done, I've done for God'" (Cameron, 2012a). Thérèse died at the Carmelite convent, Lisieux on 30 September 1897, at the age of twenty-four years. Her feastday is celebrated on 1 October.

Leadership as Service

During her brief life, Thérèse was committed to responding to the Gospel's call to service. Sister Geneviève of the Holy Face (Céline), when called to testify as a witness for the process of beatification for her sister maintained: "Therese liked to be constantly at people's service and to please them ... Her 'silences' and her Sundays ... were spent ... writing poems at the request of other sisters. She never refused anybody. Her time was so taken up with these acts of charity that she had none left for herself" (O'Mahony, 1975:129). Thérèse considered the needs of others above her own. Even though she lacked formal education, Pope St John Paul II in his Apostolic Letter *Divini Amoris Scientia* proclaiming Thérèse a Doctor of the Universal Church, refers to her "wise reflection nourished by the sources of Sacred Scripture and divine Tradition" (L'Osservatore Romano, 1997, October 29. N.44, p.2). The Pontiff stressed that she possessed a *"special charism of wisdom* ... illumined by the light of the Gospel ... [and] taught by the divine Teacher" (ibid.).

Wisdom has built her house, she has hewn her seven pillars (Proverbs 9:1, cited in Sipe & Frick, 2015:4). For the purpose of this analysis, the "Seven Pillars of Servant Leadership" (see Appendix A for the list of attributes), are outlined below, and the discussion on each pillar includes aspects of Thérèse's life and leadership practices.

Pillar 1 – "Person of Character"

If you recall Thérèse left school when she was thirteen, and even though she was then taught by a tutor prior to entering the Carmelite Order at the age of fifteen, she would not have been considered "a learned person". The theology she taught to her novices was "simple". When discussing the importance of Thérèse's contribution to the Church today O'Donnell (1997:30) emphasises her "living knowledge of the Church [which] ... is not the intellectual knowledge of the theologian." You may remember from a previous chapter that when I was in Rome in 2002, I asked the Catherinian scholar Giuliana Cavallini to compare the then three women doctors of the Church. Her wise response for the youngest doctor (I have already cited her reply for Catherine and Teresa in the respective chapters on their faith journeys): "Thérèse of Lisieux was concerned chiefly with love of God and the Church – the Heart of the Church."

Thérèse actioned her values and maintained her integrity when dealing with her duties as an assistant novice mistress. For example, Thérèse was assistant to the novice Mistress Mother Marie de Gonzague, who was re-elected to the position of Prioress in 1896, but still maintained the title of novice-mistress, even though Thérèse was often asked to deputise for her. Geneviève [Céline] recalls, "Strictly speaking, one cannot say that Sister Therese was ever novice-mistress [per se]. Because of the prioress's fickleness Sister Therese hadn't a moment's security in this so-called office, which was taken from her and given back again every two weeks or so" (O'Mahony, 1975:120; Cameron, 2012a:180). Nevertheless, Thérèse accepted her position with grace and humility.

Fink (2000b:211-212) emphasises the profound humility of this extraordinary young woman. For example, just prior to her death, Thérèse "overheard two other nuns discussing the obituary that would be written and sent to other Carmelite convents after she died. They wondered what could be written in hers, that would be of interest since [they believed] she had never done anything exceptional." Indeed, Thérèse never had cause to boast about her considerable accomplishments – she was serving a "higher purpose"!

Pillar II – "Puts People First"

Sister Mary Magdalen of the Blessed Sacrament had entered the order as a lay sister, and though she would describe herself as a problem novice, she spoke highly of Thérèse's "guidance and mentoring skills. She recalls that six months after she entered Carmel, 'at the beginning of 1893 … when Mother Agnès of Jesus became prioress and Sister Therese of the Child Jesus novice-mistress' … It was here that the tribunal judge corrected Sister Mary Magdalen pointing out that Thérèse had not been novice-mistress and that Mother Marie de Gonzague had the position."

Sister Mary Magdalen responded:

> Yes, it was Mother Gonzague, the ex-prioress, who was officially appointed novice-mistress, but ... She was not able to train novices properly, so Sister Therese was given the unofficial task of supplying for her as discreetly as possible in this service of training ... One noticed that she did everything she said, and that inspired people to imitate her ... She always arranged things with a view to pleasing God. Her decisions were clear and fair (O'Mahony, 1975:260).

Thérèse was committed to the spiritual growth of the novices. Mother Agnès (O'Mahony, 1975:135) maintains in her testimony, "This 'spiritual childhood and complete surrender' was the essential characteristic of her holiness. In the personal guidance she gave each novice individually, the same points always cropped up: humility, poverty of spirit, simplicity, trust in God." Sister Martha of Jesus (O'Mahony, 1975:222) in her testimony, emphasised that Thérèse was discreet, confidential, and "did not denigrate others": "Whenever I complained to her about other nuns, she was careful not to agree with me or follow my example. She would invariably make excuses for them and show me their good side. She was very discreet too: I could tell her anything, even my most secret thoughts, and have nothing to fear. She never repeated a single word, even to her own sisters."

Thérèse affirmed her charges, she had their interests and well-being at heart. She took her responsibilities very seriously and empowered those who sought her counsel. O'Donnell (2001:87) gives reasons for Thérèse's popularity: "[S]he admits to sharing experiences that are common to us all. We can easily identify with her struggle to love those who were difficult; we have all at some time fallen asleep at prayer; we have suffered disappointments and frustrations in trying to be good; we know what it is to fail." Thérèse was an ordinary person who became an extraordinary saint.

Pillar III – "Skilled Communicator"

Thérèse was very gifted, and she shared her talents and skills with the nuns at the convent at Lisieux, working collaboratively with them, thereby "building a sense of community". DeMeester (2002:65) elaborates: "She could paint, and she could write verses. Indeed, she became the community poet ... if a jubilee, a ceremony of vesture of a profession was planned, Therese was ready to enhance the celebrations with her poems. For the prioress's feast or that of the lay Sisters, or again for the Christmas recreations, Sister Therese was asked to compose something like a little play" (Cameron, 2012a:212). Dreyer (2014:111) refers to the "use of military imagery to describe the spiritual life ... [as being] prominent in nineteenth century France." She maintains that "Thérèse associated military imagery with Joan of Arc, whom she admired [and who] had suffered nobly" (ibid.). In a previous chapter you have read about Joan of Arc and her exploits! Dreyer refers to "the numerous poems, hymns, and plays ... about Joan [written by Thérèse saying] ... she was captivated by a desire to imitate ... [Joan's] great deeds" (ibid.). Original photos exist today, that depict the young Thérèse dressed as Joan of Arc – probably as she enacted her play on the life of Joan.

Dreyer (2014:98) refers to the writings of Thérèse and emphasises "her three-part [Manuscripts A, B, C] autobiography" *Story of a Soul* ... [maintaining] that the saint also produced "54 poems, 21 prayers, 266 extant letters, eight plays written for feast day celebrations, and her last conversations." Thérèse's autobiography owes its existence to Agnès (Pauline), who persuaded her sister some two years before Thérèse died, to write her life story. When giving testimony some years later, Agnès spoke of the enormous number of letters from all over the world, that were sent to the convent following Thérèse's death: "I can say that since the *Story of a Soul* appeared we have printed 62, 815 copies of the complete life, and 80,000 copies of the abridged edition" (O'Mahony, 1975:70-71).

In 1895 Thérèse (Clarke, 1996:276) wrote her "Act of Oblation to Merciful Love ... 'Offering of myself as a Victim of Holocaust to God's Merciful Love.'" Agnès (Pauline) recounts this 'defining' moment in the life of Thérèse:

> In the month of June 1895, she was inspired to offer herself as a victim to the merciful love of God. She came to me for permission to do so, for I was then prioress ... Then she composed the formula of her self-dedication and submitted it for my approval, expressing at the same time the desire to have it checked by a theologian. Fr Le Monnier, superior of the Missionaries of Our Lady of Ransom, examined it ... [and when he approved] the principal part of it ... she was delighted. It was on 9 June 1895, the Feast of the Holy Trinity, that she officially made this offering of herself (O'Mahony, 1975:46; Cameron, 2012a:189).

O'Donnell (1997:42-43) maintains that Thérèse's, *Act of Oblation* was, "no mere devotional action. It summarised Therese's spiritual journey to date ... The Offering summed up for her the whole meaning of her life."

Pillar IV – "Compassionate Collaborator"

As one who has lived within a community of nuns, I can identify with Thérèse in her efforts to overcome difficulties associated with having a group of people living together in harmony, while making efforts to communicate, and endeavouring to cope with any conflict that may arise, through collaboration and teamwork. Jamart (1961:112-113) discusses difficulties that Thérèse may have encountered in her community life:

> [L]ife in a religious community is one that is difficult and that the purpose of this is to have the religious emulate Christ who redeemed the world by his suffering. Whatever be the rigours or ascetical practices that are special to any particular Order, the very fact of living in community

entails certain trials, mortifications, and sufferings that are not found elsewhere. This is especially true in the cloister where one's whole life is spent with the same set of persons and in a frame of circumstances that is narrow and rigid ... the law of charity bids us love our neighbour as ourselves (Cameron, 2012a:210).

Jamart (1961:93) assures us that Thérèse did her best, and guided the novices to present a pleasant, "calm and serene demeanour for, in her opinion, nothing makes community life more depressing than sad faces and beclouded brows. She preached this by her own example. Her face was lit up with a perpetual smile" (Cameron, 2012a:211). Thérèse was known to have a sense of humour, Jamart (ibid.) tells us that there were occasions when she was absent, for example, from recreation activities after a meal, when some nuns were heard to comment, that "Well, we shall not laugh so much today!" A sense of humour is a great attribute in a leader. Laughter and smiles come from feelings within and can radiate to those around us – and being infectious cause the worries and concerns of others to dissipate.

As with Christ the servant leader, Thérèse reached out to the poor and the marginalised, even as a child. Sister Marie of the Sacred Heart (Marie the eldest Martin sister), testified that: "She loved to give alms to the poor ... When she was ten, she asked if she could go and look after a poor woman who was dying and had no one to help her. She wanted to take some food and clothing to another woman, who inspired her with particular compassion because she was burdened with several children" (O'Mahony, 1975:93; Cameron, 2012a:179).

Unlike Hildegard, Teresa, and Catherine, Thérèse did not establish any foundations. Her charism is embedded in the legacy of her autobiography, and her "Little Way." Her death heralded the beginning of her mission: "I feel that my mission is about to begin, my mission to make God loved as I love Him, to teach souls my little way" (Clarke, 1996:xi). This one life of a young Carmelite nun has made a difference in building community, not just in the Carmelite Order but in the Church.

Mother Agnès (Pauline), questioned Thérèse: "what is this little way you want to teach to souls" (Clarke, 1996:xi)? Thérèse's response: "It is the way of spiritual childhood, the way of trust and absolute surrender." St Thérèse has given the world and "the Church her 'Little Way' of holiness" (O'Donnell, 2001:13). With her simple approach to doing ordinary things in an extraordinary way, Thérèse epitomises the childlike surrender and trust that are "the foundation of ... [her] teaching ... 'Whoever is a little one, let him come to me' – Proverbs 9: 4" (Clarke, 1996:xii).

Both the Church and the Carmelite Order are custodians of the legacy of Thérèse's *Autobiography* and her *Little Way of Spiritual Childhood*. According to O'Donnell (1997:212) "It is clear that Therese has made a major contribution to spirituality. The Little Way and her Offering to Merciful Love have entered into the mainstream of Catholic spirituality." And in a letter received by Mother Agnès regarding "the sainthood and doctrinal mission of St. Therese ... [her Little Way is being] universally recognized. From now on she belongs to the Church and to history" (Clarke, 1996:xix-x).

Pillar V – "Has Foresight"

During her lifetime, Thérèse was the recipient of visionary experiences. When called as a witness, Sister Marie of the Trinity, one of Thérèse's novices, recalled that she had spoken to her about the "prophetic vision she had as a child [and also] of the trials that would accompany her father's last years. She also told me how the Blessed Virgin had miraculously cured her of a strange illness, and how on that occasion [Therese had] a clear vision of the Mother of God herself" (O'Mahony, 1975:253).

Thérèse's insight and inner spirituality gave birth to her spiritual awareness, which produced her "Little Way of Spiritual Childhood". Such awareness extended beyond her inner reality and was manifested in the outer reality. O'Donnell (2001:21) "writes of Therese's awe and wonder when she experienced her first sight of the sea, 'when she was six or seven', 'I couldn't take my eyes off it since its majesty, the roaring of its waves, everything spoke to my soul of God's grandeur and power.'" In her autobiography, Thérèse recounts a visionary experience from her childhood, when she was quite young (six or seven) and her father was not at home but away on business.

> I was all alone at the window of an attic … when I saw a man dressed exactly like Papa … The man had the same height and walk as Papa, only he was much more stooped. His head was covered with a sort of apron of indistinct color and it hid his face. He wore a hat similar to Papa's … I called out very loudly – 'Papa! Papa!' … But the mysterious personage … continued his steady pace without even turning around … the prophetic vision … vanished (Clarke, 1996:45-47; Cameron, 2012a:198).

O'Donnell (1997:195) "comments on the significance of this vision for Therese and refers to her gift of 'prophetic charism'":

> The investigations for Therese's beatification paid special attention to prophecy. There is quite an amount of evidence of the presence of the prophetic charism in Therese's life. Her first such experience was the vision at about the age of six or seven of her father bent with age, his face covered with a veil. Mother Agnes testified at the diocesan process: "She was convinced not only of the reality of the vision, but also that this vision had a significance that would be manifested later, that it foretold some trial or ill fortune" (ibid.).

Agnès (Pauline) in her testimony (O'Mahony, 1975:61): "states that when Therese called out to her father during the 'apparition,' she (Agnes) and Marie ran to her and when told about the 'vision' went outside to check the garden but found no one": "When father suffered that humiliating cerebral paralysis during the last five years of his life ... she [Therese] realised that it was these sad events that were presaged by that childhood vision" (Cameron, 2012a:199). Here Agnès is referring to the 'mental' illness, which was instrumental in Louis Martin being admitted to a psychiatric hospital in Caen, some five years before his death (Clarke, 1996:156; Cameron, 2012a: ibid.).

Mother Agnès (Pauline) in her testimony, recalls the moment when Thérèse passed to eternal life. The community of nuns were summoned:

> [They] were in time to witness her ecstasy ... Her face ... had returned to its pristine freshness and the lilywhite colouring of healthier days, her eyes stared upwards, shining with peace and joy. A sister drew near with a torch to get a better look at this sublime gaze, and the light of the torch produced no movement of the eyelids. This ecstasy lasted for the space of a Credo. Then I saw her close her eyes; she sighed several times, and rendered her soul to God (O'Mahony, (1975:69).

Those present were witnesses to the ecstatic state of the young Carmelite nun, during her final moments.

Pillar VI – "Systems Thinker"

Thérèse was aware of her shortcomings, and this knowledge was a great factor in being able to understand the sometimes-complex behaviour of her charges: "When some trouble arose ... she did her best to restore peace. The presence in a monastery of four and then five members of the same family was bound to cause certain difficulties. Therese sometimes had to suffer on this account, 'We must seek forgiveness, she told her sisters, for living under the same roof'" (Jamart, 1961:92-93).

Thérèse was a systems thinker. She was organised and had a vision for all. The big picture for Thérèse was to look after her charges, and to have them listen and learn, and for her to try to guide each novice to be the best that she could be. Her charges grew in number. As we have read previously in this chapter, Thérèse only ever held the position of acting novice mistress, though on many occasions she was considered the "mistress of novices". O'Donnell (1997:118) writes of a missionary priest, Armand Lemonnier, who had given retreats at the convent at Lisieux, and who was asked to be a witness at the beatification process for Thérèse. O'Donnell says that during his testimony, Lemonnier paid: "special tribute to her wise direction of the novices, her confidence and faith, and the high esteem in which she was held, especially by the chaplain Father Youf." O'Donnell (1997:199; Cameron, 2012a) also refers to the focus of the Diocesan process regarding Thérèse's "direction" of the novices:

> The Diocesan Process focused attention on the gifts Therese exercised in the direction of her novices. She herself describes as the "goods of heaven" those "inspirations of the mind and heart, profound thoughts" to which one can wrongly claim ownership, but which are "lent" by God. Mother Gonzague, who treated Therese with much severity, none the less recognised her qualities, even to having her function as novice mistress, albeit without the title.

Thérèse was flexible and adaptable with her charges. Her gentleness was her strength. She affirmed and reprimanded, but in a respectful and proactive way. She adapted to the situation, did not judge, and set an example for the other members in the community. Sister Martha of Jesus was described as a difficult novice (O'Mahony, 1975:217-218), but though she may have been difficult for Thérèse to manage, she had only words of praise for her former "assistant novice-mistress", when called as a witness for the tribunal:

> From the time the Servant of God joined us, I was aware that she was no ordinary person. But I found it very hard

to understand how so young a nun could be as perfect as
she was. What struck me most about her was her humility,
piety and mortification ... Like myself, all the novices felt
the need to have her opinion, to be encouraged by her, and
to follow her advice. Mother Prioress had given a general
permission to consult the Servant of God in this way, so
that in actual fact we used to deal with her as if she was a
real novice-mistress.

Thérèse was keen for her autobiography *Story of a soul to be* published without delay but accepted that if a decision was made by the prioress, to 'discard' the manuscripts, she would know that this was God's will (O'Mahony, 1975:64; Cameron, 2012a). Thankfully, Mother Marie de Gonzague organised for the manuscripts to be printed, following the approval of the Bishop of Bayeux. Initially it was circulated just to the Carmelites, and replaced the "Obituary circular", generally sent on the death of a member of the Order. "The Carmels lent the book to people, and request for it poured in from all sides" (Agnès, cited in O'Mahony, 1975:70-71; Cameron, 2012a:204-205).

Pillar VII – "Leads with Moral Authority"

Thérèse had confidence that those who were left behind, would make the right decisions regarding her writing. She accepted that all people may not be influenced by what she had to say, and she accepted full responsibility for her words and actions. O'Donnell (1997:13) maintains, "Within a year, the initial edition [2000 copies] was sold out and a second edition of four thousand copies was issued in 1899. Within seven years it had appeared in English, Polish, Dutch, Italian and Portuguese. In one year alone (1910), the Carmel received 9,741 letters. By 1914 it was getting two hundred letters daily, and the autobiography was now available in Spanish and Japanese." The ecclesiastical authorities soon realised the tremendous impact that the publication of Thérèse's autobiography had on the Church:

The local bishops of Bayeux were well disposed towards the Lisieux Carmel: they permitted the publication of the autobiography and allowed the introduction of Therese's cause. The first major statement on Therese from a Church authority was by Benedict XV who signed the formal decree about Therese's heroic virtue and spoke on her spirituality in August 1921 (ibid.).

Jamart (1961:24-25) elaborates: "her Cause of Canonization was quickly introduced, and the Process progressed with unusual rapidity ... 'Opened at Bayeux in 1910, it ended with Therese's beatification by Pius XI on April 29, 1923. Two years later, on May 17, 1925, the same Pope canonized her ... Since that time, she has grown in popularity.'" Thérèse's autobiography and writings, have empowered her followers and so impressed the Church, that it has honoured her with sainthood and doctoral status. However, the initial translation of *Story of a Soul* was not without its difficulties. Clarke (1996:ix) explains:

> Following the wishes of her superiors, Therese herself had written the story of her brief life in ink and pencil, with few emendations, at odd moments as her health declined, on whatever paper was available (often of poor quality) ... Not surprisingly ... the autograph is sometimes difficult to read, and shows countless variations in capitalizations, underlinings, the size, position, and slant of the letters and so on (with some occasional corrections in a later hand).

Realising that her autobiography would require some maintenance, Thérèse delegated her sister Mother Agnès to edit the manuscripts on her behalf, and to "have no scruples about it." Agnès fulfilled Thérèse's request, and though Clarke (above) refers to "some occasional corrections", O'Donnell (1997:10-11) states, that "there were seven thousand changes and what amounted in places to a rewriting of the text."

Values

Aspects of Thérèse's life and works are now discussed in relation to the values – dignity, respect, fairness, justness and equality (see Chapter 4 for the terms of reference).

Dignity

The Catechism of the Catholic Church states: "The dignity of the human person is rooted in his [her] creation in the image and likeness of God. It is fulfilled in his [her] vocation to divine beatitude. It is essential to a human being freely to direct himself [herself] to this fulfillment" (2000:para.1700). St Thérèse, though she was only twenty-four when she died, seemed to have reached her fulfillment as a spiritual being within her human reality. She possessed a love of God, and love of neighbour. She empowered her novices and acknowledged their right to achieve full human dignity under her care. Thérèse was humble, and she respected the dignity of others. Pope St John Paul II, when he addressed pilgrims who had arrived in Rome to attend the Proclamation Ceremony for St Thérèse stated:

> Yesterday gave you an opportunity to take part in a ceremony rare in the Church's life but richly meaningful: the proclamation of a doctor of the Church ... You have wished to come and learn from her who embodies for us the "Little Way", the royal way of Love, St Therese of the Child Jesus and the Holy Face, belongs to that group of saints whom the Church recognizes as teachers of the spiritual life (L'Osservatore Romano, No. 44, Oct. 29th, 1997:2).

There is reference here to the "Holy Face" as part of Thérèse's title. Clarke (1996:152) writes that in the 19th century there was devotion to the 'Holy Face' and that Thérèse signed her name "St Thérèse of the Child Jesus and the Holy Face", for the first time when she received the habit of the Order on 10 January 1889.

Respect

On the evening of October 11, 1962, at the Opening of the Second Vatican Council, Pope St John XXIII made what is referred to as a "famous moonlight speech". Maureen O'Riordan (2017, Oct. 11) tells us that as the Pope prepared his speech, he was inspired by St Thérèse of Lisieux stating later that "I turned to my Teresina". Undoubtedly, Thérèse had the confidence and respect of the Pope, who accepted stewardship of her "love in the heart of the Church". In the contemporary Church, she continues to have the confidence and respect of the Church, and she is one of the few saints mentioned in the Catholic Catechism (CCC, 2000:para.2558).

Sister Marie of the Trinity (O'Mahony, 1975:240) testified to the respect and importance, Thérèse placed on observing the rule, "One day I wanted to omit mental prayer because of urgent work. Thérèse said: "Unless the necessity is very great, never ask to be dispensed from community exercises for the sake of work, no matter what it is. That kind of dedication cannot be pleasing to Jesus. Real dedication is to never waste a minute, and to give oneself fully during the hours set aside for work." Thérèse was able to reprimand using gentleness and firmness. She treated her charges with respect in a sensitive and courteous manner, while guiding them in their spiritual formation.

Fairness

Sister Geneviève (Céline) recalls that some of the novices who had been admitted to the order in the early days, "were far from perfect"; however, Thérèse "never shirked her duty, and was not afraid to do battle with the defects of the novices; but she was also very gentle and compassionate when that was called for" (O'Mahony, 1975:120). According to her biological sisters and her sisters in religion, Thérèse treated her novices with great respect, and her dealings with them were fair. They acknowledged and appreciated her sense of fairness, and though there was diversity in their backgrounds and temperaments, all novices received similar treatment and training. Decisions made were in the best interests of all the members of the community. Thérèse possessed the wisdom to be able to value each person, and she "celebrated their differences with justness and fairness". Sister Geneviève (Céline) in her testimony, recalls the "wisdom and perception of Thérèse. She was faithful in keeping her emotions under control: she was always calm and serene. She had a lively imagination, yet she never got excited, and one was always sure of receiving wise and measured advice from her" (O'Mahony, 1975:143).

The Church has honoured Thérèse with sainthood and elevated her to the ecclesial ranks. However, the process leading to Thérèse being proclaimed a Doctor of the Universal Church, was not without controversy. According to Cameron (2012a:67): "The Proclamation had its detractors. One such critic was William Graham (1995), who in the article, 'Is there a case against Saint Thérèse as Doctor of the Church?', argues strongly that there is such a case, and that Thérèse did not possess the 'right stuff of which doctors are made.'" Another critic John McGee (1997:21), also maintains that "Spiritual attitude does not a doctor make." Payne (2002:91) notes, "the undue haste of promoting the cause for the doctorate of Thérèse" and states that: "One presumes that the Congregation for the Causes of Saints was 'acting on higher orders' ... [those of] Pope John Paul II" (Cameron, 2012a:68). And Pope St John Paul II did have a special devotion to the saint!

In all justice, is such a strong censure by her detractor's fair? Thérèse's beatification (1923) and canonisation (1925) occurred within 3 decades of her death, which is extraordinary. And due to the relative short span of time (in terms of history), there were many witnesses to her life and work, who were still alive at the time, and able to give testimony at the process for her beatification and later, her canonisation. Regardless of the controversy, St Thérèse of the Child Jesus and the Holy Face was declared a Doctor of the Universal Church on 19 October 1997, on the anniversary of the centenary of her death. At the conclusion of the Apostolic Letter *Divini Amoris Scientia* proclaiming Thérèse a Doctor, Pope St John Paul II declared:

> We decree that this Apostolic Letter is to be religiously preserved and to have full effect both now and in the future; furthermore, it is thus to be judged and defined as right, and whatever to the contrary may be attempted by anyone, on whatever authority, knowingly or unknowingly, is null and void. *Given in Rome, at St Peter's, under the Fisherman's ring, the 19th day of the month of October in the year of the Lord 1997, the 20th of the Pontificate.*

Justness

The Carmelite rule, pertained to all the nuns, regardless of status in religious life, or their social standing prior to entering religion. Thérèse applied justness in her dealings with her novices. She instilled in them, a love of obedience to the rule: "even if all were to fail in the observance of the rule," she said, "that would not be a reason for justifying ourselves," and, repeating the words of her holy Mother, St. Teresa, she added that "everyone should act as if the perfection of the Order depended on her personal conduct" (Jamart, 1961:84). Concerning her "Act of Oblation to Merciful Love ... 'Offering of myself as a Victim of Holocaust to God's merciful Love,'" written by Thérèse in 1895, and which was discussed in an earlier paragraph, Thérèse emphasises the justness of God in relation to souls who offer themselves to him to save others: "I was thinking of the souls who offer themselves as victims of God's justice in order to turn away the punishments reserved to sinners ... I cried out: O my God! Will Your Justice alone find souls willing to immolate themselves as victims?" (Clarke, 1996:180).

Thérèse "had a presentiment that her activity after her death would extend far beyond the influence of a book [her autobiography], that it would be worldwide" (Clarke, 1996:263). DeMeester (2002:93) states,

"Towards the end of her life, we see Therese developing a formidable prophetic awareness of a need to carry out a 'mission' to the world." Thérèse (Clarke, 1996:192) sums up her "true vocation" as: "Carmelite, Spouse, Mother, and yet I feel within me other vocations. I feel the vocation of the WARRIOR, THE PRIEST, THE APOSTLE, THE DOCTOR, THE MARTYR ... I feel in me the *vocation of* the PRIEST ... But alas! While desiring to be a *Priest*, I admire and envy the humility of St. Francis of Assisi and I feel the *vocation* of imitating him in refusing the sublime dignity of the *Priesthood*" (Cameron, 2012a:201). Geneviève (Céline) recalls of Thérèse's "priesthood aspirations":

> In 1897, but before she was really ill, Sister Thérèse told me she expected to die that year ... When she realized that she had pulmonary tuberculosis, she said: "You see, God is going to take me at an age when I would not have had the time to become a priest ... If I could have been a priest, I would have been ordained at these June ordinations. So, what did God do? So that I would not be disappointed, he let me be sick: in that way I couldn't have been there, and I would die before I could exercise my ministry." The sacrifice of not being able to be a priest was something she always felt deeply ... "Oh! What wonders we shall see in heaven! I have a feeling that those who desired to be priests on earth will be able to share in the honour of the priesthood in heaven (O'Mahony, 1975:155-156; Cameron, ibid.).

Surprisingly, Thérèse had great aspirations to be a priest, and she accepted that this was not to be her mission.

Equality

In its document *The Church and Racism: Towards a More Fraternal Society* the Pontifical Commission on Justice and peace (1988) states the following:

Equality does not mean uniformity. It is important to recognize the diversity and complementarity of one another's cultural riches and moral qualities. Equality of treatment therefore implies ... recognition of differences which minorities themselves demand in order to develop according to their own specific characteristics, in respect for others and for the common good of society and the world community. No human group, however, can boast of having a natural superiority over others, or of exercising any discrimination that affects the basic rights of the person (#23).

It is important then, for all leaders to recognise the diversity that exists within their teams and organisations, and to be prepared to cater to the needs of all, by respecting and valuing diversity, and by being inclusive of all. Many of the testimonials from the members of the Carmelite Order, who knew Thérèse stated that she treated everybody equally, and without malice, seeing God in each person and wanting to train her novices in the practice of the "Little Way of Spiritual Childhood".

Thérèse loved God and neighbour, and she adored her saintly parents. In a letter to Father Belliere the saint declares: "God gave me a father and a mother who were more worthy of heaven than of earth." These words were repeated by Father Antonio of the Mother of God, Vice Postulator (Order of Carmelites website, 2017), in reference to the Beatification of Louis and Zélie Martin in 2008. Father Antonio responds: "The beatification of Louis Martin and Zélie Guérin, whom Thérèse defined as 'parents without equal', worthy of heaven, holy ground permeated with the 'perfume of purity' is very important to the Church" (ibid.).

The parents of Thérèse are now canonised saints, and their daughter is venerated by the Church, "in the various Eastern and Western Rites". She has had "Her Little Way – the Gospel way of holiness for all ... studied by theologians and experts in spirituality." And she has been honoured with Cathedrals, basilicas, shrines and churches throughout the world ...

built and dedicated to the Lord under ... her patronage" (Pope St John Paul II, *Divini Amoris Scientia*, 1997:2). Pope St John Paul II proclaimed St Thérèse of Lisieux a doctor of the universal Church on World Mission Sunday 19 October 1997. During her lifetime Thérèse had expressed interest in being a missionary though she never left the Carmel cloister at Lisieux. Nevertheless, as a model of missionary commitment she has been given the title – *patroness of the missions* (L'Osservatore Romano, No. 43, Oct. 22nd, 1997:1).

In the following chapter we meet Blessed Frances Siedliska, Foundress of the Sisters of the Holy Family of Nazareth.

14

Blessed Frances Siedliska

My preparations for writing this chapter began with some trepidation, as the life and works of the extraordinary woman to be investigated had touched me personally, shaping my youth and initiating me into the transcendental delights of a spiritual journey, that began when I was fourteen years of age and is still going strong in the twilight years of my life. As I commenced the research and reached for a book that was a narrative of the life of Mother Mary Frances Siedliska – the very first page I accessed, had a photo of this remarkable woman known as Blessed Frances Siedliska, Foundress of the Sisters of the Holy Family of Nazareth. Though it had been many years since I had seen the image of Blessed Mother Mary Frances, my heart and emotions responded immediately. Tears gathered and threatened to fall – memories came flooding back of times past – a youth spent – memories of young teenagers gifting themselves to God, while just emerging from childhood! Echoes resounded from long ago of young voices – some coming from a dormitory whispering: "Is that the sound of rosary beads on the stairs? Perhaps it is the mistress of aspirants coming to check that we have retired for the evening – do you think she knows that we went downstairs to the kitchen in the middle of the night to eat toffee apples"?

Most of my friends and I had entered the convent at fourteen years of age as aspirants, and then what seemed to be no time at all, we were going on sixteen and already postulants. We studied, prayed, giggled and laughed together. We were novices when the Second Vatican Council was convening in Rome, and this momentous, religious event in the Church, heralded change for the Church and for all religious congregations. We quickly adapted to the new rules and regulations, and meditation and prayer guided us as we performed our everyday duties.

Consequently, during our two-year novitiate, theological studies, prayer and meditation received prominence. Meetings with our families were restricted, and we were confined to the enclosure of the convent grounds, except for medical reasons and/or emergencies. Radios and televisions were silent; our spiritual lives were nourished, and the development of our talents and skills encouraged – theological studies, sewing, music, dancing and many other activities, enriched our physical and spiritual growth into adulthood. We played the organ and arranged the flowers in the chapel, and shared cleaning and cooking duties. At Easter, we participated in the Polish custom of preparing food to be blessed; and the celebration of midnight Mass at Christmas was always magical and mystical, as we all gathered and assembled in the chapel for Mass, singing carols and giving thanks for blessings received through the year. Christmas day was filled with excitement and indeed one of the many enjoyable activities was opening mail that had been set aside during Advent as we then had the opportunity to read all the letters and cards from relatives and friends. We celebrated feast days, special days, and indeed we celebrated every day – for we were members of one family – the Holy Family of Nazareth.

And this is the reason why, more than half a century later and after many other memorable events and experiences – that my heart is still with my family of sisters. It matters little, that for some of us, our faith journey may have changed direction, and we have gone our separate ways. We are all still united by the charisma of one woman, who left a legacy for future generations – stewardship of the sacredness of her family, under the protection of Jesus the Good Shepherd. In this chapter, we honour Blessed Frances Siedliska, Foundress of the Sisters of the Holy Family of Nazareth.

Historical Background

In 2016, Poland celebrated one thousand and fifty years of Christianity (Derek Scally, 2016). Such a milestone had been reached, despite there being a communist regime in the country over many years. Indeed, during the millennium celebrations in 1966, a Polish priest ministering to a local Polish community, spoke to me of the difficulties experienced by the Polish people in their native Poland, during the communist era. For example, apart from quite serious political issues, he recalled that on important feast days such as that of Our Lady of Częstochowa, known as "The Black Madonna", public transport could be suspended at a moment's notice, but he emphasised, that this did not deter the citizens, for their faith was so strong, that they would decide instead to walk the many miles (kms) to reach the city churches in time to celebrate the special feast day of Our Lady.

Interestingly, Poland, as a country, has had a chequered history – particularly with Russia. In the 18th Century, Russia imposed a treaty on Poland and in 1815: "At the Congress of Vienna the great European powers … [partitioned] the continent. Poland was divided between Prussia, Russia and Austria. Prussia took the western and northern part of Poland while Russia took the centre and east. Austria kept Galicia" (Tim Lambert, 2018). In 1830, Poland rebelled but the Russian army proved to be too strong, and within twelve months had defeated the Polish forces. The Polish rebels tried to overcome the Russians in 1863, but after eighteen months were once again soundly defeated (ibid.). In this later insurrection, the Polish patriots had been assisted financially and provided with "safe shelter" by high-ranking members of the Polish aristocracy, who supported patriotism because of their great love for their country. One such noble was Adolph Siedliski, father of Frances Siedliska (Katherine Burton, 1951:52-53).

Profile

Frances was born in Roszkowa Wola, an "ancient manor house ... some forty miles from Warsaw" (Inez Strzałkowska, 1989:11), on 12 November 1842, the first of two children born to Adolph and Cecilia [nee Morawska] Siedliski. Frances describes her baptism: "[I was] baptized at three o'clock in the afternoon on November 20, the eve of the presentation of the Blessed Virgin in the Temple. I was given the names of Frances, Anne, and Josephine. I was to have been a weak child and destined for an early death. The attending doctors gave little hope for my survival" (Autobiography, 1997:1-2). In later years Frances thanked God for sparing her life and giving her the opportunity to grow into adulthood and serve him, "I adore and praise your mercy for all you have done for me, dear Lord, for the life you have so graciously spared me. May I use it well, living for your glory alone" (p.3). During those first early years, illness prevented Frances from sitting or standing unaided. Though she regained some strength as she grew older, she suffered from fragile health throughout her life. Her mother Cecilia also experienced chronic poor health, the symptoms of which escalated following the birth of her second child Adam in 1847.

The Siedliski household was not particularly religious. Adolph is described as being indifferent in regard to religion and its practice, and Cecilia herself in those early days was not particularly devout but did observe the basic tenets of the Christian faith. According to Strzałkowska (1989:16), Adolph and Cecilia were "no different from other contemporary Polish aristocratic families." Frances confirms this assessment: "My parents were religious according to the accepted norms of the social class. They were outstanding in their personal integrity and decency, greatly esteemed and respected, but God was not the Lord of our household. Christ's law was not the model for our daily life and activities, yet my parents, especially Mamma, observed all religious precepts" (Autobiography, 1997:3).

Strzałkowska (1989:15) maintains that though Frances was virtuous she did possess her faults, and that "she had inherited her quick violent temper and inclination to outbursts from her father", whom Antonio Ricciardi describes as also having a kind and gentle side, particularly regarding his employees (1971:3). Throughout this profile, many interesting facets to the personality of Frances will be revealed, but in her youth, she believed that she put on a façade in the presence of others: "The members of our household as well as our acquaintances considered me sensible, mature and astute beyond my years. All this behavior was merely superficial, engendered and put on by a proud ambition to give the best impression of myself" (Autobiography, 1997:5).

Frances was intelligent but delicate, and when she was about ten years of age her parents decided to employ tutors to oversee her education at home. A succession of tutors followed, including teachers of voice and music. The first was an elderly woman who had a great love of the Church, and was loyal to the Siedliski family, but whose sojourn in the household was curtailed due to her unexpected death. In later years, Frances spoke fondly of this tutor, who had made such an impression on her when she was a child:

> When I was ten or eleven years old, my parents accepted into our home a teacher of great rectitude, one truly God-centered. She was very devout, a penitent of Father O. Antoniewicz, SJ, who corresponded with her while she was with us. She attended church often and received the sacraments ... She instructed us with real charity, stressing the importance of religion lessons. She taught us how to pray and took us to church. My soul clung to all this, I yearned for it with expectation. It may well be that God's grace would have found a greater readiness in my soul, if she had not died shortly after coming to us. I experienced her death profoundly (Autobiography, 1997:4-5).

The next tutor was German, young and non-Catholic. "She was highly educated, skillful, a Protestant, also a person of the ugliest disposition. She used all means to gain my affection, but I couldn't stand either her person or her caresses and endearments … Aided by God's grace, I told Mamma everything, stating that I refuse to listen to that teacher" (Autobiography, 1997:7). Sharing unsuitable stories with her charge and having no love for the Church, this tutor was soon removed from the Siedliski household. The third tutor, referred to as a "Swiss beauty", was educated, competent and intelligent and made a favourable impression and remained with the family for some years (Burton, 1951:8). According to Frances her tutor "was a beautiful, well-educated young woman and engaged to be married. She used to tell me many things about her young man and she shared his letters with me. She was so attractive that during our walks people, even strangers, would stop and stare at her loveliness" (Autobiography, 1997: 10-11).

Unfortunately, over time Cecilia's health deteriorated, and in 1854 when Frances was 12 years old, her mother's health crisis necessitated a stay for them both at the maternal grandfather's palatial residence in Warsaw. Frances recalls, "Since Mamma was constantly ill, we lived with our grandfather Morawski" (Autobiography, 1997:9), who was the "Director of the Revenue and Finance Commission in Warsaw" (ibid:7). It was following this crisis, when Cecilia was on the road to recovery and still in Warsaw, that she became acquainted with Father Leander Lendzian, a Capuchin priest, who was to become a close friend and confidante of Frances, particularly in later years when he played a significant role in the establishment of her Congregation (Strzałkowska, 1989:19). As mentioned, Frances was twelve years old at the time, and on one occasion when occupied with a music lesson, was called to the "drawing room" to meet a visiting priest. She describes this first meeting with Father Leander as a time of conversion for her.

> After taking leave of this Father, I returned to the piano, but, my Lord and God, how different was my disposition, what a transformation in my soul! This was truly a graced

moment, an hour of conversion. I had left the piano a pagan, having no knowledge, no love for God; I returned to it in silence, strangely reflective. I daresay that already a spark of love began to glimmer in my soul. I felt something for the Jesus of whom Father spoke to me, although I had no idea where to look for him (Autobiography, 1997:16).

Burton endorses this, "it was in the winter of her thirteenth year that faith and the meaning of faith really entered Frances Siedliska's life ... This was her epiphany." (1951:15). Father Leander was commissioned to prepare Frances for her First Holy Communion, which she received on 1 May 1855. Frances had received what she referred to as her first Confession on 9 March 1855 from Father Leander. She had earlier been prepared for her first confession with a Father John Dziubacki, and she had made this confession in Warsaw "to Canon Topolski in the church of Saint Charles Borromeo" (you may recall St Charles Borromeo from previous chapters particularly the chapter on St Angela Merici), however, she was dissatisfied with the experience because she believed that she wasn't adequately prepared. "I experienced in my soul the solemn dignity of that moment without completely understanding what I was doing. My mother's aunt a devout and saintly person, took me to the church'" (Autobiography, 1997:7-8). Hence, this is the reason why Frances regarded the confession she made with Father Leander as her first confession.

Frances received the Sacrament of Confirmation on 8 June 1855, about a month after her First Communion, "in the Church of the Benedictine nuns ... [The sacrament] was administered by the Archbishop [A. Fijalkowski] of Warsaw" (Ricciardi, 1971:11). She chose the name of Mary as her Confirmation name, and recalls that: "Since my grandfather was good friends with the archbishop and a benefactor of the Blessed Sacrament Sisters in Warsaw, Mamma and I were permitted to pass through the nuns' cloister ... I saw the convent walls, the corridors, the choir, the nuns -- my dream! Had I followed my natural inclination, I would have been ready to remain there serving my Jesus in solitude and recollection, away from all else. It seemed to me that serving God in religious life was the epitome of beatitude on earth" (Autobiography, 1997:33-34).

Some months following her reception of the sacraments, Frances and her mother returned to Żdżary, as Adolph was keen for his family to return to the family estate in the country. This decision caused Frances "great pain since it meant leaving Father Leander. The trust, respect and faith I had for my confessor were different from purely natural sentiments. I considered Father Leander God's instrument in my regard, although I did not as yet understand the full meaning of this relationship" (Autobiography, 1997:37). Burton maintains that it was because Frances was separated from Father Leander, that she soon "lost the sense of the presence of God" (1951:26).

In August Adolph was summoned to Warsaw, where he was informed that his father-in-law M. Morawski had passed away. Extreme sorrow was experienced by the entire Siedliski household. Ricciardi writes that, "The death of Minister Morawski coincided with Frania's passing from childhood to adolescence" (1971:15). Frances sums up her experience, "My most honest conclusion was that all experiences are finite and transitory" (Autobiography, 1997:40). From her grandfather's estate, Frances received "a belt about 3inches wide, beautifully made, hair-thin, vari-coloured cord. I thought about what I might do with that belt and the thought came to me to use it as an instrument of penance ... [I decided to wear it] beneath my clothing ...It was something painful, as in some places on the edges, the cords were unfinished and so pierced the flesh ... I fell ill with a fever" (Ricciardi, 1971:15). Frances eventually disclosed the penitential practice to Father Leander during confession and was forbidden to continue with that or other similar penances (ibid.).

Twelve months after the demise of her father, Cecilia developed "tuberculosis of the throat" (Autobiography, 1997:55), and she and Frances returned to Warsaw. Adam was away at school and Adolph was working on the family property, but he visited his wife and daughter often. During this time Frances had renewed contact with Father Leander, and Cecilia also began to become more conscious and fervent in her religious practices. Adolph accepted his wife's recommitment to her faith, and occasionally chatted to Father Leander when he was in Warsaw, but he began to despair over his daughter's growing spiritual and religious tendencies. He wanted Frances to secure an advantageous marriage, so when they were in Warsaw, he forced her to attend balls and social events and when he urged his wife and daughter to return to their estate at Żdżary, he insisted on his daughter entertaining guests at their home. Frances was unhappy about returning to Żdżary:

> Returning to our country estate was a painful ordeal ... in doing so we were forfeiting the freedom of serving the Lord. Thank God there was a parish church with a pastor in Żdżary. Grandfather Morawski had built the church. This made it easy to practice our religion and at first everything progressed smoothly. Mamma had asked Daddy to be taken to church every day and he agreed (Autobiography, 1997:56).

Fortunately, Father Leander was appointed to Nowe Miasto which was close to Warsaw. And not far from Żdżary. Frances was elated: "It is difficult to describe my joy! I shared my happiness with Jesus alone, hiding as best I could from the others" (Autobiography, 1997:56). When Father Leander arrived in Nowe Miasto, Adolph was in Warsaw and Cecilia invited the priest to spend time at the family home. He heard their confession, and distributed communion to them at the local church, while also offering his spiritual guidance to Cecilia and Frances. Unfortunately, Frances was soon "to lose the comfort of Father Leander's direction. [For when he] ... had completed three years of superiorship in the Nowe Miasto monastery ... [he] was transferred to the monastery at Lublin" (Ricciardi, 1997:29).

Prior to the good priest's departure, Adolph became increasingly antagonistic towards him and the influence he had upon Frances. He redoubled his efforts to virtually force his daughter to participate in frivolous activities, and as a result though there were moments when Frances was strengthened by the reception of the Eucharist, she did experience some temptation and pressure, to engage in these self-indulgent pursuits organised by her father to entice her into the world of society, privilege and entitlement, "there were fleeting moments of pleasure in her distinguished life style which she later described as 'a betrayal and an apostasy'" (Strzałkowska, 1989:20).

In those days frequent reception of the Eucharist was frowned upon. Frances recalls that their local pastor was so against frequent reception of the Eucharist, that he turned Adolph against his family for their desire to regularly receive Christ in the Eucharist: "Our pastor turned Daddy against us, condemned the frequent reception of Holy Communion as unheard-of, in fact as a heresy which he will have to denounce from the pulpit, lest the faithful be scandalized. Our neighbors openly addressed Daddy with irony: 'Why do your wife and daughter have such greed for the wafer?'" (Autobiography, 1997:60). Ricciardi (1971:22) writes about the emotions Frances experienced at this time, and quotes from her autobiography:

> [I had] the opportunity to perceive people at their most ugly, at their most repulsive. Daddy enjoyed the respect of his neighbors, he was highly esteemed by his friends as a superb host, a clever and enjoyable companion. Our home was always filled with visitors and guests. These get-togethers invariably ended in eating and drinking – at times to excess. All these gentlemen ... [ladies did not attend since Mamma didn't return any of their visits] ... were for the most part unbelievers and had no religion ... "Lord, you alone know what was taking place in my heart!" ... Purposely, to irritate me they would begin talking against priests, against religion. Later after they had been drinking,

they would launch into immoral stories. Poor Mamma would try signaling to Daddy to make them stop – all in vain. Daddy enjoyed these conversations; at times he himself initiated them. He would then laugh and turning to me ask: "What does my little bigot think about all this?" (Autobiography, 1997:61-62).

These times were difficult for Frances who was fighting her "demons"! She loved her father but tried to hide her growing religious aspirations from him. Though she was in the world she was not often of the world, however as stated in an earlier paragraph, there were occasions when she experienced some attraction for the "good life", that resulted in her berating and loathing the weakness of her own human nature. "My torture – my spiritual torment at this time, consisted in the fact that I was unable to distinguish between a temptation, and evil inclination of my wounded nature and a deliberate sin" (Autobiography, 1997:66-67). Frances turned to prayer for comfort, though she was restricted in the amount of time that she was permitted to allocate to prayer. When Father Leander departed from Nowe Miasto:

> I was faced by what I feared most. Daddy wanted to move to Warsaw where he rented an elegantly furnished apartment. I was to "come out" into society and make some acquaintances with possible marriage in view. Mamma tried explaining that I wasn't inclined to pursue this, and that, furthermore, I was frail and not in the best of health. I was seventeen then and it was high time for me to choose a state in life (p.79).

On the family's arrival in Warsaw, dancing and social outings became the norm for Frances. Letters were sent to Father Leander, advising him of her spiritual progress and the perceived effect on her soul, as a result of the expectations of having to "come out into society". Frances recounts her message to Father Leander sent in January 1860, "Writing about the accolades received from my dancing teacher and others, I hastened to confess my culpability, my vainglory ... I further indicated that I was no longer repelled by dancing and that I consider this to be an indication of my carnality" (Autobiography, 1997:88). She was disappointed with her behaviour, because she had begun to entertain thoughts of entering a religious order and her present lifestyle was a huge distraction.

Father Leander replied on 16 January 1860: "I do not know what to write, I have no desire to chastise you, yet I must do so since I find it hard to recognize you; you have changed so much for the worse. I see your soul as plainly as if on the palm of my hand. Your letters, especially the last two were most revealing, a true mirror of your soul. Do not be angry if I cite your own words by way of admonition" (ibid.). Ricciardi posits that perhaps the spiritual direction of Father Leander was more suited to an experienced religious, rather than someone just starting out on their spiritual journey (1971:24); for he believes the reaction of the priest was excessive. Frances oscillated between her strong desire to unite herself to Jesus in prayer and meditation, and her need to placate her father by acquiescing to his demands, which on occasion did hold some appeal for her. Finally, she had the fortitude to arrive at a decision that would in time have consequences for all the family:

> I was afraid of Daddy, of his powerful voice, of his very demeanor, his vehemence and his attitude in general, for at that time he was suffering deeply ... fortified by prayer and possibly Holy Communion ... I begged Daddy not to force me to enter society, since I am martyred by the very thought of such a possibility. I told him, that no one will force me into marriage ... After presenting many other arguments, I added this final one – should Daddy force me to enter society, I will run away from home and no one will find my hiding place in some convent. Daddy's reply was simply that he would rather see me in a coffin than as a nun (Autobiography, 1997:96-97).

Frances fasted and prayed, particularly when the quarrels and atmosphere at home with her father grew more and more intense. Her fragile health soon deteriorated, and she was directed by the doctors to seek a warmer climate: "The doctor advised Daddy to take me abroad for I was susceptible to tuberculosis. It was too late in the season to go to a health resort, so the doctor suggested Meran in the Tyrolean Alps. This was in keeping with Daddy's plan, who decided to take my brother to the Jesuit college in Metz. The two trips could be easily combined" (Autobiography, 1997:119). Consequently, all the family, Frances, her parents and Adam, together with a group of servants, set out "by carriage and train" (Burton, 1951:48-49) for Meran. Frances describes the journey:

> We had planned to stop in Czestochowa for one day and ask the Madonna to bless our journey. I was overjoyed! To be at Jasna Gora! The Blessed Lady was always my most beloved Mother. I owe her so much, in fact everything. I was baptized during the first vespers of her Presentation in the Temple; on the first May, the month dedicated to her honor, her son Jesus entered my heart for the first time. This loving Mother was always my salvation, my deliverance, my defense. My entire childhood was spent under her loving regard. Her picture always hung in my room (Autobiography, 1997:122-123].

Finally, the group arrived at their destination and Frances opted to go on long walks but even this exercise soon became a drain on her fragile health, and she was "confined to bed" with incipient pulmonary tuberculosis (Burton, 1851:50; Autobiography, 1997:128). The time spent abroad was lengthy. In all they were away from their homeland for five years, from 1860 - 1865 (Autobiography, 1997:126). Unfortunately, on the occasions when Frances was feeling much better, her mother became ill and this state of affairs became the norm – hence, when Frances was feeling reasonably well, the health of her mother deteriorated and vice versa. During the spring of 1861, after Adolph had returned to the family estate in Poland, and while Adam was away at school, Frances and Cecilia went to Interlaken (Burton, 1851:50) under medical advice. By 1862 Adolph was still in Poland. You may recall that at the beginning of this chapter, under the title "Historical Background", mention was made of Polish rebels rising against the Czar in the early 1860s, and that Adolph was one of the aristocrats who gave shelter to the insurgents. He also provided financial backing for the rebellion.

Both Cecilia and Frances worried about Adolph, particularly as they thought that Adam might be tempted to leave his College and enrol in the "army of insurgents" (Burton, 1951:52). The worry about her husband and son, resulted in Cecilia succumbing once more to serious illness, and Frances assumed the nursing duties of her mother, but then she became ill, and this set-back necessitated spending "the winter in bed" (ibid.). Following the failure of the rebellion, Adolph was under surveillance by the Russian government, however because of his influential friends he was able to avoid the most severe of punishments, though he was prohibited at the time from leaving Warsaw. Eventually, he was given permission to leave and join his family in Interlaken.

Soon Frances was once again experiencing reasonably good health, and so she "made a pilgrimage to the well-known sanctuary of our Lady of Hermits at Einsiedeln ... At the Shrine Frances implored Our Lady for light and direction regarding the congregation she hoped to join" (pp.51-52). At Einsiedeln she:

> found an excellent confessor, a Benedictine monk, a member of the famous abbey in the town ... The monk found that his penitent wanted to enter the religious life and encouraged her to enter the convent of the Benedictines in Einsiedeln. Frances though attracted to the life of prayer and meditation of the nuns, felt it was not the will of God for her. Frances said she would make no decision until she returned to Poland and saw Father Leander (Burton, 1951:54).

During that time Adam was sixteen and on holidays with the family. Unfortunately, he became seriously ill with pneumonia, and while he was recuperating the doctor recommended that the entire family again seek a more favourable climate. Therefore, a decision was made to go to the Riviera, and to spend some quality time at Cannes (p.55). This was a critical stage for Frances and her father, "It seems to me that we spent our third winter abroad in Cannes ... where I felt better physically for a ... [short time]. I attended church and performed all my spiritual exercises, something which I had to forgo during my illness" (Autobiography, 1997:151). As her father Adolph was still keen to acquire a suitable marriage for Frances, she decided that the time had arrived for him to be informed of her plans for the future: walking along the seashore with her father, Frances disclosed "her irrevocable resolution of total abandonment to God" (Strzałkowska, 1989:24). She thought her father would be angry, but "he sobbed ... In my heart I begged Jesus to comfort father whom I consoled by telling him that Jesus would give him joy when he will see me happy" (ibid).

Towards the end of their sojourn in Cannes, Frances had an attack of acute neuralgia, which left her in continuous pain, "I recall God's goodness to me, and this helped me to endure the pain for love of Jesus" (Autobiography, 1997:158). She was also receiving treatment for a malady of the spine. Cecilia too continued to suffer, and at times was thought to be near death, so though the health of mother and daughter continued to be a cause for serious concern, both women were preoccupied with saving the soul of Adolph, and prayed for his conversion (Autobiography, 1997:167-168). Incredibly and after many years of indifference and a loathing for the religion that seemed to "obsess" his wife and daughter, Adolph approached Frances on the Virgil of the Ascension in 1864, and asked her forgiveness saying that he was on his way to make his Confession. Frances's describes her reaction:

> I began kissing Daddy's hand, looked into his eyes and asked what, was the meaning of all this. Daddy said, "I am

going to confession; you have obtained this grace for me from our loving God. Now pray for me and believe me as I have had no faith heretofore, and having refused to give in to your pleas, now fully convinced and with unaffected faith, I desire to receive the sacraments." Daddy's eyes were red from crying; he was so humbly moved that we were able to find fitting words of gratitude for God's marvelous power so visibly acting in his soul (Autobiography, 1997:169).

Though Adolph had been involved in a serious discussion and argument, followed by capitulation regarding "eternal salvation" with Father Hube, a Resurrectionist priest (Burton, 1951:60), he credited the prayers of Frances and Cecilia for his conversion.

It was towards the end of 1865, following five years abroad, that Frances and Cecilia returned to the family's estate in Poland. Frances contacted Father Leander who was once again at the Capuchin monastery at Nowe Miasto. She had written to him while she was away, but he had refrained from contact not wanting to curtail her spiritual growth, which he believed was in the hands of Jesus. She informed him of her decision to become a religious, and that she was eager to embrace the life immediately, but Father Leander's advice to her was to be patient, and to wait for God to show her the way (Autobiography, 1997:175). There was a recurrence of the spinal disease and this necessitated specialist treatment in Warsaw for Frances, who on arrival at the city was confined to bed. She wondered how she could become a religious when her health was so unpredictable (Strzałkowska, 1989:26):

> God permitted my illness and I grew worse daily, confined to bed with a stomach ailment. Moreover, I was feverish and weakened by the past spinal-aperture treatments. Daddy had procured the best doctors, but their therapy was exhausting me more and more. Jesus was present to me in this time of physical suffering and I would spend sleepless nights in quiet prayer and meditation (Autobiography, 1997:176).

Meanwhile, there was some misunderstanding with Father Leander and a woman Mme Aszberger, whom Frances had befriended but who was relating gossip to Father Leander about his protégé. Unfortunately, Father Leander was initially inclined to believe this woman and he was quite harsh with Frances, reproaching her for her insincerity to him (Burton, 1951:63). Thankfully Father Leander soon realised he had been deceived and he apologised to Frances. However, he was soon transferred to another monastery, which was some distance away and he persuaded Frances to seek another confessor. Interestingly, there were three failed attempts at securing the services of a confessor, and Father Leader returned to the Siedliski household and advised Frances not to be anxious but to be patient, for God would see to her spiritual needs. In the interim the many medical treatments were failing to produce a positive result, so Adolph sought more doctors and advice in his efforts to cure his daughter of her worsening malaise. Frances writes that Adolph eventually agreed for her to try hydrotherapy – cold water therapy, and when this treatment was administered, there was an improvement in her condition and Frances and her family were soon able to leave Moscow and return to their country estate (Autobiography, 1997:181).

Father Leander was given permission to visit Frances every two weeks. He heard her confession, administered communion and guided her spiritually. Unfortunately, over the next few months her condition deteriorated, and she was near death. Frances recalls that her father "travelled all night to bring another doctor from Warsaw" (p.188). She kept calling for Father Leander, but he was either unable to be contacted or unavailable. Another Capuchin priest arrived, and though she was disappointed, she accepted his priestly ministrations (p.190).

Over the next few years, Frances's health continued to be unpredictable. She experienced various temptations that assail human nature when it is in a weakened condition, and this affected her inner spirituality (ibid.). Father Leander was a "constant" during this time, and it was his wise advice that gave Frances the strength to accept her human frailties and come to the realisation that her fragile health was always going to be a concern. He told her that regardless, she was still favoured by God and she should remain patient and wait for Him to reveal his divine will. For now, her interior voice was telling her, "The time has not yet come" (p.198).

It was in 1867 that her father "began to manifest the first symptoms of the illness which would lead him to the grave" (Ricciardi, 1971:70-71). Frances was concerned. Apparently, the illness lasted for about three years, but the cause was unknown. Adolph was sent to Dresden for treatment, but his condition worsened. She tried to bring her father pleasure by playing his favourite music on the piano. Though her love for both her parents didn't diminish, "she never departed from her resolve to consecrate herself to God ... [and] she remained with ... [her father] until his death" (p.72). Adolph died on 18 April 1870, and was subsequently buried from the family chapel, in the cemetery at their Żdżary estate.

Frances was keen to start a life committed to Jesus, but she followed the advice of Father Leander to be patient and to wait for a sign. Her father's unsigned will stipulated that she was to receive her share of the estate on her marriage, and that Adam her brother, who worked the estate, was to draw on the capital. Frances tells us that following the death of her father, she and her mother "led a life of prayer and dedication to the corporal works of mercy. We embroidered Church vestments and sewed linens; mamma was especially dedicated to visiting the sick in the village" (Autobiography, 1997:210). Father Leander continued to celebrate Mass in the family home, and though Frances and her mother had both been admitted as Franciscan tertiaries (third order) during their time abroad, this commitment did not satisfy the yearning Frances experienced to fully consecrate her life to God.

She spent the following few years in prayer and solitude, preparing for the time when she would be able to renounce the world and live her dream of a life committed to religion (p.211). In 1872, her health suffered another setback and Frances was brought to the brink of death. She received the last rites from the local pastor, for Father Leander had been delayed and when he arrived, he spent the night in prayer, as her funeral arrangements were being organised. Miraculously, following the celebration of Mass and the reception of the Eucharist and the many, many prayers of her family and supporters, Frances began to respond to treatment and her condition showed a marked improvement.

During the following twelve months Frances experienced dreams where she was dressed in a religious habit. She shared these dreams with Father Leander, and when she was thirty-one years old, he wrote in a letter to her, "I want you to become a religious" (Ricciardi, 1971:77-78). On 8th March 1873, the "vigil of the feast of St. Frances of Rome, patroness and protectress of Frania, Father Leander came to hear her confession" (p.78), after which he told her that the Lord had revealed to another his love for her. She was encouraged by this for she believed that she was already a bride of Christ.

Now Father Lander was also a spiritual director, to a "Maria Wojewodzka, who with several other wellborn women of the city [Lublin] had formed a pious association" (Burton, 1851:69) and lived as Franciscan tertiaries. They were wealthy women, who wanted to leave their fortunes to the founding of a new congregation in honour of Our Lady, but they were no longer young, and felt that the mission of a new foundation was to be the responsibility of another. They confided in Father Leander, who sought counsel from others particularly a Brother, Stephen Rembiszewski (ibid.) who had a vision of a Mlle Kobylanska in which she stated that she had left her fortune "to the founding of a new congregation to be dedicated to Our Lady ... [and that he was to] Let Father Leander know it is to be used for this purpose. And tell him it is the will of God that Frances Siedliska head this undertaking. "

When Father Leander informed Frances that it was God's will that she found a new religious congregation, her initial response was: "Full of uncertainty and fear, I took my crucifix into my hands and implored Jesus to give me strength to fulfil his will. After a long time spent in prayer, I suddenly felt enlightenment and courage" (Strzałkowska, 1989:26). She then participated in an "intense spiritual retreat" organised by Father Leander, as part of her preparation for the religious life that awaited. This retreat was in the form of a novitiate complete with the "rigid practices" associated with training in formation. You may recall that in the early paragraphs I referred to my own novitiate training. During those two years there was a grounding in theology and scripture, associated with prayer and meditation. Speaking aloud, contact with others and leaving the enclosure were "frowned upon". However, Frances didn't have the luxury of two years of formation and her spiritual preparation was condensed to a month of intense training under Father Leander's guidance and direction. Burton tell us that it was "On 2 July 1873 [the] Feast of the visitation of the Blessed Virgin Mary [that] Frances Siedliska took the three vows of religion [poverty, chastity and obedience] in the Church of the Canonesses in Warsaw" (1951:78).

Frances began to consider the type of order she wanted to establish. There were communities – "monasteries of Benedictine and Franciscan nuns, devoted to contemplation only and [that] had strict enclosures", but she believed that her foundation should offer more than a life of prayer; hence she was considering a community of nuns who would be involved in a life of both contemplation and action, for "a life of prayer must be united [to] a catechetical apostolate for children and a program of assistance for the poor, the abandoned, and the aged" (Ricciardi, 1971:94). Shortly after her profession Frances and her mother travelled to Lublin where there were two tertiaries belonging to the order of Our lady of Loreto. The tertiaries Mme. Załoziecka and Mme. Nęcińska, welcomed Frances as a "new recruit and offered to turn over their entire work to Frances, as well as give her the management of their fortunes" (Burton, 1951:78). Cecilia Siedliska was keen to join her daughter's community, and "With Father Leander's approval, she ... made a private vow and was given the name in religion of Mary Rosalia" (ibid.).

The "political and religious" situation in Poland was deteriorating, and Ricciardi (1971:97) posits that as "Lublin was at the very center of Russian control", religious persecution was becoming the norm. Hence Frances and her small community decided to sell the house at Lublin, and in the interim, while deciding on a suitable country in which to establish a foundation they elected to move to the Siedliski estate at Żdżary. Father Leander was happy with this decision as he was again living at Nowe Miasto, which was situated just a few kilometers from the estate and hence he would be on hand to give spiritual direction to the group when required.

Frances believed that it was important to obtain "official recognition" from the Church for the foundation she was keen to establish. She knew that if she had the "assent and blessing" of Pope Pius IX, then this would be a sign from God that it was His will the foundation should go proceed (ibid.). "[T]he foundation was to be modelled on the hidden life at Nazareth; characterized by simplicity and solitude in God, [and] ... centered in some way about the blessed Sacrament; and ... consecrated to God in a spirit of reparation for outrages committed against him" (Burton, 1951:79). Frances left her mother with Załoziecka at Żdżary and went with Nęcińska to Rome to seek an audience with the Pope. However, Nęcińska was a fair age and the journey exhausted her, and so she decided on an immediate return to the estate leaving Frances alone to seek an audience with the pontiff (ibid.).

Fortunately, Frances met Father Laurençot, a French Jesuit who became her confessor and who drafted a petition in French, "which was to be signed by Siedliska and [then] presented to the Pope" (Ricciardi, 1971:97). Part of the petition reads:

> Frances Siedliski ... approaches with confidence to place before the fatherly heart of your Holiness the plan which she has devised to found a new Congregation, that of Loreto, in honor of, and under the protection of the most holy and immaculate Virgin Mary, with the purpose of

praying, working, suffering and giving itself entirely for the supreme Pontiff and the Holy Catholic Church, attempting in its hidden way of life to retrace all the virtues of the Holy Family of Nazareth. Most Holy Father, in anticipation that the rules and constitutions of the said Sisters of Loreto may be presented for examination and sanction by the Holy see, the aforesaid Frances de Siedliska, devoutly prostrate at your feet, begs in all humility that Your Holiness deign to encourage her in her holy plan with your apostolic blessing (ibid.)

The full account of the [above] *"precious document is preserved in the General Archives of the Sisters of* [the Holy Family of] *Nazareth, Rome* [italics added], (p.98).

"Approval was given for the New Foundation on 1 October 1873" (Strzałkowska, 1989:29; Ricciardi, 1971:98; Burton, 1951:81). In a Papal audience on 2 October 1873, Frances was able to thank the Holy Father for his acceptance of her new Congregation, which Burton (ibid.) maintains was then referred to as the "Sisters of Loreto" in accordance with the description in the above petition. Frances now had a dilemma on the location for the establishment of her congregation. The city of Rome was appealing but did not seem to be a practical option at this time, and Poland was a non-starter as it was still under the control of Russia.

Father Laurençot her French Confessor, suggested to Frances that she consider Lyons in France as "many Polish families had emigrated" (Ricciardi, 1971:98) to that country. He also recommended that she meet a Father Gautrelet in Lyons. This priest was the Provincial Superior for the Society of Jesus in France, and had some years previously, "founded a community of perpetual adorers of the Blessed Sacrament at Fourvières and ... [so he] would [be able to give] advice [to Frances] regarding her own plans" (Burton, 1951:81). Unfortunately, the fledgling order in France lacked funds, and depended on "God's providence" for survival.

The wealth of the Siedliski family would have been enticing and perhaps a huge factor, and an important consideration in the sisters wanting to meet Mother Frances, whom they were keen to have join their order and assume the role of leadership (ibid.) of their congregation.

Frances was reluctant and believed that this was not the path God wanted her to follow. She prayed for guidance, and in the meantime suffered a relapse "of the spinal disease" (Burton, 1951:82) which you may recall she had suffered some time before, and it had almost been fatal. Ricciardi (1971:99) writes that "Scarcely had word of her illness arrived at Żdżary ... [then] her brother Adam came to Lyons with a letter from Father Leander who ordered her to return at once" to the family estate, where she remained for the following year recovering her health and once again contemplating options for the location of her foundation. Unfortunately, the persecution of the Catholic Poles began in earnest and with the authorities watching his movements, Father Leander counselled Frances to leave Poland, and advised her that it would probably be a worthwhile initiative, to establish her congregation in Paris. Then, with the growing unrest, Frances and her nuns left Poland and went to Paris as did Father Leander who had been "threatened with arrest ... by the Russian Government" (Burton, 1951:82-83).

Father Leander arrived in Paris with Brother Stephen in June 1874 (ibid.). However, Mother Frances did not believe that the mission of her order was to dedicate themselves to the Polish families in Paris at this time, so she decided to go on a pilgrimage to Lourdes, to pray and seek God's will regarding her foundation. "Her visit to Lourdes and her fervent prayers at the Marian sanctuary convinced her that ... [her Congregation] was to be established in Rome" (Strzałkowska, 1989:31). Consequently, it was around November 1874 that "the little community accompanied by the two Capuchin exiles [Father Leander and Brother Stephen] arrived in Rome" (Ricciardi, 1971:101). Various places of residences for the Congregation are noted in the eternal city, with the frequent change of residence being due to the unsuitability of the buildings and/or environs in regard to the Sisters' health: for example, some of the buildings rented out to them were in need of repairs; other buildings had poor heating, or too much moisture; or were built on unhealthy sites; and often had rooms that were too small and did not have enough ventilation.

Strzałkowska maintains that Mother Mary recognised the "First Sunday of Advent 1875", as the official date for the actual founding of the Congregation (1989:32). A few months before this Cecilia Siedliska who was now a member of the Order, became quite ill, and Frances decided to accompany her mother and two elderly companions (Lublin Tertiaries) back to Poland. "Cecilia had to be placed in a nursing home at Kowanówek where she remained until her death" on 5 September 1899 (Ricciardi, 1971:103/443). Strzałkowska writes that during the early years "Mother wrote in her personal journal, 'The beginnings of this great work were very difficult and full of crosses, especially since the first superior was constantly ill' ... That first superior, [being] Mother Mary [herself], however she did not lose heart nor courage but with great patience guided her congregation" (p.32). Unfortunately, her fragile health was still (and would always be) an issue, but she was determined to overcome her human frailties, and oversee the growth of her fledging Congregation.

Burton (1951:89) asserts that it was in December 1877, that Mother Frances secured a second audience with Pope Pius IX and presented her then community of eight sisters with a request "to change their name to that of the Congregation of the Sisters of the Holy Family of Nazareth." In her diary she wrote: "Our aim ... is to procure the greatest glory of God by contemplating and imitating the hidden life of the Holy Family of Nazareth and by living in a spirit of prayer and sacrifice for the Church ... The Lord has chosen us, and we must serve Him" (ibid.). If you recall, in the petition presented to Pope Pius IX and approved on 1 October 1873, the Congregation was referred to as that of "Loreto, in honor of, and under the protection of the most holy and immaculate Virgin Mary", with reference to "the virtues of the Holy Family of Nazareth" (Ricciardi, 1971:97).

The Pope approved the name change and the title "the Congregation of the Sisters of the Holy Family of Nazareth" was officially adopted. The first clothing ceremony was held at Christmas 1877, when the three Lubowidzki sisters were given the names: Michael, Gabriel and Raphael (Burton, 1951:90-91). When I (the author of this book) first received the habit many years ago, I was told that Mother Foundress based the design of the habit on the clothing worn by the Pontiff at the time; for example at the clothing ceremony for the sisters, the habit consisted of a long black cassock, with a cape of the same colour falling to the waist and buttons down the centre of the habit and cape. The novices covered their heads and shoulders with a white veil, whereas though Frances was dressed in a similar habit and cape, her veil was black (ibid.).

Interestingly, on the occasion of the clothing ceremony of the Lubowidzki sisters, their young cousin Thecla Lubowidzka, entered the postulancy. In later years Thecla (as Mother Laureta) "succeeded Mother Mary as superior general of the order," (Strzałkowska, 1989:33). Ricciardi states that Father Leander presided over the clothing ceremony and that it "had been preceded by intense spiritual preparation" (1971:115). The novices Wanda, Laura and Felicia Lubowidzki were given the names Michael, Gabriel and Raphael in gratitude "to the three Archangels who in 1873 ... had promised their protection and guardianship over the new community" (p.112).

Pope Pius IX died on 7 February 1878, and Mother Frances, always keen to keep the leader of the Church informed about the current progress of her foundation, sought an audience with the newly elected Pope Leo XIII. In her diary on 10 June 1878 she wrote:

> Today at noon we were all received in audience by the Holy Father ... [who] asked whence we had come, what is the purpose of our community, and whether we already

had Constitutions, and whether that little person kneeling before him might be the Foundress. To my affirmative reply he placed his hand on my shoulder and said that he gives me a very special blessing, and then blessed our entire Congregation. He moreover gave his blessing on the compiling of the Constitutions and repeated several times: If it is pleasing to God this work will prosper; pray, pray much for us (Ricciardi, 1971:115).

With the Congregation firmly established in Rome, Mother Frances was motivated to establish the sisters in as many cities as numbers, finances and her ailing health would allow. Several foundations followed and "in 1881, [after some initial set-backs] the first Nazareth home was established at Cracow in Poland" (Strzałkowska, 1989:34). Then there was the opening of a convent in Lemberg, a second one in Cracow in 1892 (when growing numbers necessitated a bigger house), and the opening of a home in Wadowice in 1894. Strzałkowska records that "In Cracow the sisters taught catechism not only to Catholic children but also to neophytes, schismatics and Protestants." Poverty was prevalent in the community at Wadowice. Mother Foundress sent Mother Laureta to oversee the opening of the home for the poor children. She wrote of the experience of her much-loved daughter: "Laureta begins penniless, hence, all hope rests on divine Providence, and the home will be named Divine Providence" (ibid.). Mother Mary found that when she returned from some of her absences from Rome (for example after her first trip to Cracow in 1881), the Sisters had been forced to seek alternative accommodation for reasons mentioned in earlier paragraphs, "this time [they had moved] to a good location a house which ... was small but airy and full of light" (Burton, 1951:101).

It was around the early 1880s, that Mother Mary prayed at the Holy Chapel at Loreto (a place where she went often to pray), for a counsellor who would be reliable and offer sound advice to her and the Congregation. Her experiences with some of the priest advisers had thus far not been successful, due to several priests having their own personal agenda. Some were founders of orders and they tried to encourage Mother Mary to unite her fledging community with their own foundations. Ricciardi (1971:129-130) cites one example: "Father Semenenko persisted in his notion of attracting the Nazareth Sisters into the ambit of his projected foundation of Resurrectionist Sisters [and] Father Feliński, an enthusiast of Mother Marcellina Darowska's new foundation, was warmly recommending and favoring the fusion of the Sisters of the Holy Family of Nazareth with the Sisters of the immaculate Conception"; however Mother Mary knew that linking up with another community, was not in God's plan for her. Fortuitously, in 1883 she "made the acquaintance of one who seemed to be sent by Providence – Father Anthony Lechert, Procurator General of the Resurrection Fathers" (p.105).

Father Lechert was appointed confessor to the community, and this was "confirmed on January 8th, 1884" (Ricciardi, 1971:147). He was officially their spiritual guide. Interestingly, as a new community the sisters, including Mother Frances, had made private religious vows which meant that the full observance of canonical norms had not been followed. This was permissible initially for new congregations, however in due course the situation needed to be rectified. Therefore, "Among the first benefits procured for the Congregation by Father Lechert was its juridical regularization in the eyes of the Church" (p.165):

> Father Lechert saw to it that the Sisters of Nazareth would be given a firm juridical basis and began with the regular and canonical profession of its members who had previously made private vows. Having been delegated by the Cardinal Vicar of Rome, Father Lechert received in official and solemn manner the vows of the Foundress and her first companions on May 1st, 1884, the anniversary of the first communion of Mother Siedliska. On that occasion the Sisters assumed new names along with a "mystery," or title. Mother Siedliska was henceforth known as Mary of Jesus the Good Shepherd (p.166-167).

Father Lechert's friendship and respect for Mother Mary lasted throughout her lifetime and was remembered and extolled by him in the days preceding his death in 1921 (Strzałkowska, 1989:38-39).

Until this time, the houses in Rome had been rented and now with the growing numbers of young women entering the community, Mother Mary sought more permanent accommodation. According to Burton (1951:106), she "bought a freehold estate on Via Machiavelli on the Esquiline, which is one of the seven hills of Rome." The grounds were spacious, and though extensive repairs were needed, the site was ideal for it was large enough to be both "the Mother house and the novitiate" (ibid.). Burton tells us that it was "16 January 1884 that the sisters moved into their new home on Via Machiavelli" (ibid.), which Strzałkowska writes was dedicated to Jesus the Good Shepherd: "The first permanently established home of the congregation in Rome was placed under the protection of the Good Shepherd. The Good Shepherd [the chosen mystery of Mother Mary] is a symbol of God's inexhaustible mercy and reveals the deepest meaning of what it is to be a Christian, the highest form of love in action" (1989:45).

While establishing foundations in Rome and Cracow, Mother Mary was conscious of the constant fragility of her health. Burton maintains that there was "talk of establishing houses in other cities [remember the foundations at Lemberg and Wadowice were discussed in a previous paragraph] and countries, even in the New World" (1951:111). Unfortunately, on the advice of doctors she was required to leave Rome for a time, to seek a more suitable climate in which to regain her strength and well-being. Mother Mary realised that her continuing ill health could be a hindrance to the development of the Congregation, and she accepted that with continued growth, more formal processes of Canon Law needed to be followed. Thus, she became resigned to the fact that her time as Superior General was drawing to a close:

> I gave foundation to our Congregation and have done all of which I have been capable, notwithstanding my

miserableness. At this present moment, I believe that I have completed my mission of giving life to the Congregation, and it seems opportune that I resign as your superior, no longer having right to that office. Therefore, I ask you to proceed to the election of a new superior (Mother Gabriel's chronicle, cited in Ricciardi, 1971:171).

Following the submission of the resignation of Mother Mary as Superior General, a spiritual retreat was organised from 25 November to 5 December 1884, and "free" elections were held on the final day which was 5th December. Mother Frances was unanimously elected Superior General at this meeting (Burton, 1951:111), a position she accepted humbly while reminding her sisters that she was but a handmaid of the Lord whose purpose was to do his will. Over the ensuing years she retained the position of Superior General of the Congregation "being elected and re-elected … [to the position] in the respective General Chapters of 1895 and 1899" (Ricciardi, 1971:416). Mother Mary of Jesus the Good Shepherd, after a brief illness lasting a few weeks, and after a lifetime of poor health and considerable suffering, died on 21 November 1902 at the age of 60 on the Feast of the Presentation of the Blessed Virgin Mary. She was beatified on 23rd April 1989, by Pope St John Paul II. Her feast day is celebrated on 21 November.

Leadership as Service

It was essential to Mother Mary that "her Nazareth would catechize, conduct retreats, teach and guide children and youth, prepare women for the sacrament of matrimony, and care for the ill and neglected. Such ministries permitted the members of the congregation to serve God and … [humankind] in various political and social situations" (Strzałkowska, 1989:38). Hence though foundress and Superior General of her order Mother Mary lived her life in humility and in service to others. Her wise guidance "grew" a community of nuns who became custodians of her legacy for future generations to continue to serve and emulate the spirit of the Holy Family of Nazareth.

Wisdom has built her house, she has hewn her seven pillars (Proverbs 9:1, cited in Sipe & Frick, 2015:4). For the purpose of this analysis, the "Seven Pillars of Servant Leadership" (see Appendix A for the list of attributes) are outlined below, and the discussion on each pillar includes aspects of the life and leadership practices of Blessed Frances Siedliska.

Pillar 1 – "Person of Character"

Mother Mary was of noble birth – privileged and wealthy, and yet she sought a life of poverty and self-discipline. She was humble but firm, respectful and determined in her approach to the way she led her Congregation. According to Sister Augustine: "Mother was always and everywhere with us: in the chapel for all our religious exercises, in the dining room, washing dishes, and at recreation. Very often she labored until very late at night. Despite her great weakness, she rose at the same time as the other sisters so that she could participate in community life. Although overburdened with work, she found time for all this because she knew how praying and working together united the sisters with God and each other" (cited in Strzałkowska, 1989:44). Before everything else she was a mother who wanted the best for her daughters, and for her "the best" was that they love and serve God in the spirit of the Holy Family of Nazareth.

Throughout her faith journey, Mother Mary was the recipient of spiritual advice from several priest directors, and one in particular – Father Anthony Lechert who was "elected director of the Work of Nazareth and as such was confirmed by the Cardinal Vicar of Rome and entrusted with the duties of Ecclesiastical Deputy" (Ricciardi, 1971:156). There was an occasion when Father Lechert inadvertently caused some heartache for the Foundress, who stood by him and acted with integrity throughout the painful experience (see Pillar IV – "Compassionate

Collaborator"). Lechert in turn was impressed with the sanctity and impressive leadership skills displayed by the wise foundress. This is noted in the testimony for the cause of the beatification of Mother Mary given by Mother Joseph-Theresa Tyszkiewicz who observed the following:

> Before my very eyes I was witness to an undoubted proof of the sancity {sic} of Mother Foundress; it was her blind and unlimited obedience, as well as her total submission to the decisions of Father Lechert whom she regarded as God's gift in the assistance and guidance of a divine work as difficult as the foundation of a religious Congregation. She was not merely obedient to him, but in her profound humility she made herself nothing; she, as it were, vanished. Their rapport was always unstudied and had a prudent reserve about it which made me often think of the relationship which must exist among the angels (cited in Ricciardi, 1971:176).

Strzałkowska (1989:38-39) endorses these comments: "Mother benefited very much from the advice Father Lechert gave her, and although she was humble and obedient, much can be attributed to her initiative as Father Lechert stated to the sisters providing nursing care for him a few days before his death in 1921, 'Remember, Sisters, that everything you have in the congregation you owe to your mother.'" Mother Mary encouraged when it was needed. She guided and trained her daughters; she raised the bar for those in leadership positions by always being available to offer advice. She shared her vision as she led her daughters to value themselves and others. As Superior General of the Order, she wrote prolific letters to the nuns in Europe and the United States, always engaging in positive conversation while encouraging the Sisters in their ongoing formation. She expected certain standards of her Nazareth family members and was ever ready to teach them the way to holiness and truth emphasising strict adherence to the Rule and not being tempted to surrender to a mediocre spiritual life.

Her extreme fragile physical health and the huge distances between the initial foundations in Europe and the United States, didn't seem to restrict Mother Mary's constant desire to watch over her daughters. She travelled constantly back and forth to the various foundations. In 1885, there was a request to Father Lechert from a Father Vincent Barzyński a Resurrectionist priest in Chicago, who was asking for nuns to staff the orphanages and schools, but as the numbers entering the Congregation were still low, Mother Mary after giving the matter considerable thought and seeking ecclesiastical advice, opted to go herself on this, her first voyage to the United States. There were occasions when she could be broadminded and flexible, and when a proposed foundation in Paris necessitated that the sisters not wear their habits, she didn't hesitate, for to her saving souls was more important than the wearing of a habit; so she suggested that the sisters "wear secular attire during their work away from the convent" (Strzałkowska, 1989:37).

Mother Mary was charismatic, talented, empathetic and generous. She was ever ready to assist those in need. She shared her many talents while serving her vision of a united Holy Family. Father William Van Rossum (a Redemptorist) was Mother Mary's Confessor in the early days before he became Cardinal. Van Rossum was very effusive in his description of the gifts which the foundress had shared with her biological and spiritual families and emphasised that:

> In nature she was very well endowed by Providence. To great gifts of mind, she united great qualities of heart. She had a love of the sciences, of the fine arts, of literature, of poetry, of music. She loved the beauties of nature and, above all, flowers which uplifted her to God and spoke to her of His perfections and of His beauty. She had a great heart, noble, generous, full of goodness and of great compassion for those in poverty and misery, particularly, spiritual misery; she was also rich in tenderness and in gratitude. All these good qualities were perfected by a holy

formation and magnified by perfect innocence of life, of grace and of virtue (cited in Ricciardi, 1971:328).

Apparently, Van Rossum was not the only confessor during this time and more prominence seems to be given to "the role of Blessed Father Hyacinth Cormier, Dominican", who had ten years of association with the Congregation and spoke highly of Mother Mary some years after her death: "The sisters had had a holy and virtuous foundress" (Ricciardi, 1971:396; Personal Correspondence, 2019). Sister Antoinette Kalicka's testimony reveals the high regard in which Mother Mary was held by the Sisters: "She had great natural and intellectual gifts; she possessed many attractive aspects in her exterior; she had a profound intelligence and a generous spirit. It is no wonder that she was irresistible, and that she drew all to herself, and that we loved her without measure" (cited in Ricciardi, 1971:326-327). The sisters rejoiced in these "natural gifts" of Mother Mary. Sister Eugènie Roy praised her God-given talents:

> Very well instructed ... she could engage herself on all questions of science and literature ... I recall several French priests who, after a conversation [they] had with her, said to us: "Truly, your Mother General is not only a saint, but also a person of extraordinary capacities." In reality she was admirable endowed in every way. She excelled as well in the fine arts, in embroidery, in music, and so on ... God had crowned her with very rich gifts of nature (ibid.).

Because of her exceptional and outstanding qualities, much can be said about the personality of Mother Frances. You may recall that mention was made earlier in the chapter that as a child and young adult she did have her faults and possessed a "quick temper"; however, this intense expression of emotions was somewhat suppressed during her years as a religious, for she was able to channel her energy and passion into developing her spiritual awareness. Strzałkowska (1989:42) writes that Mother Mary was, "By nature ... headstrong but knew how to control herself much to the admiration of her sisters." You may remember that for some years prior to establishing the Order Frances Siedliska had virtually lived the life of a nun. In fact, when Frances and her mother had their extended stay abroad both became Franciscan Tertiaries. Burton (1951:66) maintains that at that time, by becoming a member a Third Order of a religious community "Frances felt that was close to being a nun."

We have read that Adolph Siedliski was initially opposed to his daughter entering the religious life for he hoped that one day she would marry well and live on the family estate. However, he eventually accepted her decision to seek prayer and solitude, and though a nominal Catholic during his lifetime he was converted back to the faith prior to his death. When her father died, Frances did not immediately seek admittance to a religious community. She prayed and waited for direction from her then spiritual adviser Father Leander who advised her to wait until her continuing ill-health showed improvement. Nevertheless, he assured her of his continued prayers and guidance. Hence, Frances and her mother Cecilia "remained at Żdżary and Adam took over the business ... [while mother and daughter] "devoted themselves to prayer and good works, to visiting the sick and the poor and to making vestment for neglected churches" (ibid.).

Pillar II – "Puts People First"

Charity was a virtue that Mother Mary lived and promoted her entire life. On her deathbed it is reported that she spoke and uttered the words "Charity, my sisters, charity…" Strzałkowska (1989:63) maintains that the foundress uttered the word charity in "several languages: miłość, love, amour, liebe, and carità." Burton's interpretation differs slightly, suggesting that the words "'*Charité, charité*,' [were said] first in French and then in Italian, and finally in Polish – '*Milosci, milosci*'" (1951:195). Regardless of the order or the language what is important is the emphasis on "charity" for Mother Mary believed that for true sisters of

Nazareth, "Charity must reign" (Strzałkowska, ibid.), and this was her final message to her beloved daughters.

Love of God and love of neighbour formed the *Credo* for the Congregation. Mother Mary lived this code in her daily life and works. According to Strzałkowska (1989:43-44): "Mother was especially solicitous about the sisters who were ill and sometimes served them and cared for them. Occasionally she kept an all-night vigil at the bedside of a sister who was ill. She often repeated that for the welfare of the sick she would gladly give the last cent from the savings of the convent, and they were frequently in need of these savings." And on 19 August 1879, when she was in Lyons France, she wrote to Mother Raphael and the sisters in Rome and instructed them to: "Take care of your health... rise at a later hour when it is hot... I give you permission for everything that is needed for your physical wellbeing. Enjoy the fresh air... In the evening you may eat some meat or an egg... I do not, however, dispense you from loving Jesus more and more" (ibid.). She nurtured her daughters with love, mercy and compassion, but was firm in her attitude to their spiritual formation.

Mother Mary was happy serving others. Burton (1951:101) writes that she and "the other Sisters worked with her daughters at all tasks of the house – making beds, sweeping, cleaning the rooms, cooking." This was love in action. "Mother Laureta testified at the beatification process that 'Mother took advantage of every occasion to concern herself with the good of her neighbor in order to gain souls for God'. Hence hoping to emphasize this to the novices, Mother wrote to them [from Cracow] on 31 October 1886: 'One cannot have true love for Jesus if one does not love his [her] neighbor'" (Strzałkowska, 1989:55):

> My very dear Sisters and daughters in Jesus Christ I want to write a few words to you, to send you the blessing of Jesus Christ, to embrace you in His love, and to inform you that, thanks to Him, I have arrived here safely. Moreover, I have trust in God and hope that all will work unto His greater

glory. And you, my dear daughters, how are you? I very often think about you and pray for you, asking the Lord that He might grant you to live in peace and union with Him ... Do not fail, my daughters, to nurture within yourselves the love of Jesus Christ. All that you do, do for Him. Reflect well whether your actions and thoughts conform to His holy will, and whether they give Him pleasure and consolation. And, my daughters, insofar as one cannot love Jesus Christ unless one loves one's neighbor, beg our Lord to grant you this mutual and reciprocal charity, gift of true union with God ... Put up with one another's defects and faults and help one another... (cited in Ricciardi, 1971:209).

Strzałkowska (1989:47) quotes Sister Eugenia: "Like the good Shepherd, she especially loved the souls of sinners. Once she accepted into the convent on probation a person who was condemned by the public, but who wished to return to the right path of living and who requested admission to the congregation" and so she sent this person to one of the convents and wrote to the Superior Mother Michael on 29 December 1884: "This soul whom Jesus is lifting up from the abyss of afflictions, could learn to love Him exceedingly and wants to sanctify herself. We must give her a helping hand" (ibid.). Mother Mary reached out to those in need with compassion and love.

It is mentioned in a previous paragraph that Father Lechert informed Mother Mary in 1885, that he had received communication from Father Vincent Barzyński a Resurrectionist priest in Chicago, requesting that the congregation send some Sisters to care for and teach poor Polish children from the orphanage and in the parish schools, but Mother Mary was somewhat reluctant to respond as the Congregation was just ten years old and the numbers entering were still low. According to Ricciardi:

> The Servant of God was at first somewhat timid because the community was still small and unprepared for the missions, but afterwards, following the counsel of

Cardinal Parocchi, Vicar of Rome; of Cardinal Simeoni, Prefect of the Sacred Congregation for the Propagation of the Faith; and of Cardinal Ledóchowski, one of the curial Cardinals, she accepted the invitation and herself left with ten Sisters in 1885 (1971:182).

Mother Mary was keen for the Congregation to experience expansion, and regardless of the ill-health that was a continuing concern and prevented her from visiting her European foundations as much as she would have liked, and even though her presence as Superior General was needed in Rome and Cracow, she decided to undertake the long voyage to the United States, appointing suitable replacements to the positions of superiors to ensure that all progressed smoothly in the various European communities during her absence. Burton (1851) writes that letters were left for the heads of the European houses, and these contained statements "of her own experiences as Superior", and how she would deal with "unexpected" problems. "'Study Charity,' she wrote ... It is imperative that in the person of their Superior the Sisters see God, His spirit and His works. Truthfulness, constant work, humility, straightforwardness and, above all, charity must distinguish a Sister of the Holy Family of Nazareth" (pp.114-115).

Consequently, on 13 June 1885, she sought for and obtained an audience with Pope Leo XIII, to receive his Apostolic Blessing before departing with her small group of missionaries for the United States. The travellers left Rome on 17 June and arrived in New York on their way to Chicago on 4 July 1885 (ibid.). This was the beginning of the American foundations.

Pillar III – "Skilled Communicator"

Wherever she was in the world Mother Mary was always conscious of what was happening in her convents. As mentioned previously, she was a prolific letter writer and if a situation warranted her presence regardless of her fragile physical condition, she made every effort to travel to the location of concern to check and see that her daughters were following the rule and that they were living according to the spirit of the Holy Family – a life of charity – of love for those they served. According to Strzałkowska (1989:63), her emphasis was always upon charity: "Charity, my sisters, charity ...The Incarnate Word came forth from Nazareth. Love went out into the world. And so, in us daughters of the holy Family, charity must reign; otherwise, we will never be true daughters of the Holy Family."

This important virtue was also the one that guided Mother Mary throughout her life and to her Congregation she bequeathed, "Her will [which] was her entire life, the Rule, her instructions, her letters, and her last conference to the sisters during which she spoke of her favorite subject, reciprocal charity" (ibid.) showing kindness and empathy to all – giving and accepting feedback. "Thanks to the good and wise advice of the ecclesiastical authorities she undertook to expand the influence and labors of the Congregation" (Ricciardi, 1971:188). Since her foundation in the United States in 1885, she realised that she needed to keep her finger on the pulse as it were, at all her convents, whether in Poland, Rome or America. She did not want her sisters to succumb to temptation, and to be women of the world who desired material things, she wanted them to be women of Christ – who were always keen to develop their spirituality as they went about their daily tasks. She took her duties of motherhood to her daughters very seriously, regardless of the city or country of their location.

Ricciardi maintains that Mother Mary had some serious concerns "about the Sisters in America, for she realised that the active life presented dangers; moreover, the relative prosperity [in that country] had its own way of cooling the fervor of spirit which had been nurtured in the Roman Nazareth" (1971:189). Nevertheless, she was wise in her advice to her daughters which was not to fear anything when the love of God is there to guide their actions which should mirror those of their divine teacher – love and compassion for all and a profound awareness of self and others.

There are numerous testimonials from witnesses who gave evidence at the process for the beatification of Mother Mary (Ricciardi, 1971). Because she wanted to have the novices trained in charity and love for the Congregation and its rule, when she returned from her first trip to America in 1885: "she took upon herself the demanding task of mistress of novices" (Ricciardi, 1971:189). Even though at this time she was Superior General of the Congregation, she mentored and nurtured her charges and when separated from them, due to her administrative duties she worried about their spiritual progress. This was because she was committed to their ongoing spiritual formation. She also wanted to ensure that they did not have the distractions that might be experienced when associating with other members of the community, so as novice mistress she organised for the novitiate to be located:

> on the second floor; [and] only the novices and I sleep there. A grating separates us from the rest of the house. We are totally enclosed, and no one can enter. Our recreation is apart. The older Sisters are alone, and I go there now and again to see them. The novices are learning their catechism, sacred history, and a daily lesson in the rule. They are truly good, docile, and filled with faith. I hope that the Lord will lead them along the way of His perfection, and that, with His sacred grace, they may correspond to His love (cited in Ricciardi, 1971:194).

Mother Mary showed great initiative by separating her novices from the distractions that can be found when mixing with the general community during the time of their novitiate. Her commitment to the growth of her sisters, was not just limited to the novices but to all the sisters in the Congregation, and this sense of responsibility resulted in her copious letter writing, and effective communication with all her convents in Europe and the United States – and this kept her informed and aware of issues when they arose; of successes when they were achieved, and milestones when they were reached. A decision was also made to organise for the American postulants to be brought to Rome and the "Motherhouse for their training in order to find [and ensure] the true spirit of the Congregation" (Burton, 1951:126). "At the same time under the guidance of Father Lechert ... [Mother Mary] dedicated herself to the arduous task of writing the Constitutions and the Rule" (Ricciardi, 1971:189).

In November 1887, when the strain of combining all her responsibilities became too onerous, Mother Mary reluctantly relinquished her much-loved position as novice mistress, appointing Mother Gabriel Lubowidzka to the position. However, she did in fact and for a time, assume the position of acting novice mistress during the following summer, when Mother Gabriel had taken leave for health reasons. As mentioned, it was a position in which Mother Mary rejoiced for she related well to the novices and was keen to ensure that their training was of the highest order, and that they were committed to the rule and spirit of the Holy Family of Nazareth. Sister Augustine writes of this time in the novitiate when Mother Mary was Acting Novice Mistress during the absence of Mother Gabriel: "Really, there was no unhappiness about entering the convent when one had a Mother so good and tender. During the winter she was concerned that we have sufficiently warm clothing. One time she gave me her own habit. The year of my novitiate has remained in my heart as a beautiful and happy memory" (Ricciardi, 1971:215). The foundress cultivated awareness in her treatment, not just of the novices but of all the sisters in the Congregation.

Pillar IV – "Compassionate Collaborator"

As is evident from her profile, Mother Mary showed empathy and compassion to others even from her earliest years. Strzałkowska (1989:45) emphasises that "...[she] saw in her chosen mystery/title (the

Good Shepherd) a special vocation to witness the compassion of which she gives evidence throughout her life. She followed in the footsteps of the Good Shepherd, Jesus of Nazareth, seeking the lost and giving those who were suffering or in need of help her merciful goodness." In her personal journal written on 16 October 1895 Mother Mary wrote:

> I cannot express the joy and the personal happiness I experience when Jesus in his mercy grants me what I desired most, after our life of prayer, for Nazareth. This is what I want; a way to seek the wandering sheep through the grace of God and to lead them to the sheepfold, to console the oppressed, to visit the sick and to fill their souls with the spirit of Jesus Christ (ibid.).

She did not want to judge the behaviour of her daughters, and her advice to superiors when disciplining the sisters was to trust in the innate goodness in people for, she believed that when given the opportunity they would realise their shortcomings and make the right choices. In a letter to Mother Raphael in America on 23 December 1885 Mother Mary advised:

> My dearly beloved Raphael ...
>
> Should one of the Sisters desire to accuse herself before the superior of some failings against the house rules, she may do so; *but it may not and must not be demanded of her.* She may be encouraged to do so, with an explanation of the salutary value of such a practice in assisting us to amend our lives. If some do not do so, they should not be considered less perfect, nor should such confidence be exacted from them. Leave matters to the Lord; moreover, show to such Sisters the same charity and goodness which is had towards those who open their souls in confidence. Not all souls have the same inclinations, nor the same needs. It is necessary to leave to the Lord the direction of each soul, and to limit

oneself to observing in what manner God leads souls so as to help them fulfill that which God Himself demands of them (cited in Ricciardi, 1971:195).

During my time in the religious community, it was a common practice for the sisters to gather and then individually ask forgiveness of their peers for indiscretions caused against their neighbour (at the time such meetings were referred to as "The Chapter of Faults"). Mother Mary in the above communication with Mother Raphael, is recommending that superiors do not coerce their charges to admit faults but that they should offer to support their efforts to do so at an appropriate time that is suitable for them.

As is evident from her profile, the clergy played a huge role in the life of Mother Mary, and when priests were "unfaithful" it caused her much suffering and worry for their salvation. Strzałkowska (1989:48-49) cites the foundress who wrote:

> A certain person presented himself to me at prayer for a few days – a poor person, a priest who had broken ties with God… O Lord, take possession of his soul … (Personal Journal, January 1, 1885). A Few days later she added, "Jesus gave me the grace to write to him… to this unfortunate priest, who was unfaithful to his God… Lord, how merciful and patient you are! … Forgive this soul, help him and draw him and others to you" (Personal Journal, January 15, 1885). Later she thanked God for the Priest's conversion. Mother knew that priests, the chosen ones of God, were more susceptible to trials and spiritual danger so she prayed fervently for them and directed her sisters to do the same.

She loved sinners because she believed that God was sanctifying them through her and that by showing love and compassion to the poor and marginalised, she was emulating the Divine Redeemer, who was inclusive and reached out to the needy and those souls rejected by society because of their diversity.

In 1892, besides the problems with her health, other more serious challenges arose, which led to a serious conflict for Mother Mary and her Congregation, and in contemporary terms the year could be best described as "Annus Horribilis"; in other words, "horrible year"! For it was in the summer of 1892, that Father Lechert found himself in trouble with his congregation, "because of his close connection with the Holy Family Sisters" (Burton, 1951:143). Ricciardi, (1971:245) refers to the year as "one of trial and cross" for the foundress and in fact he maintains that this was the beginning of a decade of personal suffering (emotional, physical and spiritual), when darkness enveloped her soul. Sadly, the effects of the physiological and psychological trauma lasted until her death in 1902. Burton (1951:144) states that Father Lechert was ordered to break off all contact (spiritual and material) with the Sisters. Hence, when he arrived back in Rome, he went straight to them announcing, "Te Deum Laudamus ['God we praise you'] for the Lord has sent us a great cross" (Ricciardi, 1971:245). It is my belief that both Mother Mary and Father Lechert were professional in their response to the serious allegations and accusations.

There was the insinuation that Father Lechert spent "too much time" with Mother Mary (Burton, 1951:144). And feeling the weight of the cross she wrote to Mother Laureta who was in the United States (Mother Mary held mother Laureta in high regard and as mentioned in a previous paragraph when the foundress passed away, it was Mother Laureta who was appointed as the Superior General of the Congregation a position she was to hold until her death in 1947): "I write to you, dear daughter, with great suffering of heart: and you, too, accept this cross from our Lord, because this cross touches all of us. It is to be, moreover, in the designs of the good God but another ulterior proof of the sanctity of this work which the Lord has permitted to be engulfed with so much suffering..." (Ricciardi, 1971:245).

Ricciardi (1971:248) maintains that Father Lechert had presented his petition to the Congregation for the Sacred Congregation of Bishops and Regulars, to obtain permission to found a community of Brothers of the Holy Family. Spurious allegations ensued. A Monsignor Giovanni Biasiotti, testified during the beatification process, to what was revealed to him by Blessed Father Hyacinth Cormier regarding the situation with Father Leander:

> His Resurrection Confrères ... considered him quite incapable not only of directing them, but also of directing the Religious of Nazareth. In Father Cormier's judgment they were motivated by a certain jealous spirit and obtained from the ecclesiastical authority the prohibition against his frequenting the Nazareth Community. The Servant of God greeted the decision of the ecclesiastical authority serenely, and obeyed, despite that she suffered much from it (ibid.).

Mother Mary was urged by the ecclesiastical authorities to "draw up a memorandum of protests in refutation of the calumnies brought forward in the account of the Procurator General of the Resurrectionists" (ibid.). However, she was reluctant to lay the blame directly on Monsignor Giuseppe Graniello, who had seemed to rush into responding to the allegations by the Resurrectionists without first seeking the advice of more senior ecclesial officials, who had been on leave at the time of his actions. Consequently, rather than submitting an initial formal complaint Mother Mary decided to write directly to Monsignor Graniello to inform him of her concerns in an effort to obtain a resolution. Her letter has some length, so just short excepts will be included here to provide a background for the source of the conflict and to explain the complaints:

> Your Excellency Spurred by obedience and moved by a desire to make known the truth, I dare write to Your Excellency. I do this only after prolonged reflection and much prayer. I do this at the feet of Jesus crucified, having no other purpose than to glorify God and to remove from

our Congregation the stain of suspicion with which it has been represented before Your Excellency ... (cited in Ricciardi, 1971:249).

Regarding the first complaint: "They reported to Your Excellency that we have had some internal communications and that we were not separated except by a drapery from a religious community of men being formed in the same house and under the title of the Holy Family of Nazareth. I have the obligation in conscience to protest against this falsehood..." (ibid.). Mother Mary reported that the sisters had a guesthouse outside their enclosure where on occasion a chaplain and others might stay, but she reinforced that, "A religious community of men was never established in that guesthouse"; however, "For some months there resided with the chaplain, one priest and two (afterwards three) young boarders who, desirous of consecrating themselves to the lord, were awaiting the permission of the Supreme Pontiff to begin their religious life in a house which would have to be bought for that purpose. These young men had absolutely nothing to do with us..." (ibid.).

Regarding a second complaint Mother Mary wrote, "They have reported to Your Excellency that these boarders were in the chapel together with our religious, and also in their refectory. This is another deception. Our chapel is public, it is divided into two parts by an iron grille. These boarders came to hear Mass and assist at Benediction in that part of the chapel open to the public..." (pp.249-250). (Please note that the conclusion to this letter from Mother Mary is recounted in the final Pillar VII, "Leads with Moral Authority" under the subtitle – Justness.)

Eventually Father Lechert left his religious order and became a secular priest. In early December 1892 he again resumed his duties as Director with the Sisters of the Holy Family of Nazareth – a connection that was not severed until his death in 1921. The professional attitude displayed by Father Lechert and Mother Mary in their response to extreme provocation by forces beyond their control, is a great example of valuing and respecting self and others.

Pillar V – "Has Foresight"

You may recall from her profile, that Mother Mary first met Father Leander when she was in her thirteenth year. It was from that moment of "spiritual awakening", that she entertained the idea that she might give her life to God. However, this vocation had not materialised by the time she reached the age of thirty, and because of continuing ill-health, the likelihood of her entering the religious life seemed to become more, and more remote. Interestingly, it wasn't long after Father Leander delivered a message to Mother Mary from a friend of his that she began again to reconsider that she might indeed become a nun. Apparently, Father Leander had requested prayers for a special intention from a young brother, Stephen Rembiszewski. You may recall Stephen from the profile on Mother Mary, where it was mentioned that this young man experienced visions of a Theodosia Kobylanska. Now in one of these visions Stephen recounts that he saw Mlle. Kobylanska:

> Who was walking in a flower garden and stopped to speak with Brother Stephen: "The fortune I have left is to be for the founding of a new congregation to be dedicated to Our Lady ... Let Father Leander know it is to be used for this purpose. And tell him it is the will of God that Frances Siedliska head this undertaking. If she will agree to do it, she will regain her health and will receive the necessary enlightenment to fulfil God's designs." And she added that, as a sign that this was God's will, Frances would receive the blessing of the Holy Father on her work, if only she agreed to accept it (Burton, 1951:71-72).

Accordingly, as we have seen, the vision became a reality and the rest is history. Frances participated in "an intense retreat", which had been organized by Father Leander as essential to her spiritual preparation prior to founding a new religious order. Witnesses who consisted of the first members of the soon to be foundation testified during the canonical processes that:

> [D]uring the period of prayer and spiritual preparation for her new work Mother Siedliska was privileged by a heavenly apparition or vision. They testified that Frania [Frances] had seen at her side the Archangel St. Michael and had heard these words from him "I am the archangel Michael and I take this work of God under my protection. Other souls will come together with you and will also be under my special protection and under that of the Archangels Raphael and Gabriel, and of the Evangelist, St. John" (cited in Ricciardi, 1971:91).

There is no evidence available regarding the origin of the vision said to be witnessed by Frances; however certain inexplicable signs suggest some semblance of authenticity. For example, Ricciardi maintains that the first members of the congregation, "the three Sisters Lubowidzki, on the day of their clothing received respectively the names Michael, Gabriel and Raphael. Mother Siedliska, moreover, during her entire lifetime had special devotion to St. Michael and to St. John the Evangelist" (ibid.). Mother Mary was a visionary who "engaged in transformative action to mentor and nurture her daughters, facilitating and utilising their talents and gifts, by empowering them to be the best they could be in their mission of service" (Cameron, 2018).

Mother Mary was an innovative leader who expanded her Congregation by founding houses in Europe and America. With her precarious health it would have been simple to establish houses in the countries where she spent time during her youth, and where she was reasonably certain the young women joining the order would be well versed in the spirit of the Holy Family of Nazareth. And yet she was keen to challenge the status quo. In 1885, she stepped outside her comfort zone and boarded a ship to the United States, a country which was an enigma to her and where she was to be confronted with poverty, conflict and a different way of life to that experienced in

Europe. Nevertheless, she accepted the challenge and persisted in her endeavours.

Orphanages, hospitals, schools, homes for the aged and numerous other facilities have been established over the centuries by members of the Sisters of the Holy Family of Nazareth and their forebears. Such structures are evidence of the unwavering determination of one woman who inspired her daughters to live the Nazareth spirit – if they wavered in their resolve, she was there to guide them, if they needed her, she was there for them; if they suffered, she suffered with them. Unfortunately, on occasion when she visited any of her houses whether they were in America or Europe, the weight of the responsibility often affected her health, and on her return to Rome she took what would be referred to in contemporary terms as "time out" at a sanctuary at Loreto. You may recall Loreto – a "Holy House – Marian shrine" was mentioned in an earlier paragraph and though located some distance from Rome, was quite accessible and offered a special spiritual environment where Mother Mary went regularly to recuperate, meditate and to pray as the need arose (Burton, 1951:110).

In early 1887, when the sisters had settled into their convent at Via Machiavelli in Rome, several unpleasant incidents began to occur that appeared to put the sisters at risk. They were attacked in the street as they went about their daily duties, and stones were used by vandals to damage windows and gardens. It was soon discovered that a disgruntled neighbour was behind the vandalism. Before long, his wife approached the sisters begging forgiveness for the trauma and the destructive and violent incidents. Apparently, her husband wanted to work their gardens for his own use, but when he approached Mother Mary about his plans, he was told that the sisters needed to maintain the garden for their needs. He retaliated with violence. "Now his little son, an only child was ill, and he thought God was punishing him for his misdoings. He sent his wife to ask pardon of the Sisters and to beg prayers for the sick boy. Mother Mary Frances assured the mother of her forgiveness and later in the day visited the sick child's bedside taking with her various remedies." She harboured no ill will towards her neighbour for his violent behaviour. The sisters prayed for the boy and he recovered (Burton, 1951:129-132).

A saintly life is often evidence of sainthood, but to be recognised by the Church a more formal process has to be followed. According to Ricciardi (1971:403) since the death of Mother Mary "A series of numerous extraordinary facts regarding cures have been attributed to ... [her] intercession. These, of course, must be judged by the Church so as to determine securely their extraordinary or miraculous nature." Fortunately, one such miracle has been approved and has resulted in the Servant of God, Mother Mary of Jesus the Good Shepherd, being beatified by the Church and being given the title Blessed Frances Siedliska. Strzałkowska (1989:67-68) recounts the event which involved the miraculous recovery of a mother of seven children who had just lost her eighth child at birth, and she, the mother, was not expected to survive. The sisters of the Holy Family of Nazareth prayed a novena to their foundress for this mother who was seriously ill and near death. The mother subsequently recovered:

> Upon hearing the testimonies of the witnesses and on the basis of the medical records, the illness and subsequent recovery of ... [the mother] was carefully studied by a medical commission first in Warsaw and then in Rome. On September 1, 1988, at Castel Gandolfo, in the presence of His Holiness [St] John Paul II, the Congregation for the Causes of the Saints promulgated the miraculous cure attributed to Mary of Jesus the Good Shepherd (Frances Siedliska).

The next step in the process requires a second miracle to be acknowledged before Blessed Mother Mary of Jesus the Good Shepherd is canonised a saint of the Catholic Church.

Pillar VI – "Systems Thinker"

The "Big Picture" for Mother Mary was that though the order was of Polish origin she was adamant that it should not be referred to as a Polish Order. You may recall that in earlier paragraphs I have referred to my time as a member of the community and I remember being informed that the reason Mother Mary founded the order in Rome was that she wanted it to be considered an international order. A Monsignor Vincenzo Sardi (who was the first biographer of Mother Mary's work though he did not complete the task), reinforces this statement:

> The intelligent and pious Foundress did not tolerate national exclusivism which unfortunately might be found in some religious Institutes, causing harm to mutual charity and loss of interior peace to the soul. She desired above all that her Congregation would be Catholic, that is, universal, and that all her religious, whether Poles, Americans, Englishwomen, Frenchwomen, Italians, or of any other nationality would have but one goal, one heart, that all would be viewed under one light, without regard for worldly status, origin or nationality. For that reason, she did not like that her daughters be referred to as *the Polish Sisters*, and she protested against the title and permitted no other name than that which was universal namely, *the Religious of the Holy Family of Nazareth* (Sardi, 1921:139, cited in Ricciardi, 1971:120).

As mentioned in the profile, though approval was given for the new foundation by Pope Pius IX on 1 October 1873, Mother Mary gives the official date for the founding of the Congregation as the "First Sunday of Advent 1875" (Strzałkowska, 1989:32). According to Ricciardi: "The first ten years were spent in consolidating the Roman house, establishing the first novitiate, and founding a house at Cracow in 1881 where no small number of Polish vocations were to be gathered" (1971:414).

The foundation in the United States followed in 1885 and heralded "seventeen years of progress and expansion … [and] the establishment of more than 29 houses in the United States and in Europe" prior to the death of the Mother Mary in 1902 (ibid.).

Strzałkowska (1989:50) recounts that the ministries in which the Sisters engaged included "schools, orphanages, kindergartens, hospitals and homes for the elderly." She emphasises that following the call "to serve in the USA the sisters heard from Paris, London, St. Petersburg, Sachalin, Westphalia, and Roumania. Mother even considered India and China" (ibid.). The sisters now had a global perspective and the growth of the foundations was ensuing sustainability into the future. According to Ricciardi (1971:416-417):

> One cannot say that the death of Mother Siedliska had left the Congregation in a state of unawareness or lack of order. No, to the contrary, the Foundress, as though forewarned of her premature departure from this world, left her Sisters a Congregation in running order, complete in efficiency, perfect in organization. This is the more marvelous when one notes how short a time had elapsed since the foundation of the Congregation.

Her organizational skills were excellent. In 1895 Mother Mary submitted the Constitutions for the Congregation "to the Church for approval. Permeated with the divine and Gospel-imbued, they were modern for the times" (Strzałkowska, 1989:39). In fact, the foundress was a little worried that perhaps the Constitutions were a little too avantgarde for acceptance, so she wrote to Father Lechert asking his prayers for a successful outcome. Then "[o]n September 1, 1896, the Holy See issued the decree of Praise to the congregation. The Constitutions were accepted and confirmed on August 2, 1909" (p.40), seven years after the death of Mother Mary. Monsignor Carlo Sica, who succeeded Monsignor Sardi as the biographer of Mother Foundress, stated that on the death of Frances Siedliska "a giant personality had vanished" (1925:46, cited in Ricciardi, 1971:417). The extraordinary work of an exceptional leader has left a wonderful legacy for succeeding generations. The missionary endeavours of the Congregation of the Sisters of the Holy Family of Nazareth are continuing into the twenty-first century, with foundations established on 5 continents – Europe, Asia, Africa and North America, and as recently as 2012 – in Ghana Africa, and Spain in 2018.

Pillar VII – "Leads with Moral Authority"

From the beginning of the foundation of the Congregation, Mother Mary empowered and inspirited her daughters to live a life of commitment and dedication to the Holy Family. She was their mentor and their teacher, always their teacher, guiding and showing them the way to transcend the ordinary and to achieve the extraordinary by keeping them on task and setting an example for them in the way she carried her cross and performed her duties. The fragile state of her health, and the many challenges associated with the various foundations are evidence of this and in particular, her total abandonment to the will of her divine spouse. The foundations in the United States and in Europe in response to requests from the ecclesiastical authorities, provided Mother Mary and her Congregation of sisters with the opportunity to engage in active discipleship, whereby they proclaimed the love of Christ by their very presence and in their missionary service to others. According to Ricciardi (1971:382):

> A characteristic note of Mother Siedliska's moral personality is found in her simplicity and humility. When one takes into consideration Mother Siedliska's aristocratic origin, her role as Foundress and Superior General until the day of her death, her indefatigable activity in the erection of new foundations, her contacts with highly placed ecclesiastical personalities, one might be tempted to think of her as possessed of an authoritarian streak despite

her refinements and urbanity. Instead, as Mother Clare Netkowska testifies, "humility was the most characteristic virtue in her."

This view is confirmed by the words of Sister Redempta Siefert: "Among us she did not act like a superior or a foundress, but as a co-Sister and companion" (ibid.). As a leader then Mother Mary worked collaboratively with her sisters to "build a sense of community". She was a leader, a sister, a colleague, a friend and, above all – a mother!

Values

Aspects of Blessed Frances Siedliska's life and works are now discussed in relation to the values – dignity, respect, fairness, justness and equality (see Chapter 4 for the terms of reference).

Dignity

Frances loved her father but there were occasions (as outlined in the profile) when he did not treat her with dignity and respect (Strzałkowska, 1989; Burton, 1951). Did Adolph really understand his daughter? The profile also reveals that Mother Mary was stoic in times of conflict and especially during her episodes of significant human suffering. Indeed, she had a wonderful capacity to treat aggressors during confrontational situations, with much dignity and respect, and to not complain about the failure of her body to conform to her expectations when duty called her to leave her sick bed. Her humility was admirable.

The foundress and her sisters maintained their dignity and respect in spite of constant harassment. You may recall the incident where the Sisters were attacked, and their convent vandalized by a neighbour for no other reason than that he wanted to use their garden for his purposes and when he was denied access he retaliated with violence. Ricciardi (1971:212) tells us that "Mother Siedliska lived in the Rome of anticlericalism, better put, of anti-clerical reaction, and of Freemasonry. No wonder ... she and her spiritual daughters were objects of harassment in the via Machiavelli." The Sisters treated others with dignity and respect. In Cracow poor girls who "on Sunday afternoons from all over the city – the forgotten and unloved and underprivileged – came to the convent to [spend time] with the Sisters" (Burton, 1951:103). This apostolate was replicated in other cities and in other countries in Europe, and the United States after their missionary foundation in 1885.

Even though Mother Mary had a privileged upbringing she had a great love of poverty. She trusted in Divine Providence (p.50). To Mother Mary human life was sacred – every person had rights – equal rights. Burton (1951:53) maintains that:

> Mother Mary prescribed to the members of her congregation, that the sisters show love, sacrifice, and compassion to those in need, especially those who were the most neglected, unwanted and unloved. To serve Christ in others was the service of charity, a service mother remembered daily. She showed kindness not only to the sisters for whom she was a mother ... but also to every person she met everywhere – on the train, at the station, or on the street. Whenever charity demanded it Mother responded and disregarded no one."

Ricciardi (1971:327) recounts the testimony of Mother Joseph-Theresa Tyszkiewicz, "In her exterior she joined to a profound humility a very great dignity which did not hinder or take away from her exceeding affability and her irresistible goodness which was capable of winning all hearts." According to the Catholic Catechism: "The dignity of the human person is rooted in his [her] creation in the image and likeness of God" (2000:para.1700). Mother Mary lived the Gospel with dignity and integrity.

Respect

The profound respect Frances had for her parents is evident in that when her father, Adolph passed away, she didn't immediately pursue her dream of entering the religious life, even though she had reached the age of 30. She stayed at home assisting her mother and brother to adjust to life without a father and husband. She respected her spiritual director Father Leander, to advise her when the time was right for her to begin her life of prayer and contemplation as a religious.

When writing the Foreword to the book "Where There is Love: The Life of Mother Mary Frances Siedliska of Jesus the Good Shepherd" by Katherine Burton in 1951, Thomas E. Molloy, Bishop of Brooklyn states:

> And, therefore, very eagerly do I take this occasion to offer a richly deserved tribute of respect, regard and reverence to their holy Foundress and to express my sincere approval and appreciation of her spiritual daughters. And very fervently do I pray that they continue to enjoy, in the faithful fulifllment of their vocational ideals and responsibilities, God's enlightening, strengthening and sustaining grace.

At the process for the cause of the beatification of Mother Frances Mother Laureta Lubowidzka gave testimony: "She never talked about herself, and did not tolerate being referred to as Foundress, saying that the only founder was the Lord. In correcting the Sisters for some defect or other, she took the occasion to humble herself, and although reproving and remonstrating, she would add that perhaps in similar circumstances she would have done worse" (ibid.). Mother Mary respected the integrity of those she served. She enabled them and also respected their independence. On the 14 December 1887, Mother Mary wrote to the Sisters in Poland and the United States:

> What I ask for you of the Lord, what I desire, is that

the kingdom of God flourish among you, that the spirit of the Holy Family reign in you, and that you live according to our Holy Rule. What I want for you, above all, is that you have a spirit of prayer, that we live in intimate union with Jesus; that we be mortified, destroying by the grace of God the old man in us. The Lord calls us to a fullest possible union with our superiors and to respect for their authority as coming from Himself, and to a total obedience, one that is joyous, simple and sincere (Ricciardi, 1971:387-389).

Mother Mary is advocating that her daughters look upon their superiors with respect, seeing in them the image of the Lord. For to obey is to live the vows they have taken, and to obey while respecting the person and the decisions of the leader, is to obey with love. If respect is shown to others, they in turn will respond with respect. Burton (1951:89) records the testimony of Thecla (a postulant at the time, whom you may remember was later known as Mother Laureta and appointed Mother General following the death of Mother Mary), and "not long after her arrival in Rome ... was in the convent garden when Mother Mary Frances came up to her; so much like a vision from Heaven did she seem to the young girl that she sank to her knees and kissed the older women's hand in deep respect. She had never seen any show this respect to the Superior; she was urged to it by an inner impulse of veneration."

Fairness

Mother Mary exhibited justice and fairness in her relationship and dealings with others in her mission of service. Whether she was dealing with Popes (Pius IX or Leo XIII), ecclesiastical officials, priests, religious and/or lay people, the foundress had the utmost respect for those in office and for all who were touched by the ministry of her leadership. Fairness involves making decisions in the best interests of all, but this did not seem to be the case with those who made allegations regarding Frances Siedliska and Father Lechert (see Pillar IV "Compassionate Collaborator").

At this point in our history, we find Mother Siedliska literally on the cross because of her fidelity to God, who, by means of his representatives, had called her and willed her to take upon herself the role of foundress of the Congregation of the Sisters of the Holy Family of Nazareth … We have noted that 1892 was a year of trial and cross in Mother Siedliska's life … [it] marked the beginning of the mystic passion of Mother Siedliska; it would perdure another ten years and end in her death, which came on slowly, following the peritonitis which had derived from cholescistitis. Her physical suffering was accompanied by prolonged and oppressive moral suffering which, as a consequence of the events of 1892, she was compelled to bear and which she accepted in fullest conformity to the divine will (Ricciardi, 1971:243-244).

It wasn't just Mother Mary Frances and Father Leander who suffered, it was the entire Congregation of sisters. The allegations were not substantiated with any concrete evidence; hence the lives of many people were affected. It is apparent then that the initial response by religious and ecclesiastical officials to the unfounded allegations, was not just and indeed not fair?

It was around May 1893, that Mother Mary Frances received word that her only sibling, Adam Siedliska was dying and asking to see her. She wanted to go to him. She had also received a telegram from her mother requesting that she make haste to be with Adam during his final hours. The sisters urged their foundress to go to her brother, but she felt it was important to first seek the permission of her spiritual director, Father Lechert. Surprisingly, Father Lechert "was opposed to her departure, supporting his view with the fact that it would be necessary to authorize other Sisters in the future equal facility in similar cases" (p.261).

Burton maintains that Mother Mary Frances was devastated by the decision and it was "only in prayers [that she] was with her brother in his last hours" (1951:147). Was this a form "blind obedience" on the part of Mother Mary? Though she did what she felt that she must do in fairness to all her sisters, the decision of Father Lechert perhaps needed to be tempered with compassion, which I believe is an element of fairness. Mother Mary Frances rarely asked for anything for herself and this seemed to be an occasion where a true sense of fairness was not observed! For she was not the only one affected by the decision – Adam Siedliski died without being able to bid farewell to his adored sister, and a beloved mother was obliged to suffer the loss of her son without the solace of her daughter's presence.

Justness

Justness is important in dealings with others. There were occasions when Mother Mary was accused of being unjust. One such incident occurred in Paris:

> Animated by Christian charity, she was wont to pardon the injuries perpetrated against her. At Paris, the lay directress thought she had done more than her share and duty in directing the school, and that the Servant of God had not shown sufficient recognition of the fact and used to refer to her as unjust. She repeated this accusation outside the community and to strangers. The Foundress was not perturbed by this accusation, but pardoned the woman and, moreover, made it possible for her to obtain her higher degree and wanted her to remain as head of the school (Ricciardi, 1971:381).

In Pillar IV under "Compassionate Collaborator" there is discussion on the problems that plagued Mother Mary Frances and her community in 1892, as a result of a situation in which Father Lechert had become embroiled. The following is the conclusion to the letter sent by the foundress on 19 November 1892, to Monsignor Graniello in which she is asking for justness for herself and her community (cited in Ricciardi, 1971:252):

> ... In consequence of this false information presented to Your Excellency and referred to the Holy Father, our Congregation has not only been compromised before His Holiness, but we have been hit with a decree which in one moment [according to a third complaint] takes away from us a Director, a man of God, who not only led souls along the way of religious perfection, but knowing the Institute, perfectly assisted it with his wise and prudent counsel in the difficulties and conflicts through which it must pass, and made it flourish with the grace of God, for in a few short years this little Congregation has been extended to, and already is at work in eight dioceses, both in Europe and in America, instructing and giving a Christian education to poor little boys and girls ... I will be very grateful to your Excellency if you will favor us with a visit, and then you will see with your own eyes how false the reports are that have been made against us..."

As noted in Pillar IV the situation was eventually resolved; generally, to the satisfaction of all parties, though really the damage to the reputations and health of those involved was significant and perhaps justness for all was not really served!

Equality

Equality is not about uniformity it is about diversity, inclusion, awareness and an appreciation of the dignity of all, regardless of gender. Mother Mary Frances had a great love of the scriptures and it was her living out the Gospel message that formed the Rule of life for her daughters to follow. They were to love everybody without reserve. Strzałkowska (1989:52) posits that it was:

> In the spirit of the Gospel, in imitation of the first Christians, Mother Mary sought Christ in every person and was willing to sacrifice herself for everyone without reserve. She knew there was "no Greek or Jew here, slave or freeman. Rather, Christ is everything in all men" (Col. 3,11). The Christ of Nazareth was teaching her to bend over moral and material misery. His teaching was to "do good" to everyone even to giving one's life for another. Just as she opened wide the doors of Nazareth to all true religious vocations, she also hastened with as much assistance as she could supply to all who needed it, disregarding race, nationality, or creed.

If we open the scriptures on John (15:12-13), we read Christ's message: "This is my commandment, that you love one another as I have loved you. No greater love than this, to lay down one's life for one's friends." Indeed "Christ lived His values of love of God and love of neighbour all the way to the Cross" (Blanchard and Hodges, 2003:50). To Christ, neighbour refers to all people with whom we share the sacredness of life. He does not differentiate according to gender, race or creed. Blessed Frances Siedliska taught her daughters this lesson by her life that achieved so much in such a short time, and at a cost that entailed a lifespan of extreme physical suffering and mental anguish. During the twentieth century the stewardship of her legacy has been immortalised in blood, with the slaughter of eleven sisters by order of the Gestapo on 1 August 1943, at Nowogródek, Poland. Now referred to as the "Blessed Martyrs of Nowogródek – Sister M. Stella and her ten companions were beatified by virtue of martyrdom on 5 March 2000 by Pope St John Paul II" (nazarethcsfn.org., 2019). Hence, what greater leader to emulate, than one who inspires others to follow the example of Christ and offer the supreme sacrifice for those they serve!

One final memory from my past – as a young nun in Sydney many years ago: an aged American nun arrived to commence her mission for the Holy Family in Australia. At the time in America presidential elections were being held. In my youthful naivety and in reference to American politics, I asked her if she was a Republican or a Democrat. Her response was quick and from the heart – "I am a Nazareth". In recent years the sisters have established communities in Spain and in Ghana, Africa. They are true "missionary disciples" (Pope Francis, *Evangelii Gaudium*, 2013:120). So Blessed Frances Siedliska, in the words of Matthew (25:23): "Well done, good and faithful servant"! Your message has transcended the centuries, and your daughters have listened and responded well to the Gospel's call to service. They are a credit to you and to the Congregation. You would be so proud of them!

I invite you to join with me now for the chapter on St Mary of the Cross MacKillop, who was Co-founder of the Order of the Sisters of St Joseph of the Sacred Heart.

15

St Mary of the Cross MacKillop

My first experience with the members of the Josephite Order was in 1968, when I was a young Junior Professed Religious attending the Catholic Teacher's College at Mount Street, North Sydney. Several of the lecturers at the time were Sisters of St Joseph of the Sacred Heart, otherwise known as Josephites. I was intrigued by the aura that emanated from these nuns. They were professional educators who had a spiritual presence that reached out to all who were touched by the ministry of their teaching. Over the years and as I continued to pursue my educational career, I was fortunate that my teaching and experiences as a leader were at schools that had been established by the co-founders of the Order, Mary MacKillop and Father Julian Tenison Woods. Hence, I was thrilled and excited when it was announced that Blessed Mary MacKillop would be canonised as the first Saint of Australia. This extraordinary and momentous event occurred on Sunday 17 October 2010. During his homily on this very special occasion, Pope Emeritus Benedict XVI (2010d:para.10) spoke of the achievements of this remarkable Australian woman who was being honoured with sainthood:

> For many years countless young people throughout Australia have been blessed with teachers who were inspired by the courageous and saintly example of zeal, perseverance and prayer of Mother Mary MacKillop. She dedicated herself as a young woman to the education of the poor in the difficult and demanding terrain of rural Australia, inspiring other women to join her in the first women's community of religious sisters of that country. She attended to the needs of each young person entrusted to her, without regard for

station or wealth, providing both intellectual and spiritual formation. Despite many challenges, her prayers to Saint Joseph and her unflagging devotion to the Sacred Heart of Jesus, to whom she dedicated her new congregation, gave this holy woman the graces to remain faithful to God and to the Church. Through her intercession, may her followers today continue to serve God and the Church with faith and humility!

Mary's story is one of enduring love and service to God, the Church and humanity – of self-sacrifice and extreme poverty, while meeting challenges associated with a harsh climate and land, all of which had a profound effect on the attitudes and decisions of the laity and a clerical body geographically removed from the Church in Rome, and in dioceses that were being established in fledgling colonies. The faith journey of St Mary of the Cross MacKillop began in the nineteenth century in the Australian colony of Victoria which apparently was previously a part of New South Wales until 1851; then a colony until it became a state in 1901 following Federation.

Profile

Mary was born in Brunswick Street, Fitzroy (formerly Newtown) Melbourne, on 15 January 1842 (Margaret Paton, 2010:8) to Alexander and Flora MacKillop, who were Scottish immigrants. Marie Therese Foale (1989:13) informs us that Mary was "baptised in St Francis Church, Melbourne by Father Patrick Geoghegan", who in later years was appointed as the second Bishop in Adelaide, and who "set the scene for the foundation of the [Josephite] Institute of St Joseph by his insistence that Catholics have nothing to do with government schools and establish their own instead" (ibid.). Mary was the first born in the MacKillop family, which later comprised eight children with one youngster dying before reaching his first birthday.

Mary's strong faith was nurtured by both parents. According to Paton (2010:9), in later years Mary wrote to her mother about the great trust and confidence Flora had in Divine Providence, and that this trust enabled Mary to always believe in "Divine Providence". Her father Alexander initially wanted to serve God. As a boy in his teens he had spent time in a seminary, studying in Rome, but this vocation was not to be, and he did not complete his studies. In 1840, a couple of years after his arrival in Australia, Alexander met and married Flora McDonald. Initially the family settled into suburbia in Melbourne, owning their own home and welcoming the new additions to their family. However, over time Alexander made some unwise business decisions, and in due course was declared bankrupt. This was a situation from which he never fully recovered and according to Paton (2010:8), he was unable to provide adequately for his family from that time, and in due course removed himself from the family environment to live elsewhere. Hence "Mary and her younger brothers and sisters grew up in respectable poverty, dependent on the help of relatives" (ibid.).

Foale (1989:13) tells us that though Mary was "well born in class terms, she had first-hand experience of the rigours of poverty. And because of her father's inability to provide adequately for his young wife and children ... [Mary] was obliged to go out to work at an early age and ... the family came to rely on her for both financial and moral support." She was employed as a governess on various station properties with one such property being owned by a relative living in Penola. At the time Mary was eighteen and it was during her sojourn in this small town that Mary became acquainted with Father Julian Tenison Woods, priest in charge of the parish, which stretched for thousands of square miles across desolate terrain. Father Woods was conscious of the lack of educational opportunities for the children in his parish, whose families suffered extreme poverty and hardship. He hoped to entice one of the religious orders from overseas to accept the burden of providing a religious education to the children of his parish. But no offers were forthcoming, and before long he began to envisage founding a religious institute of his own, based on his memory of an Order in France that had met the needs of the poor – the Sisters of St Joseph at Le Puy (Paton, 2010:10).

Woods discovered a kindred spirit in Mary. Her faith was strong, and she sought his counsel and listened to his plans for the future. However, Mary was recalled to Victoria to assist with the financial management and practical organisation of her family, and consequently commenced employment as a clerk "in a Melbourne business house. Then, in 1863, when she was twenty-one years of age, she gained a teaching position in the Catholic denominational school at Portland in Western Victoria" (ibid.). During this time, Mary continued to communicate with Father Woods, and in her notes Foale [1989:14] writes that "much of the Woods-MacKillop correspondence, 1861-1879, is still extant and is held in the archives of the Sisters of St Joseph." It was on 8 September 1860 that Bishop Patrick Geoghegan mandated in a:

> *Pastoral Letter* to the clergy and laity of South Australia, elaborating on the dangers of the existing state education system. He commanded all Catholics to sever every connection with it ... he implored his priests to establish independent Catholic schools, regardless of the cost, and to agitate for a better deal from the government by organising meetings and drawing up petitions for presentation to parliament (p.6).

You may recall that Father Patrick Geoghegan was the priest who baptised the infant Mary MacKillop. He became the second Bishop of Adelaide in 1859, and had arrived in Adelaide from Melbourne, where "the church there was more financially secure" (Foale, 1989:6) with the government at the time contributing to its support. Apparently, the gold rush years were lucrative for the Church in the colony of Victoria with several Churches and Catholic schools being built. Foale (ibid.) emphasises that "coming from such a background, Geoghegan was appalled at the situation he found in his new See and complained bitterly of the Church's poverty as demonstrated by its 'deplorable lack of priests' and almost non-existent Catholic school system."

In the colony there was religious tolerance, but Geoghegan did not believe that this was an acceptable situation for he believed that "religious tolerance caused indifference. This was bad enough at the best of times and was particularly dangerous in South Australian, where … the government had established and was supporting a system of 'state Protestant Schools' with the sole aim of proselytising the Catholic children from the faith of their baptism" (ibid.). Geoghegan was of the opinion that as the Catholic population "contributed an equivalent proportion of the revenue allocation for education", they should receive equal support from the government. Hence the "strongly worded *Pastoral Letter*" referred to in a previous paragraph.

Catholic schools began to emerge across the colony. Father Woods set up a school in Penola but when the lay teachers he employed resigned, he invited Mary and her sister Annie to come from Portland to teach the children. However, the families could ill-afford to pay the fees, so Father Woods offered to pay Mary and Annie, who needed the income as they were still supporting their family back home. Woods also organised for John, brother of the MacKillop sisters to assist with transforming a stable into a classroom, until such time as a school could built (ibid.).

As a result of her regular communications with Father Woods, Mary's faith commitment had grown over the years, and she became intent on devoting her life to the service of the Church as a religious. You may recall from a previous paragraph that Woods was keen to proceed with the founding of an order that would fulfil his dream of establishing a community of nuns who would live a life such as that lived by St Francis of Assisi and based on the spirit of poverty. Consequently, on 19 March 1866, on the feast of St Joseph, the Josephite Institute was established.

To consolidate his position within the diocese, and to reaffirm the "official status" of the newly formed Institute, Woods endeavoured to attend the "episcopal consecration" of Lawrence Sheil on 15 August 1866. The new Bishop was the appointed successor of Bishop Patrick Geoghegan, who had passed away a few years previously. Foale (1989:18) maintains that Woods was extremely pleased with his interaction with the new Bishop who was likewise "impressed with the enthusiasm of the young English priest …[and] he … tacitly approved the foundation of the new sisterhood even though some of his ideas as to how it should be run differed from Woods'. As well, he decided to appoint Woods Director-General of Catholic Education and Inspector of Schools and asked him to accompany him to Adelaide as his private secretary and personal chaplain."

Woods was keen for Mary to join him in Adelaide and wanted her to assist with the training of the teaching staff in the schools in the diocese. Foale (1989:27) writes that Mary and Rose Cunningham, her companion, arrived in Adelaide on Sunday 23 June and that on "2 July 1867, Mary and Rose donned the distinctive habit of the Sisters of St Joseph for the first time and they and Ellen ['McMullen, a teacher from a local Catholic school'], who was still a postulant … took charge of the St Francis Xavier's Cathedral Hall School in the centre of the city." The Rule of life for the institute was formulated and drafted by Father Woods and "approved by Bishop Sheil in 1868." Following the spirit of poverty as lived by St Francis of Assisi, the institute:

> gave prominence to no ownership. The Sisters would not own any property or material possessions and would live a life of poverty from contributions to the schools, as people could afford, or from alms. The Institute would have Central Government, which meant that, although the Sisters would work in various dioceses, they would not be under the control of the bishops but answerable to the Superior General of the Institute (Paton, 2010:11).

Foale (1989:16) states that in regard to her teaching Mary "used the monitorial system, which required that the children learn from their books and repeat each lesson by rote in answer to the teachers' questions, devoted four days each week to direct teaching and set Fridays aside for a recapitulation of the week's work." Mary integrated religion across the curriculum of the day. Poverty was everywhere – there was no financial security for Woods or for the Sisters. "all who joined this institute were to be prepared to live among and like the poor whom they were serving" (p.18). As stipulated in the Rule of Life "they were to own neither houses, land nor money in their own right and were to subsist solely on such school fees as they might receive and the gratuitous offerings of the local people" (ibid.). Because the Sisters were being sent out to teach with little or no teacher training, "Mary found it necessary to abandon classroom teaching early in 1868. Instead, she travelled from school to school, helping the sisters with the preparation and presentation of their lessons" (p.44).

As the number of schools increased, so did the poverty. Over time many of the nuns taught in mud shacks during the day and slept in these during the evenings. "The sisters made as few demands on the people as possible and indicated their willingness to live in any accommodation available, whether it was free standing or attached to the local church or schoolroom" (Foale, 1989:145). There were only enough sisters to send in twos to the distant and far reaching settlements, and this provided its own challenges particularly in regard to distance, transport, and being separated from the Mother House community. Initially lack of time and the urgency to staff the makeshift schools meant that a number of young women were accepted into the Institute who were perhaps unsuitable choices! They received little if any spiritual preparation and were not trained in teaching methods; this resulted in criticisms from several priests in the diocese regarding the competence of the sisters in the classroom (Paton, 2010:13).

Foale (1989:20) maintains that Sheil "was overly trusting by nature and a poor judge of character, was easily influenced by those closest to him at any given time and was unable to recognise an impending crisis until it had come to a head. He also suffered from chronic ill-health, which often rendered him unfit for attending to his duties." Though he was warmly welcomed by his fellow clergy, and though the diocese was without debt but "lacking in financial resources" on his appointment to the office, he soon began to spend time away from the diocese and as a result "His prolonged absences served only to exacerbate the effects of his administrative ineptitude and to open the way for the development of clerical factionalism and lay disunity" (p.21). Sheila McCreanor (2011:xvii) emphasises that:

> During the first absence of the Bishop overseas, Fr John Smyth acted as Vicar General. He supported the efforts of Fr Julian Woods and gave encouragement to Mary MacKillop. By the time the Bishop left Adelaide in October 1869 to attend the first Vatican Council, again leaving Fr Smyth as Vicar General, the diocese was in a very different and more complex state. Some of the priests who had come to the diocese were ill suited and poorly trained for missionary work in the new colony. Factions developed and many priests resented the role of Fr Woods in the development of so many small Catholic Schools. These were viewed by some priests as a financial burden rather than as an essential element in the growth of the new colony.

The first Vatican Council was held in Rome between 1869 and 1870. When Bishops went overseas generally it was for the purpose of *ad limina* visits to Rome which consisted of the Bishops having to visit Rome about every five years to report and share issues and concerns with the Pontiff. Often on their trips away the Bishops would bring home eager young men keen to be missionary priests in colonial Australia. However, many of these immigrants were not really suited to the climate or could not assimilate into the culture. In addition, during the prolonged absences of Bishop Sheil, several of the clergy in South Australia were vocal in their disapproval of the appointment of Woods as the Director-General of Education and Inspector of Schools, which enabled him to have a certain amount of control over education in the diocese and to also have the "ear" of the Bishop and/or his representative.

There was also some resentment also by members of the clergy over the fact that the young women who were encouraged to enter the Josephite Institute, were not required to have a dowry or to own property, and that the payment of school fees was not a requisite for the education being provided, particularly if poverty was an issue for the families concerned. Also, they believed that it was unacceptable that the Sisters were prepared to beg and accept what was needed for survival in the way of food and accommodation. Consequently, a number of the Irish born priests in particular, were appalled by the lifestyle of the Josephite sisters for they were not like the European nuns, who divided their members into two classes – the "Choir sisters and the Lay Sisters" (Foale, 1989). In other words, the clergy were of the opinion that Mary MacKillop's sisters were not "gentlewomen – ladies", like their European counterparts – for they did not follow the rules of enclosure and they mixed and lived with what might be described as the "riff raff" of society – the poorest of the poor:

> It was the way Mary MacKillop and Woods adapted their observance to suit the Australian environment that gave rise to conflict. Thus, the sisters' poverty, their mobility, their living in groups of two or three in places where a priest seldom visited, their independence of clerical control and their refusal to admit of class distinctions within their ranks or to cater for the needs of the rich, irked some of their contemporaries, especially among the bishops and priests (Foale, 1989:24).

According to Foale (p.37), "Woods ... later regretted that so few educated women had entered the Institute during its foundation years. Initially, however, lack of education or social standing was no bar[rier] to a girl's being admitted. In fact, the most notable characteristic of the first sisters ... was their ordinariness. Sixty-seven, or just over half of the

127 young women, who became Josephites between the foundation and September 1871, were either born or reared in the colonies."

Hence, "Life for Mary and the early Sisters was a constant challenge yet one which they approached with great trust and faith in God" (McCreanor, 2010:xviii). Nevertheless, McCreanor emphasises that *"by late 1869 there were approximately 80 Sisters engaged in working in some 23 schools as well as in social welfare through a House of Providence for* [the] *aged and homeless"* (p.xvii). It was apparent however that at this time "a perceptive observer might have noticed that Woods was very much overworked and was showing signs of the strain of his many duties ... [and responsibilities]" (Foale, 1989:55). He travelled less around the diocese and didn't hold "regular meetings of the Catholic Education Council. He also neglected to test the genuineness of the religious experiences that several mystically inclined young sisters claimed to be enjoying, and, instead, encouraged them to believe that they were specially chosen souls who were called to follow an extraordinary path to holiness" (ibid.). Mary saw the dangers but couldn't convince Woods of the potential risks associated with his encouraging these sisters in their "abnormal" behaviour.

In 1869, Bishop Sheil accepted an invitation from Bishop James Quinn to send Josephite sisters to his diocese in Queensland. *"Mary travelled to Brisbane with the first group of Sisters and stayed with them during 1870. Her absence from Adelaide left a huge gap in the leadership of the group"* (McCreanor, 2010:xviii) in South Australia. Paton (2010:12) writes that the Sisters remained "in Queensland until 1879 when Mary was obliged to withdraw them after trouble with the Bishop who wanted control over the Sisters" and wanted them to be subject to him and his diocese and to surrender their centralised form of governance. "However, Mary would not yield to his demands" (ibid.). Consequently, the Bishop asked the sisters if they wanted to leave, and if so, to go and those who wanted to stay could remain, but if they chose to remain, they had to abide by his rule of governance of the Institute. He was quite surprised when he realised that all the sisters would probably leave and that there would be about 1300 children without teachers, so he reneged on his demands and reached a compromise – a truce, but it was short-lived, and when several more Mercy Sisters arrived from overseas to staff the schools – the diocese bid farewell to the Josephites.

Now Bishop Matthew Quinn, who was the brother of Bishop James Quinn in Queensland, approached Mary MacKillop in 1871, about sending sisters to staff schools in his diocese in Bathurst. However, this Bishop "turned out to be particularly antagonistic to Central Government. Mary resisted his attempts. He tried to change their Rule so that he had power over what they taught" (Paton, 2010:12). Finally, he gave the sisters a choice, they could return to Adelaide or if they remained, they were to submit to his form of Rule. Most of the sisters returned to Adelaide – some authors state that two sisters remained (Foale, 1989:132) while others give the number as one (Paton, 2010:12). Bishop Quinn then established his own institute of sisters who, in time, became known as the "Black Josephites", because of the colour of their habits.

Over the years the unpopularity of Woods among several of his colleagues continued as did their perceived opinion of the inefficiency and incompetence of the Josephite sisters. Two priests, in particular – both Franciscans, were at the root of much of the disharmony affecting the diocese. Father Charles Horan (who saw himself as the successor to Sheil) and Father Patrick Keating (who was later dismissed from the diocese and returned to Ireland – some reports suggest there were suspected allegations regarding children in his care). Matters came to a head, when Sheil was in Rome and Mary was in Queensland: "Both leaders were now too far from Adelaide to intervene effectively in its affairs" (Foale, 1989:58). Father John Smyth was again the Vicar-General during Sheil's absence and Teresa MacDonald was acting as Superior for Mary MacKillop.

At this time, Woods' emotional state was unravelling and he "reached a point where he believed that he held the offices [of General superior and provincial of the Institute] by divine appointment" (Foale, 1989:61). He sent Teresa away to reside in the community's "Refuge", and left one of his "so-called favourites in charge" a Sister Ignatius, who was disliked by the other sisters and who claimed that "she was the recipient of remarkable spiritual and mystical favours from God" (p.62). The emotional and mental state of Woods was now near breaking point. He didn't think the behaviour of Ignatius or a couple of her followers was unusual in any way and believed that the Institute was blessed to have such visionaries in their midst.

The other members of the Institute were unhappy, and disunity became the norm. This, and the dissatisfaction of Woods' colleagues, led to an implosion in the diocese that occurred following the death of Smyth in 1870, and the return of Bishop Sheil in 1871. Horan as the leader together with members of the diocesan clergy prepared a Memorial to present to Sheil on his return. It was "a statement of their grievances … The several issues raised in this memorial can be reduced to one, namely, that the clergy had no say in the control and management of the Sisters of St Joseph in the areas of their recruitment, training, placement or teaching methods" (p.70). Obviously, there were other criticisms including, "that the general public was being scandalised by the publication of visions and other supernatural phenomena by Woods and some of the sisters … [and in addition] they wanted Woods removed from his powerful position as Director General of Catholic Education and Father Director of the Sisters of St Joseph" (p.71). The clerics were prepared to have the Institute disbanded if necessary.

Paton (2010:13) posits that on his return from overseas and being confronted with the perceived allegations, the ailing Bishop Sheil "was so influenced by what he heard about the Sisters from the priests that he excommunicated Sister Mary in the chapel at Franklin street and dispersed the Adelaide Sisters." Reasons contributing to such an extraordinary decision were that Sheil believed that as Bishop of the Diocese "he was the 'sisters' ecclesiastical superior … [and] had the right to make necessary changes to the rules and, if circumstances appeared to warrant it, the power to disband the Sisters" (Foale, 1989:91). However, Foale (ibid.) maintains that neither Sheil,

> nor any other ecclesiastic could oblige sisters who had taken vows according to one set of rules to accept another. The changes Sheil now proposed were so radical that their adoption would have altered the entire character of the Institute. The most important was that the community be divided into two classes, namely, choir and lay sisters. As well, each house was to be under the complete control of the local pastor and to have no ties beyond those of friendship with other houses of the Institute. There was to be no movement or interchange of sisters between houses. Only paying pupils were to be admitted into their schools and the sisters were to teach music, languages and other "accomplishments" if and when required. Seemingly Sheil and his advisers had expected the sisters to comply with their suggestions without demur. However, they soon discovered that these women knew their rights according to church law.

On behalf of her sisters Mary (who had returned to the diocese in early September 1871), respectfully declined Bishop Sheil's proposal and stated her position clearly. For her the rule as it was, was sacred, and when formulated had been given his approval, and she was disappointed that such decisions were being made when Woods (who had gone to Sydney in early August 1871) was absent from the Diocese. The sisters were put under review and examined for their "educational attainments and teaching ability with a view to classifying them as lay or choir sisters" (Foale, 1989:92).

In a letter dated 21st September 1871, Mother Mary MacKillop wrote to a Sister Francis Xavier: "My dear Sister – This has been a day of Crosses ... Do not be surprised, dear Sister, when I tell you that I have been excommunicated by the Bishop tonight for non-compliance … We have all good courage … All my fear is lest any of my sisters should act proudly or say some unbecoming word. Oh, let us, if we cannot agree to what our poor dear old Bishop requires, at least be humble in the way we refuse" (cited in McCreanor, 2011:269-270).

Sheil died on 1 March 1872, and some days before his passing he organised through his senior priest Peter Hughes, "to absolve Mary MacKillop from her sentence of excommunication without requiring that she formally request the absolution, without any preconditions and without imposing any penance or asking that she abjure any errors, and with the understanding that she be immediately restored to her position as superior of the Institute" (Foale, 1989:109).

In order to consolidate her position, and have her rule approved by the Holy See, so that in future there would be no doubt over her intention to have centralised governance, Mary was encouraged to travel to Rome in March 1873, by the then administrator of the South Australian diocese Christopher Reynolds (later Archbishop), and his offsider Joseph Tappeiner, a Jesuit priest. Mary went to Rome without meeting with Woods. "The officials [there] … soon realised that the rule could not be approved as it stood, because it was much too detailed in its prescription and was 'very imperfect and confused' … [hence] a new simplified constitution" (p.130) was produced, which retained the central government. However, one of the conditions for approval of the document was that the Institute "should possess money, land and income in its own right" (p.131) to ensure survival.

The rule was eventually approved, with the few minor changes concerning the necessity of the sisters at least owning some property, as they needed to have some financial independence to survive. Mary was pleased about the central governance being retained because, "as long as she was superior general, she was not prepared to make any concessions on this score because, in her view, a strong, centralised authority structure was the single most important means of preserving unity among her sisters ... These *Constitutions* gave the Superior General of the Institute full domestic authority over its government and administration and spelled out the rights and duties of the bishops in relation to it" (p.129-131).

Hence, with "the confirmation of the principle of central government, the position of ecclesiastical superior was abolished once and for all, and the Institute was placed under the care of a 'Cardinal Protector' based in Rome. The Josephites' first such protector was Cardinal Franchi" (p.131). The Institute held its first General Chapter on Mary's return from overseas in 1875. The new *Constitutions* were accepted, and Mary was elected Superior-General. Father Woods was against the acquisition of property being added to the Rule, which he had formulated in the early days of the Institute, "He was very much against the decision of Rome to make owning property mandatory" (Paton, 2010:13). Woods felt betrayed by Mary and in an emotive letter to her in June 1875 he wrote:

> *It has been almost a death blow to me to see the poverty and simplicity of the Institute of St Joseph destroyed and that without my being able to say a word in its defence. I can never get used to that and it makes me sick with sorrow whenever I think of it ... No one understands the spirit of what I consider the Institute was intended to be who does not think that the essential point of all. Unity without poverty and simplicity is a poor privilege* (cited in Foale, 1989:137).

The relationship between the two co-founders was never the same again. Father Julian Tenison Woods died in Sydney on 7 October 1889 (Deitrich Hans Borchardt, 1976), without being fully reconciled with Mother Mary or wanting to have any involvement with the Institute. Mary was never critical of his stance on the issue and always spoke of her co-founder with respect and admiration for his outstanding support during those early difficult years.

During the years 1880 – 1883, Mary was receiving requests from dioceses in New Zealand, Western Australia, Sydney and Armidale to staff their schools. She was in a quandary, as some offers had to be refused due to a lack of personnel, and she was also wary of antagonising her bishop, Christopher Reynolds, who was worried that she would remove the novitiate from Adelaide to another diocese and that he might eventually then lose the presence of the sisters altogether. Some of the sisters were also upset at the thought that this might happen. For "Reynolds … [had been] overseas when the Josephites entered the dioceses of Sydney and Armidale and Vaughan lodged his application for permission to establish a novitiate in Sydney" (Foale, 1989:154). Archbishop Roger Vaughan of Sydney had welcomed the Sisters and had no issue with their rule or their constitutions.

However, you may recall that when Bishop Sheil died, he was "succeeded by Bishop Reynolds who, at first was very well-disposed to the Josephites, but with the animosity of the priests toward the Sisters he became disaffected. He decided to set up a Commission in 1883, to enquire into the affairs of the Sisters of St Joseph in South Australia" (Paton, 2010:15). This was following allegations that Mother Mary was imbibing too much alcohol (medically approved due to serious health problems), and that there was a rapidly accruing debt on property/properties owned by the sisters in the diocese (ibid.). Reynolds also revisited the issue of their centralised governance and was determined once again to be their ecclesiastical superior even though the position had been abolished by Rome when a Cardinal was appointed as the Protector of the Institute.

The tension in the diocese began to affect the harmony and spirit of the members of the Institute in Adelaide. Foale (1989:167) asserts that Reynolds announced in 1883, "that he had instructions from Rome to make a formal visitation of all the religious communities in the diocese and was about to begin with the Sisters of St Joseph … [though as mentioned previously] no such instructions [from Rome] were ever issued" (p.173). Reynolds dismissed Mary from the diocese in November 1883, and appointed an interim Superior General, even though he did not have authority to do this, as the Institute was under "papal protection". Mary did not argue but complied with his request. In 1885 Sister Bernard Walsh was appointed Superior General and Mother Mary became her Assistant. The following years were difficult but when Reynolds died in 1893, "Mary never let … [her sisters] forget that he had been a true friend to them in their hour of need … [for] he had restored the Institute after Sheil's death in 1872, [and] had sent Mary … to Rome during the following year [to have her Rule of Life approved] …[He also] encouraged her during the time of her difficulties with the Bishops Quinn" of Queensland and Bathurst (p.187).

In a decree dated 25 July 1888, "the Institute of St Joseph of the Sacred Heart … [became] a Regular Congregation of Pontifical Right with its Mother House in Sydney. The decree stated that the then incumbent "Mother General, Sister Bernard Walsh, was to remain in office for the next ten years" (Foale, 1989:174). Paton writes that the first New Zealand foundation was made in 1883 and that it was a country that Mother Mary visited on several occasions, with the first being "in 1894-5, the second from 1897-8; the third in 1900 and the last in 1902" (2010:15-16) when she suffered a stroke and with "Her right side paralysed … she was confined to a wheelchair. She returned to Sydney at the end of 1902" (ibid.). Mother Mary of the Cross MacKillop died in Sydney on 8 August 1909 at the age of 67 years. "She is buried in the chapel at Mount Street, North Sydney". As mentioned in the Introductory paragraph Pope Emeritus Benedict XVI canonised St Mary of the Cross MacKillop on 17 October 2010. Her feastday is celebrated on 8 August.

Leadership as Service

During his Homily on the occasion of the canonisation of St Mary of the Cross MacKillop on 17 October 2010, Pope Emeritus Benedict XVI spoke of the wisdom associated with education and the faith commitment of inspired educators: "Remember who your teachers were; from these you can learn the wisdom that leads to salvation through faith [and service] in Christ Jesus."

Wisdom has built her house, she has hewn her seven pillars (Proverbs 9:1, cited in Sipe & Frick, 2015:4). For the purpose of this analysis, the "Seven Pillars of Servant Leadership" (see Appendix A for the list of attributes), are outlined below, and the discussion on each pillar includes aspects of the life and leadership practices of St Mary of the Cross MacKillop.

Pillar 1 – "Person of Character"

As a leader and co-founder of an Institute that was formed in love and the spirit of poverty, Mary MacKillop valued true humility: "It is good to suffer wrong in silence, but better to prevent wrong in others, and to make the children of Jesus and Mary what they should be – happy and charitable" (Mary MacKillop, 3 June 1870, cited in McCreanor, 2011:99). She valued the poor, and what she could offer them: "Mary MacKillop never wavered in her single-minded determination to preserve unity, regardless of the cost to her personally" (Foale, 1989:187). In a letter to Bishop Sheil, dated 10 September 1871 she emphasised: "I longed for a religious life, one in which I could serve God, and His poor neglected little ones in poverty and [have a] disregard of the world and its fleeting opinions" (cited in McCreanor, 2011:257). Mary had confidence believing that God in his providence would look after her.

Pillar II – "Puts People First"

The life and works of Mother Mary MacKillop were a testament to her great love for God, and her fellow human beings. As we read her profile, we see a person who is not self-serving for who could endure all that Mary did, and still not retain trust in God and neighbour? From the very beginning of the Institute she worked with Father Woods to provide a faith-based education for the children who were born into poverty, but who were blessed by God when they were given the opportunity to be educated by people of faith: "Woods insisted that the sisters – and, by inference, all who taught in Catholic schools – were 'bound as a duty they owe[d] to God and their neighbour' to work towards the achievement of … [the aims of the Catholic school] and urged them to remember that the Church could only succeed in keeping 'its hold against the wicked, secular instruction of the world by offering a superior education'" (Foale, 1989:17).

It is evident from reading the information on the life of Mary MacKillop, that "The sisters' personal needs were of paramount importance to her, as were the needs of the local clergy, some of whom had gone to great lengths to support the Institute in its time of trial" (p.119). In June 1872 in her report to the Apostolic Commission investigating the affairs of the Adelaide Diocese, following decisions by Bishop Sheil, who had died in the February, Mary MacKillop spoke kindly of the man who was responsible for her excommunication and separation from the Institute:

> Our late and much-loved Bishop was far too kind a Father to the children of the institute for any, much less myself, to forget his memory now. I think he thought too kindly of us – and then when some who did not understand our struggles and intentions spoke perhaps too harshly of us, he believed what he heard and consequently felt bitterly disappointed in us. He was never anything but kind, extremely kind to any of us until early in September last [when she was excommunicated], (cited in McCreanor, 2011:372).

Mary stated that she wanted to discuss the situation with the Bishop, and acquaint him with more of the details, but she did not have the opportunity to do so, and when she referred the matter to her Director Father Woods, she said that his "motive in this was one of extreme charity, and besides he thought it more pleasing to God that we should suffer ... these little annoyances in silence" (ibid.). Mary didn't really hold anyone to blame except herself for her excommunication. "From some things I heard last September, I believe that fault was found with my visiting the Convents, it appearing to some of the priests that I did so for personal gratification, or from a love of authority etc" (cited in McCreanor, 2011:378).

Mary's view was that "an Institute such as ours with its subjects in so many ways exposed to dangers from which others are exempted, it becomes the bounded duty of someone from time to time to see and encourage them, and to endeavour to keep uniformity both in the schools and in the Sisters' minds" (ibid.). Hence as the nominated Sister Guardian, Mary was required to visit the schools and convents at regular intervals, to check that everything was running smoothly, and that if there were any difficulties, she would discuss these with the parish priests, and changes would be made if needed. Mary only ever had the interests of others at heart. She "was always concerned for the Sister's welfare [particularly those] in isolated outposts" (Foale, 1989:144).

Pillar III – "Skilled Communicator"

There are volumes of books containing letters written by Mary MacKillop. She was prolific in her letter writing, particularly to Father Woods. They exchanged numerous letters that are still extant with many being published and available for the purpose of research or for those interested in the historical content. Mary listened empathetically to others, but she was not backward in coming forward, when it was warranted. She stood up for herself and her sisters. There were occasions in her life, as we have seen in the profile when she was called to justify her actions and those of her sisters. She was brought to task by Bishops (Queensland, Bathurst, Western Australia, and on occasion Adelaide) for not conforming to their perceived right to have control of her Institute, and to enforce their role as ecclesiastical superiors (or so they thought) of the Institute, when in reality, she was under "Papal protection". She showed strength and initiative by standing her ground. The rule was important to her.

Mary went to Rome to state her case, and this would have been a rare sight at that time having a woman, a leader, come before the Roman officials and not only present her argument, but also with a few modifications, gain approval for her rule, and have a Cardinal Protector appointed to offer advice regarding future decisions. She accepted the feedback, and even agreed to some minor changes in the rule, as long as the centralised form of governance stayed – this she believed was the key to maintaining unity and harmony in the Institute. In addition, she had a strong belief in the will of God. Paton (2010:43) posits that "When she wrote 'His will be done in all things,' Mary MacKillop had the Rule very much in mind ... [she] saw the Rule as she saw the later Constitutions, as an expression of the Will of God for the Sisters. In response, they were to give themselves entirely to God by living according to the Rule ... God's Will, as it was manifested in the Rule, was formative."

Mary was aware of her limitations and those of her sisters. She knew that many of the members of her Institute were colonial born like herself, and that those who entered before the novitiate had been firmly established, would need assistance to cope with the demands of religious life. For they had received virtually no spiritual preparation, and the obvious lack of initial training in the rudiments of teaching, which affected their competence in the classroom, had led to complaints from the pastors and some laity.

Pillar IV – "Compassionate Collaborator"

Father Julian Woods and Mary MacKillop built teams and communities. According to Foale (1989:12), "The Institute of the Sisters of St Joseph came into being at Penola because that township lay at the centre of Woods' mission area and because Mary MacKillop, the teacher at his local Catholic school, was prepared to throw in her lot with him and become the first Sister of St Joseph. The needs of the area gave rise to the idea of a new religious institute." (ibid.). In her letter to Bishop Sheil on 10 September 1871, Mary revisits this exciting time in her life, when she collaborated with Father Woods to build her community – her Institute:

> I went to open a school in Penola under Father Woods who gradually unfolded to me his idea of endeavouring to do something … for the neglected poor children of South Australia. The way in which he described their wants so completely agreed with all my previous desires that when he asked me whether (provided he got the Bishop's consent to commence an Institute to meet these wants) I would remain and become one of his first children in the work, I joyfully consented. From that time, I gave myself completely to the work, which almost every day seemed to confirm as the vocation I had so long sought and under the direction of my good Confessor I found true peace (cited in McCreanor, 2011:258).

The trials and tribulations that beset Mary throughout her faith journey, didn't deter her from her mission of reaching out to the poor and marginalised. Her empathy was exceptional as she valued her sisters, the clerics (even those who were so judgmental of her behaviour), and the laity whom she served with such love and compassion.

Pillar V – "Has Foresight"

Mary was a visionary, as was her co-founder of the Institute Father Julian Woods, however his:

> direct influence on Josephite affairs ceased after 1875 but Mary's involvement with them lasted throughout her lifetime. She was Superior-General until her deposition

in 1885, Assistant-General to Mother Bernard Walsh for the next fourteen years and Superior-General again from January 1900 until her death in August 1909. The credit for the idea of the Institute and its initial foundation belongs to Woods, the visionary and dreamer. However, its later development and ultimate survival were largely the result of Mary's single-minded determination to bring his ideas to fruition. It was she who held the Institute together after his departure, especially during the period 1871-1885. She did so because she commanded the sisters' loyalty and was genuinely concerned for their personal well-being (Foale, 1989:191).

Mary had a great awareness of just what was needed to justify her actions before a demanding clergy, who were confronting and even on occasion, quite abusive in their language to her; however, she knew to refrain from retaliating verbally and was prepared to move on; and after each "affront", she followed her plans and what she believed was God's will for her and her Institute. She did not falter, but proudly walked the path needed to serve her vision which in time became her legacy to future generations.

Pillar VI – "Systems Thinker"

The "Big Picture" for the Josephite Order, is its outstanding history that has weathered the enormous pressures that surrounded its essence since inception. So many trials and tribulations experienced and overcome by one leader – one woman, supported on occasion by Woods, but often left to face the vicious onslaughts on her own. What incredible courage and resilience! The charism of St Mary of the Cross MacKillop is a legacy for future generations, and is embedded in the rule, constitutions, and her writings and numerous letters. Mary gifted her sisters with the stewardship of the schools and buildings she established. She encouraged social welfare work, catering particularly to those who were ill in mind and body, and she advocated the care of the elderly, whom she believed to be wise with age and experience. As in the early days of the Institute many of the Sisters in our contemporary times, are living in small groups, providing for and serving the poor and those who are in need, both in rural and urban communities. In this they are emulating the fine example set by their foundress in another time, century and millennium.

Pillar VI – "Leads with Moral Authority"

The missionary discipleship of St Mary of the Cross MacKillop, was undertaken during her lifetime, and now in our contemporary era, she speaks to us through some of the venues dedicated to her honour many of which are visited by pilgrims from around the globe. One such location is Mary MacKillop Place "Museum" in North Sydney. It is "housed in the original 'Practice School' for novices built in the 1900s … [In addition, there is] The Mary MacKillop Memorial Chapel [which] is adjacent to the museum." Within the chapel is the tomb and resting place of Mary MacKillop.

Another important landmark was described to me by close friends and former educators' – husband and wife team, Maria and Robert McRae. Their "descriptive" narrative is as follows:

In early May 2018 we were on the Great Australian Road Trip from the Gold Coast to Western Australia and spent a few days in Mt. Gambier. The proximity to Penola and our combined 85+ years involvement in Catholic Education led us to the Mary MacKillop Interpretive Centre in Penola. The small town of Penola is attractive and busy both as a pilgrimage centre for Mary MacKillop and for being located on the southern edge of the Coonawarra region.

The Mary MacKillop Interpretive Centre, located adjacent to the attractive Parish church of St Joseph, is remarkable for the insight it provides into the life of Mary and her drive to provide an education for the children of poor families. The Centre is well set up with attractive photo/information boards and artefacts relevant to the life of

Mary. The overwhelming impression is of a woman completely dedicated to her cause, who consistently displayed strong faith, determination and resilience.

The Centre also has a very well-presented exhibition dedicated to Fr. Julian Tenison Woods, which provides an excellent insight into his life and work. His impact on the life and work of Mary MacKillop is well-documented and illustrated. The adjoining Woods-MacKillop Schoolhouse is well worth a visit as it gives a further window into the nature of the education, both religious and secular, that was provided by Mary and her Sisters. The Centre is well presented and informative, the staff of volunteers cheerful and helpful and the town itself caters for a range of visitors. It was an enjoyable and worthwhile diversion on our westward journey (Personal correspondence – 2019).

The Congregation of the Order of the Sisters of St Joseph of the Sacred Heart have indeed assumed the role of cultural custodians of the heritage of their co-founders – St Mary of the Cross MacKillop and Father Julian Tenison Woods.

Values

Aspects of Mary MacKillop's life and works are now discussed in relation to the values – dignity, respect, fairness, justness and equality (see Chapter 4 for the terms of reference).

Dignity

Mary personified dignity in the way she handled the numerous allegations and complaints against her and her institute. Pope St John Paul II in his Apostolic Letter *Mulieris Dignitatem* on "The Dignity and Vocation of Women" (1988:para.27), emphasises that "in every country we find many 'perfect' women (cf.*Prov.*31:10) who, despite persecution, difficulties and discrimination, have shared in the Church's mission." Hence while Mary MacKillop was a human being and therefore not "perfect", she nevertheless embodied the ideals of which the Pontiff speaks.

Respect

Mary had great respect for all people, and particularly the clergy: However, "As superior of a centrally governed religious institute, Mary also acted within her rights when she withdrew her sisters from Bathurst and Brisbane. Because their spiritual and physical well-being was of paramount importance to her she refused to leave them in situations where either might be compromised in any way, she found having to act against the wishes of these bishops very difficult because of her great respect for the priesthood but in the circumstances, felt that she had no choice in the matter" (Foale, 1989:136).

Fairness

When reading the life of St Mary of the Cross MacKillop, we can ask ourselves, was it fair that when her father Alexander couldn't provide for his family that she had to assume responsibility for them – was it because she was the eldest? Was it fair that she was excommunicated because of information provided by clerics who were perhaps misinformed? Why did Bishop Reynolds ask Mary to leave his diocese when she had worked so hard to consolidate her sisters in the colony? Was it fair when he appointed an interim Superior-General over Mary? Nevertheless, regardless of the negative attitudes and responses by Bishops and priests, Mary was always consistent in her dealings and responses, and didn't try to attribute blame to any her accusers. Indeed, she had a great sense of fairness, unlike her critics.

Justness

There was a definite lack of justness when Mary was excommunicated by Bishop Sheil on 22nd September 1871. She was a member of a religious community in his diocese and had a right to be protected. She was one woman who was "pitted" against many antagonists. Fortunately, Sheil corrected the situation prior to his death.

You may recall that when Bishop Reynolds was going through a crisis and he was worried he would lose the sisters, their novitiate and their Mother House to another diocese, he began to investigate various complaints that had been raised against Mary and her sisters. He organised a Visitation that he said had been authorised by Rome (which was incorrect) and during the visitations, the convent books were being examined by two priests, who refused to give Mary and her sisters "an opportunity to explain any seemingly anomalies in their pages ... The evidence indicates that the sisters were treated 'very unjustly' on this score, although it is possible that the bishop and his assistants were so frustrated by Mary's apparent naivete concerning money matters that they believed further discussion would be time wasted" (Foale, 1989:169). The Bishop sent Mary away from the diocese even though he had no authority to do this, as the Institute was under "Papal protection". There was no justness in this action.

Equality

St Mary of the Cross MacKillop certainly had her crosses to bear. She acted as a professional particularly when confronted with the often-misguided accusations that were directed at her. She treated everybody equally, whether the person was a Bishop, priest, sister or member of the laity. She was respectful of their human dignity, listened to them and responded politely though she was decisive and firm in her convictions. Mary spent her life working to improve the conditions of those in need. Her actions on behalf of the people of God, are supported in the catechism which states that in regard to human beings, "Their equal dignity as persons demands that we strive for fairer and more humane conditions" (CCC, 2000:para.1938).

According to Foale (1989:xi): "The sisters' struggle for autonomy in a male-dominated hierarchical Church touched upon and reflected many of the conflicts then wracking the wider Church in Australia and overseas. These included its struggle against the secular liberalism of the day, its members' attitudes towards social class and social mobility and its struggle for survival in a pluralist society." In our contemporary society, the Congregation of the Sisters of St Joseph of the Sacred Heart, continues to address challenges in the spirit of their co-founder St Mary of the Cross MacKillop!

The following chapter traces the life and faith journey of St Josephine Bakhita, a woman who as a child was kidnapped by slave traders, but who survived to become a member of a religious order and a canonised saint of the Catholic Church.

16

St Josephine Bakhita

The Encyclical Letter *Evangelium Vitae*: "On the Value and Inviolability of human life" (Pope St John Paul II, 1995), was written some 30 years after the Second Vatican Council (1962-1965) and emphasises the integrity and dignity of the human person. You may recall that this document and the following paragraph are both cited in Chapter 4 under the heading – "Dignity":

> Whatever is opposed to life itself, such as any type of murder, genocide, abortion, euthanasia, or wilful self-destruction, whatever violates the integrity of the human person, such as mutilation, torments inflicted on body or mind, attempts to coerce the will itself; whatever insults human dignity, such as subhuman living conditions, arbitrary imprisonment, deportation, slavery, prostitution, the selling of women and children; as well as disgraceful working conditions, where people are treated as mere instruments of gain rather than as free and responsible persons; all these things and others like them are infamies indeed. (1995:para.3).

Nearly a quarter of a century has passed since the publication of the above encyclical, and its relevance is just as applicable today in our contemporary society, as it was in the previous century and millennium. In 2015, the United Nations Congress defined "Human trafficking ... as 'the recruitment, transport, transfer, harbouring or receipt of a person by such means as threat or use of force or other forms of coercion, of abduction, of fraud or deception for the purpose of exploitation' (*Trafficking in Persons Protocol*) ... [and they emphasised that] [t]he trafficking of human beings has existed for centuries. It is a ruthless crime which mercilessly exploits millions of vulnerable women, children and men worldwide." In fact, "[a]ccording to a United Nations report, human trafficking has become the world's fastest-growing global crime. Millions of people in the world today are forced to engage non-consensually in activities such as commercial sex, street crime, domestic servitude and even the sale of organs and human sacrifice" (Priscilla Muzerengwa, 2019).

Pope Francis announced 8 February 2015 as a "Day of Prayer and Awareness against Human Trafficking … [and he called on] on governments to remove this 'shameful wound' which has no place in 'civil society.'" The Pontiff emphasised that "Each one of us feels committed to being the voice of these, our brothers and sisters, humiliated in their dignity" (ibid.). Calling "Human trafficking … [as] a crime against humanity" (Sr Bernadette Mary Reis, 2018), Pope Francis formally called for an end to the inhumane practice, by appealing "for renewed efforts to protect victims of human trafficking, and to denounce the exploitation and slavery of men, women, and children" (Christopher Wells, 10 February 2019). Muzerengwa writes that according to "the United Nations Office on Drugs and Crime Global Report on Trafficking in Persons 2016 … Seventy-nine percent of all detected trafficking victims are women and children" (2019, January 2). In 2019, Pope Francis officially declared 8 February to be a "World Day of Prayer, Reflection and Action Against Human Trafficking … [and a] time to end slavery" (Catholic Religious Australia, 2019).

The significance of the 8 February regarding "Action Against human trafficking", is that this date is the feastday of St Josephine Bakhita, who as a child, was kidnapped and sold into slavery. The following is an account of Josephine's faith journey from her origins in Africa, to her conversion to Christianity, and finally to her elevation to sainthood in the Catholic Church. Please note, that much of the information used for this Profile, has been taken from the Memoirs of St Josephine, which she completed in Schio in 1910, and which were "abstracted from 'Bakhita' by Maria Luisa Dagnino in Rome in 1991". All direct quotations of St Josephine are printed in italics, which is how her words are presented in the manuscript of her memoirs.

Profile

Josephine Bakhita was born about 1869 at Olgossa, Darfur, Sudan. According to Josephine, her family *"lived at the very heart of Africa, in a village of the Darfur region, known as Olgossa, close to Mt. Agilere"* (Maria Luisa Dagnino, 1991:5, cited in Bakhita's Memoirs, 1910). The family was relatively wealthy, with lands, crops and livestock. Josephine records, that her family consisted of her father, mother, and *"three brothers, three sisters and four others I never knew because they died before I was born. I [also] had a twin sister"* (cited in Roberto Italo Zanini, 2013:35).

Bakhita was not the name that Josephine received when she was born. The Vatican News sources (n.d.) state that "The fright and the terrible experiences she went through made her forget the name she was given by her parents. Bakhita, which means 'Fortunate [or lucky]', was the name given to her by her kidnappers." Also, it wasn't until her baptism in 1890, that Bakhita was given the name Josephine. Hence, as the faith journey of this exceptional women unfolds throughout this chapter, she will be referred to as Bakhita.

Apparently, on a day like any other, Bakhita's mother *"decided to go to the fields where we owned plantations and cattle, to make sure that the workers were doing their duty"* (Dagnino, 1991:5, cited in Bakhita's Memoirs, 1910). Bakhita admits that her life until that day was quite happy and free from worry. Her eldest sister didn't feel up to accompanying the other members of the family on their task, and hence requested permission to remain behind at home in the village to keep company with the youngest child. While the members of the family were occupied in the fields, slave traders attacked the village and kidnapped Bakhita's eldest sister. The youngest child, who had managed to hide from the raiders, reported the details of the kidnapping to the family when they returned, after hearing disturbing sounds emanating from their village (ibid.).

In his book, Zanini (2013:37) cites from the memoirs of Bakhita and provides background and historical information where warranted. He refers to Bakhita as "Mother Josephine". "We know that she belonged to a well-to-do family. Her uncle was the village chief, and her parents cultivated grain on several local farms." In his notes (ibid.), Zanini stresses that children in an African village in the 1800s, would have been unable to determine their exact age. However, at the time of her kidnapping, Bakhita gives her age: *"I was about nine years old, when, one morning after breakfast, I went with a little friend of mine, who was twelve or thirteen years of age, for a walk in the fields, not far from our home. During a pause in our games we were all intent on gathering some wild herbs…"* (Dagnino, 1991:6, cited in Bakhita's Memoirs, 1910).

While engaged and engrossed in their task, the girls were approached by two men – one had a concealed dagger, and the other – a gun (though it was hidden at the time). They persuaded Bakhita's friend to continue on her way, promising that Bakhita would meet up with her when she had completed a small task for them. After the separation of the two friends, Bakhita went to collect a "parcel" the men said they had left in the forest. Bakhita obeyed the orders of the adults, as her mother had always taught her the importance of obedience. However, she had not gone far when she sensed an uncomfortable feeling that both men had approached her stealthily from behind: *"One grabbed me roughly with one hand while he pulled out a big knife from his belt with the other. He put the point of the knife against my side and with a demanding voice said, 'If you scream, you're dead. Now move it. Follow us.' The other one pushed me, aiming the barrel of his gun at my back"* (cited in Zanini, 2013:38). Bakhita was just a young child, and she was extremely terrified. In her memoirs, she recalled that her *"little body* [was] *shaking uncontrollably. I made as if to scream, but a lump in my throat prevented me from doing so. I could neither speak nor cry"* (Dagnino, 1991:6, cited in Bakhita's Memoirs, 1910). She was ordered to move quickly and quietly.

After a time, Bakhita broke her silence and tried to call out for her parents, but her efforts were in vain – they could not hear, and her kidnappers threatened her life if she continued to cry out. They were relentless in their desire to reach their destination as quickly as possible. They *"violently dragged* [me] *along into the thick of the forest, through unbeaten tracks, I was forced to walk till evening. I felt dead tired, my feet and legs were bleeding because of the sharp pebbles and thorny bushes which pricked me all over. I burst into tears, though in no way did my sorrow touch the hearts of those cruel men"* (p.7).

Bakhita was forced to march the entire night with little food, except what was given to her in the way of leftover fruit. When the destination was reached very early the next morning, she was thrown into a room with no bed, but tools and other storage items. She was given dry bread to eat and left to sleep on the dirt floor. The Arab traders who had kidnapped her had given her the name "Bakhita" which as mentioned previously means "lucky [or fortunate]" in Arabic (Zanini, 2013:40). The implications of the meaning of the name would not become clear to Bakhita, until her years of slavery had ended, and Christianity became her focus. For then she realised that if she hadn't been kidnapped as a child, she would not have known about Christ the Lord, so she considered that she was indeed "lucky"!

After a month spent in captivity in the confined space, Bakhita was bought by a slave merchant who *"added me to the long queue of several other slaves, three men, three women and a young girl slightly older than myself ... without delay we set out on our way. Seeing the countryside, the sky and the water, being able to breathe some fresh air, restored my strength"* (Dagnino, 1991:8, cited in Bakhita's Memoirs, 1910). Bakhita writes that the journey took more than a week, and that they made very few stops. *"We always walked on foot. We crossed woods, mountains, valleys and deserts. As we reached new villages, our number*[s] *increased as more slaves were purchased"* (p.9).

When the caravan of slaves had reached the slave market, Bakhita and another (they were the youngest of the group) were separated from the others, their feet were chained together, and they were left in a room on their own. They spoke of family and in their grief also discussed ways to escape. *"The good Lord, who watched over us, even though we were unaware of it* [at the time], *offered us the chance to realize our daring feat"* (ibid.). Bakhita recalls that one evening when the Master had returned from the market, he unlocked the door, and released the chains so that the two young slaves could help with the unloading of the corn that he had bought. He wanted them to "husk the ears of corn" and feed the mule. *"He then departed, absentmindedly leaving the door unlocked. We were alone and without chains. God's providence – now was the time"* (Zanini, 2013:50). The two young slaves escaped, running as fast as they could into open country – then through woods and deserts.

As they ran through the night, the nocturnal noises and sounds of animals frightened them, as did the sounds of the passing slave caravans, from which they hid in thorny bushes. At times they also climbed trees for safety from prowling animals. Finally, they made it to a village and at first were excited, thinking that it might be the village from which they had been captured, but this was not the case. They were approached by a man who spoke kindly to them asking them their plans, and offering to take them to their parents, after they had rested. They trusted the seemingly caring nature of this stranger, but after giving them food and drink he *"led us out to a big pen full of goats and sheep. He made some space for an angareb* [Note:12 'A bed of intertwining cords on a wooden frame'] *and then tied our feet together with a big chain, telling us to stay in the pen until we were told what to do next. Here we were, slaves again"* (p.52).

The two were then sold to another slave trader, and spent some weeks with this caravan, travelling on foot to the nearest city. On arrival, Bakhita and her companion were brought to the house of an *"Arab leader. He was an extremely rich man and already owned a large number of slaves … My companion and I were destined to be handmaids of the young ladies who were his daughters, who came to like us ...* [Initially in] *that house I was treated well and lacked for nothing"* (p.55). However, Bakhita said that this situation was too good to last, and soon the son of the household turned on her:

> *He immediately got hold of the lash to beat me. Instinctively I ran to the next room to take shelter with his sisters ... He became furious, snatched me violently from my hiding place, hurled me to the floor and began to beat me ferociously both with his feet and with the lash. Finally, with a kick in my side, he left me half dead. I was completely unconscious. Some slave carried me away and lay me down on a pallet where I was to remain for more than a month"* (Dagnino, 1991:15, cited in Bakhita's Memoirs, 1910).

Some months following this violent attack, Bakhita was sold to a new master *"a general in the Turkish army. With him were his elderly mother and his wife. Both of the women were quite inhumane toward the poor slaves ... In the three years I spent in their service, I do not remember a day going by without my being hit. The wounds I received one day would not be healed before others were added the next, without my knowing why"* (Zanini, 2013:56). Reasons for the abuse and torture were negligible. Apparently on one occasion, Bakhita and her companion were in the presence of the general when he was arguing with his wife. They were forced to bear the brunt of his anger, for he wanted to take his frustration out on someone, consequently he *"ordered the two of us down to the courtyard and commanded two soldiers to throw us to the ground to be flogged. Those two [soldiers] began this cruel punishment with full force and left both of us covered in blood. I remember how they took aim at my thigh with the cane, taking away skin and flesh and giving me a long gash that left me immobile in bed for months"* (p.57). First aid was not administered to the slaves and Bakhita said that others in the household had died after receiving such blows. In fact, in her later years when her health deteriorated, she would require the use of a wheel-chair due to the many horrific injuries she had received during her years of slavery.

Bakhita recalled another extreme case of sadistic cruelty, in the form of a ritual to which she referred as "tattooing", a form of torture from which she had been previously spared *"though most of our fellow slaves had undergone it. Not only their bodies but even their faces* [and arms] *had been disfigured"* (Dagnino, 1991:18, cited in Bakhita's Memoirs, 1910). Apparently, the tattoo "marks" were to honour the owners of the slaves. Bakhita tells us that:

> *Up until now I did not have any tattoos ... Well, one day on a whim the lady of the house decided to give a gift to those who had not been tattooed ... A woman who was an expert in this cruel art was sent for. She led us beneath the portico, with our mistress behind us, whip in hand. The woman prepared a plate of white flour, another with salt, and a razor. She ordered the first among us to stretch out on the ground. Two of the strongest slaves were commanded to hold her, one by the arms and the other by the legs* (Zanini, 2013:56).

Bakhita was forced to watch as a slave was mutilated, and then had salt rubbed in the wounds. Soon it was Bakhita's turn. The whip in the hand of the "lady of the house" was a deterrent to trying to "escape", and fearful of the implications Bakhita immediately stretched herself out on the ground:

> *The woman, having been told to spare my face, began to make six cuts on my breasts and up to sixty on my stomach. Then forty-eight on my right arm. I could not tell you how I felt. It seemed I was dying at every moment, especially when they rubbed in the salt. Lying in a pool of blood, I was then carried to a bed, where I remained for hours unconscious ... the scars are still with me. I can honestly say that the reason I did not die was that the Lord miraculously destined me for better things* (pp.60-61).

The following is not mentioned in the memoirs written by Bakhita in 1910, or in Zanolini's *Tale of Wonder* on the life of Bakhita. However, it is mentioned in this account by Zanini of what occurred in the life of Bakhita, and it concerns another cruel attack on Bakhita in the home of the Turkish general in Kordofan. It is important to note that Zanini stresses that "The incident, which occurred during adolescence, was so psychologically devasting that the saint had the courage to recount it only in strict confidence in her old age ... [and that] Zanolini ... only revealed this information during the beatification process" (Zanini, 2013:61).

Apparently when Bakhita matured, her body was well-developed. However, it seems as if the Turkish general was dissatisfied with her full-bodied appearance being on display as it were. As a result, there was an occasion when Bakhita was called into his presence. She recalls that she knelt before him, and "He took the budding part of my chest roughly in his hands and began to twist my breasts as if they were dishrags" (Zanini, 2013:62). The painful process was repeated on at least two other occasions, and forever changed and deformed the shape of Bakhita's chest. Bakhita never spoke of this as she was humiliated and embarrassed at the time and in later years couldn't bring herself to mention the episode. It has only been revealed due to communication confided by Bakhita to another nun who later informed her superior and then relayed the incident to Zanolini prior to the process for beatification of Bakhita (ibid.).

During Zanolini's testimony at the beatification process for Bakhita, she also commented on the status of the future saint's virginity:

> "In response to my explicit questions on this matter, Mother Bakhita said that none of her masters, and none of the slaves either, had ever touched her." Sister Josephine always gave this same answer over the course of her life, attributing such circumstances to the intercession of Mary and to the protection of her guardian angel.
>
> When one considers the harrowing accounts of cruelty against women that have come to light, it seems impossible that, without direct divine intervention, Bakhita would have been able to preserve her virginity. And she took great pride in this fact. "Mother," she said when already very

old, speaking to her superior Martini, "I have been in the middle of mud, but I never got dirty" (Zanini, 2013:62).

Such an admission is indeed surprising, considering all the inhumane treatment that Bakhita received at the hands of her captors. Nevertheless, it would have been divine intervention that protected her purity and gave her the courage and strength to survive the torturous assaults on her body, during her many years of captivity.

Around 1882, the Turkish general, who had been away for some months, returned to Kordofan and announced that he wanted to return to his homeland – Turkey, and that he would sell some of his many slaves and keep just a small number. Bakhita was retained at that time, however the trip necessitated a stop-over at a hotel at Khartoum, and it was here that she was sold to an Italian Consul, Callisto Legnani. It was this "exchange" that was to transform Bakhita's life. Her new master was kind and generous, and her duties involved assisting with the housework and other such chores, and hence "for the first time since … [her] kidnapping", she enjoyed "peace and tranquillity" (Dagnino, 1991:20, cited in Bakhita's Memoirs, 1910).

Some two years later the consul was recalled to Italy. Bakhita said that when she heard this, she experienced a feeling like no other, as if she was meant to go to Italy, so she persuaded Legnani, who had developed a fondness for her, that he should take her with him. Despite the fact that to do so would incur financial and other obligations, Legnani eventually consented. In later years, Bakhita realised that the providence of God was in this decision though she didn't realise it at the time (ibid.).

The travellers consisted of the Consul, his friend Mr Augusto Michieli, Bakhita and a young boy, also a former slave from Africa. They set out for the port city of Suakin on the north-east coast of Sudan. During the month that the group remained in this city, news was received that Khartoum had been attacked by a "gang of rebels … [who] had carried away all the slaves" (Zanini, 2013:64). Bakhita realised that if she had stayed, she would have been kidnapped once again as she had so many years before, and unbeknownst to her at the time, the Lord had saved her again. This thought came to her in later years, when she had embraced Christianity.

The group finally set sail for the city of Genoa in Italy. On arrival at a hotel, the boy slave was assigned a new owner, and when Mr Michieli's wife saw the two slaves – Bakhita and the boy – she was keen to have a slave for herself, to assist with her expected child. The Consul then gifted Bakhita to his friends and proceeded alone on his journey to northern Italy. Bakhita recalls that *"The Michielis took me to Mirano Veneto where, for three years, I was to be the babysitter of their newly born Mimmina. The child soon came to love me very much, while naturally, I reciprocated with equal affection"* (Dagnino, 1991:21, cited in Bakhita's Memoirs, 1910).

After the passage of another three years, Bakhita travelled with Mimmina and her mother back to Sudan to the city port of Suakin. Mr Michieli was managing a hotel there, and some months after the arrival of the women, he decided that the family would settle for good in Africa. Therefore, Mrs Michieli (sometimes referred to as Lady Turina), Mimmina and Bakhita returned to Italy to finalise the sale of property, and to organise the transport of belongings back to Africa. However, as she departed from the African shores on this occasion, Bakhita was very sombre: *"Though I did not know it at the moment, this was to be my last goodbye to Africa, my native country. Something in my heart warned me that I would never set foot on that continent anymore and so it was to be"* (p.23).

The women and the child Mimmina returned to Mirano, where they had lived for some years prior to returning to Africa, and after a couple of years Mrs Michieli had finalised most of the obligations in Italy: "selling the house in Zianigo with its surrounding property" (Zanini, 2013:78), and was ready to return to Africa; however she was reluctant to take her daughter back to Suakin, and, according to Bakhita the mother wanted the child to remain in Italy and be admitted, *"into a boarding school where she would receive a good education. The Canossian Sisters in Venice agreed to give the child hospitality in their Catechumenate."* Zanini (2013:70) writes that it was Illuminato Checchini, the administrator for the Michieli's who persuaded his employers to entrust Mimmina to the Canossian Sisters, and as she adored Bakhita, to let the young woman remain in Italy as a companion for the child.

Known to be a fine upstanding Catholic, Checchini had explained the rudiments of Christianity to Bakhita, who had a positive response to his attention: *"From the very beginning he had developed a fatherly affection for me ... when he handed a Crucifix over to me, I noticed that he kissed it with great devotion. He then explained to me that Jesus Christ was the Son of God and that he had died for us. I naturally did not grasp the meaning of this"* (Dagnino, 1991:24, cited in Bakhita's Memoirs, 1910). Bakhita goes on to say, that she had never owned anything of her own, and wasn't really *"attached to anything. I remember how, as I looked at the Crucifix, I experienced a strange feeling which I could not explain"* (ibid.).

As she was leaving for Africa, Mrs Michieli told Bakhita that *"Here you are; this is your home"* (Zanini, 2013:81), and Bakhita and Mimmina were formally admitted to the Catechumenate Institute:

> We *were entrusted to the Sister in charge of the instruction of the Catechumens. Whenever I think of the loving care, she lavished on me, even now my eyes fill with tears. She wanted to know whether it was really my intention to become a Christian. In hearing that, indeed, this was my intention and the purpose for being here, she was overjoyed ... the gentle Sister responsible for all this was Sr Fabretti and she used to say that "I drank in the truth of the faith"* (Dagnino, 1991:24, cited in Bakhita's Memoirs, 1910).

Zanini (2013:82) writes that the room shared by Bakhita and Mimmina, "still exists today and is used as the bedroom for one of the Salesian Sisters who now runs the house." Because the view from the room is of "the Basilica of Santa Maria della Salute (Our Lady of Salvation) ... [it] helps explain why Mother Bakhita warmly recalled many years later that her room was nestled 'under the shadow of the Madonna'" (ibid.).

Barely a year had passed when Mrs Turina Michieli returned for her child and demanded that Bakhita also return to Africa with her. There was a position waiting for "the young African girl – behind a bar counter, serving coffee and liquor" (p.86). Bakhita had a strong reaction to the demands of her "mistress": *"I refused to follow her back to Africa, since my instruction for baptism had not yet been completed. I also knew that, if I had followed her after receiving baptism, I would not have had the opportunity to practise my new religion. That is why, I thought it better to remain with the Sisters"* (Dagnino, 1991:25, cited in Bakhita's Memoirs, 1910). The woman ranted and raved as it were, hurling verbal abuse at her servant, but Bakhita, though she had love for the woman who had looked after her, held steadfast to her convictions, and her desire to stay. She later wrote *"I am sure that the Lord gave me strength at that moment, because He wanted me for Himself alone"* (ibid.).

The matter took some resolving, and involved third and fourth parties and others – "Father Jacopo de' Conti Avogadro di Soranzo [the reverend superior of the Institute] … the Patriarch of Venice – His Eminence Domenico Agostini, … the attorney general of the king, … the President of the Congregation of Charity, … and some of the sisters of the Catechumenate" (Zanini, 2013:88). The outcome however was in Bakhita's favour, as in Italy slavery was illegal and so Bakhita was a free person. The date given was *"November 29, 1889"* (ibid.).

Then on 9 January 1890, a little over a month later, Bakhita received the sacraments of Baptism, Confirmation and Holy Communion. *"I was given the names Josephine, Margaret and Fortunata which in Arabic is Bakhita … Oh! What an unforgettable day that was!"* (Dagnino, 1991:26, cited in Bakhita's Memoirs, 1910). Bakhita remained in the Catechumenate for a few years, and then heeded a call from within her heart to enter the religious life as a Canossian nun. She maintains that it was on 7 December 1893, that *"I joined the Novitiate in the Institute of the Catechumenate in Venice where I had been instructed. After one and a half years I was called to Verona to receive the Holy Habit. A few months before the end of my third year of Novitiate I returned there to pronounce my Religious Vows"* (p.27). Josephine Bakhita made her first profession on 8 December 1896.

According to Zanini (2013:98): "From 1896 ... to 1947, the year of her death, Mother Josephine lived the life of a humble sister, almost exclusively within her convent. This long fifty-one-year period was invariably spent between Venice and Schio, except for three or four years, when she was sent throughout central Italy to promote the missions ... [p.108] These were trying days for the naturally shy and unassuming Bakhita, who was obliged to appear and speak in public." Josephine Bakhita died in Schio on 8 February 1947 at about the age of 78 years. She was beatified by the Catholic Church on 17 May 1992, with Josemaria Escriva the founder of Opus Dei, and she was canonised a saint on 1 October 2000. Her feastday is celebrated on 8 February.

Leadership as Service

Bakhita's entire life was one of service. As a child she was enslaved by traders, who tried to break her indomitable spirit by selling her to merchants, many of whom tortured her body, but not her soul. The atrocities she experienced as a slave, did not make her lose faith in her fellow human beings, for she always had hope that her life would change. While she was obedient to those who treated her so appallingly, she was always mindful of caring for the other slaves, when they were mistreated and in need of human compassion. Her courage, strength and natural insight and compassion, sustained her as she craved the light of wisdom and understanding in all the darkness!

Wisdom has built her house, she has hewn her seven pillars (Proverbs 9:1, cited in Sipe & Frick, 2015:4). For the purpose of this analysis, the "Seven Pillars of Servant Leadership" (see Appendix A for the list of attributes), are outlined below, and the discussion on each pillar includes aspects of the life of St Josephine Bakhita – a life inspired by love, forgiveness and service.

Pillar 1 – "Person of Character"

Throughout all the experiences of her early life, Bakhita valued herself and others. She was obedient to her captors. Rarely would a human being have experienced such degradation and indignity, and yet emerge physically and psychologically sound! She was deprived of her dignity and freedom, but she emerged strong and forgiving. Christopher Heffron in his article *St. Josephine Bakhita – A Model of Faith*, recounts words of Bakhita that are on record: "'If I were to meet the slave traders who kidnapped me and even those who tortured me,' she once said, 'I would kneel and kiss their hands, for if that did not happen, I would not be a Christian and religious today. The Lord has loved me so much. We must love everyone.' In the face of inhuman trials, she only saw the face of Christ" (2018, January 22). What strength of character! What faith! What love!

Pillar II – "Puts People First"

From her childhood, Bakhita put her trust in others. In her naivety, she believed what she was told and tried to see the good in everybody. Through her experiences, Bakhita put others first. However, after reading though her memoirs, there is only one occasion throughout her entire life where I noticed that Bakhita put herself first, and that was when Mrs Michieli wanted her to return to Africa, and Bakhita chose God over the love she had for the family that had nurtured her prior to her entrance to the Catechumenate Institute. For Bakhita the love of the divine was stronger than any human love!

In a Vatican News document (n.d.) Bakhita is described as a "Witness of love" to others: "Her humility, her simplicity and her constant smile won the hearts of all the citizens. Her sisters in the community esteemed her for her inalterable sweet nature, her exquisite goodness and her deep desire to make the lord known." Bakhita's advice to other people, whether those in religious life or those serving God in other ways was:

"Be good, love the Lord, pray for those who do not know Him. What a great grace it is to know God" (ibid.).

Due to injuries she received during her years as a slave, Bakhita suffered much as she aged, but she "continued to witness to faith, goodness and Christian hope. To those who visited and asked how she was, she would respond with a smile: 'As the Master desires'" (Vatican News, n.d.).

Pillar III – "Skilled Communicator"

Though she was illiterate, Bakhita managed to communicate her great faith to others, particularly when she was a member of the Canossian sisters. According to Rozann Lee (2018, February 8), "No literary works are attributed to Josephine Bakhita, few quips of theological genius carry her citation, no major religious orders or movements memorialize her earthly existence … She is a saint of almost-unnoticed holiness." As a member of the Canossian community she had her daily duties which mostly comprised "Cooking, sewing, embroidery and attending the door" (ibid.).

Josephine was asked to write her memoirs, and these were completed in 1910. They traced the story of her life from the time of her kidnapping, through to her embracing Christianity and eventually entering the Canossian Order as a religious. Her message in her memoirs to her sisters, states: "I beg of all the dear Sisters who will read these memoirs of mine to thank this generous Lord for me and to beg Him to grant me the grace to be more and more faithful to Him" (Dagnino, 1991:27, cited in Bakhita's Memoirs, 1910).

Pillar IV – "Compassionate Collaborator"

Bakhita had great empathy and love for others. Lee (2018, February 8) compares this saint with St Thérèse of Lisieux and her "Little Way". Lee also writes that: "Many of us can relate to the simplicity of this path to holiness. It hearkens back to Saint Teresa of Calcutta's words: 'In this life, we cannot do great things. We can only do small things with great love.' Our daily lives, the place wherein our vocation is actualized, provide countless opportunities to exercise this great love if we will only recognize them as such." Bakhita's life in the religious community was unremarkable, but it was memorable because she lived her life in holiness and great love for God and others. In regard to Bakhita's feastday on 8 February, Lee (ibid.) emphasises that "St. Josephine serves as a powerful intercessor for the deeply persecuted Christian population of Sudan ... [Her] feastday is a valuable reminder that the Church is constantly being persecuted. For most Christians, this state of being is the status quo. Let us fervently implore the intercession of St. Josephine on behalf of these persecuted Christians all over the world."

Pillar V – "Has Foresight"

Bakhita was keen to engage in active discipleship. She wanted to be a missionary. She was on a mission to help Africa and her family, and she realised that she could do this through prayer. Zanini informs us that:

> She possessed a keen awareness of being a missionary in and through prayer. She intuited – or perhaps she understood very precisely, since we are unable to plumb the depths of the mystery of holiness, nor can we grasp the prophetic capacities of the saints – that even though she lived a simple and, in many ways, obscure life of a nun in a little northern Italian town, despite all of this she could truly bring Christ to the world, "raising up a people to God" in her Africa (2013:198).

Since Bakhita's passing to eternal life, there have been several miracles that have been said to have occurred through her intercession. To be beatified and canonised official miracles need to be approved by the

Church. Two such miracles are listed by Zanini (p.216-217). One concerns Mother Angela Silla Mari, a Canossian nun who "was diagnosed with tubercular synovitis of the knee ..." She lost the use of her leg and after hospital stays and the need for surgery, she participated in a novena to Mother Bakhita and was fully cured just prior to surgery being organised to remove "the kneecap and a portion of the shinbone" (ibid.).

The other miracle concerned Eva Da Costa, single mother of four children, who was "diagnosed with diabetes mellitus ... [and who] fell into a hyperglycemic coma" in 1976 (p.218). She recovered from this, but her overall condition deteriorated over the years and there was the threat of amputation to at least one of her legs. In 1992, she received a visit from Mother Regina dos Santos, a Canossian nun, who encouraged Eva to attend a group meeting of women "In preparation and thanksgiving for the beatification of Mother Josephine Bakhita. The ... group prayed a novena together" (p.219). During one of the meetings Eva heard about the torture of Bakhita, and she touched her own wounds while praying to the saint. "In silence she made a humble prayer of petition: 'Bakhita, you who have suffered so much, please help me, and, for the love of god, make my legs get better.'" Her prayers were answered, and her leg/s healed (pp. 219-220).

Since Bakhita's beatification, "one can count across the globe over a hundred chapels, parishes, prayer groups and youth groups, base communities, hospitals, health centers and medical dispensaries, schools, and at least two religious communities bearing the name of Bakhita; hence there must be something exceedingly attractive and prophetic about this humble black nun who was once a slave" (p. 200). Indeed, Bakhita has inspired generations with her awareness of the importance of prayer and holiness and serving just one master – Our Lord and God, Jesus Christ.

Pillar VI – "Systems Thinker"

The "Big Picture" for Bakhita, was that after overcoming almost insurmountable odds as a victim of slavery, she then lived close to fifty-one years as a Canossian nun, in relative peace and was well-known for her simplicity, her humility and her sanctity. Zanini (2013:195) quotes Father Paolo Rocca, Director of the centre for "Migrantes Giuseppina Bakhita di Alba ... [a shelter in Italy whose entire approach is based upon the example of Bakhita] who maintains that Bakhita came to Italy as an immigrant. Therefore, she seemed to be a perfect example and model, a bridge that would enable dialogue ... Bakhita has been a real revelation." Zanini (ibid.) writes about "Another migrant center dedicated to Bakhita [that] is located in Florence." Apparently, the Director a Father Mioli, a Scalabrini priest, heard about Bakhita when he was in the seminary during the Second World War, "I remember that people often spoke about Bakhita. What they were saying had a ring of sanctity to it" (p.196).

More examples are included by Zanini, regarding the growing awareness of Bakhita and the incredible charisma that continues to surround her popularity, which is being cultivated and promoted bringing hope to many in our contemporary world. Zanini refers to a group in Turin that is committed to publishing "a magazine called *Bakhita News*" (p.197). One of the phrases on the magazine's cover echoes words of Bakhita, "'Take heart, I am praying for you' ... She is also presented as a 'luminous figure of a non-EU immigrant in Italy'" (p.197). During the process for the canonization of Bakhita, there were reports of many graces and blessings received by a large number of the faithful as they engaged in prayer, to ask this humble and spiritual nun to intercede on their behalf before the Lord.

Pillar VII – "Leads with Moral Authority"

Pope Emeritus Benedict XVI in his Encyclical Letter *Spe Salvi* on "Christian Hope" states that besides Bakhita's:

work in the sacristy and in the porter's lodge at the convent, she made several journeys round Italy in order to promote the missions: the liberation that she had received through her encounter with the God of Jesus Christ, she felt she had to extend, it had to be handed on to others, to the greatest possible number of people. The hope born in her which had "redeemed" her she could not keep to herself; this hope had to reach many, to reach everybody.

The former Pontiff's words refer to Bakhita in terms of hope – hope for the future. Bakhita's early life was almost a paradox – she lived a virtuous life in the midst of depravity. Her oppressors couldn't break her spirit or touch her soul. Her inner spirit sustained her until she was touched by the promise of a life, that could be lived serving one master, who embraced her with a love that sanctified her, and raised her to sainthood.

Values

Aspects of Bakhita's life are now discussed in relation to the values – dignity, respect, fairness, justness and equality (see Chapter 4 for the terms of reference).

Dignity

Zanini (2013:200) recalls the words of Sister Maria Lucia Tokoyo, "Bakhita embodies the dignity of Africa for all mankind to see. Africans recognize this and feel it with a sense of pride and as a sign of hope." She maintained her human dignity in the midst of degradation and extreme torture. On occasion even her colour was an issue. Zanini (p.192) tells us that she "faced the racial climate of her day" with pride in her faith and race. Italians at the time would not have seen people of Bakhita's colour. On several occasions, she was referred to as "little brown mother" (p.221). When she was in the convent:

[I]t was not only the people she met outside the convent who made comments about her skin color. It was also her own religious sisters and the priests who came to hear her confession and say Mass ... [they would comment] "How do you manage to do it Mother, with such dark hands to make such snow-white embroidery?" or "How do you keep the cloth so clean with those dark hands of yours?" Bakhita replied giving no heed to the racial allusions ... Her responses ... [were] full of humility and submission to the will of God: "The Lord wanted it this way, and it cannot be changed." Or, calling attention to the equal dignity that very human being shares in God's eyes and to the shared purity received at baptism: "What counts is that one's soul is white" (p.194).

And so, with Bakhita, let us emphasise the importance of all peoples – the poor and the marginalised and let us be inclusive of all, celebrating our differences with dignity and respect.

Respect

Bakhita lived in humility, but people loved her and sought her out. "Already when she made her perpetual vows people spoke of her as a saint, and in 1931 a book on her life was printed in thousands of copies and translated in several languages. Josephine Bakhita died on 8 February 1947 at the Canossian Institute at Schio. Immediately crowds came to pay homage to her" (Fides Newsletter, 2007, 30 November). The people paid homage to Bakhita because they respected her. She had respected her own human dignity during years of tortuous abuse, and also showed forgiveness for the perpetuators of that abuse, respecting them for being the catalyst in leading her to Christianity and the religious life.

Fairness

When reading Bakhita's memoirs of her early experiences, one might conclude that fairness is not a word that could be used to describe her ordeals. She was not treated fairly when kidnapped by the traders. During her years of slavery, the treatment she received was not "fair" and in fact the word sounds very inadequate to be even applied to a life of torture and servitude. She never complained and in later life gave thanks for the experience that led her to embrace Christianity. Bakhita's best interests were not considered in her homeland, as she was considered a slave and hence had no social status as such, and it was only when she "immigrated" to another country, that justice and fairness were extended to her allowing her to stay where she had settled, so that she was able to live a long life of service to God, as a religious – giving hope and empathy to all who sought her counsel.

Justness

Following her years of serving masters who were often men and women without mercy, Bakhita found Christianity and wanted to serve the supreme "paron" (master in the Venetian dialect). According to Pope Emeritus Benedict XVI in his Encyclical letter *Spe Salvi*, "Saved in Hope" where he refers to Bakhita:

> after the terrifying "masters" who had owned her up to that point, Bakhita came to know a totally different kind of "master", she used the name *"paron"* for the living God, the God of Jesus Christ. Up to that time she had known only masters who despised and maltreated her, or at best considered her a useful slave. Now, however, she heard that there is a *"paron"* above all masters, the Lord of all lords, and that this Lord is good, goodness in person. She came to know that this Lord even knew her, that he had created her — that he actually loved her ... Now she had "hope" —

no longer simply the modest hope of finding masters who would be less cruel, but the great hope: "I am definitively loved and whatever happens to me—I am awaited by this Love. And so my life is good" (2007:para.3).

Initially justness did not exist for the young Bakhita, because there was no rule of law to safeguard her interests. She was unaware of her legal rights, and even if she was knowledgeable about these, what could she have done? Bakhita was shown the providence of God, who in his justness brought her to a new life – serving as a religious nun and offering prayer and hope to humanity. It is important then, that in our contemporary world where human trafficking is on the increase to remember that "individual problems have now become global problems." Kimberley Motley (2016) emphasises that "By creating a global human rights economy and becoming global investors in human rights we can achieve justness together." The Archbishop of Khartoum, Gabriel Zubier Waco, spoke to the people of the Sudan "All of you who are refugees, oppressed, exhausted, and without a roof – you are 'Bakhita'. All of you who are victims of injustice and exploitation, victims of discrimination and of persecution – you are 'Bakhita'" (cited in Zanini, 2013:213). Courtney Grogan (2019, February 10) leads her article with a request from "Pope Francis… [to] Pray with St. Bakhita for the end of human Trafficking."

Equality

We read that the equality of men and women rests on their dignity as persons. As mentioned previously, every human person shares "equal dignity" in the eyes of God; however, on occasion, there can be *"Sinful inequalities* that affect millions of men and women. These are in open contradiction of the Gospel (CCC, 2000:para.1935). This has been the situation in Africa. The late Cardinal Gantin, who loved Africa and died in 2008, wrote about his thoughts on Bakhita:

Bakhita reminded me of my mother; she made me understand the huge role that women can play in Africa today. For it is not by chance that, in order to show us the way to freedom, of redemption, the Lord specifically chose a woman. African women have always been exploited. But in Bakhita, an African woman whose history is our history, the people discover a beacon of hope. She who never asked anybody for anything has obtained everything. She, a black woman who belonged to everyone, is loved by all … She is a little star capable of illuminating the entire world (Zanini, 2013: 204).

What we need to have is hope and faith in God and each other, for we are created in the image of God (Genesis 1:27). Let us heed then the call for help from all persons (regardless of gender, age, or ethnicity), who are victims of human trafficking in the twenty-first century, and pray to St Josephine Bakhita that they will be granted freedom from the scourge that condemns them to a life of slavery.

You are now invited to participate on the faith journey of Servant of God Dorothy Day, an American social activist, who experienced a spiritual awakening that transformed her life and that of the poor and destitute she served in God's name.

17

Servant of God Dorothy Day

Cardinal John O'Connor wrote to the Holy See on 7 February 2000, initiating the beatification and canonization process for Dorothy Day. As early as 1983 some three years after Dorothy's death, the Claretian missionary priests in Chicago, had begun to collect "volumes of her writing, letters and testimonies from others about her good works" (Hanna Rosin, 2000). Their efforts were supported by Cardinal O'Connor, who, after being installed as Archbishop of New York in 1984, had organised an investigation into Dorothy's life and works, to determine if she fulfilled the criteria of sanctity of life (you may recall from previous chapters that this is a requirement for a candidate to be admitted to the catalogue of saints of the Catholic Church). By 1997, the year celebrating the centenary of Dorothy's birth, the Cardinal was organising meetings with individuals who had personally known her; those who had written about her; and those who had worked with her. Most witnesses testified to Dorothy's incredible faith and commitment to the Church. They described her as an ordinary woman – a human being who though not perfect had led an extraordinary life. O'Connor (2000) referred to Dorothy as "a simple woman living the Gospel."

On 16 March 2000, and some two months before he died, Cardinal O'Connor announced with great joy that the Holy See had given its approval "for the Archdiocese of New York to open the Cause for the Beatification and Canonization of Dorothy Day." Dorothy was given the title "Servant of God". In 2012, the United States Conference of Catholic Bishops "provided its formal endorsement" (CNS, 2016) of the canonization process for Dorothy. As the Archdiocese of New York is sponsoring her cause, evidence will be now be gathered and presented to the "Vatican's Congregation for the Saints and Pope Francis. [And] after carefully examining the information presented, the Congregation and Pope Francis will determine if ... [Dorothy] will be elevated from 'Servant of God,' to 'Venerable' and so become eligible for beatification and ultimately canonization" (ibid.). Initially the process will involve interviewing witnesses still living. Those:

> who had firsthand experience of Dorothy Day ... [and then Cardinal Timothy Dolan, Archbishop of New York will] appoint a historical commission that will issue a report placing Day's life in historical context and review her unpublished writings. Theological experts [will be] appointed by the Cardinal, [to] review her published writings – two readers for each publication – with an eye toward doctrine and morals.

Who was this woman who stirred the hearts and minds of her peers so much, that at the time of her death, Catholic historian David O'Brien asserted that she was "the most significant, interesting, and influential person in the history of American Catholicism" (2011)? Her story starts over a century ago in a previous millennium.

Profile

Dorothy Day was born on 8 November 1897 in Brooklyn, New York City, the third in a family of five children (three boys and two girls) born to John Day, originally from Tennessee, and Grace Day (nee Satterlee) from New York. Though not wealthy, the family could be described as comfortable and middle-class. William D. Miller (1973:37) writes that when Dorothy was six years of age John moved his wife and family to California. He was a sportswriter and had obtained a position on a newspaper in San Francisco. Though the religion of the household was Episcopalian it was not practised, and when Dorothy was about eight years of age, she "attended a Methodist Sunday school and church with a friend, and from that visit she began to experience 'the sweetness of faith.' Her parents, not accustomed to an outward show of piety, could not answer when she asked her mother 'why we did not pray and sing hymns?'" (ibid). In later life she referred to this childhood experience as a form of "spiritual awakening" with another powerful encounter, occurring in her adult years, following the birth of her daughter (Mark & Louise Zwick, cited in Day, 1999:3)

A devastating earthquake in San Francisco in 1906 forced the Day family to relocate to Chicago with their meagre belongings. The initial twelve months proved difficult financially – John was unemployed, and the family was forced to live in substandard accommodation. However, John did try to earn an income "by writing short stories and a novel." Miller writes that "Dorothy Day, then eight years old, later recalled how ashamed she was of the apartment house on thirty-seventh Street in which the family lived" (1973:37). Fortunately the circumstances for the family improved, when John was offered a position as a sports editor for a Chicago paper, *The Inter* Ocean, and they were able to move to a "better" neighbourhood, "on Webster Avenue near Lincoln Park, and it was here that [Dorothy] spent her girlhood years" (ibid.).

During her growing years and indeed throughout her life, Dorothy was an avid reader of books, particularly those that encouraged her to think and react emotionally. Mark and Louise Zwick (1999a:3) state that she "grew up in a household in which lightweight literature was forbidden. Her adolescent reading included the New Testament, John Wesley's *Sermons*, the works of St Augustine ... St Teresa of Ávila and St. John of the Cross. In addition, she read and cherished Thomas à Kempis *Imitation of Christ*, which became a lifelong favorite; the works of Dostoyevsky, which were also significant throughout her life; and the works of Tolstoy and other classics."

A book that "stirred her conscience [was] a novel by Upton Sinclair – *The Jungle* – [it] inspired Day to take long walks in poor neighborhoods on Chicago's South Side, the area where much of Sinclair's novel was set. These long walks were the start of a life-long attraction to areas many people avoid" (Jim Forest, 2013). The images presented to Dorothy were inspirational, "Walking through the slums of Chicago ... [she was] moved by the resilience of the impoverished in their efforts to create beauty amidst squalor" (cited in Dorothy Day Exhibit, n.d.). For example, Kimberly Rae Connor (2014:29-30) states that during these walks Dorothy "asked herself: who, what, why, where, and when? As she walked, Day was practicing empathetic imagining – developing the characters, hearing their voices, sensing how they lived their daily lives ... the plight of the poor and of workers ... 'made me feel that from then on my life was to be linked to theirs, their interests were to be mine. I had received a call, a vocation, a direction in my life.'" However, though she had discovered her mission, and found "beauty in the midst of urban desolation" (ibid.), the effect on her consciousness led to periods of depression – highs and lows – resulting in feelings of "Loneliness and sadness" (Miller, 1973:38). Such was the emotional make-up of Dorothy, as she grew from adolescence into young adulthood.

During her latter high school years, Dorothy's interest in reading produced a fascination for the works of "the Russian anarchist Peter Kropotkin" (Miller, 1973:39), and other Russian revolutionaries. This interest increased her awareness of the "plight of the workers." Miller emphasises Dorothy's involvement and preoccupation "with poverty, misery, and the class war" (ibid.). Academically gifted she received a scholarship to attend the University of Illinois at Urbana but lasted just two years. Academia was not for her – she was committed to writing and doing everything she could for the workers and for the poor.

Dorothy then moved with her family to New York, where her father was given a position on the *Morning Telegraph*. She found work, reporting, initially for *The Call*, then *The* Masses, followed by *The Liberator*, with all three magazines/papers described by Mark and Louise Zwick (1999a) as being "socialist papers". However, Forest (2013), refers to *The Call* as being "the city's one socialist daily [whereby Dorothy] covered rallies and demonstrations and interviewed people ranging from butlers to revolutionaries." He also refers to Dorothy's work on *The Masses* which he describes as "a magazine that opposed American involvement in the European war ... [and that] Day's conviction that the social order was unjust changed in no substantial way from her adolescence until her death, though she never identified herself with any political party." Forest (1997) writes that he was twenty years of age when he first met Dorothy, and their friendship lasted until her death twenty-one years later.

It was during this time in New York that "Day became involved with a literary and liberal crowd in the city's Greenwich Village neighborhood. Playwright Eugene O'Neill was one of her friends at the time. Day worked as a journalist, writing for several socialist and progressive publications in the 1910s and '20s. She interviewed a number of interesting public figures of the day, including Leon Trotsky" (Biography.com Editors, 2014), who at the time was known to be a Russian revolutionary and Marxist theorist. Mark and Louise Zwicks (1999a:4) maintain that "Dorothy was very much a part of the socialist antiwar movement before World War 1. She participated in demonstrations against U. S. involvement organized by socialists, and she was clubbed, albeit accidentally, by police." When President Woodrow Wilson confirmed the entry of the United States into the First World War, there were those who agreed with the decision and others who did not. Dorothy "and a group of Columbia University students ... joined a haphazard expedition to Washington to protest the draft" (Miller, 1973:46).

It was on her return to New York that Dorothy was given a position on *The Masses* (mentioned above) – a magazine which was "Founded in 1911 ... [and] was the voice of revolution and the new freedom of the young. In 1912 it came under the capable editorship of Max Eastman and aimed its attack at the whole range of values and practices associated with middle-class America ... Eastman ... [and his writers] were all talented and joyously set against prevailing conventions" (Miller, 1973:46-47). *The Masses* took "a pacifist stand" during the First World War (Mark & Louise Zwick, 1999a:4).

After the government suppressed *The Masses* in November 2017, Dorothy and a friend "impulsively decided to go to Washington to picket the White House with a group of militant suffragists" (Miller, 1973:49). The women were arrested and jailed for thirty days. This incarceration led to the women participating in a hunger strike to protest their imprisonment. The experience devastated Dorothy who was tortured by her thoughts as she began to despair of freedom. Miller (ibid.) recounts Dorothy's feelings of distress: "I felt that we were a people fallen from grace and abandoned by God." However, after a few days, "an attendant brought her a Bible and she read it 'with the sense of coming back to something of my childhood that I had lost.'" This transcendental encounter with God was fleeting and the experience did not fully resurface again until almost a decade later, following the birth of her daughter Tamara. After about a week into their hunger strike, the women were removed from their cells and taken to the prison hospital to recover their strength. They were freed by order of the President. According to Dorothy, following her imprisonment:

> I had no [further] thought of religion these last days [out of solitary confinement]. I was very much in the world again, talking with others, reading and writing letters, and I no longer thought of the depths I had been in. To be so degraded was to be shamed and humbled, but I rejected the humiliation. I had seen myself too weak to stand alone, too weak to face the darkness of that punishment cell without crying out, and I was ashamed and again rejected religion that had helped me when I had been brought to my knees by my suffering (1999:6).

This was just the first of many arrests and incarcerations to which Dorothy would be subjected over the years, due to her continuing social activist stance. When she returned to New York she was given a position on *The Liberator*, a newspaper that had replaced *The Masses*.

Her time in prison gave Dorothy cause for reflection and wanting a change from the writing and reporting while being of service to others, she commenced a brief stint of nurses' training at King's Country hospital in Brooklyn. However, it wasn't long before she felt "the urge to write again ... and left after a year" (Miller, 1973:52). Her life then seemed to then spiral out of control. Volanth writes that it was in "the early 1920s, [that] Day conceived a child with a Lionel Moise [a newspaper man] but ended the pregnancy with an abortion" (2015:11). Apparently Moise had given her an ultimatum – him or the child? She chose the former; but he abandoned her, nevertheless. This was a dark chapter in her life and her decision to abort her child was one "she deeply regretted [and] which she described [at length] in her semiautobiographical novel, *The Eleventh Virgin*" (Vivian Cherry, cited in Peter Dreier, 2012).

In early 1921 Dorothy married Berkeley Tobey "a wealthy older man, and a founder of the Literary Guild. They vacationed for [about] a year in Europe [London and Paris and Capri], where Dorothy wrote ... her novel *The Eleventh Virgin*, a thinly veiled account of a previous tumultuous relationship [see the previous paragraph]. The marriage was brief and ended on her return to the United States" (Dorothy Day Exhibit, n.d.). Miller writes that "in *The Long Loneliness* [her autobiography] Dorothy prefers to say little [about this time in her life], which was "a time of joy she says, but also of heartbreak" (Miller, 1973:52).

Her novel *The Eleventh Virgin* was published in 1924, and Dorothy was informed that "her publishers had sold moving-picture rights for five thousand dollars ... she bought a small bungalow on Raritan Bay on Staten Island" (Miller, 1973:55). She moved into the bungalow and experienced great peace, "tranquillity and reflection in her life" (ibid.). It was during this time that she met Forster Batterham who became "the very half of my being" (cited in Dorothy Day exhibit, n.d.), and with whom Dorothy began a de facto relationship. "'I was happy', she wrote ... 'But my very happiness made me know that there was a greater happiness to be obtained from life than any I had ever known'. To her surprise she was beginning to pray daily, and when she walked to the village for the mail, she took her rosary and tried to recite its prayers … [she realised that] she prayed because she was happy" (Miller, 1973:56).

Dorothy Day's joy was complete when she gave birth to her only child, a daughter, Tamar Teresa Day, who was born on 4 March 1926: "If I had written the greatest book or composed the greatest symphony … I could not have felt more the exalted creator than I did when they placed my child in my arms" (cited in Dorothy Day Exhibit, n.d.). She experienced a "spiritual transformation" (ibid.) which did not augur well for her relationship with Batterham. According to Forest (2013), "Batterham was an anarchist who opposed both marriage and religion. In a world of such cruelty, he found it impossible to believe in a God. By this time Day's belief in God was unshakable. It grieved her that Batterham didn't sense God's presence within the natural world. 'How can there be no God,' she asked, 'when there are all these beautiful things?'" The death knell for the relationship was sounded when Dorothy organised for Tamar to be baptised a Catholic and later, she herself converted to Catholicism and was baptised. She made "a total commitment to the Church and its teaching, and gave up Batterham, whom she apparently loved until the end of her days" (Vicky Cosstick, 2016).

With the Depression looming Dorothy, as a single parent, sought work where she could. At one stage she was writing dialogue for moving-pictures in Hollywood but she didn't enjoy living there and after three months, when her contract wasn't renewed "she used her last paycheck to buy a bus ticket for herself and Tamar to Mexico City" (Miller, 1973:60-61). However, their duration there was short – just three months. While in Mexico, Dorothy wrote articles for the Catholic journal – *Commonweal*, and though there was an expectation that she would write about the "politically directed anticlericalism in Mexico", she pled ignorance regarding politics, and instead wrote chiefly about "the life of the poor among whom she lived" (ibid.). In May 1930 when Tamar became ill "from a chronic digestive disorder", Dorothy decided to return to New York.

Miller (1973:61) states that the following "two years, despite the worsening Depression were a happy time in her life. She found a library research job where she could manage her time as she wished and was thus able to read and write." Also, she moved back to her home on the bay. Then according to Forest (2013):

> In the winter of 1932 Day travelled to Washington, D.C., to report for two Catholic journals, *Commonweal* and *America*, on a radical protest called the Hunger March. Day watched the protesters parade down the streets of Washington carrying signs calling for jobs, unemployment insurance, old age pensions, relief for mothers and children, health care and housing. What kept Day in the sidelines was that she was a Catholic and the march had been organized by Communists, a party at war with not only capitalism but religion.

Dorothy was disillusioned with the poverty and injustice she witnessed around her. And so, on "December 8, the Feast of the Immaculate Conception [of Our Lady], after witnessing the march … [she] went to the Shrine of the Immaculate Conception where she expressed her torment in prayer: 'I offered up a special prayer, a prayer which came with tears and anguish, that some way would open up for me to use what talents I possessed for my fellow workers, for the poor'" (cited in Forest, 2013).

When she returned to New York the following day, it seemed as if her prayers were answered. Waiting to greet her on her doorstep was "the eccentric French itinerant philosopher Peter Maurin" (Cosstick, 2016), who was to become her inspiration, guide and friend for life. Peter was a former Christian brother who:

> had read her articles in several Catholic magazines … He was convinced that she was the person who could implement his program … opening houses of hospitality,

and especially starting a newspaper ... He began immediately on her Catholic education, which included a Catholic outline of history and the social teachings of the Church ... [he was keen to inform her of the papal encyclicals] as well as instruction about personalism, the common good, liturgy, and hospitality. Each day when he returned to continue his teaching, he brought up the idea of a newspaper (Mark & Louise Zwick, 1999a:10).

Maurin embraced poverty in the Franciscan tradition. "He had a vision for houses of hospitality ... communal farms, and ... [a] newspaper, and a deep knowledge of Catholic Social Teaching – but he was a man of theories. Day was a practical woman, the 'cipher' for Maurin's abstract ideas" (Cosstick, 2016). On 1 May 1933 Dorothy and Peter co-founded the radical newspaper *The Catholic Worker*, which is still being published today in the 21st century. At the time there were two and a half thousand copies printed and each sold for a penny a copy. "By December [1933], 100,000 copies were being printed each month. Readers found a unique voice in *The Catholic Worker*. It expressed dissatisfaction with the social order and took the side of labor unions, but its vision of the ideal future challenged both urbanization and industrialism. It wasn't only radical but religious" (Forest, 2013).

The paper didn't merely complain but called on its readers to make personal responses" (ibid.); hence the emphasis on personalism, promoted by Maurin and articulated by Emmanuel Mounier (1905-1950), "as a philosophy of engagement ... [it is] perspective, method, exigency..." (cited in Mark & Louise Zwick, 1999b). In their article the Zwicks (ibid.) quote Miller (*Image* Books, 1974:21), who "describes personalism as central to Catholic Worker thought and action: 'The theme of the personalist idea held commonly by Mounier, Maritain, and the Catholic Worker, was that the primacy of Christian love should be brought from its position of limbo where human affairs are concerned and infused into the process of history.'" They emphasised that personalism was not the same as self-centred individualism, it respected the "freedom and dignity of individuals" and encouraged them to do what they could to make a difference in the world without waiting for assistance from others, and ultimately taking personal responsibility for their actions (Mark & Louise Zwick, 1999b).

Over time, Houses of hospitality were established in many centres. Maurin emphasised the necessity that the houses have a "Christ room", for there should be a room in every house for "the ambassadors of God to share and to break bread" (Forest, 2013). Several communal farms were also established – some were productive; others were not. All depended on available finance and their success as working communities – for, with so many workers living together in relative poverty, relationships became easily frayed and occasionally bickering and infighting erupted. Dorothy spent much of her time in between writing and speaking engagements travelling across the country, and on occasion endeavouring to pacify those workers who inhabited the Houses of Hospitality in the various centres and those working on the communal farms, who had an issue with their "neighbours".

The "Catholic Worker [soon] became a national movement" (Forest, 2013). Cosstick asserts that as a radical peace activist, Dorothy "protested against the Spanish Civil War, the Second World War, the dropping of the bombs on Hiroshima and Nagasaki, and the Vietnam War" (2016). Her protests led to her being arrested and imprisoned on several occasions. Nevertheless, the Catholic Worker Movement continued to grow and "Whenever Maurin or Day went and spoke about the ... Movement, around the country further communities sprang up" (ibid.). Peter Maurin and Dorothy Day worked together until his death in 1949.

As mentioned previously Dorothy travelled extensively and was invited to numerous speaking engagements to promote the efforts of the Catholic Worker Movement. Forest (2013) refers to the occasion in 1963 when she "was one of fifty 'Mothers for Peace' who went to Rome to thank Pope [St] John XXIII for his encyclical *Pacem in Terris* [Peace on

Earth]. Close to death, the pope couldn't meet them privately, but at one of his last public audiences blessed the pilgrims, asking them to continue their labors."

Forest (2013) also discusses the tendency of many of the *Catholic Worker* communities to participate in protests which included refusing "to cooperate with conscription ... [opting instead to be conscientious objectors (CO)]." He maintains that "many went to prison for acts of civil disobedience. Probably there has never been a newspaper [that has had] so many of ... [its] editors ... jailed for acts of conscience. Day herself was last jailed in 1973 for taking part in a banned picket line in support of farmworkers. She was seventy-five" (ibid.). In his article Stephen Zunes (2014:40) refers to this incarceration of Dorothy in her twilight years, saying that at the time Dorothy was in "declining health ... [when she] was arrested ... and jailed for ten days."

Dorothy Day died on 29 November 1980 at Maryhouse, which is a Catholic Worker residence she helped to establish in the East village section of New York. She was 83. Martha Hennessy, her granddaughter – one of Tamara's nine children, repeats the adage attributed to Dorothy who was quoted as saying: "Don't call me a saint, I don't want to be dismissed that easily" (as cited in Catholic News Service, 2016). Hennessy states that her grandmother "also said we're all called to be saints ... [and] in the end it was very clear that her life took the direction that it took, because she responded to hearing the voice of God" (ibid.). Cardinal O'Connor (2000) who prior to his death fought for and was successful in initiating the cause for the beatification and canonization of Dorothy maintains that she "is a model for all in the third millennium." Indeed, she was an ordinary person who achieved the extraordinary by rising above her human weaknesses and imperfections, to engage in active discipleship and communion with others by sharing poverty, purpose and the printed word. And according to O'Brien (2011), her discipleship was "revolutionary" via her voice in "The Catholic Worker Movement."

Leadership as Service

Dorothy Day's entire life was one of service to others – to the poor, the needy and the marginalised. For "Service to all was at the base of the [Catholic Worker] movement and Day's writings from the first to the last … celebrated making Catholics and beyond aware of what was happening in their world while also directly informing and engaging everyone to help the 'other' [person] in their midst" (Volanth, 2015:31). Dorothy's actions enabled her to perform her ministry of service. Especially important to Dorothy was the printed word: "For Dorothy Day, literature was both a mirror reflecting reality, and a lamp guiding her towards a life of service" (Kimberly Rae Connor, 2014:28). Dorothy had a great respect for "Wisdom". According to Robert Ellsberg (2014:7), "Though she was offered many honorary degrees, she consistently declined them, citing her respect for 'Holy Wisdom'. As she once told me. 'Too much praise makes you feel you must be doing something terribly wrong.'" Hence Dorothy lived her wisdom humbly, serving her God and her neighbour.

Wisdom has built her house, she has hewn her seven pillars (Proverbs 9:1, cited in Sipe & Frick, 2015:4). For the purpose of this analysis, the "Seven Pillars of Servant Leadership" (see Appendix A for the list of attributes), are outlined below, and the discussion on each pillar includes aspects of the life and works of Servant of God Dorothy Day.

Pillar 1 – "Person of Character"

O'Connor (2000) emphasises the humility of Dorothy. "Her personal humility was such that she never considered herself to be holier than any other Catholic." Throughout her life she integrated faith and social justice in all she did. According to Ellsberg (2014:8), "She embodied the type of holiness most necessary for our time – a holiness that is not concerned with its own purity or perfection, but empties itself to confront the burning issues of our time: poverty, violence, the desecration of nature, the meaning of work, the yearning for community, freedom, and peace."

Dorothy was a progressive thinker of her day and a passionate Catholic. Andrei Antokhin (2014:19) maintains that while she was "socially radical and progressive ... in many ways [she] was a very traditionalist Catholic. She regularly attended Mass and made regular confessions. She also had a special admiration for many Catholic Saints, many of whom were mystics ... Her favorite saints to imitate were Francis of Assisi, Julian of Norwich, Catherine of Siena, Teresa of Ávila, and Thérèse of Lisieux". You may recall that most of these saints have been mentioned in previous chapters of this book!

Connor (2014:31) emphasises Dorothy's ability to "marry the active with the contemplative." For "when ordinary people have an awareness of a mystical reality and then translate this experience into their everyday lives they enhance their spirituality; they become aware of the importance of balancing their contemplative lives with their active lives – their private lives with their working lives" (Cameron, 2012b:5). They assume stewardship of the sacredness of life (Sims, 1997) and this is what Dorothy did when promoting the Catholic Worker Movement – she raised awareness of the importance of valuing self, others and the environment! She stood up for her convictions even if pursuing her goals meant that she would be arrested and incarcerated.

Pillar II – "Puts People First"

Cardinal O'Connor (1997) referred to Dorothy Day as a "living basilica". He believed that the following scripture reading embodies what Dorothy herself would have said to those people touched by the ministry of her leadership, "Are you not aware that you are the temple of God ... [and that God's spirit dwells in you]? (1 Corinthians 3:16). Dorothy Day has been described as "A woman of conscience, a Saint for Our Time". According to the Dorothy Day Guild (n.d.):

> [L]aywomen like Dorothy Day represent a type of vocation not often seen in the canon of the saints. Eileen

Egan, a lifelong friend and colleague of Day's, saw her as someone who "shows that ordinary people can live by the Sermon on the Mount. She tried to relate the Sermon on the Mount to everything she did. This makes her a tremendous inspiration for lay people" … she transcended the divisive boundaries of right and left, pointing to the common ground of discipleship … "her complex personality and rich life, focused however on love for God and for neighbor, make her very much a saint for our times."

Ellsberg (2014:10) writes about Dorothy's "ability to integrate a traditional style of Catholic piety with a radical style of social engagement. She said the rosary and went to daily Mass while also marching on picket lines and going to jail to protest war and injustice." But Ellsberg (ibid.) stresses that Dorothy did not regard this as a paradox: "The basis of the synthesis she had been seeking was to be found in the central doctrine of her faith: the Incarnation. Her subsequent mission was rooted in the radical social implications of this doctrine: that God had entered our humanity and our history, so that all creation was hallowed, and whatever we did for our neighbors we did directly for him." Dorothy's message was all about love – love for God; love for our neighbour and love for our enemies.

Dorothy believed in non-violence such as Jesus taught. Her manifesto was the Sermon on the Mount. "Jesus never forbade self-defense or allowing one's neighbor to be oppressed. She recognized Christ teachings were a call for individuals and popular movements to struggle on behalf of justice for themselves and for their neighbors, but to do so nonviolently" (Zunes, 2014:41). Zunes quotes historian Anne Klejment who calls "The Catholic Worker Movement the 'cradle of Catholic pacificism in the United States'" (ibid.). Dorothy was a pacifist who stood up for the workers and for all people encouraging Christians to live the Gospel and to work toward personal holiness. She embraced the life of poverty sharing what she had with her neighbours. She "realized that it is only through *agape*, the Christian notion of love of God and one's neighbor, we can hope to make this world a slightly better place" (Antokhin, 2014:18).

Pillar III – "Skilled Communicator"

Prior to the confirmation from Rome regarding approval to commence the process of beatification and canonization for Dorothy Day, Cardinal O'Connor (2000) wrote the following "I have been very much impressed by the attestations of holiness given by those who knew and worked with Dorothy Day." The testimonies of these witnesses would have had a great influence on the decision makers in Rome who approved the Cause being opened.

Cardinal O'Connor (2000) separates the life of Dorothy Day into two phases – the pre-conversion phase and the post-conversion phase. Of the latter phase and in his letter to the Vatican he writes:

> I have subjected Dorothy Day's post-conversion writings to the careful examination of a dogmatist, moralist, and canonist. All assure me that her writings are in complete fidelity to the church. Moreover, I frequently quote from her writings in my own columns and homilies. Letters continue to come to my attention from those who were introduced to her by my own efforts and from those who know well of her and are happy to see my support for her. Many letters ask that I consider a proposition of her Cause to the Holy See. Thus, in my position as Archbishop of New York, I believe it is my responsibility to promote this Cause.

As mentioned early in this chapter Dorothy was an avid reader from her girlhood. She was also a prolific writer, which enhanced her career as a journalist. Ellsberg (2014:14) writes that Dorothy continued writing "until a few days before her death." Though he does state that "through her diaries and letters we see her gradually slowing down, adjusting" (ibid.). For though the symptoms of her advancing age and heart condition were beginning to influence her ability to be as active as she was previously, just being able to read, gave her immense pleasure, "my heart can still leap for joy as I read and suddenly assent to some great truth enunciated by some great mind and heart" (Dorothy, cited in Ellsberg, 2014:14).

Antokhin (2014:23) maintains that there was just one Catholic Saint "to whom Dorothy Day dedicated a whole book." And that saint was Thérèse of Lisieux. Antokhin is quick to point out that this was not a great academic work, but that it was Dorothy's intention to reach the ordinary person, "My purpose in writing the book in the first place was to reach some of 65, 000 subscribers to the Catholic Worker, many of whom are not Catholic and not even 'believers,' to introduce them to a saint ... [Thérèse of Lisieux who] was so much like the rest of us in her ordinariness" (ibid.). Dorothy's purpose in writing the book on Thérèse was because she wanted to raise awareness in her readers that any person, however ordinary could achieve the extraordinary.

Dorothy was a journalist who wanted to reach the workers. Her contribution to *The Catholic Worker* was a column and her articles were written under the heading "Day by Day"; however, "In February 1946, she changed the name of her column. Thereafter ... [it was called] 'On Pilgrimage'" (Miller, 1973:218). According to Dorothy "We should always be thinking of ourselves as pilgrims" (ibid). She wrote several books during her lifetime and as mentioned previously she continued writing, particularly her journals until her death. One such journal that has received prominence was one published in 1948 and titled "On Pilgrimage". A paragraph on the final page of this journal dated December 1948 reads:

> And now ... I finish this long account of the year. I send the book out with diffidence. It is the work of a journalist who writes because it is her talent; it has been her means of

livelihood. And it is sent out with the hopes that it will *sell* so that the printing bill will be paid, and enough [will be] left over to bring out another book next year ... We write also to help support the work which we are doing ... It is written most personally because I am a woman who can write no other way. If it is preaching and didactic in parts, it is because I am preaching and teaching and encouraging myself on this narrow road we are treading. "Life," said St. Teresa, is but a night spent in an uncomfortable inn, crowded together with other wayfarers" (Dorothy, cited in "On Pilgrimage", 1999:256).

Dorothy lived the Gospel. Her writing reflects her commitment to a life of voluntary poverty.

Pillar IV – "Compassionate Collaborator"

When she was a child and her father was out of work for a time, following the earthquake in San Francisco and the subsequent move to Chicago, Dorothy experienced the trauma of poverty and how living in less than ideal conditions, could affect the human dignity of a person, thus leading to feelings of despair and disenchantment. From that time even though conditions improved for the Day family, Dorothy was on a mission to reach out to the "poor, the needy and the marginalised" to improve their lot and to be their voice. She was empathetic, providing food and accommodation for all – working to provide houses of hospitality, so that there would be community houses for all who were homeless and in need. Dorothy was a philanthropist. She affirmed and built up the teams working in the houses and on the farming communes. She called for volunteers and when there were arguments – she travelled – sometimes long distances, in an effort to 'right' any wrongs that may have been committed. She listened to those who felt they were being taken for granted. She believed that if given the opportunity, everybody could strive for sainthood.

When Pope Francis "addressed a joint meeting of Congress" in the United States on 24 September 2015, he quoted the names of four Americans about whom he wanted to speak – Abraham Lincoln, Martin Luther King, Thomas Merton and Dorothy Day. Of the latter the holy father said: *"In these times when social concerns are so important, I cannot fail to mention the Servant of God Dorothy Day, who founded the Catholic Worker Movement. Her social activism, her passion for justice and for the cause of the oppressed, were inspired by the Gospel, her faith, and the example of the saints."* The Holy Father also spoke about extreme poverty and the need to serve others for the common good (Laudato Si', 2015:para.129), while addressing the challenges associated with "environmental challenges" and the effect on the sacredness of life (ibid). These issues were supported by Dorothy Day.

Pillar V – "Has Foresight"

The visionary leadership of Dorothy Day and Peter Maurin in founding the *Catholic Worker* newspaper has served generations of Catholic workers and their families. The newspaper is still in circulation in the twenty-first century, having recently celebrated its 86th anniversary. Patrick Jordan, "a former managing editor of the Catholic Worker newspaper" (Catholic News Service, 2016), and a longtime companion to Dorothy referred to her as a "prophetic witness". His reasons being that "The serious issues of the times themselves – refugees, poverty and inequality, racism, massive spending on wars and developing military technologies for future wars, capital punishment, torture, and prolonged incarcerations, etc – are all issues on which Dorothy Day wrote forcefully and sought to ameliorate" (ibid.). Jordan believes as do others that by having the process of the cause for the beatification and canonization of Dorothy approved by the Holy See, her life is being given "the recognition it deserves."

Zunes (2014:37) quotes William Thorn: "the Catholic Worker movement she [Dorothy founded] 'became a voice for the powerless which challenged those who ignored or dismissed them – the wealthy, churches, government and employers.'" As a pacifist, Dorothy fought for non-violence. In Pillar IV there is reference to *Laudato Si'* – Praise be to you – *On care for our common home*, the Encyclical by Pope Francis (2015) calling for environmental stewardship. Zunes emphasises that: "Today, the world is facing ... [a] greater threat than war and poverty: the destruction of the environment, a direct result of overconsumption. Though rarely articulated in the language of the contemporary environmental movement, Dorothy Day nevertheless embraced a sense of stewardship for this planet. She advocated living simply, long before it became fashionable" (ibid). Zunes refers to Dorothy's actions as prophetic, for she advocated living a life of "voluntary poverty" – as a way of living the Gospels. In her writings she motivated people to operate in a sustainable manner, living simply, in order to minimise any impact on the environment.

Pillar VI – "Systems Thinker"

Dorothy Day was declared "Servant of God" in 2000. According to Cardinal O'Connor (2000), she held "a common respect for the poor and a desire for economic equity. In no sense did she approve of any form of atheism, agnosticism, or religious indifference. Moreover, her complete commitment to pacifism in imitation of Christ often separated her from ...[the] ideologies of the time."

In the 21st century the Catholic Worker Movement co-founded by Dorothy Day and Peter Maurin is still a formidable movement and owes it sustainability to the foresight of the co-founders and for the legacy they left to succeeding generations, who continue to share and serve their vision. The aim of the Movement continues to be to:

> live in accordance with the justice and charity of Jesus Christ. Our sources are the Hebrew and Greek Scriptures as handed down in the teachings of the Roman Catholic

Church, with our inspiration coming from the lives of the saints ... This aim requires us to begin living in a different way. We recall the words of our founders – Dorothy Day who said, "God meant things to be much easier than we have made them," and Peter Maurin who wanted to build a society "where it is easier for people to be good" (*The Catholic Worker* newspaper, 2018 – 85th Anniversary Issue).

According to Mark and Louise Zwick (1999b): "Peter Maurin introduced personalism and the ideas of Emmanuel Mounier to Dorothy Day and to the Catholic Worker movement. As Dorothy said, he brought to us "great books, and great ideas, and great men, so that over the years, we have become a school for the service of God here and now" (D. Day, "Peter's Program," *Catholic* Worker, May 1955, p.2). When "Emmanuel Mounier ... articulated the ideas of personalism, [he wrote] of human persons whose responsibility it is to take an active role in history" (Mark & Louise Zwick, 1999b). This Dorothy Day certainly did during her lifetime. Each person can "be the difference that makes a difference". Dorothy led the way!

Pillar VII – "Leads with Moral Authority"

Mark and Louise Zwick (1999a:12) posit that "Dorothy Day lived with the pain of knowing that she had not lived according to Catholic morality during the years before she became a convert ... she had made certain choices that would cause her great [pain and] concern after her conversion." Nevertheless, once she was converted to the faith and baptized a Catholic, she accepted the teaching of the Catholic Church and all that it involved. "Now the creed to which I subscribe is like a battle cry, engraved on my heart – the *Credo* of the Holy Roman Catholic Church" (1999:12). "Day's conversion to Catholicism did not hinder her growth as a radical dedicated to the equality of every human being. On the contrary ... [her] conversion bolstered her energy and resolve to commit to a life of drastic Change" (Volanth, 2015:29). She developed a profound love for the Church and lived the Gospel.

Values

Dorothy's love for the Church embraced the values of dignity, respect, fairness, justness and equality (see Chapter 4 for the terms of reference). Her entire life was spent working for equality and justness for all. In fact, Cardinal O'Connor (2000) stated that "Much of what she spoke of in terms of social justice anticipated the teachings of Pope [St] John Paul II and lends support to her cause." She had respect for the human dignity of people providing food (including setting up soup kitchens); organising accommodation (for the homeless at the houses of hospitality); and when needed, assisted with small amounts of cash for essentials.

Throughout her life Dorothy fought for the rights of her workers, the poor and the destitute. She fought for women and supported movements for women's suffrage. She was involved in civil rights activism, which on one occasion led to her life being threatened with shots fired but the bullets missed their target (Zunes, 2014:40). Dorothy chose to live in voluntary poverty as a means of living the Gospel. She was fair in her dealings with her workers and the many volunteers who comprised the Catholic Worker Movement. She spent many hours trying to sort out differences before they escalated. Most of the problems that arose were as a result of a clash of personalities; or a lack of food; and often because there were too few funds to allocate for rents/newspaper circulation/ and other expenses. Dorothy depended on the providence of God. She recognised and respected the integrity of each person and rejoiced "in the sacredness of human life and the value of human dignity" (see Chapter 4 – Dignity). Dorothy believed in the equality for all – that men and women – indeed all genders, should live together in peace and harmony (Cardinal O'Connor, 2000).

It is at this point in the chapter that I am going to digress from previous chapters and consolidate my interpretation of the application of the values to the life and works of Dorothy Day, by including a tribute to Dorothy from my cousin, Father John Daly.

I was thrilled to hear that Dorothy Day was being included in this book which celebrates and honours significant women leaders in the Catholic Church. I first came across Dorothy Day via the Catholic Worker Movement Newspaper in the 1960s. She was a co-founder in the Catholic Worker Movement in America. I next came across her in 1982, when I read her story again while working with the Young Christian Workers Movement. I and the young people I worked with were encouraged by her life to live the gospel more fully. During her youth Dorothy was a radical journalist, a member of an anarchist group, and a onetime communist.

Her life changed when she became a Catholic, being particularly attracted to Jesus' command to love as He loved: to the social justice teaching of the church: to the homeless and the landless farm labourers: and to promoting peace in the world. Time Magazine called her "the street saint". The Catholic Church is moving to canonise this radical woman. Reflecting the hardships, she endured in living her faith and life of justice, she said this of Christ's command to love, "love is indeed a harsh and dreadful thing to ask of us, each one of us, but it is the only answer." Dorothy Day was a true leader and challenger in the Catholic Church. (Personal correspondence, 18 May 2019).

Dorothy Day's faith journey has not ended with her passing, for the Church continues to investigate her life and works in light of her possible beatification and canonization. As Cardinal O'Conner (2000) emphasised – she is indeed a woman for our millennium, our century and our times.

The following chapter will introduce you to another outstanding woman of the twentieth century – Mother Teresa, who on 4 September 2016 was canonised a Saint in the Catholic Church and is now honoured as St Teresa of Kolkata.

18

St Teresa of Kolkata

During a history that has entered its third millennium, the Catholic Church has formally canonised more than ten thousand saints (Kenneth Woodward, 1990:17). You may recall from Chapter 13 that canonisation is an ecclesial process, which prior to 1969, followed strict guidelines within a lengthy and complicated procedure. However, the reforms of Pope St Paul VI in 1969, and Pope St John Paul II in 1983 paved the way for the canonisation process to be simplified (Paul Keven Meagher, Thomas C. O'Brien, Consuelo Maria Aherne, 1979:616). Significantly, the honour of sainthood for a candidate, who has led a sanctified life and has the confidence of the Church, is only awarded by the Church posthumously. And yet during her lifetime, Mother Teresa of Kolkata was referred to as "a living saint" (BBC News, 2015).

According to Kathryn Spink (2011:285): "Mother Teresa's body had scarcely been laid to rest before speculation began about whether she would be placed on the 'fast track' to sainthood. In the eyes of many for whom she was already a saint, the official process of beatification and canonization was purely academic." Who was this tiny woman, not even 5 ft (152.4 cm) tall who mesmerised the leaders of large and small nations collectively, and who has been described as "one of the 20th Century's greatest humanitarians"? (Biography.com Editors, 2014, April 2).

Unfortunately, I was never personally acquainted with the "iconic figure" of Mother Teresa during her lifetime; however, Mrs Patricia McRae the mother of a close friend and colleague Robert McRae, was at Bourke NSW Australia in the early 1980s and met Mother Teresa, who was visiting the convent of the Missionary Sisters of Charity. Mother Teresa and five of her sisters had set up a mission in Bourke in the late

1960s, to cater to the health needs of the indigenous population. Some of the recollections of Patricia include the following:

The Sisters worked with the Aboriginal Community in Bourke. There were 6 Sisters in the convent, four of these were Indian, one was from the Philippines, and one was Australian. Mother Teresa was tough and very determined. She wouldn't take 'no' for an answer. For example, during her visit to Bourke she was asked to speak at a community meeting at the local Bowling Club. On the way to the club Mother Teresa said to the Sisters that they would open the presentation with a hymn. The Sisters were reluctant for they believed that as they couldn't sing, they would be embarrassed to do so in front of all the people. Nevertheless, Mother Theresa responded that they would open with a song, and consequently the meeting opened with the Sisters singing "Something Beautiful for God".

On another occasion, Mother Teresa used the following example to illustrate the importance of being obedient and positive. One morning at the convent in Calcutta, a young Sister came downstairs looking sad. Mother Teresa asked what was the problem? The young Sister said that there was nothing wrong. Mother Teresa then told her to go back to bed and rest and when she was ready to come downstairs with a smile on her face, then she could come back down and go out to work. She told her that the poor did not need to see her looking sad, their lives were already sad enough. In another example she said that if you took a bowl of rice to a poor family in Calcutta, they would always share it with another family who were in need. It didn't matter how needy they were or their caste or religious background, they would always share what they were given.

The most significant example given by Mother Teresa, was that of a man who was dragged dying from a canal his body covered with maggots. Mother Teresa herself removed the maggots from his body and as he lay dying, he said to her, "I have lived like an animal but now I die like an angel". Patricia also said that *"Mother Theresa was very prayerful, and that the Sisters did not often engage in social interaction, as they were there for a purpose and that was to offer support to the Indigenous community."*

Almost forty years after meeting Mother Teresa, Patricia is aware that her experiences in Bourke were with a "living saint" – for Mother Teresa was canonised by Pope Francis on 4 September 2016. To trace her life story, let us turn back the hands of time to a previous century and to the former country of Yugoslavia.

Profile

Mother Teresa was born on 26 August 1910 in Skopje, "the current capital of the Republic of Macedonia", which is north of Greece. On 27 August, she "was baptized Agnes Gonxha Bojaxhiu" (Biography.com Editors, 2019, April 8). Agnes was the youngest of three children, two girls and one boy (Aga, Lazar and Agnes) born to Nikola and Dranafile (Drana) Bojaxhiu. Spink (2011:4) writes that both Nikola and Drana were Albanian, and "had come originally from Prizren, a city that during their daughter's childhood was part of Yugoslavia but had belonged at one time to the kingdom of Serbia." During those early years the family enjoyed prosperity as "Nikola was a merchant and entrepreneur", who travelled frequently pursuing his business interests. The children had a strict, but loving upbringing in a traditional household. According to Spink (ibid.): "In one of her infrequent references the adult Mother Teresa made to her family background, she remembered how, while her father was away working, her mother busied herself about the house, cooking, mending, and performing other domestic tasks, but as soon as the father returned, all work stopped. Her mother would put on a clean dress and comb her hair and ensure that the children were fresh and tidy to greet him."

The political climate at the time was volatile, with uprisings and "internal fighting ... in both Serbia and neighbouring Albania" (p.5). Spink writes that Nikola Bojaxhiu was a sympathiser "for the Albania freedom fighters by providing them not only with financial support but also with hospitality" (ibid.). When Agnes was 8 years old, her father died suddenly in unexplained circumstances, and "the family's business assets were appropriated by his Italian business partner" (p.6), leaving the family if not in a destitute state, then one that necessitated Drana setting up business for herself, sewing and "selling handcrafted embroidery" (Roger Royle & Gary Woods, 1992:10). The family was Catholic and Drana was very religious; hence her own dire situation did not influence her generosity, in sharing the little she had with the poor and the needy of the neighbourhood. Royle and Woods (ibid.) recount Mother Teresa's memory of her mother's charitable deeds:

> *Many of the poor in and around Skopje knew our house, and none left it emptyhanded. We had guests at table every day. At first I used to ask, "Who are they?" and mother would answer. "Some are relatives, but all of them are our people." When I was older, I realized that the strangers were poor people who had nothing and whom my mother was feeding.*

These experiences nurtured a life that would in time be dedicated to serving the poor – a long life that would be lived doing "Something Beautiful for God". Spink writes that though Agnes "felt herself called to the religious life" at the early age of twelve years, her health was not good, and her mother Drana believed that her daughter would not survive into adulthood (2011:8). Agnes was to struggle with the question of her vocation for six years, uncertain if she had a vocation, and so she prayed for guidance, often discussing her dilemma with her parish priest (Royle & Woods, 1992:14.

Prayers were a major feature in the home. The family were members of the local Sacred Heart Parish, and both Agnes and her older sister Aga, were members of the Church Choir. Spink (2011:8) tells us that the "The Bojaxhiu family were musical. Singing, playing instruments, and even composition was an accepted part of family life." Then in 1925, with the arrival to the parish of a Croatian priest, Father Jambrenkovic of the Society of Jesus (SJ), the lives of the young people of the parish were transformed, when he "introduced a young people's society called the Sodality of the Blessed Virgin Mary. Membership of this society was to play a very important part in Agnes Gonxha's formative years. It was a society founded in 1563, that faced its members with the challenge of answering St. Ignatius Loyola's questions, *What have I done for Christ? What am I doing for Christ? What will I do for Christ?*" (Royle & Woods, 1992:11).

Father Jambrenkovic was also keen on emphasising the incredible work of the missionaries of his order, who were working with "the poor and the lepers" (p.12). He spoke to the young parishioners of countries further afield, where such missionary activity was being undertaken. India and Calcutta (renamed Kolkota in 2001) were included in the places of reference, and in the stories, he related to them about the missionaries of his order. Agnes listened to the narrations on the missions and wondered what she could do herself for Christ. She was contemplating a vocation to the religious life, but was still unsure; however, the missionary work really appealed to her.

At the same time, she was developing and nourishing her inner spirituality – seeking answers as to how she could best serve God and her neighbour. Her mother "Drana made regular pilgrimages to the shrine of Our Lady of Cernagore in Letnice and encouraged her daughters to do the same. Set in the mountains of Montenegro, this shrine provided physical as well as spiritual refreshment for the young Agnes Gonxha" (Royle & Woods, 1992:13). It was here that Agnes often went to retreat and engage in prayer. Subsequently, "by the time she was eighteen she was convinced that her own calling was to be a missionary, to 'go out and give the life of Christ to the people'" (Spink, 2011:10).

Agnes applied for and was accepted into the Order of Loreto nuns, "whose missionaries were working in Bengal, but whose Mother House was in Dublin" (Royle & Woods, 1992:15). She was to commence part of her training in Dublin and departed from Skopje on 25 September 1928. She arrived at the Mother House with a young companion "Betika Kajnc", who was also keen on entering the Loreto Order. The two young women became postulants "at Loreto Abbey, Rathfarnham, on

12 October 1928" (Spink, 2011:12). The period of postulancy in the Mother House lasted for just six weeks, and during that time both postulants were given intensive lessons in the English language. Then, on 1 December 1928:

> [T]hey set sail for India and a new world of separation and service. By then Agnes Gonxha Bojaxhiu had chosen the name of Sister Mary Teresa of the Child Jesus – after Thérèse of Lisieux, the "Little Flower" [you may recall the chapter on St Thérèse] who had pointed the way to holiness through fidelity in small things, Mother Teresa was at pains to emphasise, not the great Teresa of Avila. Her travelling companion had taken the name of Mary Magdalene [ibid.].

Royle and Woods (1992:18) maintain that Mother Teresa, "had to adopt the Spanish spelling of the name [Thérèse], as there was already a Thérèse who was a novice in Loreto."

The voyage to India was long and arduous and the young women, who had previously led lives that were insulated and sheltered from the realities of the poor, were exposed to poverty and squalor at some of the stopovers on their way to Calcutta. Hence, with a growing awareness of what might await them in India, they arrived safely at their destination on 6 January 1929, but as their novitiate training was to be undertaken in Darjeeling, "a hill station some seven thousand feet up in the foothills of the Himalayas" (Spink, 2011:14), they stayed a week in Calcutta and then set out for Darjeeling, where they formally received the habit of the Order and became novices. "The novitiate was a period of preparation and probation for the religious life. For Loreto nuns it also involved preparation for the particular apostolate of teaching, an apostolate that suited Sister Teresa's talents" (ibid.). Teresa was instructed in other languages including Hindu and Bengali, and during those early years she was described as being "very hard working" and *"a sincere, religious type of novice"* (Royle & Woods, 1992:17).

Sister Teresa made her temporary vows on 24 May 1931, and even though she lacked formal educational qualifications, she was appointed as a teacher of geography and later history at St Mary's High School, Entally (Jean Maalouf, 2001:12), which is a neighbourhood of central Calcutta. She had a special aptitude for teaching and was popular with the students (ibid.):

> At Entally there was a Sodality of Mary that operated in a very similar fashion to the sodality to which Mother Teresa herself had belonged as a girl in Skopje. Under the spiritual directorship of a Belgian priest, Father Julien Henry, and with Mother Teresa's encouragement, its members visited patients in a local hospital and went into the slums of Motijhil, which sprawled, with its improvised shacks and its mud alleyways teeming with life, just the other side of the walls of the Entally compound. These visits to the bustees [slum areas of Calcutta] became the subject of subsequent discussion and were constantly related to the Gospel message. "Mother Teresa", one of her pupils – who would later join her in her work as a Missionary Sister of Charity – recalled, "was not only our teacher, she was all the time drawing us to Christ. Whether we were Christian, Hindu or Muslim, she used to talk to us about Jesus" (Spink, 2011:18).

Mother Teresa made her final vows of poverty, chastity and obedience at the Loreto Convent in Darjeeling on 14 May 1937. Her life settled into a routine. However, the following war years (1939-1945) were difficult: "Boats that had been used to transport rice were requisitioned for the purposes of war" (Royle & Woods, 1992:23). The many challenges of these years also included a severe famine in 1943, resulting in "several million people losing their lives"; babies and children were being abandoned on the streets and/or left at convents; and there were mass evacuations of students and the public to safer locations. During these years Mother Teresa was appointed headmistress at St Mary's school, and superior of a small group of nuns. She was extremely conscious of her responsibility in ensuring the safety and well-being of all her charges, endeavouring to shield them from the effects of war (pp.18-19).

On 11 July 1944, Mother Teresa met Father Celeste Van Exem, a Belgian Jesuit, who was to become her spiritual director and good friend, and who was to have a profound influence upon her life. However, when Father Van Exem first met Teresa, he was unimpressed, for as a young priest on a mission, he did not want to become involved with the nuns, he just "wanted to work with intellectuals" (p.20). Asked about his thoughts on that initial meeting with Mother Teresa, his response was that she was "a simple nun, very devout, with an interest in the poor but not particularly remarkable in any respect" (ibid.).

Over the years the visits to the slums near Entally, fired a flame within the heart of the little nun, and she knew that God was asking much more of her, but she didn't know what it was. Her life was full and busy, and yet she was restless. She sought inspiration from the extreme poverty that existed in *bustees*, and in many parts of the neighbourhood and surrounds. Ultimately, her heightened awareness precipitated a spiritual awakening, that occurred when she was on a trip up to the mountains, to make a retreat at Darjeeling on 10 September 1946. Mother Teresa recalls, "I heard the call of God. In quiet, intimate prayer with our Lord, I heard distinctly, a call within a call. The message was quite clear: I was to leave the convent and help the poor while living among them. It was an order. I knew where I belonged, but I did not know how to get there" (cited in Maalouf, 2001:12). Such was the importance of that occasion, that in the 21st century, more than seventy years after the event, "the Missionaries of Charity [continue to] commemorate September 10 as 'Inspiration Day'" (ibid.).

The divine message had been received, but what was this young Loreto nun to do? Her retreat was spent praying for guidance from God and working out ways that she could fulfil his mission for her, while remaining faithful to her vows. On her return to Entally, Mother Teresa confided in her spiritual director Father Van Exem, who advised her not to rush her decision but to think out and plan the best course of action. Hence when she returned to the school, she organised a retreat based on the words of "Christ from the Cross, 'I thirst' and of the request in St. John's Gospel to the Samaritan woman (4:9): 'Give me to drink'" (Spink, 2011:24). She decided that this form of spirituality would be the essence of the constitutions of the congregation she wanted to establish. Also, the Order would be "consecrated to the Immaculate Heart of Mary ... and ... its expressed aim ... [would be] to 'quench the infinite thirst of Jesus Christ on the Cross for love of souls'" (ibid.). And, "in addition to the usual religious vows of poverty, chastity, and obedience – [there would be] a fourth unique vow of 'wholehearted free service to the poorest of the poor'". Most importantly, the Order would be called "'Missionaries of Charity' – carriers of God's love". Finally, Mother Teresa was ready to embark on her mission!

However, Father Van Exem continued to persuade her to exercise restraint, and to pray and wait, and not to speak about the matter to others, even her immediate superiors. Nevertheless, as the months passed Mother Teresa was still intent on realising her goal to found a new congregation of nuns, "who would live and work in the slums of India". Father Van Exem knew that such an undertaking required much forward planning, and he was adamant that Mother Teresa, when applying to leave the Loreto nuns and commence her new foundation, should apply for "an indult of exclaustration which in allowing her to leave the convent would nevertheless enable her to continue as a religious still bound by her vows and answerable directly to the Archbishop. The alternative, an indult of secularization, would mean that she reverted to being a layperson, a fact that would render her even more vulnerable, and liable to lose the respect and confidence generally afforded to religious by the Indian people" (Spink, 2011:28). Archbishop Ferdinand Périer was kept informed of the plans and he directed Mother Teresa "to write to the Mother General of the Loreto Order in Dublin to get permission to be released from the congregation" (Royle & Woods, 1992:24). When the permission was granted, the Archbishop himself organised for the application to be sent to Rome.

Pope Pius XII approved the "Request" on 12 April 1948 (p.25). Consequently, the decree of exclaustration arrived from Rome, and the news was relayed to Mother Teresa by Father Van Exem: "You have the decree of exclaustration for one year. You can do the work. Your Superior is now the Archbishop of Calcutta. You are no Longer a Loreto nun" (Spink, 2011:30). Her sisters in religion were saddened to hear that she would be departing their midst. She was well-liked and *"Loreto meant everything to me"* (Mother Teresa, cited in Royle & Woods, 1992:25). According to Spink (2011:31):

> In readiness for her departure Mother Teresa purchased three saris from a local bazaar: white saris edged with three blue stripes, which would in time become the distinctive habit of her new congregation. The fabric was the cheapest she could find at the time, and the blue stripes appealed to her because blue was the color of the Virgin Mary. In the sacristy of St. Mary's chapel at Entally Father Van Exam blessed them ... on the evening of August 16 she exchanged the religious habit she had worn for nearly twenty years as a Loreto nun for the new habit of her future congregation, and left the Loreto convent, quietly, by taxi.

Father Van Exem advised her to undertake a certain amount of medical training prior to commencing her mission within the slums. Hence, Mother Teresa left on a train to join the "Medical Mission Sisters" at the Holy Family Hospital in Patna, "an ancient city on the Ganges, some 240 miles from Calcutta ... [for she] realised that if she was to be of any practical help to 'the poorest of the poor' it was vital that she had some medical knowledge" (Royle & Woods, 1992:26).

After just a few weeks of medical training at the hospital in Patna, Mother Teresa believed that she was ready to undertake her work in the slums. Maalouf (2001) maintains that it was in December 1948 that she returned to Calcutta, and accepted the hospitality of the Little Sisters of the Poor: "From there, she began her work at the Motijhil slum, just a few miles away ... she started by gathering children under a tree to offer lessons on the alphabet and personal hygiene ... She visited them in their homes and helped them with cleaning and with whatever they needed ... Every day their hunger was growing at the same pace as their hopelessness" (p.13).

She "started teaching, visiting the sick and elderly, instructing Christian children in the catechism, bringing comfort to Muslim and Hindu families alike in their poverty, in the slums of Tiljala (a neighbourhood of Calcutta) and Howrah (referred to as the twin city of Calcutta)" (ibid.). She even started a dispensary at St. Teresa's church. However, there were times when the work was so hard, and Mother Teresa felt so lonely and depressed, that she thought of the comforts she had enjoyed at the convent of Loreto:

> *God wants me to be a lonely nun laden with the poverty of the cross. Today I learned a good lesson. The poverty of the poor is so hard. When I was going and going till my legs and arms were paining, I was thinking how they have to suffer to get food and shelter. Then the comfort of Loreto came to tempt me, but of my own free choice, my God, and out of love for you, I desire to remain and do whatever is your holy will in my regard. Give me courage now, this moment* (Mother Teresa's diary entry, cited in Royle & Woods, 1992:27).

If she was to encourage other young women to follow her example, and assist with her work in the slums, Mother Teresa needed to find suitable accommodation, that would house a growing religious community. Father Van Exem and Father Julien Henry (whom we have met previously) set about looking for a place and it wasn't long before one was found that was ideal. The owners were Catholic, and they were happy to have Mother Teresa and any prospective Sisters occupy the rooms for "gratis", as they were not needed since members of the family had left the area. Mother Teresa moved to the property on 28 February 1949 (Spink, 2011:38). From this moment the number of young women aspiring to join Mother Teresa began to grow. Spink states that: "The first ten girls who arrived were all former pupils. One by one they began the work of serving the poorest of the poor, going begging from door to door, taking the proceeds to those who were starving in the streets, comforting the sick and the dying, and teaching the children the dignity of human life" (p.39).

During this first year (1949), Mother Teresa became an Indian citizen (Royle & Woods, 1992:29), and the Archbishop decided to set in motion, the process that would culminate in Teresa and her sisters, being recognized as a congregation. This necessitated a copy of the proposed written constitutions being received by the Office of the Propagation of the Faith in Rome. Mother Teresa had formulated a copy of the constitutions a few years earlier, however she was not versed in Canon Law, and "much had to be added by Father Van Exem under her inspiration. The constitutions were developed largely on the Loreto Rule, which had in turn been based on the Jesuit Rule ... [and] As far as the rule of poverty was concerned, Mother Teresa wanted it rigorously implemented. She wanted to stipulate that the Missionaries of Charity would not own the buildings from which they served the poor" (Spink, 2011:41). The Constitutions were "typed, copied and handed to Archbishop Périer to take to Rome in April 1950". A Decree of approval was issued from Rome, and on the Feast of the Holy Rosary, 7 October 1950, the Missionary Sisters of Charity became a recognised religious community.

Before long the numbers of young women wanting to join the order and serve the poor and needy grew. Spink (2011:44) writes that "Mother Teresa herself had become more accomplished in the art of begging, and those around her learned from her: Mother gave us a love for begging from door to door." Even though the young nuns had nothing and were "Totally dependent ... on the generosity of others" (ibid.), they did not beg for themselves, but for those less fortunate – the destitute. "The young Missionaries of Charity possessed only their cotton saris and habits, coarse underwear, a pair of sandals, the crucifix they wore pinned to their left shoulder, a rosary, an umbrella to protect them against the monsoon rains, a metal bucket for washing, and a very thin palliasse to serve as a bed" (ibid.). As the number of Missionaries of Charity grew, so did those who offered their assistance:

> Doctors, nurses, and other lay people worked with the sisters on a voluntary basis, and an increasing number of dispensaries were set up to cope with the sickness arising from malnutrition and overcrowding ... The three thousand official slums could no longer contain the two million or so destitute who sought to scratch their daily bread from the streets of ... [Calcutta] ... The Indian government, backed by international relief organizations, set up dispensaries and soup kitchens and managed to send some medicine and clothing into the slums but the flow of destitute refugees from East Pakistan was seemingly interminable, the relief efforts were hopelessly inadequate, and the starving and the disease-ridden lay dying where they fell (pp.53-53).

Mother Teresa, her group of sisters and helpers walked the streets and cradled these dying people in their arms, giving solace and being there for them as they drew their last breath. Mother Teresa approached the relevant authorities requesting provision of accommodation for the dying so that they would "die with dignity" (Royle & Woods, 1992:32-33). Eventually "She was given a pilgrim's hostel near the Temple of Kali. It was in a filthy condition, but it had everything that was required: space, gas, and electricity" (ibid). The Sisters got to work cleaning and preparing the building. It was called "Nirmal Hriday – Place of the Pure Heart".

With the passage of years, more homes for the poor were established. On 23 September 1955 "Shishu Bhavan, the first of a whole series of children's homes was opened, initially as a home for sick children … [but soon it became a] refuge for crippled and unwanted babies and children. Some of them were found in garbage cans and drains. Others were simply abandoned on the city railway platforms. Nearly all were suffering from acute malnutrition and tuberculosis … [regardless of the circumstances] No child was ever refused a home" (Spink, 2011:58-59]. The children were given the love they craved.

Mother Teresa came to realise that of all the afflictions with which she and her sisters were confronted daily, loneliness was perhaps the worst, and they endeavoured to shower the love of Christ upon the many souls who despaired, not because of the immense pain and indignities they were suffering, but often because they had a fear of dying alone. When speaking about the Sisters' efforts regarding children, and visiting the sick and lonely in New York, Mother Teresa spoke of another form of poverty, "We know now that being unwanted is the greatest disease of all" (p.87).

Mother Teresa had a profound concern for leprosy sufferers. "As a disease that ran rife in areas of great poverty, cramped living conditions, and malnutrition, leprosy constituted a particularly pressing problem in and around Calcutta, where poor nutrition, overcrowding, and inadequate medical attention determined the tragic struggle for survival of so many" (Spink, 2011:63). Her concern was for the ignorance that surrounded the disease, for in India though many of the "leprosy cases were noninfectous" (ibid), the sufferers of the disease were generally treated as outcasts.

Karl Schmude (2016, September 1) refers to a television interview in 1968, facilitated by Malcolm Muggeridge, who "was by then a world-renowned author and TV personality. He had been a newspaper correspondent and columnist in various countries". Muggeridge interviewed Mother Teresa and followed this interview with "a special

TV program he made in Calcutta called *Something Beautiful for God*" – a documentary film on her life and work. Royle & Woods (1992:35) posit that in this documentary, Mother Teresa talks about her work with the lepers. Apparently "the work started in 1957 with just five lepers who came to the Mother House. They had been thrown out of their work. Soon they were joined by a doctor, Dr. Senn, who not only treated the lepers but trained the Sisters for leprosy work. Much of this work was done through mobile clinics set up in the areas where the lepers gathered." In 1969, Mother Teresa was granted thirty-four acres of land by the government "on which she built a town called Shanti Nagar, Town of Peace, where the lepers could live in peace" (p.36); be accepted and if cured, receive the necessary "rehabilitation treatment they needed to enable them to resume their place within society" (ibid.). Mother Teresa wasn't worried about how the project would be financed, for she firmly believed in the divine providence of God, and that He would see to their monetary needs!

In 1965, the congregation of the Missionary Sisters of Charity was formally approved by the Holy See, with the granting of the Decree of Praise. The congregation was removed from Diocesan jurisdiction, and placed under papal authority, which meant that the constitutions could not be changed without approval from Rome. Soon "Mother Teresa's work with the dying, the lepers, and the children, with the poorest of the poor, had spread from its humble beginnings in Calcutta to many places throughout the world. The first foundation outside India was in 1965 in Venezuela, and this was followed by foundations in ... [far-flung places] such as Melbourne and London, Rome and New York, Peru and Manilla" and many more (Royle & Woods, 1992:39).

In addition to the religious membership, the legion of voluntary helpers was growing rapidly, reaching the hundreds of thousands in just a few years. Consequently, "[i]n 1969 Mother Teresa drew up, with the help of others, the regulations for the International Association of the Co-Workers of Mother Teresa. On March 26, as head of the Society, she presented them to His Holiness Pope Paul VI" (Royle & Woods, 1992:39). The regulations included the following:

> *The International Association of Co-Workers of Mother Teresa consists of men, women, young people, and children of all religions and denominations throughout the world, who seek to love God in their fellow man, through wholehearted service to the poorest of the poor of all castes and creeds, and who wish to unite themselves in a spirit of prayer and sacrifice with the work of Mother Teresa and the Missionaries of Charity* (p.42).

Mother Teresa believed in the providence of God, and the many awards she received were often accompanied by a monetary gift. These funds were used to enhance the conditions for the destitute, the dying and those who were afflicted with mental and physical ailments, that required long term treatment. For example, when Mother Teresa was awarded the "first Pope John XXIII Peace Prize in 1971 ... [by Pope St Paul VI] ... [she] used the $25,000 prize to establish a home for leprosy patients" (ibid.). She was adamant that the order would not be involved in activities that would permit fundraising. Mother Teresa once explained that the fourth vow they took at profession of "wholehearted and free service to the poorest of the poor", meant "that we cannot work for the rich; neither can we accept any money for what we do. Ours is to be a free service and to the poor" (Catholic News Service, cited in the Catholic Weekly, 1997, September 14).

Regarding the accolades she received – "Mother Teresa had spoken out for peace on a number of international platforms" (Spink, 2011:166), and hence, was nominated on a few occasions for the Nobel Peace Prize. However, it was not until 1979 that it was announced that she would receive this prestigious award, of which she said she was an unworthy recipient. Prior to the ceremony, she and a couple of sisters arrived in Oslo in freezing conditions:

> They were offered heavy cots and fur-lined boots to protect

them against the cold, but Mother Teresa politely refused them. It was only at the insistence of the nuns of St. Joseph, with whom the sisters stayed while in Oslo, that the three sisters from Calcutta agreed to wear woollen socks with their sandals. The usual celebratory banquet was cancelled at Mother Teresa's request. She said that she would rather the money was used for those who were really in need of a meal, and the 3,000 [pounds] earmarked for it was duly added to the prize money [90 000 pounds], together with a further 36, 000 [pounds] raised by Norwegian young people (ibid.).

All monies gifted on this occasion were used to provide housing for the poor, the homeless and for those suffering from leprosy and their families.

In time, with the responsibility of visiting foundations in over 100 countries around the world, and accepting invitations to speak on various international platforms, Mother Teresa's health began to deteriorate. Her heart which encompassed humanity, was beginning to be weighed down with the burden. Hence in April 1990, when she was in her eightieth year and at a General Chapter of the Congregation, she "announced that she was stepping down as Superior of her Order for health reasons. Her followers however refused to accept her resignation and re-elected her in September. She agreed to carry on" as Superior General (Royle & Woods, 1992:50). However, ill-health dogged her over the coming years, and she was beginning to suffer bad falls, and was admitted to hospital on several occasions. Her health became a major concern, and "in January 1997 Archbishop Henry D'Souza of Calcutta announced that mother Teresa had made it clear that she wished to resign as general superior of her order and that there was to be no repeat of 1990 when she had resumed the position" (Spink, 2011:280).

However, the elections were delayed. Spink maintains that the reasons for the delay were that "The transition from charismatic founder to successor in religious congregations was invariable problematic ... [Then on Thursday March 13] Sister Nirmala, former head of the contemplative sisters, was ... [announced as the] overall superior general ... [she] was a Hindu convert, from a Nepali family, and a profoundly spiritual, well-educated, and wise woman" (p.281). Sister Nirmala was very experienced and had accompanied Mother Teresa on several overseas trips. Then on 5 September 1997, at the age of 87, and within six months of relinquishing the leadership of her beloved Missionaries of Charity, Mother Teresa passed to eternal life. She was beatified on Sunday 19 October 2003 by Pope St John Paul II, and canonised on 4 September 2016, by Pope Francis. Her feastday is celebrated on 5 September.

Leadership as Service

You may recall that at the beginning of this chapter, one of the criterions for sainthood was that a candidate had lived a sanctified life. Because of Mother Teresa's "selfless service to Calcutta's poor" (Spink, 2011:290), she was regarded during her lifetime as a "living saint." Her service then, "in the minds and hearts of many Christians and non-Christians alike, was the most authentic indication of sanctity" (ibid.). Her leadership was love and service in action. She guided her sisters in humble service that was based on love: "*What we must do is to have and to put into the work greater love and more generous service*" (p.186). Mother Teresa taught the members of her communities to "serve the poor with tender, compassionate love" (Maalouf, 2001:140). She taught them that to engage in such service, it was important to learn how to pray, and that to learn how to pray required an awareness of the inner and out realities of self, and a focus on silence. Her mentoring emphasised that:

> The fruit of silence is faith.
>
> The fruit of faith is prayer.
>
> The fruit of prayer is love.
>
> The fruit of love is service.

And the fruit of service is silence.

(Mother Teresa, 1995, cited in Maalouf, 2001:64)

Mother Teresa's wisdom is found in her simplicity and in her humanity – she saw beauty in all of creation and particularly "in each man, woman and child" (Spink, 2011:283).

Wisdom has built her house, she has hewn her seven pillars (Proverbs 9:1, cited in Sipe & Frick, 2015:4). For the purpose of this analysis, the "Seven Pillars of Servant Leadership" (see Appendix A for the list of attributes), are outlined below, and the discussion on each pillar includes aspects of the life and works of St Teresa of Kolkata, who "made her voice heard before the powers of this world" (Pope Francis, Homily/Canonisation Mass, September 4, 2016).

Pillar 1 – "Person of Character"

At the beginning of the chapter, there is reference to Mother Teresa as being tough. Indeed, just reading the story of her faith journey, and the challenges that living in the slums entailed, gives the impression that such a lifestyle would not have been conducive to the faint-hearted or the overly sensitive. It would have taken an iron-will to cradle dying people – men, women, children and babies in a compassionate embrace, and tend them till the final breath left their bodies! Her presence and that of her sisters ensured that they did not die alone. Mother Teresa washed the filth from bodies riddled with disease and wasted from hunger – many of these human beings were near death. She sought homes for the poorest of the poor, where they could be tended to with love and compassion, by the members of her congregation. So perhaps here "tough" is an inadequate word, for Mother Teresa's toughness was not based on just being able to cope, it also enabled her to see the image of Christ in each of the suffering human beings who graced her life on a regular basis.

Mother Teresa's life could have had a very different scenario. Initially, she was settled with the Order of Loreto nuns, where she had spent over

20 years, living a life of security in a convent community, well-liked by her sisters in religion, and recently appointed headmistress at St Mary's High school. It was a life though not easy, was what could be called "safe"! She was only responsible for her charges and when on occasion she found the time to visit the slums, with her students from the school, such contact did not involve living in the slums and she was able to return to the comforts of the convent at the end of the visit. When Mother Teresa heard "the call within a call" on the train journey up the mountains to Darjeeling, on her way to a retreat, she could have ignored the message, and continued to live her "safe" life. However, this was not meant to be, because she was a person of tremendous character, and possessed a strong faith. She surrendered herself to God and trusted in his divine Providence. Maalouf (2001:18) speaks highly of the principles of this generous and gifted nun:

> By surrendering totally to God, trusting the divine providence, and just being "a pencil in the hands of God," she was able to bring hope to people, to touch their wounds, and to heal their lives leading them to Christ ... Mother Teresa was a person of principles. [Though extremely humble] she was [at the same time] straight-forward, courageous, uncompromising, bold, and challenging. She was never afraid to speak her mind before any audience, even if ... that audience disagreed with her. Wherever she went ... [she] emphasised and insisted on the unity, love, peace, and joy that must exist in the life of the family (Maalouf, 2001:17-18).

On numerous occasions Mother Teresa was invited on the international platform, to speak before audiences, and there was a time in 1985 when at the United Nations she was introduced by the "then secretary general, Javier Pérez de Cuellar ... [who said]: "I present to you the most powerful woman in the world" (Edward Le Joly, 1993, cited in Maalouf, 2001:18). Indeed, integrity and charisma radiated from this tiny self-effacing nun, who enthralled the world, but who just wanted to serve others.

Pillar II – "Puts People First"

This could be described as Mother Teresa's mantra. According to Spink (2011:283) "in celebration of the fiftieth anniversary of India's independence (1997) ... [Mother Teresa wrote]: *When I look around our country, the land God has given to each one of us to call our home, I see so much of His blessings and goodness: in the smallest flower, the tallest trees, the rivers, plains and mountains. But where do we find most the beauty of our country? We find it in each man, woman and child.*"

She believed that "We all have the duty to serve God where we are called to do so [and] I feel called to serve individuals, to love each human being. My calling is not to judge the institutions. I am not qualified to condemn anyone. I never think in terms of a crowd, but of individual persons ... I believe in the personal touch of one to one" (Mother Teresa, 1996, cited in Maalouf, 2001:35). Mother Teresa was "a voice for people who had no voice ... With a team of Sisters, Brothers, and Co-Workers ... she endeavored to respond to the ever-growing demands of the poorest of the poor. People throughout the world came to recognize this small woman, in her simple white sari with a blue border and a small black crucifix pinned to it, as a source for the powerless" (Royle & Woods, 1992:44).

Maryanne Holm & Maree Woodbury, 1997, quote "A Vatican spokesman, Father Ciro Benedettini [who] said that when Pope John Paul II heard of Mother Teresa's death ... he was deeply moved and pained ... He was very close to this Sister who dedicated her life to helping people in the world who were the poorest, the most neglected and the abandoned ... She was a glowing example of how the love of God can be transformed into love of one's neighbour." Mother Teresa inspired others to look beyond their own needs, and to see the image of God in their neighbours.

Pillar III – "Skilled Communicator"

Mother Teresa wrote many letters during her lifetime. When she was undertaking medical training at Patna, prior to commencing her work in the slums, she wrote letters back to Calcutta asking to return, as the work she was doing in Patna was not really what she thought she would be encountering back at Calcutta (Spink, 2011:34). In reality she was very keen to begin her new Order. Other letters were written over the years and documentation kept. However, at one stage during the early 1990s:

> Certain documents dating from …[when] she first ventured into Motijhil, the slum she had been able to see from the windows of the Loreto convent, Entally … were kept by Father Van Exem. There came a time, however, when Mother Teresa, adamant that the work was God's work and not her work, wanted all such documentation destroyed. The response of her spiritual director was that the documents were not her property but belonged rather to the congregation. Without the authority of the bishop he could not destroy them … Some years later, however, worn down by Mother Teresa's repeated pleading, Father Van Exem sent her the two boxes he had so carefully retained, on condition that she keep anything that rightfully belonged to the congregation.

You may recall from reading previous paragraphs that Mother Teresa was invited to speak on numerous international platforms, about her work and the dedicated people who were following her lead. She was not an orator, but spoke simply from the heart, without notes but with a message to all to care for the poorest of the poor, within their countries and communities. When accepting the Nobel Peace Prize in Oslo on December 10, 1979:

> Mother Teresa accepted the gold medal and the money, as she had accepted all other honors, "unworthily" but

"gratefully in the name of the poor, the hungry, the sick and the lonely" ... Even in the Aula Magna of the University of Oslo, with the eyes of the world upon her, Mother Teresa did not deviate from her practice of speaking without notes. Before delivering a speech prepared only with the sign of the cross, she called upon her audience to recite the Prayer of St. Francis, and in the name of peace all those present – Roman Catholics, Lutherans, Anglicans, Greek Orthodox, Baptists, Methodists, and those who had forgotten how to pray – joined in the words: "Lord, make me an instrument of thy peace that where there is hatred I may bring love." As Father Van Exem would afterward comment: "Only Mother could have got[ten] away with it" (Spink, 2011:168).

Mother Teresa wrote to presidents, prime ministers and many other leaders, asking in her own simple way for a commitment to peace. She wrote regularly to her sisters, brothers, the priests, the co-workers, the lay missionaries and others urging all to pray. *"If you pray, God will give a clean heart and a clean heart can see the face of God in the Poor you serve"* (p.269).

Mother Teresa did not give in to her own pain – be it physical or psychological. According to the News Corp Australia network (2016, August 28) "Private letters published after her death in 1997, also revealed that for the last 50 years of her life she despaired over having lost a personal connection with Jesus, while she continued steadfastly to serve his cause." She wrote "In one despairing letter to a confidant ... 'Where is my faith – even deep-down right in there is nothing, but emptiness & darkness – My God – how painful is this unknown pain – I have no Faith'" (Biography.com Editors, January 17, 2019). Such despair and mental anguish led to what has been called the "dark night of the soul". Fifty years from 1997 brings us back to 1947, a year after Mother Teresa received the "call within a call", and a year prior to her leaving the Loreto convent and founding the Missionaries of Charity! Such was the cross she bore, as she actioned her love of God in service to others!

Pillar IV – "Compassionate Collaborator"

In addition to the Co-Workers movement, which was established in 1969, Mother Teresa founded another group, which was formed to show support for the work being done by the Missionaries of Charity. This group was referred to as the "Sick and Suffering Co-workers of Mother Teresa" (p.48). The members of this group though they might have been incapacitated in some way, that would prevent actually being physically involved and assisting the Missionaries of Charity first hand, they were asked to offer their pain, suffering and prayers in support of all those less fortunate then themselves, and for the Missionaries. In addition, Mother Teresa was keen to always involve lay people in assisting her sisters with their service to the poor. Hence on 16 April 1984, the Lay Missionaries of Charity were established (Catholic Online, 2019).

Surprisingly, the presence of the Missionaries of Charity in the community, was not always met with a favourable reaction. When the Sisters first moved into the "Nirmal Hriday" building, which was used to accommodate the dying, the building was near a "holy Hindu shrine. Rumors were circulating that people were being converted to Christianity. Complaints reached the ears of the Police Commissioner, who duly inspected Nirmal Hriday. He was impressed by what he saw and said to those who brought the complaint, '*I have said that I will get rid of this foreign lady and I will do so, but you must first get your mothers and your sisters to do what she is doing. In the Temple is a black stone image of the goddess Kali. But here, we have a living Kali*'" (Royle & Woods, 1992:32-33).

Mother Teresa and her sisters were often accused of proselytising, and that their reasons for showing such compassion and love to the poor, ill and dying was because they were keen to convert those of other faiths to Christianity. Spink (2011:253-254) recounts that: "To many Bengalis she became known 'as the preacher of love who does not preach', but the allegations of 'rice Christianity' [becoming a Christian for material reasons, rather than religious] were never totally dispelled. There continued to be those who felt that she believed that Hinduism and Islam were wrong and Catholicism was right, and who questioned the validity of the fact that she was ministering to the poor of Calcutta and the world, not for their own sake but for the sake of her Catholic God." Mother Teresa argued that this was not the case and that they had never tried to force people of other religions to convert to Christianity, by providing them with nourishment and medical assistance, but then they would also not make excuses for being proud witnesses for their faith.

Pillar V – "Has Foresight"

You may recall from reading her Profile, that in her early days as a Loreto Sister at St Mary's High School, Mother Teresa and some of her students who were members of the Solidarity visited the slums of Motijhil. The purpose of the visits was to relate the experience to follow-up discussions on the Gospel message. When Mother Teresa had her "call within a call", a flame was ignited in her heart and she wanted to work and live in the slums of Calcutta. She had seen a need and now she was responding to God's will in her life. During the Homily presented at the Mass for the Canonization of Blessed Mother Teresa of Calcutta, Pope Francis likened her to a prophet hearing God's call and reaching a decision that pleased Him (*Wis* 9:18):

> In order to ascertain the call of God, we must ask ourselves and understand what pleases God. On many occasions the prophets proclaimed what was pleasing to God. Their message found a wonderful synthesis in the words "I want mercy, not sacrifice" (*Hos* 6:6; *Mt* 9:13). God is pleased by every act of mercy, because in the brother or sister that we

assist, we recognize the face of God which no one can see (cf. *Mt* 25:40). In a word, we touch the flesh of Christ ... those who put themselves at the service of others ... are those who love God ... For Mother Teresa, mercy ... was the "light" which shone in the darkness of the many who no longer had tears to shed for their poverty and suffering ... "May she be your model of Holiness" (Saint Peter's Square, 2016, 4 September).

Mother Teresa shared her vision of serving the poorest of the poor, with the world. She was inclusive of all, and she valued diversity. She didn't differentiate between "culture, race or religion ... [and she] loved to say, 'Perhaps I don't speak their language, but I can smile'" (ibid.). As part of her desire to "share the vision" Mother Teresa founded the Missionary Brothers of Charity in 1963 (see Pillar VI). She believed that there were some duties that the Sisters would not be able to perform as well as the men. "You can do what I can't do. I can do what you can't do. Together we can do something beautiful for God" (Mother Teresa, cited in Spink, 2011:103). Vivian Dyer, the then Archbishop of Calcutta was favourable in his response to the creation of a new order. "In India people have understood the vocation of a priest. They have understood the vocation of a sister. They have not understood the vocation of a Brother. Tell her to begin" (ibid.).

Mother Teresa's understanding of the needs of her religious communities, and the many foundations she served were amazing. According to Malcolm Muggeridge "Mother Teresa not only had mystical insight but also the practical acumen ... [He] was surprised – and hugely impressed – by her organisational shrewdness and efficiency, managing an order of sisters spread beyond India to various countries across the globe, including Australia. His reference to her "mystical insight", was his understanding of her experience of the "Dark night of the Soul", which you may recall from Pillar III. Such an experience is likened to the experience of St John of the Cross, and many other saints and by Christ himself on the Cross: "My God, My God, why have you forsaken me?" (cited in Schmude, 2016, September 1).

The process for beatification required a miracle for the cause to proceed. The miracle chosen was attributed to the case of "Monica Besra, an Indian woman who had a massive tumor in her abdomen. According to Besra, she was wearing a locket containing the image of Mother Teresa. A beam of light emanated from the locket at the moment the miracle occurred. All subsequent medical scans revealed she was totally cured. There was no scientific or medical explanation for the miracle" (Catholic Online, 2019). Consequently, Mother Teresa was beatified on 19 October 2003. Now for canonization to proceed, a second miracle was required. However, it was to be some years before a second miracle was announced by Pope Francis in 2015. "The miracle Involved a Brazilian man who was afflicted with tumors [and] who was miraculously cured. This cleared the way for Mother Teresa's canonization" (ibid.) ceremony, which was held in Rome on 4 September 2016.

Pillar VI – "Systems Thinker"

The "Big Picture" for the community was its global perspective. During the first ten years of the congregation, the sisters served the communities in the Diocese of Calcutta. However, with the growth in the numbers of sisters and brothers over the years the community looked further afield. Spink (2011:77) maintains that "Canon Law forbids the opening of further houses outside the Diocese by institutes less than ten years old". It was after this time had elapsed, that various houses of the Missionary Sisters of Charity were founded throughout India. In addition, new Branches of the community were also established with the founding of the Missionaries of Charity Brothers in 1963 (refer to Pillar V – "Has Foresight").

A Jesuit Priest, Father Ian Travers-Ball, who had been ordained in 1963, asked for and received permission to live with the Brothers for a time. Eventually he got permission to leave his congregation, and "accepted the call ... to serve the poor of the world. He became the male co-founder of the Missionaries of Charity Brothers". He received the title General Servant, and the name Brother Andrew (Royle & Woods, 1992:40). Spink (2011:107) asserts that "The Roman Catholic Church finally approved the Brother's institution as a diocesan congregation on March 26, 1967", thus allowing the congregation to establish a novitiate. As the order grew, other branches of the congregation were established, and apart from the Missionary Sisters of Charity and the Brothers, "there was a contemplative branch of the Sisters, founded in New York on June 25, 1976, and a contemplative branch of the brothers, established in Rome on March 19, 1979. The [Missionary] fathers were founded in the Bronx, New York on October 13, 1984" (Catholic Online, 2019).

Mother Teresa was the recipient of several Honorary Doctorate Degrees. She was uncomfortable receiving such accolades, as she believed they were not for her. They were for 'Her People'. "I don't know why universities and colleges are conferring titles on me. I never know whether I should accept or not; it means nothing to me. But it gives me a chance to speak of Christ to people who otherwise may not hear of him" (cited in Spink, 2011:163): "her aim was always to touch the hearts of those to whom she spoke with a spiritual message, to bring them the Good News." The awards she received numbered more than one hundred and included:

> The Padmashree (one of India's highest honours) medal (August 1962); John F. Kennedy International Award (September 1971); Jawahalal Nehru Award for International Understanding (November 1972); Templeton Prize for "Progress in Religion" (April 1973); Bharat Ratna [Jewel of India], (March 1980); Order of Merit [from Queen Elizabeth], (November 1983); Gold Medal of the Soviet Peace Committee (August 1987); United States Congressional Gold Medal (June 1997).

According to Catholic Online (2019), when Mother Teresa died: "The Missionaries of Charity numbered 3,914 members and were established in 594 communities in 123 countries of the world." Since that time, the numbers have grown to "over 4,000 members in 697 foundations in 131 countries of the world" (ibid.). Mother Teresa's legacy is continuing to have a huge impact around the globe.

Pillar VII – "Leads with Moral Authority"

Mother Teresa led with moral authority. "She was not always understood and ... The simplicity of her vision ... did not engage everyone's hearts. Feminists were frequently angered by her consistent exhortation for women to be homemakers and to leave men to do 'what they do best' ... Her fidelity to the traditional authority and teachings of the Roman Catholic Church was another point that provoked controversy ... At a time when some theologians, priests, and laypeople within the Catholic Church had been challenging dogma ... her firm traditional allegiances were a source of comfort to other traditionalists" (Spink, 2011:248-249). Her "vocal endorsement of some of the Catholic Church's more controversial doctrines regarding contraception and/or abortion" (Biography.com Editors, 2019) was criticised. "'I feel the greatest destroyer of peace today is abortion,' Mother Teresa said in her 1979 Nobel [Peace Prize] Lecture" (ibid.).

She travelled extensively to promote the missionary discipleship of the Order. "In 1971 ... [she] traveled to New York City to open her first American-based house of charity, and in the summer of 1982, she secretly went to [war-ravaged] Beirut, Lebanon, where she crossed between Christian East Beirut and Muslim West Beirut to aid children of both faiths. In 1985, Mother Teresa returned to New York and spoke at the 40th anniversary of the United Nations General Assembly. While there, she also opened Gift of Love, a home to care for those infected with HIV/AIDS" (Biography.com Editors, January 17, 2019). Her work did not stop there, and as the years and foundations increased so did her reputation as one of "the greatest humanitarians of all time". Mother Teresa's example has empowered generations of followers to continue her work – her communities of Sisters, Brothers, Priests, Co-Workers and Lay Missionaries, are all stewards of the legacy of her profound love for "the poorest of the poor".

Values

Aspects of Mother Teresa's life and works are now discussed in relation to the values – dignity, respect, fairness, justness and equality (see Chapter 4 for the terms of reference).

Dignity

Mother Teresa respected the human dignity of all people, regardless of their cultural or religious background. She was particularly disposed to the very poor, the helpless, the diseased and the dying. In her dealings with people from all levels of society, she always respected their human dignity. Thomas Menamparampil, (2016, 24 August) maintains that "The apostolic administrator in Jowai met the future saint in 1958, when he was in the seminary. What struck him was Mother's devotion to others, especially the poorest. Faced with the irrational process that makes humans into consuming machines, Mother Teresa cried out to the world the sacredness of the human person and soul." The soul is sacred because it is created in the image of God (Gen 1:27).

> If Mother Teresa "had a message for our time, it would be that the human person has dignity and value no matter his or her fragilities. She saw the 'glory of God' shine through the eyes of people at death's door", said Mgr [Monsignor] *Thomas Menamparampil, Archbishop Emeritus of Guwahati and current apostolic administrator in Jowai ... According to Mgr Menamparampil, Mother Teresa showed the heroic spirit that is in each of us, starting from the slums of Kolkata.*

She "had the courage to bring the lost Sense of the Sacred back into the modern world" (ibid.).

Mother Teresa saw the image of God in the poor. Her love in action respected the dignity of all people.

Respect

According to Spink (2011:177-178):

> There was between Mother Teresa and Pope [St] John Paul II clearly a relationship of reciprocal personal respect and affection. To the eyes of the general public this was particularly apparent when in 1986, during [the visit of] Pope [St] John Paul II ... to India, Mother Teresa showed him around the Home for the Dying in Calcutta, on what she described as the happiest day of her life ... [St] John Paul II spent almost three-quarters of an hour in Nirmal Hriday, feeding some of the occupants, pausing beside the low cots to hold the face of a suffering person in his hands, blessing them. He paid rich tributes to Mother Teresa's work among the poor: "For the destitute and the dying Nirmal Hriday is a place of hope. This place represents a profound dignity of every human person."

Mother Teresa's empathy and love reached out to all with whom she came in contact. She stated that: "'People throughout the world may look different, or have a different religion, education or position but they are all the same. They are all people to be loved.' Above all, fame did nothing to alter the interest, respect, and love she had for individuals, regardless of their nationality, standing or creed." Mother Teresa believed that we are all made in the image of God, and hence are entitled to a "duty of respect" (CCC, 2000:para.1738) from others. It is our inalienable right as human beings!

Fairness

Fairness involves treating others with dignity and respect. It is valuing each other and celebrating the uniqueness of all people. Mother Teresa did this, but her life was not without controversy:

> [S]he ... faced rejection ... [and] misunderstanding. It is a fact, for example, that not everyone, even in India, wanted a home for the destitute dying or a center for lepers in their neighborhoods. Even after settling in, the Missionaries of Charity were asked to leave. This happened in Northern Ireland and in Sri Lanka ... [also] she was friendly with public officials and private individuals whose values and conduct were contrary to her own. What is more, she accepted their charitable donations, regardless of their motives. In 1994, for example she and her sisters were attacked very harshly for accepting donations from individuals like Haiti's exiled dictator Jean-Claude Duvalier. Mother Teresa's argument was that "she had no more right to refuse donations given for the poor and miserable" (Mother Teresa, 1983, cited in Maalouf, 2001:19-20).

Regardless of what is done by one individual to ease the burden of others, there will always be those who disagree with actions taken. Some will do so, just to be different; others will generally believe, that things could be done another "better" way, and still others would perhaps be indifferent! Mother Teresa didn't do what she did for recognition, or for accolades, or for rewards or for praise. She silenced her critics by doing what she did best – loving and looking after the needs of the poor.

On an occasion in November 1960, when Mother Teresa went to Rome to apply for papal recognition of her Congregation, she was able to meet up with her brother Lazar, whom she had not seen since 1924. "Lazar was by then living as an exile in Italy with his wife, Maria, and their daughter, Aggi. Drana and Aga Bojaxhiu, however, were still in

Tirana [capital of Albania]" (Spink, 2011:79). Over the years Mother Teresa and her brother Lazar were unable to visit their mother and sister, in what at the time was regarded as "one of Europe's most rigorously socialist states" (ibid.). However, Mother Teresa and her brother Lazar wrote to their mother and sister in an effort to maintain contact. Spink (2011:96-97) states that Drana wrote to her son wanting to see him and his family and Teresa one last time before she died:

> Teresa did her utmost to bring about a reunion ... [and] as one who had "come from Albania and brought great honor to the country", [she] appealed to the Albanian Embassy to allow her mother and sister to leave Albania ... [for her] elderly mother ... wanted only to see her children once more before she died ... [Teresa] explored the possibility of going to Albania herself before her mother died, but was given to understand that while permission would be granted for her to go to Albania no guarantee could be given that she would be allowed to leave again afterward. [Hence Teresa, deeply aggrieved, opted not to go] ... On July 12, 1972, a telegram arrived in Calcutta announcing that Drana Bojaxhiu had died ... [and] Her daughter Aga [who had lived with her mother] ... died on August 25, 1973 ... without seeing her brother or sister again.

Some might say that the decisions made in reference to Drana and her daughter Aga were not fair; obviously, the situation could have been handled differently by the Government to obtain a more favourable outcome, however the Bojaxhiu family remained united in prayer. Mother Teresa's disappointment resulted in her spending more time with her spiritual family, ensuring that they maintained contact with their own families, for she believed that "love began in the home" (p.97).

Justness

Kimberley Motley (2016) maintains that justness is needed for all, and that "By creating a global human right economy and becoming global investors in human rights we can achieve justness together." It is my belief however, "that people need to want to achieve justness in their dealings with one another. For there may be some who would be satisfied with the status quo, and would not want change, regardless of the benefits to the majority" (Cameron, 2019). Mother Teresa definitely wasn't satisfied with the status quo, or she would have stayed in the Loreto convent early in her religious life. By answering "the call within a call", she stepped outside her comfort zone, and was prepared to address the challenges that came her way. According to Mother Teresa:

> In the world there are some who struggle for justice and human rights. We have no time for this because we are in daily and continuous contact with men, [women and children] who are starving for a piece of bread to put in their mouths and for some affection. Should I devote myself to struggle for the justice of tomorrow or even for the justice of today, the most needy people would die right in front of me because they lack a glass of milk. Nevertheless, I want to state clearly that I do not condemn those who struggle for justice. I believe that there are different options for the people of God. To me the most important is to serve the neediest people. Within the church some do one thing, others do a different thing. What is important is that all of us remain united, each one of us developing his/[her] own specific task (cited in Maalouf, 2001: 30).

Hence justness for all means believing in ourselves and doing what we can do individually, and together to make a difference. We need to be "the difference that makes a difference"!

Equality

Mother Teresa treated everybody equally. It didn't matter whether they were rich or poor. She often spoke out about "spiritual poverty" in the western nations, as being a serious problem (Spink, 2011). The Catechism of the Catholic Church emphasises that "the equality of men/[women] rests essentially on their dignity as persons and the rights that flow from it" (2000:1935). There is much to learn from Mother Teresa's simple self-analysis: "By blood I am Albanian. By citizenship, an Indian. By faith, I am a Catholic nun. As to my calling, I belong to the world" (Spink, 2011:308). She didn't think that she was any better or more important than anybody else. Mother Teresa's mission was a discipleship of service.

This chapter, which has investigated and highlighted the life and faith journey of an extraordinary woman – St Teresa of Kolkata, concludes the second millennium section of this book. Prepare now to enter the third millennium and reflect on "Current & Emerging Global Trends". Listen to the voices of selected women in the contemporary Church, and to the voices of the youth – our leaders of the future – who are challenged by the voices from the past to respond to the Spirit and to live and proclaim the Gospel, as they continue to serve those they lead.

THIRD MILLENNIUM:

Current & Emerging
Global Trends

19

Voices of Selected Women in the Contemporary Church

In December 2018 and February 2019, I attended two events in separate states of Australia that focussed on the topic "Women and Leadership in the Catholic Church" – on both occasions the numbers wanting to attend exceeded the places being offered. In recent months I have heard of similar events being organised. The message is clear – there is passionate interest in this focus on the role of women leaders in the contemporary Church. However, such passion can tend to ignite emotions in response to varying opinions on how to move forward; and regardless of our opinion, or our gender, it is important to remember that we are all Church, and that we need to treat each other with dignity and respect.

Without question women are seeking "greater involvement in leadership, decision making, and ministry roles in the [life of the] Church" (Women Matter, 2017, September 28); however, rather than just having emotions influence actions, perhaps it is best to let wisdom also lead the way! For "wisdom is radiant and unfading, and she is easily discerned by those who love her and is found by those who seek her" (Catholic Bible Press, 1990:718). Note "the female figure of Wisdom (*Hokmah* in Hebrew; *Sophia* in Greek – Proverbs 8 and 9; Wisdom 7)". You may recall reading this information about wisdom, in a quotation in Chapter 8 in reference to St Catherine of Siena.

The Church appears to recognise the invaluable contribution of its women leaders. Within the Vatican administration, in dioceses and in parishes changes are occurring albeit slowly. However, after centuries of patriarchal administration in the Church, it is obvious that change will not happen overnight. It takes time to replace structures and mindsets that have developed over many years. The existing governance in the Church is based on the hierarchical concept of authority (Cardinal Avery Dulles, 1978:43). In his chapter on "The Church as Institution" Dulles quotes from the Vatican 1 Schema: "the Church of Christ is not a community of equals in which all the faithful have the same rights. It is a society of unequals, not only because among the faithful some are clerics and some are ... [laypersons], but particularly because there is in the Church the power from God whereby to some it is given to sanctify, teach, and govern, and to others not" (ibid.). Dulles then refers to Bishop Emile De Smedt of Bruges' comments during Vatican II regarding the hierarchical nature of the Church's governance and the rights of the "faithful people of God":

> Bishop De Smedt spoke of the pyramidal pattern in which all power is conceived as descending from the pope through the bishops and priests, while at the base the faithful people play a passive role and seem to have a lower position in the Church. In contrast to this view, the bishop reminded the conciliar Fathers that in the Church all have the same fundamental rights and duties, so that popes and bishops, together with lay persons, are to be reckoned among the faithful people of God (p.44).

As members of the Church, we all belong to the "People of God" and as human beings "we are created in the image of God" (Genesis 1:27). Equality rests on our dignity as persons, "There is neither Jew nor Gentile, neither slave nor free, nor is there male and female, for you are all one in Christ Jesus (Galatians 3:28). As mentioned previously, some changes may not be immediate; indeed, for any change to occur within an administration that is hierarchical and patriarchal, including changes in traditional practice, would require "culture change and coercive persuasion", which according to Schein (1999:168) would be fraught with difficulties. Schein (ibid.) posits that one must consider the implications of dealing with an organisation "whose very essence has been hierarchy as the prime means of coordination and control ... Consider what this means to managers whose power has been based on their organizational position, whose very concept of management has been to be 'over' others, to give orders, to call the shots, to be individually accountable."

Hence is it possible for traditional practice to be changed in the Church regarding ecclesial leadership opportunities for women? I believe so, for a precedent was set as a result of a major shift in traditional practice which occurred in 1970, when St Teresa of Ávila was proclaimed the first female doctor of the Universal Church. Prior to 1970 an "unspoken" though not officially documented criterion was that the candidate should be male. There are now, in 2019, four women doctors of the Church. Consequently, change regarding the appointment of more women to senior leadership positions within the Church is possible and is happening.

Recent announcements in the LaCroix International Newspaper (9 July 2019) and The Tablet (8 July 2019) state that Pope Frances has named "the first women members of the Vatican department that oversees religious orders ... the congregation for Institutes of Consecrated Life and Societies of Apostolic Life" (Christopher Lamb, 2019, July 8). Apparently, the Pope appointed seven women (six religious superiors and a consecrated lay woman) to the board and these are the first female members to hold such a position on the body. The appointments "give the women executive rather than simply consultative roles" (Lamb, 2019). This announcement comes just weeks after the Pope appointed "four women to top Synod jobs" as consultors (CN Catholic News, 27 May 2019; The Tablet, 24 May 2019). In his article in May Christopher Lamb wrote that "Pope Francis has appointed the first women consultors to the secretariat of the Synod of Bishops, which under his pontificate has become a crucial vehicle for setting the Church's pastoral agenda. Four women – [including] three religious sisters – will be tasked with offering advice and strategic direction to the body which organises the synod of Bishops gatherings" (The Tablet, 24 May 2019). So, the voices of women are beginning to be heard!

However, if women leaders are to move forward in their efforts to have "greater female representation at senior levels in the Church" (ibid.), it is important that they exercise patience with those who may be less motivated towards change. With wisdom comes understanding and the need to listen and communicate, interacting with members of teams and/or organisations – keeping them informed and valuing each member, mentoring and nurturing individuals "to be the best they can be in their mission of service". It is a time also for leaders to step outside their comfort zone and challenge the status quo! Robert Greenleaf (cited in Fraker and Spears, 1996:4) maintained that "inspired, prophetic institutional leadership begins with one spirit-filled faithful person, who will be strong enough to strike out on a different path, leading the institution down that path."

The women leaders mentioned throughout this book were not too concerned with what the future held – they believed in the Providence of God! Perhaps we all need to step back then and reflect on the meaning of these words? When you read the following contributions by women who are expressing their voice on their particular role in the Church, you will notice that each person is being the best they can be, and they are being the difference that makes a difference within their communities. When I wrote about the women leaders throughout the centuries in the previous chapters – certain aspects of their leadership qualities emerged which could be emulated by women leaders in the contemporary church. I will explore these briefly in the final chapter. However, here I repeat a quote from Servant of God Dorothy Day (*Quotes*, n.d.):

> What we would like to do is change the world ... [and] we can, to a certain extent ... we can work for the oasis, the little cell of joy and peace in a harried world. We can

throw our pebble in the pond and be confident that its ever widening circle will reach around the world ... there is nothing we can do but love, and, dear God, please enlarge our hearts to love each other, to love our neighbor, to love our enemy as our friend.

If one person can achieve so much, imagine what the efforts of many would accomplish. However not all of us are activists like Dorothy. Some of us are content with our current status, while others are prepared to challenge the status quo. To the latter I ask the following questions – Are you content to step outside your comfort zone and be the pebble rippling out within the waters of faith and leadership, doing what you can as a leader to support the rights of others within the Church? When you ask others, what are they doing to improve the situation regarding "greater involvement of women in leadership, decision making and ministry roles in the [life of the] Church", what will be your response if they reply, "And what are you doing"? For it is everybody doing their "bit" and working together collaboratively, that will rebuild and "heal" the church community – thus leading to renewal, change and growth – particularly in regard to the ongoing appointment of female leaders to senior administrative positions. I invite you now to read the contributions of selected women leaders, who are giving voice to their role in the contemporary Church. Pease note that the contributions are listed according to the order received.

Dr Patricia Madigan OP (Ecumenical Officer in the Catholic Church in Sydney [1997 – 2013] and currently Chair of the Council for Australian Catholic Women)

These days "social location" and "intersectionality" are buzz words when it comes to describing one's opinions and/or activities. I can only explain aspects of how I have engaged in leadership throughout my life in the same way. My parents were third-generation Australians and active Catholics. Growing up in the then working-class inner-city Melbourne suburb of Brunswick in the post-World War II years, the first examples of leadership I became aware of was my mother as president of a parish women's group and my father as president of the St Vincent de Paul Society. In fact, it seems this was how they originally came to know each other.

So, it did not seem in any way unusual that at university I became involved in student politics and was a member of la Trobe University Students' Representative Council. These were the days of sit-ins and student protests – there was a sense that we could make change happen. The raised grass area in the centre of the university (the Agora), which the university administration originally planned to concrete, remains a symbol of our activity even to this day. It was while reading about Catherine of Siena in the university library, that I discovered that there were saints who had combined their spirituality with political involvement. I could connect with them! This led me into a period of discernment, and I joined the Dominicans in 1976, after completing three years teaching in Victorian government schools.

As a Dominican sister I became involved in leadership in a whole host of ways, as a Religious Education Co-ordinator in secondary schools, and later as Diocesan Ecumenical Officer in the Catholic Church in Sydney. In the latter role I found myself collaborating on various levels – with grassroots people in parishes, with faith leaders, and with organisations in the wider community. In this capacity I found myself working alongside Christian leaders from seventeen different churches who were members of the New South Wales Ecumenical Council and many leaders of other faiths. I discovered there were so many ways of exercising religious leadership, which gave me cause to reflect on the way leadership is exercised in the Catholic Church. In recent years I have been an active member of the international Ecclesiastical Investigations network and the Catholic Women Speak network and have published widely, mostly in international books and journals – another way I see of exercising leadership.

Professor Tracey Rowland (Member of the Ninth International Theological Commission)

I was educated by the Sisters of Mercy. There were two sisters whom I found to be very inspirational. One sister encouraged her Confirmation class to go to daily Mass and about 10 of us took up the challenge. That had a big effect upon my spiritual life. The other sister gave me a hard time, jumping on every perceived character defect, because, as she told my grandmother, "I think she might someday amount to something". During my teenage years I found the "hold hands around a candle" style of RE insufferable and rebelliously read theology books loaned to me by my parish priest.

As an undergraduate Arts/Law student I continued to be interested in the intellectual side of the faith and eventually I won a Commonwealth scholarship to Cambridge University where I completed a doctorate in the Divinity School. I have met many high-ranking clerical leaders and in almost all cases I have been treated with great respect as an academic colleague. I often receive letters from priests and bishops thanking me for some article I have written. I have however encountered chauvinism and endured bullying behaviour from poorly educated laymen who work in the bureaucracy of the Church. The problem here is a kind of philistinism. These types are very tribal – they think of the Catholic Church as something like their football team and they are not interested in intellectual formation or evangelisation. They are 'company men' who just want to defend the material assets of "Catholic Inc". Priests find these types problematic too – anyone who cares about spiritual things – whether they are male or female – find that these types are the biggest obstacles to the work of the Holy Spirit.

Sister Clare Condon (Former Leader of the Sisters of the Good Samaritan – Australia)

Being born into a Catholic, rural family of Irish descent, gave me the foundations for my lifelong journey of seeking God. As a young person, God was ever present in the rhythm of daily life at home, school and church. So, it was not unusual for me at the age of 20, to join the Sisters of the Good Samaritan, who had taught me from the age of 4.

These sisters who live the values of the Rule of St Benedict gave me a spiritual framework with a strong tradition of liturgy, lectio, hospitality, compassion and social justice within the church; a tradition that has traversed over 1500 years in diverse cultures and adapted to changing times and circumstances. It is these values that inform my ministry and leadership roles within the community and the broader church.

I believe that women are made in the image of God and have the right and responsibility to image their God. For us Christians that God is portrayed by Jesus in the gospel stories. For me, the opportunity to share my gifts on the Archdiocesan Pastoral Team and as a Chancellor of the Archdiocese of Adelaide reinforced for me the call for women to take greater roles of responsibility at the heart of the Catholic Church.

As leader of the Sisters of the Good Samaritan for twelve years, I sought to draw forth the many leadership qualities amongst sisters in their ministries of education, pastoral care, liturgy, and care of those most disadvantaged and so to work for the dignity and human rights of every person. Together we are called to apply the 'wine and oil' of the Parable with ever abundant compassion and mercy.

Sister Catherine Seward RSM (Parish Pastoral Director – Adelaide South Australia [1988-2000])

The Adelaide Diocese was blessed with enlightened bishops and great theologians in the years following Vatican II. Adult Education for leadership among the people of God was strongly encouraged. A diocesan team was set up including a priest, a woman religious and a lay woman. Diocesan Renewal, acting synodally, faced and implemented many of the challenges of Vatican II.

Addressing the shortage of priests and to retain viable Eucharistic communities, I was appointed Parish Pastoral Director of a newly formed parish in Mansfield Park, South Australia, with a priest as the Pastor Moderator. Mansfield Park was a 75% Housing Commission area with high unemployment and social disadvantage. The congregation had a rich mix of Australians and many European and Vietnamese migrants.

With my background in Secondary School Education, Pastoral Associate roles in various parishes and a year of theological studies in Heythrop College, London, I was very excited to accept the appointment which is covered in Canon Law, as a strategy to maintain Eucharistic communities when there is a shortage of priests.

> *Canon 517 #2 permits a bishop to appoint a person to leadership of a pastoral community, entrusted with the formal, public, responsible leadership and pastoral care of a parish community. This person exercises a leadership role of responsibility for the day-to-day operations of a parish community, in collaboration with a pastor-moderator designated by the Archbishop.*

The Priest's role was to celebrate Eucharist and affirm the gifts of the whole community to take up the Archbishop's vision of "Community for the World." At the time of my appointment, our diocese was swept up in the *"Community for the World"*, a vision of the Archbishop which invited parishioners to leadership formation for evangelisation. According to the Archbishop:

> *The Synod of Bishops has focussed attention on the formation of Christian leaders. The Synod stressed the importance of forming and supporting leaders who can bring the gospel to bear on their neighbourhood and workplace, on economic and political decisions, and on all aspects of life in the world of the late twentieth* century (Leonard Faulkner, 1988).

My role was to develop the many pastoral ministries in the community: leaders for liturgical, social, and catechetical ministries, visitation of the sick and those in prison. We worked as a team with the school principal and the appointed youth worker who shared in outreach activities through the *Young Christian Students* [YCS]. We took for our motto: "Come and see" from [John 1:46] and there was the joy each Easter of new members coming to belong. Over time other theologians followed, bringing to the people their vision for an inclusive and multicultural Church, where all gifts of the whole People of God were affirmed and flourished. My 12 years in leadership in Mansfield Park parish helped build a strong community, which is still very active today.

Sister Lois Ann Richardi CSFN (Spiritual Director)

My life is a mystery even to me as I reach seventy-seven years. I journey on with faltering steps not really knowing where I am going yet with unquestionable assurance that Someone is leading me. As a child I was imbued with a sense of belonging in the 'domestic church' where my eight siblings and I felt unconditionally loved by our parents. At the age of ten I fell in love with Jesus present in the Blessed Sacrament on the altar for adoration in our little parish church. I did not tell anybody my secret and suspect that my love affair went unnoticed until I announced it to my parents three years later.

At that time, I knew nothing about charisms, spiritualities, missions or founders. However, I did know that I wanted to be a Sister of the Holy Family of Nazareth. As life unfolded, I gradually learned that the charism of Nazareth is Love Incarnated in the Holy Family of Nazareth, and its spirituality is simply living out the mystery of Nazareth – the life of the Holy Family. This no-frill spirituality delighted me. As for our mission, our foundress Blessed Mary of Jesus the Good Shepherd clearly stated that LOVE is the first mission of Nazareth sisters. "Easier said than done", I thought and set out on a mission to learn from others how to love.

As a primary school teacher in less privileged schools in the United

States, the children taught me that they learn, grow and develop best when they feel loved. So, love became our syllabus. As a catechist in a small village cradled in the Andes Mountains of Peru, the townswomen taught me that love is a more powerful force than the cloud of evil oppression hovering over their families struggling for existence. As a member of the Archdiocesan Family Commission in India, Mother Teresa of Calcutta taught me that a joyful heart is the normal result of a heart burning with love. As a member of the Spirituality Commission in Rome, our foundress taught me that God's love freely flows through a humble merciful heart and spreads to embrace the whole human family. And now as a spiritual director in Australia accompanying others to understand and live out their unique relationship with God, I am still on a mission learning from them how to love.

Ms Jennifer M Harman B.Ec. M. Bus (Diocesan Chancellor & Financial Administrator, Diocese of Armidale NSW Australia)

My journey with the Catholic Church starts in 1987 when I became a Catholic. In 1990 I commenced with the Diocese of Armidale in the Catholic development fund; in 2000 the role of Diocesan Financial Administrator was added and in 2016 Chancellor. In a small Diocese, under the guise of promotions, you get to wear many hats and get to do a wide array of jobs!

Working within the Church has the added element of service to the people of God and of integrating your faith into your work. Often moving out of mainstream employment into the Church sector is characterized as stepping into a lesser professional role. However, that view diminishes the extraordinary efforts made by lay employees to the life and works of the Church.

So about working in Church. Is it a bed of roses? Definitely not! In any employment there are challenges, differences of opinion, jealousies and criticisms. Is it easy being a woman working in a senior role within a Diocese? Absolutely not! It is a tough gig. But I know it's just as tough for my male friends in similar roles in other Dioceses. But it does afford an opportunity for us to bring different perspectives – both masculine and feminine – to the everyday Church administration.

As lay employees we are not interested in the pursuit of power, titles or influence – we are, however, committed to doing our own jobs. We are not seeking to be someone else or to become something else. What drives us is our commitment to contributing to building the Kingdom of God and that focus is founded within faith – a faith that is deeply embedded in our DNA; it is not an optional extra. A faith which influences and informs all that we do – at work, home, with our families and in other relationships.

Faith is enriched through work just as work is enriched by faith. I know that my faith is stronger, more resilient, more assured because of my experience of working within a Diocesan structure. As a senior lay employee, I know that this is where I am meant to be – responding to the demands on the Church here and now. I am proud that I can use my God given gifts for the Church doing what God is calling me to do.

Mrs Teresa Brierley (Director Pastoral Ministries – Diocese of Maitland – Newcastle Australia)

My first profession was as a Biomedical Scientist working in hospital pathology. Prior to being appointed to my current position, I served the Catholic Church as a Pastoral Associate, a secondary school Religious Education Co-ordinator and a maths and science teacher. I remember the day in 2005 when my dad said to me; "This job has your name on it!" At the time my husband and I were living on the Gold Coast of Australia, and the position was for Vice Chancellor Pastoral Ministries in the Diocese of Maitland-Newcastle, about 800km south from where we were living with our five children. I agonised over the reality of what this meant for me, my husband, children, dad and the community in which I was in ministry, first as a high school Religious Education Coordinator, and then as a Pastoral Associate in the parish. There were many personal implications in responding to this call.

These many years later, I am convinced that dad's invitation was of the Spirit. This significant leadership role in the diocese has been very challenging, during a time of great heartache in the Catholic Church. We have undergone the scrutiny of a Special Commission of Inquiry and the Royal Commission into Institutional Responses to Child Sexual Abuse. Those who were abused have been gravely harmed and those who continue to identify as Catholic have been greatly shamed. The spiritual trauma is palpable!

As a female leader, I feel the people's pain and despair and believe that the temptation to walk away is one I am unable to consider seriously. A matriarchal figure is needed, the person who hangs in there in the good times and the not so good times. A person who tries to give an authentic voice to different ways of considering what it means to make Jesus real in this time and place. I am conscious that people of all ages look to those in leadership for stability, direction, truth, hope and trust. Deep listening, prayer and discernment are required, skills that I have acquired from the experiences over a lifetime, of trying to hear what God is asking and then sharing and testing God's response with others in leadership and with the faithful.

As a member of the Diocesan Leadership group my responsibilities include co-ordinating the Pastoral Ministries Unit along with its many diocesan councils: overseeing chaplaincies; supporting parishes with pastoral planning; and liaising with other non-diocesan Public Juridic Persons exercising ministry in the diocese. Key to this role is working with the Bishop and the Council for Mission in developing and implementing the diocesan pastoral plan.

Since my teenage years, I have sensed God's call for me to discipleship.

The great commission to go, make, baptise and teach forms the critical path of being anointed as priest, prophet and king at baptism. I have been called, formed and sent and I do this within the context of the Catholic Church, in this time and place and with the community of believers – Bishop, Clergy, those in active ministry, leaders, faith-filled disciples who believe in the Good News of Jesus Christ and those who are struggling. God's mission, as revealed through Jesus Christ, is a worthy commitment.

My family, schooling, professional life, married life, the role of being a mum and being in ministry have formed me into the person who finds herself reflecting on the complexity of what it means to be a Catholic today.

Sister Miriam Joseph Mikol CSFN (Chair of Trustees of the Charity of the Sisters of the Holy Family of Nazareth – Jesus the Good Shepherd, located in Enfield, England)

Each person's journey of faith is a story of how the *Hound of Heaven* (Christian poem by Francis Thompson) searches without end to bring human creation to the fullness of his love. In my life there was not any particular moment at which I discovered God and His calling. Instead, my vocational calling evolved through progressive reflective and dialogical experiences of God and people. Early in life I understood that what makes for a happy and meaningful life are intangible realities such as love, the quality of human relationships and being of service in community. These understandings shaped my faith, religious calling, ministerial work and how I exercised leadership in Australia in such roles as deputy principal of a teacher's college, director of planning and coordination of amalgamated tertiary Catholic colleges, policy analyst for the NSW Ministry of Education, head of a NSW university department for planning and information management and in Rome Italy as General Secretary of the International Union of Superiors General and as Coordinator of an international Master's Degree Programme funded by a European foundation for Sisters working in developing countries.

In my life, the reflective and dialogical experiences of God and people occurred in three ways, by *listening, engaging and serving*.

Listening as an active and passive process of understanding meaning contributed to my early understanding of people and the challenges faced in life's journey. Listening to God and significant others inspired me to enter religious life, and to take certain decisions and not others. Listening provides a leader with a realistic grasp of realities.

Engaging with God, individuals, communities and creation drew me into a world wider than myself. Being an only child, engagement was the manner by which my spiritual and material world was extended, my horizons widened. I learned about the richness of drawing my material reality into a spiritual world, a type of incarnation experience. Engagement provides a leader with a process for the development of people within the context of mission.

Serving God and people seems a natural overflow from engaging with others. How many times can one engage with others in challenging situations before one begins to ask what can I contribute? In Biblical terms *serving* translates to servant leadership. These leaders change systems and create new futures.

Ms Lisa Chen (A Voice for the Deaf Church)

I was christened a Catholic but at present I am not an active church goer as attending services presents many challenges for me. When I was young, I was deaf but when I turned twenty-one my vision also began to deteriorate. Due to financial constraints in parishes, particularly in New South Wales, there are no support services available to enable me to experience "Church" as a committed Catholic. This is an area where the Church needs to be more inclusive and provide support for members of the deaf community.

Admittedly some churches may organise for an interpreter to

communicate with the deaf members of the congregation by way of using sign language to interpret the readings of the day, and also to interpret the message that the priest conveys during his sermon. However, a person with my particular disability, is unable to see sign language being used from afar. As a human being I am asking for equal dignity and respect. Now deaf children are being integrated into the schools but to fully experience their faith, more must be done to support them in their faith communities.

My family have always been very supportive of me. My mother learnt sign language so that she could communicate with me, but I am frustrated advocating for support from external agencies particularly the church. If the Church supports me, it would inspire me to become an active member of the Church community and help others in the deaf community. I was raised in an environment where I was treated the same as all the other members of my family. All the children were treated equally. I wasn't treated as a deaf person. Communities consist of deaf people and as a minority group they need acknowledgement.

I am a feminist. As women, regardless of the communities to which we belong, we have rights in a "male" world. You don't have to be married for success. I am staying positive. Some people are frightened as they don't like change, but change takes time. I respect Mary. I have noticed that women generally do not receive a huge mention in the bible. I am looking for fairness and equality and hope that in the future a more equal society will exist; one that is not dominated by men and one where women also have a voice. Jesus was respectful of women. He was inclusive of all particularly the marginalised. As a person then, who cannot hear, who has failing sight and who cannot speak vocally, I give voice to the need for the Church to consider inclusivity and to support its deaf community.

Mrs Sherry Balcombe (Co-ordinator Aboriginal Catholic Ministry Victoria)

I have been associated with the Aboriginal Catholic Ministry Victoria (ACMV) before it was established in the late 1980s. Previously I was working at Victorian Aboriginal Child Care Agency (VACCA) in Foster Care, where I met the founding member of the ACMV. In 1991 I had my daughter Baptised at the ACMV. Although I was not a Catholic my husband and his family were, and so it was important that our children be baptised Catholics. My children went to a Catholic School and St Mary of the Immaculate Conception in Ascot Vale was our parish – the one that we attended as a family. I became a Catholic through the ACMV with RCIA (Right of Christian Initiation of Adults).

I heard about "The Opening the Doors Foundation" which offered support to Aboriginal children attending Catholic Schools. We were thrilled about this as I was a stay-at-home mum and my husband was a labourer, so funds were tight. I was so touched as we had never before received so much support, and it was so important for the children to start school with all new uniforms, so I called to express my deep gratitude. I spoke to the Coordinator who then offered me a part-time position.

I started at the ACMV in July 2003, and not being from the computer age I was a bit lost so the first few months were learning how to turn on a computer, do emails and just generally work a computer. In August 2003 the ACMV had their national conference with their national body NATSICC (National Aboriginal Torres Strait Islander Catholic Council). This was the first time I had been exposed to Spirituality like this, I got to learn what the ACMV and NATSICC were all about, it was amazing. I made plenty of friends with whom I am still in contact today.

I have been blessed to be mentored by some incredibly strong, amazing, tough, resilient women and I will be forever grateful for their guidance, love, support and encouragement. I am certainly doing what

God wants me to do. The Coordinator not only was my boss (Team Leader as she would remind me), but a true friend and confidante. Without her encouragement and support I would not be where I am today.

I love my job even though at times it is challenging, in both the Catholic world and the Aboriginal world. As one Bishop who told me when I asked why we have to argue with our own groups so much, he said: "Because what we are doing has not been done in this country before. We are the first and we are creating a whole culture that has not existed before." I was glad for his counsel as it made me realize the bigger picture of enculturation of the Church today. Up until 1986, Aboriginal people were invisible in the church and we still are to a great extent today. Pope St John Paul II said until our contribution is joyfully received, the Church will not be what Jesus wants it to be. But for this to happen we need the Church to accept the gifts we can offer and do all we can to find our place. But if others refuse us entrance or don't make a place for us, then it is they who must answer to our Creator. I'm doing what he asked.

I have had so many wonderful women who have inspired me and given me the courage and strength to challenge. Without the support of the religious Sisters and the constant encouragement I think I would have resigned long ago. The Sisters have always supported me even when I have made mistakes and helped me to see the right way. They have provided a very special kind of unconditional love that I will be forever grateful. Their love will always remain in my heart and soul. In the office when I started, we had five nuns who volunteered on a regular basis; one of them – a founding member, still continues to support me. I have had many times when things have gone wrong that she has been there for me and truly understands the pressures that are put on Aboriginal people especially by the Church community. We as Aboriginal people have to be more dedicated, more organised and are pulled in many directions.

Ms Kerry Alys Robinson (Global Ambassador, Leadership Roundtable)

I have worked on behalf of the Church all of my adult life. My background is in Catholic philanthropy, having been born to a family with a 75-year history of service to the Church at the local, diocesan, national and international level through the instrument of a private family foundation. Five generations of direct descendants of the founders have been invited to serve as stewards of the foundation's resources in a voluntary, non-remunerative manner. The expectation is that members of the family will fully immerse themselves in the life of the Church to better anticipate unmet needs and increase philanthropic impact.

From a very young age I was enamored of the Church through the example of women and men, ordained, religious and lay, who were at the vanguard of human suffering, injustice and inequity and responded out of faith with mercy and tenacity to alleviate human suffering, promote justice, provide healthcare and education, advance peace and offer hope.

For ten years I served as the director of development at Saint Thomas More Catholic Chapel and Center at Yale University and with the Catholic Chaplain, a priest of the Archdiocese of Hartford, expanded Catholic life on campus. Together we modeled lay – clergy collaboration and raised $75 million, introduced 14 new initiatives, built a 30,000 square-foot Catholic student center designed by Cesar Pelli and added a third Sunday liturgy to accommodate the expanding community of students and faculty.

When the revelations of sexual abuse by clergy were made evident in the U.S. in 2002, we planned and hosted a three-day conference entitled Governance, Accountability and the Future of the Catholic Church and published the proceedings. Three months later I met the founder of Leadership Roundtable, a network of senior level executive leaders which promotes best managerial practices, accountability, transparency and the expertise of the laity to strengthen the Church. I was invited to serve as the founding executive director and after 11 years was named global ambassador.

Concurrently for nearly 15 years I have been going to Rome twice a year with a small group of women who represent their respective family foundations. We meet with the prefects and presidents of the pontifical congregations and councils in order to promote the role of women in meaningful leadership in the Church and at the tables of decision-making.

We speak about concrete ways we can advance the role of women in the Church and mentor young women. Our thesis is that when a young Catholic woman looks at the landscape of her professional life, she knows that she can reach the highest levels of leadership in any sector. When that same woman discerns a vocation of service to the Church she loves, she is invariably met with limitations that prevent her from exercising her full complement of gifts and abilities. This is an untenable frustration which results in the Church losing her leadership capability to the secular world. In turn this affects her children's view of the church. Our advocacy for women in leadership in the Church is not fundamentally because this is what women deserve. Of course, it is. But rather, it is what the Church deserves and needs if it is to flourish. When women are included in greater percentages on corporate boards, the return of investment to shareholders increases. In every sector, when women share leadership with men, mission is strengthened, and reputation improves. If we care about the vitality of the Church and efficacy of its mission, we will increase the leadership roles and decision-making responsibilities of women.

Ms Audrey Brown (Director of Catholic Education, Diocese of Ballarat; Chief Executive Officer Diocese of Ballarat Catholic Education Limited; Director of Catholic Education Commission of Victoria Ltd and Catholic Capital Grants Ltd)

I had the privilege of being raised as a Christian in a small country town by a Methodist mother and Godparents who were Salvation Army Officers! An education in government, independent and Catholic schools led to me studying music and Arts before finding my niche in education. I chose from the start of my career to teach in Catholic schools because I felt a deep sense of "belonging" there.

The daily faith witness of colleagues and families I experienced in successive school communities, prompted me to seek full reception into the Catholic Church as an adult. Significantly, this was in the great year of Jubilee (2000), so I grew in understanding of Catholic social teaching as our Church community called for cancellation of third world debt. As a Catholic woman, the principles of respect for human dignity and solidarity have especially prompted me to look beyond myself as I strive to be the woman and leader God calls me to be.

My career in Catholic education has included roles as teacher, coach and principal in regional Victoria. The combined wisdom, advice, encouragement and feedback of many leaders (lay, religious and clergy) has been instrumental in shaping my leadership capability and encouraging me to imagine myself into new roles and responsibilities. Women in our Church can be particularly effective when tapping others on the shoulder, journeying with others and focusing on ways of working (together) that enable us to pursue our shared mission.

I commenced as Director of Catholic Education in 2012 at a time of great challenge in our Church and had the privilege to lead our education community during the Royal Commission into Institutional Responses to Child Sexual Abuse. Attending as many of the sessions related to the Ballarat Case Study as I could, I knew that it was important to listen to the stories of those who gave evidence, to share in the collective responsibility for our failure as a Church to protect our children, and to give whatever witness I could that our current Church is one of respect for the human person, transparency and optimism.

Responding to the demands of all the stakeholders in Catholic education now – as always – requires leadership from me that is calm, confident and consistent. I hope that this is the gift that I give both to those with whom I serve and for those who will serve after me.

Conclusion

We thank all the women for their contribution, and for the great work they are accomplishing within their parish and diocesan communities. It is evident that female leaders have been "responding to the call of the gospel and engaging in active discipleship since time immemorial, commencing with the leadership of Mary, Mother of God and Mother of the Church (CCC, 2000:para. 887). Let all of us then – all genders, for we are the Church, rejoice, celebrate, and give thanks for the sacredness and dignity of womanhood", and let us support all women in leadership positions in the Church and other faith-based organisations (Cameron, 2019).

I invite you to turn now to the following chapter which highlights the voices of the youth, as they express their thoughts and concerns regarding change and growth within the Church and discuss implications for the future.

20

Voices of the Future – The Youth of the Church

The youth of today are the leaders of the future. The legacy they have inherited from previous generations is embedded in the multi-cultural and multi-religious environments that comprise the complex world of the 21st Century. It is imperative then that as well as recognising and valuing diversity and inclusiveness, present and future leaders possess a global vision and "an awareness of the interconnectedness of spiritual, existential and cosmic realities" (Fritjof Capra, 1996). This chapter is based on the opinions and thoughts of a select group of student leaders at an Australian Catholic College (High School), who completed a survey that focussed on the topic of women and leadership in the Catholic Church. The message of these young people is relevant to all who respond to the Gospel's call to service within local, national and global communities.

Background

The project originated as a result of ongoing discussions with Ms Bernadette Harris, Deputy Principal (Identity, Mission & Administration) at St Monica's College Epping, Victoria, Australia. In our initial correspondence I discussed with Bernadette my intention to devote a chapter in this book to the youth who are the leaders of the Church of the future. I believe as did Robert Greenleaf (1977:144) that: "Leaders are needed in the contemporary [and future] Church ... who are not just content with the status quo, but who will challenge the 'establishment' ... determined builders ... who can move creatively with these times", and I believe that these leaders who will be agents of change, are the very impressive and talented youth, who are graduating from our Catholic schools and colleges. Though Greenleaf wrote of leadership in another century and time, his words are just as applicable today in a new century and as we move into the third decade of the third millennium.

An additional incentive for the chapter was that the Australian Catholic Bishops identified 2018 to be the "National Year of Youth", which commenced on 3 December 2017 and concluded at the end of November 2018. Coincidentally, the year also witnessed the convening of the Synod of Bishops in Rome for the XV Ordinary General Assembly, "Young People, the faith and Vocational Discernment", which was held from 3 October to 28 October 2018. According to Cindy Wooden (*Catholic News Service*, 2018:para.3), the Synod comprised: "267 voting members – cardinals, bishops, 18 priests and two religious brothers – and 72 experts and observers, including three dozen men and women under 30 to discuss 'young people, the faith and vocational discernment.'"

Interestingly, Wooden reports that the definitive message from the Synod of Bishops is that, "The Catholic Church and all its members must get better at listening to young people..." (para.1). Carol Glatz (*Catholic News Service*, 2018:para.1) states that during the closing Mass at the end of the Synod of Bishops, Pope Francis asked young people for their forgiveness: "Forgive us if often we have not listened to you; if, instead of opening our hearts, we filled your ears. As Christ's church, we want to listen to you with love" because young people's lives are precious in God's eyes and "in our eyes, too," the Pontiff said in his homily (para.2). The Pope's formal response to the 2018 Synod is the Post Synodal Apostolic Exhortation Christus Vivit – Christ is alive – which was published early in 2019, and which is referenced in Chapter 21, the final chapter of this book.

This chapter *Voices of the Future – The Youth of the Church* provides a forum for a select group of inspiring young women and men who are asking for their voices to be heard and their questions answered. Knowing that Bernadette would be the ideal person to discern the opinions and thoughts of her students, I encouraged their participation in the venture and after conferring with the Principal Mr Brian E. Hanley and the College community, Bernadette proceeded to organise a questionnaire (see Appendix B) with open-ended questions based on our previous discussions which had been centered on faith, service and leadership and with the focus on women and leadership in the Catholic Church. This collaboration was important for, following the publication of the results in 2017, Bernadette maintained that the project gave their community an opportunity "to support the research ... and to also gather feedback that may provide an insight into student beliefs and faith understandings."

Regarding her stewardship of the young female leaders in her care Bernadette (Personal correspondence, 2 January 2017) reflected that: "Each day I see such capable, faith-filled, young and vibrant women with limitless potential. I would dearly love for their voices to join with yours...". After some discussion a decision was made to also include male voices as well as female voices in the project, primarily to acknowledge and emphasise the importance of gender equity, in discerning the opinions and ideas of the selected group of students. For both females and males belong to the community of the "People of God" (Vatican II, 1962-1965), and form "one, holy, Catholic and apostolic" Church (Creed, CCC, 2000:para.811). Therefore, it was essential that all voices be given the opportunity to be heard!

Consequently, selected student leaders attending the College in 2017 and 2018, and a number of former students (age range 16-24) comprise the Survey Participants (see Appendix B), who were invited to participate in the consultative process by completing the questionnaire, on which the topics listed for discussion were "Faith, Service and Inspiration", "The Catholic Church", and "Voices of the Future". Several questions relating to each topic were also included. For your information, in the compilation of the students' responses some questions and answers have been combined to facilitate fluency and presentation and brief and/or repetitive replies have been omitted. I commend the students for their participation, co-operation and sincerity in raising their voices in support of all youth, both leaders and followers, who will comprise the Church of the future.

Faith, Service and Inspiration

Does your Catholic faith call you to serve or lead others?

The students who responded to the initial question, demonstrated amazing insight regarding faith, service and inspiration. They emphasised the importance of true humility and a values-based leadership that recognises the dignity of every person. There are comparisons to Christ, the Servant Leader, who "lived his values of love of God and love of neighbour all the way to the cross" (Blanchard & Hodges, 2003:50). *I was impressed with all the responses; however, I believe that the following thoughts of one student reiterate the opinions of all, regarding faith, service and inspiration:*

> The role of our Christian community is to uphold the dignity and human rights of all people. I believe that we are all made in the image and likeness of Christ, which means that we are called to look beyond our differences and see that we all have dignity and inner worth. God created us to be companions not competitors, therefore, we are called to look beyond ourselves and show love and service to others in the wider community and beyond. I also believe that God has given us life on this earth as a gift. We are each given gifts and talents to be used during our time on earth to do good in the world (MaC).

It is important to share our faith and use our talents and giftedness in the service of others!

Do you possess a desire to make the world more socially just? If so, in what ways do you think this could or should be approached by people of faith?

Here the two questions on social justice and faith are combined. The students approached these questions with honesty and a commitment to social justice issues which focus on human rights. We are reminded that Christ reached out to the poor and the marginalised (New Testament). The responses indicate that the students are aware that values and morals influence behaviour and that "people of faith" around the world should unite to make a change and to make a difference. The students list the advantages and disadvantages of social media and other forms of technology. They believe that "people of faith" are needed to work towards a sustainable future and that there should be justness when dealing with issues such as gender inequality, discrimination and all matters pertaining to human rights.

From where do you draw your inspiration and strength? Is it from inspirational women faith leaders and if so, who and why?

Again, two questions are combined. The students invariably draw their strength and inspiration from their families, teachers and friends. Mothers are cited as role models to emulate. Other significant women leaders who have had an influence on the youth include Mary the Mother of Jesus, St Monica, St Brigid, St Teresa of Calcutta (now referred to as St Teresa of Kolkata), St Joan of Arc, various members of religious Orders and others. Interestingly some of these women have received coverage in previous chapters in this book.

Other sources of inspiration include significant women in the Aboriginal and Torres Strait communities and those who are stewards of their ancestral legacies. Some male leaders who have been impressive include St Ephraim (cited by a student as being "the saint for troubled youth"); Pope St John Paul II and then the sportsman Roger Federer for his humanitarian work. In fact, multiple sources of inspiration are listed emphasising the importance of support networks and the influence of the Church and faith, Catholic Social Teaching, prayer and events such as World Youth

Day 2008. *The following statement by a student reinforces the importance of the hierarchy of the Church to formally recognise the contribution of its women leaders:*

> I think that because of the way the writings of the Bible that relate to women are interpreted and communicated in the public, schools and churches, it is often difficult for progressive women who aim to positively influence the world to strongly identify with the Catholic Church and its teachings (RD).

It is important that everyone's voice is heard and actioned, for regardless of our gender, or the role we have in our faith-based organisations, we are all part of the Church – a pulsating and Gospel inspired community of God!

Is prayer an influence in your life?

The responses to "prayer" practices show that the youth recognise that prayer is a form of communication with God. Interestingly, formal "childhood" prayers, for example, the "Our Father" and the "Hail Mary" receive little if any attention. For the majority of students, prayer is a private time that they spend with God – a time where they find peace and comfort and are able to pray for any or all of the injustices experienced by humanity. One student reflects on how prayer influences her life:

> …When I was four years old, my father questioned me, "Olivia what is prayer?" My simple heart and mind responded, "Talking to Jesus." I believe that prayer can become overcomplicated, and for a youthful person, it is something that is seen as boring, and unnecessary. I fell into this notion in my early teenage years. But reflecting on the definition of prayer that my young self-came up with, I realised that to feel enriched in my prayer life, I must in fact understand that prayer *is* a conversation with God. Although it is unlikely that God will respond to me in a literal sense, His presence and guidance in my life becomes crystal clear to me when I converse with Him through

prayer. He speaks to me through others, through nature, through the sacraments. As I grow, I believe that my prayer life should too. It strengthens my love for the Catholic faith and for God, and I feel that I have enough experience with prayer to understand that in its true and humble form, it is what ignites a strong sense of faith (OC).

For the students then, prayer nourishes their faith lives and contributes to their ongoing relationship with God.

Are you connected to parish life and/or the sacraments? Does this strengthen your faith and life in any way? In what ways has this been influenced by any formation and guidance you may have received (e.g. leadership training etc)?

The three questions regarding parish life and the sacraments have been linked and indicate general support for local parishes through family commitments and the establishment of groups such as CFC (Couples for Christ) *and YFC* (Youth for Christ). *Regular reception of the Eucharist seems to be a common practice. Faith, life and service are intermingled with a focus by some on strengthening faith and fostering the development of a relationship with God. Positive experiences with the parish and religious leaders (including members of religious orders – for example, the Capuchin and Franciscan Orders) who prepare the students to undertake leadership roles are very much appreciated together with the training to lead others which is described by a student (LL), as being able to "serve as guidance leadership in qualities I see as inspiration."*

Some students do not feel an obligation to relate to the parishes as much as when they were young children, but their solid foundation still enables them to place their trust in God knowing that He is there beside them during the good times and the not so good times. Overall the message is clear that Church and ministry are important for the students to continue living a sacramental life and to experience ongoing faith and leadership development within their parish communities.

The Catholic Church

How do you view the Catholic Church? Do you feel connected to the universal Catholic Church?

The Two questions on the Catholic Church have been combined. The responses reveal that many students have a high regard for the Church and its presence in the world. The honest opinions of these young people who are at such an exciting and wonderful stage of their lives are quite impressive. Their obvious pride in the Church is inspirational and even though aspects of its past have resulted in the Church receiving negative publicity in recent years (for example in regard to "child abuse and gender inequality"), there is a growing connection with the Church by the youth who recognise that the Church is endeavouring to respond positively to the "complexities of global issues" that have arisen, particularly those that have occurred in what could be called the "dark days" in its history.

There is a call also for the Church to become more inclusive particularly in its stance on the LGBTIQ (Lesbian, Gay, bisexual, Transgender, Intersex and Questioning) communities, by one respondent (RD) who identifies as LGBTIQ and who feels a connection to the Church because of her educational background but then feels that there is an unjustness in the way that those who may have a diverse opinion to the majority are treated – and expresses hope for an all-encompassing Church that respects and considers the needs of all its faithful equally. The response of the following student shows what it means to be a part of the contemporary Church:

> The Catholic Church is my family. I feel connected to God through His people, the Sacraments and the teachings of the Church which have been passed down for generations. I have attended Mass in foreign countries on two occasions; the Canonisation of St Mary MacKillop in Rome and World Youth Day 2016 in Krakow. On both occasions, being able to participate in the Mass with people from all over the world revealed to me how the Universal Church truly is the body of Christ (TC).

The Church is universal – one big family and we are all working together, to assist the Church in its mission of evangelisation. The Gospel "Good News" is the legacy handed down through the generations and embedded in the culture of faith-based organisations around the globe.

Who inspires you by their faith or actions within the Catholic Church?

Role models include mothers and parish leaders who make a huge impression on young people because of their empathy, compassion and service to the Church. In addition, members of religious orders, teachers and parish priests who put the needs of others before their own as they engage in sharing their faith through their prayerful actions also have a huge influence on the youth. The responses list four popes – Pope Francis and Pope St John Paul II are acknowledged and admired for their true humility, simplicity and their gentle approach to addressing contemporary issues and Pope Emeritus Benedict XVI is recognised for his intellectual acumen and contribution to the theological life and writings of the Church. Pope St Paul VI and St Francis of Assisi are commended for the inspiration of their faith ministries. One student made the following observation:

> Biographies of saints and their desire for Jesus has moved me several times, as well as many lay people of today. I've had the privilege of meeting many ordinary people who gave up their jobs and luxuries of life purely due to a strong calling they felt to evangelise the world about Christ. For a person to leave behind all the riches and happiness of this world, for a person whom they've never seen in real life but only know through others, really stirred my mind (ES).

Indeed, a special acknowledgement of ordinary people living extraordinary lives in the service of the Church!

Are there any Vatican documents you feel are relevant today?

Few students commented on the Vatican documents which are readily available on the Vatican website. The dearth of responses is not surprising as the content of the documents does not make for 'light' reading and should be read slowly and over a period of time – and not rushed. The responses of those students who addressed the question were impressive as was their knowledge of the documents. The following documents were cited:

- *Laudato Si'* – On Care for our Common Home (Pope Francis, 2015)
- *Evangelii Nuntiandi* – In Proclaiming the Gospel (Pope St Paul VI, 1975)
- *Gaudium et Spes* – Pastoral Constitution on the Church in the Modern World (Pope St Paul VI, 1965)
- *Apostolicam Actuositatem* – Apostolate of the Laity (Pope St Paul VI, 1965)
- *Lumen Gentium* – Dogmatic Constitution on the Church (Pope St Paul VI, 1964)

The following response from one student recommends his choice of document that promotes the Church's mission of evangelisation: "Personally, I also believe that major documents such as *Evangelii Nuntiandi* (1975) and the Vatican II document *Gaudium et spes* (1965) … touch upon the evangelization dimension of the Church and set out a clear manifesto for missionary outreach" (MF).

The above response reinforces the directive of Pope Francis (Evangelii Gaudium, 2013:para.120) that our baptism calls us to be "agents of evangelization" *engaged in a ministry of* "missionary discipleship" – *active discipleship!*

Have any key Church events you have attended (e.g. World Youth Day, Ministry Expos, retreats, camps etc) left any impression on you?

Retreats, camps, etc., provide opportunities for young people to engage with faith leaders and for those who are interested to receive ongoing formation in faith leadership in preparation for their response to the Gospel's call to service within their parish communities. The opportunity for youth to participate in the various World Youth Days hosted around the globe has provided many with a profound insight into their faith experiences and 'enabled' them on their faith journeys. What better forum to engage the youth of the Church than to celebrate within the global arena the manifestation of faith in a spirit-filled explosion of transcendental grace and love enveloping all participants – who then convey the message of their experiences back to their communities!

Voices of the Future

How do you feel your life after secondary school will be/ is guided or influenced by your faith?

The students wrote a positive response to the question on post-secondary 'faith' influences and their responses were sincere. They spoke of the huge influence of their Catholic school on their faith journey providing values for life and giving a 'creed' by which to live. Those who have left school wrote of the many challenges facing them but also added that their "faith [continued to ground] them" and gave them strength to cope as they endeavoured to serve justice to the poor and marginalised in society. One response that reflected the strong spiritual and faith-based foundation provided by the Monican experience was the following:

> No matter what happens in my life, God will always be there for me. People in life come and go, but God is a constant. He is not only in thought but in everything that I see around my life. I aim to work in an industry that involves helping people. Through being a Catholic, I

remind myself that there are reasons for people's actions, and that not everything is black and white. What I can take away from my faith and apply to my life outside of school is not to judge people, as that is not my role – It is God's. My role is to spread the positivity that Jesus shared with us and influence other people to do the same (GL).

What a wonderful intuitive response to the question! This young person is an inspiration not just to their own generation but to those who have commenced their faith journey and are still unaware of the inner and outer realities of their spiritual giftedness.

How may this have been shaped by your past experiences including family, parish and educational opportunities?

The focus once again is on an awareness of social justice issues. Families, schools and parish communities have all contributed to the spiritual growth and faith formation of the respondents. Educational experiences involving "Immersions" particularly in indigenous communities have been life-changing for some students who have spent time in the communities and now "champion" the rights of the poor and the disadvantaged. For some students there is a sense of God's presence in all their endeavours and they are able to locate this presence in places and people other than in Church and religious representatives. Gospel values were integrated across the curriculum in the students' educational context enabling them to action their faith and live their values at College, home and now, for some within their workplace. For others the focus may not be to develop their faith per se but to consider all faiths and their religious foundations in their search for Truth. Indeed there are times when 'Faith seeks understanding" (St Anselm, cited in CCC, 2000:para.33).

Do the Catholic Church's teachings influence your life and/or decisions?

Generally, all the responses have a positive approach to the teachings of the Church which seem to be ingrained in the faith practices of the students. This foundation has provided many of the students with a strong initiative to love their neighbour, "to be forgiving" and to pursue justice. They find that their Conflict resolution skills have also been helped as they are readily able to discern "right from wrong". One student wisely states:

> The teachings of the Catholic Church which I experienced at a young age I think have been embedded into my judgement and view of the world around me and assists me in making some moral decisions. I believe that my school community, whether it was Catholic or not, was more of a stronger influence as it offered the Church's teachings to its students in a less apparent way and accepted that not all will agree with the entirety of the Catholic church's teachings. Although I personally do not agree with all its teachings, it continues to influence my life and my milestones on a deep, intrapersonal level (MR).

Truly an honest opinion expressed in a respectful and dignified manner!

Do you aspire to be a 'Voice of the Future' for or in the Catholic Church?

The students who express their desire to be a voice of the future do so strongly and with intent. They want to make a difference and be a voice for others who may not have the strength to speak out for what is right – to ask for justness in how they are treated. The responses emphasise the need to share the faith and be active in the ecclesial and sacramental life of the Church. I was inspired when I read the words of the following student:

> I believe I need to testify to my faith and how I got it so that other young people around the world may also be moved if they are open to God. As Romans (10:14) says, "But how are they to call on one in whom they have not believed? And how are they to believe in one of whom they have never heard? And how are they to hear without someone

to proclaim him?" Therefore, if God provides and it is His will, I would take every chance I get to share my faith (ES).

Such is "Missionary Discipleship" – active discipleship, to which we are called by Pope Francis (Evangelii Gaudium, 2013:para.120).

What can the Catholic Church do for you or others?

The youth are calling for more young leaders in the Church. They want the Church to be open to this suggestion. While there is overall support and respect for the Church in the responses, the following comprises some important suggestions from our youth to the Church authorities:

> The future of our faith lies in this generation, so by making the Church more open to youth is just one thing the Church can do for all of us (CB).

> I think with its teachings or beliefs put aside, the Catholic Church can offer any individual, no matter their socio-economic, gender, age, political or even religious differences a sense of community and support. It can offer welcoming hearts and hands and assist in personal and emotional healing (MR).

> Ultimately, I think where the Catholic Church can do the most, is actively listen to people that its beliefs and practices affect (women, LGBTIQ people, people of other faiths etc.) before casting judgement on them (RD).

> The Church must make youth (and youth issues) a priority and must also focus on clearer pastoral solutions to the complex issues of the day (social or otherwise), rather than approaching them from a strictly doctrinal perspective (MF).

> Continue to be a pillar in the community for spiritual, moral and ethical guidance. Be a place that is welcoming

and not condescending. Help with the education of people in terms of social justice (MeC).

Continue to inspire people to love one another, raise awareness that times have changed now and ensure that people of faith don't let the chaos and injustices of the world today dim their faith for the future (AS).

The Preparatory Document for the XV Ordinary General Assembly of the Synod of Bishops on "Young People, the Faith and Vocational Discernment" held in Rome in October 2018 addressed many of the above issues and in the compilation of the final document, the Synod of Bishops emphasised that in future they would: "Listen to, support, guide, [and] include young people" (Wooden, 2018)!

Conclusion

I believe the outstanding contribution of the young leaders at St Monica's College has encapsulated the essence of the opinions and ideas of youth around the globe. It is interesting to note that on the website for "The Year of Youth" (2018) there are eight focus areas listed: "prayer and worship; evangelisation; catechesis; pastoral care; community life; justice and service; leadership development; and advocacy" (Year of Youth [yoy], website, 2017) and every one of these focus areas has been addressed by the Monican students in their response to the questionnaire.

In his letter to the youth of the world regarding the Synod of Bishops (October 2018) on "Young People, the Faith, and Vocational Discernment", Pope Francis (Vatican, 2017, January 13) proclaimed:

The church ... wishes to listen to your voice, your sensitivities and your faith; even your doubts and your criticism. Make your voice heard, let it resonate in communities and let it be heard by your shepherds of souls. St Benedict urged the abbots to consult, even the young, before any important decision, because "The Lord often reveals to the younger what is best" (*Rule of St Benedict,* III, 3).

And the message of the Pontiff at the completion of the Synod was to "apologize to young people who have felt ignored by the Church" and to ask their forgiveness for not listening to them (Glatz, 2018; Pope Francis, *Christus Vivit*, 2019).

The thread running through many of the responses in this chapter emphasises social justice and reaching out to the poor, the disadvantaged and the marginalised. On behalf of those who have no voice, our youth are calling for dignity and respect through fairness, justness and equality and asking all leaders regardless of faith affiliation to respect all genders and to "uphold the dignity of the human person at all times" (Pope St Paul VI, *Gaudium et Spes*, 1965:Ch.1). Our youth are challenging the status quo and giving hope for the future. Let us heed the wisdom of our young people in discerning their needs as future leaders and followers in their mission of active discipleship within the Church! May their voices be heard!

Let us turn now to the concluding chapter which references the Apostolic Exhortation – *Christus Vivit* "Christ is alive" (2019), which is the post-synodal response of Pope Frances to the XV Ordinary General Assembly of the Synod of Bishops on "Young people, the Faith and Vocational Discernment" (2018). The document itself is quite lengthy, but its message is clear – A living Church needs to change and grow! Female leaders throughout the history of the Church have shown that they have had the drive and determination to overcome adversity and to challenge the status quo of their times. They have passed on their legacy to succeeding generations. Hence in Chapter 21, each of the significant women investigated in this research, gives voice to a message of support to all women, and indeed to all leaders, who aspire to senior leadership positions within the Church in the twenty-first century and beyond.

21

A Living Church Changes & Grows

Christus Vivit "Christ is Alive", is the fourth Apostolic Exhortation of Pope Frances and is dated 25 March 2019, the feast of the Solemnity of the Annunciation of the Lord. This lengthy document is a letter to young people and to "the entire People of God" and as mentioned in the previous chapter, is the Post-Synodal response to the XV Ordinary General Assembly of the Synod of Bishops on "Young people, the Faith and Vocational Discernment" (2018). The Exhortation emphasises to the youth the importance of listening to the Spirit and giving voice to their faith.

When the youth grow into adulthood, some may be called upon to undertake leadership roles within the Church. However, as they "assume leadership positions within their organisations, ministries and communities, will they all experience equity within their working and social environments? History reveals that they may not, rather that some leaders, particularly females … will experience inequality and discrimination" (Cameron, 2019)! Such prejudice must not to be tolerated in a loving Church. Gender should not define leadership! All leaders need to feel valued and respected, and their very considerable talents and skills should be mentored and developed, thus equipping them to face the challenges of leadership within an ecclesial community – one that values diversity, has transparency and is inclusive. The Catholic Church was founded on Love – "Love of God and love of neighbour".

Christus Vivit – "Christ is alive"! The document lists two headings early on that are of particular interest to this chapter – the first refers to

"A Church [being] open to renewal" (2019:para.35); and the second calls for "A Church [that is] attentive to the signs of the times" (2019:para.39). Significantly there is acknowledgement that for the Church to be "open to renewal … [and for it to be] attentive to the signs of the times" that "some things concretely need to change" (ibid.). Hence renewal is possible if the Church "appreciates the vision but also the criticisms of young people" (ibid.). She needs to listen to others; and should not always be "on the defensive, which loses her humility" (para.41). "Christ is alive" in a living Church, that is open to change and growth as she fulfills "the missionary mandate of Jesus" to evangelise and to spread the "Good News", by promoting a discipleship of love and service (ibid.).

As mentioned in the introductory paragraph the message of *Christus Vivit* is directed chiefly to the youth, but also to all the *People of God* regardless of gender, ethnicity or age. Significantly the document acknowledges the importance of the role of women within a living Church:

> [A] Church that is overly fearful and tied to its structures can be invariably critical of efforts to defend the rights of women, and constantly point out the risks and the potential errors of those demands. Instead, a living Church can react by being attentive to the legitimate claims of those women who seek greater justice and equality. A living Church can look back on history and acknowledge a fair share of male authoritarianism, domination, various forms of enslavement, abuse and sexist violence. With this outlook, she can support the call to respect women's rights, and offer convinced support for greater reciprocity between males and females, while not agreeing with everything some feminist groups propose. Along these lines, the Synod sought to renew the Church's commitment "against all discrimination and violence on sexual grounds" (Pope Francis, 2019:para.42).

Every person mentioned in this book forms part of the tapestry of significant people and events that have contributed to a living Church changing (ever so slightly), growing and moving forward in the third millennium! Let us take the time now to retrace our steps through the chapters and select a few of the many examples of exceptional leadership practices that have been left as a legacy for female and male leaders in the contemporary Church, by the women selected for this study, who have served and graced the Church throughout its long history.

Voices from the Past to the Present – Challenge Future Leaders

Mary Mother of God and Mother of the Church

Mary, Mother of Jesus Christ with her Jewish origins and her rustic background lived in a country ruled by men of violence, and in a land occupied by a foreign army (Elizabeth Johnson, 2003). Her faith journey is interwoven within Catholic, Marian and feminist theologies. Mary was a young girl conditioned by her circumstances and who possessed an innate strength that radiated from the very core of her being across the centuries and into the hearts of popes, bishops, priests and laity. She is a woman unlike any other. God chose her, Himself and by her *fiat* "Yes" she became the Mother of God. "All generations will call me blessed (cf. Lk.1:48)", (cited in *Marialis Cultus*, Pope St Paul VI, 1974). Mary has set an example for leaders who may be called upon to say "Yes" to God, but who are hesitant to give a positive response. Mary was committed and willing to take a risk and accept the challenges ahead (Pope Francis, 2019:para.44), are we?

Eve "the first woman; wife of Adam" (CCC, 2000:877)

The biblical Eve is portrayed in the scriptures as a sinner – as betraying humanity. However, Adam was her partner in "crime" as it were and perhaps, they both should share the responsibility of their "spectacular fall from Grace". According to the Catechism "humanity was originally created in a state of holiness and justice and that the first ancestors of the human race [Adam and Eve] lost this state for themselves and all humanity by their sin (original sin)", (CCC, 2000:865). A lesson for leaders is that there is often a tendency when things go wrong to blame someone, the system or something else. There is no weakness in a leader being vulnerable and admitting a mistake. It is important to rise above the occasion and with the lesson learnt – moving on – stronger and more confident because of the experience.

Selected women leaders in the Old Testament

Heather Farrell in her blog (2013, March 23) maintains that "there are more than 317 women and groups of women in the Old Testament." In the introduction to Chapter 3, twelve women are selected as being representative of the amazing females who graced the pages of the Old Testament and whom I believe contributed immensely to the origins of Christianity. These women lived at a time when, just being female, may have hindered their efforts but nevertheless they have gone down in history as women who paved the way between the Old and the New Testaments and who achieved this against almost insurmountable odds. They never gave up when chaos seemed to reign. Leaders, in our contemporary times are often called upon to do what may seem to be impossible tasks but with application, commitment and perseverance most tasks are accomplished successfully. A leader needs to always remember to do what is most important first and then the rest generally follows.

St Mary Magdalene – Apostolorum Apostola

St Mary Magdalene is depicted in the scriptures as a sinner. However, "in recent years the Church has finally recognised the tremendous impact that Mary Magdalene had on its early history? On 10 June 2016 the Holy See Press Office announced the publication of a decree honouring St Mary Magdalene in her role of *Apostolorum Apostola* (Apostle of the Apostles)" (Chapter 3, Part I). Leaders need to have empathy. They need to see beyond the apparent, for quick judgements and rash decisions can often lead to failure and to heartache. True discernment and taking the initiative are very important skills for a leader to possess, in order to diffuse potential "volatile" situations.

Women Leaders in the early Church – Deacons

In Chapter 3, Part II, I noted that "It would be impossible to analyse the contribution of all women leaders who influenced the growth of early Christianity for though there were many who may have had ministerial roles, few have been mentioned by name in the new Testament. What is known is that some were apostles, others were prophets and still others were widows and deacons. Surprisingly, Paul refers to just one deacon by name – Phoebe". In this chapter there is mention of women deacons appearing in the Eastern Church about the third century and definitely in the Western Church from about the fifth century, and that they continue to appear in documents until the tenth to twelfth centuries (ibid.).

Phyllis Zagano (2017) in her contemporary article *On the case for Catholic Women Deacons* (2001) argues that in the twenty-first century, consideration should be given to ordaining women as deacons. However, Phyllis maintains that the debates between those who support the move to ordain women deacons and those who support the "exclusion of women from the diaconate" are currently continuing (ibid.). Phyllis argues:

> Women are now called and have been called in the past to the diaconate. There are stronger arguments from Scripture, history, tradition and theology that women may

be ordained deacons than that women may not be ordained deacons ... The ordained ministry of service by women is necessary to the church – that is, to both the people of God and the hierarchy (ibid.).

In 2016, Dr Phyllis Zagano was appointed to the gender-balanced (six males and six females) Commission created by Pope Francis to investigate the possibility of women serving as deacons. On 7 May 2019, when questioned as to the possible date of a report on the commission being issued, Pope Francis stated that "The Vatican commission studying the history of women serving as deacons in the Catholic Church has been unable to find consensus on their role in the early centuries of Christianity and is yet to give a 'definitive response'". Though "the pope made clear that he does not consider the matter of understanding how women deacons served, as closed", it is unlikely however that a decision on the issue or a report from the commission will be available in the foreseeable future.

A lesson for leaders of the future, is not to think of leadership in terms of control. Leadership "is about building consensus within groups and empowerment of individuals" (Spears:1998:5). Hence, the skill of persuasion is all important. Greenleaf (Frick and Spears, 1996:159) wrote of "the legitimate use of power; the power of persuasion." Sims (1997:ix) maintains that servant power, "functions as a two-way exchange, never as subjugating, dominance; it not only influences others, but is also open to influence." Sims (ibid.) encapsulates the essence of power as a persuasive element, "Wise power ... undergirds all that is the velvet and steel in an enduring love: gentle enough to cradle the cosmos in patient care and strong enough to outlast and forgive all assaults on its compassion."

St Monica – Mother of St Augustine – Doctor of the Universal Church

Monica never gave up on her end goal – she prayed constantly that her son Augustine would be converted to Christianity. She was organised and her leadership was relational. She had a good rapport with her son Augustine and his friends, and when they were in Italy, she not only cleaned, cooked, and kept house for them, but was also invited by Augustine to participate in their philosophical discussions. The sum of the parts of her experiences, was becoming whole, as her goal was close to being accomplished. Monica maintained equilibrium in the group of friends, and projected peace and harmony, which energised Augustine, and her contribution to the philosophical debates nurtured and tested the intellects of all who participated. She was part of the team and her contribution was valued by all. It is important for Leaders to value each member of the team for effective teamwork to occur: "Being effective in today's organizations is a team game, and without collaboration and teamwork skills, you are unlikely to be successful" (Blanchard, 2007:167). Monica believed in God and she persevered until the task was done. When the mantle of leadership becomes "heavy" – it is possible to share the load by having faith in the members of our teams. It is important for them to feel valued!

St Hildegard of Bingen – Doctor of the Universal Church

The healing remedies and music of this twelfth century nun are still very popular in the twenty-first century. Pope St John Paul II (1979) called Hildegard a "Light for her time" and Pope Emeritus Benedict XVI (Apostolic Letter, 2012a) informs us that "her authority reaches far beyond the confines of a single epoch or society; despite the distance of time and culture, her thought has proven to be of lasting relevance." Her influence has transcended the centuries. Benedict emphasises that she is "a credible witness of the new evangelization" because she is a "prophetess, who also speaks with great timeliness to us today. She was able "to discern the signs of the times" (ibid.).

All the women mentioned in this chapter could be considered

prophets. They are teachers of the faith who have set an example and their charism is embedded in the legacy they have left for succeeding generations. There are theologians today who give witness as prophets. No doubt you, the reader, have your favourites!

St Clare of Assisi – Co-founder of the Order of Poor Clares

In his video clip, Bill Short (2009) states, there are religious orders in the contemporary Church where the monks still write the rules for the nuns, and that some of these women having heard about St Clare of Assisi being the first woman in the Church to write a Rule for her community, are very interested in the methods she used to write her rule, almost eight centuries ago! However, Clare's "rule of life", was not formally approved by the Pope until Clare was on her deathbed. She and St Francis "relied on the Gospel as a pattern for life" (ibid.). In fact, Short (2009) refers to both Francis and Clare, as living lives of "radical Gospel discipleship" (ibid.). Initially, I thought that the term "radical" was a surprising choice, when applied to the lives of Clare and Francis, but when I researched their lives and found that both Clare and Francis yearned for "the privilege of poverty", and were prepared to argue their case solidly before Popes, Cardinals and Bishops, I realised that the term "radical" in this instance seemed quite apt. Would that all leaders set an example by enjoying the "privilege of poverty", being content with just what is needed for a comfortable life – serving others and living the Gospel!

St Catherine of Siena – Doctor of the Universal Church

Catherine was a visionary who possessed the gift of foresight, and the charism of prophecy. She demonstrated these skills through her intuitive insight! She was a prophet – a teacher. Interestingly, Bernard McGinn (1999:132) and Karen Scott (1992:37), both refer to Catherine of Siena as "*Apostola.*" She was a teacher and mentor responding to "direct visionary contact with God to authorise ... [her] teachings" (McGinn, ibid.). "Her leadership revolved around her ministry of discipleship" (Cameron, 2012a) and she traversed the countryside with her loyal band of followers – her disciples, proclaiming and being witness to the Good News of salvation. Giuliana Cavallini (1979, cited in Noffke, 1980:xvi) maintains that, "Today's ... [leaders are] ready to meet Catherine. Women and men ... can find [in her] an ideal model to imitate" especially in her visionary discipleship.

St Joan of Arc – Patroness of France and of soldiers

Though she was a simple peasant girl without formal schooling, Joan's inherent wisdom, was evident at her trial, and transcended that of the brilliant minds of the Church, whose representatives were often outwitted in their attempts to confuse and humiliate a young woman, who dared to be different. According to Pope Emeritus Benedict XVI (2011a):

> The words of Jesus, who said that God's mysteries are revealed to those who have a child's heart while they remain hidden to the learned and the wise who have no humility (*cf.* Lk 10:21), spring to mind. Thus, Joan's judges were radically incapable of understanding her or of perceiving the beauty of her soul. They did not know that they were condemning a Saint.

This lone girl stood before more than "131 theologians, canon lawyers, clergymen and abbots ... most of them [participated] as assessors, or advisers, all but eight of them French" (Hobbins, 2005:4). Joan stood before the tribunal, and answered questions put to her, generally in a respectful and modest manner. She was not permitted to have a lawyer, or witnesses to testify in her defence. In addition, her responses were not documented according to what she had said, but according to what the lawyers thought she should say. What chance did a nineteen-year-old girl have in such a situation? The Church of the time had abandoned her. And unfortunately, its clergy did not listen. She was "Misunderstood for her demeanour, her actions and her way of living the faith" (Pope Francis, 2019:para.53).

Listening is an important characteristic of a good leader, "When we listen, not just to what others are saying but also to our own internal voice, we create a mindset that fosters such characteristics as empathy, awareness, foresight, and commitment to others" (Don DeGraaf, Colin Tilley, & Larry Neal, 2001:3). This service towards others is the essence of servant leadership!

St Angela Merici – Foundress of the Ursuline Order

With deep faith, a profound vision, determination and inspiration, Angela established a Company, that would support an active apostolate, while its members were engaged in the mystical state. Wendy Brennan (2003, p.8) quotes Henri Bergson that "perfect mysticism is action." Angela's awareness of self and others, and her concept of the Sacred within a transcendent reality, gave her the wisdom, courage and strength to engage in active discipleship, while maintaining her independence and Christ-centred approach to life. Angela translated her personal experience into a lived reality, whereby, she chose to remain in the world, and fulfil her mission of service towards others. She offered a third option to lay single women, to follow her example. For previously the only two options available to young women in the late Middle Ages, were to be married or to enter a monastery. The idea of a virginal life consecrated to God but living at home, appealed to Angela, for it was a life lived in the world but not of the world. Angela's legacy has inspired and continues to inspire generations of independent women, determined to lead and live active lives in service to others, while developing their interior lives in contemplation of the sacredness of their union with their Divine Spouse.

St Teresa of Ávila – First woman to be declared a Doctor of the Universal Church

On March 28, 2015, Pope Francis stated that, "500 years after [her] birth, the witness of St Teresa of Avila remains strong", a powerful leader for the twenty-first century!" Over the course of her lifetime "Teresa was called upon to defend the legitimacy of her mystical experience, her reform agenda, and indeed, her very self. As she realized how rooted such criticisms were in misogynist assumptions, Teresa began to take on the defense of women in general, arguing for a greater and more explicit role for women within the Christian tradition" (Ahlgren, 1996:1, cited in Cameron, 2012a:113). Teresa was a "powerful spokesperson" (p.165) for the Church in sixteenth century Spain. And now leaders in the contemporary Church, who challenge the status quo and step outside their comfort zone, have an opportunity to become powerful leaders within the global Church of the twenty-first century!

Caroline Chisholm – Philanthropist & "Emigrant's Friend"

Stinson (2013, January) maintains that "Caroline Chisholm pioneered a new form of committed Christian discipleship: lay, married, and actively involved in the world for a fairer, better functioning society. This was a new path of social doctrine which emphasised praxis and service." It is in this way that Caroline responded to the Gospel's call to service and emulated the work of our Divine Redeemer by accepting his mandate to serve (Mk, 10:42-45). Geoghegan (2011:448) writes of "Caroline Chisholm in the context of a prophetic figure – a prophet of the laity. She was a woman ahead of her time in both the secular and the religious sphere. As a philanthropist and "Emigrant's Friend", she shared her vision and respected and valued those whose lives she worked so hard to improve. In addition, there was much mutual respect between wife and husband – Caroline and Archibald. An effective leader will share and serve vision, giving hope for the future, while creating an atmosphere of trust and mutual respect amongst the members of the team/organisation.

St Thérèse of Lisieux – Doctor of the Universal Church

According to Camilo Maccise and Joseph Chalmers (1997:9), "The experience and doctrine of Therese of Lisieux become especially significant in our day when new horizons are opening up for the presence and action of women in society and in the Church. Women are called to be 'signs of God's tender love towards the human race', and to enrich humanity with their 'feminine genius.'" Maccise and Chalmers (ibid.) maintain that Thérèse's life and works reflect these sentiments: "Today women find areas of greater participation in society and Church opening up for them ... they can find encouragement in Thérèse of Lisieux to live ... 'a culture of equality between men and women'" (Pope St John Paul II, cited in Maccise and Chalmers, 1997:10). Maccise and Chalmers (ibid.) posit that: "Hans Urs von Balthasar noted on the occasion of the celebrations for the first centenary of Therese of Lisieux's birth, that she opened the whole field of theology to feminine reflection." They then quote Guy Gaucher (1996, p. 127): "The theology of women has never been taken seriously nor integrated by the establishment. However, after the message of Lisieux, it must finally consider it in the present reconstruction of Dogmatic Theology" (cited in Maccise and Chalmers, 1997:10). How then, has "the theology of women" been incorporated into the "reconstruction of dogmatic theology"? What are the challenges for female leaders and how does this impact on a "culture of equality" between men and women in the contemporary Church?

Blessed Frances Siedliska – Foundress of the Sisters of the Holy Family of Nazareth

When Frances Siedliska (also known as Mother Mary of Jesus the Good Shepherd) founded the Congregation of the Sisters of the Holy Family of Nazareth, her intention was to establish a community that would give service to God. Consequently, "It was of great importance to Mother Mary while she was writing the Holy Rule, that emphasis should be placed on the principal purpose of the congregation, which was not only the sanctification of its members but above all, the glory of God and service to the Church and its people" (Strzałkowska, 1989:37). As Superior General of the Order, Mother Mary cultivated awareness that covered many aspects of her "deep sense of spiritual motherhood toward all the Sisters and a concern and solicitude for the spiritual good of each of her daughters. She was a team player, and this is how she built her team and her communities. She encouraged all her daughters to work together collaboratively, and with one purpose to "serve Christ in others" in the "service of charity".

At the process for the cause of the beatification of Mother Frances, Sister Augustine Pietrzykowska testified: "her authority was not cold and rigid; she was really a mother to all. The greatest testimony of her spirit and of her humility, is the respect accorded her, and even the signs of veneration expressed to her, and with which she was surrounded by high dignitaries of the Church" (Ricciardi, 1971:383). Leadership requires certain standards. It is not a time to express "mate ship' but a time to generate respect and dignity for the position, while cultivating an atmosphere of love and friendship within a collegial community.

St Mary of the Cross MacKillop – Co-founder of the Sisters of St Joseph of the Sacred Heart

Mary MacKillop served the Church and her community with extraordinary strength, purpose, and adaptability. She accepted without question the responsibilities of looking after and providing for her family and her Institute of sisters. During all her trials and tribulations with Father Woods, the clergy and the bishops she maintained her integrity, particularly during the times of personal attacks and innuendos. She did not retaliate but always acted with a sense of pride in the achievements of others and showed gratitude and respect for the outstanding support received during the seemingly never-ending period of trials. She didn't complain but got on with the job as it were. She had "Tenacity and determination of purpose", and this is what enabled her to survive the countless trials, the pain of which would have pierced her heart, as she bore their weight and bravely carried her cross. Mary possessed "spirit and prophetic vision". Greenleaf (Fraker and Spears, 1996: 181) writes "It is the spirit in the prophetic vision that will move the strong and the successful to become builders of serving institutions." St Mary of the Cross had this ability. She planned for the future! She wasn't worried about what other people said, did or thought. She had God on her side, and she acted accordingly.

St Josephine Bakhita – Patron Saint of Victims of Slavery & Human Trafficking

In 2019, Pope Francis officially declared 8 February, the feastday of St Josephine Bakhita to be a "World Day of Prayer, Reflection and Action Against Human Trafficking ... [and a] time to end slavery" (Catholic Religious Australia, 2019). How Bakhita must have felt, when she was virtually "ripped" from the security of her family and physically abused by her kidnappers, and later her masters. What psychological damage would such a brutal separation from parents and family cause, particularly, as such actions were followed by abusive behaviour towards her? Indeed, defying the odds Bakhita seemed to emerge stronger from her years of physical and psychological trauma. Her faith was simple. She asked God's forgiveness for her captors and for those who had wronged her.

In a Vatican News document (n.d.) Bakhita is described as a "Witness of love" to others: "Her humility, her simplicity and her constant smile won the hearts of all the citizens. Her sisters in the community esteemed her for her inalterable sweet nature, her exquisite goodness and her deep desire to make the lord known." Bakhita's advice to other people, whether those in religious life or those serving God in other ways was: "Be good, love the Lord, pray for those who do not know Him. What a great grace it is to know God" (ibid.). To lead is to try to understand others and to mentor them so that they acquire leadership skills. Patience, humility and forgiveness are essential virtues for leaders to cultivate.

Dorothy Day Servant of God and Social Activist

Dorothy Day loved the Church and according to Mark and Louise Zwick (1999a:16), "she was not a cafeteria Catholic ... [that is, she was] not a pick-and-choose believer. If it was Church teaching, it was her credo. This commitment and active participation in Catholicism brought Dorothy into the mainstream of a large organization together with the masses, which she called the Mystical Body of Christ." She had a great respect for the Benedictines. The spirituality of the Benedictine Order influenced Dorothy to such an extent that "In 1955 ... [she] became a Benedictine Oblate of St. Procopius Abbey, Lisle, Illinois, and she often returned ... [to the abbey] for retreats" (St Procopius Abbey, n.d.). Benedictine priests were also invited to speak at the Worker headquarters and also to give the workers retreats at Maryfarm – one of the farming communes.

Mark and Louise Zwick (1999a:19) emphasise that Dorothy, "integrated into her life the charisms of the Benedictines (e.g., hospitality, liturgy, divine office), and the Franciscans (works of mercy, voluntary poverty, pacifism), which brought her not only into the lives of the saints, but also into the lives of the many men and women of her day who were attempting to live out the Gospel." Cardinal O'Connor (2000) said that Dorothy Day was "a model for all in the third millennium", hence her life is a relevant study for leaders in the 21st Century.

St Teresa of Kolkata – Foundress of the Missionaries of Charity

What a woman! What a saint! Mother Teresa mentored the Missionaries of Charity, including the sisters, brothers, co-workers and lay missionaries, and all who sought her advice. She taught and she loved. She set an example by actioning her love. She saw a need and she acted – she didn't wait to see if someone else would come and save her from having to do the lowest or the most unpleasant and menial of tasks, be it cleaning toilets, cleaning buildings, cooking and/or begging. According to Spink (2011:135), "Even as she became increasingly internationally acclaimed, she continued to roll up her sleeves and scrub floors as required." It was she who nursed and cradled babies, children, adults and the dying in her arms, and loving them till they died, or were admitted to the homes she had established for the purpose of healing.

In his Homily during the Beatification ceremony for Mother Teresa, Pope St John Paul II (2003, October 19) stressed, that she empathised with the poor: "she bent down to those suffering various forms of poverty. Her greatness lies in her ability to give without counting the cost, to give 'until it hurts'. Her life was a radical living and a bold proclamation of the Gospel." Mother Teresa was described as "one of the 20th Century's greatest humanitarians"? (Biography.com Editors, 2014, April 2). Who will be identified as representative of the next generation of philanthropists – will their humility equal that of the saint of Kolkata?

Finale

Leaders in the contemporary Church may not possess all the qualities of the extraordinary women mentioned above, however there are many, including those women who have given voice in this book, to the experiences of their role in the Church in the 21st Century, who are well on the way to engaging in active discipleship in their mission of service, as they continue their faith journey and live the Gospel. And now hopefully with the recent Vatican appointments of several women to senior leadership/executive positions (see Chapter 19), this recognition will soon lead to "greater female representation at [more] senior levels in the Church" (Lamb, 2019).

The Spirit is "moving" and the "times are changing"; however, before becoming overcome with excitement, let us remember the length of time it has taken for even slight changes to occur! The movement of change within the Church must accelerate. As leaders, we need to step up, and be and do, what God wants us to be and do. We have listened and the Spirit is with us! Consequently, as the third decade of the third millennium approaches, it is timely to herald a renaissance for women leaders in the Catholic Church! "So, what are we waiting for?" (Pope Francis, *Evangelii Gaudium*, 2013:para.120). Let us step forward now with pride and confidence and embrace the future!

References

Abbott, G., 2014, "Hildegard of Bingen", *ABC Classic FM: Keys to Music*, September 28. Retrieved 15 January 2015 from http://www.abc.net.au/classic/content/2014/09/28/4047546.htm

Abbott, W. M. (ed), 1967, *The Documents of Vatican II*, Chapman, London.

Agenzia Fides, 2007, 30 November, "Vatican – Josephine Bakhita the slave who became the first Sudanese saint, cited as an example in Benedict's new Encyclical, Spe Salvi" in *Fides Newsletter*. Retrieved 20 March 2019 from http://www.fides.org/en/news/10916-VATICAN_Josephine_Bakhita_the_slave_who_became_the_first_Sudanese_saint_cited_as_an_example_in_Pope_Benedict_XVI_s_new_encyclical_Spe_salvi

Ahern, P., 1999, *Maurice & Therese: The Story of a Love*, Darton, Longman and Todd Ltd., London.

Ahlgren, G.T., 1996, *Teresa of Avila and the Politics of Sanctity*, Cornell University Press, U.S.A.

Antokhin, A., 2014, "Dorothy Day's Thérèse of Lisieux: Ad Majorem Dei Gloriam", cited in Lane Center for Catholic Studies and Social Thought, 2014, "Dorothy Day: A Life and Legacy" in *The Lane Center Series*, vol. 1, (Summer), University of San Francisco. Retrieved on 28 April 2019 from https://www.usfca.edu/sites/default/files/pdfs/cas-lane-center-lecture-series-01.pdf

Armstrong, R.J., 2006, "The Lady" *Clare of Assisi: Early Documents*, New York Press, U.S.A.

Ashley, B., 1981, "St Catherine of Siena's Principles of Spiritual Direction", in *Spirituality Today*, vol.33, (March), pp.43-52.

Associated Press, 2017, September 6, *Vatican Declares Mother Teresa A Patron Saint of Calcutta*. Retrieved 7 April 2019 from https://www.voanews.com/a/vatican-declares-mother-teresa-a-patron-saint-of-calcutta/4017426.html

Athans, M.C., 2013, *In Quest of the Jewish Mary: The Mother of Jesus in History, Theology, and Spirituality*, ORBIS Books, New York.

Atkins, R., 2013, May 23, "Dorothy Day's Social Catholicism: the formative French influences", in *International Journal for the study of the Christian Church*. Retrieved 20 April 2019 from https://doi-org.ezproxy2.acu.edu.au/10.1080/1474225X.2013.780400

Aumann, J., 1985, *Christian Spirituality in the Catholic Tradition*. Retrieved 29 February 2012 from http://www.domcentral.org/study/aumann/cs/cs09.htm

Australian Catholic Bishops, 2017, *A National Year of Youth*. Retrieved from http://www.youth.catholic.org.au/year-of-youth/what-is-yoy

Australian Catholic Bishops Conference & Catholic Religious Australia, 2011, *Integrity in the Service of the Church: A Resource Document of Principles and Standards for Lay Workers in the Catholic Church in Australia*. Retrieved 11 March 2018 from https://www.catholic.org.au/documents/1345-integrity-in-service-of-the-church-1/file

Australian Catholic Bishops Conference, 2018, *Catholic Social Teaching*. Retrieved 12 March 2018 from http://www.socialjustice.catholic.org.au/social-teaching

Australian Catholic University, 2016, *Caroline Chisholm House officially opens* (Staff News). Retrieved 26 January 2019 from https://staff.acu.edu.au/our_university/newsroom/new_archive/acu_officially_opens_caroline_chisholm_house_in_north_sydney

Bada, F., 2018, *What were the Great Italian Wars?* (July 20). Retrieved 16 October 2018 from https://www.worldatlas.com/articles/what-were-the-great-italian-wars.html

Baird, J.L., 2006, *The Personal Correspondence of Hildegard of Bingen*, Oxford University Press Inc., U.S.A.

Bass, B.M., 1981, *Stogdill's handbook of leadership*, (rev. edn), the Free Press, New York.

Batten, J., 1998, "Servant-Leadership: A Passion to Serve", in *Insights on Leadership: Service, Stewardship, Spirit, and Servant-Leadership*, (ed) L. C. Spears, John Wiley & Sons, Inc., U.S.A., pp. 38-53.

BBC News, 2015, December 18, *Profile: 'Living Saint', Mother Teresa*. Retrieved 8 May 2019 from https://www.bbc.com/news/world-asia-india-35130795

Beattie, T., 2002, *God's Mother, Eve's Advocate: A Marian Narrative of Women's Salvation*, Continuum, Great Britain.

Beckwith, R.T., 2015, September 24, "Transcript: Read the Speech Pope Francis Gave to Congress" in *Time*. Retrieved 30 April 2019 from http://time.com/4048176/pope-francis-us-visit-congress-transcript/

Benedict XVI, 2007, "Spe Salvi", Encyclical Letter on *Christian Hope*, 30 November. Retrieved 20 March 2019 from http://w2.vatican.va/content/benedict-xvi/en/encyclicals/documents/hf_ben-xvi_enc_20071130_spe-salvi.html

Benedict XVI, 2010a, "Saint Hildegard of Bingen", *General Audience*. Papal Summer Residence, Castel Gandolfo, (September 1). Retrieved 8 March 2013 from http://www.hildegard.org/BenedictXVI/BenedictXVI.html

Benedict XVI, 2010b, "St Hildegard of Bingen (2)", *General Audience*. Paul VI Hall, (September 8). Retrieved 8 March 2013 from http://www.hildegard.org/BenedictXVI/BenedictXVI.html

Benedict XVI, 2010c, "St Clare of Assisi", *General Audience*. Paul VI Hall, (September 15). Retrieved 10 July 2018 from https://w2.vatican.va/content/benedict-xvi/en/audiences/2010/documents/hf_ben-xvi_aud_20100915.html#

Benedict XVI, 2010d, *Homily of Pope Benedict XVI on Canonization of Six New Saints*, (October 17). Retrieved 2 February 2019 from http://www.superflumina.org/PDF_files/BenedictXVI_homily_on_canonisation.pdf

Benedict XVI, 2010e, "Sala Regia", *Address of His Holiness Benedict XVI on the occasion of Christmas Greetings to the Roman Curia* (December 20). Retrieved 30 January 2019 from http://w2.vatican.va/content/benedict-xvi/en/speeches/2010/december/documents/hf_ben-xvi_spe_20101220_curia-auguri.html

Benedict XVI, 2011a, "Saint Joan of Arc", *General Audience* (Jan 26). Retrieved 21 October 2018 from http://w2.vatican.va/content/benedict-xvi/en/audiences/2011documents/hf_ben-xvi_aud_20110126.html

Benedict XVI, 2011b, "Saint Teresa of Avila", *General Audience* (Feb 2). Retrieved 3 June 2018 from http://w2.vatican.va/content/benedict-xvi/en/audiences/2011/documents/hf_ben-xvi_aud_20110202.html

Benedict XVI, 2012a, "Proclaiming Saint Hildegard of Bingen, professed nun of the Order of Saint Benedict, a Doctor of the Universal Church", *Apostolic Letter* (October 7). Retrieved 9 January 2013 from http://w2.vatican.va/content/benedict-xvi/en/apost_letters/documents/hf_ben-xvi_apl_20121007_ildegarda-bingen.html

Benedict XVI, 2012b, "The Opening of the Synod of Bishops and Proclamation of St John of Avila and of St Hildegard of Bingen as 'Doctors of the Church'", *Holy Mass*, (October 7). Retrieved 9 January 2013 from http://www.news.va/en/news/holy-mass-for-the-opening-of-the-synod-of-bishops

Bennis, W., 2009, "On Becoming a Leader". *The Leadership Classic Revised and Updated*. Basic Books, Perseus Books Group, New York.

Bennis, W. & Nanus, B., 1985, *Leaders: The strategies for change*, Harper and Row, New York.

Betti, U., 1988, "Preserve the True Meaning of the Canonical Requisites", *L'Osservatore Romano*, English Language edn (1981, June), no. 3.

Bible Gateway, 1988, *Mary Magdalene: The Woman who Had Seven Devils*. Retrieved 20 March 2018 from https://www.biblegateway.com/resources/all-women-bible/Mary-Magdalene

Biography.com.Editors, 2014, April 2, *Mother Teresa Biography: Saint Nun (2010-1997)*. Retrieved 8 April 2019 from https://www.biography.com/people/mother-teresa-9504160

Biography.com Editors, 2018, February 27th, "Joan of Arc Biography" *A&E Television Networks*. Retrieved 13 August 2018 from https://www.biography.com/people/joan-of-arc-9354756

Biography.com.Editors, 2014, April 2, *Dorothy Day Biography*. Retrieved 30 April 2019 from https://www.biography.com/writer/dorothy-day

Bishops of Australia, 2017, *The Year of Youth*. Retrieved 26 February 2018 from http://www.youth.catholic.org.au/year-of-youth/what-is-yoy

Blanchard, K. & Hodges, P., 2003, *The Servant Leader: Transforming Your Heart, Head, Hands & Habits*, Countryman, Tennessee U.S.A.

Blanchard, K., 2007, *Leading at a Higher Level*, Prentice Hall, New Jersey.

Blanchard, K. & Broadwell, R., 2018, *Servant Leadership in Action. How You Can Achieve Great Relationships and Results*. Berrett-Koehler Publishers, Inc., U.S.A.

Borchardt, D.H., 1976, "Tenison-Woods, Julian Edmund (1832-1889)", *Australian Dictionary of Biography, National Centre of Biography*, Australian National University. Retrieved 17 February 2019 from http://adb.anu.edu.au/biography/tenison-woods-julian-edmund-4700/text7787

Bottum, B. & Lenz, D., 1998, "Within Our Reach: Servant-Leadership for the Twenty-first Century", in *Insights on Leadership: Service, Stewardship, Spirit, and Servant-Leadership*, (ed) L. C. Spears, John Wiley & Sons, Inc., U.S.A., pp. 157-169.

Bradley, Y., 1999, "Servant Leadership: A Critique of Robert Greenleaf's Concept of Leadership", *Journal of Christian Education*, vol. 42, no. 2 (September), pp. 42-54.

Bradstock, A. & Rowland, C. (eds), 2008, *Radical Christian Writings: A Reader*, Blackwell Publishers Ltd., Oxford UK. Retrieved 21 April 2019 from https://ebookcentral-proquest-com.ezproxy2.acu.edu.au/lib/acu/reader.action?docID=351392#

Branson, C., 2009, *In Search of Authentic Leadership*. Retrieved 17 March 2018 from https://leo.acu.edu.au/course/view.php?id=23589&section=6

Brennan, W., 2003, *Women Mystics of the Modern Era*, Thierry Gosset (trans), St Paul's Publication, USA.

Brown, R.E., 1977, *The Birth of the Messiah: a commentary on the infancy narratives in Matthew and Luke* (1928-1998). Doubleday, Garden City, New York.

Buby, B.A., (n.d.), *The Use of Biblical Methodologies in Marian Theology Today*. Retrieved 10 February 2018 from https://udayton.edu/imri/mary/b/biblical-methodology-and-mariology.php

Burns, J.M., 1978, *Leadership*, Harper & Row, New York.

Burton, K., 1951, "Where There is Love" *The Life of Mother Mary Frances Siedliska of Jesus the Good Shepherd*, P.J. Kenedy & Sons, New York.

Butcher, C., 2013, *A Spiritual Reader St Hildegard of Bingen Doctor of the Church*, Paraclete Press, Brewster, Massachusetts, U.S.A.

Bynum, C.W., 1987, *Holy Feast and Holy Fast: The Religious Significance of Food to Medieval Women*, University of California Press, U.S.A.

Bynum, C.W., 1990, "Preface", in *Hildegard of Bingen: Scivias*, Hart, C. & Bishop, J. (Trans.), Paulist Press, U.S.A.

Cameron, C., 2009, "Women Doctors of the Catholic Church: A Study in Servant Leadership", *PhD Thesis*, CD-ROM, University of New England, Armidale, Australia.

Cameron, C., 2012a, *Leadership as a call to service The lives and works of Teresa of Ávila, Catherine of Siena and Thérèse of Lisieux*, Connor Court Publishing, Ballarat, Victoria.

Cameron, C., 2012b, "The Realism of Mysticism: St Teresa of Ávila through the eyes and reasoning of Simone de Beauvoir" in *ACU Newsletter Golding Centre for Women's History, Theology and Spirituality*, vol. 12, no. 2.

Cameron, C., 2014a, "Stewardship as Service", *Mission and Spirituality eNewsletter*, Broken Bay Institute, March 3, 20th edn. Retrieved from: http://www.bbi.catholic.edu.au/e-news/bbi-mission-and-spirituality-e-news/133-2014-02-28.html

Cameron, C., 2014b, "Leadership as Service", *Catholic Viewpoint*, vol. 23, no. 1, autumn, Diocese of Armidale.

Cameron, C., 2015a, *Leadership as a call to service The life and works of Hildegard of Bingen*, Connor Court Publishing, Ballarat, Victoria.

Cameron, C., 2015b, "EDLE 638 Faith Leadership" *Lumen Fidei – Light of Faith* [PowerPoint Presentation – Slide 13], Australian Catholic University, Sydney.

Capra, F., 1996, *The Web of Life*, p. 295, Doubleday, New York.

Catechism of the Catholic Church, 2000, *pocket edn*, 2nd edn, St Pauls Publications NSW.

Catechism of the Catholic Church, (n.d.), *Respect for the Human Person*. Retrieved 9 May 2018 from http://www.vatican.va/archive/ccc_css/archive/catechism/p3s1c2a3.htm

Catholic Bible Press, 1990, *Holy Bible: The New Revised Standard Version*, Thomas Nelson, Inc., U.S.A.

Catholic Charities of St Paul & Minneapolis, 2018, *Racism, Inclusion and Diversity*. Retrieved 12 March 2018 from https://www.cctwincities.org/education-advocacy/catholic-social-teaching/notable-quotations/racism-inclusion-and-diversity/

Catholic News Agency, 2018, *Women in the Catholic Church, Women in the Church – Latest News*. Retrieved 20 August 2018 from https://www.catholicnewsagency.com/tags/women-in-the-church

Catholic News Agency, 2018, April 11, *Papal Commission asks Francis for Synod on the Role of Women in the Church*. Retrieved 8 January 2019 from https://www.catholicnewsagency.com/news/papal-commission-asks-francis-for-synod-on-the-role-of-women-in-the-church-43751

Catholic News Agency, 2017, July 26, *Sts. Anne and Joachim*. Retrieved 7 December 2017 from https://www.catholicnewsagency.com/saint.php?n=313

Catholic News Agency, *The Four Marian Dogmas*. Retrieved 29 November 2017 from https://www.catholicnewsagency.com/resources/mary/general-information/the-four-marian-dogmas

Catholic News Service, 1997, September 14, "Mother Teresa (1910-1997) 'The Greatest evil is the lack of love and charity'" in *The Catholic Weekly*, vol. 56, No.3175, Petersham, Sydney, Australia.

Catholic News Service, 2016, April 20, "Next step in Dorothy Day canonization process initiated in New York" in *America the Jesuit Review*. Retrieved 23 April from https://www.americamagazine.org/issue/next-steps-begin-dorothy-day-canonization

Catholic News Service, 2016, April 26, "Friends of Dorothy Day applaud progress in sainthood cause", in *Crux*. Retrieved 23 April 2019 from https://cruxnow.com/church/2016/04/26/friends-of-dorothy-day-applaud-progress-in-sainthood-cause/

Catholic Online, 2019, *Mother Teresa Fact File*. Retrieved 7 April 2019 from https://www.catholic.org/life/teresa/quotes.php

Catholic Online, (n.d.), *St. Clare*. Retrieved 13 July 2018 from https://www.catholic.org/saints/saint.php?saint_id=215

Catholic Online, (n.d.), St. Agnes of Assisi. Retrieved 20 July 2018 from https://www.catholic.org/saints/saint.php?saint_id=1179

Catholic Religious Australia, 2019, January 31, *8 February 2019 – World Day of Prayer, Reflection and Action against Human trafficking – time to end slavery*. Retrieved 15 March 2019 from https://www.catholicreligious.org.au/media-releases/2019/1/31/8-february-2019-world-day-of-prayer-reflection-and-action-against-human-trafficking-time-to-end-slavery?fbclid=IwAR0LmghIHnxJEs6CFRGCuzzITCQ0xCNtfTSKSnwTPEPkq_jxhEWQ8BlJpYI

Catholic Saints Info, 2018, June 4, *St Ursula*. Retrieved 20 October 2018 from https://catholicsaints.info/saint-ursula

Catholic Worker Movement, 2018, May, "The Aims and Means of the Catholic Worker", in *The Catholic Worker*. Retrieved 18 May 2019 from https://www.catholicworker.org/cw-aims-and-means.html

Cavallini, G., 1998, *Catherine of Siena*, Chapman, London.

Chaignot, M.J., 2018, *Mary Magdalene and Seven Demons*. Retrieved 25 March 2018 from http://www.biblewise.com/bible_study/questions/mary-magdalene-seven.php

Chisholm, C., 2015, "The Easter Vow" in *Female Immigration*. Retrieved 18 January 2019 from https://mrschisholmdotcom.files.wordpress.com/2015/11/fear-left-me.pdf

Chisholm, C., 2015, "Fear Left Me" in *Female Immigration*. Retrieved 18 January 2019 from https://mrschisholmdotcom.files.wordpress.com/2015/11/the-easter-vow.pdf

Chisholm, C., 2015, "Heart Speaks to Heart" in *Female Immigration*. Retrieved 18 January 2019 from https://mrschisholmdotcom.files.wordpress.com/2015/11/heart-speaks-to-heart.pdf

Chisholm, C., 2015, "Seeking the Girl's Good" in *Female Immigration*. Retrieved 18 January 2019 from https://mrschisholmdotcom.files.wordpress.com/2015/11/seeking-the-girls-good.pdf

Chisholm, C., 2015, "A Sure Judge of Character" in *Female Immigration*. Retrieved 18 January 2019 from https://mrschisholmdotcom.files.wordpress.com/2015/11/a-sure-judge-of-character.pdf

Chopra, D., 2002, "The soul of leadership", *School Administrator*, vol. 59, iss. 8, p. 10. Retrieved 17 August from ProQuest database.

Clark, E. A., 1983, *Women in the Early Church: Message of the Fathers of the Church*, Michael Glazier, Inc., Delaware U.S.A.

Clark, G., 2015, *Monica An Ordinary Saint*, Oxford University Press, New York, U.S.A.

Clarke, J., 1996, *Story of a Soul: The Autobiography of St Therese of Lisieux*, ICS Publications, Washington.

Clissold, S., 1979, *St Theresa of Avila*, Sheldon Press, London.

CN CathNews, 2019, May 27, *Pope Appoints four women to top Synod jobs*. Retrieved 28 May 2019 from http://www.cathnews.com/cathnews/35062-pope-appoints-four-women-to-top-synod-jobs

Coleridge, M., 2017, "Time for Change". A paper prepared by the Council for Australian Catholic Women (June). In *Women Matter* 2017 28 September. Retrieved 10 December 2017 from http://www.opw.catholic.org.au/latest-news/the-participation-of-women-in-the-2020-plenary-council.html#.WiyQKExuJPZ

Commission on the Franciscan Intellectual Tradition, 2017, "Clare of Assisi" in *The Acts of the Process of Canonization (1253)*. Retrieved 10 July 218 from https://www.franciscantradition.org/clare-of-assisi-early-documents/78-the-acts-of-the-process-of-canonization-1253

Commonwealth of Australia, 2010, *Handout: Simplified Version of the universal Declaration of Human Rights*. Retrieved 11 March 2018 from www.civicsandcitizenship.edu.au/verve/_resources/FQ2_Simplified_Version_Dec.pdf

Congregation for the Clergy, 1997, *General Directory for Catechesis*. St Paul's Publications, Strathfield N.S.W. Australia.

Congregation of the Sisters of the Holy Family of Nazareth, 2016, "Way of Love", *Ration of the Congregation of the Sisters of the Holy Family of Nazareth*, Rome.

Connolly, M., 2016, May 15, "Did you Know the Catholic Church has a birthday?" [video file] on the *California Network*. Retrieved 29 March 2018 from https://www.catholic.org

Connor, K.R. "Dorothy Day, Restless Reader", cited in Lane Center for Catholic Studies and Social Thought, 2014, "Dorothy Day: A Life and Legacy" in *The Lane Center Series*, vol. 1, (Summer), University of San Francisco. Retrieved 28 April 2019 from https://www.usfca.edu/sites/default/files/pdfs/cas-lane-center-lecture-series-01.pdf

Cosstick, V., 2016, November 19, "A Saint for our time, now in the making", in *The Tablet*. Retrieved 16 May from https://www.thetablet.co.uk/features/2/9189/a-saint-for-our-time-now-in-the-making

Council of Nicea (325), 1996-2007, *Canon 19*. Retrieved on 5 July 2019 from www.intratext.com/IXT/ENG0425/_P6.HTM

Council of Chalcedon (451), 1996-2007, *Canon 15*. Retrieved on 5 July 2019 from http://www.intratext.com/IXT/ENG0428/_P7.HTM

Covey, S., 2004, *The Seven Habits of Highly Effective People*, Simon & Schuster, New York.

Covington, R., 2008, Jan.25, "Mary Magdalene was None of the Things a Pope Claimed", in *U.S. News*. Retrieved 25 March 2018 from https://www.usnews.com/news/religion/articles/2008/01/25/mary-magdalene-was-none-of-the-things-a-pope-claimed

Cowley, R. & Parker, G., 1996, "Hundred Years' War" in *The Reader's Companion to Military History*. By Houghton Mifflin Harcourt Publishing Company. Retrieved 13 August 2018 from https://www.history.com/topics/hundred-years-war

Cunneen, S., 1996, *In Search of Mary: The Woman and the Symbol*, Ballantine, New York.

Cunningham, L.S., 2005, *A Brief History of Saints*, Blackwell Publishing, U.S.A.

Dagnino, M.L., 1991, "Bakhita" in *Bakhita an Inspiring life*, (Memoirs, 1910). Canossian Daughters of Charity, Canossian Generalate Rome.

Daneault, S., 2008, "The wounded healer: Can this idea be of use to family physicians?" *Canadian Family Physician*, vol. 54, p. 1218. Retrieved 20 March 2009 from ProQuest database.

Day, D., 1999, *On Pilgrimage*, William B. Eerdmans Publishing Company, Grand Rapids, Michigan.

De Beauvoir, S., 1953, *The Second Sex*, translated and edited by H.M. Parshley, (1972 edn) Penguin Books, Great Britain.

De Chardin, P. T., 1960, *The Divine Milieu*, p. 138, Harper & Brothers, New York.

De Chardin, P. T., 2004, in Stephen R. Covey, *The Seven Habits of Highly Effective People*, p. 319, Simon & Schuster, New York.

Degler, T., 2007, "Kundalini Awareness: St. Hildegard of Bingen", *Institute for Consciousness Research*. Retrieved 6 July 2014 from http://www.readbag.com/icrcanada-documents-sthilbingen

DeGraaf, D. & Tilley, C. & Neal, L., 2001, *Servant Leadership Characteristics in Organizational Life*, The Greenleaf Center, Indiana, U.S.A.

Delhaye, P., 1972, "A View of the Past and Future of Feminine Ministries within the Church", in *Women Deacons? Essays with Answers*, 2016, (ed), P. Zagano, Michael Glazier/Liturgical Press, Collegeville, Minnesota.

DeMarco, D., 1999, "The Virtue of Fairness", *Lay Witness* (September). Retrieved 11 March 2018 from https://www.catholiceducation.org/en/culture/catholic-contributions/the-virtue-of-fairness.html

DeMeester, C. & Conroy, S., 1998, *The Power of Confidence: Genesis and structure of the 'Way of Spiritual Childhood' of Saint Therese of Lisieux*, Alba House, New York.

DeMeester, C., 2002, *With Empty Hands: The Message of St Therese of Lisieux*, Burns & Oates, London.

Desmarchelier, D., 2000, *Voices of Women: Women and the Catholic Church*, Spectrum Publications Pty. Ltd., Australia.

De Vinne, C., 2009, "Live a New Life: Innovation and intuition in the Rhetoric of Angela Merici", in *Magistra*, Atchison, vol. 15, Iss.2., (Winter), pp.39-60. Retrieved 13 September from https://search-proquest-com.ezproxy2.acu.edu.au/docview/216916830?accountid=8194&rfr_id=info%3Axri%2Fsid%3Aprimo

Dorothy Day Exhibit, (n.d.), *Dorothy Day: A Life Lived*. Retrieved 16 May 2019 from http://www.dorothydaydoc.com/pdf/Timeline_A.pdf

Dorothy Day Guild, (n.d.), *Process of Canonization*. Retrieved 23 April 2019 from http://dorothydayguild.org/the-cause/process-of-canonization/

Dorothy Day, (n.d.), *Quotes* (Author of the Long loneliness). Retrieved 21 May 2019 from https://www.goodreads.com/author/quotes/119043.Dorothy_Day

Dossier, F., 2008, August, "The Role of the Woman in the Life of the Church", in *FIDES News Service*, Rome. Retrieved 8 January 2019 from https://www.catholicculture.org/culture/library/view.cfm?recnum=8422

Dreier, P., 2012, *The 100 Greatest Americans of the 20th Century: a social justice hall of fame*. Nation Books, New York. Retrieved 2 April 2019 from https://search-credoreference-com.ezproxy1.acu.edu.au/content/entry/persgreatest/dorothy_day_1897_1980/0

Dreyer, E.A., 2014, *Accidental Theologians: Four Women Who Shaped Christianity*, Franciscan Media, Cincinnati, OH., U.S.A.

Drucker, P.F., 2001, *Management Challenges for the Twenty-First Century*, Harper Business, New York.

Dulles, A., 1978, *Models of the Church*, Doubleday, New York.

Editors Encyclopaedia Britannica, 2018, *Saints Anne and Joachim*. Retrieved 10 December 2017 https://www.britannica.com/biography/Saint-Anne

Editors Encyclopaedia Britannica, 2018, *Italian Wars. European History*. Retrieved 16 October 2018 from https://www.britannica.com/event/Italian-Wars

Editors Encyclopaedia Britannica, 2018, *Counter-Reformation*. Retrieved 18 September 2018 from https://www.britannica.com/event/Counter-Reformation

Egan, K.J., 1998, "The ecclesiology of Teresa of Avila: Women as church especially in the book of her foundations", in *Theology: Expanding the Borders*, (eds) M. Aquino & R. Goizueta, "The Annual Publication of the College Theology Society", vol. 43, pp.145-161.

Egan, K.J., 2011, Oct.13., "St. Teresa of Avila – First Woman Doctor of the Church" in *McGrathMD* [video file]. Retrieved on 2 June 2018 from https://www.youtube.com/watch?v=gd77qwAwkfc

Eisen, U.E., 2000, *Women Officeholders in Early Christianity: Epigraphical and Literary Studies*. A Michael Glazier Book, The Liturgical Press. Collegeville, Minnesota.

Ellsberg, R., 2014, "Dorothy Day: A Radical Saint" cited in Lane Center for Catholic Studies and Social Thought, 2014, "Dorothy Day: A Life and Legacy" in *The Lane Center Series*, vol. 1, (Summer), University of San Francisco. Retrieved on 28 April 2019 from https://www.usfca.edu/sites/default/files/pdfs/cas-lane-center-lecture-series-01.pdf

Erhard, E., 2017, June 22, "Léonie Martin, Disciple and Sister of St. Thérèse of Lisieux" In *Crisis Magazine*. Retrieved 17 June 2018 from http://leoniemartin.org/my-blog-about-st-therese/

Falbo, G., 2007, *St. Monica: The Power of a Mother's Love*, Pauline Books & Media, Boston, U.S.A.

Farrell, H., 2017, March 27, "List of All the Women in the Old Testament", *Women in the Scriptures*. Retrieved 26 May 2019 from http://www.womeninthescriptures.com/2017/03/list-of-all-women-in-old-testament.html

Feely, K., (n.d.), "Human Dignity" in *Education for Justice*. Retrieved 9 May 2018 from http://www.caritas.org.au/docs/cst/education-for-justice-dignity.pdf?sfvrsn=dd1f90aa_0

Fierro, N., 1997, *Hildegard of Bingen: Symphony of the Harmony of Heaven*. Retrieved 23 January 2014 from http://hildegard.org/music/music.html

Fink, J.F., 2000a, *The Doctors of The Church: Doctors of the First Millennium*, vol. 1, Alba House, New York.

Fink, J.F., 2000b, *The Doctors of the Church: Doctors of the Second Millennium*, vol. 2, Alba House, New York.

Fiorenza, E.S., 2009, "Abstract" in *Mace, E.R.*, 2009, "Feminist Forerunners and a Usable Past: A Historiography of Elizabeth Cady Stanton's *The Woman's Bible*", in *Journal of Feminist Studies in Religion*, vol. 25, no. 2, (Fall), pp.5-23.

Fisher, A., 2015, August 11, *Mass at Sancta Sophia College*, Sydney University Sydney. Retrieved 11 July 2018 from https://www.sydneycatholic.org/people/archbishop/homilies/2015/2015811_1756.shtml

Flanagan, S., 1995, "Hildegard von Bingen (1098-1179)", In *German Writers and words of the Early Middle Ages: 800-1170*, vol. 148. University of Adelaide. Retrieved 23 January 2014 from http://hildegard.org/documents/flanagan.html

Flanagan, S., 1998, *Hildegard of Bingen (1098-1179): A Visionary* Life, (January 2nd edn), Routledge, New York.

Foale, M.T., 1989, "The Josephite Story", *The Sisters of St Joseph: their foundation and early history 1866-1893*, St Joseph's Generalate, Sydney.

Foale, M.T., 1997, "Mary Mackillop: a woman of her time" [online], *Journal of the Australian Catholic Historical Society*, vol. 18, pp. 25-34. Retrieved 11 February 2-19 from https://search-informit-com-au.ezproxy2.acu.edu.au documentSummary;dn=980201674;res=IELAPA

Fordham University, *The Life and Works of Hildegard von Bingen (1098-1179)*. Retrieved 16 July 2014, from Internet History Sourcebooks Project. http://www.fordham.edu/halsall/med/hildegarde.asp

Forest, J., 1997, October 10, "Dorothy Day – A Saint for Our Age?" in *The Catholic Worker Movement*. Retrieved 23 April 2019 from https://www.catholicworker.org/pages/forest-saint-our-age.html

Forest, J., 2013, "Servant of God Dorothy Day", in *The Catholic Worker Movement*. Retrieved 23 April 2019 from https://www.catholicworker.org/dorothyday/servant-of-god.html

Franciscan Intellectual Tradition, 2017, "St Clare of Assisi" in the *Acts of the Process of Canonization*. Retrieved 10 July 2018 from https://www.franciscantradition.org/clare-of-assisi-early-documents/78-the-acts-of-the-process-of-canonization-1253

Franciscan Media, 2018, *Celebrating St Clare of Assisi* by a Guest Author – Sister Claire André Gagliardi. Retrieved 20 July 2018 from https://www.franciscanmedia.org/celebrating-saint-clare-of-assisi/

Freely, K., (n.d.), "The Principle of Human Dignity" in *Education for Justice*. Retrieved 30 July 2018 from https://www.caritas.org.au/docs/cst/education-for-justice-dignity.pdf?sfvrsn=dd1f90aa_0

French, M., 2015, "The Carthaginian Case and Private Prosecutions" in *Friends of Caroline Chisholm Newsletter* #11, (July). Retrieved 17 January 2019 from

French, M., 2016, *Caroline Chisholm: The Carthaginian Case and Private Prosecutions in Mid-Nineteenth Century New South Wales*. Retrieved 17 January 2019 from https://mrschisholmdotcom.files.wordpress.com/2016/02/private-criminal-prosecutions_-matthew-french1.pdf

Fraker, A.T. & Spears, L.C. (eds), 1996, *Robert K. Greenleaf: Seeker and Servant: Reflections on Religious Leadership*, Jossey-Bass Publishers, San Francisco.

Frankl, V., 1959, *Man's search for meaning*, Simon and Schuster, New York.

Frick, D.M. & Spears, L.C. (eds), 1996, *Robert K. Greenleaf: On Becoming A Servant-Leader*, Josey-Bass Publishers, San Francisco.

Furlong, M., 1987, *Therese of Lisieux*, Virago Press Limited, London.

Gardiner, J., 1998, "Quiet Presence: The Holy Ground of Leadership", in *Insights on Leadership: Service, Stewardship, Spirit, and Servant-Leadership*, (ed), L. C. Spears, John Wiley & Sons, Inc., U.S.A., pp. 116-125.

Gaucher, G., 1996, "Actualité de Sainte Thérèse de Lisieux", in *Thérèse de Lisieux et les missions. Mission et contemplation* (Kinshasa, p.127).

Geoghegan, C., 2011, "Caroline Chisholm – A Prophetic Voice in Church and Society", *The Australasian Catholic Record*, Strathfield, (October), vol.88, iss.4, pp.447-461. Retrieved 25 January from https://search-proquest-com.ezproxy2.acu.edu.au/docview/963553335/fulltextPDF/57857BD0ACF7421FPQ/1?accountid=8194

Geoghegan, C., 2014, "Caroline Chisholm: A prophet of the laity" (July 27), [Cradio] *New Media*. Retrieved 19 January 2019 from https://cradio.org.au/topics/christian-living/discipleship-virtue/caroline-chisholm-a-prophet-of-the-laity/

Geoghegan, C., *Caroline Chisholm – advocate for women and prophet of the laity*, (n.d.). Retrieved 18 January 2019 from https://www.cam.org.au/News-and-Events/Reflections/Article/7884/caroline-chisholm-the-emigrants-friend#.XEGZTfZuJPY

Giangravè, C., 2018, March 8, "Signs suggest a turning point on the role of women in the Church", in *Crux*. Retrieved 8 January 2019 from https://cruxnow.com/vatican/2018/03/08/signs-suggest-turning-point-role-women-church/

Giles, K., 1989, *Patterns of Ministry Among the First Christians*, Collins Dove, Melbourne Australia.

Glatz, C., 2018, "Pope apologizes to young people who have felt ignored by the church", in *Catholic News Service*, 2018, October 28. Retrieved 11 November 2018 from http://www.catholicnews.com/services/englishnews/2018/pope-apologizes-to-young-people-who-have-felt-ignored-by-the-churc.cfm

Glazier, M. & Hellwig, M. (eds), 1994, *The Modern Catholic Encyclopedia*, E.J. Dwyer, Newtown, NSW.

Glossary of Jewish Terminology, (n.d.), *Betrothal*. Retrieved 10 February 2018 from https://udayton.edu/imri/mary/b/bethrothal-meaning-in-luke.php

Goldman, S., 2017, *Caroline Chisholm: An Irresistible Force*, HarperCollins*Publishers*, Australia.

Got Questions, 2018, *What are the Gnostic gospels?* Retrieved 7 April 2018 from https://www.gotquestions.org/Gnostic-gospels.html

Got Questions, 2018, *What was the Protestant Reformation?* Retrieved 25 September 2018 from https://www.gotquestions.org/Protestant-Reformation.html

Graham, W.C. 1995, "Is there a case against St Therese as doctor of the church", *Sisters Today*, vol. 67, (January), pp. 56-58.

Green, D., 2015, October, "7 Facts about the Hundred Years' War", in *History Extra*. Retrieved on 21 August 2018 from https://www.historyextra.com/period/medieval/7-facts-about-the-hundred-years-war/

Greenleaf, R., 1977, *Servant Leadership: A Journey into Legitimate Power and Greatness*, Paulist Press, New York.

Greenleaf, R., 1991, *Servant Leadership: A Journey into the Nature of Legitimate Power and Greatness*, Paulist Press, New York.

Greenleaf, R., 1998, "Servant-Leadership", in *Insights on Leadership: Service, Stewardship, Spirit, and Servant-Leadership*, (ed), L. C. Spears, John Wiley & Sons, Inc., U.S.A., pp. 15-20.

Greenleaf, R., 2002, *Servant Leadership: A Journey into Legitimate Power and Greatness*, 25th edn, Paulist Press, New York.

Greto, V., 1999, "Scholars taking a new look at Mary Magdalene", in *The Gazette*, Colorado Springs. Retrieved 20 March 2018 from http://www.thenazareneway.com/new_look_at_mary_magdalene.htm

Gronau, E., 1996, *Hildegard. Vita di una donna profetica alle origini dell'eta moderna*, Milan, pp.402-412.

Guardian News & Media, 2016, *Who Were the Popes?* "Datablog – List and Spreadsheet". Retrieved 9 July 2018 from https://docs.google.com/spreadsheets/d/12BaspZ1dyJ_16BF8AXvy3obr34H9_n011x5jfiqRafk/edit#gid=0

Hackman, M. & Johnson, C., 2009, *Leadership: A Communication Perspective*, 5th edn, Waveland Press, Inc., Illinois.

Haines, R. F., 1997, *Emigration and the Labouring Poor – Australian Recruitment in Britain and Ireland 1831-60*, Macmillan Press Ltd, Basingstoke, 1997. First published USA, St. Martin's Press, Inc. 1997.

Hamilton, J.W., 2006, "The Critical Effect of Object Loss in the Development of Episodic Manic Illness", *American Academy of Psychoanalysis and Dynamic Psychiatry*, vol. 34, no. 2, (summer), p. 333. Retrieved 2008 from ProQuest database.

Hann, R. (n.d.), *Martin Sisters, Sister Genevieve of the Holy Face, Marie Céline Martin*. Retrieved 17 June 2018 from http://www.martinsisters.org/sister_genevieve_of_the_holy_face.html

Hart, C. & Bishop, J. (trans), 1990, *Hildegard of Bingen: Scivias*, Paulist Press, U.S.A.

Hayton, M.S.J., 2015, "Inflections of Prophetic Vision: The Reshaping of Hildegard of Bingen's Apocalypticism as Represented by Abridgments of the *Pentachronon*", *Centre for Medieval Studies*, University of Toronto. Retrieved 13 May 2015 from http://www.academia.edu/10763619/Dissertation_Abstract_Hayton

Heffron, C., 2018, January 22, "St Josephine Bakhita – A Model of Faith", in *St Anthony Messenger*. Retrieved 15 March 2019 from https://blog.franciscanmedia.org/sam/st.-josephine-bakhita-a-model-of-faith

Heider, J., 1985, *The Tao of Leadership. Lao Tzu's Tao Te Ching: Adapted for a New Age*, Humanics Ltd., U.S.A.

Hesse, H., 1956, *The Journey to the East*, Peter Owen, London.

Hines, M.E., 1991, "Mary and the Prophetic Mission of the Church", *Journal of Ecumenical Studies*, 28:2, (Spring).

Hobbins, D. (trans), 2005, *The Trial of Joan of Arc*, Harvard University Press, Massachusetts, U.S.A. [Online]. Retrieved 6 August 2018 from https://ebookcentral-proquest-com.ezproxy1.acu.edu.au/lib/acu/detail.action?docID=3300538

Hodges, P., 2003, *The Servant Leader: Transforming Your Heart, Head, Hands & Habits*, Countryman, Tennessee U.S.A.

Holda, C., 1978, "Return to Nazareth", *Retreat Reflections for Religious Renewal based on the personal journals of Mother Mary of Jesus the Good Shepherd, Foundress of the Congregation of the sisters of the Holy Family of Nazareth*, Rome.

Holy See Press Office, 2016, June 6, *Mary Magdalene, apostle of the apostles*. Retrieved 20 March 2018 from https://press.vatican.va/content/salastampa/en/bollettino/pubblico/2016/06/10/160610c.html

Holm, M. & Woodbury, M., 1997, September 14, "Mother Teresa (1910-1997): A Life of Love" in *The Catholic Weekly*, vol.56, No.3175, Petersham, Sydney, Australia.

Holmes, J.D. & Bickers, B.W., 1983, *A Short History of the Catholic Church*, Burns & Oates, Tunbridge Wells, Kent.

Howard, J., 1989, *Angela: A woman faced with two alternatives, she saw and chose the third*, Australian Province of Ursulines, Lyneham ACT Australia.

Hoyle, J.R., 2007, *Leadership and Futuring: Making Visions Happen*, 2nd edn, Corwin Press, California.

Hugo, J., 1996, April 1, "Dorothy Day: Driven by Love", in *Houston Catholic Worker*. Retrieved 11 May 2019 from https://cjd.org/1996/04/01/dorothy-day-driven-by-love-fr-john-hugo/

Huizenga, L., 2012, *St Hildegard of Bingen, Doctor of the Church*, (October 4). Retrieved 17 January 2014 from Http://www.firstthings.com/onthesquare/2012/10/st-hildegard-of-hingen-doctor-of-the-church.

Hunt, M., 1998, *Dream Makers: Putting Vision and Values to work*, Davies Black Publisher, Palo Alto, CA.

Hunter, J.C., 2004, *The World's Most Powerful Leadership Principle: How to Become a Servant Leader*, Crown Business, New York.

Iitis, J., 1966, "Caroline Chisholm (1808-1877)", in *Australian Dictionary of Biography*, vol.1, (MUP). Retrieved 12 January 2019 from http://adb.anu.edu.au/biography/chisholm-caroline-1894

Inman, A., 2017, "Women deacons in Anglo-Saxon England", *The Pastoral Review*, vol.13, iss. 1, (January/February), pp. 42-46.

Irarrazabal, D., Ross, S. & Wacker, M-T. (eds), 2008, "The Many Faces of Mary", in *Concilium*, SCM Press, London.

Irenaeus, (n.d.), *Against Heresies* 3.22; *Sources Chrétiennes*, vol.34, p.378, cited in Hines, Mary and the Prophetic Mission of the Church, *Journal of Ecumenical studies*, 28:2, Spring 1991, p.283.

Isbouts, J-P., 2016, "Jesus and the Origins of Christianity", in *National Geographic*, 9 January, National Geographic Partners, LLC, Washington, D.C. USA.

Iuventus, P., 2015, April 9, "The Truth about Mary Magdalene" in *Catholic Herald*. Retrieved 20 March 2018 from http://catholicherald.co.uk/issues/april-10th-2015/the-truth-about-mary-magdalene/

Jamart, F. (Trans, De Putte, W. V.), 1961, *Complete Spiritual Doctrine of St Therese of Lisieux*, Alba House, New York.

Jankiewicz, D., 2013, "Phoebe: Was she an early church leader", in Ministry *in Motion*. Retrieved 31 March 2018 from https://www.ministrymagazine.org/authors/jankiewicz-darius.html

Johnson, E. A., 2003, *Truly Our Sister A Theology of Mary in the Communion of Saints*, Continuum, New York.

Joly, E.L., 1993, *Mother Teresa: A Woman in Love*, Ave Maria Press, Notre Dame, Ind.

Jusino, R.K., 1998, *Mary Magdalene: Author of the Fourth Gospel?* Retrieved 20 March 2018 from http://ramon_k_jusino.tripod.com/magdalene.html

Justice & Peace Office, 2018, *Catholic Social Teaching and Housing and Homelessness*. Retrieved 12 March 2018 from http://justiceandpeace.org.au/catholic-social-teaching-and-housing-and-homelessness/

Kavanaugh, J.A. & Rodriguez, O. (trans), 1987, revised, *The Collected Works of St Teresa of Avila*, vol. 1, ICS Publications, Washington.

Kavanaugh, J.A. & Rodriguez, O. (trans), 1980, *The Collected Works of St Teresa of Avila*, vol. 2, ICS Publications, Washington.

Kavanaugh, J.A. & Rodriguez, O. (trans), 1985, *The Collected Works of St Teresa of Avila*, vol. 3, ICS Publications, Washington.

Kearns, C. (trans), 1980, *The Life of Catherine of Siena by Raymond of Capua*, Dominican Publications, Dublin.

Kessler, A., 2016, December 3, "Remembering Dorothy Day", in *Benedictine History*. Retrieved 11 May 2019 from https://www.benedictinehistory.com/blog-sisterann-dorothy-day/

Key to Umbria: Assisi, (n.d.), *History of Assisi*. Retrieved 21 July 2018 from http://www.keytoumbria.com/Assisi/History.html

King, K.L., 1998, April, "Women in Ancient Christianity: The New Discoveries", in *Frontline: From Jesus to Christ*. Retrieved 20 March 2018 from https://www.pbs.org/wgbh/pages/frontline/shows/religion/first/women.html

Klosko, G., 1997, *The Blackwell Encyclopedic Dictionary of Business Ethics*, P. Werhane & R. E. Freeman, (eds), Malden, MA and Oxford: Blackwell Publishers, 1997, pp. 272-3.

Kneipp, P., 1982, *This Land of Promise: The Ursuline Order in Australia 1882-1982*, University of New England Publishing Unit, University of New England, Armidale, NSW, Australia.

Knight, K. (ed), 2017, "Saint Agnes of Assis" in *New Advent*. Retrieved 28 August 2018 from http://www.newadvent.org/cathen/01213a.htm

Komonchak, J.A., (ed), 1995, *History of Vatican II: Announcing and Preparing Vatican Council II Toward a New Era in Catholicism*, vol. I, Orbis, New York/Peeters, Belgium.

Komonchak, J.A., (ed), 2000, *History of Vatican II: The Mature Council: Second Period and Intersession September 1963 – September 1964*, vol. III, Orbis, New York/Peeters, Belgium.

Komonchak, J.A., (ed), 2003, *History of Vatican II: Church as Communion; Third Period and Intersession September 1964 – September 1965*, vol. IV, Orbis, New York/Peeters, Belgium.

Kouzes, J.M. & Posner, B.Z., 1987, *The Leadership Challenge*, Jossey-Bass, San Francisco.

Kraemer Jr, H.M., 2011, *From Values to Actions: The Four Principles of Values-Based Leadership*. Jossey-Bass. San Francisco, U.S.A.

Krohn, A., 2012, *Friends of Caroline Chisholm Newsletter*. Retrieved 18 January 2019 from https://mrschisholmdotcom.files.wordpress.com/2015/11/friends-newsletter-4-jan-2012.pdf

Lacoste, J.Y., (ed), 2005a, *Encyclopedia of Christian Theology*, vol. 1, Routledge, New York.

Lacoste, J.Y., (ed), 2005c, *Encyclopedia of Christian Theology*, vol. 3, Routledge, New York.

La Croix International Staff, 2019, July 9, "Pope names women to congregation for consecrated life" in *LaCroix International Newspaper*. Retrieved 10 July 2019 from https://international.la-croix.com/news/pope-names-women-to-congregation-for-consecrated-life/10490

Lad, L.J. & Luechauer, D., 1998, "On the Path to Servant-Leadership", in *Insights on Leadership: Service, Stewardship, Spirit, and Servant-Leadership*, (ed), L. C. Spears, John Wiley & Sons, Inc., U.S.A., pp. 54-67.

Lamb, C., 2019, July 8, "First women members of Vatican department that oversees religious orders appointed" in *The Tablet*. Retrieved 10 July 2019 from https://www.thetablet.co.uk/news/11848/first-women-members-of-vatican-department-that-oversees-religious-orders-appointed-

Lamb, C., 2019, May 24, "Pope appoints four women to top Synod jobs" in *The Tablet*. Retrieved 26 May 2019 from https://www.thetablet.co.uk/news/11724/pope-appoints-four-women-to-top-synod-jobs-

Lambert, T., 2018, A Brief History of *Poland. Poland in the Middle Ages*. Retrieved 27 November 2018 from www.localhistories.org/poland.html

Lane Center for Catholic Studies and Social Thought, 2014, "Dorothy Day: A Life and Legacy" in *The Lane Center Series*, vol. 1, (Summer), University of San Francisco. Retrieved on 28 April 2019 from https://www.usfca.edu/sites/default/files/pdfs/cas-lane-center-lecture-series-01.pdf

Lauter, W., 1996a, *The Hildegardis Reliquary in the Eibingen Parish Church*. Retrieved 23 January 2014 from http://hildegard.org/wirk/eschrein.html

Lauter, W., 1996b, *The Old Convent of Eibingen*. Retrieved 23 January 2014 from http://hildegard.org/wirk/eeibing.html

Ledochowska, T., 1968, *Angela Merici and the Company of St. Ursula According to the Historical Documents*, M. T. Neylan (trans), vol. 1, Ancora, Rome.

Ledochowska, T., 1968, *Angela Merici and the Company of St. Ursula According to the Historical Documents*, M. T. Neylan (trans), vol. 11, Ancora, Rome.

Lee, R., 2018, February 8, "St. Josephine Bakhita and the Door to Holiness" in *Word on Fire*. Retrieved 16 January 2019 from https://www.wordonfire.org/resources/blog/st-josephine-bakhita-and-the-door-to-holiness/1323/

Leedy, P.D. & Ormrod, J.E., 2005, *Practical Research: Planning and Design*, 8th edn, Prentice-Hall, New Jersey.

Lewis, J. J., 2012, *Hildegard of Bingen Visionary, Composer, Writer.* Retrieved 20 December 2012 from Http://womenshistory.about.com/od/hildegardbingen/a/hildegard. htm

L'Osservatore Romano, 1970a, *Doctor of the Church: A Reflection on Saint Teresa*, no. 40, (1 October), p. 1, p. 12.

L'Osservatore Romano, 1970b, *St Catherine – Doctor of the Church*, no. 42, 15 October, p. 6, p. 7.

L'Osservatore Romano, 1997a, *Love was the key to her vocation*, no. 43, 22 October, p. 1, p. 4.

L'Osservatore, 1997b, *Therese: model of a life offered to God*, no. 44, 29 October, p. 1, p. 2, p. 4.

L'Osservatore Romano, 2012, *What is Equivalent Canonization?* May 12.

L'Osservatore Romano, 2012, Weekly Edition in English, no.20 [2246], 16 May, p.11.

Maalouf, J. & Teresa, Mother, 2001, *Mother Teresa: Essential Writings*, Orbis Books, Maryknoll, New York.

Maccise, C. & Chalmers, J., 1997, "A Doctor for the Third Millennium", *Letter from the O. Carm and O.C.D. Superiors on the occasion of the Doctorate of Saint Therese of Lisieux*. Retrieved 6 June 2018 from https://pdfs.semanticscholar.org/dbd6/d91f17075ee7b5d3eb70b3ba466c2aca6f52.pdf

McCreanor, S. (ed), 2009, "Mary Mackillop On Mission To her last breath", *Correspondence about the Foundations of the Sisters of St Joseph in Aotearoa New Zealand and Mary's final years 1881-1909*, Sisters of St Joseph of the Sacred Heart, North Sydney Australia.

McCreanor, S. (ed), 2011, "Mary Mackillop and a Nest of Crosses", *Correspondence with Fr Julian Tenison Woods 1869-1872*, Sisters of St Joseph of the Sacred Heart, North Sydney Australia.

McElwee, J.J., 2019, May 7, "Francis: Women Deacons Commission gave split report on their role in early church", in *National Catholic Reporter*. Retrieved 26 May 2019 from https://www.ncronline.org/news/vatican/francis-women-deacons-commission-gave-split-report-their-role-early-church

Mace, E.R., 2009, "Feminist Forerunners and a Usable Past: A Historiography of Elizabeth Cady Stanton's *The Woman's Bible*", in *Journal of Feminist Studies in Religion*, vol. 25, no. 2, (Fall), pp.5-23.

Macy, G., 2013, "Get the facts in order: A History of Women's Leadership", (U.S. Catholic interview) in *U.S. Catholic Faith in Real Life*. Retrieved 2 October 2017 from http://www.uscatholic.org

Macy, G., Ditewig, W.T. & Zagano, P., 2011, *Women Deacons: Past, Present, Future*, Paulist Press, New Jersey.

Magdala, 2018, "Timeline" in *Crossroads of Jewish and Christian History*. Retrieved 26 March 2016 from http://www.magdala.org/about/the-story/timeline/

Marius, R. & Page, M.E., 2007, *A Short Guide to Writing About History*, Pearson Education, Inc., U.S.A.

Margolis, N., 2004, "Merici, Angela St (1470/75-1540)", in K.M. Wilson & N. Margolis (eds), *Women in the middle ages: an encyclopedia*. [Online]. Santa Barbara: ABC-CLIO. Available from: https://search-credoreference-com.ezproxy2.acu.edu.au/content/entry/abcwma/merici_angela_st_1470_75_1540/0 [Accessed 11 September 2018].

Martín, I.S., 2017, Oct. 5, "Pope defends male/female differences as well as women's equality", in *Crux*. Retrieved 10 June 2018 from https://cruxnow.com/vatican/2017/10/05/pope-defends-malefemale-differences-well-womens-equality/

Martin, I.S., 2015, March 9, "The Vatican opens the door to a debate on women's roles in the Church and the world", in *Crux*. Retrieved 9 January 2019 from https://cruxnow.com/church/2015/03/09/vatican-opens-doors-to-debate-on-womens-role-in-the-church-and-the-world/

Marucci, C., 2010, "History and value of the Feminine Diaconate in the Ancient Church" in *Women Deacons? Essays with Answers*, 2016, (eds), P. Zagano, Michael Glazier/Liturgical Press, Collegeville, Minnesota.

Mauriello, M.R., 1996, "Mary Mother of the Church" *Mater Ecclesiae*. Dayton University Marian Library. Retrieved 10 December 2017 from https://udayton.edu/imri/mary/m/mother-of-the-church.php

Mazzonis, Q., 2004, "A female idea of religious perfection: Angela Merici and the Company of St Ursula (1535-1540)", in *Renaissance Studies*, (September), vol.18 (3) pp.391-411. Retrieved 12 September 2018 from https://doi-org.ezproxy1.acu.edu.au/10.1111/j.0269-1213.2004.00068.x

Mazzonis, Q., 2007, *Spirituality, Gender, and the Self in Renaissance Italy – Angela Merici and the Company of St. Ursula (1474-1540)*. Catholic University of America Press, Washington DC, U.S.A.

McBride, T.M., 2003, *Marian Theology up to Vatican II*. Our Lady of Grace Monastery. Retrieved 29 November 2017 from http://www.christendom-awake.org/pages/mcbride/marian-upto2vat.htm

McBrien, R., 1981, *Catholicism*, Study Edition, Winston Press, U.S.A.

McCauley, A., 2017, June 6, *Francis and Clare: Faithful friends, Simple Saints*. Retrieved 13 July 2018 from https://www.archmil.org/ArchMil/ArchbishopListeckiLetters/Synod-2014/Post-Synod-/Lay-Ministry/FrancisandClare.pdf

McCuddy M.K. & Pirie, W.L., 2007, "Spirituality, stewardship, and financial decision-making Toward a theory of intertemporal stewardship", *Managerial Finance*, vol. 33, no. 12, pp. 957-969. Retrieved 16 September 2008 from Emerald database.

McElwee, J.J., 2017, "New Swedish Cardinal suggests high-level advisory group of women", in *National Catholic Reporter*, (June 28). Retrieved 23 January 2019 from https://www.ncronline.org/news/people/new-swedish-cardinal-suggests-high-level-advisory-group-women

McElwee, J.J., 2018, "Francis challenges anti-human trafficking alliance to examine society's complicity", *NCR Forward*, (February 9th). Retrieved 11 March 2018 from https://www.ncronline.org/news/vatican/francis-challenges-anti-human-trafficking-alliance-examine-societys-complicity

McFadzean, M., 2013, "Remnants of a life's work: Caroline Chisholm [online]", *Agora*, vol. 48, no. 1, (Feb), pp.17-19. Retrieved 25 January 2019 from https://search-informit-com-au.ezproxy2.acu.edu.au/documentSummary;dn=246330436048280;res=IELAPA, ISSN: 0044-6726. [cited 25 Jan 19].

Mc Gee, J., 1997, "Therese a Doctor!" *National Catholic Reporter*, vol. 34, (31 October), p. 21.

McGinn, B., 1999, *The Doctors of the Church: Thirty-Three Men and Women Who Shaped Christianity*, Crossword Publishing Company, New York.

Meagher, P.K. & O'Brien, T. C. & Aherne, C.M. (eds), 1979, "Encyclopedic Dictionary of Religion", *Corpus Publications*, Washington (vol. 1, vol. 2, vol. 3).

Menamparampil, T., 2016, 24 August, "Humans have Dignity and Value, Mother Teresa's Message for our Time", *AsiaNews.it*. Retrieved 16 April 2019 from http://www.asianews.it/news-en/Humans-have-dignity-and-value,-Mother-Teresa's-message-for-our-time-38390.html

Merici, A., 2011, in L. Rodger & J. Bakewell, *Chambers Biographical Dictionary*, 9th edn. [Online]. London: Chambers Harrap. Available from: https://search-credoreference-com.ezproxy1.acu.edu.au/content/entry/chambbd/angela_merici_st/0 [Accessed 11 September 2018].

Middle Ages, 2015, *Anchoress*. Retrieved 29 March 2015 from http://www.middle-ages.org.uk/anchoress.htm

Miller, J.D., (n.d.), "What can we say about Phoebe?" In *the Priscilla Papers the Academic Papers of CBE International*. Retrieved 31 March 2018 from https://www.cbeinternational.org/resources/article/priscilla-papers/what-can-we-say-about-phoebe

Miller, L.L., 2012, "The Charism of Saint Angela Merici Ursuline as Safe Harbour for Adolescent Development", *Dissertation* [Online], St Mary Seminary and Graduated School of Theology. Retrieved 11 September 2018 from https://search-proquest-com.ezproxy2.acu.edu.au/docview/1024339053?pq-origsite=primo

Miller, W.D., 1973, *A Harsh and Dreadful Love: Dorothy Day and the Catholic Worker Movement*, Darton, Longman & Todd Ltd., Great Britain.

Miravalle, M., 2007, *Meet Mary Getting to Know the Mother of God*, Sophia Institute Press, Manchester, New Hampshire.

Montagna, D., 2016, June 10, *Mary Magdalene, 'Apostle to the Apostles,' Given equal Dignity in Feast*. Retrieved 20 March 2018 from https://aleteia.org/2016/06/10/mary-magdalene-apostle-to-the-apostles-given-equal-dignity-in-feast/

Mother Teresa, 1996, *In My Own Words*, comp. José Luis González-Balado, Liguori Publications, Mo.

Mueller, J., 2006, *The Privilege of Poverty*. Penn State University Press. Retrieved 30 July 2018 from http://www.psupress.org/books/titles/0-271-02893-9.html

Mueller, J., 2010, *A Companion to Clare of Assisi: Life, Writings, and Spirituality* [Online]. Retrieved 9 July 2018 from https://ebookcentral-proquest-com.ezproxy2.acu.edu.au/lib/acu/detail.action?docID=583755

Muzerengwa, P., 2019, January 2, "United Methodists fight human trafficking", in *UM News*. Retrieved 15 March 2019 from https://www.umnews.org/en/news/united-methodists-fight-human-trafficking

NCR Staff, 2013, "Early women leaders: from heads of house churches to presbyters" in *National Catholic Reporter*, (January 8). Retrieved 16 April 2018 from https://www.ncronline.org/news/theology/early-women-leaders-heads-house-churches-presbyters

Nazarethcsfn.org., 2019, "Blessed Martyrs of Nowogródek". Retrieved 8 June 2019 from https://nazarethcsfn.org/about-us/spirituality/blessed-martyrs-of-nowogrodek

Newman, B., 1990, "Introduction", in *Hildegard of Bingen: Scivias*, Hart, C. & Bishop, J. (trans) Paulist Press, U.S.A.

Newman, B. (ed), 1998, *Voice of the Living Light, Hildegard of Bingen and Her World*, University of California Press, California. U.S.A.

News corp Australia Network, 2016, August 28, *Pope Francis to canonise Mother Teresa during Vatican mass on September 4*. Retrieved 8 April 2019 from https://www.news.com.au/world/pope-france-to-canonise-mother-teresa-during-vatican-mass-on-september-4/news-story/07259868d5039980541d14b312a975f0

Noffke, S., 1980, *Catherine of Siena: The Dialogue*, Paulist Press, New Jersey. U.S.A.

Noffke, S., 2000, *The Letters of Catherine of Siena*, vol. 1, Center for Medieval and Renaissance Studies, Arizona, U.S.A.

Noffke, S., 2001, *The Letters of Catherine of Siena*, vol. 2, Center for Medieval and Renaissance Studies, Arizona, U.S.A.

Norris, K., 1999, *Meditations on Mary*, pp.16-17, Viking Studio, New York.

Nouwen, H., 1979, *The Wounded Healer*, Image, Doubleday, New York.

O'Brien, D., 2015, "Popular Poetry and Devotions" in *Friends of Caroline Chisholm Newsletter*. Retrieved 17 January 2019 from https://mrschisholmdotcom.files.wordpress.com/2016/02/friends-newsletter-10-jan-20151.pdf

O'Brien, D.J., 2011, April 8, "Dorothy's Days: letters from a saint." *Commonweal*, p.16+. *Literature Resource Center.* Accessed 18 Feb. 2019. http://link.galegroup.com/apps/doc/A253928067/LitRC?u=acuni&sid=LitRC&xid=409a1ca6

O'Connor, J., 1997, "On the Idea of Sainthood and Dorothy Day" in *The Catholic Worker Movement.* Retrieved 29 April 2019 from https://www.catholicworker.org/pages/o'connor-sainthood-homily.html

O'Connor, J., 2000, March 16, "Dorothy Days Sainthood Cause begins" in *The Catholic Worker Movement.* Retrieved 23 April 2019 from https://www.catholicworker.org/pages/o'connor-cause-begins.html

O'Donnell, C., 1997, *Love in the Heart of the Church*, Veritas, Dublin.

O'Donnell, C., 2001, *Therese of Lisieux*, Veritas, Dublin.

O'Mahony, C., (ed & trans), 1975, *St Therese of Lisieux by those who knew her: Testimonies from the process of beatification*, Veritas Publications, Dublin.

O'Riordan, M., 2017, Oct.11, *Moonlight Speech* – Pope St John XXIII – inspired by St Therese of Lisieux. Retrieved 28 June 2018 from http://www.thereseoflisieux.org/my-blog-about-st-therese/2017/10/11/st-john-xxiiis-famous-moonlight-speech-october-11-1962-on-th.html

Order of Carmelites, 2017, "Saints Louis and Zelie Martin, Parents of Thérèse of Lisieux (M)" in *CITOC News.* Retrieved 16 June 2018 from http://www.ocarm.org/en/content/liturgy/saints-louis-and-zelie-martin-parents-therese-lisieux-m

O'Toole, J., 1996, *Leading Change: The Argument for Values-Based Leadership*, Jossey-Bass Inc. U.S.A.

Palmer, P.J., 1998, "Leading from Within", in *Insights on Leadership: Service, Stewardship, Spirit, and Servant-Leadership*, ed L. C. Spears, John Wiley & Sons, Inc., U.S.A., pp. 197-208.

Palmer, R., 1969, *Hermeneutics*, North Western University Press, Evanston, IL.

Tanner, N.P. (ed), 2017, "First Council of Nicea – 325 A.D", *Papal Encyclical Online.* Retrieved 23 January 2019 from http://www.papalencyclicals.net/Councils/ecum01.htm

Tanner, N.P. (ed), 2017, "Council of Chalcedon – 451A.D", *Papal Encyclical Online.* Retrieved 23 January 2019 from http://www.papalencyclicals.net/Councils/ecum04.htm

Patenaude, W.L., 2014, "The 'Green Pope' and a Human Ecology", *The Catholic Report*, April 22. Retrieved 15 May 2015 from: http://www.catholicworldreport.com/Item/3087/the_Green_Pope_and_a_Human_Ecology

Paton, M., 2010, *Mary MacKillop The Ground of her Loving*, Darton, Longman and Todd Ltd., London.

Patton, M.Q., 2002, *Qualitative Research and Evaluation Methods*, 3rd edn, Sage Publications Inc., California.

Payne, S., 2002, *Saint Therese of Lisieux: Doctor of the Universal Church*, Alba House, Washington.

Peters, M.D., n.d., *Bible Quotes by Mary*. Retrieved 10 February 2018, from https://udayton.edu/imri/mary/b/bible-quotes-by-mary.php

Peers, E.A. (ed & trans), 1963a, *Saint Teresa of Jesus: The Complete Works*, vol. 1, the New Ark Library, Great Britain.

Peers, E.A. (ed & trans), 1963b, *Saint Teresa of Jesus: The Complete Works*, vol. II, the New Ark Library, Great Britain.

Peers, E.A. (ed & trans), 1963c, *Saint Teresa of Jesus: The Complete Works*, vol. III, the New Ark Library, Great Britain.

Phillips, F., 2017, May 22, "What Mary Magdalene can teach us about adoring the Lord" in *Catholic Herald*. Retrieved 20 March 2018 from https://aleteia.org/2016/06/10/mary-magdalene-apostle-to-the-apostles-given-equal-dignity-in-feast/

Piccarreta, L., 2019, *Lists of American Saints, Blesseds, Venerables, and Servants of God as recognized by the Roman Catholic Church*. Retrieved 12 January 2019 from https://luisapiccarreta.com/other-category/saints/list-of-american-saints-blesseds-venerables-and-servants-of-god-as-recognized-by-the-roman-catholic-church/

Pontifical Justice and Peace Commission, 1988, *The Church and Racism: Towards a More Fraternal Society*. Retrieved 29 June 2018 from https://scholarship.law.stjohns.edu/cgi/viewcontent.cgi?article=2292&context=tcl

Pontifical Council for Justice and Peace, 2004, Compendium of the Social Doctrine of the Church. *To his Holiness Pope John Paul II Master of Social Doctrine and Evangelical Witness to Justice and Peace*. Retrieved 12 March 2018 from http://www.vatican.va/roman_

curia/pontifical_councils/justpeace/documents/rc_pc_justpeace_doc_20060526_compendio-dott-soc_en.html

Pope Francis, 2013, "Apostolic Exhortation", *Evangelii Gaudium – on the proclamation of the gospel in today's world*. Retrieved from http://www.vatican.va/holy_father/francesco/apost_exhortations/documents/papa-francesco_esortazione-ap_20131124_evangelii-gaudium_en.html

Pope Francis, 2014, "500 years after birth, witness of St. Teresa of Avila remains strong, says Pope" in *Catholic News Agency*. Retrieved 10 June 2018 from https://www.catholicnewsagency.com/news/on-500th-birthday-st-teresa-of-avila-remains-strong-witness-of-consecrated-life-says-pope-91722

Pope Francis, 2015, "Encyclical letter" *Laudato Si'* – Praise be to you – *on care for our common home*. Retrieved from http://w2.vatican.va/content/francesco/en/encyclicals/documents/papafrancesco_20150524_enciclica-laudato-si.html

Pope Francis, 2016, September 4, "Holy Mass and Canonization of Blessed mother Teresa of Calcutta", Jubilee for Workers of Mercy and Volunteers, *Homily of His Holiness Pope Francis*, St Peter's Square. Retrieved 15 April 2019 from http://w2.vatican.va/content/francesco/en/homilies/2016/documents/papa-francesco_20160904_omelia-canonizzazione-madre-teresa.html

Pope Francis, 2017, January 13, "Pope's Letter to Young People" on *the Occasion of the Presentation of the Preparatory Document* of the XV Ordinary General assembly of the Synod of Bishops.

Pope Francis, 2019, March 25, "Apostolic Exhortation", *Christus Vivit* – Christ Lives. Retrieved 25 May 2019 from http://w2.vatican.va/content/francesco/en/apost_exhortations/documents/papa-francesco_esortazione-ap_20190325_christus-vivit.html

Pope Leo XIII, 1891, "Encyclical", *Rerum Novarum – on Capital and Labor*. Retrieved 12 March 2018 from http://w2.vatican.va/content/leo-xiii/en/encyclicals/documents/hf_l-xiii_enc_15051891_rerum-novarum.html

Pope Pius XI, 1926, April 30, "Encyclical", *Rite Expiatis – on St. Francis of Assisi*. Retrieved 20 July 2018 from http://w2.vatican.va/content/pius-xi/en/encyclicals/documents/hf_p-xi_enc_30041926_rite-expiatis.html

Pope Pius XII, 1947, "Papal Directives for the Woman of Today" in *Papal Encyclicals Online*. Retrieved 20 August 2018 from http://www.papalencyclicals.net/pius12/p12woman.htm

Pope Pius XII, 1950, Nov. 1," Apostolic Constitution" *Munificentissimus Deus – defining the dogma of the Assumption*. Retrieved from http://w2.vatican.va/content/pius-xii/en/apost_constitutions/documents/hf_p-xii_apc_19501101_munificentissimus-deus.html

Pope Pius XII, 1957, "Apostolic Letter", *LETTRE APOSTOLIQUE PROCLAMANT Ste CLAIRE PATRONNE CÉLESTE DE LA TÉLÉVISION*. Retrieved 30 July 2018 from http://w2.vatican.va/content/pius-xii/fr/apost_letters/documents/hf_p-xii_apl_21081958_st-claire.html

Pope St John XXIII, 1963, "Encyclical" *Pacem in Terris – on Establishing Universal Peace in Truth, Justice, Charity, and Liberty*. Retrieved from http://w2.vatican.va/content/john-xxiii/en/encyclicals/documents/hf_j-xxiii_enc_11041963_pacem.html

Pope St John Paul II, 1983, January 25, "Apostolic Constitution", *Divinus Perfectionis Magister*. Retrieved 19 June 2018 from http://w2.vatican.va/content/john-paul-ii/en/apost_constitutions/documents/hf_jp-ii_apc_25011983_divinus-perfectionis-magister.html

Pope St John Paul II, 1988, "Apostolic Letter" *Mulieris Dignitatem – on the Dignity and Vocation of Women on the Occasion of the Marian Year*. Retrieved from http://w2.vatican.va/content/john-paul-ii/en/apost_letters/1988/documents/hf_jp-ii_apl_19880815_mulieris-dignitatem.html

Pope St John Paul II, 1989a, *Homily of our Holy Father John Paul II during the Beatification ceremony*. Retrieved 15 November 2018 from https://i.b5z.net/i/u/6148531/f/Homily_of_John_Paul_II_during_beatification.pdf

Pope St John Paul II, 1989b, "Apostolic Exhortation", *Redemptoris Custos – on the Person and Mission of Saint Joseph in the Life of the Church*. Retrieved from http://w2.vatican.va/content/john-paul-ii/en/apost_exhortations/documents/hf_jp-ii_exh_15081989_redemptoris-custos.html

Pope St John Paul II, 1994, May 22, "Apostolic Letter", *Ordination Sacerdotalis – on Reserving Priestly Ordination to Men Alone*. Retrieved 23 June 2018 from https://w2.vatican.va/

content/john-paul-ii/en/apost_letters/1994/documents/hf_jp-ii_apl_19940522_ordinatio-sacerdotalis.html

Pope St John Paul II, 1995a, March 25, "Encyclical", *Evangelium Vitae – on the Value and Inviolability of Human Life*. Retrieved 12 March 2018 from http://w2.vatican.va/content/john-paul-ii/en/encyclicals/documents/hf_jp-ii_enc_25031995_evangelium-vitae.html

Pope St John Paul II, 1995b, June 29, *Letter of Pope John Paul II to Women*. Retrieved from https://w2.vatican.va/content/john-paul-ii/en/letters/1995/documents/hf_jp-ii_let_29061995_women.html

Pope St John Paul II, 1997, October 19, "Apostolic Letter", *Divini Amoris Scientia*. Retrieved 29 June 2018 from https://w2.vatican.va/content/john-paul-ii/en/apost_letters/1997/documents/hf_jp-ii_apl_19101997_divini-amoris.html

Pope St John Paul II, 2003a, April 26, *MESSAGE OF JOHN PAUL II TO PROFESSOR GIULIANA CAVALLINI OF THE MISSIONARIES OF THE SCHOOL*. Retrieved 11 May 2018 from https://w2.vatican.va/content/john-paul-ii/en/speeches/2003/april/documents/hf_jp-ii_spe_20030426_prof-cavallini.html

Pope St John Paul II, 2003b, August 22, "St Clare's Message is More Important Than Ever, says Pope", in *Zenit*. Retrieved 11 July 2018 from https://zenit.org/articles/st-clare-s-message-is-more-important-than-ever-says-pope/

Pope St John Paul II, 2003c, October 19, "Homily of His Holiness John Paul II" on the *Beatification of Mother Theresa of Calcutta*. Libreria Editrice Vaticana.

Pope St Paul VI, 1964, "Dogmatic Constitution on the Church", *Lumen Gentium* (Nov.21). Retrieved from http://www.vatican.va/archive/hist_councils/ii_vatican_council/documents/vat-ii_const_19641121_lumen-gentium_en.html

Pope St Paul VI, 1965, "Pastoral Constitution", *Gaudium et Spes* (December 7). Retrieved 23 January 2019 from http://www.vatican.va/archive/hist_councils/ii_vatican_council/documents/vat-ii_cons_19651207_gaudium-et-spes_en.html

Pope St Paul VI, 1969, "Apostolic Constitution", *Sacra Rituum Congregation* (May 8). Retrieved 19 June 2018 from http://w2.vatican.va/content/paul-vi/la/apost_constitutions/documents/hf_p-vi_apc_19690508_sacra-rituum-congregatio.html

Pope St Paul VI, 1974, "Apostolic Exhortation", *Marialis Cultus for the Right Ordering and Development of Devotion to the Blessed Virgin Mary* (Feb.2). Retrieved from http://w2.vatican.va/content/paul-vi/en/apost_exhortations/documents/hf_p-vi_exh_19740202_marialis-cultus.html.

Posa, C., 2012, "Hildegard: a woman for women and men of our times", *The Good Oil*, 20 November.

Pullella, P., 2018, October 28, *Vatican meeting ends with call for greater role for women in Church*. Retrieved 8 January 2019 from https://news.yahoo.com/vatican-meeting-ends-call-greater-role-women-church-214619860.html

Rath, P., 1996a, *Hildegard of Bingen Prophetess of her Time*. Retrieved 23 January 2014 from http://hildegard.org/wirk/ehilde.html

Rath, P., 1996b, *The New Abbey of St. Hildegard*. Retrieved 23 January 2014 from http://hildegard.org/wirk/eabtei.html

Regina, E., 2013, October 5, *Poor Clare Heart Ponderings*. Retrieved 20 July 2018 from http://pcheartponderings.blogspot.com/2013/10/pope-francis-at-st-clares-monastery-in.html

Régine, P. & Clin, M.V., 2000, *Joan of Arc: Her Story*, trans & rev, Jeremy du Quesnay Adams, Phoenix Press, Great Britain.

Reid, B., 2006, "Leading Ladies of the Early Church" in *U.S. Catholic*, vol.71 (2) p.28 (4). Retrieved 27 March 2018 from http://gp/galegroup.com.ezproxy2.acu.edu.au/ps/i.do?&id=GALElA141437762&v=2.1&u=acuni&it=r&p=AONE&sw=&authCount=1

Reis, B.M., 2018, February 12, "Pope Francis: Human trafficking is a crime against humanity", in *Vatican News*. Retrieved 10 March 2019 from https://www.vaticannews.va/en/pope/news/2018-02/pope-world-day-trafficking-young-people.html

Rengers, C., 2000, *The 33 Doctors of the Church*, Tan Books and Publishers, Inc. Illinois, U.S.A.

Research Management Group, 1999, "Woman and Man One in Christ Jesus", *Report on the Participation of Women in the Catholic Church in Australia*.

Ricciardi, A., 1971, "His Will Alone", *The Life of Mother Mary of Jesus the Good Shepherd Foundress of the Congregation of the Sisters of the Holy Family of Nazareth* (Frances Siedliska), Castle-Pierce Press, Wisconsin U.S.A.

Richey, S.W., 2003, *Joan of Arc The Warrior Saint*, Praeger Publishers, Westport, Connecticut, U.S.A.

Ristine, J., 2016, July 22, "Why Pilgrims are Flocking to St Mary Magdalene's Hometown", in *Catholic Herold*. Retrieved 2 March 2018 from http://catholicherald.co.uk/commentandblogs/2016/07/22/why-pilgrims-are-flocking-to-st-mary-magdaleneshometown/

Roach, D., 2016, *The Servant-Leadership Style of Jesus: A Biblical Strategy for Leadership Development*, West Bow Press, Bloomington, U.S.A.

Rosica, T., 2006, "Mary Magdalen …" in *Toronto Sun*, 16 April 2006, pp. 1-2. Retrieved 21 Jan 2009 from http://www.ccrl.ca/doc/1Fr.%20Rosica%20re%20Da%20Vinci.doc

Rosin, H., 2000, March 17, "Vatican to Weigh Sainthood for Reformer Dorothy Day" in *The Washington Post Company*. Retrieved 23 April 2019 from https://www.washingtonpost.com/wp-srv/WPcap/2000-03/17/074r-031700-idx.html

Rost, J.C., 1993, *Leadership for the Twenty-First Century*, Praeger Publishers, U.S.A.

Royal Commission into Institutional Responses to Child Sexual Abuse, 2017, Dec. 15, *Final Report*. Retrieved from https://www.childabuseroyalcommission.gov.au/final-report

Royle, R. & Woods, G., 1992, *Mother Teresa: A Life in Pictures*, Bloomsbury Publishing Ltd., London.

Russell, R.F., 2001, "The role of values in servant leadership," *Leadership and Organization Development*, vol. 22, no. 2, pp. 76-83. Retrieved 2008 from Emerald database.

Sackville-West, V., 1948, *Saint Joan of Arc* (rev. ed), Michael Joseph Ltd., London.

Saint Making, 2015, printed from www.mrschisholm.com Retrieved 18 January 2019 from https://mrschisholmdotcom.files.wordpress.com/2015/11/saint-making.pdf

Saints and Heroes Resources, 2018, "St Clare of Assisi A Bright and Shining Light" in *The Word Among Us*. Retrieved 11 July 2018 from https://wau.org/resources/article/saint_clare_of_assisi/

Salai, S., 2011, "Teaching the Catholic View on Justice" in *Journal of Religious Education* 59 (1). Retrieved 9 May 2018 from https://www.acu.edu.au/__data/assets/pdf_file/0010/418447/2010-59-1-Complete.pdf

Salai, S., 2017, "St. Clare of Assisi: a saint … with or without Francis" in *America The Jesuit Review*. Retrieved 11 July 2018 from https://www.americamagazine.org/faith/2017/08/04/st-clare-assisi-saintwith-or-without-francis

Sardi, V., 1921, *Vita della Servadi Dio Maria Francesca De Siedliska, fondatrice della Congregazione della Sacra famigliadi Nazaret*, Opera postuma, Grottaferrata, Scuola tipografica Italo-Orientale "S. Nilo", (Out of print).

Saunders, W., 2004, July 22, "Who Really Was Mary Magdalene?" In the *Arlington Catholic Herald*. Retrieved 25 March 2018 from https://www.catholicculture.org/culture/library/view.cfm?recnum=6091

Scally, D., 2016, April 16, *Poland marks 1,050 years of Christianity*. Retrieved 28 November 2018 from https://www.irishtimes.com/news/world/europe/poland-marks-1-050-years-of-christianity-1.2612466

Scaraffia, L., 2012, "The Equivalent Canonization of Hildegard of Bingen", *L'Osservatore Romano*, May 11.

Schein, E.H., 1999, "Empowerment, coercive persuasion and organizational learning: do they connect?" *The Learning Organization*, vol. 6, no. 4, pp. 163-172. Retrieved 10 September 2008 from Emerald database.

Schlumpf, H., 2000, "Who Framed Mary Magdalene?" In *U.S. Catholic Faith in Real Life*. Retrieved 7 April 2018 from http://www.uscatholic.org/articles/200806/who-framed-mary-magdalene-27585

Schmude, K., 2016, September 1, "Malcolm Muggeridge, the Journalist who met his match in Mother Teresa" in *The Catholic Weekly*. Retrieved 13 April 2019 from https://www.catholicweekly.com.au/malcolm-muggeridge-the-journalist-who-met-his-match-in-mother-teresa/

Schneible, A., 2015, "Pope Francis' tough words against horrors of human trafficking", in *Catholic News Agency (CNA)*. Retrieved 15 March 2019 from https://www.catholicnewsagency.com/news/pope-francis-tough-words-against-horrors-of-human-trafficking-99070

Scott, K., 1992, "St Catherine of Siena", in *Church History 'Apostola'*, no. 61, pp. 34-46.

Senge, M. P., 1996, "The Ecology of Leadership", *Leader to Leader*, no. 2, (Fall). Retrieved 19 February 2015 from: http://www.scribd.com/doc/95654454/Peter-Senge-Articles#scribd

Sequentia, 1994, "Canticles of Ecstasy: Hildegard of Bingen", *CD* BMG Music, New York, U.S.A.

Serle, P., 2015, *Caroline Chisholm* (1808-1877). Retrieved 18 January 2019 from https://mrschisholmdotcom.files.wordpress.com/2015/11/adb_1949_serle.pdf

Sheppard, F., 2016, September 10, *Mother Teresa: When the saint came marching into Bourke*. Retrieved 6 April 2019 from https://www.abc.net.au/news/2016-09-10/mother-teresa-in-bourke/7822916

Short, B., 2009, *Spirituality of Francis and Clare of Assisi* [Video File]. Retrieved 10 July 2018 from https://www.franciscantradition.org/resources/video-clips

Sica, C., 1925, *La Congregazione della Sacra Famiglia di Nazareth nel primo cinquantenario della sua Fondazione* (1875-1925), Roma, Tipografia Poliglotta, Vaticana.

Siedliska, M.F., (n.d.), "Counsels from the Heart", *Extracts from the intimate letters of spiritual guidance and religious formation*. Mother M. Medarda, CSFN., 1976, Rome.

Siedliska, F., 1997, *An Autobiography*. Pennsylvania: CSFN. VIII-IX.

Silvas, A., 1998, "Jutta and Hildegard: The Biographical Sources", *Medieval Women: Texts and Contexts*, University of Liverpool, Turnhout: Brepols, Belgium.

Silvas, A., 2012, "Saint Hildegard: Teutonic Prophetess, Sybil of the Rhine, Doctor of the Church", Talk given at the *Anima Conference*, November 3, 2012, Melbourne.

Sims, B.J., 1997, *Servanthood: Leadership for the Third Millennium*, Cowley Publications, U.S.A.

Sipe, J.W. & Frick, D.M., 2015, *Seven Pillars of Servant Leadership: Practicing the Wisdom of leading by Serving*. Paulist Press, New York.

Sisters of the Holy Family of Nazareth, 2014, *25th Anniversary of the Beatification of M. Frances Siedliska*. Retrieved 15 November 2018 from https://www.nazarethfamily.org/eng/25th_anniversary_of_the_beatification_of_m__frances_siedliska

Spears, L.C. (ed), 1998a, *Insights on Leadership: Service, Stewardship, Spirit, and Servant-Leadership*, John Wiley & Sons, Inc., U.S.A.

Spears, L.C. (ed), 1998b, "Tracing the Growing Impact of Servant-Leadership", in *Insights on Leadership: Service, Stewardship, Spirit, and Servant-Leadership*, John Wiley & Sons, Inc., U.S.A.

Spears, L.C., 2010, "Character and Servant Leadership: Ten Characteristics of Effective, Caring Leaders", *The Journal of Virtues & Leadership*, vol.1, issue 1, pp.25-30. Retrieved 5 February 2015 from: http://www.regent.edu/acad/global/publications/jvl/vol1_iss1/Spears_Final.pdf

Spink, K., 2011, *Mother Teresa: An Authorized Biography*, revised & updated, HarperCollins Publishers, New York.

Stanton, E.C., 1895, *The Woman's Bible 1895/1898* (Parts I and II), reprinted edn, 1972, Arno Press, New York.

Stinson, R., 2013, *Friends of Caroline Chisholm Newsletter*. Retrieved 18 January 2019 from https://mrschisholmdotcom.files.wordpress.com/2015/11/friends-newsletter-6-jan-2013.pdf

Stinson, R., 2015, *Caroline Chisholm's Sydney: Self-Guided Walk*. Retrieved 18 January 2019 from https://mrschisholmdotcom.files.wordpress.com/2015/11/walking_tour.pdf

Stinson, R., 2015, *Caroline Chisholm A Saintly Model*. Retrieved 18 January 2019 from https://mrschisholmdotcom.files.wordpress.com/2015/11/a-saintly-model.pdf

Stinson, R., 2017, December 29, "Historical Gaucherie, Inaccuracy and Error" in *An Irresistible Force – A Book Review*. Retrieved 17 January 2019 from https://mrschisholmdotcom.files.wordpress.com/2018/09/historical-gaucherie-inaccuracy-and-error-in-an-irresistible-force.pdf

Stodart, R., (n.d.), "Mary Magdalen Apostle to the Apostles", in *The Nazarene Way*. Retrieved 20 March 2018 from http://www.thenazareneway.com/mary_magdalene.htm

Stogdill, R., 1974, *Handbook of Leadership: A survey of theory and research*, The Free Press, New York.

Stogdill, R., 1981, "Traits of leadership: A follow-up to 1970", in B. Bass (ed) *Stogdill's handbook of leadership*, pp. 73-97, Free Press, New York.

St Procopius Abbey, (n.d.), *Dorothy Day Oblate*. Retrieved 16 May 2019 from https://www.procopius.org/dorothy-day-oblate

Strange, R., 2017, "Teresian Quartet", *The Pastoral Review*, vol. 13, iss. 1, January/February, pp. 21-26.

Stringer, B., 2016, "Desperately Seeking Phoebe", *The Pastoral Review*, vol. 13, iss. 1, (January/February), pp. 15-20. Retrieved 30 March 2018 from https://www.thepastoralreview.org/issues/223-past-issues/2017/january-february-2017

Strzałkowska, I., 1989, "Blessed Mary of Jesus the Good Shepherd Frances Siedliska" *Foundress of the Congregation of the Sisters of the Holy Family of Nazareth*, Romagrafik Printers, Rome.

Sutherland, E., 2010, "Hildegard of Bingen: Entry into Disibodenberg" [online], *Parergon*, vol.27, no.1, 2010:53-66. Retrieved 28 March 2015 from: _http://search.informit.com.au/documentSummary;dn=201007767;res=IELAPA_ISSN: 0313-6221.

Synod of Bishops, 2018, "XV Ordinary General Assembly" *on Young People, the Faith and Vocational Discernment – Preparatory Document*. Retrieved 11 November 2018 from http://www.vatican.va/roman_curia/synod/documents/rc_synod_doc_20170113_documento-preparatorio-xv_en.html

Taulbert, C.L., 2008, "Slow Down to Lead", *Leader to Leader*, vol. 2008, iss. 49, summer, pp.36-40. Retrieved 19 September 2008 from ProQuest database.

Teresa, Mother, 1995, *Mother Teresa: A Simple Path*, compiled by Lucinda Vardey, Rider, Random House, London.

Teresa, Mother, 1983, *Words to Love By …,* Ave Maria Press, Notre Dame, Ind.

Tertullian, (n.d.), "The Dress of Women" ("De Cultu Feminarum"), in *Corpus Christianorium, Series Latina*, vol. 1 (Turnholt: Typographia Brepols Editores Pontificii, 1954), p.343. Cited in Hines, Mary and the Prophetic Mission of the Church, *Journal of Ecumenical studies*, 28:2, Spring 1991, p.283.

Thomas, K., 1981, June 25, "A Working Girl Review of Joan of Arc: The Image of Female Heroism" by Marina Warner, in *The New York Review*, June 25, vol.28, Issue 11, p.7. Retrieved 15 July 2018 from https://www-nybooks-com.ezproxy1.acu.edu.au/articles/1981/06/25/a-working-girl/

Throop, P. (trans), 1998, "Hildegard von Bingen's PHYSICA", *The Complete English Translation of Her Classic work on Health and Healing*, Healing Arts Press, Rochester, Vermont.

Thorn, W.J., Runkel, P.M. & Mountin, S.(eds), 2001, *Dorothy Day and the Catholic Worker Movement: Centenary Essays*, Marquette University Press, Milwaukee U.S.A. Retrieved 21 April 2019 from https://ebookcentral-proquest-com.ezproxy2.acu.edu.au/lib/acu/reader.action?docID=3017071

Thurston, A., 1998, *Knowing Her Place: Gender and the Gospels*, Paulist Press, New York.

Tierney, Tadgh, 2015, *Zélie and Louis Martin: Parents of St Thérèse of Lisieux*. Retrieved 17 June 2018 from http://www.infantjesusparish.org.au/wp-content/uploads/Therese-Parents_IJP.pdf

Tobin, M.L., 1986, November 1, *Women in the Church Since Vatican II: from November 1, 1986*. Retrieved 8 January 2019 from https://www.americamagazine.org/issue/100/women-church-vatican-ii

Toews, J.E., 1980, "The Role of Women in the Church: The Pauline Perspective", in *Direction A Mennonite Brethren Forum*, January, vol.9, No.1, pp.25-35.

Tromberend, T., 1996, *Bermersheim*. Retrieved 23 January 2014 from http://hildegard.org/wirk/ebermer.html

Trotta, Margarethe Von, 2010, *Vision – From the Life of Hildegard von Bingen*, DVD Zeitgeist video, Germany.

Unam Sanctam Catholicam, 2015, *Canonization: Old vs. New Comparison*. Retrieved 19 June 2018 from http://www.unamsanctamcatholicam.com/theology/81-theology/555-canonization-old-vs-new.html

United Nations Congress (13th), 2015, April 12-19, "Human Trafficking", *On Crime Prevention and Criminal Justice*. Retrieved 19 March 2019 from http://www.unis.unvienna.org/unis/en/events/2015/crime_congress_human_trafficking.html

United Nations, 1948, *Universal Declaration of Human Rights*. Retrieved 11 March 2018 from http://www.un.org/en/universal-declaration-human-rights/

United States Conference of Catholic Bishops, 2019, *History of the Catholic Church in the United States*. Retrieved 22 April 2019 from http://www.usccb.org/about/public-affairs/backgrounders/history-catholic-church-united-states.cfm

Unnamed Source (n.d.)., Retrieved 18 October 2018 from https://www.lsrhs.net/departments/science/faculty/Rami/Forces%20of%20Change/FOC_PDFs/Typhus_p26-30.pdf

University of Maryland Medical System, 2013, *Thoughts and Reflections*, pp.1-4. Retrieved 5 February 2015 from: http://umm.edu/patients/pastoral/thoughts-and-reflections

Ursulines of the Roman Union, 2018, *History of the Serviam Badge*. Retrieved 21 October 2018 from https://www.ursulines-ur.org/index.php/menu-detail-serviam/899-serviam

Vatican Document, 2000, Dec 8. *Mary a Disciple of Christ by St Augustine*. Retrieved 18 Nov. 2017 From http://www.vatican.va/spirit/documents/spirit_20001208_agostino_en.html

Vatican Information Service, 2010, Sept. 15, "Clare of Assisi: a decisive Impulse to Church Renewal" in *The Catholic News, Archdiocese of Singapore*. Retrieved 11 July 2018 from https://catholicnews.sg/index.php?option=com_content&view=article&id=4923:clare-of-assisi-a-decisive-impulse-to-church-renewal&catid=196:vis-vatican-information-service&Itemid=525&lang=en

Vatican Information Service, 2011, October 28, "May Religions bring Justice and Peace Upon Earth" in *The Catholic News, Archdiocese of Singapore*. Retrieved 11 July 2018 from https://catholicnews.sg/index.php?option=com_content&view=article&id=6725:assisi-may-religions-bring-justice-and-peace-upon-the-earth&catid=196:vis-vatican-information-service&Itemid=525&lang=en

Vatican Information Service, 2012, March 31, "The Undying Allure of St. Clare of Assisi" in *The Catholic News, Archdiocese of Singapore*. Retrieved 11 July 2018 from https://catholicnews.sg/index.php?option=com_content&view=article&id=7337:the-undying-allure-of-st-clare-of-assisi&catid=196&Itemid=525&lang=en

Vatican News, (n.d.), *Josephine Bakhita (1869-1947)*. Retrieved 13 March 2019 from http://www.vatican.va/news_services/liturgy/saints/ns_lit_doc_20001001_giuseppina-bakhita_en.html

Vatican Radio Announcement, 2016, *Pope institutes commission to study the diaconate of women*, 2 August. Retrieved 10 Feb. 2017 from http://en.radiovaticana.va/news/2016/08/02/pope_institutes_commission_to_study_the_diaconate_of_women/1248731

Vatican Radio Announcement, 2017, *Pope: Women bring harmony that makes the world beautiful*, 9 Feb. 2017. Retrieved 10 Feb. 2017 from http://en.radiovaticana.va/news/2017/02/09/pope_women_bring_harmony_that_makes_the_world_beautiful/1291436

Volanth, A, 2015, *Dorothy Day and the Catholic Worker Movement: Social Transformation and Feminist Legacies*, Thesis, Master of Arts, Southern Connecticut State University, New Haven, Connecticut, (December). Retrieved 21 April 2019 from https://search-proquest-com.ezproxy2.acu.edu.au/docview/1754639700?pq-origsite=primo

Volckmann, R., 2005, "An Interview with Joseph Rost", *Integral Leadership Review*, vol. 5, no. 3, July 2005, pp. 1-15. Retrieved 3 Dec. 2007 from http://www.integralleadershipreview.com/archives/2005_07/2005_07_rost.html

Volckmann, R., 2012, January/February 2015, "Integral Leadership and Diversity—Definitions, Distinctions and Implications", *Integral Leadership Review*. Retrieved from http://integralleadershipreview.com/7046-integral-leadership-and-diversity-definitions-distinctions-and-implications/

Walcot, P., 1996, "Plato's Mother and Other Terrible Women". In Ian McAuslan and Peter Walcot, (eds), *Women in Antiquity*, pp.114-33.

Walker, A. (trans), 1886, "The Protoevangelium of James" in *Ante-Nicene Fathers*, vol. 8. A. Roberts, J. Donaldson, & A. Cleveland Coxe (eds). Christian Literature Publishing Co., Buffalo, New York. Revised and edited for New Advent by Kevin Knight. Retrieved 13 December from http://www.newadvent.org/fathers/0847.htm

Walker, C.A., 2001, "Caroline Chisholm, 1808-1877: ordinary woman - extraordinary life, impossible category", *Dissertation*. Downloaded 19 January 2019 from https://dspace.lboro.ac.uk/2134/8035

Walker, C.A., 2018, January, "Dr Carole Walker's Review of Sarah Goldman's Biography" in *Friends of Caroline Chisholm Newsletter*, # 16. Retrieved 17 January 2019 from https://mrschisholmdotcom.files.wordpress.com/2018/01/friends-newsletter-16-jan-2018.pdf

Warner, M., 1981, *Joan of Arc The Image of Female Heroism*, Weidenfeld and Nicolson, London.

Warner, M., 1983, *Alone of All Her Sex: The Myth and Cult of the Virgin Mary*, Vintage, New York.

Wayman, B.D., 2014, "Ordaining Women and The Woman's Bible: Reading the Bible with B.T. Roberts and Elizabeth Cady Stanton", *Women's Studies*, 43:5, pp.541-566 DOI: 10.1080/00497878.2014.914391

Weber, A., 1990, *Teresa of Avila and the Rhetoric of Femininity*, Princeton University Press, New Jersey, U.S.A.

Weinstein, D. & Bell, R.M., 1982, *The Two Worlds of Western Christendom. 1000-1700*. University of Chicago Press, Chicago.

Wells, C., 2019, February 10, "Pope at Angelus: Join forces to end human trafficking", in *Vatican News*. Retrieved 15 March 2019 from https://www.vaticannews.va/en/pope/news/2019-02/pope-francis-angelus-josephine-bakhita-end-human-trafficking.html

Williams, K., 2017, *The gospel of Mary Magdalene and Her Near-Death Experience*. Retrieved 20 March 2018 from https://www.near-death.com/reincarnation/history/gospel-of-mary.html

Wojtatowicz, N., 2014, "The Word of God" in *the Life and Writings of Blessed Mary of Jesus the Good Shepherd Frances Siedliska*, Rome.

Wooden, C., 2018, "Synod document: Listen to, support, guide, include young people", in *Catholic News Service*, October 27. Retrieved 11 November 2018 from http://www.catholicnews.com/services/englishnews/2018/synod-document-listen-to-support-guide-include-young-people.cfm

Woodward, K.L., 1990, *Making Saints: How the Catholic Church Determines Who Becomes a Saint, Who Doesn't and Why*, Simon and Schuster, New York.

Zagano, P., 2003, "Catholic Women deacons", in *America Magazine*, February 17, Issue 422. Retrieved 5 March 2017 from http://www.americamagazine.org/voices/135079

Zagano, P., 2011, *Women & Catholicism: Gender, Communion, and Authority*, Palgrave, Macmillan, New York, U.S.A.

Zagano, P. (ed), 2016, *Women Deacons? Essays with Answers*, Michael Glazier/Liturgical Press, Collegeville, Minnesota.

Zanini, R.I. (Author) & Matt, A. (trans), 2013, *Bakhita From Slave to Saint*, Ignatius Press, San Francisco.

Zunes, S., 2014, "Dorothy Day's Active Nonviolence", cited in Lane Center for Catholic Studies and Social Thought, 2014, "Dorothy Day: A Life and Legacy" in *The Lane Center Series*, vol. 1, (Summer), University of San Francisco. Retrieved 28 April 2019 from https://www.usfca.edu/sites/default/files/pdfs/cas-lane-center-lecture-series-01.pdf

Zwick, M. & Zwick, L., 1999a, cited in "Day, Dorothy", *On Pilgrimage*, William B. Eerdmans Publishing Company, Grand Rapids, Michigan.

Zwick, M. & Zwick, L., 1999b, August 1, "Emmanuel Mounier, Personalism, and the Catholic Worker Movement", in *Houston Catholic Worker*, July-August. Retrieved 9 May from https://cjd.org/1999/08/01/emmanuel-mounier-personalism-and-the-catholic-worker-movement/

Appendices

Appendix A

Attributes for Servant Leadership & Values-Based Leadership

The following attributes, found to be most beneficial to my own leadership practices, are analysed in relation to the seven pillars of servant leadership, as identified by James W. Sip & Don M. Frick in "Seven Pillars of Servant Leadership: Practicing the Wisdom of Leading by Serving" (2015:4-6). Consequently, and according to my own interpretation of data researched, the attributes that I believe best suited to the individual leadership practices of the fourteen selected women leaders in the Catholic Church throughout the centuries, are addressed in the "Leadership as Service" section of the written text, within Chapters 5 through to 18.

Wisdom has built her house; she has hewn her seven pillars (Proverbs 9:1, cited in Sip & Frick, 2015:4)

Pillar 1 – "Person of Character"

- Is Christ-centered
- Is wise
- Acts with integrity
- Is honest and humble
- Is not self-serving
- Is disciplined
- Values self and others

Pillar II – "Puts People First"
- Leads to serve
- Mentors and nurtures
- Builds mutual trust
- Loves God and neighbour
- Is empathetic
- Allows those served to grow as persons
- Builds consensus

Pillar III – "Skilled Communicator"
- Listens Empathetically
- Listens to what is said and *not* being said
- Influences with persuasion
- Shows initiative
- Cultivates awareness
- Gives and accepts feedback
- Promotes effective communication

Pillar IV – "Compassionate Collaborator"
- Affirms others
- Is discerning
- "Builds teams and communities"
- Values conflict resolution
- Is inclusive
- Is collaborative and collegial
- Values diversity

Pillar V – "Has Foresight"
- Is a visionary
- Is prophetic
- Has spiritual awareness
- Inspires and serves vision
- Encourages innovative thinking
- Uses creativity as a strategic tool
- Foresees and anticipates "potential" situations

Pillar VI – "Systems thinker"
- Considers the "Big Picture"
- Manages strategically
- Is flexible and adaptable
- Engages in ethical behaviour
- Has a global perspective
- Promotes change management
- Encourages sustainability

Pillar VII – "Leads with Moral Authority"
- Empowers and inspirits
- Promotes active discipleship
- Is a cultural custodian
- Is accountable
- Values stewardship
- Has principles and makes moral choices
- Calls for dignity and respect through fairness, justness and equality

"Knowing yourself is the beginning of all wisdom" – Aristotle

Appendix B

St Monica's College, Epping (SMC)
Survey Participants

(I acknowledge and applaud the outstanding efforts of Ms Bernadette Harris and the following students for their impressive and inspirational responses to the Survey Questions)

SMC: 2013-2018

Melissa Eyles (ME), Larissa Liberatore (LL)

SMC: 2012-2017

Chloe Bowen (CB), Sonia Carneiro (SC), Olivia Chamoun (OC), Nicola Depangher (ND), Luke Fontinovo (LF), Michael Kundevski (MK), George Lai (GL), Leonard Mammolitti (LM), Sia'a Sooaemalelagi (SS)

SMC: 2011-2016

Makayla Rao (MR), Evelyn Sebastian (ES)

SMC: 2010-2015

Michael Fontinovo (MF), Rachael Davies (RD)

SMC: 2009-2014

Maree Chamoun (MaC), Melvyn Charan (MeC), Jessica Provenzale (JP)

SMC: 2007-2012

Alvina Stowers (AS)

SMC: 2006-2011

Theresa Chamoun (TC)

Survey Questions

Participants were invited to reflect on the following questions:

Faith, Service and Inspiration

Does your Catholic faith call you to serve or lead others?

Do you possess a desire to make the world more socially just?

If so, in what ways do you think this could or should be approached by people of faith?

From where do you draw your inspiration and strength?

Is it from any inspirational women faith leaders and if so, who and why?

Is prayer an influence in your life?

Are you connected to parish life and/or the sacraments? Does this strengthen your faith and life in any way?

In what ways has this been influenced by any formation and guidance you may have received

(e.g. leadership training etc)?

The Catholic Church

How do you view the Catholic Church?

Do you feel connected to the universal Catholic Church?

Who inspires you by their faith or actions within the Catholic Church?

Are there any Vatican documents you feel are relevant today?

Have any key Church events you have attended (e.g., World Youth Day, Ministry Expos, retreats, camps etc) left any impression on you?

Voices of the Future

How do you feel your life after secondary school will be/is guided or influenced by your faith?

How may this have been shaped by your past experiences including family, parish and educational opportunities?

Do the Catholic Church's teachings influence your life and/or decisions?

Do you aspire to be a 'Voice of the Future' for or "in" the Catholic Church?

What can the Catholic Church do for you or others?

(Full transcripts of responses are available upon request from the author Dr Christine Cameron)

www.ingramcontent.com/pod-product-compliance
Lightning Source LLC
Chambersburg PA
CBHW052040290426
44111CB00011B/1563